Praise for James B.

"[A] hugely engaging book that sign... ...g of how, in each instance, the mighty fell. ... ...riter is that he is both exhaustive and engrossing. The onrush of facts somehow never overwhelms a steady narrative current. . . . Mr. Stewart has done a grand job . . . which is distinguished by indefatigable reporting, consistent narrative drive, and admirable balance. I loved it."   —Scott Turow, *The New York Times*

"An extraordinary forensic analysis of the high-stakes American liar. . . . Much will be made of the bombshells contained within *Tangled Webs*. . . . The book is most impressive, however, on the granular level."   —*BusinessWeek*

"Remarkable . . . His quartet illustrates the ripple effects of lying on friends, associates, investors, voters, and society."   —*Bloomberg*

"*Tangled Webs* is an exquisitely written book that strings together four extraordinary cases from the past decade. . . . The 'tangled webs' of which Stewart writes had to be written about, and no one writes about them better than Stewart."
—*New York Law Journal*

"*Tangled Webs* is the rare book in which the parts are greater than the sum. Pulitzer Prize–winning journalist James B. Stewart proves to be a gifted reporter who can dig up facts on complicated legal cases *and* assemble them in a concise and engaging way."   —*The Columbus Dispatch*

"Stewart has a prosecutor's ability to reconstruct dizzyingly complicated stories about who said what to whom and to organize them as intelligible narratives."
—*The New York Times Book Review*

"Through three decades, eight books, and countless articles, James Stewart has made exposing liars the touchstone of his career. In *Tangled Webs*, he focuses on a particular type of lie—perjury—and blows open the stories of four blockbuster trials, with previously secret testimony, investigators' notes, and a bevy of exclusive interviews. . . . The results . . . are startling—and so is the backdrop. Stewart raises the specter of 'a surge of concerted, deliberate lying' by the nation's loftiest citizens."   —*The Daily Beast*

"Good thing . . . that we have Stewart to play The Ethicist, retrying Bonds but also Martha Stewart, I. Lewis "Scooter" Libby, and Bernie Madoff—and nailing some ears to the post."   —*Newsweek*

"James B. Stewart dives deeply into four recent cases of high-profile conspiracies of lies. What he finds does not say good things about us. . . . Ultimately, Stewart's book is less about his voluminous details than it is about the pervasiveness of lies, and, to borrow an Al Franken phrase, the lying liars who tell them."   —*Los Angeles Times*

"Timely."   —*The Portland Oregonian*

PENGUIN BOOKS

TANGLED WEBS

James B. Stewart is the author of *Heart of a Soldier*, the bestselling *Blind Eye and Blood Sport*, and the blockbuster *Den of Thieves*. A former Page One editor at *The Wall Street Journal*, Stewart won a Pulitzer Prize in 1988 for his reporting on the stock market crash and insider trading. He writes the weekly "Common Sense" column for *The New York Times*, and is a contributor to *The New Yorker*.

Tangled Webs

HOW FALSE STATEMENTS ARE UNDERMINING

AMERICA: FROM MARTHA STEWART

TO BERNIE MADOFF

JAMES B. STEWART

PENGUIN BOOKS

PENGUIN BOOKS
Published by the Penguin Group
Penguin Group (USA) Inc., 375 Hudson Street, New York, New York 10014, U.S.A. • Penguin Group
(Canada), 90 Eglinton Avenue East, Suite 700, Toronto, Ontario, Canada M4P 2Y3 (a division of Pearson
Penguin Canada Inc.) • Penguin Books Ltd, 80 Strand, London WC2R 0RL, England • Penguin
Ireland, 25 St Stephen's Green, Dublin 2, Ireland (a division of Penguin Books Ltd) • Penguin Books
Australia Ltd, 250 Camberwell Road, Camberwell, Victoria 3124, Australia (a division of Pearson Australia
Group Pty Ltd) • Penguin Books India Pvt Ltd, 11 Community Centre, Panchsheel Park,
New Delhi – 110 017, India • Penguin Group (NZ), 67 Apollo Drive, Rosedale, Auckland 0632,
New Zealand (a division of Pearson New Zealand Ltd) • Penguin Books (South Africa) (Pty) Ltd,
24 Sturdee Avenue, Rosebank, Johannesburg 2196, South Africa

Penguin Books Ltd, Registered Offices: 80 Strand, London WC2R 0RL, England

First published in the United States of America by The Penguin Press,
a member of Penguin Group (USA) Inc. 2011
Published in Penguin Books 2012

1 3 5 7 9 10 8 6 4 2

Copyright © James B. Stewart, 2011
All rights reserved

THE LIBRARY OF CONGRESS HAS CATALOGED THE HARDCOVER EDITION AS FOLLOWS:
Stewart, James B.
Tangled webs : how false statements are undermining America: from Martha Stewart
to Bernie Madoff / James B. Stewart.
p.   cm.
Includes bibliographical references and index.
ISBN 978-1-59420-269-8 (hardback)
ISBN 978-0-14-312057-5 (pbk.)
1. Perjury—United States.   2. False testimony—United States.
3. Truthfulness and falsehood—United States.   I. Title.
HV6326.S74 2011   2010049339
364.1'34—dc22

Printed in the United States of America
DESIGNED BY AMANDA DEWEY

To all who seek the truth

Contents

Introduction xi

PART ONE: MARTHA STEWART

ONE. "Can I Go Now?" 3

TWO. "Everyone Is Telling the Same Story" 45

THREE. "A Conspiracy of Dunces" 85

PART TWO: I. LEWIS "SCOOTER" LIBBY

FOUR. "This Is Hush-Hush" 123

FIVE. "All the Reporters Know It" 154

SIX. "Double Super Secret Background" 203

SEVEN. "A Cloud over the White House" 220

PART THREE: BARRY LAMAR BONDS

EIGHT. "I'm Keeping My Money" 265

NINE. "Everybody Is Doing It" 303

TEN. "You're a Snitch" 331

PART FOUR: BERNARD L. MADOFF

ELEVEN. "Keep Your Eyes on the Prize" 363

TWELVE. "Some People Feel the Market" 392

CONCLUSION. 433

Acknowledgments 443

Notes and Sources 445

Index 455

Introduction

Perjurii poena divina, exitium; humana, dedecus
(The crime of perjury is punished by heaven with perdition, and by man
with disgrace.)

—Cicero, derived from the Twelve Tables
of Roman Law, circa 450 bc

Oh! What a tangled web we weave
When first we practice to deceive!

—Sir Walter Scott, "Marmion" (1808)

We know how many murders are committed each year—14,299 in 2008. We know the precise numbers for reported instances of rape, robbery, aggravated assault, burglary, larceny, and vehicle theft. No one keeps statistics for perjury and false statements—lies told under oath or to investigative and other agencies of the U.S. government—even though they are felonies punishable by up to five years in prison. There is simply too much of it, and too little is prosecuted to generate any meaningful statistics.

Although lying seems to be an inherent part of human nature, the narrow but serious class of lies that undermines the judicial process on which government depends has been a crime as old as civilization itself. Originally prosecuted in England by ecclesiastical courts, by the sixteenth century perjury was firmly embedded as a crime in the English common law. The offender was typically punished by cutting out his tongue, or making him stand with both ears nailed to the pillory. False testimony that resulted in the execution of an innocent person was itself punishable by death. Exile, imprisonment, fines, and "perpetual infamy" were meted out as the centuries passed.

Perjury was a crime in the American colonies and has been a crime in the

United States since independence. Today perjury and false statements are federal offenses under U.S. criminal code Title 18, and perjury is also outlawed by statute in all fifty states. The obligation to appear as a witness if summoned and to provide truthful testimony has been inculcated in generations of Americans through civics and history classes. "I swear to tell the truth, the whole truth, and nothing but the truth" is a phrase nearly every American knows by heart.

Yet lying under oath is a subjective crime. It requires the person telling the lie to know that the statement is false and to intend to lie. The subject of the lie must be "material," of some importance, and not a trivial irrelevancy. Guilt or innocence turns not on accuracy, but on state of mind. For that reason, it is an extremely difficult crime to detect, prosecute, and prove.

Mounting evidence suggests that the broad public commitment to telling the truth under oath has been breaking down, eroding over recent decades, a trend that has been accelerating in recent years. Because there are no statistics, it's impossible to know for certain how much lying afflicts the judicial process, and whether it's worse now than in previous decades. Street criminals have always lied when confronted by law enforcement. But prosecutors have told me repeatedly that a surge of concerted, deliberate lying by a different class of criminal—sophisticated, educated, affluent, and represented in many cases by the best lawyers—threatens to swamp the legal system and undermine the prosecution of white-collar crime. Perjury is committed all too often at the highest levels of business, media, politics, sports, culture—even the legal profession itself—by people celebrated for their achievements, followed avidly by the media, and held up as role models.

"It's nearing a crisis," James Comey, the former deputy attorney general and U.S. Attorney who prosecuted Martha Stewart, told me. "People think the government is omnipotent. The truth is, this is an honor system. We count on the fact that witnesses will testify, produce documents and other evidence, and tell the truth. If not, the whole system is reduced to nothing but perjury and obstruction prosecutions."

I have written for many years about business and politics, and as the scandals of the last decade mounted—Enron, WorldCom, Adelphia, Tyco, culminating in the shocking Bernie Madoff Ponzi scheme—it occurred to me that they shared a common thread: lying. Sometimes it wasn't labeled perjury per se, but the essence of fraud is false statements, whether they're accounting statements, SEC filings, or briefings to Wall Street analysts and investors. So many false statements were made in financial statements by business executives that the

Sarbanes-Oxley reforms passed by Congress in 2002 require that chief executives and chief financial officers swear to the accuracy of their financial reports, and if they prove to be false, the executives face criminal prosecution. That such a law would even be necessary would surely have shocked earlier generations of American business leaders.

Lying in politics is hardly novel, but lying under oath by politicians has taken on new dimensions. It's not necessarily a crime to have extramarital sex or to lie about it in press conferences. It is a crime to make false statements under oath. A grand jury investigated former vice presidential nominee and presidential candidate John Edwards, who repeatedly denied having an affair or fathering a child with Rielle Hunter, a woman on his campaign staff, after the *National Enquirer* broke the story in 2007. He eventually issued a press release admitting the allegations. The grand jury is reportedly examining a wide array of potential crimes, including whether Edwards induced an aide to submit a false affidavit claiming that he, not Edwards, was the father of Hunter's child. (The investigation was ongoing and no charges had been filed by the end of 2010.)

In 1999 Arkansas federal judge Susan Webber Wright ruled that President Bill Clinton gave "false, misleading, and evasive answers that were designed to obstruct the judicial process" in the Paula Jones sexual harassment case when he said in sworn testimony that he had never been alone with Monica Lewinsky and had never engaged in any sexual activity with her. (Jones's lawyers had asked Clinton about Lewinsky and other women in order to show a pattern of such behavior.)

Judge Wright issued thirty-two pages of findings and held Clinton in contempt. She referred the matter to the Arkansas Committee on Professional Conduct, which suspended Clinton's license for five years and fined him $25,000. The U.S. Supreme Court subsequently barred him from appearing before the high court. In resolving the criminal investigation against him, Clinton acknowledged that he "knowingly gave evasive and misleading answers" in a sworn deposition, and said, "I tried to walk a fine line between acting lawfully and testifying falsely, but I now recognize that I did not fully accomplish this goal and am certain my responses to questions about Ms. Lewinsky were false." Special Counsel Robert Ray, successor to Kenneth Starr, closed the case without seeking an indictment or further penalties.

Perjury has infected nearly every aspect of society. Consider a sampling from recent years, in roughly chronological order, all involving prominent, successful people:

- Former Los Angeles detective Mark Fuhrman was convicted in 1996 of perjury during the O. J. Simpson trial for testifying that he never used the word "nigger" after an audiotape and numerous witnesses contradicted him.
- British novelist Lord Jeffrey Archer was convicted of perjury and perverting the course of justice in 2001 after he sued the *Daily Star* for libel and testified that he hadn't slept with a prostitute. He also created a fake diary and asked a friend to provide a false alibi for the night in question. The judge called it "as serious an offense of perjury as I have had experience of and have been able to find in the books." Archer was sentenced to four years in prison.
- Merrill Lynch executive James A. Brown was convicted in 2004 of perjury and obstruction of justice for false testimony that he didn't know important details of a Nigerian barge investment that enabled Enron to book a fake profit and falsify its financial results, defrauding investors. He was sentenced to three years and ten months in prison. Three other Merrill Lynch executives were also convicted in the Enron barge scheme and given prison sentences.
- Recording star Kimberly Jones, the rapper known professionally as Lil' Kim, was convicted of perjury and sentenced to a year in prison in 2005 after testifying to a grand jury about a shooting outside radio station Hot 97 FM in New York. She testified she didn't know her manager and a friend were at the site; a videotape showed them there together.
- In 2006, the powerful Milberg Weiss law firm, which made its name representing plaintiffs in large class-action suits, and four of its long-term partners pleaded guilty to federal charges of obstructing justice, perjury, bribery, and fraud. The complaint accused the partners of paying three plaintiffs $11.4 million in illegal kickbacks in about 180 cases spanning twenty-five years, and then repeatedly lying about it to the courts.
- Lord John Browne, the chief executive of international oil giant BP, abruptly resigned in May 2007, after a forty-one-year career at the company. He admitted that he lied in a deposition to the court when he said he met his former lover, Jeff Chevalier, while exercising in London's Battersea Park. They had actually met through an escort service.
- In March 2008, the mayor of Detroit, Kwame Kilpatrick, and his chief of staff, Christine Beatty, with whom he denied having a long-running affair, were charged with multiple felony counts including perjury,

misconduct in office, and obstruction of justice. Kilpatrick pleaded guilty to obstruction of justice and served ninety-nine days in jail. He was subsequently convicted of lying under oath about his affair with Beatty and sentenced to up to five years in prison.

- The former Chicago police commander Jon Burge was convicted in June 2010 of perjury and obstruction of justice for lying in a 2003 civil lawsuit about his use and knowledge of torture of criminal suspects.
- John McTiernan, the director of *Die Hard* and *Predator*, pleaded guilty in July 2010 to two counts of making false statements to the FBI, and one count of perjury for lying to a federal judge. McTiernan denied hiring private investigator Anthony Pellicano, the mastermind of a long-running wiretap conspiracy on behalf of his famous Hollywood clients. Pellicano is currently serving a fifteen-year prison term.
- In August 2010, the baseball legend Roger Clemens was indicted on three counts of making false statements, two counts of perjury, and one count of obstruction of Congress. Prosecutors allege Clemens lied repeatedly to Congress, particularly when he stated under oath, "Let me be clear, I have never taken steroids or HGH [human growth hormone]." He pleaded not guilty and a trial was set for July 2011.
- The governor of New York State, David Paterson, was accused of lying under oath to a state commission about whether he had solicited free tickets to a Yankees baseball game. In August 2010, an independent commission, chaired by Chief Judge Judith Kaye, found that Paterson gave "misleading and inaccurate" testimony, and referred the case to the Albany prosecutor for possible perjury charges.
- Robert Allen Stanford, chairman of Texas-based Stanford Financial Group and the first American to be knighted by the Caribbean nation of Antigua and Barbuda, was accused in June 2009 of running an $8 billion Ponzi scheme and indicted on numerous counts of mail fraud, wire fraud, and obstruction of justice, including making numerous false statements. Laura Pendergest-Holt, his chief financial officer and a Stanford board member, was charged with obstruction and conspiracy and with lying to the SEC in sworn testimony in February 2009. Stanford's knighthood was revoked in 2010.

This surge of perjury cases at the highest levels of business, politics, media, and culture poses some fundamental questions: Why would people with so much to lose put so much at risk by lying under oath? Whatever they may have done, why would they compound their problems by committing an independent felony, punishable by prison? What were the consequences? And what price are all of us paying for their behavior?

I set out to answer these questions by examining recent cases of perjury by people at the pinnacle of their fields. They come from the worlds of media, business, politics, sports, law, and Wall Street—just about every center of power and influence in American society. They enjoyed money, fame, power, and celebrity to a degree that most people can only dream of. Yet they shattered their lives and those of people around them while inflicting untold damage on society as a whole. I believe that only by exploring these fascinating cases in depth do the answers to my questions emerge.

Most instances of perjury are very difficult to assess, because sworn testimony is often delivered in secrecy, before a grand jury, or as part of a confidential investigation. All of the lies in these cases were told in circumstances that at the time were veiled in secrecy. In each of these cases, I was able to obtain transcripts of such testimony or notes taken by FBI agents or other investigators. They provide a rare look at the very moment these people made the fateful choice to lie.

That a witness will raise his hand, swear to tell the truth, and then do so is a breathtakingly simple proposition on which the entire American legal system rests. These cases tell us what happens when that proposition breaks down.

Tangled Webs

Part One

MARTHA STEWART

ONE

"Can I Go Now?"

Douglas Faneuil hurried into the Merrill Lynch office, on the twenty-second floor of 1251 Avenue of the Americas, one of the large office towers across from the Radio City Music Hall. It was December 27, 2001, and Rockefeller Center was still decked in its holiday decorations, but the midtown streets had a subdued post-holiday feel. Faneuil was looking forward to a quiet week; his boss, Peter Bacanovic, was away on vacation. Merrill Lynch's Rockefeller Center offices had the dark paneling and conservative decor common to investment banks and trust companies, suggesting nothing reckless would ever happen there.

Faneuil had neatly cropped dark blond hair, a slender build, and boyish good looks. He wore a suit and tie, both to emulate his boss, who was always impeccably dressed, and to appear professional.

From his cubicle Faneuil could see through the interior glass wall of Bacanovic's office and out the windows to the neighboring skyscrapers. Faneuil knew little about Bacanovic's life outside the office, and Bacanovic rarely discussed it. Bacanovic was thirty-nine years old, handsome, often sought after as a desirable single man for society dinner parties. His name regularly appeared in society columns. He'd been educated at a Swiss boarding school and spoke fluent French.

Since Bacanovic was on vacation in Florida, Faneuil was answering all calls and handling anything that came up. He and Bacanovic had split the Christmas holiday period; Faneuil had taken off the week before Christmas. Faneuil thought it was typical of Bacanovic's thoughtfulness. Indeed, Faneuil considered Bacanovic the best boss he'd ever had, the first who seemed genuinely interested in him as a person.

Sometimes Faneuil wondered how he'd ended up with a budding career in the financial industry. At Vassar College he'd studied art and wanted to be a sculptor. After he graduated, he moved to Brooklyn, hung out with other artists, and struggled to make ends meet. He couldn't count on any assistance from his divorced parents. His father lived in Boston on a modest inheritance that left little for his son. Faneuil wasn't quite sure why his father had never held a regular job. His mother had remarried and lived on Cape Cod. Pressed for funds, Faneuil had responded to an ad for artists looking to supplement their income. D. E. Shaw, a hedge fund, had placed the ad in a quest for some people with unconventional backgrounds, people with interests outside of finance. When told the salary was $38,000 a year, Faneuil laughed. It seemed like a fortune. After he took the job, his mother baked a sheet cake, which she decorated like a dollar bill.

Faneuil began with relatively routine back-office accounting tasks, but within a few years was compiling and delivering to Shaw the firm's daily profit-and-loss statement. While he still lacked any burning interest in finance, he found he had a knack for it. He worked hard and tried to do a good job. He got steady raises and by 2001 was earning $60,000. Compared with his artist friends, he was wealthy.

Faneuil was at a birthday party for a coworker when he ran into Zeva Bellel, a friend from Vassar who had moved to Paris. She in turn introduced him to Rob Haskell, who was working as an editor at *W* magazine, a spin-off from *Women's Wear Daily* that chronicled the fashion and society elite. Haskell had grown up in Brookline, Massachusetts, close to Faneuil. He'd graduated from Yale, and their paths had crossed briefly when Haskell visited Bellel at Vassar. The two agreed to have lunch. That same week, Faneuil was devastated by news that his sister had committed suicide. Haskell was sympathetic and supportive. Soon they were dating.

Haskell seemed enamored of the glamorous, wealthy Manhattan lifestyle chronicled by *W*. He kept encouraging Faneuil to become a trader and make even more money. Haskell knew a stockbroker who needed an assistant. By chance they met at the ballet, and Haskell introduced Faneuil to Peter Bacanovic. He seemed charming; Faneuil followed up with a call, and then an interview at Bacanovic's office. Bacanovic confided that he hadn't really planned on being a stockbroker either and always thought he wanted to be a

Hollywood agent or film producer. Bacanovic told Faneuil that if he got the job, he'd take him under his wing, and eventually Faneuil could have clients of his own.

Faneuil didn't say much. He listened, but he had other ideas. He thought about starting a nonprofit to help struggling artists find affordable studio space. His ambitions were vague but altruistic.

Deeply shaken by his sister's death, and still unsure about his career choice, Faneuil quit his job at D. E. Shaw in April 2001. With his savings, he and Haskell took a trip to Paris, where they visited Bellel. Faneuil continued on his own to Spain. He figured he'd ponder his future while traveling. One evening he climbed a hillside outside Toledo and sat looking down on the beautiful old city. He watched the sunset. Later he wrote about his thoughts in his diary: "What is this inclination of mine to help other people before I have a life or any money of my own?" Haskell was right. He should make some money and then help others. When he got back to New York, his savings exhausted, there was a message from Bacanovic's assistant: "Congratulations! You got the job."

When Faneuil got in that morning, December 27, he already had phone messages. Even before he could retrieve them, the phone started ringing. When he answered, a woman identified herself as Aliza Waksal. She sounded a little groggy, as if she'd just been awakened from a sound sleep. Faneuil had never spoken to her before, but he knew she was the daughter of Sam Waksal, one of Bacanovic's most important clients and the chief executive of ImClone Systems. Aliza, a graduate student at New York University and an aspiring actress, had never called the office or executed a trade, so far as Faneuil knew, but now she was interrupting a ski vacation in Idaho, where it was just 7:00 a.m. "I want to sell all my ImClone shares," she said.

Faneuil looked at her account on the computer and saw she owned 39,472 shares, worth over $2.5 million. He wasn't sure he could simply sell the shares when her father was the company's CEO. Still, they didn't seem to be restricted. He said he'd get back to her.

The phone rang again. "Did you get my fax?"

It was Alan Goldberg, Sam Waksal's accountant. Faneuil rarely dealt with Goldberg himself. He usually spoke directly with Bacanovic, who'd often said he was pushy and offensive.

"No, I haven't had a chance to check the fax machine."

"Is Peter there?"

Faneuil said he was on vacation.

"Then we've got a lot to do today," Goldberg said. "Ignore your other business. I want you to act like I'm Peter's only client."

Faneuil wasn't sure what to say.

"Here's what I want you to do: Sell all of Sam's [ImClone] shares right away."

Faneuil hadn't been sure about Aliza, but he was all but certain he couldn't just sell Waksal's shares. On the computer screen they were designated with "R" for restricted, in red. Restricted shares can only be sold pursuant to SEC Rule 144, which sets certain conditions and usually requires that a lawyer certify the conditions have been met.

"Alan, I can't just put in the trade," Faneuil said, mentioning Rule 144.

"Okay," Goldberg said. Faneuil was surprised he seemed to accept this without argument. "The fax instructs you to transfer all of Sam's shares to Aliza's account. You've got to do this immediately. Then sell them once they're in her account."

Faneuil doubted this brazen attempt to evade the restriction would work, but he stayed calm. He prided himself on his cool demeanor in crises. "Alan, you can't just do that. The shares are still restricted, even if they're in Aliza's account."

"Do me a favor and ask Peter," Goldberg said, sounding annoyed. He hung up.

Faneuil hated calling Bacanovic so soon; it was barely nine-thirty, and Bacanovic hadn't even been in Florida twenty-four hours. But this was one of Bacanovic's biggest accounts, the transaction was large (Sam Waksal had nearly 80,000 ImClone shares worth nearly $5 million in his account at Merrill, although they were margined, since Waksal had borrowed heavily against them), and it raised all kinds of issues. Faneuil reached Bacanovic on his cell phone, and briefed him on the Waksal activity.

Bacanovic seemed to take the unusual developments in stride, told him to execute the trade for Aliza—the shares weren't restricted—but to check with a manager about Sam Waksal's request. Faneuil put through the order for Aliza, realizing a total of $2.46 million. Then he found Julia Perez, the only manager in the office that day, and told her about Waksal's request to transfer the shares to his daughter. "We can't do that, right?" he asked.

"Absolutely not," she concurred.

On the way back to his desk, Faneuil stopped at the fax machine. There was the fax from Goldberg:

"Urgent: Immediate attention required. Dear Peter: Please transfer the entire balance in the above referenced account to the account of my daughter, Aliza Waksal . . . including all shares of ImClone and the related margin balance. It is imperative that this transfer take place tomorrow morning, December 27, first thing." The last sentence was underlined.

Faneuil called Goldberg, told him he received the fax but that his manager had blocked the sale. Goldberg ordered him to transfer the shares to Aliza's account anyway. Faneuil said he'd see what he could do. Aliza called again, asking if he'd gotten the fax and was making the transfer.

He'd barely hung up when another Waksal called, Elana Waksal Posner, Waksal's sister.

"What's ImClone at? What's the stock at?" she demanded. She sounded like she was on a cell phone in her car.

Faneuil said it was just above $60.

"Shit," she said. "It's already going down." She hung up, but called back soon after. Her husband was in the background, and they argued about whether to sell her ImClone shares. Faneuil listened patiently. Finally she said, "I'm selling." But when Faneuil checked, he discovered she didn't have any ImClone shares in her Merrill account with Bacanovic. "Oh, they must be in my other accounts," she said, and hung up. (They were in her online Merrill account.)

Faneuil kept looking for a way to transfer or sell Sam Waksal's shares, but the legal department blocked him, reporting that there was "news pending" on the company preventing any sales by officers. It was the first Faneuil had heard about any news. He relayed this development to Goldberg, who seemed annoyed. Shortly after, Sam Waksal himself called, demanding to know why he couldn't sell his shares. When Faneuil mentioned there was news pending, he shouted, "That's ridiculous! There's no pending news!" Then he slammed down the phone.

Faneuil reached Bacanovic again.

Faneuil said Goldberg was really pressing him, wouldn't take no for an answer. "Take it with a grain of salt," Bacanovic told him. "He's always very demanding, but don't worry about it."

Faneuil also described the calls from Aliza and Elana. "Why is [Goldberg] so frantic? Why are they acting so crazy? What do you think is going on?" Faneuil asked.

There was a pause. Suddenly Bacanovic interjected, "Oh my God! We've got to get Martha! Get her on the phone."

From humble beginnings in New Jersey, Martha Stewart had vaulted from stockbroker, to caterer, to cookbook author, to Kmart spokeswoman, to magazine creator and editor, to a one-woman lifestyle conglomerate. She was indisputably talented, with a keen aesthetic sensibility, unerring taste, and an encyclopedic command of household skills. She was also ambitious, a perfectionist, a workaholic, stubborn, and, at times, a harridan.

Through sheer drive, determination, hard work, and an unerring instinct for self-promotion, Stewart had transformed herself into a ubiquitous one-woman brand—"Martha"—and her name into a widely used adjective, as in "That holiday centerpiece is so Martha."

Stewart and Bacanovic had struck up a friendship while Stewart's only child, her daughter, Alexis, was dating Sam Waksal. Bacanovic had worked at ImClone for two years, had stayed in contact with Waksal, and Waksal had introduced him first to the younger Stewart, then to her mother. The photogenic Bacanovic showed up in several spreads in *Martha Stewart Living*, including a brunch feature in which he, Stewart, and other guests were pictured wearing bathrobes. A framed photo from the shoot was the only personal photo Bacanovic had in his office.

When Waksal learned that his former employee had become a stockbroker, he opened an account with him at Merrill Lynch, as well as one for his daughter, Aliza. Stewart had steered her company's pension account to him and had recently consolidated more of her accounts with him. With clients like the Waksals and Stewart, Bacanovic was a rising star at Merrill Lynch, his future secure.

Bacanovic and Waksal seemed to have much in common besides their mutual friendship with Stewart, at least on the surface. Like Bacanovic, Waksal could be charming and charismatic. Both were children of immigrants: Greek in Bacanovic's case, Polish in Waksal's. Waksal's father fought in the Polish resistance during World War II, and his mother was a concentration camp survivor. Waksal grew up in modest circumstances in Ohio, where he attended public schools and Ohio State. He earned a PhD in immunology, did research in Israel, and landed a postdoctoral position at Stanford. He had become enormously wealthy, and often hosted glamorous, celebrity-studded parties in his sprawling loft in Manhattan's trendy SoHo neighborhood. His rise had seemed meteoric.

Despite his financial success, Waksal's career had been shadowed, though never derailed, by allegations of a series of disturbing and at times bizarre ethical lapses. The *Wall Street Journal* reported that Waksal was asked to leave Stanford after the doctor in charge of the lab concluded Waksal had lied about the source of antibodies he'd obtained from the Sloan-Kettering Institute in New York. Waksal subsequently apologized and told another doctor that he "was seeking psychiatric help and had changed," according to the *Journal*.

Waksal moved to the prestigious National Cancer Institute. But his colleagues there reported a disturbing pattern: "When the critical time came to deliver his part of the collaboration, there would be a catastrophe of some sort—a tissue culture would become contaminated or the mice would develop an infection and have to be killed," the supervising doctor told the *Journal*. His research fellowship was not renewed.

Nonetheless, Waksal moved to Tufts University, outside Boston, where his brother Harlan was a medical resident. There allegations were even more serious: that Waksal fabricated laboratory results. In one bizarre episode he was accused of impersonating his brother, while Harlan himself was arrested in the Fort Lauderdale airport carrying more than two pounds of cocaine. In 1982 Harlan was convicted of possession of a controlled substance with intent to distribute and sentenced to nine years in prison. On appeal, the search was deemed illegal because Harlan hadn't consented to it, and his conviction was overturned. Still, no one disputed that Harlan was carrying a large quantity of cocaine through an airport.

Sam Waksal's ouster by Tufts didn't prevent him from securing yet another prestigious medical position, this time at New York's Mount Sinai Hospital (Tufts officials later said no one from Mount Sinai conducted any reference checks). Waksal was soon fired amid recurring allegations of fabricated lab results, financial irregularities, and ownership disputes over technology. (Waksal's files at Mount Sinai were sealed as part of a termination settlement the hospital reached with Waksal.)

In part due to Sam Waksal's prestigious résumé, and in part due to an investment frenzy for anything in the biotech field, the Waksal brothers successfully raised $4 million to launch ImClone Systems in 1994 despite their checkered careers. As Waksal told *BusinessWeek* in 2001, he and Harlan "thought we'd focus on infectious diseases, cancer, and diagnostics, make some products, get rich, and retire early." With the money they raised they opened a research lab on the site of an abandoned shoe factory in Manhattan. The company never earned a profit, but in the biotech-crazed 1990s, that hardly mattered. It went public in 1991 at $14 a share, and Bacanovic was one of the employees of the fledgling company who received a few hundred shares in the initial public offering.

Despite many fruitless efforts to develop new drugs, ImClone was essentially a one-drug enterprise, focused most recently on the development of Erbitux, a genetically engineered treatment for colorectal cancer. The Waksals had little to do with developing the drug; they had acquired rights to it. Dr. John Mendelsohn at the University of California developed it, and over the years Erbitux had emerged as the company's leading (indeed, only) potential blockbuster drug. Early trials were so promising that the Food and Drug Administration put Erbitux on a fast-track approval schedule. ImClone's stock price soared, and in September 2001 pharmaceutical giant Bristol-Myers Squibb agreed to pay $2 billion for a 40 percent stake in the company, valuing ImClone at an astonishing $5 billion. This assumed, of course, that Erbitux would be approved by the FDA. The company filed for FDA approval, and on December 20, the FDA said it had reached a decision, which would be announced eight days later, on December 28, 2001.

On Christmas Day a Bristol-Myers executive called Harlan Waksal, who was spending the holiday skiing in Colorado, to report that he'd spoken with an FDA official, and the Erbitux application looked "doomed." Harlan conveyed the news to Sam the next morning, and the brothers embarked on a frantic round of calls to get the FDA to reconsider. But the decision was final, and the next day, when Sam Waksal returned to his office in Manhattan, the company was already drafting a press release to convey the bad news, which would be released after the stock market closed on December 28.

With his lavish standard of living, Sam Waksal gave the appearance of great wealth. He was indeed rich by most standards but lived far beyond his means and was heavily indebted. He had $75 million in personal debt, $50 million of it secured by his ImClone stock. Waksal had taken out a $44 million loan from Bank of America secured by a warrant to purchase ImClone shares. (A warrant is the right to buy shares, in this case, 350,000 shares at $5.50 a share. The warrant was potentially valuable: with ImClone trading at $60 a share, it would be worth over $19 million.) But unknown to Bank of America, Waksal had already executed the warrant by mid-2000. Once exercised, the warrant expired and had no further value. Using it as collateral for a loan was a fraud. When Bank of America asked for verification that the warrant remained in effect, Waksal provided a document with a forged signature of ImClone's general counsel. Like so much about his life and career, when it came to his personal finances Waksal demonstrated an astonishing recklessness and disregard for any legal or ethical constraints.

Should ImClone's price fall—as it surely would on the news that the FDA was denying the Erbitux application—Waksal faced margin calls, forced selling of other assets, and huge potential losses, as well as problems if Bank of America discovered that the warrant no longer existed. And the stock's plunge would not only affect Waksal himself. His family members and friends had also invested in the stock.

As chairman and chief executive, Samuel Waksal was barred by the securities laws from selling stock while possessing inside information, such as the still-secret FDA decision on Erbitux, or from leaking the information to anyone else.

The moment Bacanovic ordered Faneuil to "call Martha," Faneuil had figured out what was going on. Something bad was about to happen to ImClone.

Faneuil placed the call to Stewart's office, with Bacanovic on the line in Florida. The phone rang, and then Stewart's assistant of four years, Ann Armstrong, answered. Stewart was away, traveling. They all hung up, then Bacanovic called Faneuil back. Bacanovic was going to be unreachable for a few hours; Faneuil thought he said something about going out on a boat, though he wasn't sure. Then Bacanovic said, "Listen, Martha's going to call and you've got to tell her what's going on."

Faneuil felt uneasy. He assumed Bacanovic meant that he should tell Stewart about the Waksals' attempts to sell their shares. But he had never discussed one client's transactions with another. He'd only been working at a brokerage firm for six months, and he didn't recall being told anything specifically, but wasn't this possibly illegal insider trading?

"What can I say?" he asked Bacanovic. "Can I tell her about Sam? Am I allowed to?"

"Of course!" Bacanovic sounded irritated at his naiveté. "You must. You've got to. That's the whole point!"

At 1:18 p.m. Faneuil got an e-mail from Bacanovic. "Has news come out yet? Let me know. Thanks. P."

Faneuil replied, "Nothing yet. I'll let you know. No call from Martha either."

. . .

Armstrong, known to everyone in the office as Annie, was intelligent, efficient, organized, and reassuring. Many thought she was too well qualified to be Stewart's assistant, while recognizing that she helped hold the office together. She was middle-aged, slender, with shoulder-length hair streaked with gray. She avoided the limelight surrounding Stewart, and the two didn't socialize outside the office. Still, probably no one on the staff knew Martha—her strengths and weaknesses—better than Armstrong.

Armstrong worked at the magazine headquarters on West Forty-second Street, where Stewart usually spent Mondays and Wednesdays. On Tuesdays and Thursdays Stewart filmed her television show at her studio in Westport, Connecticut, near her home there. She had other assistants, but whenever Bacanovic felt he needed her, he called Armstrong.

When she answered the phone, just after 11:00 a.m. on the twenty-seventh, Armstrong recognized Bacanovic's voice. "I need to speak to Martha."

It had been a quiet morning, so close to Christmas and with Stewart out of the office. Armstrong told Bacanovic that Stewart was en route to a vacation in Mexico, traveling by private jet.

"Can I call her on the plane?" Bacanovic asked. "I need to speak to her about ImClone."

"It's not that easy," Armstrong said. She'd tried on other occasions, and she had to reach the private jet company, which had to phone the pilots, who had to get a message to Stewart. It could take over an hour to get a reply. "She's going to be touching down and I'm sure she'll call the office for messages."

"Tell her, when she calls, that I think ImClone is going to start trading downward," he said. Armstrong carefully wrote the message in a blue notebook she kept at the ready for messages. Then she turned to her computer and typed the same message into Stewart's phone log: "Peter Bacanovic thinks ImClone is going to start trading downward."

"Ask her to call my office," Bacanovic concluded, and then hung up.

Armstrong thought the message was "fishy." She knew to a near certainty that Stewart would act on Bacanovic's information, whatever it was. The stock market in general, and ImClone in particular, was a near obsession with Stewart, who had earlier worked as a stockbroker before quitting to launch her catering business. She had been furious with Bacanovic a few weeks earlier, after ImClone shares rose a few dollars shortly after she sold a large block, on

Bacanovic's recommendation. Armstrong's father had been an active investor, and she knew a good deal about the market and its workings, and what kind of information drove stock prices. She wondered what Bacanovic knew.

Stewart had the peculiar fixation with money that is common to many self-made entrepreneurs, no matter how wealthy they've become. Born in 1941 in Nutley, New Jersey, to working-class Polish Catholic parents and an alcoholic father, she had worked as a housekeeper on Park Avenue to help pay for college at Barnard. One employee recalled that after a photo shoot for the magazine in North Carolina, Stewart insisted that all the food be wrapped and flown home with her. Her personal expenses were often billed to the company; after one half-day photo shoot in her Westport home, Turkey Hill, the company paid for nine days of housekeeping expenses. One year, the company paid Stewart $2 million in "rental fees" for the use of her various homes as sites for photo shoots, the *New York Times* reported. After the 1999 public offering of shares in Martha Stewart Living Omnimedia, Stewart was indisputably wealthy, with a fortune estimated at $1 billion by *Forbes* magazine in August 2000.

Little more than an hour after Bacanovic's call, Stewart phoned from an airport in San Antonio, Texas, where the jet had stopped to refuel. Her companions on the flight and vacation—her close friend Mariana Pasternak and Kevin Sharkey, interior decorating editor at the magazine and a favorite decorator of Stewart's—noticed that she grabbed a phone from a desk as soon as they arrived in the waiting area. Armstrong relayed several messages from magazine staff members as well as Bacanovic's, which Armstrong read to her in its entirety. Stewart didn't react. But after Armstrong patched her into her employees, she told Armstrong to call Bacanovic. "Merrill Lynch, Peter Bacanovic's office," Faneuil answered.

There was a slight pause as Armstrong got off the phone. "Hi, this is Martha," Stewart said.

Given his prior experiences with her, Faneuil was nervous. All of their brief conversations—there had been three or four—had been unpleasant. Bacanovic didn't want Faneuil to talk to Stewart if it could be avoided, and had given him strict instructions to get him ASAP when Stewart called. One time Faneuil put her on hold, and Bacanovic told him to pick up and make conversation while he gathered some information. Faneuil returned to Stewart's line, but before he could say anything, Stewart had erupted. "Do you know what I've just had to listen to? I can't believe people have to put up with this shit."

Merrill Lynch's phone system played classical music whenever someone was put on hold.

"You tell Peter that if I ever have to put up with this shit again I'm taking my money elsewhere." She slammed down the phone without saying good-bye.

On another occasion, Stewart's call was transferred to the receptionist, who answered it and sent it back to Faneuil. The receptionist spoke with a mild speech impediment. When Faneuil picked up the phone, Stewart yelled at him, "Do you know who the hell is answering your phones? You call and you know what he sounds like? He says this . . ." Stewart, as Faneuil later wrote in an e-mail describing the incident, "made the most ridiculous sound I've heard coming from an adult in quite some time, kind of like a lion roaring underwater."

Faneuil laughed. He thought she was joking.

"This is not a joke!" Stewart shouted. "Merrill Lynch is laying off ten thousand employees because of people like that idiot." She slammed down the phone.

Faneuil e-mailed a colleague: "I have never, ever been treated more rudely by a stranger on the telephone."

That Stewart could be rude, profane, impatient, self-centered, mercurial, and dictatorial was documented in best-selling books like *Martha Inc.* by Christopher Byron and *Just Desserts* by Jerry Oppenheimer. Nearly everyone working at Martha Stewart Omnimedia had witnessed, or been subjected to, one of her fits of anger. So far as anyone knew, she never apologized or acknowledged she might be wrong. As one longtime employee put it, "She has her ways of trying to make amends, but they do not include the words 'I'm sorry.'"

Over the years, she had left a trail of discarded and disaffected former friends, business associates, and employees. By the time she sold her ImClone shares, she had only a handful of people who could reliably be considered friends. These included the Waksals, Johnny Pigozzi, Mariana Pasternak, and Charles Simonyi, the wealthy former Microsoft executive she was widely reported to be dating. She was also close to Susan Magrino, her longtime public relations adviser; Sharon Patrick, the chief executive of Martha Stewart Living Omnimedia; and Sharkey, all of whom also had a business relationship with her.

Still, there were many loyal and longtime employees, and thousands more who sent résumés and wanted to work for her. Stewart had made many people rich beyond their dreams.

For a while Bacanovic had seemed on the brink of joining the charmed

circle of people who were genuinely close to Stewart. But recently the relationship between Stewart and Bacanovic had become strained as technology stocks
plunged and the September 11 attacks had sent the economy deeper into recession. One e-mail began:

> Peter: do nothing. The account is a mess, as is the pension account.
> I think we need to go over each and every item and evaluate the entire
> scenario. I think it's time for me to give my money to a professional
> money manager who will watch it when I'm too busy and will take a bit
> more care about overall market conditions and political and economic
> problems. We have just watched the slide and done nothing, and I'm
> none too happy. I've made two or three horrendous mistakes and not sold
> when I was still far ahead. Please call me and I'll work with you.

Other Martha Stewart employees who were using Bacanovic because of
the pension accounts were also starting to complain. Apart from his undeni-
able ability to attract and charm clients, it's not at all clear that Bacanovic was
a particularly good stock picker or financial planner. He was swept up in the
technology and telecommunications mania of the late 1990s, and some of his
favorite stocks, former clients recall, were AOL and Amazon.com, both hard
hit in the crash, and Urbanfetch, which went bankrupt. One Stewart employee
recalls asking Bacanovic what would happen in a downturn. "Don't worry, I'm
really good at managing a down market," Bacanovic had replied. But he had
only been a broker since 1992—and there hadn't been any down markets since,
until the tech bubble burst in 2000. Apart from a few tech favorites, Faneuil's
impression was that Bacanovic simply followed the recommendations of Merrill's research department. But he had Faneuil buy expensive leather binders to
dress up his clients' account reviews.

That year Stewart certainly had plenty of losses she could blame on Bacanovic. Among them were losses of $59,931 in Amazon, $77,200 in Digex,
$113,490 in Lucent, and $65,000 in Sunbeam. All had once been market favorites; only Amazon survived.

As the market continued to drop precipitously from its March 2000 peak,
Faneuil knew Bacanovic was under mounting stress, especially from Stewart, his
most important client by far. In Faneuil's presence he often referred to Stewart
as "the blonde," "the bitch," or the "blonde bitch." In one e-mail to Faneuil he
referred to her as "that witch."

Faneuil had been dreading yet another direct encounter with Stewart, and now one was at hand.

"What's going on with Sam?" Stewart demanded impatiently, with no preliminaries.

Despite what Bacanovic had told him, Faneuil was determined to say as little as possible. "Well, we have no news on the company, but Peter thought you might like to act on the information that Sam Waksal was trying to sell all of his shares." So were Aliza and Elana, he added.

"All of his shares?" Stewart sounded incredulous.

"Well, I'm sure he doesn't have all of his shares here at Merrill, but what he does have he is trying to sell."

"Where is ImClone now?"

Faneuil told her it was at $58, down two points. There was a brief pause, and then Stewart erupted.

"It's unbelievable I wouldn't get a call! What kind of program are you running over there? It's down $2 and no one calls me?"

Faneuil's heart was racing. Then he realized she'd misunderstood him. "I'm sorry, it's down 2 percent, not $2. I'll never say points again."

Now Stewart was screaming as she berated him for this display of incompetence. Finally she paused, her anger seemingly spent.

"I want to sell all my shares."

"Do you want to place a limit?" Faneuil asked. Since it was a large trade, he thought she might not want to sell below a certain point. "You might want to protect yourself on the downside."

"No. I want to sell at the market. How am I going to find out about the sale?"

"Well, Ms. Stewart, I could e-mail Annie . . ."

Stewart erupted again, shouting at him, "Absolutely not! You have no right to tell Annie Armstrong about my personal transactions!"

"I'm sorry," he stammered. "I didn't mean to imply I'd send the details, just that the trade was executed."

"Absolutely not! You can't do that. You can't tell Annie anything about what goes on in my account." Faneuil couldn't believe he had again managed to set off Bacanovic's most important client. She told him to e-mail the results to her personal e-mail account, and then abruptly hung up without saying good-bye or giving him the chance to ask for her personal e-mail address. Faneuil's heart was pounding.

Faneuil placed the sell order at the market price. Stewart's 3,928 shares were sold in two blocks, one at 1:51 p.m., and the other a minute later. But without her e-mail address, he couldn't report the transaction. He'd have to wait for Peter.

S till at the airport in San Antonio, Stewart immediately placed a call to Waksal at ImClone headquarters. Emily Perret, his secretary, answered.

"Get Sam. This is Martha." Even by Stewart's standards, she sounded abrupt and impatient.

Perret said Waksal wasn't there.

"There's something going on with ImClone. Do you know what it is?" Stewart asked.

"No," Perret said.

"I need you to go find him."

Perret said she couldn't do that, but would give him her message as soon as he returned. Stewart didn't sound satisfied, but told her to have him call her at the Las Ventanas resort in Cabo San Lucas, Mexico.

B acanovic finally called the office at about 3:30 p.m. "Did she call?" he asked Faneuil.

Faneuil told him everything that had happened, including that he'd angered Stewart with his suggestion that he confirm the trade through Armstrong. Bacanovic seemed to take the news in stride and gave him Stewart's personal e-mail address. Faneuil wrote her that the shares had been sold at an average price of $58.4325. "As always feel free to call me with any questions at Peter's number. Sincerely, Douglas Faneuil."

That evening, Faneuil met his boyfriend, Rob Haskell, at Haskell's apartment in Chelsea. Faneuil lived nearby, and although they had separate apartments, they spent most nights together. "You wouldn't believe what happened today," Faneuil told him, recounting the day's saga. Haskell seemed impressed that Faneuil had been at the center of so much activity, talking directly to a celebrity like Martha Stewart.

Later that evening, Faneuil called his father and recounted the same story. But his father reacted differently from Haskell. "Should you be telling people about this?" he wondered, sounding somewhat worried. Faneuil didn't see why not. What was the harm?

. . .

The luxury resort Las Ventanas is perched on the southern tip of the Baja California peninsula with spectacular views of the Pacific. Stewart and Pasternak
had checked into a suite with its own butler service. Stewart had forgotten to
make a reservation for Sharkey, so she had ordered a roll-out bed for the living
room. The three had been relaxing around the pool, going to the beach, frequent-
ing the spa, and enjoying the resort's vaunted cuisine. Stewart had bumped into
financier Steve Schwarzman, the cofounder and chief executive of Blackstone
Group, a big private equity and investment advisory firm. Schwarzman wasn't a
close friend, but the two knew each other socially in New York, and they had a
brief conversation. On Sunday, Stewart and her companions took an organized
hike through the rocky, desert terrain on the peninsula. Afterward, Stewart and
Pasternak spent the evening relaxing on chaises on the terrace, drinks in hand.
"Well, here we are again," Stewart said. "Just the two of us on a holiday with no
male companionship." (Sharkey evidently didn't count.)

Pasternak commiserated, and the two began discussing what various friends
were doing for New Year's Eve.

"What's Sam doing?" Pasternak asked, referring to Waksal.

"He disappeared again," Stewart replied. She added that he'd been "walking funny" at a Christmas party, and that he was selling his ImClone stock. So
was his daughter, Aliza. But Merrill Lynch wouldn't sell it, Stewart reported.
Then "his stock went down." Fortunately, Stewart had sold her ImClone shares
before the Erbitux announcement. "Isn't it nice to have brokers who tell you
these things?" she commented—or so Pasternak later recalled. She really wasn't
all that interested in ImClone.

As soon as he got home from work on December 28, Brian Schimpfhauser
turned on his television to CNBC to check on that day's market news, as
he did on most days. Schimpfhauser worked at Merrill Lynch, but downtown
at 222 Broadway, far from the glamour of Rockefeller Center. He worked in
compliance, as a surveillance officer, looking for evidence of improper or illegal trading. As he tuned in that Friday afternoon, he heard the news that the
FDA had rejected ImClone's application for Erbitux. Schimpfhauser had never
heard of ImClone, but he knew the likely impact of a decision like that on a

biotechnology stock. He made a mental note: "That stock is going down when it opens on Monday."

As soon as he arrived at the office Monday, New Year's Eve, Schimpfhauser made a list of ImClone's top officers, including Sam and Harlan Waksal. He read a summary of its business, and examined recent trading patterns. They already looked suspicious: that Thursday and Friday, just before the Erbitux news, ImClone stock had been trending down on heavier than usual trading volume. When the market opened that morning, Schimpfhauser's prediction was confirmed: ImClone shares opened sharply lower at $45.39, down nearly $10 from Friday's closing price. Schimpfhauser ordered a computer run on ImClone trading by Merrill Lynch clients during the two weeks preceding the announcement.

When Schimpfhauser glanced over the results, he immediately noticed the name Waksal: both Aliza and Elana. Besides the trading, he saw the transfer of Sam's shares to Aliza's account. This was startling. In his six years at the firm, he'd never seen activity like this in the family of a chief executive the day before an important, market-moving announcement. This was obviously a potential legal problem. As Schimpfhauser later recalled, "Some bells and whistles went off in my head." The results also showed that Aliza Waksal had traded through the Rockefeller office; Elana, however, had executed her trade without a broker, using a Merrill Lynch online account. Then he noticed the name directly above Aliza's on the computer printout: Martha Stewart. She, too, had traded through the Rockefeller Center office. This was getting too big for Schimpfhauser alone. He took the information to Stephen Snyder, his immediate supervisor, who in turn notified David Marcus, Merrill Lynch's associate general counsel.

Later that morning, Judy Monaghan called Bacanovic's office and Doug Faneuil answered the phone, explaining that Bacanovic was on vacation. Monaghan was a compliance officer and also handled personnel matters in the Rockefeller Center office. She was warm, direct, and down-to-earth, and Faneuil liked her. She told him to have Peter give her a call.

"I got a call from our surveillance unit," she told Bacanovic. "We need to ask some questions about trades on the twenty-seventh." It was Bacanovic's first official query about the ImClone trading. Bacanovic said she should speak to Faneuil, since he had handled the Waksal trades. "What about Martha Stewart?" Monaghan asked. Bacanovic said somewhat vaguely that the sale was a "follow-up" to an earlier conversation about selling the shares.

Monaghan walked over toward Faneuil's cubicle, where Faneuil was standing. "What's up?" he asked.

"What's going on with these ImClone trades?" She said she was fielding some questions from surveillance, and Faneuil went through the events of the twenty-seventh involving the Waksals, but didn't say anything about Martha Stewart. He said he'd been consulting with Julia Perez, the manager he'd asked about the Waksal sale. Then Monaghan looked directly at him. "Was the Martha Stewart trade solicited?" (A solicited trade is one in which the broker suggests the transaction; an unsolicited trade is one in which the client initiates the order.)

"No," Faneuil answered quickly, even though he wasn't entirely sure. Bacanovic had initiated the call to Stewart, but she had called back and made the decision to sell. Since being told by Bacanovic to disclose the information to Stewart, he'd assumed everything was okay. But now some of his earlier doubts came back.

Monaghan left. Slightly panicked, Faneuil asked to borrow a cell phone from a coworker. He didn't want to call Bacanovic on the Merrill line, which would leave a record.

"Peter," he began, "Judy just asked me all sorts of questions about the ImClone trades. She asked me if the Martha trade was solicited. I said no. Was it?"

Bacanovic, who tended to speak at a rapid-fire pace under normal circumstances, now started yelling, the words pouring forth in a torrent. "It was tax-loss selling! It was tax-loss selling!" He said he and Stewart had a preexisting plan that had to be executed before the end of the year.

Faneuil tried to interrupt, but he couldn't say anything, because Bacanovic talked right over him. "It was tax-loss selling. Right? Right? Right?" Faneuil still hadn't been able to get an answer as to whether the trade was solicited or not. Faneuil was silent.

"Okay?" Bacanovic asked. Faneuil still didn't answer. "Okay?" Bacanovic pressed.

"Okay," Faneuil finally mumbled.

Faneuil tried to calm himself. So this is how it's going to be, he thought. His mind was reeling. Bacanovic wasn't dealing with reality. He, Faneuil, had conveyed the Waksal news to Stewart and she decided to sell. No other explanation was even remotely true. The tax-loss-selling explanation was preposterous. Tax-loss selling requires selling shares at a loss to offset gains, and these shares had been sold at a gain. He thought he and Bacanovic could have dealt with the situation, but he hadn't been able to get a word in. He was worried, but surely, he thought, Bacanovic would come to his senses.

That night, New Year's Eve, Faneuil went out with Haskell and some friends and started drinking. Eventually he and a few others, all "wasted," as Faneuil put it, ended up at a Brooklyn club called Luxx. Faneuil took some of the recreational drug Ecstasy, something he almost never did, hoping to erase from his memory the previous day's events. He stayed out until 6:00 a.m.

The day after New Year's, Monaghan summoned Faneuil to her office at 10:00 a.m. Jim Porz, head of the Rockefeller branch office, was there, so he knew this was a big deal. Snyder, the compliance officer, was on the phone. "This is a big deal," Snyder said, raising his voice. "I don't know what the hell happened, but someone is going down for this. Heads are going to roll! You are going to be questioned by law enforcement. This is huge." Faneuil was terrified. Monaghan tried to reassure him, and said she'd go with him to Merrill's compliance offices on lower Broadway and that Merrill Lynch lawyers would be there to represent his interests. "Doug, just tell the truth," Porz told him once he calmed down. "Everything will be all right. Just make sure you tell the truth and you'll be fine. It'll be simple, a walk in the park. I know you're a little bit nervous, but you'll be fine."

Faneuil immediately returned to his cubicle and again called Bacanovic. "Jesus, Peter. They sat me down. Porz said heads are going to roll. I've got to testify."

Bacanovic started repeating the tax-loss-selling story. Once again, he spoke in such a rapid-fire style that Faneuil couldn't say anything. Bacanovic never said that this is the story Faneuil should tell the SEC, but to Faneuil, the implication was obvious. Then Bacanovic hung up.

Moments later Bacanovic called Faneuil with some routine questions about other accounts and what was happening at the office. He made no mention of Stewart or the SEC. It was as if their earlier conversation had never happened.

Faneuil was torn. He decided he would do his best not to lie. He was certainly not going to repeat the tax-loss-selling explanation, which made no sense. He wasn't going to tell Bacanovic's lies for him. On the other hand, he didn't want to get Bacanovic into trouble. Bacanovic had done so much for him. He'd treated him well. He was his boss and he felt he owed him a duty of loyalty. It was becoming obvious that telling Stewart about the Waksal trading was improper at best, possibly illegal. He didn't want to get into that. He decided he'd be as truthful as possible, short of implicating Bacanovic in something bad.

The next morning, when Faneuil got into the office, he was shocked when Monaghan said they were going downtown and he'd be testifying that very day. He thought he had at least another twenty-four hours to prepare himself. They took the subway, and when they arrived at 222 Broadway, an array of lawyers was waiting: Marcus, Snyder, and two others. Faneuil was terrified, but he managed to repeat his story, leaving out the details about the Stewart trade. When they finished questioning him, Marcus said they were going to call the SEC. He had his hand on the speakerphone ready to place the call, and then stopped. "Before we do," he said, "we want you to know you don't have to go through with this. You don't have to talk to the SEC if you don't want to. We can all go home right now. And you can get your own lawyer too." He said Merrill would pick up the fees.

The offer was tempting. But to stop now and ask for a lawyer would be like waving a red flag, immediately implicating himself. He didn't really have a chance to think. "No, it's okay," Faneuil said.

Marcus placed the call. Helene Glotzer, the SEC's regional director in New York, and Jill Slansky, senior counsel, came on the line. They introduced themselves, and Slansky explained that this was just a preliminary investigation into ImClone trading, and that Faneuil was not a target. They asked him to answer to the best of his recollection and not to speculate. And he must answer truthfully. Even though the interview wasn't under oath, failure to do so was a federal crime. Did he understand that? Faneuil said he did.

Faneuil felt he was truthful—up to a point. He answered everything they asked about the Waksal trading and events leading up to it, which by his estimate accounted for 98 percent of the interview. There were only a couple of questions about Martha Stewart. He said she'd called, asked for a quote on ImClone, and after he provided it, told him she wanted to sell her shares. That was all. They didn't ask any follow-up questions. What he said was true in the narrowest sense.

Everyone congratulated Faneuil when the interview was over. The SEC didn't seem interested in Martha Stewart! He didn't care about the Waksals. Bacanovic wasn't involved in that and Faneuil had told the truth. Maybe he didn't have to worry.

That evening Bacanovic called. "What did they ask about?"

"You know, Peter, they really didn't focus on Martha at all. They mostly asked about Sam. But they did ask me about Martha."

"What did you say?"

"I just told them that Martha asked for a quote and sold her stock."

"Good," Bacanovic said.

The next day, Faneuil was trying to put the whole Martha Stewart mess out of his mind. Then Heidi DeLuca called. She was Stewart's personal accountant, and she sounded annoyed.

"Doug, what's up with this ImClone trade?"

Faneuil felt a sinking feeling. Now what? He tried to sound nonchalant. "I don't know. What's up?"

"Well, this ImClone trade completely screwed up our tax-loss-selling plan. We had everything down perfectly, and this screwed it all up! What happened?"

If he'd needed any further evidence that Bacanovic's insistence about the tax-loss selling was a fabrication, this was it. Of course the trade had screwed things up, because the whole point of tax-loss selling was to generate losses, and ImClone was a gain. "I don't know," he told her. "You'll have to speak to Peter," who was still on vacation. As soon as he finished, Faneuil put his head in his hands. He looked so devastated that an intern working nearby came over to console him. He insisted he'd be okay, but then again borrowed someone else's cell phone and called Bacanovic.

"Peter, what the hell is going on? Heidi DeLuca just called me." He told him how upset she was that the ImClone sale had screwed up the tax-loss-selling plan.

Bacanovic erupted again. "Martha Stewart sold that stock because there was a predetermined price at which we decided to sell!" It was a replay of their conversation about the tax-loss selling, with Bacanovic talking rapidly and constantly, only this time the alibi was that Stewart had decided to sell if ImClone shares hit $60. Faneuil wanted to interrupt. He felt like screaming, "This story is utter bullshit and you're acting like an idiot." Once again, he couldn't find an opening.

"Okay?" Bacanovic breathlessly concluded. "Okay? Okay?"

Faneuil grudgingly acceded, just to get off the phone. He was stunned that Bacanovic had changed his story without even acknowledging the prior tax-loss-selling rationale. Faneuil knew the $60 story was equally false. He'd never heard a word from Bacanovic about any decision to sell ImClone at $60, as he surely would have, since Bacanovic was away and Faneuil was monitoring the markets.

Besides, when he spoke to Judy Monaghan, she, too, told him that Bacanovic had ascribed the trade to tax-loss selling.

Faneuil's anxiety came back in full force. He was haunted by Slansky's warning that failure to tell the truth was a crime. He felt he'd never seriously done anything wrong in his life. He thought of himself as a good citizen, a moral person. Until his testimony, he'd done nothing wrong in the ImClone trading. Now he felt he'd lied, or at least failed to tell the whole truth. Bacanovic had thrust him into the middle of this. So why was he protecting him now? He wasn't sure. He thought about Marcus's offer to get him a lawyer. Now that he had some time to think about it, and wasn't flanked by four Merrill lawyers, it seemed appealing. He began calling lawyers he knew, asking if they'd represent him. One by one, they turned him down. He called six, exhausting his list of possibilities. They were all in firms with some ties to Merrill Lynch, and said representing him would pose a conflict. He began to wonder, Would anyone risk a clash with powerful Merrill Lynch? He felt increasingly alone.

That evening Faneuil was in Haskell's apartment when Zeva Bellel, his old friend from Vassar, now living in Paris, walked in. She was staying with Haskell while she was in New York. She could tell something was wrong, and when she asked him, Faneuil told her the story of the Waksal and Stewart trades and subsequent events. The Waksals "were in a heated rush to sell because they thought the FDA was not going to approve a drug that ImClone was promoting at the time," he told her. He was upset about his SEC testimony. He told her he'd never been contacted by the SEC before, never had to testify, so he'd had no experience with that kind of thing. Later he elaborated on his frustrations with Bacanovic. As Bellel recalled the conversation, Faneuil told her he'd called Bacanovic. He was "looking for advice, he was looking for support, and said, 'What happened? What's going on? Why are they interested in the sale?'" Bellel recalled. "And Peter responded very firmly and very forcefully and said, 'Listen, nothing happened. There was nothing wrong with the sale. This is how it all happened. End of story.' And he told me he was at a loss. He felt totally abandoned, betrayed and frightened, because he knew very well that what Peter had just described as the sequence of events that took place that day leading up to this sale was totally inaccurate."

The next afternoon, Monaghan thought Faneuil looked so nervous and stressed out that she asked if he was feeling okay. He said he was. "Why don't you take a friend out to dinner, and we'll pick up the tab," she suggested.

That Friday, Faneuil went to see his therapist. The stress was intolerable. He asked if client-therapist conversations were confidential, protected from disclosure in court, and when assured they were, he poured out the entire story. It felt good getting it off his chest to a sympathetic listener. His therapist seemed shocked. "I wouldn't normally say this, but I do know a lawyer who might be able to help you. We'll get to how you feel about all this, but you need a different kind of help first." The name she offered was Jeremiah Gutman.

Gutman was an unusual choice, with virtually no experience in securities matters and insider trading, but at least he had no conflict with Merrill Lynch. He was a well-known civil rights lawyer, a founder of the New York Civil Liberties Union and a board member of the American Civil Liberties Union. Among his clients were antiwar activists Abbie Hoffman and Jerry Rubin as well as the Reverend Sun Myung Moon and the Hare Krishnas. Faneuil called Gutman right after his therapy session and made an appointment for the following week. On Sunday evening, he took up Monaghan's offer for a dinner on the firm. He and Haskell went to Gramercy Tavern, a popular—and expensive—restaurant in the Flatiron district.

Martha Stewart returned from vacation on Sunday, January 6. From Las Ventanas, she and Pasternak had flown to Panama, where they celebrated the fiftieth birthday of Jean (Johnny) Pigozzi on Pigozzi's yacht. Among the guests was Sam Waksal, and Stewart had gotten her chance to quiz him about the ImClone situation. He filled her in on the FDA decision, ascribing it to bureaucratic problems and not a clinical failure of Erbitux. The cost of the trip amounted to $17,000—the private jet, helicopters to get Stewart to and from Pigozzi's yacht, Las Ventanas, where the suite alone was $1,500 a night. Stewart told DeLuca, her accountant, to charge the entire amount to Martha Stewart Living Omnimedia as a business expense. The expense report said only "meeting with Steve Schwarzman," as if their chance and brief encounter amounted to a business meeting. (A Blackstone spokesman said that Schwarzman recalls a brief encounter, which was "accidental, and purely social.") Even though the company reimbursed her for the full cost of the trip and Pasternak was facing financial pressures, Stewart ordered DeLuca to have Pasternak "kick in" her "fair share," money that went to Stewart, not the company.

The next day, January 7, was Bacanovic's first day back in the office. He looked tanned and relaxed despite the tumult of the previous week. He made no mention of the Stewart situation, although Faneuil saw him huddling with Monaghan in her office. At 11:22 a.m., Bacanovic called Stewart at her office, but she was en route to her Connecticut TV studio, and Armstrong didn't answer. At 11:44 a.m. there was a call from Stewart's Connecticut studio to Bacanovic, which lasted twenty-two minutes, phone records show. During that twenty-two minutes, they would certainly have had the opportunity to talk about the investigation and what Bacanovic was going to tell the SEC later that day.

Soon after that call, Bacanovic and Monaghan left for Merrill's downtown offices and met with Marcus and the other Merrill Lynch lawyers, who debriefed him and gave him the same advice they'd given Faneuil, which was to tell the truth. At 1:00 p.m. they placed a call to the SEC, and Glotzer and Slansky again came on the line. They, too, reminded Bacanovic that he was obliged to tell the truth and that failure to do so was a crime. They added that if at any time he wanted to end the interview, he was free to do so.

The SEC lawyers asked Bacanovic about his background, his relationships with Stewart and the Waksals. Bacanovic described his calls from Faneuil reporting the Waksals' attempts to sell their shares. Then Glotzer asked him to tell them about Stewart's trading.

"About a week before, on December 20 or so, she and I decided that if ImClone stock fell below $60, she'd sell it."

"Who is 'she'?"

"I'm sorry, Ms. Stewart. And that day [the twenty-seventh] ImClone was dropping, so I called her . . . I told her it was falling below $60 a share, and she sold it."

So it was Bacanovic—not Faneuil—who spoke to Stewart and took the order to sell? That seemed to be what Bacanovic was saying, but Glotzer asked for clarification to make sure.

"Who placed the order for Ms. Stewart?"

"I did."

This must have come as a surprise to the Merrill Lynch lawyers and Monaghan. Bacanovic had already told Monaghan that Faneuil had handled the trade and that the selling was part of a tax-loss-selling strategy. But no one said anything.

That same morning, Faneuil had approached Monaghan and said he wanted to take Merrill Lynch up on its offer for him to hire his own lawyer. Monaghan seemed surprised. "Well, Doug, if you feel that it is necessary to do that, yes, we will fulfill our commitment as we offered it to you, but I'm a little surprised. I mean, all you need to do is—you answered the questions and you were direct. So if you feel the need to go and speak to an outside counsel, then I'll support you. Go ahead."

The next afternoon Faneuil arrived at Gutman's office at 11 Park Place. Gutman wore a beard, was heavyset, and sported a cape. As he had with his therapist, Faneuil unburdened himself, telling Gutman the entire story. He sensed his job might be in jeopardy at Merrill Lynch. He didn't feel anyone really cared about him, notwithstanding Monaghan's support for his getting a lawyer, which seemed lukewarm, in his view. "I don't have any dreams of being an investment banker," Faneuil told Gutman. "If I lost my broker's license I wouldn't really care."

Gutman swept those concerns aside. "You have no choice but to come forward and correct your testimony," he said. "The minute you leave this office I'm going to call the SEC and we'll go down there tomorrow. This is absolutely what you have to do. You made a mistake, but nothing will happen to you if you admit it now. They'll understand."

Faneuil started to sob. "I can't believe this is happening," he said. "Peter is my friend. I mean, I know he put me in this awful position, but I just can't believe this is happening."

"He's not your friend," Gutman said sharply. "He did a horrible thing to you. He doesn't care about you at all."

On some level Faneuil knew Gutman was right. He had to correct his statement and implicate Bacanovic. And yet the prospect seemed overwhelming. He had to admit he lied. He felt physically sick. "I can't do it," he finally stammered, wiping away tears. "I can't go down there tomorrow. I just can't even envision it. I'm not saying no, I won't do it, but I just need a few days to let this sink in and face the decision."

Gutman seemed disappointed, but didn't press him. "I'll wait to hear from you."

A couple of days later, Faneuil was still wrestling with his dilemma when Gutman called him and told him to come to the office. Gutman's demeanor seemed to have changed. "I had a very interesting conversation with Dave Marcus," Gutman said, referring to the Merrill Lynch lawyer who was handling the matter. "He told me you did a great job with your SEC testimony. He felt there was really nothing to add and hoped you didn't do anything drastic." Obviously Marcus suspected there was more to the story than Faneuil had divulged, and Marcus wanted Faneuil to keep his mouth shut.

"Do lawyers really talk that way?" Faneuil asked.

Gutman shrugged and chuckled. "I can't tell you exactly what Marcus said to me, but what he said in so many words was that Merrill Lynch has reached a deal with the government in which Merrill Lynch will hand over the Waksals on a silver platter. In return, the government will look the other way with regard to the Martha Stewart situation."

Faneuil struggled to absorb the implications. The notion of some kind of deal between Merrill Lynch and the government struck him as far-fetched, but what did he know? Marcus and Gutman were the lawyers. "Does this change your advice?" Faneuil asked.

"Yes, it does. I think you should lie low. If Merrill Lynch asks you any more questions about what happened, you can continue to answer. Just don't offer them anything. Try to be as brief as possible. Stick to yes-or-no answers if you can."

"What if they ask me pointed questions? What if they ask specifically what I said to Martha?"

Gutman leaned back in his chair and put his hands behind his head. "Then don't lie." He was smiling. "But if the government ever tries to speak to you again, call me first."

Faneuil left the meeting feeling a mixture of relief and confusion. The painful confrontation with the government was now postponed, perhaps forever. On the other hand, he wasn't supposed to lie but he wasn't supposed to change his story either. He wasn't sure how he was going to manage such a balancing act. But for now, he was supposed to "lie low." That's what he intended to do.

A few days later, on January 10, Armstrong handed Martha Stewart a message that had come in that morning:

"Peter Bacanovic would like to speak to MS about the money in the accounts and the status of it, and would like to have dinner alone with her next week, maybe Tuesday (National Retail Federation) or Wednesday (Lillian Goldman) or Thursday (nothing on calendar)." Armstrong had added prior commitments for Stewart's reference. Like the earlier message from Bacanovic, Armstrong thought this one was odd. There was nothing pressing about Stewart's portfolio with Bacanovic that she knew of. It was also unusual for Bacanovic to ask for a dinner alone with Stewart.

After Stewart read the message, she was dismissive. Bacanovic, she told

Armstrong, didn't merit a dinner, or even a lunch. If she had to meet with Bacanovic alone and in person, they could meet for breakfast. Armstrong mentally dropped Bacanovic a notch in Stewart's social and business hierarchy.

Stewart's driver dropped her off at Le Gamin, a small French restaurant on Ninth Avenue and Twenty-first Street, at 9:15 a.m. on January 19. Bacanovic was waiting.

At the U.S. Attorney's office in lower Manhattan, Steve Peikin, deputy head of the securities fraud unit, was startled as he read a January 19 front-page article in the *New York Times*, "House Panel to Investigate a Cancer Drug and Its Maker."

> Saying it had "serious concerns" about how ImClone Systems had communicated with investors, a House committee said yesterday that it would investigate whether the company had covered up problems involving its cancer drug.
>
> The House's investigation hinted at the possibility of securities fraud, and the U.S. Attorney for the Southern District of Manhattan, which covers Wall Street, traditionally prosecutes securities crimes while the SEC handles civil cases.

But what really struck Peikin was another aspect of the story:

> Panel members were also concerned about stock sales by ImClone executives. Samuel D. and Harlan W. Waksal, the chief executive and chief operating officer of ImClone, together sold more than $150 million of ImClone stock at peak prices in the months before the FDA action.

The story continued:

> ImClone's stock, which was trading above $70 in early December before rumors of the FDA problems began surfacing, has lost more than two-thirds of its value since then and some shareholder lawsuits have been filed against the company. Yesterday the stock fell $8.93, or about 30 percent, to $21.15.

ImClone, Bristol-Myers and the FDA all said they would cooperate with the House committee. ImClone also said in a statement that it
"remains fully confident" in Erbitux.

One hundred fifty million dollars in insider sales before the release of bad
news? The situation reeked of possible insider trading by the two top officers in
the company. Though the SEC investigation was already under way, it hadn't
progressed to the point where possible criminal charges were being considered,
and so the U.S. Attorney's office hadn't been notified. But Peikin saw no reason to delay. He hurried through the office looking for an available assistant.
Everyone was busy on other cases, but finally he found Michael Schachter, who
said he'd get on the case.

Schachter, age thirty-three, had recently joined the office after working at
a Chicago law firm. He'd attended Indiana University and DePaul law school,
and spoke with a trace of his native midwestern accent. He'd been so eager to
be a federal prosecutor that he applied to fifteen U.S. Attorney's offices around
the country. New York had been the first to respond.

Schachter called the SEC and got the trading records. Obviously all the
Waksals would be called in for questioning. Schachter wondered who else Waksal might have tipped. It was no secret that he and Martha Stewart were close,
and the timing of her trade looked highly suspicious. A week later, on January
25, Schachter called Martha Stewart Living's general counsel, Greg Blatt, to say
that the Justice Department was investigating trading in ImClone and would
like to interview Stewart—that very day, if possible.

It was the first anyone at Stewart's company, apart from Armstrong and
Stewart herself, knew anything about the suspicious ImClone trading. The
implications, to which Stewart herself had seemed oblivious, were profound.
Stewart was the chief executive of a publicly traded company, held to strict standards of conduct and disclosure. She was also chief executive of a company in
which she herself—as an executive, a talent, a personality, and a brand—was the
company's most valuable asset. Without Stewart, there was no Martha Stewart
Living.

Stewart was in Los Angeles that day filming her television show. Blatt
immediately called Andrew Nussbaum, a lawyer at Wachtell Lipton Rosen &
Katz, the prominent firm that had long represented Stewart's company and
had successfully steered it through its initial public offering in 1999. Wachtell

is one of the most prestigious firms and has long specialized in mergers, acqui-
sitions, and corporate law. Its lawyers are perennially ranked as the nation's
most highly paid in the *American Lawyer*'s annual survey of partnership
incomes. It also has a small but highly regarded white-collar crime practice,
headed by Lawrence Pedowitz, former chief of the criminal division of the
Manhattan U.S. Attorney's office. Nussbaum in turn contacted John Savarese,
a former Supreme Court clerk and lecturer on white-collar crime at Harvard
Law School.

After learning about the call to Blatt, Stewart called John Cuti, a lawyer who
was married to her daughter, Alexis, or "Lexi," as she was known. Even though
Alexis and Cuti had virtually separated and were contemplating a divorce, Stewart and Cuti had remained friends and she called him as soon as she heard
about the call from the U.S. Attorney's office. Cuti wasn't unduly concerned;
he assumed that the government was interested in the Waksals, not Stewart. But
he agreed she needed a criminal lawyer, and at her request, checked on Savarese.
All the reviews were glowing.

Stewart's status as chief executive of a publicly traded company posed an
unusual dilemma for her lawyers. The prudent course would have been to delay,
to become thoroughly familiar with all the evidence, and only then—perhaps—
allow Stewart to be questioned by prosecutors. But Stewart was no ordinary
defendant. Because she was chief executive, any criminal investigation of her
activities, even if unrelated to the company itself, might have to be disclosed
as a "material" fact that might affect investors' decisions about whether to buy,
sell, or hold stock in her company. And anything short of a declaration that
Stewart was cooperating fully with the investigation could be devastating for
the stock price, affecting the company's financial health as well as Stewart's own
personal fortune, most of which was in her company's stock.

The phone records Armstrong maintained reflect a flurry of calls from
Savarese to Stewart beginning Monday, January 28. What Savarese asked and
what Stewart said has never been disclosed, since the conversations are protected by the attorney-client privilege. But people close to the Stewart defense
team maintain that Stewart insisted that she hadn't spoken to Waksal before
selling and that she didn't know about the FDA's Erbitux ruling. This was the
essence of any potential insider trading case from the lawyers' perspective: Did
Waksal tip Stewart? The answer was no. However, Stewart also told them the
$60 story, which is what Bacanovic had said in his statement to government

lawyers. She didn't volunteer anything about the call from Faneuil reporting that the Waksals were dumping their shares. In other words, Stewart failed to tell them that she'd been told the Waksals were dumping their shares—the real reason she sold.

Savarese also called Merrill Lynch, where Marcus reassured him that Stewart "had nothing to worry about," according to lawyers familiar with the call. According to these lawyers, Marcus told Savarese that Bacanovic had also offered the $60 explanation, which corroborated Stewart's account. Remarkably, Marcus never mentioned Doug Faneuil. Nor did he say that Bacanovic and Faneuil had given contradictory versions of who actually spoke to Stewart and took the order that day, let alone that phone records established that it was Faneuil who took her call. Instead, he stressed that Merrill had no phone records or any other physical evidence suggesting any contact between Stewart and Waksal. (A Merrill Lynch spokesman said Marcus wouldn't comment on his discussions with Stewart's lawyers.) Marcus also didn't reveal that Bacanovic was Waksal's broker.

Savarese also spoke to Stewart's employees, including Ann Armstrong. According to Savarese's notes of the conversation, Armstrong told him that Stewart had indeed spoken to Bacanovic and that she had stayed on the line to say, "Martha, you're on with Peter, and Peter, you're on with Martha." Savarese thought he now had three sources—Stewart, Bacanovic, and Armstrong—all telling the same story. (What Armstrong actually told Savarese remains in dispate since Armstrong maintains she told Savarese the same thing she did anyone else who asked, which was that she connected Stewart to Bacanovic's office.)

Should Savarese have been more skeptical? The timing of Stewart's trade was, on its face, highly suspicious. The absence of a stop-loss order confirming the $60 story should also have been troubling. On the other hand, the lack of any direct contact between Waksal and Stewart prior to her trade seemed to prove her contention that she hadn't acted on any inside information. Moreover, the Wachtell lawyers had no way of knowing that Bacanovic was also Waksal's broker. And they didn't even know Faneuil existed. Without this crucial information, the possibility that another form of inside information—that the chief executive was dumping all of his shares—was transmitted to Stewart by her broker's assistant at Merrill Lynch didn't occur to Savarese or any of the other lawyers representing Stewart.

In any event, by Thursday, Savarese had concluded that Stewart should submit to questioning at the U.S. Attorney's office as soon as possible, which turned out to be the following Monday, February 4. Not only would she cooperate, but she should do so with no strings attached. Potential targets of investigations often make a "proffer," a description of their likely testimony, and reach an agreement that nothing disclosed can be used in any subsequent prosecution. (Such agreements, however, never provide any immunity for perjury or false statements.) Evidently so confident was Savarese in Stewart, and so eager to make a favorable impression on the government lawyers, that he made no proffer on her behalf and sought no protection for anything she might say. And it did make an impression: the prosecutors thought it was an extraordinary assertion of Stewart's innocence.

Armstrong noted in Stewart's phone log that day: "John Savarese would like you to call him sometime around 4:30, 5 o'clock. Won't be long. He'd also like to meet you at Starrett for an hour or so before heading downtown on Monday." Armstrong knew by this point that Stewart was going to be questioned by law enforcement officials, but Stewart hadn't told her anything beyond that.

Shortly after that message, Armstrong noted that Bacanovic had called.

Then, at five, Stewart spoke on the phone to Savarese for about half an hour. As soon as she finished, she told Armstrong that Savarese wanted to see all of her messages from Wednesday, December 26, through Monday, January 7, and that she should fax copies to him. Armstrong started scrolling through the message log in her computer and had gotten to December 26 when Stewart walked over to Armstrong's desk and said she wanted to see the messages herself.

Stewart took Armstrong's seat, while Armstrong leaned over her and continued scrolling. When she got to Bacanovic's message of the twenty-seventh about ImClone trading downward, Stewart leaned over her and grabbed the computer mouse from her hand. She used it to highlight the entire message after Bacanovic's name. Stewart typed over it: "re imclone," which had the effect of deleting the prior message. She got up from the computer, and Armstrong dutifully corrected the capitalization and punctuation: "Re: ImClone." Then Stewart had second thoughts. "Put it back," she said. Armstrong had no idea how to do that. Stewart walked to her office door, turned, and told Armstrong, "Get my son-in-law on the phone."

. . .

John Cuti was startled by the call. He told Stewart, "Don't touch anything." He immediately called Savarese and left a message. Then he called Armstrong. "Don't touch anything. Just stop in your tracks."

"I'm glad to hear from you," Armstrong said. She'd become friendly with Cuti from his many calls to Stewart's office. Though she had simply followed Stewart's orders and hadn't erased the message herself, Armstrong was nervous that she was getting enmeshed in something that might be illegal. That Stewart had enlisted Armstrong in altering the message suggested that Stewart herself thought she'd done something wrong. Why else would she tamper with potential evidence? Cuti suggested to Armstrong that they meet for dinner that evening at a restaurant in Greenwich Village.

Stewart left the office for a hair appointment, and afterward was flying to Germany for the weekend. As soon as she got into her car, she called Armstrong. "Were you able to get it back?" she asked, obviously referring to the phone message.

"No, but I'll keep trying."

Stewart was silent.

Later, at the restaurant, Cuti tried to reassure Armstrong. He told her he had a call in to Savarese, that they'd find a way to retrieve the message, and that she shouldn't worry. Armstrong found his advice and demeanor comforting, but still, when she got home that night, she wrote everything that had happened that day in a notebook.

The following week, Armstrong enlisted a young writer for the magazine and together they examined the trash folder on her computer. It turned out that the computer had crashed on January 4, and Stewart's message log had been open on the screen at the time. It was automatically saved in the trash folder, and it included the message from Bacanovic before it was altered. Armstrong immediately made copies. She faxed one to Stewart's lawyers at Wachtell. Just to be safe, she put another in an envelope, sealed it, and placed it in a locker down the hall from Stewart's office. "I hope we never need this," Armstrong said.

Martha Stewart arrived at the Manhattan U.S. Attorney's office in lower Manhattan on Monday afternoon. She was accompanied by two of her lawyers from Wachtell, John Savarese and Steven Pearl.

Michael Schachter represented the Justice Department and did the questioning. Also present were the SEC lawyers Helene Glotzer and Jill Slansky, as well as an FBI agent, Catherine Farmer, who took notes. In keeping with standard policy of the Department of Justice, this voluntary interview—one that, unlike Bacanovic's, had not been compelled by subpoena—was not recorded and Stewart wasn't sworn to tell the truth. Still, Schachter began by reminding her that she was obliged to tell the truth and that making a false statement to law enforcement officials is a crime. She was free to consult her lawyers at any point and the government wouldn't draw any inference if she did so. She was also free to end the interview at any time. Stewart nodded in agreement.

Initially, the questions seemed innocuous. Stewart described her investment approach, her fondness for biotech and technology stocks, and ImClone in particular. She'd met Sam Waksal through her daughter and they'd become friendly, with houses near each other in East Hampton. She attended the wedding of one of his daughters, and met other family members, including his brother Harlan. She liked ImClone's prospects, especially because at one point it was researching a cure for AIDS, and she first bought the stock in the mid-1990s when it was selling for about 60 cents a share.

Though Stewart saw Waksal socially and the two spoke two to three times a month, he didn't tell her anything specific about ImClone, Stewart said. Although he was often optimistic about the company and its prospects, he didn't tell her when Bristol-Myers Squibb was going to launch a tender offer for a stake in the company, and hadn't told her anything about the status of its Erbitux application.

And then the questions became specific. Schachter asked her what, if any, conversations about ImClone she'd had with Bacanovic. According to Helene Glotzer's sworn recollection of what Stewart said, "They decided that if ImClone stock fell below $60 a share, she would sell the remaining stock out of her personal account. She said that Mr. Bacanovic believed that at that point she had made a profit, and she should just take the money and run."

Stewart recalled that on the day of the sale, en route to Mexico, "she called in to her assistant, Ann Armstrong, for her messages. Ms. Armstrong told Ms. Stewart at this point that Mr. Bacanovic had left a message and wanted to speak to her hopefully before the end of the day, and she asked to be patched through to his offices. And when she was put through to him, he told her that the price of ImClone had fallen to $60, and she at that point told him to sell all of her shares."

According to Farmer's notes, Schachter asked if there was a written record of the message that Bacanovic had left for her. A Wachtell Lipton memorandum, however, written by Steven Pearl, an associate who took notes at the interview, reads: "AUSA: at what time had PB [Bacanovic] left a message for MS [Stewart] to call him on December 27? MS: does not know. JFS [Savarese]: Agrees to send them the phone log."

"She said she didn't know," Farmer's notes continued. "I believe at that point her attorney offered to check and get back to us with that message, if one existed."

Schachter asked why she sold then.

"She was on her way to vacation. She didn't want to be bothered over her vacation with it. . . . She said that they also briefly discussed Martha Stewart Living's stock price as well as Kmart."

At this point Glotzer herself asked Stewart if she was sure she spoke to Bacanovic and placed the order through him that day. After all, Doug Faneuil had already told the SEC lawyers that it was he, not Bacanovic, who spoke to Stewart. Glotzer mentioned Faneuil by name and asked Stewart if she was sure she didn't speak to him.

According to Glotzer, "She said she spoke with Mr. Bacanovic and didn't recall who his assistant was then." Stewart added that "she doesn't trade on information she's not supposed to know about."

Stewart continued that at the party in Panama, after news of Erbitux's rejection was public, Waksal explained what had happened with the ImClone application, mentioning "someone at ImClone had botched up with the filing with the FDA. It would take them about six to eight weeks to refile the application, but that, you know, he was very optimistic that everything with the drug trials was going very well." Otherwise, she said, she didn't discuss the matter with Waksal, and he didn't say anything about trying to sell his shares.

When Schachter asked Stewart about any conversations with Bacanovic between the time of the sale and the interview, she recalled that they spoke just "two or three times." In only one of those conversations, which took place on the phone, was ImClone mentioned, she said. "Mr. Bacanovic had told her that the SEC was asking Merrill Lynch some questions about trading in ImClone," but he "didn't tell her whether he had been asked any questions or whether any of the questions involved her at all."

Stewart also volunteered that she'd discussed the ImClone trade with her bookkeeper Heidi DeLuca, who also remembered that Stewart had an agreement with Bacanovic to sell ImClone at $60. "All three of them—Mr. Bacanovic, Ms. DeLuca and Ms. Stewart—all had the same recollection," Stewart said.

But how could she know Bacanovic's recollection if she'd only had one conversation with him—one that didn't mention her trading?

Schachter pounced on the inconsistency, and Stewart hastily tried to recover. "Well, I don't know what his recollection is. I only know that my bookkeeper and I have the same recollection."

The obvious gaffe seemed to put Stewart on edge. "Can I go now?" she testily asked. "I have a business to run." Shortly after, she ended the interview. She and her lawyers left the room, the atmosphere strained.

The government lawyers were baffled by Stewart's performance. On the one hand, she didn't say anything incriminating. Her story was consistent with their phone interview with Bacanovic; she knew nothing about the FDA's decision on Erbitux and had sold because the stock dropped below a prearranged target of $60. And yet her story suffered from the same weaknesses. There was no stop-loss order, and Stewart had been unable to recall even one other instance where she'd made such an arrangement to sell a stock. She had sold her entire position the day before a major public announcement, which remained highly suspicious. And then there were the curious inconsistencies: the lawyers knew that it was Faneuil, not Bacanovic, who took the order and spoke to Stewart that day. But when pressed on the issue, Stewart insisted she'd spoken to Bacanovic and didn't even know Faneuil's name. Why would she lie about Faneuil? Moreover, too much of her story was self-serving: the convenient alibi from the bookkeeper; the claim that she would "never" trade on improper information. And then there was her gaffe about Bacanovic supporting her story, when allegedly she'd never discussed the investigation with him. As she was represented by some of the finest lawyers in the country, it was little short of incredible.

Given Stewart's performance, Schachter thought it essential that they question Bacanovic again—as soon as possible, and this time under oath. At four-thirty that afternoon, the SEC issued a subpoena calling for Bacanovic to appear on February 6, just two days later. Merrill's lawyers managed to put it off a week.

. . .

Peter Bacanovic arrived at the Woolworth Building's ornate, vaulted lobby on February 13, 2002. He was dressed in an expensive, well-tailored dark suit, white shirt, and tie. His thick hair was carefully groomed. He had the polished, affluent look of the successful Manhattan stockbroker he was.

Bacanovic was accompanied by Marcus, the Merrill Lynch lawyer. The two took the elevator to the sixteenth floor, which was serving as the temporary offices in New York for the Securities and Exchange Commission.

Bacanovic and Marcus were shown to room 16042, where they were greeted by three SEC lawyers: Glotzer, Slansky, who'd earlier interviewed Bacanovic on the phone, and Laurent Sacharoff, a young lawyer in the office.

"Do you promise to tell the truth, the whole truth, and nothing but the truth?" Slansky asked him.

"I do," Bacanovic replied.

Jill Slansky began the questioning for the SEC.

"Let's go to December 27," she said. "Let's start when you woke up that morning . . . as much as you can recall the specifics of conversations with Aliza Waksal, Alan Goldberg [Waksal's accountant], Sam Waksal, Martha Stewart, Doug Faneuil, and anyone else who was attempting to sell ImClone stock on that day."

Bacanovic was poised and exuded self-confidence. He hadn't traded any ImClone shares for himself and wasn't even in the office that day. "Starting at the beginning of the day, I received a phone call from my assistant [Doug Faneuil] in the morning, and . . . he had received a phone call from Alan Goldberg, the accountant of the Waksal family, and the nature of the phone call was, as described by my assistant, that we were to expect additional phone calls from members of the Waksal family, most importantly, Aliza Waksal had an intention to sell all the shares in her account, and Sam Waksal would like to transfer shares from his account to her account. . . . I was on holiday in Florida . . . at a borrowed apartment in Miami Beach, where I had been staying.

"At that point I asked [Doug], I wanted to make sure that's what he was saying. And I said, 'I would like to speak to Alan Goldberg myself to understand exactly what this is about.' . . . I believe I spoke with Alan Goldberg that morning . . . to just confirm what he had said. And that was that . . . Doug had only been in my employ about six months, and I was away, and this was a large transaction, and [I] also wanted to make sure that he knew what to do in such a case. . . .

"I must have spoken once or twice with Doug about other matters. At some point, on one of those phone calls, I said, 'I would like to call Martha Stewart, and I would like to apprise her of the price of the stock, please.'"

"Do you remember what the stock was trading at, at that point?"

"I believe the stock was approximately $60 a share, or something close to it. Slightly above or slightly below. And I don't recall whether I placed the call from my cell phone or, once again, Doug and I placed the call together. And we did not reach her, so we simply left a message with her assistant, who explained to us that she was in transit."

"When you were calling her, did you call her at home? At work?"

"We only call the office."

"Do you know who you spoke with?"

"Yes. Annie, who has been her assistant for several years, and with whom we speak all the time . . ."

"And what was the message?"

"The message was to please call us back, and also to please advise her that ImClone stock was at whatever the price was at that time."

"'Please call us back'?"

"Yes . . ."

"And you specifically told Annie that ImClone stock was dropping?"

"No. We just gave her the price of the stock."

"Okay, I'm sorry . . ."

"Then I get another call from Doug, and this call came in after lunch. And that call was that Martha had returned the phone call from an airport, that she was in transit, and he had given her the price of the stock. And, based on the price of the stock, she elected to sell her shares, her remaining shares, in ImClone Systems from her account, her personal account."

"So Martha called Doug."

"Correct."

"You did not speak with her?"

"I did not speak with her that day."

Helene Glotzer interrupted.

"When you called Annie, can you just try and think, to be as specific as possible, when you asked her to ask Ms. Stewart to please call you back, did you say, 'It's urgent, call me back immediately'? Something like that?"

"No. I said, 'I would like to speak with her, if possible today, regarding

ImClone and what the current price of the stock is.' Understanding that she was in transit and that she sometimes is very, very difficult to reach."

By way of further explanation, Bacanovic described in detail an earlier phone conversation he had had with Stewart on December 20. "We reviewed each and every position in the account. And we discussed the fundamentals of all the positions. We discussed the overall status of the portfolio, and included in that discussion was ImClone. And so we reviewed ImClone and discussed what her intentions were for ImClone at that time versus my recommendations. . . . And she wanted to hold the stock. And I challenged that by saying, 'The stock has been clearly declining. Why would you hold it?' And she goes . . . and at that point, we determined that if, in fact, it fell much further, then we would sell it."

"Did she give you any indication as to why she wanted to hold the stock?" Glotzer continued.

"Many of my clients invest in certain companies out of loyalty and friendship and they like to say they own each other's stock."

"And so your recommendation to her was to sell because the price was declining?"

"Correct."

Slansky continued the questioning. "Did you hear any rumors on Wall Street or by analysts that, you know, this drug wasn't going to be approved?"

"None whatsoever."

"So, going back, she didn't really want to sell it; you recommended that she sell it. You can continue on from there."

"So, we made a deal. I said, 'Okay, if you would not like to sell the stock now, how low are you going to wait before you sell this stock?'"

"I'm sorry, on December 20, when you had this conversation, do you remember what the price of the stock was?"

"It was in the mid-60s. And at that point we determined that $60 a share would be a suitable share price, should it ever fall that low. Of course, she never thought it would."

"And did she place a limit order [an order to sell that would automatically be executed if the price hit $60]?"

"[She] did not. We did not put an order into the system. She does not like doing that . . . so I said, 'We'll watch the stock for you.'"

Glotzer jumped in. "So, I mean, every day, then, would you basically look at the price of ImClone?"

"Well, while on vacation, this is a little . . . here we have a problem. I mean, I cannot keep up with all my prices during that time. And I was a little bit alarmed on the morning of the twenty-seventh. I hadn't really thought about ImClone on the twenty-sixth or twenty-seventh, to be honest. I was really relieved, in fact, not to be thinking about ImClone. And when my assistant called me that morning, and all of a sudden ImClone was on my mind again, and I got a price on the stock, I thought, Oh, I better find Martha now. I just had this conversation with her a week ago, and here we are."

Slansky continued: "You recommended that she sell, you picked a price of $60."

"Yes."

"Is that correct?"

"Yes. Yes. Back on the twentieth."

Slansky asked him to continue.

"In answer to your question, I had not looked at the price of ImClone since I left the office at 1:00 p.m. on the twenty-fourth, which was Monday. The holiday was Tuesday, and Wednesday I was in transit to Florida. So, it is now Thursday. I'm still—I'm just getting settled in for this holiday. This phone call comes in the morning. I haven't been out of the office for more than a day at this point, and all of a sudden, you know, sooner—much sooner—I didn't expect ImClone to move that quickly, at least in a decline. And my assistant was telling me, 'Well, the price of this stock is now at . . .' lower than when I last looked at it."

"Do you remember if it was about $60 at this point?"

"I believe it was just at $60. I believe. You know, within pennies of $60. And at that point, I thought, you know, I just had this conversation. This is someone who gets irascible. And I thought, So much for the vacation. Let's try and track down Martha, find Martha, which is the process I normally go through, and I've had to call her all over the world with conversations like this. And you initiate the process, which is calling the office. 'Is Martha findable?' Martha got back to us, spoke to my assistant. We did the trade."

"Did you ever tell Martha Stewart that the SEC had been speaking with Merrill Lynch about sales in ImClone at the end of the year?"

"I said that we had . . . we had been reviewing this internally. And that was all."

"In other words, you didn't mention that the SEC was looking into this?"

"No."

"Did you tell her that anyone was asking questions about her transactions specifically?"

"I did not."

"Did she ask you that?"

"She did not."

"Did you say anything that would give her cause for concern, the fact that she sold on December 27?"

"No, because she had no cause for concern. Because we had reviewed this position. I have notes of this conversation. It was completely typical, and she would have had no cause for concern. So, no."

"And you have notes of that conversation?"

"Well, I mean I have a work sheet that I worked from that day, that we did on the twentieth, where all of this stuff, which is a printout of the screen, with all sorts of markings on it. And so, I mean, all of this was discussed at the time, long prior. And so she had no reason for concern."

"And the information about her selling—her possibly selling ImClone at 60 would be reflected on that work sheet."

"Yes. I mean, reflected on the work sheet in a very loose way. I mean, things are highlighted, marked for sales. Some things are circled. I mean, it's scribbled on."

Slansky asked how he and Stewart came up with the $60 sales price.

"She didn't really have a price," Bacanovic testified. "I said, 'Listen, what will you settle for? How low does this have to go before you're prepared to part with this?' She said, 'I don't know.' I said, 'Well, how about $60 a share? Does that sound reasonable?' And the conversation was something like that. She said, 'Yes, sure, $60.'" . . .

"Did you ever tell Martha Stewart that Sam Waksal was attempting to sell his shares on December 27 and 28?"

"I must discuss my business in general in order to reply to that question. I do not discuss other clients' affairs with other clients."

"So, are you saying that you know for certain in this instance you didn't do it?"

"Inasmuch as I make a practice of not discussing any client's business with another client, I would have to assume that in this case as well. So, the answer to your question would be yes. I would not discuss his transactions with her, in the same way I would not discuss her transactions with him, or even with her own daughter, for that matter." Bacanovic elaborated: "I don't like discussing clients' business, even if they're people like the Waksals. And I did not get to be a first vice president at Merrill Lynch by discussing other people's business and by being indiscreet."

"And Doug Faneuil, have you had conversations with him about the investigation?"

"I told him, he knows that I'm here right now, because I'm out of the office for a day. That's it."

"You haven't talked about the investigation?"

"No. Not only did I not talk to him about it, we gave him a week off because the stress levels were so high, and we felt sorry for him, and we gave him a week off. Which, of course, only made my situation that much worse, because I've got big business, and my very smart assistant was out on vacation at the beginning of the year. So, no."

And there the deposition ended. Bacanovic had spoken with confidence and poise, showing none of the stress he'd attributed to Faneuil. Bacanovic hadn't even hired his own lawyer, although Merrill Lynch had offered to pay for one. Marcus, the Merrill Lynch lawyer, had only spoken a few times. Stewart, in Bacanovic's telling, had a solid alibi: with Bacanovic's encouragement, she'd decided to sell the shares for $60 on December 20, and did so on December 27 when told they were trading at or near that price. Bacanovic said he had written notes of the December 20 conversation, which Merrill Lynch had already produced to the government. Bacanovic knew nothing about the FDA's adverse ruling on Erbitux and hadn't spoken to any of the Waksals.

The SEC lawyers were impressed. It was hard not to like Bacanovic. He and the lawyers even managed a few laughs in the course of the questioning. True, a few of his answers seemed curiously elliptical, especially the discussion of whether he mentioned the Waksal trading to Stewart. They'd had to pry a simple denial out of him. It was also curious—and too bad for Stewart—that no stop-loss order to sell ImClone at $60 had been entered into the system. That would have been irrefutable proof of the alibi. And then there was the timing. Stewart sold on the same day that the Waksals were dumping their shares, and a day before the FDA made its announcement. But perhaps it simply was a remarkable coincidence. In all major respects, his story aligned with Stewart's: neither knew anything about the FDA's negative decision on Erbitux. He'd agreed with Stewart that she'd sell her ImClone shares if they fell below $60, which they did on that day.

There was simply no evidence to support the SEC lawyers' initial suspicion that a tip from Waksal had prompted Stewart's sale. When the lawyers in the

U.S. Attorney's office subsequently reviewed Bacanovic's testimony for possible criminal charges, they essentially halted the investigation into Stewart's trading for lack of any proof, while continuing their investigation into the far more promising Waksal case.

And there the investigation might have languished, with no one ever knowing—or caring—that Martha Stewart showed uncanny timing in disposing of a few hundred thousand dollars of ImClone stock or that Peter Bacanovic was her stockbroker. Throughout her life and career, Stewart had shown herself to be a consummate risktaker, always coming out ahead. As of February 2002, she had done so again.

TWO

"Everyone Is Telling the Same Story"

O ver a month had passed since Faneuil's interview with the SEC, for which he'd received such praise from the Merrill officials. He'd heard nothing further from the government. He'd been trying to follow his lawyer's advice to keep his head down. He knew Bacanovic had traveled downtown for another interview (though not that Bacanovic had been subpoenaed), but Bacanovic acted like nothing had happened, and told Faneuil nothing about it. At the office, the usual routine reasserted itself. Faneuil wondered if Merrill Lynch had indeed reached that "silver platter" deal with the government to implicate the Waksals in return for dropping the Stewart matter.

Then one day Bacanovic called Faneuil into his office and brandished a computer printout. "Look what I found," he said. Faneuil examined the document and saw that it was a list of all Stewart's stock holdings from December. It seemed to be the same list that Bacanovic had used to discuss the end-of-year tax-loss selling in Stewart's account. Faneuil noticed the ImClone entry and, right next to it, "@ $60," in ink, evidently in Bacanovic's writing. "See," Bacanovic said. "Proof!"

He didn't say proof of what. Was this supposed to be confirmation of the now-discarded tax-loss-selling theory? Or the agreement to sell at $60? Or some new hybrid of the two: that the decision to sell at $60 was made during a discussion of tax-loss selling? Faneuil had no idea.

"Okay?" Bacanovic asked. When Faneuil remained silent, he repeated it. "Okay?"

"Okay," Faneuil said, as he had in the past. He felt the web tighten around him.

Faneuil was having trouble sleeping. One night, exhausted and worried, he unburdened himself to Rob Haskell, breaking down and crying. He couldn't figure any way out except to come forward and tell the truth. Bacanovic didn't seem to show any appreciation for Faneuil, or awareness of the terrible situation he'd put him in. The constant pressure to acquiesce in what Faneuil knew to be lies was insulting and draining. If Bacanovic would just level with him, maybe they could figure something out.

Haskell argued that Faneuil should stick to his story and protect Bacanovic, but he could tell that Faneuil's loyalty was wavering. Finally, at about 8:30 p.m., Faneuil went to bed.

Haskell decided to take matters into his own hands. He considered Bacanovic a friend, and he'd introduced him and Faneuil. Haskell thought Faneuil was "freaking out," as he later recalled, and was on the brink of coming forward and confessing his lie. In Haskell's opinion, this would be bad for both Faneuil and Bacanovic. Haskell and Bacanovic hadn't spoken since the Stewart trade and the ensuing chill between Faneuil and his boss, but now he called Bacanovic.

"Doug's stressed out," he told Bacanovic. "You need to make Doug feel a lot better about not coming forward, and that he'll be safe. I think he feels the only person you're thinking of is yourself."

"Doug cannot tell them what happened!" Bacanovic insisted, sounding panicked. "It's important to me." Speaking at his usual rapid rate, he continued, "Do you realize how much I have to lose? I pay for my mother's life. I live paycheck to paycheck." Haskell sensed how fragile Bacanovic's aura of money, success, and status was, how important it was to him to remain a part of the glamorous, wealthy, sophisticated world he inhabited but wasn't really a part of.

"He essentially acknowledged that what happened, happened," Haskell later recalled. "It's not as if we needed to review the circumstances. He knew or feared they were incriminating circumstances."

Haskell knew Faneuil well enough to know that all he really needed was some attention and understanding. Faneuil, in Haskell's view, was "a humanist. If anything was going to allow him to subsume his values [to be truthful], it had to be love for that person," meaning Bacanovic. "Doug makes decisions for other people that are against his own self-interest and well-being," Haskell warned Bacanovic. "I need this to be a good decision for Doug."

"What can I do?" Bacanovic finally asked.

"Take him to lunch. Treat him gently. Let him know how hard this is for him. Be his shrink."

The next morning, when Haskell told him he'd spoken to Bacanovic after he'd gone to bed, Faneuil was furious. He felt betrayed that Haskell had called Bacanovic without asking his permission. He stormed out without even asking Haskell what they had discussed.

When Faneuil arrived at work that morning, still angry at Haskell, Bacanovic called him in. "Let's go to breakfast." Faneuil was surprised; nothing like this had ever happened.

The two went to Dean & DeLuca, a gourmet café in Rockefeller Center. Faneuil ordered a hot chocolate. "I had no idea you were so upset," Bacanovic said soothingly. "I'm sorry. But I really don't understand your concern. I have everything under control. You have absolutely no reason to worry. This isn't about you." Bacanovic continued in this vein, stressing that it was the Waksals being investigated, not Bacanovic or anyone at Merrill Lynch, and certainly not Faneuil. In Bacanovic's view, Faneuil hardly mattered.

Faneuil feared he wasn't going to get a word in, just as in his previous exchanges with Bacanovic. But the more Bacanovic talked, stressing that none of this was about Faneuil, the angrier he became. It certainly was about Faneuil, or at least it was now that he had been enlisted in a false version of what happened. Finally he burst out, "Peter, I know what happened!"

Bacanovic was silent for a moment. He leaned forward and put his hand on Faneuil's shoulder, looking him in the eye. "With all due respect, Doug, no, you don't," he said.

Faneuil was trembling. Bacanovic lifted his hand and leaned back. Faneuil didn't know what had happened or why, Bacanovic insisted. Only he and Stewart did. "I spoke to Martha. Everyone is telling the same story," Bacanovic assured him. So Bacanovic and Stewart were coordinating their accounts, Faneuil realized.

Bacanovic launched into a long account of his relationship to Stewart. How she'd allocated "friends and family" stock in Martha Stewart Living to Bacanovic and his clients when her company went public. "She could have given them to much bigger fish than me," Bacanovic said. How, with Stewart's backing, he'd gone from obscurity to being one of the most successful people in the office. He and Stewart "are close. We're loyal. We are not going to betray each other," he concluded.

With only the briefest mention of Faneuil and a perfunctory apology, Bacanovic had, once again, steamrolled over his assistant. Despite Haskell's admonition to be sensitive and show he cared, Bacanovic had launched into another monologue that focused only on himself.

Far from reassuring or comforting Faneuil, the excursion to Dean & DeLuca made things worse.

Faneuil felt increasingly angry at Bacanovic for putting him in this excruciating position and then showing no empathy for what he was going through. After the call from Haskell and the breakfast, Bacanovic demanded constant reassurances that Faneuil was on the team. Sometimes it was just a knowing smile when they passed. Other times Bacanovic would repeat the $60 story and demand that Faneuil agree with him. He often repeated that "Martha is telling the same story."

Periodically Bacanovic offered Faneuil something of value. Bacanovic suggested he take an extra week of paid vacation, and offered him a free plane ticket anywhere in the United States. After Bacanovic learned that Haskell was traveling to Argentina on an assignment from his magazine, he offered to buy a ticket for Faneuil so he could go along. Faneuil didn't take any of it. They struck him as the equivalent of bribes. It was insulting that Bacanovic thought he could be bought off. And Faneuil hated Bacanovic's constant need for reassurance.

Monaghan, Faneuil's supervisor, commented frequently that he seemed under stress, but she never asked Faneuil why. Instead, she kept reassuring him that everything would be all right. She offered him coveted tickets to a New York Knicks game, which he declined. Finally she told him to take a week off with pay, and gave him no choice in the matter. He had nowhere to go, and spent most of the week at his apartment, brooding about his plight.

Bacanovic and Stewart were obviously discussing and coordinating their stories. Compared with Bacanovic and Stewart, he was a nobody. What if they decided to blame him for divulging the information that the Waksals were trying to sell? Who would believe his version, even if it was the truth? Especially since he'd already lied to protect them? Already thin, he lost much of his appetite and lost weight. He felt increasingly isolated and vulnerable.

Then, during the first week in March 2002, Dave Marcus, the Merrill lawyer, called Faneuil to say that the SEC wanted to interview him again. This time, it would be in person, with an assistant U.S. Attorney present. Marcus said he couldn't go, but would send another Merrill lawyer, Rick Weinberg, to represent Faneuil. Faneuil immediately called Gutman, his lawyer.

It should have been obvious that the SEC's investigation had advanced considerably, with potential criminal charges signaled by the presence of someone from the U.S. Attorney's office. But Gutman's advice remained the same: he told Faneuil not to lie, but not to volunteer anything either. Gutman didn't seem unduly concerned. Indeed, when Faneuil told him the interview was scheduled for March 7 and gave him the time, assuming that Gutman would accompany him, Gutman dismissed the idea. "You don't need me there," he said. "You'll have a Merrill attorney with you, right?"

"Yeah," Faneuil said, mentioning Weinberg.

"Then you don't need me. You'll be fine."

Just weeks earlier Gutman had told him to notify him immediately if the government called him again and not to answer any questions without Gutman being there. Faneuil didn't know what to think.

On March 6, the day before the interview, Faneuil went back to Merrill's downtown offices. Marcus introduced him to Weinberg, who would now be handling the matter. Then Marcus went over Faneuil's earlier testimony in great detail in order to get Weinberg up to speed. Or so he said. Faneuil interpreted the exercise as a way to make sure he didn't change his story. Marcus and Weinberg didn't ask him any questions.

The next day Faneuil met Weinberg outside the federal courthouse in downtown Manhattan. Schachter met them in the lobby of the U.S. Attorney's office, then took them to a conference room upstairs. Glotzer and Slansky, who had questioned him on the phone, were already there.

The interview was remarkably similar to their earlier conversation. Once again, he was warned that failure to tell the truth is a crime. By Faneuil's estimate, 98 percent of the questions were about the Waksals and his dealings with them on December 27. At one point Schachter played a recording of Faneuil's discussion with Merrill Lynch compliance officials. In the call, Faneuil mentioned speaking to ImClone officials about whether any news was pending. He'd completely forgotten that; indeed, he still didn't remember it. But he conceded that the recording indicated he must have had such a conversation.

There were questions about Martha Stewart, but they seemed perfunctory. Faneuil simply repeated his earlier story: that Stewart called; he gave her the price of ImClone; she decided to sell; he executed and confirmed the order. No one pressed him or asked him to elaborate. They did ask quite a few questions about Heidi DeLuca, Stewart's bookkeeper. Faneuil wondered why, but didn't have much to add. He didn't say anything about DeLuca's later call, and how annoyed she was that the ImClone sale had upset their tax-loss-sale planning.

All in all, Faneuil felt he had handled the interview well, successfully carrying out Gutman's advice not to volunteer anything. Of course, Gutman had also told him not to lie. But by withholding crucial evidence he hadn't told the truth either. Still, he was feeling pretty good until the very end. Schachter concluded the interview by telling Faneuil he'd be receiving a subpoena to testify under oath before a grand jury. He added that this was confidential information, and Faneuil couldn't tell anyone.

Faneuil was startled. A grand jury? He felt it was one thing to tell his admittedly incomplete and misleading story on the phone or even at the U.S. Attorney's office. Although the government lawyers had told him to tell the truth, he'd never had to take an oath. But a grand jury: he'd have to place his hand on the Bible and swear to tell the truth in a court of law. He knew he couldn't make such an oath and then lie. It went against everything he'd been taught and believed in.

"How did I do?" he asked Weinberg as they left the building. He tried to contain a mounting sense of panic. He desperately needed someone to talk to and wanted reassurance.

"What do you mean?" Weinberg asked, giving Faneuil a hard look, according to Faneuil. "I don't understand the question." Weinberg turned and walked briskly away, leaving Faneuil alone on the sidewalk.

Faneuil frantically called his therapist. She was out; he left a voice message. Minutes later his father called.

"How did it go?"

"Fine," Faneuil said, trying to keep up a front. He didn't mention the grand jury.

Then he went to a bar. He gulped several drinks. Worried he was getting drunk, he called a friend to come get him. He just wanted to make everything go away.

The next morning he was a wreck. Bacanovic was away, so Faneuil went into Bacanovic's office and closed the door. He called his father. "It is *not* okay," he said, and then burst into tears.

"Pull yourself together!" His father sounded both angry and alarmed. "What the fuck is wrong with you?"

Faneuil just cried harder.

"Everyone has to deal with this kind of shit," his father said.

"What are you talking about?" Faneuil managed to stammer. What did his father know? How dare he talk to him like that? Furious, he slammed down the phone.

As soon as he got back to his cubicle, Faneuil typed an angry e-mail: "Do not talk to me that way or you won't have a son."

There's only one way out, he concluded. I've got to tell the truth.

Despite Schachter's warning, no grand jury subpoena materialized. As Faneuil steeled himself to confess, life went on at Merrill Lynch. He heard nothing further from the government lawyers.

The grand jury turned its attention back to the Waksals. As one government lawyer put it, "I thought it was over for Doug." The prosecutors assumed Faneuil was an innocent bystander who had simply taken and executed the order from Stewart, a transaction so insignificant that Stewart herself had forgotten she'd spoken to him.

After Faneuil's interview, ImClone responded to government subpoenas for phone records and phone logs. As the lawyers pored over the data, they noticed calls from prominent financier Carl Icahn and Jason Bonadio from legendary hedge fund SAC Capital along with a call from Stewart at 1:34 p.m., just minutes after selling her stock. The message entered by Waksal's secretary read: "Martha Stewart. Something is going on with ImClone and she wants to know what. She is on her way to Mexico. She is staying at Los Ventanos [*sic*]."

The lawyers were startled. This seemingly shattered the $60 story and the idea that Stewart and Bacanovic had tried so hard to project, which was that Stewart's sale the day before a major announcement was coincidence. Stewart knew that "something is going on with ImClone." At the same time, she didn't know exactly what was going on. She evidently didn't know that Erbitux had been rejected by the FDA, but she knew something.

It finally dawned on the lawyers that the information might be that the Waksals were selling their shares—not that Erbitux had been rejected by the FDA. After all, the Waksals and Stewart used the same broker. Bacanovic knew about their efforts. His insistence that he would never reveal one client's trading to another hadn't rung true. But how had Bacanovic conveyed this information to Stewart? Bacanovic was now saying he never spoke to her that day. Stewart said she did speak to him, but there were no phone records to support her claim. Had she used another as-yet-undiscovered phone at the airport to call Bacanovic?

Even more incriminating than the message itself was Stewart's failure to mention it during her testimony. In narrating the events of that day, she had conveniently deleted the call to Waksal from her recollection of events at the airport. On the strength of this single message, Schachter called Stewart's lawyers and said they needed to question Stewart once again, this time by phone. They agreed to a date of April 10.

The day before, on April 9, Stewart's lawyers at Wachtell Lipton finally responded to the government's request for records of calls to Stewart's office on December 27, and specifically if Bacanovic had left a message. Less than twenty-four hours before her second interview, Stewart's lawyers produced the phone log.

"Martha Stewart/NYC Messages. Thursday, December 27, 2001" was the heading. The log, in its entirety, read:

> Plum pudding was excellent!
>
> Thank Mariana for Hanro!
>
> Peter Bacanovic thinks ImClone is going to start trading downward.
>
> Jean Pigozzi's office asked if Daniel Wolf could be on your helicopter
>   to the boat.
>
> Find fact sheet.
>
> Momoko wants to confirm a new date of Sunday, March 24, for shopping
>   center opening in Japan.
>
> Jen Conine: source of 4 tabletop lamps and chaise longue in Starrett
>   office.
>
> Gift of $25,000 to Barnard Annual Fund?

The government lawyers were electrified when they finally saw it. "Peter Bacanovic thinks ImClone is going to start trading downward."

There was no mention of $60. Why did Bacanovic think ImClone would start trading downward? And why had both he and Stewart covered this up? Bacanovic had mentioned leaving a message with Stewart's assistant, but nothing like this. Nor had Stewart said anything of the sort. The discovery only heightened the significance of Stewart's second interview. Schachter and the other lawyers from the earlier interview were on the conference call, along with

FBI agent Catherine Farmer and Laurent Sacharoff, the other SEC lawyer on the investigation. Stewart was again represented by John Savarese from Wachtell.

The government lawyers focused on the revelations in the two phone logs, starting with the one from Bacanovic. Stewart said "she didn't recall seeing it, or that wasn't the message that she recalled getting," according to Helene Glotzer's notes. "She said that she merely recalled Ms. Armstrong telling her that Mr. Bacanovic had called and wanted to speak with her before the end of the day." Stewart then reiterated her earlier story about their conversation and her decision to sell when the stock dropped below $60.

Schachter asked specifically if Stewart knew that the Waksals were selling their shares. "Did you hear that any of the Waksals were selling their stock?"

"No, I have no recollection of being told that," she replied.

"Do you have any recollection of calling and leaving a message for Sam Waksal?"

"No, but when I saw the message I realized I was calling him just to see how he was doing and make sure everything was okay."

Schachter asked Stewart if she'd discussed the sale with anyone else on the trip to Mexico—either Pasternak or Sharkey—and she said she might have told Pasternak. She didn't think she'd mentioned it to Sharkey.

Given the opportunity to correct earlier testimony and set the record straight, Stewart had dug herself in even deeper. But why? What were she and Bacanovic hiding? The government lawyers still lacked any direct evidence that Stewart had been tipped by Bacanovic. The government lawyers agreed to continue the investigation by interviewing Armstrong and Pasternak. In the meantime, the Waksal branch of the investigation was heating up.

On April 18, little more than a week after Stewart's second interview, Sam Waksal arrived at the SEC's New York offices for questioning. He'd been issued a subpoena, and was sworn to tell the truth. Earlier, his father, Jack Waksal, and his daughter, Aliza, had testified that neither had discussed ImClone shares with him. On March 5, Aliza maintained that she hadn't spoken to her father on December 26 or 27 before placing her order to sell ImClone shares, hadn't discussed any investment issues with him during her vacation in Sun Valley, and had interrupted her vacation (not to mention her sleep) to sell when she did because she needed $1.7 million for an apartment she was buying in Manhattan.

Also under oath, Waksal's father insisted that he hadn't talked at all to his son on December 26, "never had a conversation about stock" with him, and "never spoke" to him "about ImClone."

The phone records produced to the SEC told another story: Sam Waksal and his father exchanged five phone calls between 9:52 p.m. and 11:11 p.m. the night of December 26. The next morning, there were four calls between Waksal and Aliza between 6:27 a.m. and 7:46 a.m. (mountain time). Aliza called Merrill Lynch at 7:01 a.m. and 7:49 a.m., in both cases just minutes after hanging up with her father.

The SEC lawyers as well as Schachter at the U.S. Attorney's office recognized that both the senior Waksal and Waksal's daughter had likely committed perjury. Would Waksal himself, already deeply enmeshed in the insider trading scheme, now compound his difficulties by also lying under oath?

Glotzer handled the questioning.

"Dr. Waksal, I'm handing you what's just been marked as Exhibit 114. Have you ever seen this document before?"

"Yes."

"What is it?"

"It's a request to transfer my Merrill account and shares of ImClone to Aliza."

"And the second paragraph says, 'It's imperative this transfer take place tomorrow morning, December 27, first thing.' Do you see that?"

"Yes."

"Why was it so imperative that the transfer take place?"

"I believe this was just the way this was written, just to make sure that they would do it very quickly. Alan Goldberg [the accountant] was going away and I was making sure it was done immediately. I don't believe that there was any imperative associated with it."

Glotzer continued, "Why did you want to give [ImClone] shares to Aliza?"

"I had told Aliza that I was going to do that for her," Waksal said. "I had told Aliza a couple of weeks before that—Aliza lived off of her ImClone. Aliza had no other real means of support, and I had told her when we talked earlier in December about her financial situation, that I was going to give her more ImClone stock that she could use to live on."

"Did you ever instruct Jack Waksal or Aliza Waksal to sell their shares of ImClone?"

"No."

"Did you ever suggest to any of them that they sell their shares of ImClone?"

"No."

As the Waksal criminal investigation was nearing a climax, the House Energy and Commerce Committee announced it would hold hearings on the FDA's handling of the Erbitux application, and specifically whether the secretive approval process and apparent leaks had fostered stock manipulation and insider trading. In May, Sam Waksal resigned as ImClone's chief executive and a director, citing "recent events and the distractions they've caused." He was succeeded as CEO by his brother Harlan. Then, on June 5, Theresa Agovino of the Associated Press reported that Sam Waksal had been subpoenaed and that "four of Waksal's relatives sold a total of $400,000 in company stock before the news of the [Erbitux] rejection emerged, a source close to the investigation said, on condition of anonymity. Also, one of Waksal's daughters reportedly sold $2.5 million in ImClone shares before the rejection." The article continued, "Legal documents given to the committee show that domestic doyenne Martha Stewart also shed 3,000 ImClone shares. . . . Stewart's spokesman said Stewart didn't receive any inside information on ImClone."

Buried in the story, with an offhand reference, it was the first public mention of any link between Stewart, Waksal, and trading in ImClone before the announcement.

The next day the *Wall Street Journal* picked up on the story, though it ran deep in the "Marketplace" section. "Martha Stewart Sold ImClone Shares—Timing Raises Questions, but There Is No Indication She Knew of FDA's Decision," the headline read.

The *Journal* article, by reporters Chris Adams and Geeta Anand, contained a detailed rebuttal of any insider trading suspicions from Savarese, Stewart's lawyer:

Stewart's sale, involving about 3,000 shares of ImClone, occurred on December 26 or 27. The sale was executed, he said, because Ms. Stewart had a predetermined price at which she planned to sell the stock. That determination, made more than a month before that trade, was to sell if the stock ever went less than $60, he said. At the time of the sale, the stock was trading at about $60. As of 4:00 p.m. yesterday, ImClone shares tumbled $1.28, or about 15 percent, to $7.40 on the NASDAQ stock market.

"There is absolutely no evidence whatsoever that she spoke to Sam, or had any information from anybody from ImClone during that week," said the attorney, who added that he examined the trades when earlier news reports talked about the social connections between Ms. Stewart and Dr. Waksal. "I am absolutely sure that there was no communication of any kind between her and Sam, no passing of any information from him to her."

This surprised Schachter and other lawyers in the Justice Department and at the SEC, since ordinarily lawyers decline comment on pending investigations or make a vague statement of innocence, preferring to develop the facts within the still private confines of the investigation. Here Savarese had denied any communications between Stewart and Waksal that week, which was technically true, although he made no mention of Stewart's insistent call and message demanding to know what was going on with ImClone.

The *Journal* article quoted subcommittee chairman James Greenwood, Republican from Pennsylvania: "Our level of interest is very high. We've been tracking the precise chronology of the sales, and how that compares to who knew what and when. What we know is that if you make a trade because you know something that is not public and that other stockholders don't know, that's insider trading. And that's what we want to take a look at."

The story was a bombshell at the offices of Martha Stewart Omnimedia, where until then practically no one knew anything was amiss. When Stewart herself arrived that day, Sharon Patrick, the company's chief executive, intercepted her and gave her a big hug in the corridor just outside her office, a conspicuous show of support. Now, suddenly, some employees were being told to get lawyers, including Ann Armstrong and Kevin Sharkey. Sharkey was spotted sobbing in Stewart's office, his head on her desk.

Until then, it was ImClone's stock price that had been getting all the attention. But the *Journal* article suddenly thrust another stock into the spotlight: Martha Stewart Omnimedia (MSO). To investors, Martha Stewart, the person, was indistinguishable from Martha Stewart, the brand, and Martha Stewart, the company. Few businesses relied so heavily on the talents and image of a single person. Should Stewart face criminal charges, the consequences could be dire.

The day the AP article appeared, on June 6, MSO shares closed at $19.01, just 22 cents lower than the day before. The Stewart news had been buried, and the impact was minimal. But the day of the *Journal* article they plunged, closing at $17.39 after dropping as low as $16.80.

At 6:30 a.m. on June 12, four FBI agents converged on Waksal's SoHo loft. He was arrested, handcuffed, and later arraigned on charges of insider trading, perjury, obstruction of justice, and fraud.

A t Merrill Lynch, the mounting publicity over the Waksal charges and the revelation that Martha Stewart had sold her ImClone shares had no evident effect on Peter Bacanovic. Periodically, he'd look to Faneuil for reassurance. "We're on the same boat, right, Doug?" he'd ask. Faneuil would nod or answer, "Yeah," but he did so halfheartedly. But there were no more invitations to breakfast or lunch, and no more offers of free airline tickets.

With Waksal's arrest and insider trading charges, the scrutiny of Martha Stewart quickly intensified. MSO stock plunged again the day of Waksal's arrest, dropping 12 percent. Stewart was deluged with media inquiries about her sales of ImClone shares and ties to Waksal. She had her longtime public relations adviser and close confidante Susan Magrino issue a statement, carefully reviewed by her lawyers. The statement reiterated the points that Savarese had shared with the *Journal* and concluded, "In placing my trade I had no improper information. My transaction was entirely lawful."

The statement seemed to stabilize the stock, but it unleashed a storm of media coverage. The irreverent *New York Post* launched a steady stream of headlines: "Martha's Prison Everyday Collection," "Martha's Stewing," and "Martha in Hell's Kitchen." The *Daily News* countered with "Diva Martha's Now in the Soup." The story vaulted to television, with *Good Morning America* taking it up on June 17. David Letterman joked, "I was watching her show and she had to accept a subpoena wearing an oven mitt."

The next day Stewart knew she would face intense questioning at a long-scheduled investor conference. She couldn't further rattle the markets by canceling; indeed, she had to act as though nothing significant were happening. As Wall Street analysts and MSO shareholders gathered, she distributed another statement in an effort to ward off further questioning, adding a new dimension to her public defense:

"Earlier this year, I spoke with the SEC and the U.S. Attorney's office and have cooperated with them fully and to the best of my ability. I am also cooperating with the House Energy and Commerce subcommittee."

The next day MSO shares rallied strongly, jumping from $14.40 to $16.45.

I n many ways, the intense press coverage and public mention of Stewart's involvement came as a relief to Faneuil. He didn't feel so alone. It wasn't just him against Peter and Martha. This thing was much bigger. Even Congress had gotten interested. Though no grand jury subpoena had materialized, and he'd stopped expecting one, Faneuil talked to his friends about what to do next. He asked his father for suggestions about a new lawyer. He'd lost all confidence in Jeremiah Gutman.

Soon after the first articles reporting Stewart's involvement, Faneuil picked up the phone and called Marc Powers, a lawyer suggested by a friend of his father's, who in turn sent him to Marvin Pickholz, a criminal lawyer.

"You know the story that's been all over the news, Sam Waksal and Martha Stewart and trading in ImClone?" Faneuil asked Pickholz. "Well, I'm the broker's assistant. I did the trade."

"Really?" Pickholz seemed surprised but also pleased. A high-profile case had just walked in the door. Faneuil told Pickholz the entire story, including the pressure he felt from Bacanovic, and his incomplete and misleading testimony. Pickholz said he needed to ponder the situation, and suggested Faneuil continue to lie low for a few days.

Soon after, however, with press coverage of Stewart intensifying, Pickholz asked him to come in again. This time Powers joined him. "This is heating up," Pickholz observed. "We've got to act now, and you have to come forward."

Faneuil asked how that would work. "We're going to figure that out," Pickholz said. "Give us a few days."

The next day Faneuil answered the phone at his desk. It was Rick Weinberg, the Merrill Lynch lawyer who'd questioned him earlier. "How's it going?" Weinberg asked. "We have a few more questions we'd like to go over with you."

What a coincidence, Faneuil thought. Or was it? Had Pickholz said something? Faneuil said he had new lawyers, and would have to consult them first. He immediately called Pickholz. "Let's see what he has to ask, where he's going with this," Pickholz suggested.

"But what if he asks about Martha?"

"We'll cross that bridge when we come to it." Pickholz said he'd be present, and would interrupt if necessary.

The next morning Pickholz came to the Merrill office. Broker's assistants like Faneuil rarely had visitors on the floor, and Faneuil felt everyone was staring as Pickholz, wearing bright suspenders for the occasion, walked in and proceeded to make himself at home in Bacanovic's office. Bacanovic was away, so Faneuil joined him and sat in Peter's chair behind the desk. Still, it felt weird doing what he was about to do in Bacanovic's own office, with the picture of Bacanovic from *Martha Stewart Living* so close by. "Let's get Rick on the phone and see what he says," Pickholz said.

"What if he asks about Martha?"

"Tell the truth," Pickholz advised. "If he asks, 'Did you tell Martha?' say yes. Then I'll jump in."

Faneuil reached for the phone, but his hand froze. Surely this was a big mistake. His name hadn't surfaced, and now he'd be the center of a raging national controversy. Why him? It didn't seem fair. "Wait," he said. "Tell me again. Why am I doing this?"

Pickholz's voice rose. "Because if you don't, you're going to end up in an orange jumpsuit."

Faneuil was stunned. He'd never really considered the possibility of prison. He quickly dialed Weinberg's number using the speakerphone so Pickholz could participate.

There were barely any pleasantries before Weinberg asked, "Tell me what you said to Martha that day."

Faneuil was amazed at the speed with which the subject had come up. He looked at Pickholz, who nodded encouragement. This was it.

"She called"—Faneuil took a deep breath—"and she asked about Sam."

"What?!" Weinberg sounded incredulous.

Faneuil was silent.

"That's not what you said before! That's not in your testimony!" Weinberg sounded agitated and accusatory.

Pickholz stepped in. "Rick, my client has more to say. But he's not going to say it now. Let's work something out."

Pickholz motioned for Faneuil to leave the room. Why couldn't he stay and listen? He didn't know, but he did as he was told. Pickholz stayed on the phone with Weinberg for about twenty minutes as Faneuil watched through the glass wall of Bacanovic's office. When they finished, Pickholz told him he'd be meeting with the Merrill lawyers the next day, and Faneuil should tell them the whole story.

Faneuil was confused. "Aren't we going to the government first?"

Pickholz patted him on the shoulder. "You've got to trust us on this. You won't lose any advantage with the government. Merrill has promised that they'll hold off and won't say anything until you speak with the government." In return, Pickholz thought he might still be able to salvage a job for Faneuil at Merrill Lynch, though he realized it would be a long shot.

The next day, June 21, Faneuil and his lawyers gathered in a conference room at Pickholz's office, where Marcus and Weinberg from Merrill Lynch joined them. Faneuil was nervous, but he narrated the full story of his dealings with Stewart and Bacanovic on December 26. It didn't take him very long to correct his earlier statements. He filled in the crucial details he'd omitted before: that Stewart had called and demanded to know what was happening with Sam, and that Faneuil told her Waksal was selling all his shares. Everything else was what he'd already told them. But those two facts changed everything. They showed that Stewart already knew something significant about Waksal, and that Faneuil had conveyed confidential information about Waksal's trading. Marcus and Weinberg were scribbling furiously as he spoke, but didn't show any reaction. Under questioning, Faneuil said he was never aware of any agreement to sell Stewart's shares if the price hit $60, nor did Stewart or Bacanovic mention any such agreement that day, which undermined the linchpin of Bacanovic's and Stewart's explanation for the trade. Faneuil said he'd withheld the full account of what happened because he felt "pressured" by Bacanovic.

When Faneuil was finished, Pickholz asked him to step outside. Powers accompanied him into the hallway. "I don't know what's going to happen," Faneuil told his lawyer, "but I don't want to see Peter again. I can't see him." He was frightened and didn't feel safe.

"Don't worry, it will be fine," Powers assured him.

When they returned to the conference room, Marcus said, "Don't go back to the office. We're not firing you; we'll pay you. But we don't want you going back to the office just yet." Faneuil had no desire to go back to the office; he was already thinking about other job possibilities. If nothing else, this experience had already convinced him that he'd made a grave mistake taking a job on Wall Street.

After the Merrill lawyers left, Faneuil felt drained, but also relieved. He'd told the truth at last to people in authority, and a weight was lifted from his shoulders. "Keep your head down and try to relax," Pickholz urged. "Don't worry about work. Maybe you should go to a movie."

Faneuil had nothing better to do. He went to a showing of *The Ring*, a horror film. The next day he noticed there was an urgent message on his cell phone from his father: CNBC was reporting that Faneuil and Bacanovic had been suspended by Merrill Lynch.

His life as he'd known it was over.

On June 25 Martha Stewart appeared for her regular cooking segment on the CBS *Early Show*. CBS News officials warned her before she went on the air that the network couldn't ignore the mounting controversy over her stock trade. Still, she was determined to proceed. As she plunged a sharp knife into a head of cabbage, host Jane Clayson rather awkwardly changed the subject to the ImClone investigation. "I have nothing to say on the matter," Stewart retorted. "I'm really not at liberty to say. And, as I said, I think this will all be resolved in the very near future and I will be exonerated—"

"I know that . . ." Clayson tried to interrupt, but Stewart kept talking.

"—of any ridiculousness. And I want to focus on my salad because that's why we're here."

It was Stewart's last appearance on *The Early Show*.

The next morning, Faneuil arrived at St. Andrew's Plaza with his two lawyers. He wore his best suit and a tie. He was nervous. His lawyers had made clear that his future depended on this performance. He would finally be telling the truth to the people who really mattered—the prosecutors. He didn't expect them to treat him as any kind of hero for coming forward—he didn't even think of himself in those terms—but he did think they'd understand what he'd been through.

His lawyers hadn't told him much about what to expect. All they'd stressed was that he couldn't just walk in and say he'd lied. Pickholz had told him, "They really didn't press you on Martha. You really didn't answer them untruthfully. Tell them what you remember, but don't say you lied."

Wasn't this just semantics? Wasn't the whole point of this to be honest? Faneuil wasn't sure, but he agreed to follow his lawyers' advice. When they arrived, Faneuil signed a written cooperation agreement providing that anything he disclosed would not be used against him in any subsequent prosecution, a form of partial immunity.

When they came into Steve Peikin's large office, Faneuil was confronted by a crowd gathered for the occasion: Peikin, two or three FBI agents, and several others Faneuil had never seen before. Schachter was in a trial, so Peikin explained the terms of the cooperation agreement and asked if he understood. Faneuil nodded. Then he started talking. He felt slightly sick, his stomach in knots. When he got to Stewart's call, he said that she'd asked him about Waksal—"what was going on with Sam"—a departure from his earlier statements.

"But we asked you about that," Peikin interrupted.

"I don't know, there were so few questions about Martha," Faneuil said, evading the question. He was trying to follow his lawyers' advice. "There was so little time; I never really got a chance to finish . . . Nobody really asked. All I remember is I said she asked for a quote, and I gave it to her, and I sold her stock."

Peikin leaped to his feet. "You lied!" he shouted. "If you think you're going to sit here and try to tell us this was just two ships passing in the night, or some such bullshit, and we were foolish enough not to ask the right question, then you have another think coming! You're a liar. You'll never get away with this."

"Okay, hold on . . ." Pickholz tried to interject.

"No!" Peikin yelled. "We've got your notes from Merrill Lynch."

Everyone started talking at once. His lawyers told Faneuil to leave the room. FBI agent Catherine Farmer followed him outside. He got a soda from the machine in the hallway. He could hear everyone shouting and yelling in the conference room. He didn't know what was going on, but obviously it was a disaster. He started to cry.

Finally his lawyers told him to return. The government lawyers had agreed that for now, they would put aside the issue of whether Faneuil had lied or misled the government in his prior statements or would accept responsibility for that. Faneuil told his story in detail and answered all their questions.

The prosecutors were furious over what they saw as Faneuil's continuing evasions. Still, Faneuil had come forward. He wasn't going to retreat now. The Stewart-Bacanovic story was crumbling, and not just because of new information from Faneuil.

Lawyers involved say that Faneuil's change of heart came as a "bombshell" to Savarese, Pedowitz, and the other Wachtell lawyers involved in the case. When they learned the news, their first question was, "Who is Faneuil?" With the possibility of a trial suddenly more likely, and considering that Wachtell lawyers themselves might be called as witnesses, they deemed it prudent to reach out to Robert Morvillo. (Under the disciplinary codes, lawyers may generally not act as advocates at a trial in which they are likely to be called as witnesses.) Morvillo had been head of the criminal division in the U.S. Attorney's office and a law review editor at Columbia; with his portly figure and down-to-earth manner, he looked like he'd stepped out of a television law drama. He was especially effective with juries.

Now that Faneuil had changed his story and agreed to cooperate, and as the Stewart publicity mounted, Karen Seymour, the head of the criminal division at the U.S. Attorney's office, assumed a more active role in the case. Seymour had recently returned to the office at U.S. Attorney Jim Comey's request to head the criminal division, a post she considered her "dream job." Seymour had worked at the office before with both Comey and Patrick Fitzgerald, now the U.S. Attorney in Chicago; she had enormous respect for Comey's dedication and integrity. She left a lucrative partnership at Sullivan & Cromwell to take the job. When she'd arrived, the Waksal investigation was in progress. It had seemed straightforward, a brazen example of insider trading and perjury at the highest level of ImClone. She'd watched as the Stewart dimension, at first barely a footnote, had inflated into a scandal involving another publicly traded company and was now swallowing the entire case. With Faneuil's revelations, Stewart's story no longer held together. Seymour felt Stewart needed to be questioned again, this time, like Bacanovic, under oath.

Schachter contacted Stewart's new lawyer, Morvillo. This time, he flatly refused to make Stewart available for more questioning. If subpoenaed, he said, she would invoke the Fifth Amendment and refuse to testify.

This was Stewart's right, of course, but the prosecutors were free to draw their own conclusions.

With Stewart and Bacanovic balking, or worse, providing false testimony, the government lawyers turned to other potential witnesses. The SEC's Helene Glotzer arranged to question Ann Armstrong, still working as Stewart's assistant. Like other MSO employees swept into the investigation, Armstrong was told to hire her own lawyer at company expense, and was strongly encouraged to choose someone from Wachtell Lipton or Morvillo's firm, the same firms representing Stewart. But Armstrong didn't like the idea. There were too many potential conflicts, and she felt Stewart's interests would inevitably take precedence over hers. Armstrong was friendly with Stewart's personal assistant in Connecticut, whose husband was a white-collar defense lawyer. He recommended Susan Brune, a lawyer in Manhattan.

Stewart never said anything about Armstrong's decision, but the moment she hired a lawyer from outside the Stewart defense team, her attitude and demeanor changed. She was distant toward Armstrong.

Armstrong's friendship with Cuti also waned. In one phone conversation, Cuti had dismissed Faneuil's apparent decision to cooperate with prosecutors. "We're going to get Doug Faneuil, make mincemeat of him, put him through the wringer," he said, according to Armstrong.

"How dare you say that," Armstrong replied. Like her, Faneuil was a bystander dragged into the affair by his boss. "I feel closer to Doug than anybody else," she added, although the two had never met. (Cuti denies making such a comment about Faneuil.)

Finally, at a meeting in Morvillo's office, matters reached the boiling point. Armstrong got so angry that she left the meeting and sat in the firm's library to collect herself. Cuti followed her in, trying to make amends, but Susan Brune was upset when she found her client alone with one of the defense lawyers. Armstrong insisted that she was going to tell the truth, whatever the consequences for Stewart.

Glotzer began by asking about the phone calls on December 27, and Armstrong explained the sequence of events: the message from Bacanovic about ImClone "trading downward"; the subsequent call she had placed from Stewart to Faneuil. This, of course, contradicted Stewart's testimony that she had placed the order with Bacanovic directly.

"Was it possible to mistake Faneuil's and Bacanovic's voices?" Glotzer wondered.

Absolutely not, Armstrong said. She wondered why Glotzer was even asking.

Armstrong narrated the entire story of the erased message, Stewart's order to put it back, and Armstrong's subsequent efforts to retrieve the original from the computer system, all of which had happened just days before Stewart's testimony in which she claimed to have no memory of any phone message.

The government lawyers were startled. Stewart's decision to destroy crucial evidence—and then resurrect it—didn't seem to be, on its face, a smoking gun. And yet it spoke volumes about Stewart's state of mind at the time—and even more powerfully, to her truthfulness when she was interviewed just days later. Stewart had asked to see the message log and then altered it right after talking with her defense lawyer. Its existence was inconsistent with her statement in her first interview that the message was to call her broker. It also conveyed information—possibly inside information. And the information rendered utterly incredible Stewart's testimony that she "didn't recall" if there was any written record of Bacanovic's call—just days after she'd erased it.

And how could Stewart's lawyers have said nothing when she gave such an answer, when they had just spent the weekend discussing the incident and trying to retrieve the message?

Stewart's lawyers later pointed to the Steven Pearl memorandum in their files—which, contrary to FBI agent Farmer's notes, said that Schachter had asked Stewart what *time* a message from Bacanovic had come in (not whether there was a written record of the message)—to maintain that Stewart had responded truthfully when she said that she didn't remember. The lawyers didn't know either, and said they'd check to see if there was a time on the message log.

Schachter later disputed this, saying his question, Stewart's answer, and the lawyers' response clearly related to the existence of such a message, although there may also have been a follow-up question about its timing. (Notes taken by FBI agent Farmer and the SEC lawyers supported Schachter's recollection.)

In any event, the lawyers had finally produced the critical evidence. Armstrong had turned into a far more important witness than anyone had guessed. Glotzer quickly passed on the news to Schachter, who in turn conveyed it to Karen Seymour and Jim Comey. Other lawyers on the investigation called Armstrong, and she repeated the story. Finally they asked her to testify before the grand jury. They wanted this under oath, on the record. The prosecutors knew that Armstrong might come under intense pressure to change her story. Armstrong complied.

The government lawyers had also received test results from the work sheet containing the handwritten "ImClone @ $60" reference that Bacanovic had testified about, and that he was so sure was contemporaneous evidence supporting the story that he and Stewart had agreed to sell her ImClone shares if they reached $60. They'd sent the work sheet to the chief forensic scientist for the U.S. Secret Service, which specializes, among other things, in detecting counterfeit currency. They'd always felt the "@ $60" reference was curious, and the Secret Service had tested the ink. It turned out to be a unique sample; all other handwritten references on the work sheet were in a different ink. The results weren't dispositive, but were certainly consistent with the possibility that

Bacanovic had later altered the document to support his story, using the same color ink but a different pen from the one he'd used for the other entries. If so, it was a blatant attempt to obstruct justice.

The Justice Department lawyers had barely absorbed these developments when Schachter burst into Comey's office one morning, Catherine Farmer beside him. He was pumping the air with his fist.

"What's up?" Comey asked.

"Pasternak just told the truth!"

Pasternak, Stewart's self-described best friend and companion on the trip to Las Ventanas, had been a reluctant witness, to put it mildly. But the prosecutors sensed she knew something. Stewart herself had acknowledged that she "might" have said something about her ImClone trade to Pasternak during the trip. Finally they had issued a grand jury subpoena requiring her to testify. To avoid having her take the Fifth Amendment and refuse to answer their questions, they gave her full immunity, on only one condition: that she tell the truth.

Even so, Schachter had low expectations. Sharkey, for example, the other companion on the trip, had insisted he knew nothing. (He later told other MSO employees that prosecutors "hadn't asked the right questions.") So Schachter and Farmer were ecstatic when Pasternak recalled the scene on the resort terrace, where Stewart had described Waksal's attempt to sell his shares, culminating in her remark "Isn't it nice to have brokers who tell you these things?"

As Pasternak put it in a subsequent memoir about her life and friendship with Stewart, *The Best of Friends*, "I decided to follow the rules because after careful consideration, as much as I loved Martha, I could not sacrifice myself in service to her devastating problems."

No wonder Schachter was excited, since in its way this revelation was even more electrifying than Armstrong's testimony. When Stewart and Pasternak were in Mexico, there was no way Stewart could have known that Waksal was trying to sell his shares unless someone told her—and with her seemingly offhand remark to Pasternak, Stewart had acknowledged that that someone was her broker. It was now obvious that this was the reason Stewart sold so precipitously—not that she had any agreement to sell if the stock fell below $60. Did the fact that the chief executive of ImClone was trying to sell his shares meet the legal definition of inside information? That remained to be determined. What was now obvious was that Stewart and Bacanovic thought it did—and had tried to cover up the real reason for the trade.

. . .

A s the days passed after his visit to the U.S. Attorney's office, Faneuil waited anxiously for news of his fate. He thought coming forward was going to solve his problems and calm his anxiety. So far it had had the opposite effect. One day he got a call from Pickholz, asking if he'd be willing to take a lie detector test. "People are having some problems with your story," he said, specifically Faneuil's claim that Marcus had assured Gutman that Faneuil, Bacanovic, and Stewart would be fine, since Merrill Lynch was delivering Waksal on a "silver platter," and that Bacanovic had initially attributed Stewart's ImClone sale to "tax-loss selling." Pickholz sounded like even he found the account far-fetched.

Faneuil recoiled at the idea. He was telling the truth, but he knew polygraphs could be inaccurate, and given his emotional state, he thought there was a good possibility he'd fail. Still, he agreed. "I'll do what I have to do," he said. "I don't know that I trust them."

Afterward he called his father, who was incensed at the notion that even Faneuil's lawyers seemed to be doubting him. Faneuil called Pickholz, indignant. "What the hell is going on?" Pickholz told him to relax, not to worry about it.

Several weeks later, Faneuil again met with Pickholz and Powers at Powers's office. The bottom line, they said, was that the government wanted him to plead guilty to two felonies: making a false statement and obstruction of justice. Faneuil knew the government had been pushing for a felony plea, but he'd assumed this was just a tough negotiating tactic. "What about immunity? What about a misdemeanor?" he asked. Prosecutors often go along with a plea to a lesser offense if a witness is cooperating.

Immunity was "off the table," Pickholz said. The government wouldn't even discuss it. "The problem," Pickholz explained, "is that we've tried, we've looked, but we can't find a lesser crime for you to plead to." It seemed ironic that Faneuil's problem was that he hadn't committed any other crimes.

"So what does that mean, pleading to a felony? How will it affect my life?"

"There's a possible jail term," Pickholz said. "And you'd lose your right to vote."

Faneuil was stunned. "No!" he said. "I won't do it."

His lawyers stressed that he could go to trial, but that the government, they said, won 90 percent of the time, which was why most people pleaded guilty. They added that the federal prisons weren't so bad, especially for white-collar offenders. There wouldn't be any walls or fences; he could go somewhere near his parents in Massachusetts. "You wouldn't have to worry about your personal safety," Pickholz added.

Faneuil felt a surge of fear. What did that mean? He was afraid even to ask.

Faneuil left dejected. It had been horrible seeing the devastating impact of his sister's suicide on his parents. Now they would be losing their son to jail. As the prospect sank in, he started to sob.

That night Faneuil's despair turned to anger. It seemed surreal. What had he done to deserve this? After brooding about his fate, he called Powers. He was surprised by the anger in his own voice. "If you and Marvin ever mention me going to jail again I'm going to fire you. It's like a doctor telling a cancer patient to get ready to die. I'd hire a new doctor. I never want to hear another word about my going to jail."

The next day he returned to his lawyers' office. "This is insane," he told them. "You keep talking about Karen Seymour and Jim Comey. These people want to decide my fate and throw me in jail. They haven't even met me. They don't know me, the kind of person I am. I want them to see me before they decide to ruin my life."

Pickholz and Powers looked at each other. It wasn't a bad idea. Could Faneuil prepare a written statement? If so, they'd try to set up a meeting.

Faneuil threw himself into the task.

Faneuil and his lawyers returned to the U.S. Attorney's office, this time to Karen Seymour's office. Though spartan, it was large, with a sofa and several chairs in addition to her desk. Most of the lawyers who'd attended the previous session had crowded in. Seymour stood behind her desk. Pickholz was eager for Seymour to meet Faneuil in person. He thought she might relate to Faneuil's plight.

Once Faneuil was settled on the sofa, she said, "I understand you have something to say to us. But first, you need to understand the position you're in." She went around the room and introduced each person there. "If you take this to court, we're going to get on the stand, each one of us, and call you a liar. Who do you think the jury will believe? The ten of us, or you?"

Seymour outlined the case against him, which sounded only too compelling. She gestured at the notes from the Merrill Lynch lawyers. These, too, supported the case. "You have to understand the consequences of saying no to this deal," she said, referring to the plea to two felonies.

Faneuil didn't care. By now he was sure that if he did go to trial, he'd lose.

That wasn't the point. He didn't care how much pressure they put on him. He was going to stand up for himself.

Faneuil started to read his statement. He planned to stay strictly to the script. But a few words in, he was overcome by emotion and couldn't speak. He sobbed; he felt he'd never cried so hard in his life. He struggled to pull himself together and finally made it to the end. No one said anything, but even Pickholz was wiping away tears.

Finally his lawyers suggested he leave the room. With FBI agent Catherine Farmer behind him, he walked out and took a seat on a bench in the corridor. Farmer sat next to him. Just then an inmate walked by in an orange jumpsuit, handcuffs on his wrists, shackles on his legs, armed guards at his side. Farmer noticed the stricken look on Faneuil's face. She put her arm around him. "We don't get many people like you around here," she said gently.

Faneuil felt a surge of emotion. He felt it was the only nice thing anyone had said to him since he decided to come forward and tell the truth. It was the only time he felt like anyone in the government had treated him like a human being.

Back in Seymour's office, the government lawyers were weighing Faneuil's performance. Seymour had seen plenty of defendants cry. Tears alone didn't impress her. But Faneuil had seemed sincere. He was a young kid; this was his first job; he was pressured. This was hard on him. He was emotionally distraught. Could he stand up to the pressure of the witness stand? Was he a little unstable?

Faneuil was in the men's room when Pickholz burst in. He flashed him a smile and gave him the thumbs-up sign. "Immunity came up!" he said. He didn't want Faneuil to get his hopes up, but at least the government didn't reject the idea out of hand. He thought Faneuil had been great. He'd made an impression on the government lawyers. Pickholz returned to the negotiations, but they left without any resolution.

Seymour and her colleagues faced a dilemma. However sympathetic Faneuil might be, the U.S. Attorney's office followed strict guidelines about charging a cooperating witness, which did not permit pleas to reduced charges. The reason was trial strategy: if a cooperating witness guilty of a crime was offered too lenient a plea bargain or immunity, it might appear to a jury that he was simply telling prosecutors what they wanted to hear in exchange for favorable treatment. Unfortunately for Faneuil, the more serious the charges against him, the more credible he was as a witness. Of course, should Stewart or even Bacanovic decide to cooperate themselves and plead guilty, the need for Faneuil's testimony would vanish. In that case, any charges against him might well be dropped.

But there were no signs of any weakening on the Stewart-Bacanovic front, and neither had demonstrated any concern for Faneuil's fate beyond Bacanovic's efforts to keep him "on board." Schachter, Peikin, and other supervising lawyers in the office were adamant that Faneuil had to plead guilty to a felony, admit guilt, and face the likelihood of jail time.

Seymour felt differently. She felt on a gut level that making him plead to a felony was wrong. They could have given him a grand jury subpoena and he could have invoked the Fifth Amendment and remained silent. Instead he told the truth. It was a brave thing to do. He was just a kid. He'd been taken advantage of, pressured by powerful people. But this was not standard policy.

Seymour and her colleagues debated the issue for hours. Ultimately the decision was referred to Comey and his top deputy, David Kelley. They, too, felt that Faneuil deserved a break, although they recognized that any leniency might weaken his credibility as a witness. It was a tough call.

When Pickholz called to summon Faneuil to his office, he sounded pleased: The government had made a new offer. It wasn't immunity, but it was better than he'd hoped for.

Once Faneuil arrived, Pickholz explained that Faneuil would have to plead guilty to a single misdemeanor. He wouldn't lose his right to vote. "A misdemeanor is not a big deal," Pickholz said. "There is a jail term, but the government has assured us they'll recommend a departure from the sentencing guidelines. You won't go to jail."

So what was this misdemeanor? Faneuil was curious to know, since his lawyers had insisted they couldn't come up with one. It turned out to be a rarely invoked corner of the criminal code: receiving something of value in consideration for not informing law enforcement officials of a crime.

Faneuil was taken aback. What did that mean? It sounded like some kind of bribery. What of value had he taken? The dinner at Gramercy Tavern? Knicks tickets? The hot chocolate Bacanovic had bought him? Surely they weren't serious. He had rejected nearly everything offered him. He had lied out of loyalty to Bacanovic, not because he was offered anything. The very idea was insulting. "I can't do this," Faneuil said, shaking his head.

His lawyers seemed shocked. "Look, Doug, we're doing the best we can. You want to walk away from this deal? Then you're a complete and total idiot.

This is the best deal you're ever going to get." (Pickholz later said he wouldn't have used the word "idiot.")

Finally Faneuil gave in. He'd take the plea. His lawyers explained that he'd have to appear in court, enter the plea, and deliver a statement admitting guilt and assuring the judge he understood the consequences. He went home and started working on his statement. It wasn't easy. He looked up the word "consideration" in the dictionary. It confirmed his suspicion that he was being asked to admit to something that was essentially a bribe. Yes, he had misled the government. He had, in effect, lied. But that was a felony. He had not taken a bribe, but that was a misdemeanor. What Monaghan had offered him—the dinner, the tickets, the week off—were simple acts of kindness toward an employee under obvious stress. They hadn't bought his silence. It seemed incredible that he was being asked to admit something he didn't believe to be true in a case that was supposed to be about honesty.

So he wrote a statement he believed to be accurate, insisting he had not been bribed to be untruthful.

I'd just like to apologize and get this thing over with. But something tells me to speak up . . . One of the saddest ironies of this depressing circus is that lessons I've learned have not served me well (not yet). Things that I did wrong—like bow to intimidation—were things that often I had to repeat. In turning to the government, I had fears, but I expected to be treated with a sense of justice. Regrettably, it met with more disrespect, more intimidation, and more careerism.

I did not accept any gifts in exchange for my silence; in fact, none were offered. Merrill Lynch did shower me with rewards for "good behavior." Out of disgust, I turned many of them down (like a free plane ticket to Argentina). Out of sheer misery, I accepted others (like a free dinner for two). My story hasn't changed. The government will attest to that.

The government asked me some questions, and I didn't answer them fully. I was hiding—hiding behind my age and inexperience, hiding behind my sense of fairness, and hiding behind a life I thought was in my hands . . . Sometimes it seems easier to go with the flow, don't rock the boat, etc. I never wanted to be part of any of this. Since the very beginning, the behavior of all those involved disgusted me. I saw myself as an outsider, "just a kid"—certainly not an aspiring broker. And so, too easily, I tried to extract myself from the situation.

Yes, there was a conspiracy to obstruct justice. I never imagined—I never feared—that I was part of it. I felt betrayed, disappointed, and hurt by those involved from the start. They were not my friends, not any-more, and certainly we did not have the same interests. But in keeping quiet—in not coming forward with all I knew—I unwittingly embraced that conspiracy.

The thought of this makes my blood boil. I am angry with myself, among others. I never wanted to be part of any of this. I see now how I achieved less than that. To the government, to so many investors, to my family and friends, I am sorry. I should have come forward immediately.

If I take only one lesson from this mess, it will be this: if you're called to bat, you must step up to the plate. Merrill Lynch, in making me witness to its crimes, placed upon my shoulders a great responsibility. I shirked my duties to a lawful, right society—something I believe in passionately—with the naive assumption that new responsibilities are like new people: that we can decide which ones to take on. This is not true of course. And I have learned that lesson with as much force as any other in my entire life.

Faneuil's lawyers were apoplectic when they read it. "What the hell do you think you're doing? You can't say this!" Pickholz insisted. The whole point was to admit guilt to the misdemeanor, not deny it. "Just plead guilty." Ultimately they wrote a statement for him, and he grudgingly agreed to read it in court.

On September 24, Faneuil signed a letter from the Department of Justice, specifying that he would plead guilty to one count of "receipt of money and other valuable things in consideration for not informing law enforcement authorities of criminal conduct." The letter continued, "It is understood that, should Douglas Faneuil commit any further crimes or should it be determined that he has given false, incomplete or misleading testimony or information, or should he otherwise violate any provision of this agreement, Douglas Faneuil shall thereafter be subject to prosecution for any federal criminal violation of which this office has knowledge, including perjury and obstruction of justice."

Faneuil's life as a government witness was about to begin.

On October 2, Faneuil met his lawyers at Pickholz's office and they got into a Lincoln Town Car. Faneuil was nervous. His lawyers told him something about what to expect, but he was distracted and didn't remember much of what they said. They stressed that he had only two objectives: to plead guilty and to read the statement they'd written for him. He was not to say anything else.

The car stopped near some FBI offices in a building a few blocks away from the federal courthouse. As they approached the entrance, a CNBC reporter and cameraman intercepted them, thrusting the camera into Faneuil's face. Faneuil said nothing and they kept moving, with the cameraman walking backward. Pickholz reached out to stop him from running into a pole. "The U.S. Attorney must have tipped him," Powers surmised, once they were inside. "It's not unlike them. But it could have been worse. There was only one."

Catherine Farmer met them in the lobby, accompanied by two more agents. Faneuil's lawyers said they'd meet him in the courtroom, and the agents took him to a garage in the basement, where a black SUV was waiting. As they were about to get in, Farmer said, "You know, there are certain rules we have to follow, and this is one of them. Please don't take this personally." One of the other agents took out a pair of handcuffs. Faneuil raised his arms and they snapped them onto his wrists. They were much heavier than he expected.

When they got to the courthouse, Faneuil and the agents entered through a side door. A federal marshal met him and, after patting him down, started asking questions that seemed curiously personal: Who were his closest friends? Where did he hang out? Did he go to bars? Which ones? As Faneuil rattled off the names of various bars, he realized he'd been drinking far more than usual. He felt embarrassed. Farmer explained that the marshals needed the information in case he fled, though she assured him they didn't think of him as a flight risk. It was just another formality. Then they led him into a nearby jail cell. Faneuil had never realized there were cells right in the courthouse. Everything in it was painted white. There was no furniture other than a small bench protruding from the wall. He sat on it. The door slid shut. "Don't worry, we're not going to lock it," Farmer said.

Time passed. Faneuil felt disconnected from his body. How had he ended up here? Finally the marshal came for him. He removed the handcuffs. Walking into the courtroom was like passing through the looking glass. Everything about it was much nicer, brighter, more normal. He joined his lawyers at a table. "If you need to speak we'll tell you," Pickholz warned him. "Do not say anything else."

The proceedings began. Faneuil's mind again drifted. He felt like he was starring in an episode of the TV drama *L.A. Law*. Suddenly there was silence. His lawyers were nodding encouragement. He stood and said, "Guilty."

"He's a little nervous, Your Honor," Pickholz said. "Is it all right if he reads from a prepared statement?"

Faneuil began, trying to keep his voice steady. "I did not truthfully reveal everything I knew concerning the actions of my immediate supervisor . . . and the true reason for the 'tippee's' sale of ImClone stock," he said, without identifying either Bacanovic or Stewart by name. He said he'd accepted a free dinner for two, a week's extra vacation, and received a raise in return for remaining silent. It was brief, over in minutes. He would be sentenced at a later date. For now, he was free to go.

Faneuil's lawyers led him through the courtroom to the main door. "I thought we were going out the way I came in," he said. "No, we're going out this way," Pickholz said. "There will be a sea of people, more reporters than you've ever seen."

"For me?" Doug asked, incredulous.

"No, of course not. Because the main suspect is Martha Stewart. We'll make a quick statement and then go home."

When they stepped outside, they were at the top of a broad flight of stairs leading to the sidewalk. Faneuil noticed five or six reporters off to the right. Maybe it wouldn't be so bad. But then he saw them gesturing and calling, "He's here." Suddenly a horde of people rounded the corner and started surging toward him and his lawyers. Some carried heavy camera equipment. He saw several trip; the crowd kept surging forward. Flashbulbs were popping. The front rank got within two feet of him and would have come closer if his lawyers hadn't held out their arms and stopped them. The reporters yelled questions and tried to get his attention. "Doug," "Doug," he heard everywhere, as if he was on a first-name basis with any of these people. "What are you, a pussy?" someone yelled. "Aren't you going to stick up for yourself?"

"I'm very sorry, but under the circumstances I can't say anything," Faneuil said, over and over.

"Would that goddamned kid stop being so polite?" a reporter griped.

"Keep your head high," Pickholz whispered to Faneuil.

There were hundreds of reporters—more, the *New York Post* reported the next day, than for any other proceeding except the trial of mob boss John Gotti.

Faneuil and his lawyers moved slowly forward, pushing back the crowd. The flashbulbs kept popping. Finally they reached a podium that had been set up on the steps. Each of his lawyers read a prepared statement. They stressed that Faneuil had come forward to tell the truth of his own volition, that he was trying to do the right thing. Faneuil stood by, wondering what to do with his hands, which were clasped behind his back.

"Is Martha Stewart the 'tippee'?" someone called out.

Pickholz said he couldn't answer that, but added, "If you guys read this information and can't fill in the blanks, then you're in serious trouble."

Finally it was over, and they reached the waiting Town Car. The lawyers dropped Faneuil off in the Village, then continued up Sixth Avenue. Faneuil walked to Haskell's apartment—his own was staked out by photographers—and changed out of his suit. He was walking to meet Haskell for lunch when his cell phone rang.

"Douglas Faneuil, this is Jim Porz of Merrill Lynch. I have Judy Monaghan with me."

"Hi, Doug. It's Judy. How are you?"

What a ridiculous question, Faneuil thought. How did she think he was?

"We understand that you pleaded guilty today to a federal crime," Porz said.

"Yeah, that's right."

"You're fired. Doug, you broke the rules and disappointed everyone here. You shared information about a client's activity with another client. You know that's forbidden. You've proven yourself unworthy of Merrill Lynch," Porz continued, his tone grave and, Faneuil thought, pompous. "And so we have no choice."

The press release had already been written. Bacanovic, too, was fired, for allegedly failing to cooperate with a federal investigation—not for lying to Merrill Lynch. The release stressed that Merrill Lynch itself was cooperating fully with the ongoing investigation.

Now that he'd been fired, Merrill Lynch stopped paying Faneuil's outstanding legal bills. They were now approaching six figures, and Faneuil didn't have the money. But Merrill Lynch continued to pay Bacanovic's legal fees. When Faneuil's lawyers threatened to reveal this to the press, Merrill Lynch relented and resumed paying his bills.

Faneuil's picture was everywhere, on television, in the tabloids. An ex-boyfriend sold an old photo of Faneuil flexing his biceps to the *New York Post*, which emblazoned it on the cover, touting its "photo exclusive" of the "preening broker." Faneuil got calls from people he hadn't heard from in years, expressing varying degrees of sympathy, curiosity, and titillation. Journalist Christopher

Mason, a self-described "close friend" of Bacanovic's, wrote in *New York* magazine that Faneuil was a "jittery Judas" who had "shifted the blame to Bacanovic" by tattling to Merrill Lynch officials.

Meanwhile, Mason wrote, high society friends were rallying to Bacanovic's side. "Some threw him quiet dinners and lunches. The list of hosts included Nan and Tommy Kempner, Rufus and Sally Albemarle, and Louise Grunwald, who says the support for Peter has been unbelievable."

Faneuil stayed away from his apartment for six months. It was under constant surveillance by photographers. While living at Haskell's, he sent hundreds of letters looking for work. He was on the brink of being hired several times, until he explained he'd pleaded guilty and was a cooperating witness in the Martha Stewart investigation.

Eventually he landed a job at a Chelsea art gallery. It was temporary—the gallery was slated to close in a year—but having a job again made all the difference to his self-esteem. He steadily got more responsibilities and felt appreciated. Customers didn't recognize him or, if they did, said nothing.

As a cooperating witness, Faneuil was always on call if government lawyers needed him. He made many trips to the U.S. Attorney's office for meetings with Schachter, Seymour, and other lawyers on the Stewart investigation. The meetings began to blur in his mind. Sometimes he'd be there several days in a row; other times, a week or more would go by. He estimated he had fifteen to twenty meetings. He was asked to repeat every aspect of his story in painstaking detail. The prosecutors remained determined to get him to admit that he knew he did something wrong when he told Stewart about Waksal's attempt to sell his shares. This had been the sticking point before, and Faneuil still refused. Having been told to do so by Bacanovic, Faneuil had assumed it was okay. Given Merrill Lynch's policy on confidentiality, should he have known better? Perhaps, but the fact was that he hadn't known.

At first the government lawyers seemed to accept his account, but they kept returning to it. Faneuil did some research on the law of insider trading and could see why they did. For Stewart to be guilty of insider trading, she had to know that Faneuil was breaching a duty of confidentiality. If Faneuil himself didn't realize that, how could she be expected to? As Faneuil stood his ground, the lawyers were more insistent. "Are you sure? I mean, honestly, Doug, you say that's what you remember, but does that make any sense?" Finally, Seymour confronted him. "Doug, we've talked to all your friends, and they say you told them you did something wrong."

Seymour was skeptical that Faneuil didn't know he was doing anything wrong. It seemed obvious. Faneuil was smart enough to know better. She worried that if he insisted on his innocence, he'd be eviscerated on cross-examination. She and her colleagues pressed him hard on the issue, but he wouldn't budge.

The prosecutors also had problems with Faneuil's version of the $60 story. In Faneuil's account, Bacanovic had first told him the ImClone sale was part of a tax-loss-selling strategy, and only after Heidi DeLuca called him did Bacanovic shift abruptly to the $60 story. To Schachter this made no sense, since Bacanovic had testified to the $60 story in his first interview with the SEC, which was before DeLuca's call to Faneuil. Faneuil's version indicated Bacanovic was telling one story to Faneuil, and an entirely different one to others. Bacanovic may not have had a keen criminal mind, but surely he wouldn't have been that inconsistent. Under repeated questioning, Faneuil began to doubt his memory, conceding that maybe he'd gotten confused.

But by far the most troublesome of Faneuil's recollections was Marcus's assurance that Stewart and Bacanovic had nothing to fear if Merrill Lynch delivered the Waksals "on a silver platter." Faneuil was not a party to any such conversation. But his lawyer at the time, Jeremiah Gutman, was, and it was this assertion that had caused him to recommend that Faneuil "lie low" rather than come forward with the truth. From the government's point of view, this was not only far-fetched, but it put the government in a bad light, seeming to bargain with Merrill Lynch over the fate of prominent potential defendants. And it seemed self-serving, a ready excuse for Faneuil's failure to come forward sooner. Faneuil's own lawyers had made clear that they had trouble believing the story. They worried that Gutman was unpredictable, and might say anything on the stand. From a practical standpoint, if Gutman testified that no such conversation had taken place, Faneuil's credibility would be destroyed. But Faneuil held his ground. On this his memory was perfectly clear. After all he'd been through, he wasn't going to lie now.

On October 15, just weeks after Faneuil entered his plea, Sam Waksal pleaded guilty to six felonies: perjury, obstruction of justice, securities fraud (two counts), bank fraud, and conspiracy. The pleas weren't the result of any bargaining with the government, as is often the case. The evidence was so over-whelming that Schachter had refused to enter into any plea negotiations.

Waksal finally admitted that he knew the FDA was going to reject the Erbitux application and as a result told both his father and daughter to sell their ImClone shares. In an apparent effort to spare them insider trading charges, he insisted he never told them why they should sell. Still, he contradicted their sworn testimony that neither had spoken to him before selling. His admission along with the phone records all but proved that the two had committed perjury.

Indeed, Aliza Waksal, now with a new lawyer, had come forward and cor-rected her earlier testimony, conceding that her father had told her to sell her shares and had asked her to lie on his behalf, which she did. As one govern-ment lawyer put it, "What father would do that? She's twenty-four years old, a student, and he puts her in criminal jeopardy. When a father asks his daughter to lie for him, this is despicable."

Ultimately prosecutors exercised their discretion and decided not to bring criminal charges against either Aliza or Waksal's eighty-year-old father, who was a concentration camp survivor. Both were as guilty of false statements as Faneuil, arguably more so. Yet neither was needed as a witness, and thus had no further strategic importance to the government.

Besides the insider trading charges, Waksal also admitted defrauding Bank of America and forging the name of ImClone's general counsel on a letter to the bank. Waksal had shown utter indifference to the law and a willingness to drag his own family members into the conspiracy.

"I have made terrible mistakes," Waksal said outside the courthouse. "I deeply regret what happened. I was wrong."

Waksal was sentenced to seven years, three months in prison, and paid fines and restitution of $3 million. The night before he reported to a federal prison in Pennsylvania, he threw a party in his SoHo loft and handed out magnums of Château Lafite Rothschild from his cellar, *New York* magazine reported. Martha Stewart didn't attend, but phoned to offer her best wishes.

Waksal's professed remorse didn't extend to naming anyone else he tipped or cooperating with the government. Schachter told the court that there was "compelling evidence that Dr. Waksal may have tipped others," evidently refer-ring to Waksal's friends Sabina Ben-Yehuda and Zvi Fuks. Ben-Yehuda was dat-ing Fuks, who was a member of ImClone's scientific advisory board and the head of the department of radiation oncology at Memorial Sloan-Kettering

Cancer Center. Ben-Yehuda and Fuks sold all their ImClone shares just before the FDA announcement; in Fuks's case, worth $5.37 million. (They later paid fines of $2.77 million to settle insider trading charges filed by the SEC without admitting or denying guilt.)

But the big news was that Schachter didn't mention Martha Stewart. Martha Stewart Living Omnimedia shares jumped over 12 percent after her lawyers issued a statement that Waksal's plea had nothing to do with Stewart. By now the possible involvement of Stewart had overshadowed anything else connected to ImClone, including the brazen criminal behavior of its chief executive. The irony was that there never would have been a Martha Stewart investigation had Waksal not set the case in motion when he had his accountant phone Merrill Lynch to sell his shares.

With the testimony of Faneuil, Pasternak, and Armstrong, as well as the phone records, the deleted e-mail, and the doctored reference to "@ $60," the government had the makings of a sweeping case against Martha Stewart: insider trading, false statements, obstruction, conspiracy. Apart from the merits, however, the prospect of a trial of a high-profile celebrity like Stewart and her powerful broker Bacanovic was the last thing Jim Comey and his office of assistants were looking for in 2002. The office was already embroiled in investigations of massive frauds at Enron and WorldCom and a high-profile prosecution of Frank Quattrone, the Credit Suisse First Boston banker who brought dozens of companies public during the dot.com explosion. By comparison, Stewart's potential insider trading and her and Bacanovic's subsequent perjury, false statements, and obstructions paled in significance. Yet the overwhelming press interest had already shown that any Stewart prosecution would be the office's highest-profile case. She had some of the country's best and most expensive lawyers. She had a large and rabid popular following. No matter what the evidence, it was a case the lawyers felt they might well lose.

Comey desperately wanted the case to reach a settlement with guilty pleas from Stewart and Bacanovic. He couldn't understand Bacanovic's obstinacy. After all, he hadn't traded and didn't even face potential insider trading charges. In return for the truth, and testimony against Stewart, he probably could have reached a reasonable outcome with very low risk of any jail time. The incentives to do so seemed so compelling that Comey bet that Bacanovic would come forward, testify truthfully, and the case would be over. Faneuil obviously hoped for the same thing, sparing him the ordeal of testifying and allowing him to be sentenced and move on with his life.

All of their hopes proved in vain. Bacanovic, through his lawyer, never indicated any willingness to even discuss a potential plea. The loyalty to Stewart he'd expressed to Faneuil proved insurmountable, as well as the likelihood that his career would be ruined if he turned against her. And perhaps there was an element of guilt. After all, he may have felt he was doing Stewart a valuable favor, but by having Faneuil tell her about the Waksal selling, it was Bacanovic who had put Stewart in jeopardy. And in contrast to Faneuil, there was never any indication that Bacanovic felt any moral or civic duty to tell the truth.

Stewart's lawyers mounted a strenuous effort to persuade Comey, Seymour, Schachter, and the others not to bring charges. They spent many hours in presentations at the U.S. Attorney's office and submitted voluminous factual and legal analyses to support their arguments. Much of their efforts focused on the insider trading charges. The law of insider trading is complicated, and everyone agreed this was an unusual case. Criminal insider trading requires three major elements: the sale or purchase of a security, in breach of a fiduciary duty or relationship of trust, while in possession of material, nonpublic information about the security. Waksal's trading and attempted trading obviously met all three criteria: he was an ImClone officer with a duty to shareholders and he knew about the adverse Erbitux decision.

Stewart clearly sold shares. But she owed no duty to ImClone shareholders. She had been tipped by Faneuil acting on Bacanovic's instructions. Did she know, or should she have known, that Bacanovic was breaching a duty of confidentiality imposed upon him by Merrill Lynch—in legal terminology, that Bacanovic had "misappropriated" the information? Nor did Stewart know about the Erbitux decision. She was essentially copying, or "piggybacking," Waksal's trades. The fact that he was trying to sell all his shares was clearly nonpublic. But was it material? Would other ImClone investors have been likely to act on that information?

The Wachtell lawyers debated these issues at length. The prosecutors were convinced the information was material—sale of stock by corporate insiders is deemed so important that it must be reported to the SEC and publicly disclosed. Moreover, Stewart learned that Waksal was trying to sell *all* his shares and was doing so precipitously. Most if not all investors would have reacted as Stewart did to the news of Waksal's sales. And obviously Stewart knew that Bacanovic had done something wrong, and by acting on his information, so had she. Why else would she have tried to delete the e-mail message that "ImClone is going to trade down"? And why else would she and Bacanovic have lied to cover the real reason for her trade?

But Stewart's lawyers made more headway by arguing that no one had ever been charged with a crime for "piggybacking" on a trade by someone else, although the SEC had pursued numerous such civil cases. Perhaps there should have been some criminal charges in piggybacking cases, but there hadn't been. It wouldn't be fair to charge Stewart with a crime when no one else had been, and it would likely fuel suspicions already surfacing in the press that she was being persecuted because she was a successful woman in business.

Schachter and several others in the office didn't buy that argument. If the material, nonpublic information was Waksal's hasty attempt to sell all his shares, then Stewart wasn't piggybacking on someone else trading on that information. Stewart herself knew that Waksal was selling—and that's what motivated her decision. The inside information was Waksal's selling, not the Erbitux decision.

The discussions became heated at times, with Schachter and securities fraud chief Richard Owens adamant that Stewart should face insider trading charges, and Seymour leaning the other way. The SEC's head of enforcement was also urging them to indict Stewart in order to send a message to other potential inside traders. That decision, too, finally went to Jim Comey.

"I almost didn't indict this case," Comey later recalled. "It might have obscured everything else we were doing: WorldCom, Adelphia, ImClone. If we charged Martha Stewart, it would be a media circus. Would people say I did it just because I wanted to become famous? Did I need this? And it was a close case. We might have lost given the legal talent she mustered and her celebrity."

As Comey reflected on the facts, especially the obvious lies that Stewart and Bacanovic had promulgated, he remembered one of his earliest cases, when he was a young prosecutor in Richmond, Virginia. He was investigating a Baptist minister named James Miller. At the time, the mayor of Richmond encouraged people who wanted to curry favor with him to patronize various friends and family members who in turn paid kickbacks to the mayor. A company that wanted to privatize the city cemeteries was told to pay Miller, who cashed the check and then paid the mayor. "Please don't lie," Comey all but begged him. "You're a young man. The mayor will plead guilty, and he'll turn against you. Please don't do this to yourself." Miller continued to insist he hadn't paid the mayor anything.

As Comey had predicted, the mayor did plead guilty and turn against his minister. "We indicted James Miller for perjury. He went to jail," Comey said. "I was thinking about Martha, and then I got angry with myself. I was hesitating because she was rich and famous. People said the opposite about me—that I prosecuted her because she was rich and famous, but it's not true. And I asked myself, if I could prosecute James Miller, how could I *not* indict Martha Stewart?"

Before making any final decision, Comey asked Dave Kelley to do some research on recent perjury and false statement cases. It was widely perceived—and Stewart's lawyers had argued—that perjury and false statements are crimes that are rarely prosecuted. But Kelley came back with statistics that showed two thousand such cases had been filed in just the past year. Perjury was not only being prosecuted, it was threatening to become an epidemic.

Comey also wanted to know how many insider trading convictions had been obtained against someone who, like Stewart, was a "tippee" with no fiduciary relationship to the company. Schachter and Owens couldn't produce any. They found numerous SEC cases, but no criminal ones. "There's no way I will use Martha to push the boundaries of the law," Comey insisted. "This case cannot be a laboratory for developing an insider trading theory."

During their next meeting, Comey asked Morvillo to concentrate on the evidence of Stewart's false statements and not to address the insider trading issues. Morvillo rose to the occasion with a simple argument: "She's incredibly wealthy!" he said. "Why would she lie to save a few thousand dollars?"

"If she was picking up her *New York Times* and saw a $5 bill lying nearby, would she pick it up?" Comey asked. His point was that many rich people had gotten rich by caring about every penny. He already knew enough about Stewart to know she fit the pattern.

Morvillo didn't answer.

Schachter and the other prosecutors were also arguing for a count of securities fraud. Stewart had misled investors in her company by peddling a false story of innocence. She hadn't simply denied guilt and declined further comment. She had manufactured a false story and used it to prop up her stock price. Indeed, the stock had often rallied on days when Stewart had proclaimed her innocence and reiterated the $60 alibi.

"They argued I was indicting her for protesting her innocence," Comey said.

"But she went further. She made misstatements to shareholders. The more I thought about this case, the gravamen was her lies. The security count fit in with this."

That spring, Stewart's lawyers and the prosecutors launched into intense plea negotiations, with Karen Seymour the lead negotiator for the government. Given the intense media scrutiny, Comey was anxious to resolve the case with a plea, preferably before indictment. Stewart's lawyers were insistent: they'd consider a plea, but only if there was a guarantee that there would be no jail time. Comey refused. He'd never made such a deal, and Martha Stewart was not going to be the first. He continued to walk the sometimes fine line between giving Stewart uniquely favorable and unduly harsh treatment because of her celebrity and the visibility of the case.

Talks dragged on for months, with growing complaints from Schachter and others who felt Stewart and Bacanovic's lawyers had had more than an adequate chance to make their arguments. Seymour didn't want anyone to feel they'd been pressured by arbitrary deadlines. By Memorial Day, they'd pretty much reached their final negotiating stances: Stewart would plead guilty to one count of making a false statement, the least serious of the potential felony charges against her and, according to the sentencing guidelines, the one with the least chance of a jail sentence. Comey, in return, agreed that the Justice Department wouldn't seek a jail term. It wouldn't guarantee she wouldn't get one. But if the judge decided to impose a jail term, Stewart would have the right to withdraw her guilty plea. Under these circumstances, Comey felt the possibility of jail to be extremely remote. "That's a deal breaker," Seymour warned, urging that he go ahead and give the guarantee. But Comey wouldn't go any further.

That weekend Comey and David Kelley were playing golf as Seymour delivered the ultimatum to Morvillo and Stewart's lawyers. They were on the tee when Comey's cell phone rang. Seymour was ebullient: Stewart had accepted. At least, Pedowitz had indicated she would. "We'll get there," he'd said. The clear understanding was they had a deal. Stewart would plead to one felony as long as she could withdraw the plea if the judge sentenced her to prison. The SEC would allow her to remain a director of her company. Beyond the mechanics of the plea, the deal was a breakthrough: Stewart was finally accepting responsibility and admitting guilt. To the prosecutors, that was far more important than any jail term.

The prosecutors were relieved. The negotiations had been tough. Given Stewart's celebrity, everything about them had brought intense scrutiny. A settlement would save the enormous costs of a trial as well as the risk of losing.

They felt the facts were compelling, but who knew how a jury would react to Stewart? None of them had tried a case against a defendant so visible, whom everyone thought they knew, and who was beloved by many.

Little more than forty-five minutes later, Pedowitz called Seymour again. "Martha won't do it," he told her. Seymour's heart sank. Stewart had decided, according to Pedowitz, that "her business and reputation couldn't take any admission of guilt." The lawyers had pressed her, pointing out the risks of trial and trying to disabuse her of any notion that she'd get an even better deal by holding out. But Stewart had stubbornly resisted. Seymour thought it significant that Pedowitz didn't make any further claims that Stewart was innocent, only that she had made the decision for business reasons.

Seymour's primary reaction was one of sadness, not just for Stewart, but for Bacanovic, who'd obviously tethered himself to her fate; for Faneuil, who would now have the ordeal of a trial; for the other witnesses; for Stewart's employees and shareholders, for whom the ordeal would be vastly prolonged. Seymour felt like she was watching a train wreck unfold that she was powerless to stop. She felt no good would come of Stewart's decision. But at this juncture the Justice Department had no alternative but to try the case.

On June 4, 2003, the grand jury indicted Stewart on eight counts of lying, obstruction, and conspiracy and one of securities fraud. She wasn't charged with criminal insider trading, as Comey had decided, but the SEC filed a related civil suit that did. The grand jury indicted Peter Bacanovic for obstruction, perjury, and an additional count of making and using a false document. After entering a not guilty plea, Stewart resigned as chief executive and a director of Martha Stewart Omnimedia and assumed the title of "creative director." She stepped down as a director of the New York Stock Exchange. She faced a maximum sentence of thirty years in prison and a fine of $2 million if convicted on all counts. "This criminal case is about lying–lying to the FBI, lying to the SEC and investors," Comey told the horde of reporters gathered outside the courthouse. "That is conduct that will not be tolerated. Martha Stewart is being prosecuted not because of who she is, but what she did."

THREE

"A Conspiracy of Dunces"

T he trial of *United States of America v. Martha Stewart and Peter Bacanovic*
began on January 27, 2004. Karen Seymour, the lead trial lawyer, dressed
in a sober light gray suit and one strand of pearls, looked like she could
have stepped from the pages of *Martha Stewart Living*.

Stewart herself had already managed to put her distinctive stamp on the
courtroom. Her personal bodyguard was present each day, and had been granted
an exemption so he could carry a gun into the courtroom. Stewart had special
cushions made in navy fabric with contrasting stitching, embroidered with her
monogram, which were placed each morning on the first three rows of benches
reserved for her entourage. Several celebrities turned out to show their support
by sitting through at least some of the trial, among them Bill Cosby and Rosie
O'Donnell. Martha Stewart employees were assigned rotating trial duty so the
Stewart benches were always full. Stewart had even baked and delivered a chocolate cake for FBI agents who worked in the building above the underground
garage where she arrived each day. Lunch for Stewart, her lawyers, and supporters was catered by Russ & Daughters, a legendary delicatessen on the Lower
East Side often featured in Stewart's publications. Stewart's hair was styled each
day by celebrity hairdresser Eva Scrivo, who'd appeared on Stewart's TV show.

Eight women and four men filed in to take their seats in the jury box. U.S.
District Judge Miriam Cedarbaum had shrouded their selection in secrecy. Their
names were unknown. Among them were a pharmacist, an art director, someone
who worked at a law firm who traveled frequently for business (and whose husband worked at the *Wall Street Journal*), and someone whose best friend worked

at Merrill Lynch, according to potential juror questionnaires. They were all employed and seemed well educated and relatively affluent. In short, they were a sophisticated jury that would be unlikely to hold Stewart's success against her.

Seymour went straight to the point, without preliminaries: "This is a case about obstruction. It is about lying to federal agents. It is about perjury. It is about fabricating evidence, and it's about cheating investors in the stock market." After an overview of the expected testimony, she returned to the same theme: "Before I sit down I want to talk briefly about where I began, and that's when I told you that this case is about obstruction and lying to federal agents. . . . In a sense this case is about something much bigger than that, bigger than those lies and bigger than any lie. Because this case is about the truth. The truth is what our nation's investigators are entitled to hear. The truth is what our nation's investigators need so that they can conduct their investigations fairly and so that justice may be done."

Richard Strassberg, Bacanovic's lead defense lawyer, made the opening statement for Bacanovic, who sat calmly on the other side of the courtroom from Stewart. Besides reiterating many of the facts not in dispute (that it was Faneuil, not Bacanovic, who fielded the calls from the Waksals and handled the trading that day), he took aim at the core of the government's case: Faneuil's credibility. "Mr. Faneuil is the one who lied to the government. He is an admitted liar, not Peter. . . . Mr. Faneuil is the one who got the deal. He has got the deal with the government to save himself, not Peter.

"What else does Mr. Faneuil say? Because he doesn't stop there. What Mr. Faneuil says about Peter, the reason Peter has been dragged into this case, is that Doug Faneuil says, 'I told Martha Stewart about the Waksals selling, but I did it because my boss told me to do it.' That's what he says. And you are going to assess that statement . . . if it makes any sense to you at all.

"The evidence is going to show you that it's illogical, that it's contradicted and that it makes no sense. First of all, you're going to see it's illogical because Mr. Bacanovic was available on 12/27. He was in Florida. He wasn't across the world. If he wanted to tell Ms. Stewart about what another client was doing with their stock, sure, he would have done it himself. He would not have introduced his inexperienced, new assistant, ladies and gentlemen . . . he barely knew him. There is no way he would have put Mr. Faneuil in the middle of anything like that. It defies common sense. It didn't happen. . . .

"The evidence is going to show you that Peter Bacanovic never asked Doug Faneuil to lie to anybody, to the SEC, to the government, to Merrill Lynch, to anybody; no evidence. . . . Doug Faneuil admits that. He will admit Peter never asked him to lie.

"What you're going to see—and your common sense is going to tell you—is that Mr. Faneuil found himself caught in his own lies. And in an attempt to deflect—reduce his responsibility, minimize what he had done, he looked to blame his boss . . . the evidence is going to show you that he did it on his own. He did it to impress her [Stewart] because she was a celebrity.

"You are going to hear he was fixated with Ms. Stewart. You are going to hear how he talked to coworkers and his friends whenever he had limited contact with her. . . . He did it because he was trying to be the big man, because he was trying to impress her. Perhaps because he was trying to impress Peter. He did it on his own. He did it out of inexperience. He did it out of foolishness. But he did it, not Peter. Peter has been falsely accused."

Morvillo, by contrast, barely mentioned Faneuil. "What is this case about? It starts and finishes with Martha Stewart. Not much more. Most of us know who Martha Stewart is, so I will not linger on her accomplishments. . . .

"Martha Stewart has devoted most of her life to improving the quality of life for others. And because she stressed the notion of making things as good and as perfect as possible, she has often been ridiculed and parodied." The ImClone trading involved "far less than one percent of her net worth."

Morvillo conceded that Stewart "may have actually made some mistakes" while answering questions from federal investigators. But "how is the government going to prove what was in her mind and what she recalled and what she didn't recall on April 10 of 2002? How many meetings did she attend? How many projects did she initiate? How many television programs did she perform on? How many articles did she write? Is there no erosion to recollection over that period of time?

"As you can see, this really is a very unusual case and the charges are unusual. Again, I submit to you, the evidence will establish that Martha Stewart is totally innocent and is indeed a victim more than a defendant."

Douglas Faneuil waited nervously for his turn on the witness stand. He'd been told not to read about the case, so what little he knew came from his lawyers. Still, he knew much of the government's case rested on his shoulders, and he'd been told he'd be an early witness. The prosecutors asked Faneuil to come in for a one-day mock trial exercise.

One of the prosecutors played the role of Morvillo, cross-examining Faneuil and trying to poke holes in his story. Faneuil didn't recognize him, but others from the team were there. Faneuil thought he was holding up pretty well.

"Have you used any drugs?" His lawyers had told Faneuil to expect this.

"Yes. I smoked pot."

"Have you used any drugs since you signed your cooperation agreement?" In the agreement Faneuil had explicitly pledged to obey the law. But now he was taken aback. He'd gone on a vacation to Jamaica, and while there, someone had offered him a joint. He'd smoked it.

"I went to Jamaica and smoked pot," he answered.

"You *what*? Are you kidding?"

There was an uproar in the room. He was starting to panic. "But it's not illegal in Jamaica," he protested. "At least, I don't think it is. Everybody smokes pot in Jamaica." The group took a break, and when they returned, the incident was dropped. Someone said they'd research the question of whether smoking pot in Jamaica was in fact illegal. Still, they told him he'd been "stupid" to do it.

But then the questions took another tack. "What would you say if anyone asked whether we'd pressured you to change your story?" Seymour asked.

Faneuil froze. After getting him to admit his guilt, challenging him on the tax-loss story, and the "silver platter" reference, that's exactly what he thought they'd done. He said nothing.

"Because we didn't try to pressure you," Seymour continued. "If you try to insinuate that we did, the whole thing will fall apart."

Faneuil was shocked and upset. Was he supposed to say he hadn't been pressured? He was disillusioned that it had come to this. But he realized this wasn't about his integrity. He decided to "play the fucking game," Faneuil recalled. "I'd go to bat for them." (Prosecutors stressed that they simply needed to test Faneuil's memory and were not pressuring him to change his story.)

Faneuil was slated to appear on February 3. The night before, he and his father booked rooms at the City Club Hotel, compliments of one of the owners, who was a friend of Haskell's. Faneuil was grateful for the generosity. That afternoon he had a last session with his lawyers, Powers and Pickholz. Afterward they arranged a car service and rode with him back to his hotel. "We've done all we can," Powers said. "We're confident in you. You've done a great job." They had only one lingering concern, which was his account of the "silver platter" episode. "Listen, Doug," Pickholz said gently. "The silver platter sounds far-fetched. No one is going to believe you if you tell that the way you say it happened. Maybe you don't have to use the words 'silver platter.' Maybe you can soften the language."

"Guys, it's what happened. It's what I remember. Maybe I'm wrong. Maybe I'm crazy. But this is what I remember."

"We just hope you do the right thing," Powers added.

Faneuil knew that the right thing—from their point of view—was to give it up, to forget the silver platter episode.

Faneuil got out of the car and went to his father's room. He started to tell him what had just happened and burst into tears. "They're telling me the only way people will believe me is if I lie. I can't believe it."

His father didn't know how to advise him. "Listen, Doug. You do whatever you think is right. But if you lie on the witness stand tomorrow don't tell me, don't tell anyone—ever."

FBI agents picked Faneuil up the next morning and drove him to the courthouse. His parents were already there; they were planning to watch the trial but in the end were too nervous, and so sat in a room nearby. Rob Haskell didn't attend. He had to work, and in any event the prosecutors didn't seem to want him to be on hand. They'd never told Faneuil to lie about their relationship, but had suggested he might simply want to refer to Haskell as his "friend" if asked. Haskell promised to meet Faneuil at the hotel afterward. "Please don't be late," Faneuil pleaded.

When he arrived, Faneuil was taken to a room just off the courtroom. He was startled to see Judy Monaghan, the previous witness, sitting there. He hadn't seen her or heard from her since he was fired. Their eyes met, and he thought she looked sympathetic. "How are you?" she asked.

"I'm fine."

Seymour had told him that the jury wouldn't be in the room when he walked in, and that he'd be asked some questions about drug use before beginning his testimony in the case. "The defense is trying to make a big deal out of it, but it's not relevant," she'd said.

Then an agent took Faneuil's arm and led him to the door. "The government calls Douglas Faneuil, Your Honor," Seymour intoned as the packed courtroom stiffened with eager anticipation. It was midafternoon, February 3. The door opened and Faneuil could see what looked like a huge space, almost like a cathedral. He'd never seen the courtroom where he'd be testifying. The agent pointed him toward the witness stand, and he walked forward. His suit looked too big on his slender frame; he'd lost weight from the stress. He looked younger than his twenty-eight years. Off to the side he saw the jury. What were they doing there?

He was sworn in. The clerk began, "State your full name and spell your last name slowly for the record."

He didn't feel ready. His knees were hitting the partition in front of him. His voice quavered and he was barely audible. The judge urged him to move closer to the microphone. "My knees are so long . . ." Faneuil explained, prompting laughter in the courtroom. It made him feel a little better. Seymour began her questioning and it was obvious that there'd been some change of plan.

Had Faneuil done something wrong while at Merrill Lynch? Seymour asked, after establishing his background and employment history.

"Yes."

"What did you do?"

So here it was, practically the first question. Out of his peripheral vision he could see Stewart and Bacanovic. Of course, he'd known they'd be there, but the reality was jarring. He could feel their presence even though he avoided any eye contact. Then he spotted *Vanity Fair* correspondent Dominick Dunne scribbling notes. Dunne looked up and stared intently at Faneuil. Faneuil found Dunne's presence strangely comforting. He took a deep breath and began to speak.

"I told one client what another client was doing and then lied about it to cover it up."

At last he'd said it: he'd done something wrong, and he took responsibility for it. It wasn't so hard, really. From then on, whenever he wasn't making eye contact with Seymour or one of the defense lawyers questioning him, he looked at Dominick Dunne. It calmed his nerves and helped him focus. Seymour led him through the fateful events of December 27, leading to the moment that had set everything in motion, the phone call that morning with Bacanovic:

"And then we just started talking about the morning's events and how crazy it was and suddenly Peter said, 'Oh my God, get Martha on the phone.'"

And then the whole story emerged, one he'd told so many times before, but now under oath, in a courtroom, for all the world to hear. By the end of his first day of testimony they'd gotten to the point where Bacanovic had called Stewart's office and left a message about ImClone. Faneuil said he'd been on the call, but didn't remember what Bacanovic had said. And then court was adjourned. Faneuil had survived. He embraced his parents, and then hurried back to the hotel.

The next day Faneuil got the cross-examination on drug use that he'd expected the day before. The jury waited outside. "Mr. Faneuil, do you know—do you understand the term 'drugs,' 'illegal drugs'?"

Faneuil conceded that prior to his cooperation agreement he'd smoked marijuana with friends about once a month, and had used Ecstasy, a popular amphetamine, on two or three occasions at nightclubs. Morvillo zeroed in on his admission that he'd smoked marijuana in Jamaica after entering into his agreement.

"When you used drugs in April, were you violating what the government requested that you do?"

"I absolutely did not believe I was violating my cooperation agreement by smoking marijuana in Jamaica."

"You thought that by smoking marijuana in Jamaica it was perfectly all right?"

"No—yeah, I thought—I assumed that it was legal in Jamaica."

"What was that impression based on?"

"I'm not familiar with Jamaican law. I would say it was based on the ubiquity of marijuana use in Jamaica."

Faneuil was excused, leaving the lawyers to argue heatedly about the relevance of his drug use. Curiously, no one seemed to know the legal status of marijuana use in Jamaica. (Morvillo later reported correctly that it is illegal.) Seymour stressed that Faneuil, through his lawyers, volunteered the information, and that otherwise the government would have known nothing about it. Morvillo countered that he'd violated his agreement, which went to his credibility. In the end the judge agreed that defense lawyers could ask Faneuil about his drug use prior to entering into his agreement, but not about smoking marijuana in Jamaica.

When Faneuil returned to the stand, Seymour asked him to resume his narration: the call from Martha Stewart, his disclosure of the Waksal trading, her order to sell. He discussed his ensuing discussions with Bacanovic, the strange breakfast with Bacanovic at Dean & DeLuca, and then the convenient discovery of the work sheet with "@ $60" written on it. Faneuil testified he thought it was "fabricated," which triggered a chorus of objections from defense lawyers. Finally Seymour got around to Faneuil's decision to come forward with the truth and his dealings with his lawyers. This, more than any other testimony, would establish—or destroy—Faneuil's credibility. He was, after all, an admitted liar. And because of the controversial "silver platter" reference that had already caused him such trouble, it was the aspect that made Faneuil most nervous.

"Did you meet with Mr. Gutman?"

"I did."

"Did you tell him what happened on December 27?"

"I did. I told him the truth."

"Did you tell him about your SEC interview?"

"I did."

"What did he tell you to do?"

"He told me I had no choice but to come forward immediately and that I should go down to the SEC the next morning and correct my testimony."

"What did you say to him when he gave you this advice?"

"Well, I was extremely upset. So, I said to him—I was crying, and I said to him, I can't do it, I can't go down there tomorrow, I just can't even envision it. I said, I'm not saying no, I won't, because in my heart I really knew it was the right thing to do. . . . So I said, just give me a few days to let this sink in and sort of face the decision."

"Did there come a time when you spoke to Mr. Gutman again?"

"Yes."

"When was that?"

"Before I got back to him, as I told him I would, he called me, I believe. I went to his office. . . . He said, I had a very interesting conversation with Dave Marcus—Dave Marcus being a Merrill Lynch lawyer. He said that Dave Marcus had said to him that I did a great job with my SEC testimony, and there was nothing more to add, and that he certainly hoped I didn't do anything drastic. I said to Mr. Gutman, 'Do lawyers really talk that way?' He sort of chuckled, raised his shoulders. Then Mr. Gutman said, 'But let me talk to you really about what Dave Marcus said in detail.' He said, 'I can't tell you exactly what Mr. Marcus said, but what he said in so many words was the government had reached a deal—or Merrill Lynch had reached a deal with the government whereby Merrill Lynch would hand over the Waksals on a silver platter in exchange for looking the other way with regard to the Martha Stewart situation."

"What did you say?"

"I said, 'So, does that change your advice?' He said yes."

"What advice did he give you then?"

"He said, I think you should lie low. If Merrill Lynch asks you any more questions about what happened, you can continue to answer, but if the government ever speaks to you again, call me first."

"Did you know whether in fact it was true that the government had cut some deal with Merrill Lynch about the Waksals and Martha Stewart?"

"I certainly didn't believe there was a signed contract. It seemed a bit far-fetched to me. But I didn't know how these things worked. I had no idea."

So it was out. Faneuil took a deep breath. He'd used the words he'd remembered: "silver platter." He'd told the truth. It was strangely exhilarating.

Seymour continued to explore Faneuil's change of heart.

"After your SEC interview, did you talk to Peter Bacanovic?"

"Yes."

"Can you tell us about your conversation?"

"Yes. After the interview, I believe it was in his office, he just asked me how it went."

"What did you say?"

"I said they really didn't focus on Martha Stewart very much, but I told them she called and asked for a quote and decided to sell. And he said, 'Good' again . . . I had many conversations with Peter over the course of the year before I came forward. It was always basically the same conversation. I would say it probably occurred five times. I really couldn't say when exactly they happened, but it was spread out."

"Could you tell us the substance of the conversation?"

"Yes. In that conversation, he reiterated what he had said previously: He has spoken to Martha, everyone is telling the same story, the $60 stop-loss story, that story is the truth, we are all on the same page. That was the extent of the conversation. There was one conversation in particular that was different. I was reluctant always to do so, but for some reason during this conversation, which I would say came late, not too soon before I came forward, in which out of frustration I just said to Peter: 'Peter, I spoke to Martha on the phone—'"

Morvillo objected but was overruled. Faneuil continued:

"So out of frustration, I said, 'But Peter, I know, I spoke to Martha, I know what happened. I know what I said and I know what she said.' Peter just said, 'Don't even say that, just don't even say that.' And that was it."

Faneuil explained his decision to come forward: "There came a point in time where I just couldn't continue to lie, and I felt, of course, that not only had I lied to the SEC on two occasions but I felt the cover-up was part of my daily existence, and I just couldn't take it anymore."

Seymour showed Faneuil a copy of his plea agreement, which he acknowledged signing. "What are your obligations under that agreement?"

"First and foremost to tell the truth. Not to break the law. To attend all the meetings that are asked of me to attend, and be basically where the government wants me to be, and to plead guilty to the crime . . ."

"Mr. Faneuil, in the course of your cooperation with the government, did you tell the government about drug use that you had done?"

"Yes."

"At the time were you being investigated at all for any drug use?"

"Not that I know of."

Faneuil's direct examination was over. As former Merrill Lynch analyst Henry Blodget, covering the trial for *Slate*, observed, Faneuil's testimony

amounted to a demonstration of the art of effective storytelling. Faneuil anchored his descriptions with vivid, specific details. He used language that was forceful and direct. He appeared sober, serious, and—without being pathetic about it—contrite. He was never defensive: His body language said, "I am sorry for what I did, but I am taking responsibility for it, and I am relieved that I no longer have anything to hide." He considered his answers carefully and provided several that didn't help the government.

In short, Faneuil was credible.

Faneuil posed a serious threat to the defense's strategy. If he was, in fact, telling the truth, then Bacanovic and Stewart had lied repeatedly, concocted a cover story, and then obstructed justice to maintain it.

So why might Faneuil be lying? The obvious defense strategy in dealing with anyone who has a cooperation agreement with the government is to suggest that the witness has made up the story the government wants to hear in order to strike a lenient plea bargain. Another is to suggest the witness is a congenital liar. By his own admission, Faneuil had lied (or at least withheld the truth) and he had entered into a plea agreement that spared him a felony conviction. Having done something wrong, he was trying to shift blame to his boss. He resented Stewart and wanted to blame her too. They were successful professionals and he was a young, nightclub-crawling drug user.

Still, the defense faced the problem that having a motive to make up a story and then lie on the witness stand isn't the same as actually doing it. This was especially true for Faneuil, who had, after all, corrected his earlier lies and omissions and told the jury he "just couldn't take it anymore." And if he was making up a story to please the government, why wasn't it more damning to Bacanovic and Stewart? Faneuil never testified that Bacanovic told him explicitly to lie. He never claimed that Stewart told him why she was selling her ImClone shares. Had he wanted to curry favor with the government, he presumably would have told them what they wanted to hear about the tax-loss selling and the silver platter. He did not.

David Apfel, another lawyer for Bacanovic, began his cross-examination. "Mr. Faneuil, let's get a few things straight right away. First of all, on December 27, 2001, you spoke personally to Martha Stewart, is that correct?"

His tone was aggressive and hostile. He spoke with rapid-fire precision. When he addressed Faneuil as "sir," there was a hint of a sneer.

"That's correct."

"The stock price that you gave her over the phone was below $60, isn't that true, sir?"

"Most probably."

"Most definitely, isn't that true, sir? After you told Martha Stewart that the stock was trading below $60 a share, it was only then, sir, that she told you to sell, isn't that true?"

"She told me to sell after I gave her the quote, yes."

"When you first spoke to the government about the December 27, 2001, ImClone trades, you lied, isn't that correct, sir?"

"That is correct."

"You lied to cover up what you had done, isn't that true, sir?"

"In part, I would say, yes."

"When you next spoke to the government about the December 27, 2001, ImClone trades, you lied once again, isn't that correct?"

"That is correct."

"Peter Bacanovic never specifically told you to lie to anyone, isn't that true, sir?"

"Not explicitly."

"He never point-blank told you you should lie to anybody, isn't that correct, sir?"

"That's correct."

"He never told you to lie to the SEC, true?"

"True. . . . He never explicitly said lie."

"He never explicitly told you to lie to anybody, correct, sir?"

"That is correct."

Faneuil thought Apfel was being so aggressive and such a jerk that everyone, including the jurors, would recognize it. Oddly, he felt more relaxed, more at ease.

Apfel made what he could of the drug use issue.

"And what illegal drugs did you tell the government that you used . . ."

"Marijuana."

"Anything else?"

"No."

"That was simply a lie, was it not, sir?"

"Did you say a lie?"

"A lie."

"Was that a lie? No, of course not . . ."

"On December 3 of 2001, you acknowledge having used Ecstasy, right?"

"That is correct. Can I explain why I answered that way?"

"I will give you a chance. Just answer my questions."

"Okay."

"When you spoke this morning under oath and you were given an opportunity to say any other drugs you ever used or told the government about, you limited it to marijuana, isn't that right, sir? Wasn't that your answer?"

"That was my answer."

"And it was only moments or minutes later, when confronted with an FBI interview report, that you acknowledged having used Ecstasy . . ."

Seymour objected, and the judge terminated the line of questioning. But Faneuil never got his chance to explain his answer, which would have been that during the time period he was questioned about, he answered accurately that the only drug he'd used was marijuana.

When Apfel resumed his questioning on Thursday, he dropped the sledge-hammer approach. He worked methodically through the critical events and Faneuil's motives to lie, but never demonstrated that Faneuil had actually lied in his direct testimony. Morvillo began his questioning for Stewart on

Monday morning. By now, having survived round one of cross-examination, Faneuil had gained confidence. Morvillo adopted a more avuncular tone. He established (and Faneuil readily agreed) that Martha Stewart had never asked him to lie. Otherwise, he covered many of the same themes. But again, he uncovered nothing new, nothing that cast doubt on the truth of Faneuil's earlier testimony. Faneuil could hardly believe it when, just after lunch, he heard the words "No further questions."

"Very well, Mr. Faneuil. You may step down."

Michael Schachter handled the direct examination of Ann Armstrong. He'd just gotten to the critical events of December 27 when he asked her to describe the first phone call from Stewart that day.

"It was the first time I talked to her since Christmas, and we talked about the holidays. She had been up in Maine. I thanked her for the plum pudding that she had sent home."

Mention of the plum pudding caused Armstrong to pause. Tears welled up.

"Now I'm going to cry." She started to sob quietly, then pulled herself together. "I thanked her for the plum pudding that she sent home." Then Armstrong broke down again.

The judge called a recess.

The next morning she had fully regained her composure. She testified in meticulous detail about the call from Bacanovic and the fateful message "ImClone is going to start trading downward." But her most electrifying testimony was the account of Stewart's attempt to erase the message, just moments after a lengthy conversation with her lawyer John Savarese.

Armstrong had provided crucial evidence for the government and damaging testimony for Stewart. Bacanovic had called and left an incriminating message that neither he nor Stewart had disclosed. In fact, Stewart had tried to erase it, and the message had been produced *after* Stewart's testimony in which she claimed not to remember whether such a message even existed. Armstrong's touching display of emotion on the stand also undermined any idea that she disliked her demanding boss and might be trying to incriminate her.

As Stewart's self-described best friend, Mariana Pasternak was obviously a risk for the government. She hadn't wanted to testify. She had to be immunized, her testimony compelled. Still, Schachter had been elated by her grand jury testimony, however grudging. Schachter handled the questioning.

After establishing that at the end of 2001 they'd traveled together to Mexico, Pasternak volunteered, "I remember a conversation we had, we were on a terrace, which was part of the suite, adjacent to the suite . . . we did not go down for dinner, and we were tired, and I believe it was the day when we took a hike.

"We were talking about what our friends were doing for the end of the year, and we named a few friends. I asked Martha about her friends, Martha asked me about my friends, and I said, 'What is Sam doing?'"

"What did Ms. Stewart say?"

"He disappeared . . . He disappeared again. . . . I remember Martha saying that Sam was—that Sam was walking funny at a Christmas party, that he was selling or trying to sell his stock, that his daughter was selling or trying to sell her stock, and Merrill Lynch didn't sell. That's how I recall it."

"What if anything do you recall Ms. Stewart saying about her own stock?"

"I recall Martha saying that his stock is going down, or went down, and I sold mine."

"Do you have any other recollection of speaking with Ms. Stewart on the subject of brokers while you were in Mexico?"

"I remember one brief statement, which was, 'Isn't it nice to have brokers who tell you these things?'"

The judge interrupted. "I'm sorry, I didn't hear you."

"'Isn't it nice to have brokers who tell you these things?'"

"'Who tell you these things?'"

"Yes."

Morvillo jumped up. "Your Honor, I am going to move to strike. . . . That conversation is absolutely meaningless. It could mean anything. Therefore, it is not relevant. I move to strike it."

"Overruled."

The defense lawyers were apoplectic. They'd been told specifically by Pasternak's lawyer that she wasn't sure whether Stewart had said, "brokers who tell you things." Now she had attributed it to Stewart—twice—without any qualification. They confronted him after trial adjourned that day, and he suggested they ask her again on cross-examination. Morvillo did his best:

"Can you tell me anything about the context of that conversation, how that one remark came up?"

"I do not remember anything about the context. I just see a scene that was somewhere on the grounds of that hotel."

"Now, is it fair to say you are not even sure that that statement was made or whether it was just a thought in your mind?"

"It is fair to say. I don't know if that statement was made by Martha or just was a thought in my mind."

"And you have previously told that to the government, have you not?"

"Yes, I have. . . ."

"But you don't remember whether that statement—'Isn't it nice to have a broker tell you things?'—was actually something that was said to you by Martha Stewart?"

"A statement is just a way of defining that. I would [be] much more comfortable defining that as words than a statement. It is just a string of words that I recall. . . ."

"You are not sure that the words were actually spoken by Martha Stewart or whether they were words that just are somehow embedded in your mind as one of your thoughts?"

"Exactly. I do not know if Martha said that or it's me who thought those words."

Morvillo moved again to strike the testimony.

"Mr. Morvillo, I think you should ask the witness what her best recollection is on the subject," the judge suggested.

But Morvillo didn't want to take the risk. "I am not going to ask that. If they want to ask that on redirect, they will ask that," he replied.

Which is precisely what Schachter did. "Ms. Pasternak, you stated that you were not precisely sure whether this was something that Martha Stewart said or something that you thought."

"Yes."

"You said that your belief was that Ms. Stewart said it?"

"Yes."

"What is your best belief, sitting here today?"

"That Martha said it."

"I have no further questions, Your Honor."

Morvillo jumped up. "Is that a guess?"

"The recollection is extremely vague. All I remember are—a string of words. I remember looking at Martha. While those words appeared, I do not know if Martha said them or I said them, but I believe Martha is the one who said them."

"Still, as you sit here now . . ."

"Yes."

"You really can't remember precisely whether she said it or whether you just thought it?"

"I cannot remember precisely. My best guess—my best belief is that she said it."

But whether Stewart said the statement, or whether Pasternak thought it, hardly mattered. If Pasternak had such a thought, what could have prompted it other than an admission from Stewart? Far more incriminating was the evidence—uncontested by the defense—that Stewart told Pasternak that ImClone was going down and the Waksals had sold or were trying to sell their shares. On the date of that conversation in late December 2001, the Waksals' ImClone trading was not public knowledge. Unless Faneuil told Stewart, and Stewart told Pasternak, how could Pasternak know that?

Schachter tried to avoid looking at the spectators in the courtroom, but one day he noticed that Rosie O'Donnell was glaring at him, and later waved her finger, motioning him over. He shook her hand. "Do you have children?" she asked him.

"Yes."

"Do you want them to grow up knowing you as the man who took down Martha Stewart?"

Of Faneuil's many friends, the prosecution settled on two: Zeva Bellel and Eden Werring. Rob Haskell was on deck if necessary, but never called, even though he could corroborate almost everything Faneuil had said. Seymour didn't want the jurors distracted by a gay relationship, and also worried about how they would interpret Haskell's own involvement. His phone call to Bacanovic urging him to "do something for Doug" as well as his advice to Faneuil to keep silent brought him perilously close to the conspiracy himself.

Bellel and Werring were young, attractive, articulate, and well educated, Bellel at Vassar and Werring at Yale. Like Seymour, they also helped redress any perception that a group of men had ganged up on an attractive, successful woman defendant.

Bellel described her visit to Faneuil over New Year's 2002 and described him as "obviously very upset about something that had taken place at work."

"He said that he had a very busy morning and that it was very stressful, that he, you know, was fielding all these calls, and that he succeeded in getting his boss on the phone and asked him what he should do at that point. And his boss said, 'Please call Martha Stewart and let her know about Sam Waksal's family and himself selling their shares in ImClone.'"

"Did he tell you anything—did Mr. Faneuil tell you anything else in that conversation?"

"He said he asked his boss, 'Can I do that? Is that OK?' And his boss responded by saying, 'It is not a question of whether or not you can do it or not, just do it.'"

In a second conversation, several days later, just before she returned to Paris, Faneuil told her "that he had a conversation with his boss, Peter, basically trying to elicit some kind of direction from him about how to handle himself during the SEC investigation, and he was looking for advice, he was looking for support, and said, you know, what—what happened? What's going on? Why are they interested in the sale? And Peter responded very firmly and very forcefully and said: 'Listen, nothing happened. There was nothing wrong with the sale. This is how it all happened. End of story.' And he told me he was at a loss. He felt totally abandoned, betrayed and frightened, because he knew very well that what Peter had just described as the sequence of events that took place that day leading up to this sale was totally inaccurate."

Apfel made no headway on cross-examination and Morvillo asked no questions.

Werring was even more succinct.

"What, if anything, did Mr. Faneuil tell you about his job?" Seymour asked.

"He was—I remember I was in the apartment and he came in with Rob and he was very stressed out and he said that something had happened at work. And that he had had to lie for his boss."

"No further questions, Your Honor."

Richard Strassberg attempted to shake her memory in cross-examination until the judge stepped in.

"What's your best recollection of what was actually said?" Judge Cedarbaum asked.

"He said I had to lie for my boss."

Strassberg and Morvillo had no questions, and the prosecution rested.

As the government had feared, one of the first witnesses the defense lawyers called was Jeremiah Gutman, Faneuil's former lawyer, the eccentric civil rights lawyer who, according to Faneuil, had told him to "lie low." No one knew what Gutman would say. He had declined to be interviewed by either prosecution or defense. Would he demolish Faneuil's credibility by denying the silver platter story?

Strassberg handled the questioning for Bacanovic.

"Mr. Gutman, did you ever tell Mr. Faneuil that David Marcus of Merrill Lynch had told you that Merrill Lynch had a secret deal with the government to hand over Sam Waksal on a silver platter and to look the other way with respect to Ms. Stewart?"

"I told him something like that, but certainly not in the detail and with the language that you have phrased it."

"Could you tell us what it is you told him?"

"I told Faneuil, after having a conversation with Marcus, who represented Merrill Lynch, that Marcus had told me that he thought he was working something out with the government by which the whole investigation would go away and that there would be nothing to worry about. . . . I told him that Marcus had told me that he was working on making a deal, not that he had one, and that the deal would involve getting all the Merrill Lynch people off the hook and then let the chips fall where they may."

Gutman also recalled his advice to Faneuil to correct his testimony. "I recommended that he have independent counsel who will advise him on whether or not he should take the Fifth Amendment. He should go with him rather than have Mr. Marcus go with him, whose interest was conflicted with his, and that he should explore that way of proceeding. He told me that he was afraid of them all, that they were merciless and immoral people and he started to cry. And he said, no, I can't do that. I'm afraid to do that."

The Gutman gambit had clearly backfired for the defense; it also put Marcus and Merrill Lynch in an unflattering light.

Faneuil was back working at the art gallery that afternoon when an excited Pickholz called him. "You won't believe it! Gutman took the stand and corroborated everything you said! You did it!" Faneuil was pleased and felt vindicated. But what if he had lied on the stand, as he thought everyone wanted him to, and then Gutman had contradicted him? Where would they be now? He thought his lawyers and the prosecutors owed him an apology for trying to get him to change his story. (They maintain they were pressing him to test his memory, not to get him to change his story, and certainly not to lie.)

The star witness for the defense was Heidi DeLuca, Stewart's personal accountant, who'd called Faneuil about messing up the tax-loss selling with the ImClone trade. DeLuca was the sole witness prepared to support Bacanovic's and Stewart's testimony that they had an oral agreement to sell ImClone if it dropped below $60 a share. She said she had discussed the agreement with both Bacanovic and Stewart. Moreover, she had a document to support the claim: a spreadsheet of Stewart's positions she'd printed off the Internet, with the notation in her handwriting, "ImClone. $61.52. Wednesday, tender offer, not responding."

The note referred to the fact that Bristol-Myers Squibb had made a tender offer for a minority stake in ImClone at $70 a share. The offer expired on October 31. Since ImClone traded below $70 at the time, shareholders had a clear incentive to tender their shares for an above-market price. Stewart tendered all 5,000 ImClone shares in her own account as well as all the shares in the company's pension account. Bristol-Myers ended up buying just under 21.5 percent of those offered. Stewart and the pension fund got $70 a share for that percentage, and kept the rest. In late October, the pension fund sold all its remaining shares at $61 a share. Stewart kept the rest of hers. So the timing of DeLuca's conversations and her notes were critical. If before October 31, they clearly related to the pension fund sales at $61, and the evidence was all but worthless from the defense perspective. If after November 1, they could only have applied to Stewart's remaining shares in her personal account, which supported the notion that she had an agreement with Bacanovic to sell if they dropped below $60.

DeLuca emphasized this in her direct examination by Apfel:

Asked about her handwritten note "ImClone. $61.52, Wednesday," she explained, "That would be November 7, 2001."

"I believe November 8 would have been Wednesday, isn't that right?"

"I don't remember . . . I had called Peter the next day . . . I had asked him a couple of questions about tendering and about ImClone."

"Can you tell the jury what he said on the subject of tendering ImClone shares?"

"He explained to me tendering 101, what tendering was all about. He told me that he felt ImClone was a dog, although he felt there was still a possibility that the ImClone market share price would surpass the $70 a share and that the stock was volatile . . . and that he felt he could set a floor price of $60 or $61, just in case the stock continued to fall, as like, a safeguard. . . . He said that he would speak to Martha Stewart personally about it."

Later, in January, DeLuca said she was with Stewart in the Connecticut TV studio. DeLuca knocked on Stewart's door and went in; Stewart was on the phone. DeLuca was about to leave when Stewart asked, "What do you remember about ImClone?"

"What did you say in response?" Apfel asked.

"I said, I remember we sold shares out of the pension. I remember that she had tendered all her shares out of her personal account, and I remember Peter wanting to talk to her about setting some kind of a bottom price, $60 or $61, in ImClone to try to sell it . . . That was it."

Finally, the testimony that Bacanovic and Stewart must have been longing for: something to corroborate their alibis. Stewart and Bacanovic had discussed selling ImClone at $60 or $61 on November 7 or 8. True, the date didn't coincide with either Bacanovic's or Stewart's testimony, but that seemed a minor issue. Surely it would at least establish a reasonable doubt in the jurors' minds.

On cross-examination, Schachter immediately focused on the date. Referring to the computer-generated spreadsheet and her notes, he asked, "There is nothing on this document itself which contains the date November 8, 2001, is that right?"

"That's correct."

"Isn't it true, Ms. DeLuca, that you could be mistaken about that date?"

"No."

"Isn't it true, Ms. DeLuca, that these are notes of a conversation that you had with Peter Bacanovic on October 24 about selling the 51,800 shares from the pension account at $61?"

"No."

"And isn't it true that this note has nothing to do with setting a floor of ImClone at $61 or $60 for any future sales?"

"I don't understand the question."

And then Schachter pulled off the greatest coup in his career as a prosecutor: He produced the original of the spreadsheet with DeLuca's handwritten notes rather than the copy she and her lawyers had been using. DeLuca acknowledged that this was the original.

Perhaps sensing what was coming, Apfel frantically objected.

"Overruled," the judge firmly replied. "The witness testified this is the original of the document that you offered in evidence."

"Looking at the lower-right-hand corner of the original document, do you see a date which is printed on this document?"

"Yes."

"What is that date?"

"October 24, 2001."

"And, Ms. DeLuca, October 24, 2001, that was a Wednesday, was it not?"

The defense lawyers had apparently failed to examine the original document, which contained a date reference that is routinely included on a computer-generated printout. Either it didn't register on the copy or, more likely, it was located off the edge of what was copied. Phone records also showed that DeLuca spoke to Bacanovic for twenty-one minutes on October 24. The discussion of selling ImClone at $60 or $61 could not have happened on November 7 or 8.

DeLuca's credibility lay in shreds. Suddenly the facts fell into place. Bacanovic *had* discussed selling ImClone if it fell to $60 or perhaps $61—but the conversation occurred in October, and it was about the pension shares—not Stewart's personal shares, the ones she sold on December 27. Like many lies, embedded in the $60 stop-loss-order story, the linchpin of the defense, was a kernel of truth.

Schachter proceeded to further undermine DeLuca's integrity. Although 70 percent of her work was personal work for Martha Stewart, the company paid her entire salary. Moreover, "You submitted an expense report to the company charging Martha Stewart Living Omnimedia for the cost of this vacation [to Mexico], did you not?"

"Based on the information that I was given, as a business expense, yes."

"Now, Ms. DeLuca, even though this vacation was billed as a business expense, you called Mariana Pasternak and asked her to put in her share for the cost of the vacation, isn't that right?"

"I don't recall."

The judge jumped in. "Whatever you are asked to do, you do, regardless of whether it is true or not true?"

"Correct. I am given information. I submit it. Somebody else is the one who reviews it and would reject or accept."

"Let's move on," the judge concluded, getting DeLuca off the hook. Still, Schachter had established that DeLuca was only too willing to submit a questionable expense report on Stewart's behalf. (DeLuca's lawyer, David Fein, didn't respond to requests for comment.)

There was little the defense lawyers could do to rehabilitate her. Called to support the Stewart-Bacanovic cover story, she had instead discredited it even further.

The defense called no further witnesses.

The entire defense case had lasted less than three days. Neither Stewart nor Bacanovic testified, which was their constitutional right. The jury was instructed to draw no negative inferences from their failure to take the stand.

The burden was on the government to prove its case, not the defense to disprove it. Of course, had they taken the stand, they would have been obliged to tell the truth or risk compounding their predicament with further allegations of perjury.

Seymour was the lead prosecutor, but she stepped aside so that Schachter could deliver the government's closing argument. Schachter had been immersed in the facts of the case for over three years. In contrast to the often-interrupted and sometimes disjointed testimony and exhibits, he was able to provide a coherent narrative, one in clear chronological order, with cause and effect and motivations artfully woven together.

"On the afternoon of February 4, 2002, as Martha Stewart walked up the steps to the United States Attorney's office, she had firmly fixed in her mind two things. One was that she was going to tell the FBI and the SEC that before selling her ImClone stock she had not spoken to Sam Waksal. And he had not tipped her that the FDA was rejecting ImClone's drug application. Martha Stewart knew she could say that with defendants because it was true, and telephone and other records would back that up.

"The other thing fixed in Martha Stewart's mind was that she would conceal from the FBI and the SEC the true reason for her sale: that she had sold her ImClone shares because she had been tipped off by Doug Faneuil, that Sam Waksal and members of his family were dumping their ImClone stock on the eve of an expected critical announcement from the FDA.

"Martha Stewart would lie about this. And Martha Stewart probably thought that she would never get caught. She knew she could count on Peter Bacanovic to tell investigators the same story. But Martha Stewart and Peter Bacanovic were wrong. Because as they attempted to obstruct the SEC and FBI investigations they made a series of mistakes and they left behind a trail of evidence that exposed the truth about Martha Stewart's sale and exposed the lies that they would tell, mistakes like leaving a trail of evidence of e-mails and phone records, mistakes like Martha Stewart's admissions to her friend, Mariana Pasternak, mistakes like Martha Stewart's message for Sam Waksal that she left immediately after getting off the phone with Doug Faneuil, Martha Stewart's effort to tamper with a critical piece of evidence, and Peter Bacanovic's fabrication of another—evidence just like the documents that completely undermine the story that Heidi DeLuca told you and, most importantly, the evidence provided by Douglas Faneuil from that witness chair.

"Those mistakes and that evidence conclusively prove, ladies and gentlemen, that Martha Stewart and Peter Bacanovic are guilty of the crimes of obstructing an SEC investigation, making false statements to federal agents, and conspiracy. And Peter Bacanovic is also guilty of the crimes of making a false document and perjury."

Did Schachter really know what Martha Stewart was thinking when she walked up the steps of the U.S. Attorney's office? Perhaps not. But it was a plausible guess. So were other aspects of his summation. Why had Bacanovic first told Faneuil that Stewart's sale was part of a tax-loss-selling plan, then change the story to the $60 stop-loss order? Because when confronted with Judy Monaghan's unexpected questions to Faneuil on December 31 about the sale, Bacanovic said the first thing that popped into his mind. His last conversation with Stewart probably *had* been about tax-loss selling. But then Bacanovic must have realized that the explanation made no sense, because the ImClone sale was a gain—as DeLuca had complained to Faneuil after the trade. In fact, it had "screwed up" the tax-loss plan. Significantly, when asked by both Faneuil and Monaghan about the reasons for the sale, Schachter pointed out that Bacanovic said "nothing—nothing—about any $60 price agreement. Four days after the sale Peter Bacanovic didn't say a word about what is now the cornerstone of his defense."

Later, as the investigation intensified, "Bacanovic had worked out a better story than the relatively silly tax-loss-selling story, and this was the new story that Peter Bacanovic hammered into Doug Faneuil"—the $60 story.

Schachter also tackled another puzzling switch by Bacanovic: his initial testimony that he handled the ImClone trade for Stewart and later, when questioned under oath, that Faneuil handled the trade. "Why the switch?"

Because Judy Monaghan and Dave Marcus at Merrill Lynch mentioned that the SEC was getting phone records. "Peter Bacanovic knows that phone records would prove he was not the person who spoke to Martha Stewart. So that story falls by the wayside." Yet another mystery is why Bacanovic never conveyed the new story to Stewart. In her interview on April 10, Stewart alone was still telling the thoroughly discredited story that she placed the ImClone trade through Bacanovic, even when pressed on the statement by the SEC's Helene Glotzer.

That wasn't the only discrepancy. Stewart had said Bacanovic told her the SEC was asking Merrill Lynch questions about ImClone trading. But Bacanovic testified that he never mentioned the SEC to Stewart in connection with any investigation. "That, ladies and gentlemen, is not worthy of your belief. They, again, just did not get their stories straight about what they discussed together about the investigation."

In fact, the evidence strongly suggested that Stewart and Bacanovic not only discussed the investigation but hatched the $60 cover story. The two had breakfast at Le Gamin, alone, on January 19. The following week, when Faneuil returned from a vacation, Bacanovic called him in to report that "everyone is telling the same story. This was a $60 stop-loss order." And yet Bacanovic had also denied discussing the investigation with Faneuil.

Schachter thoroughly demolished the $60 story. Some of the most persuasive evidence was that at 10:04 a.m., the precise time when Bacanovic left the message for Stewart that ImClone was "trading downward," ImClone was *not* below $60—it was trading at $61.52, where it had already been trading for a full week. Indeed, it was lower than that on December 19, before Bacanovic's vacation, and yet that trading had not prompted any call to Stewart.

As for DeLuca's testimony, it "was not true. . . . Heidi DeLuca was at best confused." Her notes were from October 24, and related to the pension fund's sale of ImClone for $61 a share on October 25 and 26—not Stewart's sale on December 27. Moreover, Schachter replayed the recording of Bacanovic's testimony in which he said he had never discussed Stewart's personal ImClone trading with DeLuca. In this instance, Bacanovic was telling the truth.

In sum, "Defendants are guilty for lying about what they did on December twenty-seventh. Defendants are guilty of lying about the reasons for Martha Stewart's sale, for lying about the message that Peter Bacanovic left, and that Martha Stewart received, for lying about who Martha Stewart spoke with and what they discussed on December the twenty-seventh. They are guilty of obstruction for lying about the phony cover story and for lying about speaking about the investigation of Martha Stewart's ImClone sale, for lying about talking to Doug Faneuil about the investigation, and by pressuring Doug Faneuil to lie."

A t this juncture, the defense team had an unenviable task, especially with neither Stewart nor Bacanovic taking the stand to present a coherent, plausible, and innocent alternative. They were stuck with Bacanovic's and Stewart's prior testimony, which was riddled with inconsistencies. While they could and did argue that Glotzer and Farmer had misheard or made mistakes in their note taking, Bacanovic's sworn testimony had been recorded. Their testimony had been inconsistent on such fundamental facts as whether Stewart did or did not speak to Faneuil on December 27.

They had to demolish Faneuil's credibility about almost everything he'd said. More important, they had to cast doubt on those parts of his testimony that had been corroborated by records as well as by Pasternak's testimony that Stewart knew the Waksals had sold their shares.

As was the case throughout the trial, Bacanovic's team went first, in a closing argument presented by Strassberg. His argument essentially boiled down to an argument that the government's case "makes no sense" and thus, it couldn't have happened. "It makes no sense that Peter Bacanovic would have asked his brand-new assistant to pass confidential information about Sam Waksal along to Martha Stewart. It makes no sense. It makes no sense that Peter Bacanovic, after having been told that Mr. Faneuil had gone down, spoke to the SEC and told them, I, Doug Faneuil, spoke with Martha Stewart on the twenty-seventh, that then, three or four days later, Mr. Bacanovic would have gone down and said, no, forget what you just heard, I, Peter Bacanovic spoke to Martha Stewart on the twenty-seventh when I was on vacation. It makes no sense because it didn't happen. It makes no sense, ladies and gentlemen, that Mr. Bacanovic, who had built his career, his reputation, his lifeblood, really, on his integrity and his ability to have people trust him, would jeopardize it all by doing something so untrustworthy as sharing client confidences between one client and another. It makes no sense. It didn't happen.

"We are going to talk quite a bit about Mr. Faneuil, but where do we start with Mr. Faneuil? . . . We already know that his inferences are from a person who has an extreme motivation to shade the truth when he speaks to you. . . . We know he is a convincing liar. Remember, he sat before the SEC, sat before Merrill Lynch, talked to them and lied to them, and no one suspected a thing. Certainly not at first. No one suspected a thing. So we know he is able to look people right in the face and lie to them and have them believe him. . . . We all saw him on the witness stand. And what did we see? He answered the questions like a pro. Do you remember that? He was determined to say what he wanted to say, regardless of what the question was. He was even correcting the judge at one point. . . . And the answer often ended with him blaming Peter Bacanovic for something or other."

For Strassberg to say that he would be talking "quite a bit" about Faneuil proved an understatement. He went on for hours, even attacking his credibility for maintaining he had a 3.5 grade point average—when it was actually 3.44. Even the judge admonished Strassberg that he had reached the point of "diminishing returns." Still, despite the extensive questioning while Faneuil was on the stand, there was no mention of any drug use.

Spending so much time on Faneuil left Strassberg little time to rebut the actual charges against Bacanovic. All but conceding the gaffe over Heidi DeLuca's work sheet and notes, he did his best to rehabilitate her—"The date doesn't really matter" and "It doesn't make any sense that it would have happened the last week in October. . . . Her testimony, no matter when the date is of that note, undermines their whole case . . . it is not good enough for them to just raise questions about the date on a note. . . . It doesn't dispel substantial doubts, a lot of doubts. Certainly it doesn't dispel all reasonable doubt."

Although the argument had consumed many hours, that was pretty much it: Faneuil could not be believed or trusted; witnesses had misheard or misunderstood when Bacanovic initially told the SEC he spoke to Stewart; DeLuca's testimony proved or at least raised doubts about whether they did have a $60 stop-loss agreement. It didn't make sense that Bacanovic would lie to protect his most important client.

"In many ways he [Bacanovic] has been the victim," Strassberg concluded. "He has been caught in the crossfire here between the government's attempt to make a case against Ms. Stewart, caught in the crossfire about what happened on a phone conversation that he wasn't part of between Mr. Faneuil and Ms. Stewart, caught in the crossfire but not willing to cut a deal and take himself out by falsely implicating Ms. Stewart. And make no mistake about it, ladies and gentlemen, this has been a nightmare for him. He has lost his reputation, he lost his career, he lost everything that he had built up over almost nine years at Merrill Lynch and now it's even worse because the nightmare continues. His life, his very liberty, is in your hands."

Morvillo is legendary in the courtroom, but in many ways he had an even more difficult task, since Stewart's allegedly false statements were less artful than Bacanovic's, who had at least had the common sense to change his story about speaking directly to Stewart on the twenty-seventh. Morvillo, too, had to rely heavily on a variation of the "it makes no sense theory" put forward by Strassberg.

"If two very bright, successful people like Peter Bacanovic and Martha Stewart . . . We know that they are smart people. We know that they are successful people. We know that they pay attention to detail on their everyday lives. We know they have risen up the ladder from a job point of view, from an economic point of view by dint of hard work and by dint of doing things the right way. If those two people want to sit down and rig a story, wouldn't they make a story consistent on at least the major aspects of it? If you and I were conspiring to fool the government, to fool the SEC when we sat down on January 16, wouldn't we get our stories straight? Well, of course we would. Let's see whether that's what Peter Bacanovic and Martha Stewart did. Look at the gaping inconsistencies in the recollections they had when they testified . . . they fall down on the very first important element of this story, when did it [the $60 conversation] take place?"

Stewart had said the $60 conversation took place in October or November; Bacanovic recalled it on December 20 or 21. "Guess what else they forget to tell each other as they sit there rigging a story. They forget to tell each other who took the order on December 27 . . . how was it that something as elemental as who took the order on December 27, the very next date here, is not something that meshes?"

And then Bacanovic changed his testimony, saying Faneuil took the order. "Did he tell Martha Stewart that he changed his story? Did he tell his conspirator that he changed his story? Because you know on April 10 she is re-interviewed. And on April 10 she still says it's Peter Bacanovic that she talked to. So what kind of conspiracy is this? It's a conspiracy of dunces."

Morvillo took a somewhat softer line with Faneuil, though he covered much of the same ground impugning his credibility. "Doug Faneuil carries more baggage with him than a cargo handler loading a cruise ship for an around-the-world voyage," he said at one point. But Morvillo also faced the more daunting task of discrediting Mariana Pasternak and Ann Armstrong. Stewart had testified point-blank that she wasn't told the Waksals were selling, and yet she'd told Pasternak she knew they were.

Remarkably, Morvillo didn't dispute Pasternak's recollection, but claimed that Stewart had simply forgotten when she said she wasn't told. "Nobody is disputing whether or not Ms. Stewart was told that the Waksals were selling on December 27. What we are disputing is that it made a difference to her. What we are disputing is that it had so much business significance to her that she would have retained it in her mind and on April 10, when she is finally asked the question about it, directly, that she would have remembered. Four months and some two thousand phone calls later, they finally get around to asking her the question. They ask it in a misleading fashion. She tells them what her recollection is, and whammo, she is indicted for it."

As for Armstrong, "Annie Armstrong and the alteration . . . you understand my position that it is much ado about nothing.

"When Martha Stewart went to the computer on the 30th of January and she saw the message, ImClone is going to start to trade down, she didn't remember that as the message that she got about it. And so momentarily she was startled and she changed it to 're: ImClone.' Re: ImClone is significant because there was nothing in that message that was inconsistent with the fact that they had had a $60 conversation. If she had changed that to re Kmart, to re IBM, to re MSO, then it seems to me somebody could argue she was trying to mislead somebody. But she changed it to re: ImClone . . . even if she was attempting to alter the message in accordance with her recollection . . . she wasn't trying to do anything deceptive. . . . She immediately changed it or ordered that it be changed back so it could read correctly. She never asked Annie to conceal it. She never asked Annie to forget it. She never asked Annie to lie. She never asked Annie to mislead anyone. She never asked Annie to destroy it. She just simply made that brief, quick decision because she was startled about the substance of the message and wanted to make it reflect a little bit more accurately [Stewart's recollection]."

But how could Stewart have been unable to recall the message from Bacanovic just days after this incident? Morvillo made the same argument as the Wachtell lawyers, that Glotzer and Farmer were wrong about Stewart's interview: that Stewart wasn't asked "whether" there was a written record of Bacanovic's call, but "when" he called, and that's what Stewart couldn't remember—the precise time of his call.

Morvillo also tried to explain away Stewart's statement that she spoke to Bacanovic and placed the ImClone trade through him by arguing that she had mistaken Faneuil's voice for Bacanovic's. "If Martha Stewart . . . had understood that she was talking to Doug Faneuil on December 27, the first thing she would have said was: 'Where's Peter? Please get Peter for me on the telephone. I want to talk to Peter about ImClone. I don't want to talk to you.'" This, to put it mildly, stretched credulity, since several witnesses had attested to the fact that Faneuil's and Bacanovic's voices sound nothing alike. It was also nothing but speculation by Morvillo.

But what options did Morvillo have? He needed to plant a reasonable doubt in jurors' minds and put Stewart in a sympathetic light.

"This has been a two-year ordeal for this good woman," Morvillo concluded. "It's an ordeal based on the fact that she trusted her financial adviser not to put her in a compromising position. It's an ordeal based on the fact that she voluntarily submitted to a government interview. And it's an ordeal that is in the process of wiping out all the good that she has done, all her contributions, all her accomplishments."

Karen Seymour had the last word before the case went to the jury, and her final words spoke to the cost of perjury. "The heart of this case is the fact that Peter Bacanovic caused Martha Stewart to be tipped about the Waksals selling. What flowed from that was a series of lies and deceptive acts, and part of this was the $60 cover story. . . . When I started this case and I spoke to you probably five weeks ago, I told you this case was about something larger than the lies that are at issue here. I told you it was about the truth. . . . From the moment that they were first asked about this stock sale, the evidence shows that they were not truthful. They did their best to hide and suppress the truth about the tip. And it's that effort which brings us here. And the truth, if you think it's not important, it is important. It is the foundation of how our law enforcement officers and our federal agencies do their jobs. It is incredibly important to them. . . . If you think about the victims in this case, I don't want you to think about the government. Don't think about the SEC. Don't think about the FBI, though they certainly were victimized. It's really our entire nation, our country, that is victimized. The laws that are being enforced in this case are designed to make sure that investigators can fairly evaluate facts based on the truth. That is the point. It is important. And those laws must be enforced to keep the integrity of government investigations."

On Friday at 2:49 p.m., Judge Cedarbaum announced to a packed and buzzing courtroom, "We have received a verdict," and directed that the jurors be brought back. They filed in, stood in their places, and the foreman handed a paper to the judge. She glanced over it, then said, "Please be seated, members of the jury. I have received your verdict, and I will now read it.

"Defendant Martha Stewart:

"Count one, guilty.

"Count three, guilty.

"Count four, guilty.

"Count eight, guilty.

"Defendant Peter Bacanovic:

"Count one, guilty.

"Count two, guilty."

Both Stewart and Bacanovic sat impassively, betraying no emotion. Stewart's daughter, Alexis, seated directly behind her, started to sob, and murmurs swelled in the courtroom as several spectators rose. "Please be seated," Judge Cedarbaum ordered. "This is a courtroom proceeding." Then she continued:

"Count five, not guilty.

"Count six, guilty.

"Count seven, guilty."

Stewart and Bacanovic were convicted on all counts save one, which was the charge that Bacanovic had concocted a false document by adding the "@ $60" notation in a different ink.

Doug Faneuil was working at the art gallery when one of his lawyers called with the news. From what his lawyers had told him, his sense was that it had been going badly for Stewart and Bacanovic. That evening, Karen Seymour left a message on his voice mail: "I just wanted to call after the verdict today to say this really is a vindication of everything that you did. It took a lot of integrity and the jury's verdict clearly reflects that. So thanks so much for all that you've done." But since getting off the stand, he'd felt more detached from the proceedings. He was thinking more about his own future. He still had to be sentenced.

Moments after the sentence was announced, a letter from Stewart appeared on her website, Martha Talks. It was singularly unrepentant. "I'm obviously distressed by the jury's verdict, but I continue to take comfort in knowing I have done nothing wrong and I have the enduring support of my family and friends." But evidently her lawyers intervened, since acknowledging guilt is a factor to be considered in sentencing. Within an hour, the statement "I have done nothing wrong" vanished.

Jurors in the case were avidly courted by the media, and several appeared on the *Today* show and *Good Morning America* on Monday morning, and later on *Dateline NBC*. Delivering the verdict had been an emotional moment, because they liked and sympathized with Stewart. In many ways they had wanted to acquit her and hoped the defense would raise doubts about the government's case.

The jurors confirmed what was evident at trial: that the testimony of Ann

Armstrong and Mariana Pasternak was devastating to Stewart and Bacanovic, and that Faneuil was credible.

Perhaps the greatest weakness in the defense was its failure to produce evidence supporting the $60 stop-loss order as well as evidence and testimony that Stewart and Bacanovic had been truthful. The jurors felt the defense never delivered the evidence to support the claims they'd made in the opening statements. No matter how the jurors had considered the evidence, they arrived at the guilty verdicts. "We just could not have done anything else," said juror Meg Crane.

As the July 16 date for her sentencing approached, Stewart filed a letter with the judge arguing for leniency, also posted on Martha Talks.

> It is very important for me to inform you that I never intended to harm anyone and I am dreadfully sorry that the perception of my conduct has caused my family, my friends and especially my beloved company so much damage.

In her view, it was the perception of her conduct, presumably by overzealous prosecutors, rather than the conduct itself, which had caused the damage. And she also made perfectly clear that in her own mind, she had done nothing wrong.

> I sold my remaining shares of ImClone not because I had inside information, not because I was secretly tipped, but because I set a price, made a profit and knew I could always invest if I wanted to. To believe that I sold because Sam was trying to sell is so very, very wrong. To believe that I would sell, to avoid a loss of less than $45,000, and thus jeopardize my life, my career, and the well-being of hundreds of others, my cherished partners and colleagues, is so very, very wrong. [This paragraph was subsequently deleted from her letter, apparently again at the insistence of her lawyers.]

Judge Cedarbaum said she believed that Stewart had already suffered and would continue to suffer, and that the highly publicized case had already served the purpose of deterrence. Though she declined to waive the sentencing guidelines as requested by the defense, the judge gave Stewart the minimum sentence under the guidelines: five months in prison, five months of home detention at her Bedford estate, two years of probation, and a $40,000 fine. Still, Martha Stewart would have to spend time in jail.

Stewart emerged from the courthouse to cheers of "We love you, Martha" from two dozen supporters. "Today is a shameful day," she said on the courthouse steps.

> It is shameful for me, for my family, and for my beloved company and all of its employees and partners. What was a small personal matter became over the last two and a half years an almost fatal circus event of unprecedented proportions spreading like oil over a vast landscape, even around the world. I have been choked and almost suffocated to death.
>
> I'll be back. I will be back, whatever I have to do in the next few months. I hope the months go by quickly. I'm used to all kinds of hard work, as you know, and I'm not afraid. I'm not afraid whatsoever. I'm just very, very sorry that it's come to this. That a small, personal matter has been able to be blown out of all proportion and with such venom and with such gore. I mean, it's just terrible.

Peter Bacanovic, nearly forgotten in the media frenzy over Stewart, was sentenced later that afternoon. He, too, acknowledged no wrongdoing and said that he regretted the "pain and suffering this has caused my family" rather than any conduct by him. Judge Cedarbaum gave him the same sentence—five months in prison and five months of home detention—but a smaller fine of $4,000.

That same night, Stewart appeared on *20/20* with Barbara Walters and compared her situation to that of South African president Nelson Mandela, who spent twenty-seven years in prison, much of it on South Africa's notorious Robben Island.

His cooperation complete, Faneuil was finally sentenced on July 23, 2004. The government lawyers gave him a glowing recommendation:

"Faneuil faced the same choice that Stewart and Bacanovic had to make—hold firm to the lies he had told investigators or tell the truth, no matter the consequences. Perhaps the most extraordinary aspect of Faneuil's decision to tell the truth is that he came forward for only one reason—because he knew it was the right thing to do. . . . Douglas Faneuil's cooperation has been truly extraordinary. While Faneuil's role in the conspiracy to obstruct justice cannot be condoned,

Faneuil's decision to come forward and admit his crimes and, most extraordinarily, to do so voluntarily, speaks volumes to his courage and integrity."

In sharp contrast to Stewart and Bacanovic, Faneuil acknowledged his crimes and fought back tears as he apologized for initially lying to investigators. "This ordeal has been a tragic disappointment for too many people, including myself," he told the judge. "If I were given the opportunity to prevent it happening again, I would choose to do so every single time."

"You are in many ways a very lucky young man," Cedarbaum said as she sentenced him to probation rather than the six months in prison indicated by the sentencing guidelines. "I am giving you enormous credit for your assistance." She also sternly admonished him that if he ever appeared in court again as a result of any wrongdoing, she would personally see to it that he was punished to the full extent of the law.

When it was over, Karen Seymour smiled, shook his hand, and patted him on the shoulder. His lawyers were ecstatic that he'd gotten probation. His estranged parents attended and seemed relieved. Everyone seemed happy, except Faneuil. He felt depressed and looked miserable.

"What the hell is wrong with you?" Pickholz asked. "You should be happy!"

"This was three years of my life," Faneuil responded.

"You got off scot-free!" Powers added.

"What are you talking about? I've been paying for this for three years!"

"We did the best we could," Powers said. "It took some pretty good lawyering to get you here."

"Then why didn't you get me immunity?" Faneuil took a roll of mints Powers had given him and threw them at his lawyer.

M artha Stewart never spoke to Mariana Pasternak again. Pasternak maintains that her high-profile real estate business in Westport collapsed under the notoriety of the trial. She had to sell her jewelry and eventually lost her house to foreclosure.

After her testimony, Ann Armstrong took several weeks off to recover, and when she returned to the company, she moved to a position on a different floor from Stewart. One afternoon she went upstairs to see her replacement, and was startled to see Stewart herself sitting at her computer, her back turned. Stewart heard Armstrong's voice and asked a brief question; Armstrong answered. Stewart kept her back turned and didn't look at her. It was their only encounter after the trial, and Stewart never spoke to her again. Armstrong was dropped from Stewart's holiday card and gift list, and she subsequently left the company.

Kevin Sharkey remains on the staff of Martha Stewart Living and, his blog suggests, he continues to be one of Stewart's closest friends and traveling companions. He lives in a multimillion-dollar, 2,500-square-foot apartment in a Richard Meier–designed apartment building in Greenwich Village owned by Stewart. His decorating of the apartment has been the subject of ongoing coverage in *Martha Stewart Living.*

Martha Stewart reported to the federal prison camp for women in Alderson, West Virginia, cofounded by Eleanor Roosevelt in 1927. She was assigned to a cottage where she shared a room with a woman convicted of selling cocaine. She was by all accounts as perfectionist a prisoner as she was a chef, decorator, and media executive. Stewart worked on a cleanup crew, led yoga classes and sessions on weaving, arranged flowers, and lectured on starting a business.

Stewart was released to home confinement in March 2005. She resumed her syndicated daytime television program, *The Martha Stewart Show,* and launched a spin-off of the reality show *The Apprentice,* which lasted one season. She threw herself into public appearances, becoming a fixture of celebrity magazines, gossip columns, and television interview shows. By September 2006, when she was featured in *Harper's Bazaar,* the entire affair had nearly been erased from Stewart's memory, or so she claimed. "I honestly don't remember exactly what I was prosecuted for," she told the magazine.

At the time she turned down the plea bargain, Pedowitz claimed Stewart was making a business decision. The prosecutors never bought that rationale. They thought it was an emotional decision. Stewart the perfectionist simply couldn't admit wrongdoing. But if it was a business decision, it was a singularly bad one, for the adverse impact of her conviction may have been most severe at her company. Martha Stewart Living Omnimedia shares continued to rise on news of her release from prison, hitting a high of $33 in September 2005. But the company's most lucrative deal, a licensing and merchandising arrangement with Kmart (subsequently merged with Sears), was terminated in 2009. Ad sales and circulation at her flagship magazine plunged. The company reported an operating loss of $12 million for 2009 and its shares sank to just over $2 in the wake of the 2008 financial crisis, far lower than at any time during Stewart's investigation, trial, or incarceration. (They recovered along with the market in 2009–10, but by late 2010 were less than $5 a share, a small fraction of their former value.)

Though Stewart remains very wealthy, she is nowhere near the billionaire she once was. Her company's share plunge seriously dented her net worth, since she owned 50 percent of the stock and 90 percent of the voting shares, which represent the bulk of her fortune. By mid-2010 the market capitalization of the company was $300 million, valuing Stewart's stake at $150 million.

Of course, there's no way to know how Martha Stewart Living would have fared had Stewart pleaded guilty and avoided a prison term, as seemed possible, or had she never acted on the Waksal tip in the first place, which would have freed her to devote all her considerable energy to promoting her business. At one point Stewart herself estimated the cost of her ordeal at $1 billion; counting total shareholder losses, it surely is much more. Given that Stewart saved herself just $46,000 on the trade, the sale of ImClone and subsequent cover-up surely ranks as one of the most ill-fated white-collar crimes ever.

Peter Bacanovic served his sentence at Nellis Air Force Base, which houses a minimum-security federal prison fifteen miles north of Las Vegas. He was released to home confinement in his Upper East Side apartment in June 2005. Like Stewart, Bacanovic has continued to assert his innocence and maintains he was wrongly convicted. In late 2006, he told *New York Times* reporter Landon Thomas, referring to prosecutor Michael Schachter, "I'm not interested in lying to serve an overzealous thirty-two-year-old prosecutor. I stood by my friend and client and told the truth."

It cannot be said that Stewart has stood by him. As with Armstrong and Pasternak, she never spoke to him again, and dropped him, too, from her Christmas card list. As the SEC's civil charges of insider trading neared a trial date, and Stewart's refusal to settle forced Bacanovic to face the prospect of another expensive trial, this time without Merrill Lynch to pay his bills, Bacanovic swallowed his pride and called his old friend Alexis Stewart to ask for financial assistance, the *Times* reported. "No one here feels we owe you anything," Alexis replied.

Indeed, people close to Stewart emphasize that it was Bacanovic who dragged her into the entire mess by instructing Faneuil to tell her about the Waksals' trading. If not for Bacanovic, she would have continued her vacation trip to Mexico blissfully unaware that the Waksals were in trouble or that the FDA had turned down the Erbitux application. And one of the ironies of the case is that ultimately the FDA did approve Erbitux for treatment of colon cancer. In October 2008 Eli Lilly acquired ImClone for $70 a share—more than $10 a share higher than when Stewart sold. Had she simply held her shares she would have earned a significant profit.

On the other hand, from Bacanovic's point of view, had he failed to tell

Stewart that the Waksals were selling, she would have been furious and would likely have fired him as both her broker and the broker for the pension account. Given the losses in her account, Bacanovic was already on thin ice. That, of course, is no justification for violating Merrill Lynch's policy of confidentiality or for passing on inside information. Bacanovic might have lost Stewart as a client and celebrity friend, but he'd still have his career and reputation.

In August 2006, Stewart and Bacanovic resolved the SEC case by neither admitting nor denying they had engaged in insider trading and conspiracy, as is common in SEC civil suits. They received the same penalties they would have had they admitted the charges. Stewart disgorged the losses she avoided and a penalty of three times that amount, or $195,000. Bacanovic was fined $75,000 for his role in the conspiracy. Stewart was banned from serving as a director of a public company, including her own, for five years, a term that expires in 2011. From the SEC's point of view, Stewart had indeed engaged in insider trading, even if she'd never faced criminal charges for it.

Bacanovic told friends he planned to become a Hollywood producer, something he'd mentioned to Faneuil that he'd always wanted to do. He rented an apartment in Los Angeles and divided his time between there and New York. But no producing career materialized. In 2008 he was hired to be chief executive of vintage jewelry retailer Fred Leighton, a fixture on Madison Avenue that was expanding in Las Vegas and Beverly Hills. Merrill Lynch, which had financed the company's acquisition and expansion, objected to hiring a felon. Bacanovic was fired in 2009 after Leighton entered bankruptcy proceedings. In 2010 he appeared on a television reality show, *High Society*, seated next to aspiring socialite Tinsley Mortimer, the star of the series.

In part due to strains that had developed during the three-year investigation and trial, Douglas Faneuil and Rob Haskell ended their relationship about the time Faneuil was sentenced. Haskell subsequently enrolled in medical school at Brown University. Faneuil left Manhattan and moved to the Sunset Park neighborhood in Brooklyn. When the gallery where he was working closed in 2004, he continued to manage the owner's personal art collection. He has also been raising money and working on a documentary film about how suicide affects the people left behind, inspired by the death of his sister. Though struggling to make ends meet, he's been able to live the more creative existence he now feels he should have embraced from the start.

Part Two

I. LEWIS "SCOOTER" LIBBY

FOUR

"This Is Hush-Hush"

On January 28, 2003, President George W. Bush arrived at the Capitol for his third and most eagerly anticipated State of the Union address. A year before, just four months after the attacks on the World Trade Center transformed his administration into a wartime presidency, he had proclaimed the war on terror, identified the "axis of evil," and vowed to bring Bin Laden to justice. Now, a year later, Bin Laden was still at large and the administration's attention had shifted from Afghanistan to Iraq. As he reminded Congress, the millions watching on television and, for the first time ever, on a webcast:

> Today, the gravest danger in the war on terror, the gravest danger facing America and the world, is outlaw regimes that seek and possess nuclear, chemical and biological weapons.

Frequently interrupted by applause, Bush laid out the broad rationale for war, then turned specifically to the threat posed by Iraq, leaning heavily on intelligence that Saddam Hussein was developing and possessed weapons of mass destruction.

President Bush laid out a chilling inventory of Saddam's suspected deadly weapons: 25,000 liters of anthrax; 38,000 liters of botulinum toxin; 500 tons of sarin, mustard, and VX nerve agents; and "30,000 munitions capable of delivering chemical agents." But none of these were more deadly or posed a more serious threat than nuclear weapons:

The International Atomic Energy Agency confirmed in the 1990s that Saddam Hussein had an advanced nuclear weapons development program, had
a design for a nuclear weapon and was working on five different methods of
enriching uranium for a bomb.

The British government has learned that Saddam Hussein recently
sought significant quantities of uranium from Africa.

Our intelligence sources tell us that he has attempted to purchase high-
strength aluminum tubes suitable for nuclear weapons production.

It was not only that Saddam Hussein was pursuing and might possess
nuclear weapons. It was what he was likely to do with them:

Before September the 11th, many in the world believed that Saddam Hussein could be contained. But chemical agents, lethal viruses and shadowy
terrorist networks are not easily contained.

Imagine those nineteen hijackers with other weapons and other plans,
this time armed by Saddam Hussein. It would take one vial, one canister,
one crate slipped into this country to bring a day of horror like none we
have ever known.

We will do everything in our power to make sure that that day never
comes.

The president was interrupted by resounding applause. This, in essence, was
the American brief for war.

Soon after, on February 5, 2003, President Bush dispatched his secretary of
state, Colin Powell, to the United Nations to make the case to the international
community. Powell, the general and war hero who had led U.S. forces in the
first Gulf War, Operation Desert Storm, had won an important tactical victory
over the Defense Department by persuading Bush to seek UN support before
invading Iraq. Unlike that of some in the administration, Powell's credibility
and integrity were unquestioned, and he was determined not just to assert the
Iraqi threat but also to document it.

In a televised address to the United Nations Security Council in February,
often compared to Adlai Stevenson's galvanizing UN speech during the Cuban
missile crisis, Powell used previously secret intercepted communications and
satellite photos to document Iraq's alleged mobile chemical weapons facilities
and nuclear weapons program.

"Saddam Hussein already possesses two out of the three key components needed to build a nuclear bomb," Powell told the UN. "He has a cadre of nuclear scientists with the expertise, and he has a bomb design. Since 1998, his efforts to reconstitute his nuclear program have been focused on acquiring the third and last component, sufficient fissile material to produce a nuclear explosion. To make the fissile material, he needs to develop an ability to enrich uranium. Saddam Hussein is determined to get his hands on a nuclear bomb."

Powell did not repeat the president's assertion that Iraq was seeking uranium in Africa. But Powell knew his reputation and credibility were on the line. He insisted that CIA director George Tenet sit directly behind him during the speech, visible to the cameras, to demonstrate that the CIA stood behind Powell's claims.

However eloquent, Powell's efforts didn't result in any UN resolutions in support of war. On March 19 U.S. forces began an air bombardment of Baghdad and invaded the next day. Bush famously declared an end to hostilities on May 1 in a speech from the deck of the aircraft carrier USS *Abraham Lincoln*. Attention shifted immediately to the search for Iraq's weapons of mass destruction. There were several false alarms, such as the discovery of the suspected mobile facilities described by Powell. But they turned out to be for making hydrogen or weather balloons, not biological weapons. When no evidence of any weapons of mass destruction surfaced after a month of intense searching by U.S. and coalition forces, the mission was handed over to the Iraq Survey Group. It ended its work in 2004, concluding that there was no evidence that Iraq had produced or stockpiled WMD since UN sanctions were imposed in 1991. President Bush, Vice President Cheney, and their advisers were shocked and disappointed. The credibility of the CIA, which had assured them such weapons existed, plummeted.

However monumental this failure of intelligence, it still seemed to most to be an honest mistake on the part of the nation's leaders, which included many congressional Democrats as well as administration supporters. They began to emphasize other reasons to depose Saddam Hussein, such as bringing democracy to the long-oppressed Iraqi people. It didn't seem to occur to the president or his advisers that they might be accused of deliberately falsifying or manipulating intelligence to deceive the electorate and justify a predetermined decision to go to war.

Then, on May 6, 2003, *New York Times* columnist Nicholas Kristof wrote a column titled "Missing in Action: Truth." It focused not only on the discredited claim that Iraq had tried to buy uranium in Africa, but leveled the far more serious accusation that the Bush administration had "souped up" intelligence in order to "deceive people at home and around the world."

> I'm told by a person involved in the Niger caper that more than a year ago the vice president's office asked for an investigation of the uranium deal, so a former U.S. ambassador to Africa was dispatched to Niger. In February 2002, according to someone present at the meetings, that envoy reported to the CIA and State Department that the information was unequivocally wrong and that the documents had been forged.

Coming from a journalist of Kristof's stature, with two Pulitzer Prizes, the column had an enormous impact, including on other journalists, and elevated the notion that intelligence had been deliberately manipulated or distorted. The column was also the first public mention of a former ambassador and his trip to Niger. But in the White House, Kristof's column at first generated curiously little reaction, given the gravity of the charges. Vice President Cheney's chief of staff, I. Lewis "Scooter" Libby, thought it was a "sleeper," saying, "I noted it; I didn't pay much attention to it; and then it sort of built momentum as it went along."

Libby's position was too lofty for routine media operations, but Cheney relied on him for high-level media contacts on subjects of national importance, such as security and antiterrorism. At age fifty-four, Libby was graying but still trim and athletic. He was born in Connecticut but grew up in Florida before being sent to the elite New England boarding schools Eaglebrook and Andover at an early age. He was named after his self-made father, who didn't graduate from college, although he never used his given name, which was Irve, preferring Scooter, his childhood nickname, which followed him to boarding school.

Although active in public life since serving in the State Department in the Reagan administration, he had successfully cultivated a low profile. He had three titles in the Bush White House: assistant to the president, chief of staff to the vice president, and national security adviser to the vice president, with a top-secret security clearance. Occasionally, he said, part of his job was to convey the vice president's or White House's views to the press. He spent much of his day dealing with intelligence and national security issues, and each day received a briefing from the CIA.

Libby was one of the Vulcans, a small but influential group of neoconservative intellectual policy makers that included Paul Wolfowitz, Condoleezza Rice, and Donald Rumsfeld, all of whom landed prominent roles in the Bush administration. Libby took a class taught by Wolfowitz as an undergraduate at Yale, where he graduated in 1972. Wolfowitz remained a mentor, and after Libby graduated from Columbia Law School, repeatedly lured him from private law practice to work with him in government: at the State Department from 1982 to 1984, and at the Defense Department in 1989. Libby worked closely with both Wolfowitz and Cheney while Cheney was secretary of defense.

Wolfowitz also influenced Libby's intellectual transformation from a typically liberal Vietnam-era college student (at Yale he belonged to the student Democrats) to a hawkish neoconservative preoccupied by national security issues. Still, no one thought of Libby as all that ideological or partisan. He married Harriet Grant, a lawyer who worked as the Democratic staff member for the House Judiciary Committee, and helped air Anita Hill's challenge to Clarence Thomas's nomination to the Supreme Court. Libby also had a literary bent. While a Yale undergraduate he'd began work on a historical novel about a group of travelers stranded by a snowstorm at an inn in Japan in 1903, just before the Russo-Japanese War. It took twenty years of intermittent effort, but he finally published *The Apprentice* in 1996. Vice President Cheney and his wife, Lynne, threw Libby a book party for the 2002 paperback publication, and the guests included the Washington media elite such as the *Washington Post*'s Ben Bradlee and Sally Quinn as well as columnist Robert Novak.

For many it was hard to reconcile the romantic novelist with the sober, cerebral architect of the war with Iraq. Though he was a lawyer by training (he once represented pardoned fugitive Marc Rich), Libby's passion was foreign affairs, and he was a key advocate of the sweeping, ambitious, and muscular U.S. foreign policy doctrine that held sway in the Bush administration, especially after September 11, 2001. But he was also a consummate bureaucrat: thorough, methodical, careful, with a lawyer's tendency toward verbal precision. Although part of his job was to cultivate and brief reporters, almost always on an unidentified, background basis, he showed little natural aptitude or enthusiasm for this; he was not a natural gossip or raconteur, except on the relatively rare occasions—like a White House Correspondents' Association dinner—when he would toss back several shots, usually of tequila.

Kristof's claim that the vice president's office had asked for an investigation of the purported uranium deal caught Libby's attention "because that basically had to do with us." Libby didn't think that the vice president or anyone in the office had asked about a uranium deal.

Cathie Martin, the assistant to the vice president for public affairs, was still relatively new in her job, which included handling press inquiries. Kristof hadn't called their office for comment, and she didn't pay the column much attention.

Martin had worked as Mary Matalin's deputy, and ascended to Matalin's position when she left at the beginning of the year. Trained as a lawyer, Martin was relatively new to the media. She was a Texas native, a graduate of the University of Texas and Harvard Law School, someone friendly with many in the Bush inner circle. Her husband, Kevin Martin, was chairman of the Federal Communications Commission, a connection that gave her some added clout within the White House. She was thoughtful, thorough, and level-headed.

Within the vice president's office, Eric Edelman, a career foreign service officer who was the deputy national security adviser to the vice president, seemed most upset about the column and said he'd look into it. Edelman told vice presidential press secretary Jennifer Millerwise that the column "isn't right," "didn't make sense," and he "wasn't aware" of sending anyone on a fact-finding mission. Ordinarily, someone would have contacted Kristof to point out these issues, but no one had a relationship with Kristof, and since they considered him openly hostile to the administration, they didn't give it a high priority. Edelman said he'd deal with the matter, but left the office soon after to become ambassador to Turkey.

But the questions raised by the column lingered. Several weeks later, on May 29, Libby attended a regular weekly meeting of the Deputies Committee, consisting of the chief deputies to the nation's top officials. Marc Grossman, the under secretary of state for political affairs, was representing the State Department, and Libby asked him if he knew anything about a retired ambassador who'd been sent by the CIA to Africa. Grossman told him he didn't, and later recalled that he was a little "embarrassed" because he couldn't answer Libby's questions and didn't know anything about it. He told Libby he'd find out and get back to him. A couple of days later Grossman called Libby to report that he had "some" of the answers, and that it was true that a former ambassador—Joe Wilson—had been sent by the CIA to Niger. Grossman said he knew Wilson, and thought it "best to go directly to the source." He had spoken to Wilson, who described the trip and said he thought it had been requested by the vice president. Grossman apologized for not knowing more, and said he'd report again when he had a fuller explanation. In the meantime, he asked the State Department's bureau of intelligence and research for a written report summarizing everything the department knew about Wilson's trip and its origins.

The Kristof article was still stirring controversy. Kristof's assertions had developed into a steady drumbeat of articles questioning the accuracy of the State of the Union address, and specifically the sixteen words about uranium in Africa: "The British government has learned that Saddam Hussein recently sought significant quantities of uranium from Africa." It was as if all doubts about the candor of the Bush administration, which by now were legion, were focused on that one sentence. Libby's notes from June 9 indicate that President Bush himself was now asking about it. Apparently in response to a request from Libby, the CIA faxed him a classified report discussing Wilson's mission. It referred to Wilson only as a former ambassador, but Wilson's name was written in the margins, in what appears to be Cheney's handwriting. That Sunday on *Meet the Press* National Security Adviser Condoleezza Rice had been questioned about the uranium claim, and had come across as uncertain and badly prepared. The Kristof column had touched a raw nerve of suspicion among the White House, the State Department, the CIA, and the Defense Department, each fearful that another arm of the administration would try to blame it for the intelligence failure and resulting war.

As one White House official recalled at the time, the issue had rapidly become "an obsession" in the White House. "Condi [Rice] was calling me at home every night from all over: what was the press, what were they saying? She was worried. She knew that once it was obvious there were no WMD, someone was going to be blamed. Bush didn't care that much about the sixteen words, but Cheney was obsessed. So were Libby and Rove."

That same week, Cathie Martin told Libby that the *Washington Post*'s senior national security reporter, Walter Pincus, was calling, and was "sniffing around" about the trip to Niger and the sixteen-words controversy. Maybe this might prove an opportunity to correct the record. Libby discussed this in a phone call with Vice President Cheney, and during the conversation they talked about the Kristof article and what they considered its inaccuracies. Cheney had apparently spoken to someone at the CIA–presumably Director George Tenet–and told Libby there had been "strong interest" at both the State and Defense departments in the uranium issue, suggesting that they–not the vice president's office–might well have been behind the mission. Wilson had been debriefed by the CIA "here," meaning in Washington. Then, Cheney said–in an "offhand, sort of curious, curiosity-type manner," according to Libby–that Wilson's wife worked at "the agency" in counterproliferation, all of which Libby wrote in his notes of the conversation. Libby interpreted this to mean that Cheney found this interesting but wasn't sure how significant it might be. The conversation turned to the "talking points" Libby should use with Pincus: that the vice president didn't know about Wilson's mission, that he didn't get a report on it, and that he didn't know any documents were forged. A possible fourth point was that State or Defense had asked for the mission, but Cheney had cautioned Libby that such an assertion should come from them, not his office.

With Pincus's deadline approaching, Libby called Robert Grenier at the CIA at 1:15 p.m. on June 11. Grenier worked in clandestine operations, and was the Iraq mission director. He knew Libby from Deputies Committee meetings, but Libby had never called him before. Libby said "Joe Wilson" was "going around town" telling his Niger uranium story, and Libby wanted to know if he had in fact been sent by the CIA and if the CIA had indicated this was because of interest on the part of the vice president's office. Grenier thought Libby sounded "aggrieved" and "slightly accusatory" that anyone at the CIA might have told Wilson such a thing.

This was all new to Grenier, but after speaking to an agent in counterproliferation, he thought he had the answers to most of Libby's questions. He told Libby, "Yes, in fact, it was true that the CIA had sent Ambassador Wilson to Niger" and "It wasn't only the office of the vice president that was driving all this. There had been inquiries as well from State and Defense."

Would the CIA state this publicly? Libby asked.

Grenier said he thought so, although he'd have to check.

Then, in passing, Grenier added that "Wilson's wife works there [in counterproliferation] and that's why–that's where the idea came from." Almost as soon as he said this, Grenier felt guilty, he recalled. Even though he hadn't used her name, he worried that "by saying Joe Wilson's wife was working in the CIA, in effect, I was revealing the identity of a CIA officer. That is information that we normally guard pretty closely."

Libby returned Pincus's call late that afternoon, apparently just after speaking to Grenier. He conveyed the points he'd discussed with the vice president, but didn't say anything about Wilson's wife. Pincus's article ran the next day: "CIA Did Not Share Doubt on Iraq Data." From the vice president's narrow perspective, the article was a success. A "senior administration official" made clear the CIA never informed the White House about Wilson's trip or any doubts about the uranium story, and the article quoted a "senior intelligence official" saying the CIA's failure to do so was "extremely sloppy." In this sense it largely corrected the impression from the Kristof article that the vice president had deliberately suppressed intelligence. But while critical of the CIA, the article was hardly flattering to the Bush administration, with a quote from a "senior CIA analyst" that "information not consistent with the administration agenda was discarded and information that was [consistent] was not seriously scrutinized."

That same day, Grossman and Libby were attending back-to-back Deputies Committee meetings, one at noon, on Indonesia, and another at 12:45, on Iraq. They'd also met the day before for a meeting on Afghanistan. Grossman had received and read the report he'd commissioned on the Wilson mission, which revealed that Wilson's wife, Valerie, worked at the CIA and had chaired a meeting to organize Wilson's trip. Grossman found it "odd" and "remarkable" that his wife worked at the CIA and was involved in organizing his trip. He thought it "didn't seem right somehow, that the spouse of someone would be organizing their spouse's trip." Grossman felt it was his responsibility to Libby to give him the full context, so at one of those meetings (he couldn't remember exactly which), Grossman reminded Libby about the Wilson mission, and said, "There's one other thing you've got to know," which was that "his wife works at the agency."

Libby thanked him for the information and said there was also something he wanted Grossman to know, which was that the office of the vice president had "nothing" to do with organizing Wilson's trip. That was the end of their relatively brief exchange.

Libby also took up the issue with Craig Schmall, the CIA official responsible for briefing Libby and the vice president, mentioning Wilson and his wife, and asking for an explanation of why Wilson had been told the vice president's office had asked for the mission. Schmall made notes of the conversation.

The day after the Pincus article implicitly criticizing Kristof's assertions about the vice president's involvement in Wilson's mission, Kristof weighed in with another column, "White House in Denial," which the vice president's staff found even more vexing and hostile. It flatly repeated that the vice president had sent Wilson to Niger and disputed the notion that the White House had never been briefed on his findings, essentially undoing everything Libby had accomplished in the *Post*. Kristof concluded, "I don't believe that the president deliberately lied to the public in an attempt to scare Americans into supporting his war. But it does look as if ideologues in the administration deceived themselves about Iraq's nuclear programs—and then deceived the American public as well." It was clear who those "ideologues" were—Cheney and his staff.

Much to Cathie Martin's frustration, this version of events—that the vice president sent Wilson on the mission and then ignored his findings—was becoming conventional wisdom. Reporters weren't even bothering to call for comment. On June 19 the *New Republic* ran a cover story on the sixteen-words controversy, quoted the unnamed ambassador saying that administration officials "knew the Niger story was a flat-out lie," and repeated that he had undertaken his mission at the request of the vice president. "This had just become sort of . . . you know, true in the press," Martin recalled. "Just everyone that wrote the story just picked up on it, kept writing it. They didn't call and ask me for comment."

After the *New Republic* article appeared, Eric Edelman, the deputy national security adviser to the vice president, phoned Libby and asked if the fact that Wilson's wife worked at the CIA "should be shared with the press." Libby said that would cause "complications" with the CIA and cautioned they shouldn't discuss the matter further, because they were speaking on an unsecured phone line. Edelman took that to mean that the subject of Wilson's wife was classified, and showed that Libby recognized then that her identity raised security issues. After all, exposing the identity of a CIA agent could have dire consequences . . . and might well violate federal law.

Afterward, Libby was on the phone with someone at the CIA, and told Cathie Martin, who was standing nearby, to get in touch with Bill Harlow, the press spokesman for the CIA, who might be able to help rebut the story.

Her mounting frustration was evident in her subsequent conversation with Harlow:

"We didn't send him. What are you saying? I mean, if we didn't send him, you must have sent him. Who sent him? Who is the guy? What are you saying to the press? Because it keeps getting reported that we sent him. They are not taking my word for it [that we didn't]."

"You know," Harlow replied, "I didn't know who he was either when they [the press] first called. They knew more about this guy than I did." But then he added, "His name is Joe Wilson. He was a chargé [d'affaires] in Baghdad, and his wife works over here."

Martin kept notes of the conversation (though she didn't date them), and she deemed the information important enough that she immediately asked to see the vice president. When she went into his office, Libby was already there. Martin reported on her conversation with Harlow at the CIA, mentioning Wilson's name and that his wife worked at the CIA. Of course, both already knew this, but Martin didn't recall their saying anything.

Libby's mounting frustrations about allegations the administration—and specifically the vice president—had ignored or manipulated intelligence on the uranium issue were in full view on June 23, when *New York Times* reporter Judith Miller visited Libby in his office in the Executive Office Building. Miller was fifty-five, a slender, attractive reporter whose specialty as a reporter for the *Times* had long been the Middle East, terrorism, and weapons of mass destruction. Over her twenty-six years at the *Times*, she'd evolved from a liberal antiwar activist into an equally vocal neoconservative. She was married to Jason Epstein, the longtime editorial director of Random House, and the pair circulated in high-level literary and political circles in Manhattan, Washington, and Sag Harbor, on Long Island just north of the Hamptons. Miller was determined, competitive, aggressive, and was also personally close to *Times* publisher Arthur Sulzberger Jr. (they'd once shared a summer house)—qualities that annoyed many of her colleagues but also landed many of her stories on the front page.

Miller had called Libby sometime after the September 11 attacks, and they'd met for the first time in his office. Libby told her he admired the book she'd coauthored on bioterrorism, *Germs*, and she promised to send him a signed copy. He also liked her reporting on weapons of mass destruction and the threat of terrorism. He agreed they could meet periodically, as long as his name never appeared as a source and he was referred to only as an administration official or a senior administration official. In short, he found her a rare kindred spirit in the press.

Now Miller was researching a story as part of a team of reporters asked to find out why no weapons of mass destruction had been found in Iraq. Miller had been embedded in a military unit looking for WMD and reported from Iraq during the war. She was also the foremost reporter on the threat Iraq posed before the war, writing or reporting dozens of stories about Iraq's weapons capabilities, including groundbreaking stories on the purported mobile bioterrorism labs and Iraq's procuring metal tubes for nuclear enrichment—two of the factual foundations for war against Iraq that now looked increasingly dubious. Miller's journalistic reputation was plummeting as she faced allegations she was little more than a mouthpiece for the Bush administration and, like the administration itself, had deliberately ignored or manipulated evidence that undercut her conviction that Iraq posed a serious threat. In this regard she and Libby had much in common.

Miller was surprised that the normally "low-key and controlled" Libby seemed "agitated and frustrated and angry." He was especially angry with the CIA. He was convinced that the agency, which was responsible for the intelligence that went into the State of the Union address, was trying to distance itself and blame the White House through what he called a "perverted war of leaks." He said, "Nobody ever came to the White House from the CIA and said, 'Mr. President, this is not correct. This is not right.'" If the CIA had such doubts, "they should have shared them with the president."

Libby went into considerable detail with Miller about Wilson's mission to Niger, indicating that his efforts through Grossman and others had yielded a good deal of intelligence. At first he referred to the former ambassador as a "clandestine guy," but quickly referred to him by name, Joe Wilson, which Miller wrote in her notes. Libby also indicated that the vice president had been involved, unwittingly, in sending Wilson because he had asked the CIA, in 2002, for more information about a report from Congress that Iraq had been seeking uranium in Africa. But the CIA had "taken it upon themselves" to send Wilson, and the vice president never knew about the mission or its results.

Almost as an aside, Libby added that "his wife works at the bureau." Miller thought for a moment he meant the FBI, but quickly realized it was the CIA. She was taking notes, and put the the comment in parentheses. Wittingly or not, Libby had just exposed the identity of a CIA agent to a reporter.

Libby continued fuming about the CIA and its tactics. The issue wasn't Wilson, who was being used as a "ruse." He was an "irrelevancy."

When the interview ended, Miller still hadn't had a chance to ask Libby about her assignment, which was to write about the failure to discover WMD.

O n July 6, 2003, Robert Novak walked into the greenroom at NBC's studios in northwest Washington, DC, nodded to his fellow guests on that week's *Meet the Press*, and looked for a seat. There weren't any available, so he remained standing and picked up one of the thick summaries of the Sunday papers and newsweeklies prepared by the *Meet the Press* staff for its guests.

Novak was at the studio for a roundtable discussion on gay marriage–to which the conservative Novak was implacably opposed. He didn't like to waste his time on small talk while waiting to go on air, nor, in his experience, did other participants. But this morning someone in the room, only vaguely familiar to Novak, was loudly holding forth, boasting about his work for the Clinton administration's National Security Council and its superiority to President Bush's.

What an asshole, Novak thought.

Novak had been on *Meet the Press* many times–236, to be precise. He kept careful track of such things. A ubiquitous presence on TV, he had become one of the nation's best-known and most readily identifiable political columnists, one of the first to recognize the power of television to advance his career in print. In addition to *Meet the Press* (known to regulars like Novak simply as *Meet*), he was a regular on CNN, both on his own interview show and on *The McLaughlin Group* and *The Capital Gang*. Novak, with his dark looks, furrowed brow, and three-piece suits, was neither telegenic nor charming. But his combative style, glowering visage, and willingness to interrupt and confront his fellow guests made him a natural for television talk shows, which thrived on conflict.

Meet the Press was then hosted by NBC Washington bureau chief Tim Russert. Few realized how close Russert was to Novak: both were devout Roman

Catholics (Novak having converted from Judaism) and Russert had often and anonymously fed Novak material for his columns.

Novak's four-times-a-week column, "Inside Report," initially written with coauthor Rowland Evans, was the country's longest-running syndicated political column, running in as many as 150 newspapers, including the influential *Washington Post*. Novak blended scoops with a conservative editorial spin, emerging as one of the earliest of the newspaper pundits who came to dominate television news. He seemed to know everyone in Washington, was a fixture at media and political social events, and had pursued his craft with a singular and relentless energy. His conservative, often pessimistic political views had earned him the nickname "Prince of Darkness" among his colleagues, a name he relished and later used as the title for his autobiography.

To his detractors, Novak was little more than a Republican lapdog, his "scoops" self-serving leaks from members of the Republican inner circle. But despite his conservative credentials and support for George W. Bush's campaign, he wasn't a party hack. Novak had broken with the party faithful by opposing the invasion of Iraq. As a result, many of the party faithful and the White House inner circle shunned him. Still, he had influential contacts, especially top Bush adviser and political strategist Karl Rove. They spoke on the phone two or three times a month, and Rove always returned Novak's calls.

In the makeup room, Novak learned that the guest he found so annoying was Joseph C. Wilson IV, a fifty-four-year-old retired diplomat who, in 2002, at the request of the CIA, had gone to Niger to investigate reports that Saddam Hussein was trying to procure yellowcake uranium in an effort to develop a nuclear weapon. Wilson had grown up in California, attended the University of California at Santa Barbara, and spent several years surfing and playing beach volleyball before returning to school and embarking on a diplomatic career. He'd led a glamorous diplomatic life and had married three times. He was posted to both Niger and Iraq, where he was deputy chief of mission at the time of the first Gulf War. His successful effort to evacuate Americans and others led President George H. Bush to praise him as a "true American hero." He was subsequently named U.S. ambassador to the African nation of Gabon, and in his last assignment he worked as a special assistant to President Bill Clinton, specializing in African affairs. Wilson retired from the State Department in 1998 and became a consultant on foreign business issues.

Despite his CIA-sponsored trip, a mission he described as "discreet but by no means secret," Wilson had gone public that weekend with an op-ed piece in the *New York Times*, "What I Didn't Find in Africa." Novak started reading it while his makeup was being applied.

Did the Bush administration manipulate intelligence about Saddam Hussein's weapons programs to justify an invasion of Iraq?

In Wilson's view, the answer was "yes." Wilson wrote that the CIA told him that Vice President Cheney's office had asked about Iraq's alleged activities in Niger. His piece went on to describe his arrival in Niger ("Seasonal winds had clogged the air with dust and sand"), his attempts to determine if Iraq had obtained uranium from Niger, and his eight days "drinking sweet mint tea and meeting with dozens of people. . . . It did not take long to conclude that it was highly doubtful that any such transaction had ever taken place."

Wilson hadn't prepared a written report, but had delivered a briefing to CIA officials upon his return. He assumed that the agency reported his findings to the vice president's office, either orally or in writing.

The vice president's office asked a serious question. . . . I have every confidence that the answer I provided was circulated to the appropriate officials within our government. . . . If, however, the information was ignored because it did not fit certain preconceptions about Iraq, then a legitimate argument can be made that we went to war under false pretenses.

When Novak got back to the greenroom, he looked for Wilson, but he'd already left for his interview with NBC correspondent Andrea Mitchell, who was sitting in for Russert that Sunday while Russert watched the Wimbledon tennis matches (Russert always took time off for Wimbledon and the U.S. Open). Novak watched the program on the monitor. Wilson looked good on TV; he still had the tan, slightly weathered good looks of a former surfer.

"Let's put this in context for our viewers," Mitchell said, and showed a clip of President Bush's State of the Union address, with Bush speaking the now controversial sixteen words. "What did you think when you first saw the president making that comment in the State of the Union?" Mitchell asked.

"I assumed they were talking about one of the other countries and not Niger since we had, I believed, at the time effectively debunked the Niger arms uranium sale."

"So they knew months and months before they passed on these allegations that, in fact, that particular charge was not true. Do you think, based on all this, that the intelligence was hyped?"

"My judgment on this is that if they were referring to Niger when they were referring to sales from Africa to Iraq, that information was erroneous and that they knew about it well ahead of both the publication of the British white paper and the president's State of the Union address."

Wilson's comments and delivery annoyed Novak, who later called it an "obnoxious performance." Novak thought Wilson was reveling in the attention and controversy, which Novak found distasteful in someone who'd been entrusted with a presumably confidential CIA mission. Given Wilson's self-aggrandizing personality and apparent hostility to the Bush presidency and the war in Iraq, Novak wondered, Why on earth had the CIA chosen Wilson for such a sensitive assignment? That was exactly the kind of unanswered question he liked to write about.

Any hopes on Cheney's or Libby's part that the record would get corrected were dashed by Wilson's op-ed piece and his appearance on *Meet the Press* on July 6. Wilson said explicitly that his mission had been requested by the vice president. He had delivered his report to the CIA and, based on his experience in government, assumed it had been conveyed to the source of the request, which was the vice president.

To Libby, Wilson's conclusions were flatly wrong. Wilson had no actual knowledge that the vice president had requested his mission, nor did he know what the CIA did with his findings. He was speculating and making unfounded assumptions. Libby was "upset," "disturbed by the article, didn't like the article. Upset's a fair word, I guess," he recalled. Still, he thought if the administration could just get the facts out, Wilson might recant, and the record might be corrected.

The vice president was at his home in Jackson Hole, Wyoming, for the Fourth of July weekend. Cheney read Wilson's article in the *Times* on Air Force Two while flying back to Washington. He underlined several passages and wrote alongside them, "Have they done this before? Send an ambassador to answer a question? Do we ordinarily send people out pro bono to work for us? Or did his wife send him on a junket?" Cheney folded the page and, back in Washington, placed it in the small safe in his office.

The vice president was "upset," Libby recalled, and he and Libby spoke about Wilson and his claims every day that week. The vice president was "very keen to get the truth out," Libby recalled. "He wanted to get all the facts out about what he had or hadn't done, what the facts were and were not. He was very keen on that and said it repeatedly."

Cheney's and Libby's determination to get the facts out caused the vice president's press office to redouble its efforts. Early Monday morning Cathie Martin e-mailed White House press secretary Ari Fleischer a list of talking points—essentially the same ones Cheney had already dictated to Libby—on the assumption that reporters would ask Fleischer about Wilson at that morning's White House "gaggle," or press briefing. The vice president told Martin he wanted the press closely monitored, including network and cable television, for any mention of Wilson and the vice president. The press office ordinarily prepared a daily written summary of print articles mentioning the vice president, but this effort was now expanded, with a press assistant watching and then transcribing broadcast reports.

The vice president also dictated to Martin the specific talking points he wanted disseminated on his role in the Wilson affair, which had now expanded to eight.

"Not clear who authorized his travel," Martin wrote. "2. He did not travel at my request. Don't know him. 3. He was apparently unpaid. 4. Never saw the document he was allegedly trying to verify. 5. Said he was convinced Niger could not have provided uranium to Iraq, but, in fact, they did in 1980s, 200 tons, currently under IAEA seal. 6. No written report. 7. V.P. was unaware of Joe Wilson, his trip or any conclusions he may have reached until spring '03 when reported. 8. As late as last October, the considered judgment of the intel community was that Saddam Hussein had indeed undertaken a vigorous effort to acquire uranium from Africa . . . according to NIE." Martin added a question mark to the last item, since the NIE (National Intelligence Estimate) was classified, and she wasn't sure she could mention it.

Martin was again dispatched to ask the CIA's Bill Harlow what he was hearing. He seemed less cooperative this time, but told her he knew NBC's Andrea Mitchell and David Martin of CBS were working on stories about the Wilson mission. Martin reported this to Cheney and Libby, asking whether they wanted to "make sure we are a part of the story," to "make sure they don't repeat the stuff that we thought was false," and Cheney asked Libby to call both reporters. Increasingly, Cheney was insisting Libby handle the Wilson issue. Libby went into his small White House office just off the vice president's, and called both as Martin stood by.

The next day, on July 7, the White House conceded that the State of the Union address had been flawed, and that the sixteen words should not have been included in President Bush's address, or relied upon as a justification for invading Iraq. The concession only heightened media interest in Wilson's allegations.

That same Monday, July 7, Libby had lunch with press secretary Ari Fleischer in the White House mess. Libby had scheduled it as a farewell lunch, since Fleischer had announced his departure and was leaving at the end of the week. Fleischer reported that he'd been asked questions about Wilson's op-ed piece. He'd dismissed it as old news, saying there was "zero, nada, nothing new here," other than that Wilson had come forward as the previously unnamed ambassador. He assured Libby that he'd followed the talking points from the vice president, and said that the CIA had sent Wilson on the mission "on their own volition."

Libby emphasized again that the vice president had not sent Wilson to Niger, and Fleischer said he understood that; it was in Martin's talking points, which he'd used that morning. But Libby continued anyway. "Ambassador Wilson was sent by his wife. She works at the CIA." He added that she worked in counterproliferation and used her name, Valerie Plame. "This is hush-hush," Libby cautioned. "This is on the QT. Not very many people know about this."

This was news to Fleischer. So it was nepotism at the CIA; that's why Wilson was sent to Africa. It was another "nugget," he thought, that backed up the vice president's claim that he didn't send Wilson on the mission.

Other than describing it as "hush-hush," Libby didn't say anything about the information being classified or say that Fleischer couldn't use it. Fleischer's experience was that when administration officials told him something, they wanted him to pass it on. After all, his job was to talk to the press. But he didn't think the revelation about Wilson's wife was all that important, or that anyone in the press would be very interested. Reporters were focused on whether the president had deceived the American public, not who sent Wilson to Africa.

Later that day, on his last foreign trip as press secretary, Fleischer accompanied the president, Colin Powell, Condoleezza Rice, and a large entourage on a five-day goodwill trip to sub-Saharan Africa. Even on the plane, reporters kept asking about the accuracy of the State of the Union address. After sidestepping the question, Fleischer that night finally conceded, "Now, we've long acknowledged—and this is old news, we've said this repeatedly—that the information on yellowcake did, indeed, turn out to be incorrect."

As the Wilson-fueled controversy continued unabated, the mounting frustrations within the administration were evident at the next morning's senior staff meeting back in Washington. Libby's notes indicate that the Wilson story was "becoming a question of the president's trustworthiness" and was "leading all the news." Rove complained that "now they have accepted Joe Wilson as [a] credible expert" and "we're one day late with getting [the] CIA [to] write [a] response." Cheney and Libby were among those in the White House insisting that the CIA, and George Tenet in particular, accept responsibility for the intelligence on which the president had relied. High-level efforts were under way to get Tenet to make a public statement, which they hoped would take the pressure off the vice president's office.

Among the galling misperceptions, in their view, was that Wilson's findings actually rebutted the idea that Iraq was trying to procure uranium in Niger. On the contrary, Wilson had reported that an Iraqi delegation had tried in 1999 to establish "commercial relations," which in Niger could mean only one thing: yellowcake uranium. The CIA report based on Wilson's debriefing made this clear. Wilson hadn't mentioned anything about forged documents. Moreover, the NIE—the intelligence community's most authoritative report—stated unequivocally that Iraq had tried to buy uranium. Cheney felt that getting these documents to reporters would lay the issue to rest. As he said to Libby and Stephen Hadley (the president's deputy national security adviser) that week, "Anything less than full and complete disclosure is a serious mistake." Both were classified, secret intelligence documents, but Cheney said he'd get President Bush to declassify them. Libby checked with David Addington, Cheney's counsel, who assured him the president had the legal authority to do so.

Cheney and Libby selected Judy Miller of the *Times* as the recipient of the newly declassified documents. It isn't clear who first suggested her, but Cheney explicitly authorized Libby to call her and give her the classified National Intelligence Estimate. Plans for the meeting were shrouded in secrecy. Neither Cheney nor Libby told Cathie Martin or anyone else in the office about it. Libby arranged to meet Miller away from his office, at the St. Regis hotel on K Street. He'd suggested lunch, but they settled on coffee at 8:30 a.m. His calendar said only "office time," but someone wrote in "Private meeting @ St. Regis."

When they met in the hotel's dining room, Miller found Libby to be "frustrated and somewhat quietly agitated." Unlike their prior meeting, where Libby was content to be identified as an administration official, he now wanted more protection. She could refer to him only as a "former Hill staffer." Libby reviewed for Miller in exhaustive detail the evolution of the administration's belief that Iraq was pursuing uranium in Africa, referring often to both the CIA report of Wilson's debriefing and the NIE. In response to her questions, he stressed that the classified version of the NIE was unequivocal. As he had in their earlier conversation, Libby mentioned that Wilson's wife worked at the CIA, this time referring to her job at WINPAC, an acronym for Weapons, Intelligence, Nonproliferation, and Arms Control. Even though her pen wasn't working very well, Miller made note of this, which to her was a new detail.

Andrea Mitchell delivered her report on the NBC *Nightly News* that evening, emphasizing the CIA's lapses, and the next morning Stephen Hadley told the senior White House staff that CIA director Tenet was "not happy" with it, and that trying to blame the CIA for the uranium controversy was "not helpful" and they should stop doing it. As he made this point, Hadley turned and stared directly at Cathie Martin, clearly marking her as a suspect; Libby, who had actually spoken to Mitchell and blamed the CIA, said nothing and "looked down," Martin noticed. Hadley asked Martin and other press aides to join him in his office after the meeting, and again stressed that "we shouldn't be making any suggestion that this was the CIA's fault in any way, shape or form." Martin promptly reported this to Cheney; Libby was again with him in his office. But their attention was now focused on influencing the upcoming Tenet statement, a process from which Martin was excluded.

Meanwhile, thanks to the intensified monitoring in the office, the vice president was receiving a stream of transcripts from broadcast reports on the Wilson issues. Especially annoying were several from *Hardball*, hosted by Chris Matthews. Matthews was hammering away on the uranium issue, repeating without any qualification that the vice president had requested the mission, even alleging that Libby himself was responsible for the sixteen words: "Why would the vice president's office, Scooter Libby or whoever is running that office, why would they send a CIA effort down to Niger to verify something, find out there wasn't a uranium sale, and then not follow up by putting that information—or correcting that information—in the president's State of the Union?" Matthews demanded.

Libby felt Matthews had to be reined in, but he didn't know him, so he spoke to Adam Levine, who'd worked as producer for Matthews before coming to the White House. Levine called Matthews, but Matthews ended up yelling at him. Libby also called Mary Matalin for advice. She warned that "the story has legs" and that the White House needed to address Wilson's motivation. She suggested Libby call Tim Russert, NBC's Washington bureau chief: "Call Tim. He hates Chris. He [Russert] needs to know it all. He needs to know the whole story and that Chris Matthews is not getting it right." Libby left word for Russert, who returned his call on July 10. They were interrupted, but continued the next day.

Libby was unusually direct. "What the hell is going on with *Hardball*?" he said. "Damn it, I'm tired of hearing my name over and over again. What's being said is not true." Libby seemed "agitated," Russert thought.

But Russert proved to be little help. He hadn't seen the programs, and said he didn't have any management authority over Matthews. If Russert disliked Matthews, as Matalin had suggested, he gave no sign of it to Libby. Russert was courteous, and suggested Libby call Matthews directly, or one of his producers. He even gave Libby a direct number for Neal Shapiro, the head of NBC News, and alerted Shapiro that Libby might be calling. But Libby asked Adam Levine in the press office to call, since Levine had worked at NBC and knew Shapiro, but Levine didn't get anywhere.

Late that afternoon Libby went to Karl Rove's office, hoping to find out what was happening with the Tenet statement. Rove mentioned that he'd gotten a call from Bob Novak, who was writing a column about Wilson. Rove reported that Novak had run into Wilson at the NBC greenroom, and Wilson had "sort of turned him off." Novak had "concerns" about how Wilson came to be chosen, since he "might have an axe to grind." And then Novak had told Rove that Wilson's wife worked for the CIA.

The much-anticipated Tenet mea culpa finally emerged on Friday, July 11–days late, in Libby's view—and too late to make the television evening news broadcasts, which meant it would be relegated to Saturday's papers. "Legitimate questions have arisen about how remarks on alleged Iraqi attempts to obtain uranium in Africa made it into the president's State of the Union speech," Tenet began. "Let me be clear about several things right up front. First, the CIA approved the president's State of the Union address before it was delivered. Second, I am responsible for the approval process in my agency. And third, the president had every reason to believe that the text presented to him was sound. These sixteen words should never have been included in the text written for the president."

Tenet then gave his detailed account of the statement, which touched on many of the vice president's talking points. Tenet dismissed Wilson's conclusions as not having resolved the issue, and said the report based on Wilson's findings didn't get briefed to the president or vice president. Tenet also said that CIA counterproliferation experts had sent Wilson "on their own initiative."

Tenet concluded, "From what we know now, agency officials in the end concurred that the text in the speech was factually correct—i.e., that the British government report said that Iraq sought uranium from Africa. This should not have been the test for clearing a presidential address. This did not rise to the level of certainty which should be required for presidential speeches, and the CIA should have ensured that it was removed."

Still, he didn't shoulder the blame for the broader intelligence failure, and made clear that at various times the CIA had raised questions about the accuracy of the uranium claims. Libby felt the statement "wasn't all that we had hoped for" but, on balance, was "helpful."

The next day was hot and sunny in Norfolk, Virginia. A crowd of twenty thousand gathered for the festive commissioning of the navy's newest carrier, the USS *Ronald Reagan*. Former first lady Nancy Reagan issued the traditional command, "Bring her to life," and the ship's crew raced up the gang-plank. Reagan "came to the presidency with a clear understanding of the tools our navy would need to protect the American people," Cheney told the crowd, which included most of his staff. Libby brought his two children; it was his young son's birthday.

It didn't take long for the Iraq uranium controversy to reassert itself. As they were flying back to Washington on Air Force Two, Libby walked back to the rear of the plane where Martin was seated. "What do you need to talk to me about?" he asked.

Martin reported that Glenn Kessler of the *Washington Post* had called, and Matt Cooper, at *Time*, had sent a detailed e-mail with questions about the vice president's role in the Wilson mission.

"Well, let me go talk to the boss and I'll be back," Libby said. Cheney was sitting in a separate compartment at the front of the plane.

Now that the Tenet statement had been released, Libby had been wanting to discuss with Cheney how they should proceed, and had jotted down on a card a few points to bring up. Cheney said he felt there was still some ambiguity in the Tenet report, and he wanted to make clear that six months after Wilson's trip, the NIE stated that Iraq was vigorously pursuing uranium in Niger and other African countries. He dictated a statement for Libby to read to reporters that would be on the record, meaning attributed to Libby. This was a rare step, but Cheney thought it would have more impact and be taken more seriously. He didn't want Cathie Martin to make the calls or read the statement. Libby copied the statement as well as another point, which was to be on "deep background," referring to Wilson's report that Iraq had approached Niger officials in 1999.

When the plane landed at Andrews Air Force Base, Libby and Martin asked to borrow a phone and went into an office off the lounge. Libby wanted to make the calls and get home for his son's birthday party. He called *Time* reporter Matt Cooper and reached him at home. Cooper was not just another *Time* reporter; he was married to Mandy Grunwald, the daughter of legendary Time Inc. editor in chief Henry Grunwald, and a media consultant close to the Clintons, especially Hillary. Still, Cooper was new to the White House beat, so Martin got on the phone and made an introduction. Libby said he had an on-the-record quote for *Time*, and read the statement the vice president had dictated, making the point that the vice president hadn't asked for or known about Wilson's mission. "Then why does Wilson keep saying it?" Cooper asked.

Libby was "taken aback" and somewhat annoyed. The director of the CIA had said publicly that Cheney didn't send him. The vice president's chief of staff had just said the same thing. So why was Cooper still asking about Wilson? Why didn't he say, "Oh, I see, the vice president didn't send him"?

Libby stayed calm. "I don't know why he keeps saying it," he said, then went on "background" to speculate that someone at the CIA had given Wilson misinformation. Toward the end of the conversation, they talked briefly about Wilson's wife. Cooper recalled that he brought it up, asking about whether Wilson's wife had been involved in sending him to Africa. "I've heard that too," Libby said, or words to that effect. In Libby's version, he replied, "Off-the-record, reporters are telling us that Ambassador Wilson's wife works at the CIA and I don't know if it's true." Whatever Libby's exact words, Cooper didn't write anything in his notes.

Martin was listening to Libby's end of the conversation. She didn't recall hearing him say anything about Wilson's wife, but she did take another call at one point and could have missed it. When Libby finished with Cooper, Martin suggested they make the rest of the calls from the van taking them back to the capital, which would save time. They reached the *Post*'s Kessler, who was with his family at the zoo, and left a message for Evan Thomas at *Newsweek*. Libby also called Judith Miller, who was en route to her weekend home in Sag Harbor and said she'd call him back. He didn't say anything further about Wilson's wife while in the van.

When Libby and Miller did speak that evening, the topic of Wilson's wife apparently again surfaced. Libby recalled a longer conversation about the Tenet statement and telling Miller that reporters were saying Wilson's wife worked at the CIA. But by this point Miller's interest in Wilson had waned, and she didn't remember much about the conversation. She told Libby she didn't think her editors at the *Times* were interested, and she wasn't pursuing the story. Libby's efforts to use Miller to get the story out had come to nothing.

As the furor over Wilson's op-ed piece intensified, Novak had turned to the question that occurred to him that Sunday on *Meet the Press*, which was how Wilson, of all people, had been chosen for the assignment. As his call to Rove indicated, he'd learned that Wilson's wife worked for the CIA, which helped solve the mystery. He finished writing his column by noon on Friday, July 11, and went over the editing. That afternoon Novak's publisher,

Creators Syndicate, transmitted the column to a hundred subscribers, including the *Washington Post*. On Monday, July 14, 2003, Novak's column "Mission to Niger" appeared in print. It dismissed Wilson's mission as a "low level" operation and stressed that its conclusions never reached the White House, or even Tenet, the CIA director.

It was only in the sixth paragraph that Novak got to the scoop:

> Wilson never worked for the CIA, but his wife, Valerie Plame, is an agency operative on weapons of mass destruction. Two senior administration officials told me that Wilson's wife suggested sending him to Niger. . . . The CIA says its counterproliferation officials selected Wilson and asked his wife to contact him. "I will not answer any question about my wife," Wilson told me.

That Joe Wilson's wife, Valerie Plame, worked for the CIA as an "agency operative on weapons of mass destruction," and suggested her husband for the Niger mission, added little, on the face of it, to the public debate over Wilson's allegations. Even that was qualified, since the CIA official asserted that the agency chose Wilson, not his wife, and merely asked his wife to contact him. Novak rightly noted that the real issue was whether the administration had ignored facts and misled the public about the justification for war.

Only in the hothouse atmosphere of a White House desperate to salvage its reputation could Novak's column be seen as a public relations coup, and none seemed more impressed by it than Rove and Libby. Libby later maintained he never considered the column all that important, but others in the White House at the time dispute that. "Karl [Rove] and Scooter [Libby] were like cats who swallowed the canary," recalled one administration official. "They went around all day, saying 'look who sent him; look who sent him.'"

The column did advance several facts important to Libby and others in the administration: It said it was not Vice President Dick Cheney or anyone else in the White House who asked for such a mission, rendering it more plausible that they wouldn't have known about it or received any report. And by suggesting that it was Wilson's wife who chose him, the column raised the possibility that nepotism got him the assignment. This, too, suggested his report wouldn't have been taken all that seriously. Yet that conclusion seemed something of a stretch, one likely to be made only by those avidly looking for a reason to discredit Wilson, who was, after all, a former ambassador to Africa with experience in Niger.

The column seemed the classic kind of inside baseball that obsesses a small group of politicians and journalists in Washington but baffles almost everyone beyond the Potomac.

In the avalanche of coverage that Monday about the Wilson controversy, it's not surprising that Novak's column and his scoop about Wilson's wife attracted little attention. *Time* devoted its cover to the Wilson affair, with the sweeping headline "Untruth and Consequences." The lead article, "Follow the Yellowcake Road," with reporting by Cooper, began:

> How did a story that much of the national-security apparatus regarded as bogus wind up in the most important speech of Bush's term? The evidence suggests that many in the Bush Administration simply wanted to believe it.

No wonder Libby was, to put it mildly, disappointed. The CIA director had denied that the vice president was behind Wilson's mission. Libby had gone on the record at the vice president's behest, something he almost never did, so that his denial would have the added credibility of attribution. Yet Cooper had used a fragment of the quote to reinforce the perception that Cheney was behind the Wilson mission:

> When it got to Washington, the Iraq-Niger uranium report caught the eye of someone important: Vice President Dick Cheney. Cheney's chief of staff, Lewis Libby, told TIME that during one of his regular CIA briefings, "the vice president asked a question about the implication of the report." Cheney's interest hardly came as a surprise: he has long been known to harbor some of the most hard-line views of Saddam's nuclear ambitions. It was not long before the agency quietly dispatched a veteran U.S. envoy named Joseph Wilson to investigate.

On Tuesday, Libby asked Cathie Martin to call Cooper. She complained that the full quote wasn't used, so Cooper agreed to insert it into the online version of the story. Cooper also decided to use Libby's quote in full in another piece, "A War on Wilson?" that he cowrote for *Time*'s website, referring to it as an "exclusive" interview with *Time*. The article appeared on July 17, and did convey the administration's view of the Wilson trip, including the point Libby had made to Cooper about Wilson's wife:

And some government officials have noted to TIME in interviews (as well as to syndicated columnist Robert Novak) that Wilson's wife, Valerie Plame, is a CIA official who monitors the proliferation of weapons of mass destruction. . . .

In an interview with TIME, Wilson, who served as an ambassador to Gabon and as a senior American diplomat in Baghdad under the current president's father, angrily said that his wife had nothing to do with his trip to Africa. "That is bulls__t. That is absolutely not the case," Wilson told TIME.

The article seems to have been a classic case of Libby getting more than he bargained for when he called Cooper to complain about the first article. For Libby was the only administration official in the story quoted by name. Although he wasn't explicitly identified as one of the government officials who told Cooper about Wilson's wife, he might as well have been: all signs pointed to him.

Remarkably, it apparently didn't occur to anyone at a White House purportedly focused on national security that identifying a CIA officer might be a breach of security. It took two *Newsday* reporters, Timothy Phelps and Knut Royce, to point out that naming a CIA operative might put that person in danger, compromise U.S. intelligence efforts, and undermine national security. It might also be a crime. "Columnist Blows CIA Agent's Cover" ran in *Newsday* on July 22, more than a week after Novak's column:

Wilson and a retired CIA official said yesterday that the "senior administration officials" who named Plame had, if their description of her employment was accurate, violated the law and may have endangered her career and possibly the lives of her contacts in foreign countries. Plame could not be reached for comment. . . .

"If what the two senior administration officials said is true," Wilson said, "they will have compromised an entire career of networks, relationships and operations." What's more, it would mean that "this White House has taken an asset out of" the weapons of mass destruction fight, "not to mention putting at risk any contacts she might have had where the services are hostile."

Novak himself told *Newsday* that his sources in the administration had pushed the story on him. "I didn't dig it out, it was given to me. They thought it was significant, they gave me the name and I used it," he said.

Washington loves a mystery, and this was the biggest leak mystery since the identity of Watergate's Deep Throat: Who had revealed Plame's identity and CIA role to Novak?

This was no ordinary leak either. Novak had identified his sources as "two administration officials," and given the subject's position as a covert CIA agent, the leak might well be a federal crime under the Intelligence Identities Protection Act.

> Whoever, having or having had authorized access to classified information that identifies a covert agent, intentionally discloses any information identifying such covert agent to any individual not authorized to receive classified information, knowing that the information disclosed so identifies such covert agent and that the United States is taking affirmative measures to conceal such covert agent's intelligence relationship to the United States, shall be fined under title 18, United States Code, or imprisoned not more than ten years, or both.
>
> –U.S. Code Title 50, Section 421(a).

Congress called for an inquiry and the rest of the media jumped on the story. On August 21, at a public conference on the handling of intelligence, Wilson said that the leak of his wife's name should be investigated, and added, "At the end of the day, it's of keen interest to me to see whether or not we can get Karl Rove frog-marched out of the White House in handcuffs. And trust me, when I use that name, I measure my words." He didn't elaborate, but fingering Karl Rove, Bush's senior political adviser in the White House, and the architect of Bush's successful campaign, had the effect of pouring fuel on the media fire. White House press secretary Scott McClellan said allegations of any involvement in the leak by Rove were "totally ridiculous."

The CIA, its relations with the White House already strained over its role in Iraqi intelligence, responded with a formal request to the Department of Justice to investigate the possible criminal offense of revealing Plame's identity. On September 26, the Department of Justice formally launched its investigation, which triggered another wave of media attention and speculation about the identity of Novak's two sources. Novak himself said nothing further, intensifying the mystery.

That week White House press conferences were consumed by more questions about the leak investigation and the identity of the leakers. McClellan said repeatedly that the "president believes the leaking of classified information is a very serious matter," that it should be "pursued to the fullest extent," and that no one in his administration was authorized to do such a thing. Asked about Rove as a possible source, he reiterated that the president "knows" Rove wasn't involved, and added, "It's a ridiculous suggestion in the first place. . . . I said that it's not true. And I have spoken with Karl Rove." Then a reporter asked McClellan about I. Lewis "Scooter" Libby, the vice president's chief of staff.

"If you have any specific information to bring to my attention—like I said, there has been nothing that's been brought to our attention. You asked me earlier if we were looking into it, there is nothing that's been brought to our attention beyond the media reports. But if someone did something like this, it needs to be looked at by the Department of Justice, they're the appropriate agency charged with looking into matters like this. . . . I think we could go down the White House directory of every single staff member and play that game. I'm not going to do that. What I've made clear is that if anybody has information relating to this, they need to report it to the Department of Justice, and the Department of Justice should pursue it to the fullest. It is a serious matter. But I'm not going to go down a list of every single staffer in the White House."

But Libby subsequently complained to Andrew Card, Bush's chief of staff, and McClellan, saying it wasn't fair to exonerate Rove and not him. As Libby recalled, "There was no list to go down. The only people they were really talking about was me. . . . I felt it was unfair they were saying that about Karl and not about me when there was no long list, it was just . . . as far as I was concerned there were only two of us that were getting a lot of attention in part because of this, you know, the one time I had gone on the record at the vice president's request, put my name on something." But Card and McClellan disagreed.

Later in the summer, Libby was with the vice president in Wyoming, where he rented a condo to be near Cheney's home. Speculation that he was a Novak source had continued unabated, but White House press secretary Scott McClellan refused to clear Libby's name, telling reporters he wasn't "going to go down a list of every single staffer." Libby called McClellan. "Look, there is no list.

There's not a long list, there's just the two of us and I think you ought to be saying something about me too."

Back in Washington, Libby went to the vice president, who was sitting at his desk. "You know, I was not the person who talked to Novak."

"You don't have to tell me. I know you were not the source of the leak," Cheney replied.

Libby had gone so far as to draft some talking points for McClellan, writing about himself in the third person:

"I said it was ridiculous about Karl and it's ridiculous about Libby. Libby was not the source for the Novak story, period. And he did not leak classified information, period." Libby handed his notes to Cheney.

"Let me take it," Cheney said.

The vice president subsequently added his own notes to Libby's:

"Has to happen today. Call out to key press saying same thing about Scooter as Karl. Not going to protect one staffer and sacrifice the guy that was asked to stick his neck in the meat grinder because of the incompetence of others."

At Cheney's behest, McClellan spoke directly to Libby. According to McClellan, he called Libby in Jackson Hole, where he was with the vice president, and asked, "Were you involved in the leak in any way?"

"No, absolutely not," Libby replied.

"All right. I plan to tell reporters that you did not leak the classified information, nor would you condone doing so. Is that correct?"

"Yes."

(McClellan later described Libby as "never one for many words.")

On October 4, the *New York Times* reported, "2 Disclaim Leaking Name of Operative":

The White House on Saturday added to the list of senior officials who it said had disclaimed responsibility.

Spokesmen said I. Lewis Libby, the chief of staff for Vice President Dick Cheney, and Elliott Abrams, the director of Middle East affairs at the National Security Council, were not sources of the leak. The White House has said the same of Karl Rove, the president's chief political adviser.

Scott McClellan, the White House spokesman, said that Mr. Libby "neither leaked the classified information, nor would he condone it."

It was a small story and ran deep in the paper. But Libby had gotten the official vindication he'd asked for.

That same week, President Bush flew to Chicago, where he, too, was dogged by questions about the leak. During a news conference with Mayor Richard Daley, the president turned to the subject:

"Let me just say something about leaks in Washington. There are too many leaks of classified information in Washington. There's leaks at the executive branch; there's leaks in the legislative branch. There's just too many leaks. And if there's a leak out of my administration, I want to know who it is. And if the person has violated law, the person will be taken care of.

"And so I welcome the investigation. . . . I have told . . . people in my administration to be fully cooperative. I want to know the truth.

"If anybody has got any information, . . . it would be helpful if they came forward with the information so we can find out whether or not these allegations are true and get on about our business."

A reporter interrupted: "Yesterday we were told that Karl Rove had no role in it."

"Listen, I know of nobody–I don't know of anybody in my administration who leaked classified information. If somebody did leak classified information, I'd like to know it, and we'll take the appropriate action. And this investigation is a good thing. . . . I want to know who the leakers are."

FIVE

"All the Reporters Know It"

F BI special agent John C. Eckenrode's wife, Linda, sounded excited when he answered her call on September 28, 2003. "Are you watching the news?" He wasn't. "It's about a CIA agent who was outed. There's going to be an investigation. The Justice Department may be involved," she continued. "Is this going to be assigned to you?"

"I haven't heard anything," he said.

But Jack Eckenrode was an obvious choice. At age fifty, he was the only senior agent in Washington who already had experience in a sensitive leak case with national security overtones. That afternoon, Bruce Gebhardt, the FBI's deputy director, stopped by his office in the sprawling FBI headquarters building. "Do you want it?" Gebhardt asked, referring to the Plame case.

"Sure," Eckenrode replied. You don't turn down the deputy director.

"Then you got it. What do you need for resources? You can have anybody from the Washington field office."

Despite all the media attention, it wasn't exactly a plum assignment. Leak cases had a notorious reputation within the FBI for never getting resolved, which generally seemed to be the way the Justice Department wanted it. That way there were no political repercussions, no embarrassment to high-level officials caught leaking, and above all, no clashes with the press over sources, with the inevitable criticism that would result. Eckenrode often wondered why they bothered to investigate these cases at all. He couldn't think of a single leak case that had been successfully prosecuted, including the last one he'd worked on, the leak of a confidential congressional briefing to a CNN reporter. Evidence had pointed to Senator Richard Shelby of Alabama as the source, but the Justice Department didn't want to issue subpoenas to reporters or pursue the case. The matter was referred to the Senate ethics committee, where it languished. "At no time during my career as a United States senator and, more particularly, at no time during my service as chairman of the Senate Select Committee on Intelligence have I ever knowingly compromised classified information," Shelby said in a carefully worded statement.

Eckenrode looked the part of a senior FBI agent: tall, square-jawed with dark hair, in good physical shape. He'd grown up in the Lehigh Valley of Pennsylvania, graduated from St. Francis College, and as an FBI agent helped investigate fraud after the savings-and-loan crisis. He was quietly determined that this new case, the Plame leak, not suffer the same fate as the Shelby investigation.

Of the dozen or so agents offered him from the DC field office, Eckenrode settled on Deborah Bond and several other younger agents, those he felt had energy and determination, who weren't jaded by the failure of previous leak investigations. Their mandate was to investigate a possible violation of the Intelligence Identities Protection Act prohibiting disclosure of the identity of a covert agent and any related crimes.

Their primary focus was the two sources mentioned in Novak's column, which had triggered the investigation. But the agents also had a copy of Matt Cooper's online article for *Time* reporting that "some government officials" had leaked Plame's identity to him as well. Who were these administration officials, and how many were leaking Plame's name to *Time*? Eckenrode wondered. Was the Novak leak part of a broader White House effort to "out" Plame and discredit her husband? All Eckenrode and his team had to go on were the Novak and Cooper articles.

On September 28, the same day the FBI investigation got under way, *Washington Post* reporter Mike Allen wrote that "before Novak's column ran, two top White House officials called at least six Washington journalists and disclosed the identity and occupation of Wilson's wife," attributing this to a senior administration official. "Clearly, it was meant purely and simply for revenge," the official added. They were "wrong and a huge miscalculation, because they [the leaks] were irrelevant and did nothing to diminish Wilson's credibility."

Were these the same two officials who had leaked to Novak? To *Time*? Or were there four or more potential suspects? And instead of one journalist who received the leaks, they now had to consider at least seven—Novak plus six.

The next Monday, October 1, Novak weighed in again, claiming his role had been "distorted." He seemed defensive about having compromised a covert agent and possibly damaging national security as well as having been a "pawn" of the administration, not to mention a second or even third choice to disseminate the leak of Plame's identity. Without naming his sources, he elaborated in "The CIA Leak" on how he learned Plame's identity:

> During a long conversation with a senior administration official, I asked why Wilson was assigned the mission to Niger. He said Wilson had been sent by the CIA's counterproliferation section at the suggestion of one of his employees, his wife. It was an offhand revelation from this official, who is no partisan gunslinger. When I called another official for confirmation, he said: "Oh, you know about it." The published report that somebody in the White House failed to plant this story with six reporters and finally found me as a willing pawn is simply untrue.

Novak added yet another possible source: a CIA official who had confirmed her identity.

> At the CIA, the official designated to talk to me denied that Wilson's wife had inspired his selection but said she was delegated to request his help. He asked me not to use her name, saying she probably never again will be given a foreign assignment but that exposure of her name might cause "difficulties" if she travels abroad. He never suggested to me that Wilson's wife or anybody else would be endangered. If he had, I would not have used her name. I used it in the sixth paragraph of my column because it looked like the missing explanation of an otherwise incredible choice by the CIA for its mission.

The next day, the *New York Times* called for a vigorous and independent investigation of the leak:

> As members of a profession that relies heavily on the willingness of government officials to defy their bosses and give the public vital information, we oppose "leak investigations" in principle. But that does not mean there can never be a circumstance in which leaks are wrong; the disclosure of troop movements in wartime is a clear example. . . .

If someone at the White House, perhaps acting with institutional sanction, revealed the name of a CIA operative to undermine the credibility of Mr. Wilson and thus stifle dissent over Iraq policy, that in itself would be a serious assault on free speech and an egregious abuse of power. In such a case, the blanket denial that Mr. Bush issued this week would put him dangerously close to the territory in which the cover-up eclipses the offense.

But short of a public confession, how can the source of a leak to the press be identified and convicted without testimony from journalists? As the newspaper responsible for the fabled Vietnam-era Pentagon papers case, and a party to numerous First Amendment cases, the *Times* surely recognized that Novak and any other reporters who were leaked Plame's CIA status were witnesses to a potential crime. The Supreme Court ruled in a landmark 1972 case that the First Amendment does not prevent journalists from being compelled to testify before grand juries investigating crimes. In calling for an investigation and, if warranted, prosecution, the *Times* was helping make it inevitable that journalists would be subpoenaed to reveal both the identities of their sources and what those sources told them.

On October 1, John Dion, the head of the Justice Department's counterespionage division, who was overseeing the Plame case, called Dave Szady, his counterpart at the FBI. Dion had just gotten a call from Will Taft, general counsel at the State Department, regarding Novak's source. Szady sent Dion's call to Eckenrode, and after speaking briefly, Eckenrode got an FBI car, picked up Dion at Justice, and headed straight for the Harry S. Truman State Department headquarters building, popularly known as Foggy Bottom. There was no time to lose. They went to the fifth floor, where Secretary of State Colin Powell and top officials had their offices.

A secretary showed them to Richard Armitage's office, where they met his assistant. Shortly after Taft escorted Armitage in and Eckenrode and Dion rose to greet him. Armitage's sheer physical presence made an impression; he reminded Eckenrode of General George Patton. About five-foot-ten and 250 pounds, he had a wide face, and a broad chest from weight lifting, his physique emphasized by his dark, well-tailored suit. A prominent Defense Department official under Ronald Reagan, Armitage was now deputy secretary of state, perhaps best known for having allegedly threatened to bomb Pakistan "back to the Stone Age" if President Pervez Musharraf didn't support the United States in its post-9/11 war on terror. Though Armitage denied using those words, he acknowledged having such a conversation and was known in diplomatic circles for his sometimes blunt, profanity-peppered assertions.

After some pleasantries and small talk, Eckenrode asked, "What is it you'd like to tell us?"

Armitage said he'd never met with Novak before the summer, although Novak had tried to contact him many times. He'd basically told Novak to stop trying; he wasn't interested in seeing or talking to him. But then he'd relented, and had his assistant schedule a meeting for July 8. "I didn't think anything of it, until this morning," he said, when he'd read Novak's column in the *Washington Post*. It was the reference to a "long conversation," with a "senior administration official," he said, that jogged his memory, and made him worry that he might have been Novak's source. The two had been talking about other things, primarily the appointment of Fran Townsend as a homeland security adviser to Bush. Townsend's Democratic ties troubled Novak—she'd worked in the Clinton Justice Department and was close to former attorney general Janet Reno—and he wondered why someone whose loyalty was questionable would be named to a sensitive intelligence post. This was similar to Novak's concerns about the choice of Wilson for the Niger mission, given that Wilson had also worked in the Clinton administration, and this may be why Novak shifted to the Wilson affair. Armitage had offered as a possible explanation that Wilson's wife worked for the CIA and had suggested sending him.

Armitage said he realized now that this might have been what inspired Novak's column. He was so upset he had canceled a trip to Pakistan scheduled for that day. He'd gone to Powell that morning, told him what happened, and had tendered his resignation in writing. Powell had taken it, put it in his desk drawer, and called Taft, who recommended they contact the Justice Department. "I feel I failed my president and I failed my country," Armitage said with a dramatic flourish. "What can I do to make amends?"

"How did you know about Wilson's wife?" Eckenrode wanted to know.

"I read a memo," Armitage said.

"What memo?"

Armitage was vague. "Something that was kicking around." He said he didn't really remember and couldn't be more specific.

"Do you have a copy?"

"No."

"Can you get one?"

Taft said he'd look for it.

Armitage stressed he didn't know Plame was a covert agent. "I thought she was some kind of analyst," he said. "I didn't know she was an agent, covert or otherwise. I never mentioned her name. I just referred to her as Wilson's wife."

Eckenrode asked if Armitage or Taft had contacted the White House or told the president. Taft said he'd contacted White House counsel Alberto Gonzales, but only told him that the State Department had "relevant information" about the Plame leak. Given that the matter was under investigation, Gonzales had indicated he didn't want to hear any more, and so Taft had said nothing further.

"Is there anything else we need to know to help us in this investigation?" Eckenrode asked.

"No, that's it," Armitage said.

The mystery of at least one of Novak's sources was already solved, almost before the investigation had begun. Still, Eckenrode had misgivings. Why had Armitage suddenly scheduled a meeting with Novak if not to discredit Wilson? What was his motive? Perhaps it was to absolve Powell's failure to heed Wilson's warnings, although there was no evidence he was privy to them. Surely it wasn't to protect Cheney, or even the president. Armitage and Powell, along with the State Department generally, had often been at odds with the vice president. And did Armitage really not know Plame's status at the CIA? It was obviously in his interest to insist that he had no idea she was a covert agent, since a conviction under the statute requires "access to classified information that identifies a covert agent" and knowing that the United States is taking "affirmative measures" to conceal the agent's covert status.

Afterward, Dion, Eckenrode, and other agents and lawyers met for a postmortem in a Justice Department conference room to map out their next steps. Obviously they'd need to interview Powell. Did this pose possible conflicts for the Justice Department? This was getting to a pretty high level, and might ultimately reach the vice president and even the president, who'd appointed Attorney General John Ashcroft. For now, they decided to postpone that discussion. If they concluded there was no case, they wouldn't have to reach that issue. Eckenrode wanted to subpoena Novak right away, but the Justice lawyers were cool to the idea, as they had been in the Shelby investigation.

The next day, October 3, Eckenrode and his colleagues arrived at Wilson's office on the first floor in a building near Georgetown. They waited in an area with his secretary, who indicated Wilson was in the midst of yet another press interview. After waiting nearly a half hour, they asked if she'd interrupt. They did have an appointment. But just then the door opened and a television crew emerged with their cameras and equipment. Wilson was in an expansive mode and seemed to be basking in his sudden celebrity. His outrage over the outing of his wife seemed to be gaining steam, fueled by the mostly positive press he was getting. Wilson narrated the by-now-familiar story of his mission to Niger, stressing that he had volunteered for the assignment because of his ties in Niger and not because his wife had recommended him. He'd gone without pay, out of a sense of patriotism; nobody who'd been to Niger would ever consider a trip there a "boondoggle." Nor was he an antiwar fanatic; he'd long been critical of Saddam Hussein and, based on his years in Iraq, believed he probably did have hidden chemical and biological weapons.

Wilson said he never wrote a report on his trip, instead delivering his findings orally to a group at the CIA. Since it was the vice president's office that had asked for the information, he assumed his findings had been conveyed to Cheney and his staff, and on that basis had alleged that the White House had ignored information inconsistent with its case for war. Eckenrode had some sympathy for the White House's frustration with Wilson's claims. All Wilson really knew was what he was told in Niger and his subsequent debriefing at the CIA. He did not know Novak's sources, which didn't stop him from continuing to cast suspicion on Karl Rove. Indeed, he seemed angrier than ever at Rove, convinced he was behind the smear campaign against him and his wife.

For the first time Wilson detailed the basis for his claim that Rove should be "frog-marched" out of the White House in handcuffs. Wilson said he had gotten a call from MSNBC talk show host Chris Matthews, whose comments had so agitated Libby, who told him, "I just got off the phone with Karl Rove. He says, and I quote, 'Wilson's wife is fair game.' I will confirm that if asked," Matthews added, then hung up.

Wilson seemed to think that that settled the matter, and that Rove was the leak.

Maybe, but it was hardly conclusive. Rove's comment was secondhand hearsay. It hardly justified Wilson's public accusations that Rove should be handcuffed. Still, there were witnesses—and Eckenrode added Matthews's name to the list of journalists they'd need to contact.

Wilson also told the agents that a few days after his op-ed piece had run in the *Times*, a friend, Howard Cohen, had rushed in to see him at his office. He'd breathlessly told Wilson that he'd just had a chance encounter with Novak, and they'd been discussing the uranium controversy. Cohen had asked Novak what he thought of Wilson, and Novak had replied, "Wilson's an asshole. The CIA sent him. His wife, Valerie, works for the CIA. She's a weapons of mass destruction specialist. She sent him." This was days before Novak's column had appeared.

Wilson asked Cohen to write down his recollection of the conversation, then called CNN, telling the head of the news division that it was the "height of irresponsibility" for Novak to be discussing his wife with a near stranger. Novak himself returned his call the next day and apologized. Novak also seized the opportunity to interview Wilson for his column, but Wilson told him he wouldn't answer questions about his wife.

Obviously Eckenrode had to talk to Novak. Although subpoenaing journalists was only a last resort, he saw no reason not to call him. Eckenrode left a message, and Novak's lawyer James Hamilton returned his call. Hamilton was famously discreet with such high-profile clients as Vince Foster, who had committed suicide during the Clinton administration amid a welter of rumors about the Whitewater land deal and his relationship to Hillary Clinton. This didn't bode well in Eckenrode's experience, but to Eckenrode's surprise, Hamilton said Novak would meet with him at the firm's offices. Hamilton said Novak wouldn't reveal his sources, nor would he disclose any notes or other documents. He'd cooperate with the investigation, but the FBI would have to ask questions; he wasn't going to volunteer anything.

Eckenrode didn't have such good luck with Chris Matthews. He called Matthews directly, using his cell phone, but Matthews ended up asking all the questions: "How did you get my number? Why do you want to talk to me?" Eckenrode got nowhere before Matthews referred him to NBC's lawyers.

Eckenrode and two other agents met with Novak and his lawyers on October 7. Eckenrode mentioned that he'd sometimes seen Novak attending mass at St. Patrick's Church, which did little to dispel the sense that Novak was deeply uncomfortable about being interviewed by law enforcement agents.

Novak stated at the outset that he wouldn't disclose his sources; he hadn't even told his lawyers their identity. Eckenrode said nothing about his interview with Armitage. But Novak seemed happy to discuss the genesis of his columns. He described his observations of Wilson in the greenroom of *Meet the Press*, his reactions to Wilson's column, the encounter where he'd indiscreetly called Wilson an "asshole" and then his subsequent phone conversation with Wilson, where Wilson apologized for his friend having accosted him, and Novak apologized for having used such a vulgar phrase to describe Wilson. Novak pointed out that the choice of Wilson for the mission to Africa was the kind of political mystery that had long intrigued him and had formed the basis for many columns. The fact that Wilson's wife worked for the CIA explained why a former Clinton appointee and someone obviously hostile to the Bush administration had been entrusted with such a sensitive task. No one had told him Plame was a covert agent or might be endangered if he named her. If anyone had, he wouldn't have used her name. Nor did he think anyone was trying to retaliate against Wilson. He felt the whole affair had been seized upon by the left wing and turned into a cause célèbre to undermine the Bush administration.

The interview lasted about two hours. As they were preparing to leave, Eckenrode said, "You know, you could have written this column without using her name. Why was that so important?"

Novak looked sheepish, almost as though he were willing to admit it had been a mistake. Then he shrugged. "She was his wife, her name was in *Who's Who*. I didn't think there was anything wrong with this." But Eckenrode got the impression that, if he were to do it over again, Novak would have left out her name.

Armed with a copy of Karl Rove's telephone log showing several calls to and from Novak, Eckenrode and his team arrived for their first interview with a White House official. They met Rove on October 10, at his small office in the West Wing of the White House. At the suggestion of a friend, Rove had hired Robert Luskin, a partner at Patton Boggs and a veteran white-collar defense lawyer and former Justice Department official and Rhodes scholar. Rove wasn't put off by Luskin's shaved head and earring; he liked his "calming," "clear, persuasive demeanor," and came to admire Luskin's attachment to his cat. Luskin had urged Rove to delay the interview to give them more time to prepare and review all his e-mails and phone logs, but Rove was eager to get it over with and, he assumed, dispel speculation that he was the source for the Novak column.

When the agents arrived, Rove seemed friendly and relaxed. He said he was eager "to help in any way I can." Eckenrode was still following his tactic of offering an open-ended question, and began with, "It sounds like there's stuff you want to tell us."

Rove said his memory was a little "fuzzy," but acknowledged he had played what he considered a "small part" in Novak's column. Rove said Novak had called on July 7, the day after Wilson's op-ed piece and appearance on *Meet the Press*, and left a message saying he wanted to discuss Fran Townsend. Rove asked an assistant to prepare some "talking points" in defense of Townsend, and Rove returned the call late the following day. Rove said they did discuss Townsend—he felt he made no headway in rebutting Novak's criticisms—and then Novak had brought up Wilson's column and television appearance, commenting on how pompous and self-centered Wilson was, with Novak specifically using the word "asshole" to describe Wilson. Rove had agreed with Novak's assessment. Rove had then told Novak "off-the-record" that the CIA statement being prepared taking responsibility for the sixteen words was likely to assert that part of Wilson's report—the finding that an Iraq delegation had tried to establish commercial relations in Niger—actually supported the president's claim, since the only commercial activity of any significance in Niger was uranium exports.

Novak had agreed with Rove that Wilson's failure to mention this showed a clear bias against the Bush administration. Novak then mentioned that Valerie Plame worked at the CIA in counterproliferation, although Rove said the name didn't mean anything to him. Novak went on, saying Plame, not the vice president, had sent her husband to Niger. Rove realized then that Plame must be the name of Wilson's wife. "Oh, I've heard that too," Rove said he'd replied. Novak gave Rove the impression he'd already spoken with someone at the CIA, who'd confirmed Plame's role and job at the agency. The conversation wound down, and Rove didn't recall any further discussion of Wilson or his wife.

Eckenrode asked how Rove had heard about Wilson's wife, and Rove said he couldn't remember. He wasn't sure if he'd heard it from someone in the White House, at a social event, or in a phone call from another journalist. In any event, he didn't know what she did at the CIA, and certainly didn't know or suspect she was a covert agent.

Eckenrode took Rove through each of the Novak entries in his phone log, dwelling especially on a call at 3:00 p.m. on September 29, just a day after news of the Justice Department investigation broke. Rove said Novak had called to assure him he was not the source for his column and that "I protect my sources." Rove didn't think he was the source, or even a source, since Novak clearly knew all about Plame by the time they spoke.

Eckenrode asked him why he thought Wilson was so insistent that Rove was the one who had outed his wife as a CIA agent. Rove replied that he didn't know, but assumed it had something to do with Chris Matthews. Rove said he'd run into Matthews at the Bohemian Grove, the northern California site of the annual gathering of members of the all-male Bohemian Club and their guests, which have included a long list of prominent politicians, businessmen, journalists, musicians, writers, and artists. Matthews had brought up the subject of Wilson and the Novak column. Rove had tried to press the administration's view, but realized Matthews knew "squat" about the subject and they turned to other subjects. The following Monday, Rove had called Matthews about something else, and Matthews again brought up Wilson and his wife. This was the call that had prompted Matthews's call to Wilson saying that Wilson's wife was "fair game."

Eckenrode asked Rove about the comment; Rove insisted it wasn't a phrase he'd use.

"Are you saying you never used those words?" Eckenrode asked.

Rove said it was Matthews who had used those words to describe Plame. "He uses the words 'fair game' all the time," Rove said. "He used them just last week. Search his newscasts and you'll find he says it all the time." Rove said that if he had used the phrase, it was only because he was repeating what Matthews had said, and that he had never suggested Plame was "fair game." (A search revealed that Matthews had used the phrase once, on July 16.)

Eckenrode turned to the Mike Allen story in the *Washington Post*. Had Rove spoken to any other journalist about Wilson's wife before Novak's column?

No, he insisted. The subject had only come up with Novak.

Had he discussed Wilson's wife with anyone else in the administration? Rove said his memory was hazy, but he thought he had discussed it with Scooter Libby. He and Libby were discussing CIA director Tenet's statement the Friday before Novak's column, and Rove had mentioned that Novak had called and was working on a column about Wilson. Rove said he might have talked about Wilson's wife with Libby.

What about the president? Eckenrode asked.

Rove said that at the height of speculation in the media and at press conferences that he was Novak's source, Bush had called him and asked, "Are you the one behind this Novak column?"

Rove had said he wasn't. Rove later described the phone call in his memoir: "He called me from the Oval Office, where he was meeting with Card and Gonzales, and I explained to Bush that I'd talked to Novak and said 'I've heard that too' when the reporter told me about Wilson's wife, whose name and role I didn't know. Bush sounded a little annoyed but took my word."

Now the president himself was a potential witness. Would he corroborate Rove's version?

Did Rove know anything about the basis for the assertion that two White House officials had called six journalists about Wilson's wife? Rove didn't, but he told the FBI agents that he strongly suspected that Allen's source for the story was Adam Levine, a member of the communications team in the White House who acted as a liaison with the television networks. Levine was a former producer for Chris Matthews and was friendly with many journalists, including Mike Allen at the *Post*. Moreover, Rove thought Levine was disgruntled because he'd been passed over for the number two job as deputy press secretary after Ari Fleischer left. Rove gave the impression he was trying to shift the spotlight to Levine, someone he clearly distrusted. (Though he was friendly with Mike Allen, Levine denied he was the source, who he thought was at the CIA.)

"Would you be willing to take a lie detector test?" Eckenrode asked.

"Of course," Rove replied.

Luskin volunteered that Rove would sign a waiver releasing journalists like Novak from any promise of confidentiality they might have given him. Eckenrode thanked Rove for his time, and the three agents left. Eckenrode prepared a waiver with the help of Justice Department lawyers and sent one to Rove, which Rove signed. It was a waiver form he used in all his subsequent interviews with White House officials.

When they met to discuss Rove's statements, the agents felt pretty confident Rove was Novak's second source. Rove said Novak had assured him he wasn't "the" source, leaving open the possibility he might be "a" source. Why else would Novak need to protect him? Rove had only said he'd "heard" about Wilson's wife when Novak brought up the subject, but he conceded speaking to Novak and mentioning the wife. Eckenrode suspected Rove's involvement might be much deeper than he'd acknowledged. The Chris Matthews encounter suggested Rove was actively pushing the Plame story, and he might well have been a source for other reporters besides Novak. His annoyance with Adam Levine and the *Post*'s column suggesting other leaks pointed in that direction.

Rove himself couldn't tell how it had gone. He found himself obsessing about the Wilson affair and his role in it, however peripheral he may have been. He later said he was sure in his own mind he hadn't committed any crime, but as speculation continued to focus on him as a potential leak, he felt drawn into something beyond his control. He was determined to be tough, to show no reaction, to act as though nothing was bothering him—the unspoken code of the Bush White House. Yet, he later confided, "the whole thing was scaring the hell out of me."

Although Wilson had pointed the finger directly at Rove, speculation continued to swirl that Scooter Libby was the second source referred to in Novak's column, as evidenced by the persistent questions at Scott McClellan's press briefings. McClellan's belated denial that Libby was involved had done little to stop the speculation. So Libby was already someone the FBI agents were planning to interview, even before Rove's account of their conversation made him an important witness. Eckenrode scheduled an interview with Libby for October 14, just four days after Rove. In the interim he and other agents interviewed Cathie Martin, the communications director for the vice president.

Martin had readily agreed to the interview and didn't bring a lawyer. She seemed frustrated by the investigation and the leaks that had triggered it, in part, she made clear, because the vice president and Libby had decided to bypass her in her role as communications director and wage their own public relations campaign. She noted that she'd been explicitly excluded from the Air Force Two meeting where Cheney and Libby had formulated their talking points to rebut Wilson. She didn't understand the intensity with which Libby and the vice president were pursuing the story or why it was such a priority. She felt marginalized by Libby on important aspects of the story and felt relegated to mundane tasks like getting phone numbers and setting up interviews. She had spoken to reporters, mostly to schedule calls or to point out articles or facts that contradicted Wilson. She didn't say so, but she seemed worried that Libby might have gone too far in his efforts to discredit Wilson. Eckenrode was impressed by her candor. Inadvertently or not, she had also focused their attention on Libby, who by her account was the administration official most preoccupied by Wilson's allegations and the need to rebut them.

Although Scooter Libby often used an anteroom outside the vice president's office in the West Wing of the White House, he had a larger office as part of the vice presidential suite in the Old Executive Office Building next door, where he met Eckenrode and the FBI agents Deborah Bond and Kirk Armfield. Unlike many in the White House, Libby had hired an outside lawyer: Joseph Tate, from the Philadelphia office of Dechert LLP, where Libby had been the managing partner in the DC office during the Clinton administration.

Tate opened the session with a statement: "My client is here to cooperate; the president has asked for the full cooperation of everyone in the administration, and that's what my client is here to do." The FBI agents thought it was peculiar that he kept referring to him as "my client," and Libby looked slightly uncomfortable, unlike Rove and Armitage. Eckenrode said there might well come a time when they'd need to discuss classified documents or other information, and at that point Tate would have to leave the room. But as with the other interviews, Eckenrode asked Libby an open-ended question, suggesting he share whatever information he considered relevant to their inquiry into the possibly unauthorized disclosure of Valerie Plame's name and identity.

Libby began by emphasizing that he was only motivated by the truth. He and the vice president had simply wanted to "set the record straight" because what Wilson wrote was "totally inaccurate and unfair." In preparation for the interview, Libby had prepared a list of points, which he had typed and now handed to the agents:

AMBASSADOR WILSON'S CLAIMS

1. The VP asked the CIA to investigate a particular Niger report.
2. Ambassador Wilson's report shows that Iraq did not seek to acquire uranium from Niger.
3. Because the VP asked and the report of Ambassador Wilson's trip showed that Iraq had not sought to buy uranium from Niger the VP would have seen the report.
4. Because the VP/White House must have seen the report resolving that Iraq had not sought uranium from Niger the VP/White House twisted the intelligence to support the statement in the State of the Union.

Libby went over them one by one, insisting that each was false and thus Wilson's conclusions were drawn from false premises. It was as if Libby were still pleading the case for the administration, one that he'd never managed to get into the mainstream press. Eckenrode had to gently steer him back to the purpose of the interview, which was the source of administration leaks—not the accuracy or fairness of Wilson's column.

Unlike Armitage or even Rove, Libby was not a natural narrator. Eckenrode had to interrupt frequently with questions; Libby seemed to like specific questions to which he could give precise answers. He said he hadn't even known Wilson had a wife; he didn't know her name, let alone that she worked at the CIA, until NBC's Tim Russert told him on July 10 or 11. At least, that's what he'd thought until the week before, when he went through his notes to prepare for the FBI interview. He seemed eager to show the agents a note, written in his distinctive narrow, slanting script, filled with odd shorthand symbols.

6/12/03 Telephone—VP re "Uranium in Iraq"—Kristof NYT Article
1) Took place at our behest—functional office
    CP/- his wife works in that division
    debriefing took place here
    & was mtg in region
    VP hold get agency to answer that 1) didn't know about mission
2) didn't get report back
3) didn't have any indication of forgery was from IAEA [International Atomic Energy Agency]
4) OVP and Defense and State—expressed strong interest in issue

Eckenrode and the agents hadn't seen this; document production from the White House was proceeding sporadically through the White House counsel's office, and this hadn't yet been produced. Libby explained that the note indicated that the vice president had told him during a phone conversation in June that the wife of the ambassador sent to Niger worked at the CIA. The letters *CP* stood for the counterproliferation division of the CIA. The date had a squiggle over it, meaning that he'd written it sometime after the conversation, so it could be off slightly. Most likely the conversation had occurred a day or two earlier, since he and Vice President Cheney had been discussing how to respond to questions from *Washington Post* reporter Walter Pincus, who was following up on Nicholas Kristof's *Times* article questioning the accuracy of the State of the Union and whether "deceit" had been employed in building the case for war with Iraq. Pincus's article had run on June 12.

Eckenrode asked if the vice president had mentioned how he knew that the ambassador's wife worked at the CIA.

Yes, Libby said. The vice president had learned it from someone at the CIA. Libby believed Cheney's source was Director Tenet, but it might have been someone else.

Libby stressed that even then he didn't know the name of the ambassador sent to Niger, whose name doesn't appear on the note. Wilson wasn't named in either Kristof's or Pincus's article, and Libby said he didn't know his name until he read Wilson's op-ed piece in July. By then he'd forgotten the conversation with Cheney and the reference to Wilson's wife. Libby said again that when Tim Russert told him that Wilson's wife worked for the CIA, it was as if he were hearing it for the first time.

Eckenrode asked why Libby was talking to Russert, and why the subject of Wilson's wife would have come up.

Libby explained that at least twice during the week after Wilson's op-ed appeared, *Hardball* host Chris Matthews had repeated the false claim that the vice president's office had asked the CIA to send Wilson to Niger. Libby had called Russert, NBC's Washington bureau chief, to complain about Matthews and see if Russert could make him correct the record or at least stop saying that Cheney and Libby were behind Wilson's trip to Africa. Russert had returned his call on July 10. He'd listened to Libby's concerns, but said he wasn't Matthews's supervisor, so there wasn't anything he could do about it. Russert suggested Libby call Matthews's producer.

Then Russert had volunteered: "Do you know that Ambassador Wilson's wife works for the CIA?"

Libby said no, he didn't.

Russert answered, according to Libby, "Yeah, all the reporters know it."

Libby said he wasn't aware of that either.

Eckenrode asked what Libby thought Russert meant by "all the reporters," and he said he assumed Russert meant reporters in Washington, DC.

The FBI agents scribbled furiously. Libby was suggesting that even before Novak's column, many reporters knew Wilson's wife worked for the CIA.

Eckenrode asked if he'd discussed Wilson's wife with other administration officials, Karl Rove in particular, and Libby confirmed that he and Rove had spoken the Friday that Tenet issued his statement. Rove had told Libby he'd spoken to Bob Novak, that Novak had encountered Wilson in the greenroom at *Meet the Press*, wasn't impressed by him, and was going to write an article on

Wilson. Rove told him that Novak already knew that Wilson's wife worked for the CIA, which prompted Libby to tell Rove about his phone call with Russert, in which Russert told him the same thing.

The agents recognized this was critical evidence—that Libby had learned Plame's identity from Russert and then told Rove about it. It was the first indication that Libby had told the Russert story to someone right after the call occurred, as opposed to FBI agents months after the fact. Rove might be a corroborating witness—but Rove had said nothing about Libby saying this during their interview with him.

Besides Russert, Eckenrode asked Libby what other reporters he'd talked to during the June-July time frame. Libby said he didn't often speak to the press, but had several contacts related to the serious charges about the State of the Union address and then the Wilson op-ed piece. He mentioned David Sanger from the *New York Times*, to whom he'd spoken on July 2, four days before Wilson's piece, and Judith Miller two days after, on July 8. He'd met Miller at the dining room of the St. Regis hotel to discuss the contents of the National Intelligence Estimate (NIE) from October 2002, which supported the notion that Saddam Hussein was pursuing nuclear weapons and other WMD. Before the meeting, the vice president had told Libby he wanted the contents of the NIE disseminated to the press to counteract the notion that the administration had deliberately misled the public. The NIE was classified, but Cheney had told him the president had declassified it, and Libby had checked with vice presidential counsel David Addington to make sure the president had that authority and it was okay for him to disclose its contents to a reporter. They also spoke more generally about Iraq's weapons of mass destruction. The Wilson affair had come up, but Libby said he had "no recollection" of discussing Wilson's wife with Miller then (consistent with his statement that he'd forgotten about the connection until he was told by Russert on July 10 or 11).

Libby said he'd had a follow-up conversation with Miller again on July 12. This time Miller had asked, "Why did they send this guy?" It isn't clear exactly what Libby answered. Agent Bond scribbled in her notebook, "Ambassador Wilson's wife—may have mentioned indirectly. (?)" Bond meant to follow up with another question, but the interview moved on, and she never got back to it.

That conversation with Miller was the same day as the trip to Norfolk,

Virginia, for the commissioning of the USS *Ronald Reagan*. Libby described the trip and his conversation on the plane during which the vice president encouraged him to get out the story and use an on-the-record quote. Libby had taken "verbatim" notes of what the vice president wanted him to say, and as soon as they landed, he and his assistant, Jenny Mayfield, and Cathie Martin had gone to an office just off the lobby at Andrews Air Force Base. They'd called reporters Matt Cooper of *Time*, Evan Thomas of *Newsweek*, and Glenn Kessler of the *Washington Post*.

When Cooper answered, Libby said he wanted to give him an on-the-record quote, and read the words he'd written down from the vice president. Cooper asked why Wilson kept saying the office of the vice president had sent him to Africa, and Libby said he told him—off-the-record—that reporters were saying Wilson's wife worked for the CIA and she had suggested him for the trip, but that he, Libby, didn't know if that was true.

Eckenrode was startled: Libby had just acknowledged that he had disclosed Plame's identity to a reporter, although he was attributing his knowledge to unnamed reporters.

Libby had left a message for Evan Thomas, and had reached Glenn Kessler at the zoo, where he was spending the afternoon with his children. Kessler had said he'd call him back.

Later that week, Libby said he and Andrea Mitchell of NBC exchanged several messages and spoke at some point after July 10. Libby was upset because Mitchell was also making negative comments about the vice president. Like Cooper, she had wanted to know why Wilson was insisting the vice president's office had sent him. Libby said this posed a dilemma for him: he could have told her about Wilson's wife, but he didn't want to have to tell her how he knew that, because Russert was his source and Russert was her boss. Libby thought it would be "awkward" if he told her Russert had told him about Plame's identity, but hadn't confided in his own reporter. Still, he thought he "might" have told her that other reporters were saying that Plame worked for the CIA without saying who those reporters were.

And what about Novak? Eckenrode asked.

Libby had spoken to Novak, but only after July 14, when the column appeared, and not about Wilson's wife. Libby was certain he was not a source for the Plame column.

At this point Tate indicated that the ninety minutes allotted for the interview was over, and Eckenrode asked if they could schedule another session. Tate said yes, but that he and Libby wanted some time to review documents before they spoke again. Like Rove, Libby agreed to submit to a lie detector test if asked. When Libby was asked for a waiver releasing journalists from any promise of confidentiality, Tate intervened and said he'd have to review it before Libby signed anything. The FBI agents closed their notebooks and left.

As they had after the other major interviews, the agents met with Dion and other lawyers working on the investigation for a postmortem at the Justice Department. As trained investigators, they felt they had witnessed a remarkable performance. Their instincts told them that something was awry. They were surprised that Tate had allowed his client to go on at such length and in such detail with the Russert story, when it had already been contradicted by the notes Libby produced indicating the vice president, not Russert, had first told Libby about Plame's role and identity. Indeed, it was hard to recall another instance of a witness immediately undermining his own alibi. Libby knew Plame's identity before Novak disclosed it, and he had a motive to discredit Wilson. He was eager to "set the record straight," which meant refuting Wilson. He had discussed Wilson's wife with at least one reporter—Matt Cooper—and might have done so with Judith Miller and Andrea Mitchell. Still, they were trying to give him the benefit of the doubt. Was Libby's story plausible?

One thing was clear: as Cathie Martin had already suggested, Libby was deeply enmeshed in the damage control over Wilson's allegations, which had touched him personally. For someone who said he rarely spoke to the press, he was in nearly constant contact with them over that period, and initiated many of the calls. They'd have to try to interview all of these reporters, which would be no easy task. Libby must have known that leak investigations usually foundered when journalists refused to cooperate, and that his story would be difficult to corroborate—or refute.

O ver the next month, the agents turned their attention to the question of who knew about Plame's identity before the Novak column made it public, and how they knew it, focusing on officials at the State Department and CIA who dealt with the White House. The source of the information about Plame remained elusive: Armitage had spoken vaguely about "some report";

Rove couldn't remember how he'd "heard" it; Libby thought the vice president had learned it from Tenet or "someone at the CIA"; Libby thought he'd first heard it from Russert until his notes indicated the vice president had told him. Who else knew about her, and when?

The agents interviewed Marc Grossman, the under secretary of state for political affairs, on October 17, three days after Libby. As the third-ranking State Department official after Powell and Armitage, Grossman worked closely with both men.

Eckenrode asked Grossman if he had any idea who might have told Novak about Wilson's wife.

"Actually, I do," Grossman answered. He told the FBI agents that the night before, or perhaps the same morning, Armitage had come to see him and said there was something he wanted Grossman to know before he spoke to the FBI. He then confessed that the FBI had interviewed him, and he told them, "I told Novak about Joe Wilson's wife."

Grossman said he was shocked and disappointed to learn of this breach of confidence.

Armitage had continued, "It's sort of unbelievable. . . . It's the dumbest thing I've ever done in my life." He said he'd revealed the information just as Novak was leaving, and hadn't mentioned any names, but still, he'd told Novak that Wilson's wife worked for the CIA. He said he'd tendered his resignation to Powell.

Eckenrode wondered why Armitage had felt the need to confess to Grossman. His account was consistent with what he told the FBI; was he trying to make sure Grossman's version was as well?

Grossman recalled that he'd asked Armitage about Wilson's trip to Africa after meeting with Libby on May 29. Libby wanted to know if the State Department was involved, and Grossman said he'd find out and report back. Armitage hadn't known anything about it either, but two other State Department officials confirmed that Wilson had gone and said they knew about the trip. "Look," Grossman had told Armitage. "I happen to know Joe Wilson. Maybe I'll just call him up. Is that okay with you?"

"Sure," Armitage had replied.

Grossman and Wilson had both attended the University of California at Santa Barbara, and had attended some alumni events together. When Grossman called, Wilson filled him in on the trip, which Wilson said had been requested by the office of the vice president. Grossman called Libby to report on his conversation with Wilson, and said he'd try to get a fuller report.

Grossman felt the story about why Wilson had been sent still didn't "add up." So he asked the State Department's research department, the Bureau of Intelligence and Research (INR) for a written report. He'd gotten the report on June 11. It had contained this passage:

> From what we can find in our records, Joe Wilson played only a walk-on part on the Niger/Iraq uranium story. In a February 19, 2002, meeting, convened by Valerie Wilson, a CIA Weapons of Mass Destruction manager and the wife of Joe Wilson, he previewed his plans and rationale for going to Niger but said he would only go if the [State] Department thought his trip made sense.

In Tab 1, attached to the report, prominently labeled "secret," were the State Department's notes of the meeting at the CIA to discuss Wilson's mission. It read: "Meeting apparently convened by Valerie Wilson, a CIA WMD managerial type and the wife of Amb. Joe Wilson with the idea that the agency and the larger USG could dispatch Joe to Niger to sort out the Niger/Iraq uranium sale question."

This was how Grossman learned that Wilson's wife was involved, and he thought it was "not appropriate" that someone's wife was planning his trip. Armitage had gotten a copy of the report, and it's obvious that was how he, too, learned about Valerie Wilson. It seemed odd that Armitage hadn't remembered this.

Grossman had also passed on this information to Libby. They were at meetings together on both June 11 and 12, and at one or both of those they'd discussed Wilson's trip and the report. "There's one other thing you should know," Grossman had told Libby. "Joe Wilson's wife works for the agency." Libby had thanked him for the information.

To the FBI agents, this was a startling disclosure: Libby had learned about Wilson's wife, identified in this context only as Valerie Wilson, from Grossman on June 11 or 12, about the same time his notes indicate the vice president also told him she worked at the CIA. Libby had asked Grossman for more information. Yet Libby had made no mention of any conversation with Grossman. Could he have forgotten both references to Wilson's wife by the time he spoke to Russert? It hardly seemed credible.

. . .

In mid-October, Adam Levine, White House deputy press secretary, returned to his small apartment near George Washington University and found Eckenrode's card slipped under the door. On it was a note saying he wanted to meet Levine at his apartment. Levine didn't want the FBI in his apartment, which was a mess, but he agreed to join Eckenrode for a beer at Bertucci's, a nearby bar. Levine had already been into the Washington field office the first week in October, and told two other agents that he didn't know the identities of Novak's sources. But since then, Rove had cast suspicion on Levine as Mike Allen's source for the *Post* column, and at the bar Eckenrode produced an e-mail from Allen to Levine dated September 27 that read "Great to see you." Allen's article had run the next day. Was Levine the source for the column?

This put Levine in an awkward position, since he had talked to Allen. But he maintained he was not the White House official who had said the Plame leak "was meant purely and simply for revenge." Such a rash comment, even if he agreed with it, would likely end his White House career. Levine acknowledged talking to Allen, but not that he was his source. He realized he was treading a thin line, and Eckenrode seemed skeptical.

By mid-November, Eckenrode and his team had exhausted their possible sources in the administration, which included a lengthy list of assistants and others at the White House, the CIA, and the State Department. Everyone had cooperated, or had said they would cooperate, except for two former officials: Levine left the White House at the end of 2003 without signing a waiver or agreeing to further interviews. Ari Fleischer, now working in New York, retained a lawyer and flatly refused to be interviewed or to sign a waiver.

Apart from Novak, whose column had prompted the investigation, no reporters or press sources had yet been approached. In a sense they were the elephant in the room, especially Russert. If Russert corroborated Libby's account of their phone conversation, it would go a long way toward buttressing Libby's credibility.

On November 14, Eckenrode placed a call to Russert using his cell phone number. He didn't expect Russert to answer questions, but he figured he had nothing to lose by asking. He and Russert had a mutual friend, a Catholic priest who ran a leadership forum in Washington for high school students. Eckenrode had given the group a tour of the FBI and then had joined them to watch a taping of *Meet the Press*.

Russert was at home and answered his phone.

"Tim, this is Jack Eckenrode. Remember me? We met when I was at *Meet the Press*. I brought a church crew with my son and Father Mike. You were kind enough to talk to us afterward and take a picture."

"Yeah, now I do," Russert replied.

"I'm working on this CIA leak you may have read about." Eckenrode got right to the point, anxious to keep Russert on the phone. "Look, this is what Libby told us: that [you] told [him] that Wilson's wife worked for the CIA and that 'all the reporters know it.' Is this plausible?" Eckenrode knew the investigation might turn on Russert's answer.

Russert paused for a moment, then seemed puzzled. "I don't recall any conversation along those lines," he said. He said he clearly remembered Libby's call to complain about Matthews, and he seemed slightly bemused at the idea that he'd take Matthews to task for something Matthews said on his program. Libby seemed naive about how television journalism worked. But he'd referred Libby to Matthews's producer and other NBC executives, and didn't think much more about it. As for Wilson's wife, he didn't remember saying anything about her, or that she had even come up in the conversation.

"Would you have remembered something like that?" Eckenrode asked.

"Absolutely. It just didn't happen," Russert insisted.

"Is it possible? Do you need some time to think about it?"

"I don't think so," Russert said.

"Are you 100 percent certain?" Eckenrode pressed.

"Well, I guess it's possible . . ." Russert's voice trailed off.

Eckenrode asked Russert to see if he had any notes from Libby's call, and Russert said he'd check. Eckenrode said he'd call him back. He wanted to keep the channel open.

Eckenrode was elated. He'd been able to question Russert, who didn't invoke any issues about confidential sources or refer him to NBC's lawyers. Russert had not only spoken freely—he'd refuted Libby's alibi.

Eckenrode immediately briefed the lawyers and his fellow agents. At the very least there was a major conflict between Libby and Russert—and Russert had no apparent reason to lie. Was it possible Libby had fabricated the Russert story—and lied to FBI agents? Until now, Eckenrode suspected that the Justice Department lawyers thought this case would end up where all other leak cases had—nowhere. Suddenly that had changed. "Game on!" exclaimed one of the lawyers when he heard the news.

Eckenrode called Russert on November 24 to see if he had located any notes and to ask some more questions. This time Russert said he'd been told not to speak further, and all contacts with the FBI would have to go through NBC's lawyers. Still, Eckenrode knew what Russert had said—and might say again if he could be induced to testify. Eckenrode drafted a report on his earlier call: "Russert does not recall stating to Libby, in this conversation, anything about the wife of former ambassador Joe Wilson. Although he could not completely rule out the possibility that he had such an exchange, Russert was at a loss to remember it."

Eckenrode made no headway with any other reporters. At NBC, Chris Matthews and Andrea Mitchell both declined to be questioned and referred calls to the network's lawyers. Matt Cooper referred the call to *Time*'s lawyers.

Eckenrode and the other agents interviewed Libby again on November 26, right before Thanksgiving. Much had changed in the intervening weeks since their first interview. More documents had been produced, which both Libby and the FBI agents had reviewed. But much more dramatic was the shift in Libby's status from witness to suspect. Russert had flatly contradicted the centerpiece of Libby's story. Rove had failed to corroborate it. Grossman made clear that Libby was the driving force behind the White House effort to get to the bottom of Wilson's trip. Grossman had told Libby about Wilson's wife even before the vice president. Could Libby have forgotten all that, yet have retained a clear and detailed memory of a conversation with Russert in which he allegedly learned Plame's identity?

The FBI agents, Libby, and Tate, his lawyer, took the same seats as before. Libby again seemed somewhat uncomfortable, but perhaps that was simply his reserved demeanor. The picture emerging from interviews and his notes was of a meticulous, detail-oriented, lawyerly personality. Eckenrode asked him to tell them again about his conversation with Russert. Libby told the same story, mentioning again that they had gone "off-the-record" for that part of the discussion. Eckenrode pressed him: was he sure it was Russert who told him, and not some other reporter? Libby said he was sure.

"Well, I checked with Tim Russert," Eckenrode said. "What would you say if I told you he didn't remember saying this?" Ordinarily Eckenrode wouldn't have revealed information from another interview, but his instinct told him to get this out.

Both Libby and Tate looked stunned. Libby hesitated, but then said, "That's funny. I always knew Tim to be a stand-up guy. We had this conversation, but maybe Tim just doesn't remember it."

The news that Russert didn't support his story could have been a golden opportunity for Libby. He could have said he might have been mistaken; maybe it was some other reporter; his memory was vague. Eckenrode was amazed that Libby kept giving such a detailed, specific account. He had to have known Eckenrode would go to Russert, but perhaps he was counting on Russert to invoke the First Amendment and refuse to answer questions. Libby had emphasized that their conversation was off-the-record—another part of Libby's story that Russert didn't mention.

The interview continued, and Libby repeated much of his earlier testimony. There weren't any significant inconsistencies, but he added some telling details. Libby said that during his conversation with Vice President Cheney on Air Force Two about how to respond to the continuing reports that the vice president was behind the Wilson trip, they had debated whether to tell the press that Wilson's wife worked for the CIA. But then Libby said he "wasn't sure" they'd actually discussed that. But he added that at some point he had told the vice president he'd learned about Plame from Russert.

The FBI's notes from the interview read: "Libby had conversations with V.P. about the wife after July 10. The issue remained around awhile. Libby thinks that he may have mentioned to the V.P., do you want me to get something out on Wilson's wife? Libby does not recall."

That meant there was another possible corroborating witness to the Russert conversation—Vice President Cheney. And it was possible Cheney had told Libby to leak Plame's identity.

Libby also added some nuance to his account of the phone call to *Time* reporter Matt Cooper. Libby said that after reading the on-the-record statement authorized by the vice president, Cooper had asked—off-the-record—about Wilson's trip. Libby had told him that reporters were saying that Wilson's wife worked for the CIA, but that he didn't know that, and it might not be true.

Eckenrode asked Libby to describe a lunch he'd had with White House press secretary Ari Fleischer on July 7. Given that the lunch was the day after

Wilson's op-ed piece, and Fleischer would have been the logical person to lead efforts to counteract it, it seemed highly likely that the two would have discussed it. Libby said he'd asked to have lunch with Fleischer, since Fleischer was leaving his White House post the following week. Libby thought it was "possible" they had discussed Wilson, but that wasn't the purpose of the lunch. They had mostly talked about Fleischer's future plans and the Miami Dolphins. Both were fans.

Eckenrode asked specifically—and repeatedly—if he and Fleischer had discussed Wilson's wife and her status as a CIA officer. Each time Libby said no, he didn't recall anything like that, and in any event, he couldn't have discussed it with Fleischer on July 7, since he hadn't yet learned it from Russert.

The agents also pressed Libby on whether he discussed Wilson's wife with any other administration officials. Their notes read: "Libby does not recall any conversations with any administration officials concerning the exposure of Wilson's wife's identity or employment in the public domain." And except for Rove, "Libby said he would have only had discussions with the vice president or Cathie Martin concerning Wilson's wife, but he does not recall the specifics of those conversations." As for Marc Grossman, Libby said he seldom spoke to him. Eckenrode showed Libby a copy of the INR report containing the discussion of Wilson's wife, and Libby said he'd never seen it, nor had the vice president, nor had he discussed it with Grossman.

At the end of the interview, the agents gave Libby a copy of a waiver releasing reporters from any promises of confidentiality. Libby signed it and sent a copy to the FBI.

By Thanksgiving, working without subpoenas, Eckenrode and his team had made remarkable progress in what had developed into a complex and sensitive matter that touched the highest levels of the White House, the State Department, and the CIA. They had largely solved the central mystery, which was the identity of Novak's administration sources. But while the press continued to focus on Novak, the agents had moved on to broader and, in some ways, more important questions: Who else might have violated the protected identities act? Was this part of a broader administration campaign to discredit Wilson? And were the people they had questioned being truthful? Obstruction of justice now loomed as a major threat.

At the center of this dimension of the case was Libby. All indications were that he had concocted an elaborate story that was false in nearly all its most important details. Questioned a second time, confronted with Russert's response, and given an opportunity to correct any misstatements, he had repeated his story and even elaborated on it. Why? What was he trying to conceal? Nor was Libby the only person the agents suspected of being less than candid. Rove and Armitage had obvious motives to minimize their roles. Fleischer had refused to cooperate. Their net was widening.

Despite their considerable progress, at this juncture Eckenrode recognized that they had pretty much exhausted their leads. Further progress would depend on the power of subpoenas issued by a grand jury. In the case of journalists, a clash over First Amendment privileges loomed. And with the vice president and president, both important witnesses, there were potential issues of executive privilege. These were matters well beyond the powers of the FBI.

That fall, James Comey, the U.S. Attorney in New York who made the decision to prosecute Martha Stewart, was nominated to become deputy attorney general. He started commuting to Washington, handing most of his U.S. Attorney duties in New York to his deputy David Kelley. Comey read a thick binder of the FBI's interview reports, including those on Armitage, Rove, Libby, and Russert. Armitage had already admitted being Novak's original source, and Rove was a suspect. Comey had two reactions: this was a serious investigation, and it would be increasingly awkward for Attorney General Ashcroft to stay involved. He kept his thoughts to himself.

At the annual conference of U.S. Attorneys, held that year in Philadelphia, Comey pulled aside Patrick Fitzgerald, the U.S. Attorney in Chicago. They'd worked together in New York at the U.S. Attorney's office and had often sought each other's advice once they'd become U.S. Attorneys themselves. Fitzgerald was godfather to Comey's son, and there was no one Comey trusted more; plus, he understood high-profile, politically sensitive cases. Fitzgerald was forty-two, the son of Irish immigrants who'd grown up in Brooklyn. His father worked as a doorman at a Manhattan apartment building. He had been an outstanding student at Regis High School, a prestigious parochial school in Manhattan, and attended Amherst College and Harvard Law School, working as a doorman and a deckhand to help pay his way. He was tall and imposing, but had a boyish look and often-tousled sandy hair.

Fitzgerald had been hired by the then U.S. Attorney Rudolph Giuliani, and during thirteen years as a prosecutor in the Southern District, successfully handled a series of high-profile cases, including a Gambino crime family case and the 1993 World Trade Center bombing. Since arriving in Chicago as U.S. Attorney in 2001, Fitzgerald had investigated then-governor George Ryan, who abandoned a bid for reelection in 2002 and was subsequently convicted of racketeering, bribery, and false statements. Fitzgerald seemed dedicated to his work, so busy that he'd never married.

That afternoon he and Comey stepped outside into a cold rain. Comey swore him to secrecy, then briefed him on the case. Fitzgerald agreed that the investigation put Ashcroft and the department in an awkward situation. Comey said he might want to consult him again before making any decisions.

Later, in December, Comey approached Ashcroft's chief of staff, David Ayres. "I'm at the point where I feel the attorney general has to get out of the CIA leak case," Comey said. Ayres seemed shocked. The two went into his office and closed the door. Comey felt awkward. He'd just been confirmed as Ashcroft's deputy, hardly knew him, and already he was urging him to step aside in the highest-profile investigation in the department. Anything Ashcroft did would be distorted and attacked because of his ties to the administration and especially Rove. Rove had worked on Ashcroft's U.S. Senate campaign in Missouri. What if he decided not to bring charges against Rove? There would be an uproar. Ashcroft could recuse himself and delegate his authority to Comey. Comey, in turn, would name a special prosecutor. "I'm viewed differently," Comey said, since he had no political career. "It will be better received." Even if Ashcroft named a special prosecutor, the choice might be tainted by partisan suspicion.

Comey met with Ashcroft alone to discuss the situation. "Fairly or unfairly, the department cannot credibly make the decision about what to do. My recommendation is that you should step aside and leave it to me." Ashcroft called in Solicitor General Ted Olson for further advice. They agreed that Ashcroft's involvement didn't pose an actual conflict. Indeed, he'd done nothing to impede the investigation of Rove or anyone else in the White House. But they felt the appearance of a conflict amounted to the "extraordinary" circumstances called for in the regulations, and that the public interest would be served. This was especially true if no charges resulted. Ashcroft seemed uncomfortable, concerned that stepping down would be a tacit admission that he shouldn't have been involved from the beginning. But he agreed.

Just before Christmas, Comey approached Fitzgerald to head the leak investigation, choosing him over two other finalists. Fitzgerald was non-partisan; even Comey didn't know his political affiliation, if any (he was not registered with any party). He was thorough and fair. Most important, Comey thought he could credibly close the case without bringing charges. At this juncture Comey was still focused on potential violations of the pro-tected identities act rather than perjury or obstruction. He knew that the language of the statute—actual knowledge that an agent was covert and that the CIA was protecting the agent's identity—made conviction extremely difficult.

Ashcroft's decision to step aside and Fitzgerald's appointment were both announced on December 30, and Fitzgerald spent the New Year's holiday read-ing briefing materials.

Fitzgerald promptly asked to interview Novak again. After all, he was the source of the investigation, and hadn't revealed his sources. As before, Novak's lawyers didn't want to antagonize the special counsel, nor did they want to litigate a privilege issue they felt sure they would lose, at great personal and financial cost to Novak. They agreed to a meeting. Novak was equally determined not to reveal confidential sources, especially since he'd declared on national TV that to do so would end his career as a journalist.

When Novak arrived at his lawyers' offices on the afternoon of January 12, two days before his scheduled interview with Fitzgerald, his lawyer James Hamilton dropped a bombshell: Fitzgerald had just told him that he would be bringing two waivers releasing sources from any promise of confidentiality. Richard Armitage and Karl Rove had signed the waivers.

As Novak later described his reaction, the revelation "constituted a shock too severe for a seventy-one-year-old man." He tried to stay calm.

"They have succeeded in identifying my sources," he said.

Hamilton warned Novak that efforts to resist testifying would likely fail in the courts and would be costly, both in financial terms and in the resulting opinions likely to damage the scope of a reporter's privilege. In any event, it was clear Fitzgerald already knew his sources. Novak decided there was no further point in resisting. He would identify Armitage and Rove.

When Fitzgerald arrived for their interview two days later he brought three waivers: Armitage, Rove, and also Bill Harlow, Novak's source at the CIA. With a flourish he placed them on the table and encouraged Novak to read the waivers. Novak did, and then looked up. He swallowed visibly and looked pale. "Okay, let's go," he said.

As he later described it, Novak felt miserable, and declined to discuss conversations with these sources about anything except the leak of Plame's identity. Eckenrode asked how the meeting with Armitage came about, and initially Novak said no intermediaries were involved. Later he corrected that, saying that Kenneth Duberstein, Reagan's former deputy chief of staff and now a consultant and confidant of Armitage, had called that week to say that Armitage was "interested" in meeting with Novak. Novak was surprised, since Armitage had never responded to any of his calls before and had given the impression he didn't like Novak. There was no proposed subject for the interview; Novak said he considered it "wildcatting," hoping for a scoop but with no agenda in mind. He didn't take notes or record the interview.

The subsequent FBI notes of the interview indicate that Novak was following the Kristof story, and he asked Armitage why Joe Wilson, "a partisan Democrat and former Clinton official," would have been dispatched to Africa. Armitage replied, "His wife, Valerie, works in counterproliferation at the CIA and she was the one who suggested to superiors that Wilson make the trip." Armitage "smiled," and added, "sounds like typical Evans & Novak, doesn't it?" Novak had smiled in return. "He assumed he was getting privileged or exclusive information" from Armitage.

There were some critical differences from Armitage's account: according to Novak, Armitage had used a name—Valerie—which was how Novak recognized the name Valerie Plame in Wilson's *Who's Who* entry. He specified that she worked on counterproliferation, and the reference to Evans & Novak suggested he wanted the information to appear in print. Using Duberstein to set up the interview also suggested that this might have been Armitage's goal from the outset.

Novak said he didn't think Armitage would give him "bad dope," but he decided to check out the information with Karl Rove. He and Rove had known each other for twenty-three years, and Novak spoke to Rove two to three times a week. He called him later that day or the next and Rove had returned the call. Novak repeated the information about Wilson's wife working at the CIA, and Rove had said, "Oh, you know about that too." Novak took that as explicit confirmation; Rove was indeed Novak's second source. He asked Rove about Wilson's report, to which Rove responded that "it lacked meaning and was inconclusive." Rove added that it was oral, that Wilson had briefed the CIA, which summarized it in a report that the White House would like to declassify. Novak thought it was significant that the report was oral; no other reporters had that fact. Their discussion had shifted to the slowness of the White House to respond to the episode, and the conversation lasted a total of about ten minutes. Novak said Rove never told him not to use any of this information.

There were also critical differences between Novak's version and Rove's: Rove had said he'd "heard" about Wilson's wife; "you know about that too" implied he knew it. He'd also described a classified document. Fitzgerald and Eckenrode felt that neither Armitage nor Rove had been entirely forthcoming.

D espite his lack of cooperation, former press secretary Ari Fleischer hadn't been a high priority for the investigators. Other than his lunch with Libby the day after Wilson's op-ed piece, there was nothing to link him to Libby or Rove or any leaks to reporters. Still, Fitzgerald obtained a subpoena and Fleischer came before the grand jury in January. He invoked the Fifth Amendment and refused to testify. What was Fleischer holding back? Fitzgerald negotiated with his lawyer, Robert Barnett of Williams & Connolly (who'd also negotiated a book deal for Fleischer). Barnett indicated that Fleischer would answer all questions if he was granted immunity—and that it would be worth it to the prosecutors. He made a proffer describing what Fleischer could say, and they quickly reached a deal. Fitzgerald granted Fleischer immunity on February 16. Immediately after, they met for a preliminary debriefing. To avoid detection, Fitzgerald and Eckenrode met Fleischer and Barnett at an apartment Williams & Connolly keeps in Manhattan.

Fleischer described his lunch with Libby on July 7, which he thought was unusual, even "weird." Libby had told Fleischer that Wilson's wife worked for the CIA, and that this information was "hush-hush" and "on the QT." Fleischer was sure this was the first he'd heard this. Fleischer didn't think the press would be all that interested. "The press would not find it interesting one way or another if his wife sent him. . . . It just didn't strike me as news about whether the CIA had nepotism, or in this case was incompetent, was relevant to whether or not the president's statement about Iraq seeking uranium from Africa was germane."

Eckenrode had long suspected that there was more to the Fleischer lunch than Libby had ever admitted, but this was much more than he expected. Libby had told Fleischer about Valerie Wilson three days before his alleged conversation with Tim Russert.

Fleischer said he was on the presidential trip to Africa on Air Force One later that week, and there was further discussion of Wilson's wife on the plane. He had also read some classified documents on the flight about Wilson's mission, including the CIA report summarizing Wilson's trip. Fleischer also recalled presidential lawyer Dan Bartlett "venting" about Wilson's wife and the "incompetence" of the CIA.

The presidential party arrived in Uganda on July 11, and at one point Fleischer was standing along a road with several reporters, including John Dickerson of *Time* and David Gregory of NBC. They were talking about what a bad week it had been for the White House. Here they were in Africa, and all anyone asked about was Wilson and the sixteen-words controversy. "If it wasn't this crap, it would be some other crap," Fleischer said, immediately regretting his choice of words. Then he'd volunteered, "If you want to know who sent Ambassador Wilson to Niger, it was his wife. She works there." He hoped it might "make the controversy go away," but the reporters didn't even take out their notebooks. "It was a big 'so what.' "

The next day Fleischer had returned a call from Walter Pincus of the *Washington Post* from the plane, but he couldn't recall if they'd discussed Wilson's wife. He didn't think so.

None of those reporters followed up on the information or wrote a story about it. But Fleischer had leaked a CIA agent's identity to at least two reporters, possibly three. He was clearly one of the two officials referred to in Allen's *Washington Post* article. Fleischer insisted that never in his "wildest dreams" did he suspect that Plame was a covert agent, but he had reason to believe her status was classified: Libby had told him the information was "hush-hush" and he'd read about her in classified documents.

As Fleischer described his reaction to the leak investigation, "I thought, Oh my God, did I play a role in somehow outing a CIA officer? . . . Did I do something that I could be in big trouble for?" No wonder he had demanded immunity.

At least Fleischer had been truthful, acknowledging the facts and not hiding behind an alleged failure of memory. He was swiftly brought before the grand jury on February 24, repeating what he'd told Fitzgerald and Eckenrode. He dealt Libby's credibility another serious blow. As one agent put it, Fleischer's testimony all but "clinched" Libby's indictment–unless Libby was prepared to recant and correct his story. It was time to bring Libby before the grand jury.

O n March 5, 2004, I. Lewis Libby and his lawyer, Joseph Tate, arrived at the E. Barrett Prettyman Federal Courthouse on Pennsylvania Avenue. They were escorted to a small, windowless room where members of the grand jury sat at small desks and Fitzgerald and his staff worked from an L-shaped table at the back of the fluorescent-lit room. Libby testified alone while Tate waited in the corridor, although Libby was free to consult him at any time.

It was a critical moment for Libby and the investigation. He had been formally notified that he was a "subject" of the investigation, as opposed to simply being a witness. That meant he was being investigated, suggesting evidence of a crime. Clearly, Libby had talked to reporters and discussed Plame. There were glaring inconsistencies between his version of how that might have happened and others' testimony. He had told the FBI that he thought he'd learned Plame's identity from Tim Russert; the discovery of his notes indicated the vice president had told him already, but he'd forgotten that. With reporters he was careful to say he'd only heard about Plame from other reporters and didn't know if it was true she worked at the CIA. By now Fitzgerald knew from other administration officials–Martin and Grossman–that Libby had been told about Wilson's wife repeatedly. He could not have heard it for the first time from Russert, even if he had forgotten the Cheney instance. And the most glaring contradiction was with Russert, who denied ever discussing Wilson's wife with Libby.

Would Libby now try to correct the record? To admit lying to the FBI would end his career and be admitting a crime (as Doug Faneuil discovered), but perhaps he could say he'd been confused, or had misremembered. But that begged the question: If the Russert story (and perhaps others) was false, what was Libby concealing?

"Let me just introduce myself again. My name is Pat Fitzgerald. I'm a special counsel in this matter, joined by other attorneys with the special counsel's office seated at the table. And this grand jury is investigating possible offenses of different laws that include Title 50 of the United States Code, Section 421, which concerns the disclosure of the identity of a covert agent; Title 18 of the United States Code, Section 793, which is the illegal transmission of national defense information; . . . or Title 18, Section 1001, false statements. . . . Do you understand the general nature of the investigation?"

"I do, sir."

"I should tell you that you have a constitutional right to refuse to answer any question if a truthful answer would tend to incriminate you. Do you understand that you have that right?"

"I do, sir. . . ."

"Are you an attorney yourself?"

"I am."

"And do you understand that any testimony you give is under oath and that if you make any deliberate false statement about a material or important fact, you could be prosecuted for perjury? Do you understand that?"

"I do understand that."

"And what that means is that if someone were to make a false statement they should assume that anything we ask about during the course of today's grand jury is something that is material or important to the investigation. You understand that?"

"Yes, sir."

"And if someone does make a false statement or commit perjury, they could be prosecuted [and sentenced to] up to five years in jail for each such false statement. Do you understand that?"

"Yes, sir . . ."

"And I will also tell you, as you were advised prior to coming in, in the presence of your attorney, that based on your conduct in this investigation and in particular, [your] contact with reporters, you, among others, are a subject of the investigation. And that does not mean anyone has decided to charge you with any crimes, but just is to advise you of the serious nature of the proceeding. Do you understand that?"

"I do."

"And do you have any questions about the nature of the proceeding?"

"No, sir."

"And are you prepared to proceed?"

"I am."

After some background questions, Fitzgerald started with the Kristof column and steered Libby through the events leading up to the Novak column pretty much in chronological order. The first area of conflicting testimony involved Libby's dealings with the State Department's Marc Grossman. Libby said he didn't recall any discussions with Grossman about Wilson's trip or other issues in Kristof's column.

"Do you recall any conversation with Secretary Grossman about who was responsible for sending Wilson on this trip to Niger?"

"I don't recall a conversation with him about it."

"And do you know if you ever discussed with Secretary Grossman whether Wilson's wife worked at the CIA?"

"No, I don't recall ever discussing that."

After covering the events of early June in detail, including Libby's recollection of the crucial conversation in which Cheney mentioned that Wilson's wife worked for the CIA, Fitzgerald again asked about Grossman:

"As you sit here today, do you know whether or not you ever spoke to Secretary Grossman about having him find out information about what caused this former ambassador to be sent to Niger?"

"I don't recall it."

"And do you recall ever having a discussion with Marc Grossman before, during, or after a Deputies Committee meeting where Marc Grossman told you that he had learned the former ambassador's wife had worked at the CIA in the counterproliferation division?"

"No, I don't."

"Do you recall any conversation at any time when Secretary Grossman told you that the former ambassador's wife worked at the CIA?"

"I don't recall."

"You have no memory of that whatsoever?"

"Sorry, sir, I don't."

Fitzgerald wasn't subtle. It must have been obvious at this point that Grossman had said something to Libby about Wilson's wife. Fitzgerald had given Libby every opportunity to remember something about it, but Libby had insisted he had no recollection.

Fitzgerald moved on to the Wilson op-ed piece, and showed Libby the copy that Cheney had saved and annotated, including the reference to the wife's "junket." But Libby said he didn't recall discussing the wife with the vice president, or anyone else for that matter, since he only learned it when he spoke to Tim Russert. Fitzgerald leaped on this, which was the heart of Libby's alibi:

"Is it your testimony under oath that you don't recall discussing Wilson's wife working at the CIA between the July 6 date when the Wilson op-ed appeared and your conversation with Tim Russert?"

"That's correct, sir . . . I don't recall discussing it. What I do recall is being

surprised when I talked to Mr. Russert on the 10th or the 11th, and I am inferring from that surprise that I hadn't talked about it earlier in the week."

"Let me ask you this: Do you recall going to lunch on July 7 with Ari
Fleischer?"

Libby remembered the lunch, and said they discussed Fleischer's plans and
the Miami Dolphins, "and we probably discussed the uranium business because
it was a very hot topic at that point." But Libby couldn't remember if they had
or not.

"And you recall that you had lunch with Mr. Fleischer?"

"Yes."

"And you recall discussing Mr. Fleischer's future, correct?"

"Yes, sir."

"And you recall discussing the Miami Dolphins, correct?"

"Yes, sir, I recall all that quite clearly . . ."

After establishing that Libby "clearly" remembered something as trivial as
the Dolphins, Fitzgerald moved aggressively for the jugular.

"Do you recall telling Mr. Fleischer that Wilson's wife worked for the CIA
in the counterproliferation division?"

"No, I don't."

"And is it possible that you told Mr. Fleischer during that lunch that Wilson's
wife worked at the CIA in the counterproliferation division?"

"It's possible . . . well, I don't recall it and I recall being surprised by Russert, so I tend to think I didn't know it then, but that's all I really recall."

"Isn't it a fact, sir, that you told Mr. Fleischer over lunch that this was 'hush-
hush' or 'on the QT' that Wilson's wife worked at the CIA?"

"I don't recall that."

Fitzgerald shifted immediately to others who contradicted Libby's story:

"Prior to your conversation with Tim Russert on July 10 or 11, do you ever
recall a conversation where Cathie Martin told you that Wilson's wife worked
at the CIA?"

"No, sir."

"And do you recall an occasion on or about July 8 where Cathie Martin
came into the vice president's office with you present, the vice president, and
indicated that Wilson's wife worked at the CIA, that she had learned that?"

"July 8?"

"Yes."

"I . . . again, sir, I don't recall. What I recall . . . all my recollection on this point is hinged on my surprise when I heard it from Tim Russert and I'm inferring the rest from that."

Prompted by Fitzgerald, Libby gave a lengthy description of events leading up to his July 8 meeting at the St. Regis with *Times* reporter Judith Miller. As with the others, he didn't recall discussing Wilson's wife, and said he inferred he didn't, since he was surprised when Russert told him two or three days later.

In any event, Libby suggested he didn't think the fact that Wilson's wife worked for the CIA was all that big a deal.

"Is it fair to say that many would think that if Joe Wilson were hired because of nepotism, because of a contact he had at the agency, that might undermine his credibility as an expert?"

"Some people may have taken it that way. That was never what I took out of it . . . because what he did he was perfectly competent to do. He went and he sat down with the people from Niger . . . he sat down and had tea with them and asked them what they had done or hadn't done, and ambassadors do that all the time. So I thought he was very competent to do that mission."

"Sir, are you telling us under oath that you never thought Mr. Wilson was hired because of nepotism?"

"I didn't know why he was hired and I did not know at this point . . . how he came to be hired . . . as I've tried to make clear, the best of my recollection is that I was surprised when I learned from Tim Russert that his wife worked there."

Fitzgerald said he'd get to Russert in a minute, but first asked Libby about the vice president's interest in getting the full story of Wilson's mission to the public.

"Fair to say," Fitzgerald asked, "that you went through the notes and there's a number of times when the vice president during that week has said you need to get everything out?"

"Yes, sir."

"Tell the whole story. The whole truth has to get out. Anything less than that is a big mistake?"

"Yes, sir. That's exactly what we wanted to do."

"And that was a constant thing that week?"

"Yes, sir."

"And the vice president, to be blunt, was frustrated that it wasn't all getting out there and it wasn't sort of putting the story to rest, and he was sort of getting ticked off that we needed to resolve this issue?"

"I'm not sure I would use the word 'ticked off,' but he was frustrated. Yes, sir, that's a fair statement."

"Now, tell me about the circumstances of your conversation with Tim Russert."

Despite his many memory lapses from the period, Libby recalled and described the conversation and its genesis in great detail:

"Chris Matthews, who is an NBC correspondent, had been—has a TV show at night, and he is a rather outspoken fellow," Libby began. "And he was saying on this television show that the vice president sent Joe Wilson out on this mission, that the vice president got a report back from Joe Wilson on this mission, that the vice president therefore knew that the uranium report was false and should have stopped the president from putting it in the State of the Union." Libby wanted Matthews to at least acknowledge that the administration had denied Wilson's allegations. He called Mary Matalin, Cheney's communications person for the first two years in office, to ask how to approach Matthews, and she suggested Libby call Tim Russert.

"Do you want me to continue?" Libby asked.

Fitzgerald hesitated momentarily; there were some things he wanted to follow up on. But Fitzgerald figured it was best to just keep out of his way. "Yes, continue."

"Okay. So I called Tim Russert. I can't recall whether I got him on the phone right away or whether he had to call me back . . . I think I called Mr. Russert sort of late-ish on the 10th . . . I got him on the phone." After some pleasantries, "I turned to our issues. And I said, I had two things that were bothering me. One is some things that Andrea Mitchell was saying . . . but I said, 'I'm not really calling you tonight about what Andrea Mitchell is saying. I'm calling you about what Chris Matthews is saying.' And then I ran through with him what it was that Chris Matthews was saying and why it was wrong and on the public record wrong . . . that he at least had to say that the White House has denied this, the CIA has denied this, the vice president's office has denied this."

Libby explained that at this point, Russert interrupted and said he'd have to call Libby back, a call which "came only after a long-ish delay which I was uncomfortable with," probably the next day. "He told me, you know, he understood what I was saying, [but] that there wasn't much he could do about what Chris Matthews was saying. He [Russert] understood that it was not complete given that the public record was the other way. And then he said, 'You know, did you know that . . . Ambassador Wilson's wife works at the CIA?' And I was a little taken aback by that. I remember being taken aback by it. And I said . . . 'No, I don't know that.' And I said 'No, I don't know that' intentionally because I didn't want him to take anything I was saying as in any way confirming what he had said, because at that point in time I did not recall that I had ever known this, and I thought this is something that he was telling me that I was first learning. And so I said, 'No I don't know that' because I wanted to be very careful not to confirm it for him, so that he didn't take my statement as confirmation for him.″

This was pretty much the same story that Libby had told Eckenrode. But this time he said, not once but three times, that he'd told Russert he didn't know Wilson's wife worked at the CIA, and was taking great care not to give any impression he was confirming the identity of someone working for the CIA.

Libby kept talking, noting, "I omitted to tell you . . . as always, 'Tim, our discussion is off-the-record if that's okay with you,' and he said, 'That's fine.'"

"So then, he, Mr. Russert, said to me, 'Do you know that Ambassador Wilson's wife works at the CIA?' And I said, 'No, I don't know that.' And then he said, 'Yeah, all the reporters know it.' And I said, again, 'I don't know that.' I just wanted to be clear that I wasn't confirming anything or him on this. And you know, I was struck by what he was saying in that he thought it was an important fact, but I didn't want to be digging in on him, and he then moved on and we finished the conversation, something like that.″

But Russert didn't agree to speak to Matthews. "In short," Libby concluded, "I struck out trying to get Mr. Russert to intercede . . . he was unwilling or unable. In any case, he didn't do that. He said we should call his producer.″

From Libby's point of view it's understandable that he would have seized upon such a memory. It established that he couldn't have leaked Valerie Plame's identity to Robert Novak, since he didn't even know it until he spoke to Russert on July 11, the same day Novak's column was disseminated to subscribers, embargoed for release until the following Monday. By then, her identity and the fact that she worked for the CIA were already widely known in the press, according to Russert. If Libby subsequently mentioned this to other reporters, always careful to stress that he was just passing on what he'd heard from others outside the White House, he may have been gossiping, but he wasn't leaking anything. He couldn't have violated the protected identities act and, more broadly, couldn't be accused of leaking any confidential information.

If Libby thought he was hearing about Wilson's wife for the first time on July 10 or 11, surely he would have mentioned it to someone at the White

House—or so Fitzgerald assumed. "Did you tell the vice president about Russert informing you this curious fact that Wilson's wife worked at the CIA?"

"I don't recall if I told the vice president at that time what had been told me. I'm not sure if I saw him at that time and had a chance to tell him. I don't recall telling him at that time."

But Libby did recall with some clarity discussing it with Karl Rove. He'd gone to see Rove about the Tenet statement, and Rove had told him about the call from Novak. "Novak had told Karl that Ambassador Wilson's wife worked at the CIA. So this was confirmation of a sort from what I had heard from Tim Russert that all the reporters know that Ambassador Wilson's wife works at the CIA. I told Karl that I had heard from Tim Russert . . . the same thing, that the ambassador's wife works at the CIA and . . . that Tim Russert had told me that all the reporters know this. I don't remember the exact order of the conversation, but that's the sum and substance of what we talked about with regard to that."

So Rove was a corroborating witness—a possible contemporaneous account of the revelation from Russert. And Libby was potentially a key witness to Rove's exchange with Novak. But he said Rove didn't mention what, if anything, he'd told Novak.

Fitzgerald asked Libby about his conversation with NBC's Andrea Mitchell, and Libby described the "awkward moment" when he feared mentioning Wilson's wife might reveal that Russert had told him about her CIA status, but not his own reporter—an account Libby conceded was "convoluted."

"And do you remember thinking about the dilemma, that you're concerned that you may reveal to Ms. Mitchell that Russert told you what reporters know about Wilson's wife?"

"That's what stuck in my mind. Yes, sir."

"And, as you sit here today, you don't know whether you discussed Wilson's wife with Ms. Mitchell?"

"I don't recall . . . what I recall for sure was this dilemma about it. That's what I recall."

"And as you sit here today you're obviously saying that as of that time you didn't recall learning this fact from the vice president even though it had happened earlier. Correct?"

"Correct. Yes, sir."

"And you don't recall any conversation with either Grossman, or Fleischer, or Cathie Martin concerning Wilson's wife. Correct?"

"Correct."

"But you do recall having a thought during a conversation with Andrea Mitchell that if this comes up, it could put me in an awkward position because I learned this from Russert and not from any of these people that I may or may not have talked to. Correct?"

"Correct."

Libby described the trip to Norfolk on July 12, when he and the vice president discussed in some detail how to respond to Matt Cooper's questions and more broadly how to build on Tenet's statement. This may have been their first private conversation after the call to Russert, but Libby didn't recall mentioning it—or the revelation about Wilson's wife—to Cheney. Libby described taking the vice president's dictation for an on-the-record statement from Libby, and then making calls from Andrews Air Force Base. Libby conceded that he had discussed Wilson's wife with Cooper, putting it in this context:

"I said, you know, off-the-record, reporters are telling us that Ambassador Wilson's wife works at the CIA and I don't know if it's true. As I told you, we don't know Mr. Wilson, we didn't know anything about his mission, so I don't know that it's true. But if it's true, it may explain how he knows some people at the agency and maybe he got some bad skinny, you know, some bad information. So that was the discussion about Ambassador Wilson's wife. . . . I was very clear to say reporters are telling us because in my mind I still didn't know it as a fact."

Libby recalled making a similar point that day to Judith Miller; he was "pretty sure" he also discussed it with the *Post*'s Glenn Kessler and did not bring it up with *Newsweek*'s Evan Thomas.

It was late in the afternoon, and at about 4:30 p.m. Fitzgerald suggested they adjourn, but Libby interrupted. "Can I just make one other comment about this stuff? I get a lot of information during the course of a day. I probably get . . . I tend to get between a hundred and two hundred pages of material a day that I'm supposed to read and understand and I, you know, I start at six in the morning and I go until eight or eight-thirty at night, and most of that is meetings. So a lot of information comes through to me, and I can't possibly recall all the stuff that I think is important, let alone other stuff that I don't think is important. . . . What I'll normally do is I'll gather my staff together and say, Hey, what happened here? . . . What did people say, or what happened last week when we had that meeting? Did State agree to do something, or was the Defense Department supposed to do something? And we'll sort of pool our recollections of it and that almost always brings me a fuller recollection of what's happened.

"I haven't done that here because, as I understand it, you don't want me to do that here. I'm happy to do it at some point, but I haven't. So I apologize if my recollection of this stuff is not perfect, but it's not in a way that I would normally do these things. . . . And I apologize if there's some stuff that I remember and some I don't, but it's—I'm just trying to tell you what I do in fact remember."

Libby was excused from what had been, at times, a grueling ordeal. Fitzgerald's skepticism at Libby's testimony had been all too evident. The proceeding was adjourned, and Fitzgerald made clear he wasn't finished; members of the grand jury filed out of the room. Libby was no doubt exceptionally busy, preoccupied by the weightiest affairs of state, the war in Iraq, and international terrorism. But he and the vice president had spent what seemed an inordinate amount of time on the issue of Joe Wilson's mission to Niger: who inspired it, why he was chosen, and what he found there. Libby's memory about that was clear. So was his recollection of his conversation with Tim Russert, during which he learned that Wilson's wife worked for the CIA, something "all the reporters" knew about. Libby was at pains not to confirm this to other reporters, even inadvertently, insisting that he didn't know this, or didn't remember it, and in fact believed he was hearing it for the first time from Russert. He had made this point at least eight times in the course of his testimony.

Libby returned to the grand jury a few weeks later, on Wednesday, March 24. His lawyer, Joe Tate, had called Fitzgerald to say Libby wanted to correct his earlier testimony in two respects, and Fitzgerald said Libby could do so, inviting him to "forget" his earlier testimony and start over. This, too, was an opportunity for Libby to change his story, or at least suggest he might have been confused. But Libby added little of substance. He now recalled bantering with Marc Grossman about sending an ambassador to Niger, but reiterated that they hadn't discussed Wilson's wife. And he now recalled that at his lunch with Ari Fleischer, he'd thanked Fleischer for mentioning the vice president's talking points at that morning's press gaggle. So they had definitely discussed the Wilson affair. But he again denied discussing Wilson's wife with Fleischer.

Fitzgerald reminded Libby that in his FBI interview, he'd said it was "possible" he'd discussed Wilson's wife with the vice president during their talk on Air Force Two. "It's possible that would have been one of the times I could have talked to him about what I learned from Russert and what Karl Rove had told me about Novak."

"And as you sit here today, do you recall whether you had such a conversation with the vice president on Air Force Two on July 12?"

"No, sir. My best recollection of that conversation was what I had on my note card which we have produced which doesn't reflect anything about that."

Throughout his second grand jury appearance, Libby's testimony was consistent with his earlier testimony, especially that he thought he had first learned about Wilson's wife from Russert. But in one critical regard, his recollection was much better and more detailed: he clearly recalled that he had told Cheney about his conversation with Russert—making Cheney another witness to the purported conversation with Russert. Fitzgerald was asking Libby about his calls to reporters on July 12 when Libby volunteered:

"I went to the vice president and said, 'You know, I was not the person who spoke to Novak.' And he said something like, 'I know that.' And I said, 'I learned this from Tim Russert.' And he sort of tilted his head to the side a little bit." He continued, "I told him [the vice president] about Russert, that I had learned it from Russert. And I think at that point I may have told him that I had talked about the wife to Cooper. I just don't recall that. But what was important to me was to let him know I wasn't the person who leaked the information to Mr. Novak, and that in fact I had heard it from Russert, at which point . . . Mr. Russert told me it was well known, known to all the reporters."

Considering that less than three weeks earlier Libby had no memory of telling Cheney about his conversation with Russert, he now had a surprisingly vivid recollection. This conversation was "in person"; "at his [Cheney's] desk in the White House"; the vice president had "tilted his head."

Fitzgerald asked about the significance of the head gesture. "The Tim Russert part caught his attention. . . . He reacted as if he didn't know about the Tim Russert thing or he was rehearing it, or reconsidering it, or something like that."

Fitzgerald also questioned Libby at considerable length about his efforts to clear his name as a potential source for Novak or, more broadly, as a source for any classified information. Libby acknowledged that he never told McClellan or the president that he had spoken to Cooper and Miller about Wilson's wife or that he might have been one of the two White House officials described as sources in the *Washington Post* article. Nor was it clear he had disclosed this to his immediate boss, the vice president. "I would have been happy to unburden myself of it," Libby told Fitzgerald, "about all of this, and I went to the vice president and offered to tell him everything I knew, and he didn't want to hear it, and I assumed that I should not go into it, and that if he wanted to hear it, I would be happy to tell him."

Libby was vague about when this might have happened. "I had a second conversation with him [Cheney], or maybe it's a third. In my first conversation with him, I told him, 'Look, I wasn't the source of the leak of this. In fact, I learned it from Tim Russert. And, you know . . . by that point lots of reporters knew, he told me all the reporters knew,' something like that. So that it was Russert, but it wasn't just Russert. And as I say, that was most of the conversation." Then Libby had discovered his June 12 notes. "And so I went back to him and said, you know, I told you something wrong before. It turns out that I have notes that I had heard about this earlier from you and I didn't want to leave you with the wrong statement that I heard about it from Tim Russert. In fact, I had heard about it earlier, but I had forgotten it."

"From me?" Cheney had asked. And then he had again "tilted his head."

Libby hadn't said anything then about speaking to other reporters, but he offered to tell Cheney on another occasion. "He said, 'Fine,' and held up his hand. 'I understand.' I took from it, we shouldn't talk about the details of this."

Libby insisted that he never knew Valerie Plame was a covert agent; he said he played softball and basketball with CIA employees who readily volunteered they worked for the agency, and he assumed the vast majority of its employees weren't covert agents. In this regard, it didn't matter whether he'd first heard the information from the vice president or other reporters. In neither case did he suspect her identity might be classified.

Before adjourning, Fitzgerald asked if any of the grand jurors had any questions for Libby, and one followed up on this point:

"If you did not understand the information about Wilson's wife to be classified and didn't understand it to be classified when you heard it from Mr. Russert, why was it that you were so deliberate to make sure that you told other reporters that reporters were saying it and not assert it as something you knew?"

"I didn't know if it was true, and I didn't want the reporters to think it was true because I said it," Libby answered.

Eckenrode, agent Tim Fuhrman, and Fitzgerald interviewed Vice President Richard Cheney on May 8. As he was both a potential subject of the investigation and an important witness, his testimony was critical. No one had implicated Cheney in any crime, but there was circumstantial evidence. Had he directed Libby to leak Valerie Wilson's identity or any other classified information to reporters? As a witness, he could corroborate Libby's alibi, which was that Libby learned about Wilson's wife from Tim Russert and reported this to the vice president.

Like many of the witnesses, Cheney began with a broad statement, saying the president had directed him and all White House employees to cooperate fully and he would do so, consistent with any privileges that might arise. He said he had "no idea" who disclosed Plame's identity to Robert Novak. Nor did he know of any other reporters who might have been given that information, either before Novak's column on July 14 or afterward. No one ever told him they talked to any other reporters and provided the information about Mrs. Wilson's employment. "Furthermore, he has no personal knowledge of anyone having provided this information to Robert Novak, or any other reporter, and he has never been advised by anyone to that effect," the FBI agent wrote.

Consistent with others' recollections, Cheney remembered asking about Iraq's possible purchase of uranium in Niger at an intelligence briefing in 2002, but knew nothing about Wilson's mission until he read about it in Kristof's column in the *Times*. About that time Cheney had spoken to CIA director Tenet using the direct phone line in his office, and Tenet identified the former ambassador as Joe Wilson and mentioned that his wife "worked in the unit that sent him." Cheney thought Tenet sounded "defensive and embarrassed" and "had not known what was going on with this mission."

So Libby had been correct in surmising that Cheney learned Plame's identity from Tenet and it was plausible that Cheney had discussed this with Libby before the June 12 Pincus article. Cheney recalled the article, and that Pincus had called with questions. He didn't remember any conversation with Libby in which he mentioned what he'd learned from Tenet, but conceded "if he shared it with anyone, it would have been Libby." Cheney said he had "no recollection" of Cathie Martin coming into his office to tell him and Libby that she'd heard from the CIA about Wilson's wife.

Cheney recalled cutting out the Wilson op-ed piece, but didn't remember underlining portions or making notes on it. Asked for his reaction to it, Cheney thought it made the CIA look like "amateur hour," and Wilson's conclusions were so sloppy and unfounded that his mission "was not really a serious enterprise," reactions that caused him to question the previous high regard in which he held the agency and its employees. He reiterated all the complaints familiar to the agents from the talking points: that he hadn't sent Wilson or known about the mission and that he never saw the report. He didn't remember discussing Wilson's op-ed piece with Tenet, other than sarcastically suggesting, when Tenet asked about another intelligence question, that he "ought to send Joe Wilson to check it out."

The issue of Wilson's wife, and whether she sent him, "was just not a big deal," Cheney said, and "did not figure prominently" in his thinking, despite his note asking "Did his wife send him on a junket?" He said he never discussed either of the Wilsons with President Bush.

Cheney said he "assumed" he'd discussed Joe Wilson and his mission with Libby around the time of the Kristof and Pincus articles. But his memory of those conversations was largely a blank slate. He didn't recall discussing Valerie Wilson with Libby before Novak's column appeared; he didn't remember Libby complaining about Chris Matthews, and he didn't recall hearing about Libby having any contact with Tim Russert. Cheney said he "clearly remembered" the trip to Norfolk to commission the USS *Ronald Reagan*, and had been "pleased" that the president declined the opportunity so Cheney could appear in his stead. He "was particularly looking forward to spending some time with former first lady Nancy Reagan," and took his wife with him, but didn't recall that Libby had brought his family. He had no specific memory of discussing the Wilson affair with Libby on the flight home, dictating a statement, or asking Libby to call reporters, but it was "possible," and "he would not be surprised" if he had done so. The FBI agent noted that Cheney "cannot recall if he and Scooter Libby talked about Valerie Wilson's CIA position as a data point."

The last issue was significant, since both Libby and Cheney, the only two participants, had now said it was "possible" they discussed disclosing the identity and role of Wilson's wife to the press. Still, neither recalled actually doing it.

Since it was critical testimony, the agents returned to how and when Libby learned about Valerie Wilson's identity.

"Although the vice president has no specific memory of such a conversation, Libby may have told him he was not Novak's source. In any event, the vice president did not suspect Libby of being Novak's source. He cannot recall Scooter Libby telling him how he first learned about Valerie Wilson. It is possible Libby may have learned about Valerie Wilson's employment from the vice president after the vice president's phone call with George Tenet, but the vice president has no specific recollection of such a conversation. The vice president also cannot recall ever waving Libby off, at a certain point in time, when Libby offered to tell him everything he knew about the Wilson matter. The vice president has no recollection of Libby saying that he'd learned about Valerie Wilson from a reporter. . . . Moreover, Vice President Cheney does not have any recollection of Libby indicating that reporters with whom Libby was speaking about the Wilson matter ever informed him of Valerie Wilson's employment with the CIA."

Asked specifically about Judith Miller and Matt Cooper, Cheney said he wasn't aware of any meetings or conversations between Libby and Miller and said he didn't even know who Matt Cooper was.

So much for Libby's alibi, or at least any possibility that the vice president would support it.

Cheney answered their questions, but gave the impression that he disliked every minute of the interview and resented being there. He finally said he was pressed for time, and the agents wrapped up their questions. They offered him the standard waiver releasing any reporters from promises of confidentiality. Although Cheney said he'd never spoken to reporters other than in some TV appearances, he declined to sign it until his lawyers had reviewed it. Fitzgerald asked him not to discuss the interview so as not to influence other witnesses' recollections, and his lawyer said they understood the request.

Fitzgerald and the investigators were understandably frustrated by Cheney's performance. It was extraordinary that Cheney purported to remember almost nothing of relevance to the investigation, especially anything that had to do with Libby. The closest he would come was that something was "possible" or that he "wouldn't be surprised." What was that supposed to mean? That it had happened? Cheney thought it was possible he had dictated a statement to Libby on the flight back from Norfolk. In fact, he had done so, and they had Libby's notes to prove it. But this was still only a possibility. Nor would Cheney say something didn't happen. He had "no recollection" that Libby told him he had heard about Wilson's wife from other reporters. Did that mean it didn't happen? And Cheney's claim that Wilson's wife was "no big deal" was hard to swallow given the vice president's own handwriting on the Wilson op-ed clip.

His testimony was a masterpiece of defensive maneuvering. Cheney had added almost nothing to the investigation, which may have been his intent. He had certainly said nothing to incriminate himself. Also, unlike Libby, he had said virtually nothing that could be disproved or contradicted. His lack of memory may have strained credulity, but he didn't fabricate evidence, so far as they could tell. Cheney may have been wrong about Iraq's weapons of mass destruction. But details aside, his overarching story—that he was wronged by Wilson's allegations, was unfairly tarred with concealing important intelligence, and had misled the American people—was consistent with everything else they'd heard.

Fitzgerald had been cautious about approaching the president for an interview, saving this task until all other White House officials had been interviewed. The history of investigations that touched upon the Oval Office had been fraught with conflict and constitutional issues over executive privilege, a doctrine that Bush had jealously guarded, and an issue that the Supreme Court had ruled "should be avoided whenever possible." But from the outset, the president had championed the leak investigation, ordering all White House employees to cooperate and making clear that those who didn't would be fired. He had readily agreed to an interview with Fitzgerald and the FBI agents.

The investigators arrived at the White House on June 24, where they met the president in the Oval Office. In contrast to Cheney, Bush seemed very affable and relaxed. James Sharp, a well-known Washington criminal defense lawyer, represented him rather than counsel to the president Alberto Gonzales, who was a potential witness. Sharp's presence reflected an abundance of caution; Bush wasn't a subject or target, and he quickly established that he had no role in leaking Plame's identity or suggesting that anyone else do it. In contrast to Cheney and Rove, he had paid scant attention to the Wilson op-ed piece and didn't remember any conversation about Wilson's wife until the Novak column and subsequent speculation about who had leaked her identity. He was annoyed by the breach of confidence and wanted to get to the bottom of it.

Had the president discussed the leak with any members of his administration? Fitzgerald asked.

Bush said that Gonzales had told him not to, but that with speculation swirling about Karl Rove, he'd picked up the phone and called Rove. He'd asked if Rove had "any involvement" in the disclosure of Plame's identity.

What was Rove's answer?

The president said Rove had acknowledged speaking to Novak, but said the topic of their conversation "had nothing to do with Valerie Plame"; the subject of Wilson's wife "had never come up." Bush said he'd asked Rove directly if he was a source for Novak's column, and Rove denied that he was. The president said he took him at his word. He characterized Rove as a "dear friend," someone he'd known for years, but said he "wouldn't tolerate these kinds of leaks even if it was his good friend." There would be "consequences," and he'd dismiss him. But "if Rove said he didn't do it, then he didn't do it. If he was involved, he'd tell me. I trust him."

It was an awkward moment, since Fitzgerald and the agents already knew that Rove had discussed Plame with Novak, and had acknowledged confirming her identity. Rove had also given an entirely different description of this conversation to the FBI, saying he'd told Novak, "I've heard that too," and had reported that to the president. But no one said anything.

The interview lasted just over an hour, and the president made no effort to cut it short, answering all their questions. He knew nothing about any involvement by Libby and wasn't involved in McClellan's statement exonerating him. As with others questioned, Eckenrode handed the president a waiver releasing any journalists from any promises of confidentiality. "Sure, I'll sign that," Bush said immediately, taking the paper. He read it quickly, then signed with a flourish despite Sharp's efforts to intervene.

When they discussed the interview, the investigators were struck by the president's recollection of his conversation with Rove. Bush did not corroborate Rove's recollection of the exchange; indeed, he contradicted it. Rove had told the president the subject of Wilson's wife hadn't even come up in his discussion with Novak. If Bush was correct—and he had no reason to lie about it—his trusted political adviser and "dear friend" had lied to his commander in chief. Was lying to the president of the United States a false statement punishable under Section 1001 of the criminal code?

SIX

"Double Super Secret Background"

F itzgerald had never wanted a showdown with the press, even while recognizing that one might be inevitable. Justice Department guidelines state that "the prosecutorial power of the government should not be used in such a way that it impairs a reporter's responsibility to cover as broadly as possible controversial public issues" and that "the approach in every case must be to strike the proper balance between the public's interest in the free dissemination of ideas and information and the public's interest in effective law enforcement and the fair administration of justice." Here the two were on a collision course, with reporters arguing that testifying would impair their ability to obtain information from confidential sources, while at the same time, only their testimony could establish the guilt—or innocence—of Libby and Rove.

In this regard, testimony from Russert, Cooper, and Miller was essential. Russert was the pivotal figure in Libby's alibi and had already contradicted it. Cooper had written that he'd learned Plame's identity from several administration officials and could confirm or contradict Libby's and Rove's versions of their accounts. Miller could do the same for Libby's versions of their three conversations about the Wilson mission.

Justice Department guidelines also require prosecutors to negotiate with reporters and news organizations before issuing subpoenas, and Fitzgerald had had extensive conversations with the *New York Times* and Time Inc., both represented by renowned First Amendment specialist Floyd Abrams, and NBC, represented by Lee Levine. In both instances, Fitzgerald had argued that this was a uniquely weak case on which to stake an absolute privilege against testifying. Even if there had been a promise of confidentiality, both Libby and Rove had waived any privilege and expressly asked the reporters to testify. There was no coercion; they had been free to sign the waivers or not, with guidance of counsel, and the FBI didn't disclose who did or didn't sign them. They had also gone before the grand jury and testified that they had spoken to the reporters, voluntarily identifying themselves as sources. Finally—and perhaps of most importance—Rove and Libby were "sources" not in the sense that they were whistle-blowers exposing wrongdoing in government, but because they were attempting to discredit another source—Wilson—who arguably was a whistle-blower on the question of whether the administration misled the public on Iraq's weapons of mass destruction. Fitzgerald argued that protecting Libby and Rove would likely chill future whistle-blowers like Wilson, which wasn't in either the press's or the public's interest.

From the press point of view, their reporters had to varying degrees made promises of confidentiality, promises sacred to the news-gathering process. The promises had to be honored, no matter the identity of the sources or their motives for seeking anonymity. But such promises could be abrogated by the sources. Did the waivers absolve the reporters from honoring their commitments? In each case, and in contrast to the advice Hamilton had given Novak, they concluded they did not. The negotiations went nowhere.

Ordinarily the attorney general must explicitly approve any grand jury subpoenas to reporters, but since that authority had been vested in Fitzgerald, he made the decision. The grand jury issued subpoenas to Russert and Cooper on May 21, 2004. Both were narrowly drawn to limit their intrusion into the news-gathering process. Cooper's was restricted to his conversations with Libby and related documents. Nonetheless, lawyers for both NBC and Cooper tried to quash the subpoenas on First Amendment grounds, a move rejected by federal district court judge Thomas Hogan, who was overseeing the investigation. At that juncture, NBC's lawyers reached an agreement in which Russert would give a sworn deposition—but not appear before the grand jury—and testify about his conversation with Libby.

Russert was in a unique situation: Libby had called him to complain about Matthews, and although Russert subsequently maintained that he treated all such calls as confidential, he said they had no explicit agreement or understanding to that effect (even though Libby had claimed the call was "off-the-record").

It was hard to argue the call was off-the-record or confidential when Libby wanted Russert to use the information to take Matthews to task. Moreover, Libby wasn't telling Russert anything new; he was simply reiterating the standard administration position that the vice president's office hadn't sent Wilson to Africa. He hadn't imparted any new information, confidential or otherwise. Russert had also freely answered questions from the FBI without invoking any privilege.

Under the agreement with Fitzgerald, Russert gave a deposition on Saturday, August 7. It lasted just twenty-two minutes. On the critical issue of the phone call with Libby, he was even more emphatic than he'd been with Eckenrode.

"Did you have any understanding from anyone else that Mr. Wilson's wife worked at the CIA?" Fitzgerald asked. That is, did "all the reporters" know about her?

"No," Russert flatly replied.

On August 9, NBC News announced that Russert had been interviewed by Fitzgerald under oath and he had testified that he was not the recipient of a leak about the identity of Valerie Wilson, had not known about her identity until he read the Novak column, and had not said anything to Scooter Libby about her status.

NBC's summary of Russert's testimony didn't seem significant to anyone outside the investigation. Indeed, it was puzzling to the lawyers for other reporters. Libby and his lawyer, of course, were on notice that Russert had now contradicted him under oath.

Notwithstanding Libby's signing of a blanket waiver releasing all journalists from a promise of confidentiality, Matt Cooper felt he needed a "specific" waiver releasing him by name. He felt he needed to find out if the waiver had somehow been coerced, or if Libby was truly freeing him from any restrictions. Curiously, no one seems to have pressed Cooper on just what commitment to confidentiality he had made to Libby. After the on-the-record statement, Libby had shifted to "background," but background generally means that information can be used but not attributed to a source—not that a journalist will refuse to answer questions in a criminal investigation. Still, such ground rules were notoriously vague, and Cooper and his lawyers interpreted their conversation as requiring confidentiality.

On advice of *Time*'s counsel, Cooper spoke to Libby by phone on August 5, and Cooper told Libby that his recollection of their conversation was "basically exculpatory." Did Libby have any objections to Cooper testifying? Libby said he had "no objection" and suggested their respective lawyers discuss Cooper's testimony. Libby's lawyer, Tate, assured Abrams that Libby was releasing Cooper from any promise of confidentiality.

However sincere in their belief that Cooper would be helping Libby by testifying, Cooper and his legal advisers arguably had no basis for telling Libby that his testimony would be "basically exculpatory." True, Libby hadn't used Plame's name. But Libby had confirmed Wilson's wife's status, which was potentially incriminating. Moreover, Cooper wasn't privy to Libby's grand jury testimony, so he had no way of knowing if his version of the conversation corroborated Libby's. Given Libby's detailed version, in which he claimed to have told Cooper he'd only heard the information from other reporters and didn't know if it was true, Cooper's testimony was in fact damning.

Based on Tate's reassurance, Cooper agreed to answer questions related to Libby, but not about any of his other sources. The reporter met Fitzgerald at his lawyer's offices on Monday, August 23. Cooper confirmed that he spoke with Libby on July 12, and that Libby dictated the on-the-record statement. Then Libby suggested they speak "on background," and they had talked more generally about Wilson's trip and the uranium issue. Toward the end of the conversation, Cooper had asked Libby "What have you heard?" or "What do you know?" about Wilson's wife sending him to Niger. "I've heard that too," Libby had told him. Libby didn't say where he'd heard it.

As Fitzgerald later summarized Cooper's testimony, "Libby did not say he had heard the information from reporters," and he "neither vouched for the accuracy of the information nor expressed doubts." Nor did he say he didn't know Wilson had a wife. Unknown to Cooper, and contrary to his reassurance to Libby, he had flatly contradicted Libby's sworn account.

Cooper had indicated he had two other sources besides Libby, so Fitzgerald told Abrams he needed more testimony from Cooper as well as his notes. Cooper and his lawyers were disappointed, hoping that the Libby testimony would be the end of it. They knew that Cooper's testimony about Rove was potentially damaging. Should Cooper approach Rove for a specific waiver, as he had Libby?

At this juncture, Cooper, *Time*, and their lawyers decided it would be inappropriate to approach Rove on grounds that to do so would be inherently coercive. Given that they'd already done so with Libby, the logic of that decision is hardly self-evident. *Time*'s lawyers argued at the time that Cooper's Libby testimony was exculpatory, while the Rove testimony would be incriminating. But just as they had no basis for knowing if Cooper's testimony was exculpatory for Libby, they couldn't know if his testimony was incriminating for Rove. They weren't privy to Rove's prior testimony. Nonetheless, *Time* and Cooper dug in.

Having reached an impasse, on September 13 Fitzgerald issued another, broader subpoena calling for testimony and documents "between Matthew Cooper and official source(s)" related to "any affiliation between Valerie Plame Wilson and the CIA." Time Inc. was also subpoenaed for documents.

On August 12 and 14 the grand jury issued similar subpoenas to Judith Miller of the *New York Times* (but not the *Times* itself, which said it didn't have any relevant documents in its possession). With guidance from *Times* lawyers, Miller authorized Floyd Abrams to find out from Libby's lawyer, Tate, the circumstances of Libby's waiver and whether it was voluntary or coerced. As with Cooper, there seems to have been scant effort to determine from Miller what her actual promise to Libby had been. His request to be identified only as a "former Hill staffer" suggests a not-for-attribution arrangement, but not necessarily a promise of confidentiality if subpoenaed. But as with Cooper, that was Miller's interpretation of their arrangement. She felt he'd made it clear from their earliest contacts that Miller was never to identify him as a source.

The ensuing conversation between Tate and Abrams has been the subject of bitter disagreement. Tate's view is that he assured Abrams that the waiver was voluntary and encouraged Miller to testify. Abrams told him that Miller's refusal to do so was based on journalistic principles that had nothing to do with Libby. But in a subsequent letter to Tate, Abrams flatly denied that account:

> You did not say that Mr. Libby's written waiver was uncoerced. In fact,
> you said quite the opposite. You told me the signed waiver was by its
> nature, coerced, and had been required as a condition for Mr. Libby's
> continued employment at the White House. . . . You persuasively mocked
> the notion that any waiver signed under such circumstances could be
> deemed voluntary.

This seems odd, given that the same waiver had been deemed voluntary for purposes of Cooper's testimony. (Abrams didn't respond to requests for comment.)

In any event, Miller now knew that her testimony would be damaging to Libby, although she had no way of knowing how damaging. She would testify, as her notes indicated, that Libby had disclosed Wilson's wife's name and identity to her. She concluded that despite the language of the waiver and whatever double-talk Abrams had heard from his lawyer, Libby did not want her to testify. She would fight the subpoena, and the *Times* honored her decision.

Negotiations with Fitzgerald soon broke down. The standoff moved into the courts.

That same month, James Comey announced his resignation to join defense contractor Lockheed Martin as its general counsel. At a farewell dinner at a Thai restaurant, Fitzgerald asked him to step outside on the patio at the rear. True to his word, Comey hadn't interfered in any way with Fitzgerald's investigation, but Fitzgerald had given him periodic briefings. Comey was startled by the looming First Amendment showdown; he hadn't anticipated it, although perhaps he should have. He'd thought the case would be wrapped up in six months; it was going on two years.

"When are you no longer Deputy AG?" Fitzgerald asked.

"Midnight," Comey said.

"Then this will be our last conversation [about the leak case]," Fitzgerald said.

Fitzgerald outlined the case against Armitage: He had by his own admission identified Valerie Wilson as a CIA agent to Novak. He claimed not to know she was covert or even how he knew the information, but he had read the classified INR report identifying her, which was almost certainly his source. What did Comey think?

It was a tough call. Armitage had surely violated the spirit of the protected identities act. But the letter of that law set a very high bar: knowledge of covert status and that the CIA was concealing her identity. Could that knowledge be proved beyond a reasonable doubt? Since there had never been a prosecution under the act, the standards were uncertain. And while Armitage may have been evasive in the details of his testimony, attempting to minimize his role, he had truthfully admitted telling Novak. Comey concluded that Armitage should not be charged, although subsequent developments could always change that.

Rove had already spent two days testifying before the grand jury in February, an experience that left him, he later recalled, "mentally beaten to a pulp." He'd largely repeated his earlier account to Eckenrode, and described the phone call from Novak and their subsequent conversations, as well as his conversation with the president. Fitzgerald had also asked if Rove had spoken to *Time*'s Matt Cooper; Rove said he didn't recall talking to him.

That fall, Rove was again subpoenaed to the grand jury, and this time Fitzgerald told his lawyer that his status had changed. Rove was now a "subject." After his last appearance, the White House had produced more e-mails and other documents related to Rove. Luskin was sitting on the floor of his office sifting through three or four boxes of records, trying to immerse himself in Rove's correspondence, when he came across an e-mail dated July 11, 2003, to Stephen Hadley:

> Matt Cooper called to give me a heads-up that he's got a welfare reform
> story coming. When he finished his brief heads-up, he immediately
> launched into Niger/isn't this damaging/hasn't the president been hurt? I
> didn't take the bait but said, if I were him, I wouldn't get TIME far out in
> front on this.

This clearly meant that Rove had talked to Cooper at a critical time in the Wilson controversy—something Rove hadn't recalled in his earlier testimony. It was, Luskin later recalled, a "holy shit moment."

Rove testified again on October 15, and at the outset said he wanted to "correct the record." He said he still didn't recall speaking to Matt Cooper, but had discovered the e-mail indicating he had. Rove later wrote, "It was as if I'd detonated a bomb in the shabby little room." Fitzgerald was evidently unaware of the e-mail (though it had been produced by the White House along with all Rove's e-mails). The lawyers convened in the hallway, out of hearing of the grand jurors, and Fitzgerald seemed so upset that he was "quivering," Luskin later said. But Rove still recalled nothing about his conversation with Cooper, other than the reference in the e-mail to welfare reform.

Given the timing of Rove's conversation with Cooper—July 11, the day before he spoke with Libby and already knew about Wilson's wife—it seemed likely that Rove was one of Cooper's other sources, even though Rove claimed not to remember saying anything about Wilson's wife. This made Cooper's testimony even more important.

On February 15, 2005, the U.S. Court of Appeals for the District of

Columbia Circuit upheld the subpoenas and contempt citations against Cooper and Miller in a sweeping victory for Fitzgerald. In many ways the opinion illustrated the gulf that had developed between many members of the press and their lawyers, with their inflated sense of their special legal status and privileges, and the judiciary, the Justice Department, legislators—just about everyone else. The media chorus egging on Cooper and Miller seemed to take an absolute position—that no one, not even a grand jury investigating a crime, could order a reporter to testify if to do so would violate a promise of confidentiality.

But did that absolutist stand really make any sense? Did a promise of "not for attribution" or "background" without being more explicit mean that reporters would defy court orders and engage in civil disobedience? Even if such agreements were deemed contracts, the law offers no protection, since contracts contrary to public policy, and specifically those that "pervert or obstruct justice," are void and unenforceable. Otherwise every Mafia pledge of silence would stand in the way of testifying.

Reporters, of course, represent a higher, and to them, even sacred cause: the First Amendment. But even free speech has been subjected to many exceptions deemed in the public interest. (Perjury itself is, of course, a restriction on free speech.)

The appeals court judge most sympathetic to the press, Judge David S. Tatel, made short shrift of that argument: "Protection for source identities cannot be absolute. Leaks similar to the crime suspected here (exposure of a covert agent) apparently caused the deaths of several CIA operatives in the late 1970s and early 1980s, including the agency's Athens station chief. Other leaks—the design for a top secret nuclear weapon, for example, or plans for an imminent military strike—could be even more damaging, causing harm far in excess of their news value. In such cases, the reporter privilege must give way." The *Times* itself conceded such a privilege could not be absolute.

The issue that consumed the reporters themselves—whether the waivers were voluntary—was deemed irrelevant by all three judges. Two didn't even address the issue, because they flatly rejected any reporters' privilege. Judge Tatel wrote that to the extent a common-law privilege might exist, "only reporters, not sources, may waive the privilege," explaining that "because the government could demand waivers—perhaps even before any leak occurs—as a condition of employment, a privilege subject to waiver may, again, amount to no privilege at all, even in those leak cases where protecting the confidential source is most compelling. . . . The reporter privilege safeguards public dissemination of information—the reporter's enterprise, not the source's."

Tatel wrote a concurring opinion, so it may have little standing as precedent. Still, it outlines an approach that is probably as favorable to the press as any press advocate could reasonably hope for. By this logic, Cooper and Miller were free to waive the privilege, much as Novak had determined that it made no sense to protect his sources once they had identified themselves and Fitzgerald knew who they were. But if the reporters decided they could not waive the privilege, they (and their lawyers) then had to weigh the news value of the disclosure (in this case that Wilson's wife was a CIA agent) against the importance of law enforcement. As Judge Tatel wrote:

> The question in this case is whether Miller's and Cooper's sources released information more harmful than newsworthy. If so, then the public interest in punishing the wrongdoers—and deterring future leaks—outweighs any burden on news gathering, and no privilege covers the communication. . . .

The *New York Times* and *Time* didn't focus on the importance of the information whose source they were seeking to protect. Had they done so, the answer surely would have been: not very. The *Times* never ran a story. *Time* ran it on its website, after Novak had already identified Plame. "The law can't distinguish between good leaks and bad," Floyd Abrams had told the *New York Observer*. But that's exactly what Judge Tatel said the press itself must do. Instead the *Times* and its lawyers saw the issue strictly as a question of a reporter's promise. As *Times* executive editor Bill Keller told the *Washington Post*, "The simple fact is that Judy made a promise to a source that she would protect his anonymity. . . . She feels that, if she breaks that pledge, she will compromise her ability to do her job in the future."

Miller, Cooper, and Time Inc. appealed to the Supreme Court, which on June 27 declined to hear the case. Judge Hogan later said that not a single justice wanted to reconsider the ruling. Their appeals exhausted, the question now for both news organizations was whether their reporters would defy the ruling and engage in civil disobedience, punishable by jail. Time Inc. faced the prospect of a $1,000-a-day fine. (Since the *New York Times* itself didn't receive a subpoena, it wasn't a defendant.)

Time Inc. editor in chief Norman Pearlstine called the decision "the most difficult I have made in thirty-six years in the news business." He replaced Floyd

Abrams, whose legal advice had brought the company to this juncture, and on June 30, Time announced that it would comply with the subpoena. "The same Constitution that protects the freedom of the press requires obedience to final decisions of the courts and respect for their rulings and judgments," Time said. "That Time Inc. strongly disagrees with the courts provides no immunity. The innumerable Supreme Court decisions in which even presidents have followed orders with which they strongly disagreed evidences that our nation lives by the rule of law and that none of us is above it."

Pearlstine was excoriated by many in the media. The *San Diego Union-Tribune* ran a mock cover of *Time* magazine, with Pearlstine on the cover and the headline "Wimp of the Year." Cooper himself said he disagreed with the decision. The *Times* said it was "deeply disappointed" by Time Inc.'s decision and took the opposite stand.

Judy Miller appeared in court on July 6, and told Judge Hogan that she would not comply. "If journalists cannot be trusted to guarantee confidentiality, then journalists cannot function and there cannot be a free press," she said.

"I have a person in front of me who is defying the law," Judge Hogan said. He ordered her held in a "suitable jail" until she agreed to testify. Miller was taken to the Alexandria Detention Center, across the Potomac.

At the same hearing, Cooper announced that he had reached an agreement to testify. That morning he'd told his son good-bye, expecting to go to jail. Then, "a short time ago," he told the court, "in what can only be described as a stunning set of developments, that person agreed to give me a personal, unambiguous, uncoerced waiver that I could speak to the grand jury." Judge Hogan said Cooper could remain free but he would leave the contempt citation in place until Cooper had testified.

Cooper didn't name his source, but of course it was Karl Rove, who was instantly deluged with calls from the press amid renewed speculation that he was the source of the Plame leak. Rove was furious, and later called Cooper's statement to the court a "bald-faced lie." He insisted there was no new waiver; Rove's lawyer had merely confirmed that the existing waiver dating from January 2004 applied to Cooper–"what anyone with a basic understanding of the English language would have known from reading the blanket waiver," as Rove scathingly put it. In Rove's view, Cooper "needed cover" for abandoning his supposedly principled defense of source confidentiality.

Cooper, however, maintains that this was the first time anyone representing

him or Time had approached Rove to clarify that the waiver was voluntary, and
this was the dramatic development to which he truthfully referred. In any case,
the real source of Rove's anger may have been Cooper's decision to testify at all,
given what Cooper was likely to say.

The spectacle of a *New York Times* reporter being thrown in jail for refusing
to testify swamped the actual investigation into the Plame leak. The Miller
story was front-page news across the country, led the network broadcasts, and
dominated cable news and radio talk shows. It was the subject of the *New York
Times*'s lead editorial, "Reporter Jailed":

> This is a proud but awful moment for *The New York Times* and its employ-
> ees. One of our reporters, Judith Miller, has decided to accept a jail sen-
> tence rather than testify before a grand jury about one of her confidential
> sources. . . . We wish she did not have to make this choice, but we are
> certain she did the right thing.
>
> She is surrendering her liberty in defense of a greater liberty, granted
> to a free press by the founding fathers so journalists can work on behalf
> of the public without fear of regulation or retaliation from any branch of
> government.

It was an eloquent testimonial to the press, but on what basis was the *Times*
"certain" that Miller was doing the right thing? The *Times* ignored the reasons
that three federal courts, including the Supreme Court, had rejected Miller's
arguments: Miller was invoking a reporter's privilege to protect someone who
may have violated the protected identities act and may have committed perjury.
Libby wasn't a whistle-blower, risking a career to report government misconduct. Miller's testimony could establish whether he was a criminal—or an innocent bystander to the Plame affair.

None of this was a secret to the judges involved in deciding the case. Nor
would it have been a secret to the *Times* had its top officials asked to see Miller's
notes or asked her directly if anyone had leaked Plame's identity to her. But
they didn't. As Fitzgerald argued in his affidavit to the court:

> To deprive the grand jury of the ability to hear and assess Miller's account
> of what Libby told her is to ask the Special Counsel and the grand jury to

make a decision on prosecution partly in the blind—where it is unknown whether the information will be inculpatory or exculpatory. The possible consequences of a mistake—either the failure to charge what would otherwise be determined to involve a crime carried out to discredit a source who was a whistle-blower or, worse, charging a confidential source in good faith with a crime where the claim of "reporter's privilege" deprived the investigation of exculpatory information—could do far more to undermine both First Amendment interests and the fair administration of justice than could enforcement of the subpoenas.

That Friday, *Time* had handed over a critical e-mail from Cooper to his editors at *Time*, dated July 11, 2003, 11:07 a.m.:

> Spoke to rove on double super secret background for about two mins before he went on vacation . . . his big warning . . . don't get too far out on Wilson . . . says that DCIA didn't authorize the trip. It was, KR said, wilson's wife, who apparently works at the agency on wmd issues, who authorized the trip. Not only the genesis of the trip is flawed ans [*sic*] suspect but so is the report. He implied strongly there's still plenty to implicate Iraqi interest in acquiring uranium from Niger. . . . some of this is going to be declassified in the coming days, KR said. Don't get too far out in front, he warned. Then he bolted . . . will include in next file . . . please don't source to rove or even WH but have TB check out with Harlow.

To the investigators, this suggested a much more significant conversation than the one Rove had belatedly told them about, and made even more suspect Rove's failure to remember anything about the substance of the conversation. Rove had clearly identified Wilson's wife to a reporter and discussed a still-classified report.

Cooper spent two and a half hours before the grand jury on July 13. Most of the time was spent elaborating on his e-mail and notes of his conversation with Rove. He'd called the White House switchboard and was transferred to Rove's office, then Rove himself got on the phone. "I'm writing about Wilson," Cooper recalled saying. Rove had interrupted, saying, "Don't get too far out on Wilson."

On "deep background," Rove had told him what was reflected in the e-mail, mentioning that Wilson's wife worked at the "agency" on "wmd," but that he didn't use her name or indicate she was covert. This was the first time Cooper had heard anything about Wilson's wife. As for his reference to "double super secret," he explained it as a playful reference to "double secret probation," the penalty imposed on the wayward Delta House fraternity in the film *Animal House*.

Fitzgerald asked if Cooper had asked Rove about "welfare reform," a question that puzzled him. Not that he recalled, he said. About two months later, Cooper did write a short story about welfare reform, and Fitzgerald asked him about it. Cooper speculated he might have left a message for Rove saying he wanted to discuss that topic, but he didn't believe they did. One thing he did clearly remember, though it wasn't in his notes: Rove ended their conversation by saying, "I've already said too much."

Miller might have taken a courageous stand for press freedom by going to jail, but the reality was far less heroic or dramatic. She shared a small, two-person cell in a crowded wing that housed twenty-four women. She worked in the laundry. She considered the food inedible and lost twenty pounds. She received a stream of high-profile visitors, including NBC anchor Tom Brokaw, but had no Internet access. Each day she eagerly searched newspapers for articles about herself. She was disappointed. Although the *Times* kept up a steady stream of editorials—about one every two weeks—her cause was inexorably fading from public view, and with it any public pressure on Fitzgerald to release her.

From Fitzgerald's point of view, he was sympathetic to Miller's circumstances, but argued that she held the keys to her release. He couldn't understand why the *Times* hadn't been more rational in reaching an accommodation with him, as other news organizations had. He felt bad that Miller was in jail, but, as he put it, "If you feel bad, and just walk away, then what?" To do so would render a court order upheld by the Supreme Court meaningless—and with it the rule of law.

Even before she went to jail, Miller had added legendary Washington defense lawyer Robert Bennett to her team; Bennett had navigated President Clinton through the Starr investigation and Lewinsky scandal. Bennett urged

Miller to approach Libby to clarify the nature of his waiver. After two months in jail, Miller decided she "owed it to myself" to allow Bennett to contact Tate, Libby's lawyer, which he did on August 31. On September 12, Fitzgerald also wrote Tate, saying that a misunderstanding over Libby's waiver might be the cause of Miller's refusal to testify.

Soon after, Bennett received a personal letter from Libby to Miller:

Dear Judy,

Your reporting, and you, are missed. Like many Americans, I admire your principled stand. But, like many of your friends and readers, I would welcome you back among the rest of us, doing what you do best— reporting.

Libby professed surprise that Miller might have thought his waiver was coerced, noting that his lawyer had called lawyers for every reporter he'd spoken to in July 2003 and assured them that "my waiver was voluntary" and that Miller's lawyer had assured him that her refusal to testify was based on principles "unrelated to us."

I would like to dispel any remaining concerns you may have that circumstances forced this waiver upon me. . . . Why? Because, as I'm sure will not be news to you, the public report of every other reporter's testimony makes clear that they did not discuss Ms. Plame's name or identity with me, or knew about her before our call. I waived the privilege voluntarily to cooperate with the grand jury. But also because the reporters' testimony served my interests. I believed a year ago, as I do now, that testimony by all will benefit all.

I admire your principled fight with the government. But for my part, this is the rare case where this "source" would be better off if you testified. That's one reason why I waived over a year ago, and in large measure, why I write again today. Consider this the Miller corollary: "It's okay to testify about a privileged communication, when the person you seek to protect has waived the privilege and would be better off if you testify." If you can find a way to testify about discussions we had, if any, that relate to the Wilson-Plame matter, I remain today just as interested as I was over a year ago.

You went into jail in the summer. It is fall now. You will have stories
to cover—Iraqi elections and suicide bombers, biological threats and the
Iranian nuclear program. Out west, where you vacation, the aspens will
already be turning. They turn in clusters, because their roots connect
them. Come back to work—and life.

It was a strangely eloquent, almost elegiac plea, perhaps drawing upon
the novelist in Libby. For he must have known that Miller's testimony would
uniquely implicate him as leaking Plame's identity and shatter his Russert alibi,
already discredited by Russert himself. Libby would not be "better off" if Miller
testified. So what was Libby really saying? That he wanted Miller to say that
they hadn't discussed Plame, consistent with his reference to other reporters'
testimony? And what was the meaning—or relevance—of the aspens' roots being
interconnected?

In an accompanying letter to Fitzgerald, Tate expressed some exasperation
that Miller had suggested Libby didn't want her to testify. "We encouraged her
to testify—over a year ago—believing that her testimony, when added to those
of other reporters who have testified, will benefit my client." Bennett, too, said
that in their conversations Tate "could not have been clearer" that Miller was
free to testify—in stark contrast to the ambiguous reaction Abrams had reported.
Even then, Miller said she wanted to hear Libby's voice. They had a conference
call on September 19, with her lawyers and Libby's listening.

The call lasted ten minutes. Miller subsequently told the *Times* that Libby
said how unhappy he was that she was in jail because of him, and that he'd
assumed there were other people she was protecting. She had "pushed him
hard," asking, "Do you really want me to testify? Are you sure you really want
me to testify?" He'd replied, "Absolutely. Believe it. I mean it." In his tone she
heard "genuine concern and sorrow" that she was in jail. All of her lawyers,
including Abrams, now agreed that the waiver was voluntary.

On September 29, after eighty-five days in jail, Miller was released. *Times*
publisher Arthur Sulzberger Jr. and executive editor Keller took her to the Ritz-
Carlton hotel in Georgetown for a massage and manicure followed by a martini
and steak dinner. The next day she spent three hours before the grand jury.
Fitzgerald agreed to restrict his questions to her conversations with Libby.

When Miller finally testified, she described how she'd come to know Libby,
mentioning his interest in her book *Germs*. She described their meeting at the

St. Regis, observing that Libby seemed "agitated" by Wilson's op-ed piece, which had just run that Sunday. Libby had given a detailed account of his version of the Wilson saga, and mentioned that Wilson's wife worked at "the agency." She had made a note that she worked at WINPAC. Miller thought this was the first time she'd heard anything about Wilson's wife, although she had a "vague" recollection she might have heard it before this. Libby hadn't used her name. Miller also described the July 12 phone call, although her memory was hazy. They had again discussed Wilson's wife in passing, although by then Miller thought she had discussed Wilson's wife with others as well, though she couldn't remember whom. She remembered telling Libby that she didn't think she'd be writing a story about Wilson's wife and the *Times* didn't seem interested. Fitzgerald asked if she could pinpoint the date of that conversation, and she said she wasn't sure, but she'd check her notes, which were still in New York. She said Libby had never suggested Vice President Cheney knew about their conversations and never indicated he thought the information about Wilson's wife was classified.

Fitzgerald asked for Miller's reaction to the Novak story, and she said she was "annoyed" that Novak broke the story. She said she'd proposed a story, but her editor, evidently distracted by the replacement of former executive editor Howell Raines by Keller, hadn't seemed interested. He also read the letter from Libby, and she conceded that the reference to other reporters' testimony might be interpreted as an attempt to get her to say they hadn't discussed Wilson's wife. As for the cryptic reference to the "aspens," Miller explained that she had attended a national security meeting in Aspen, then visited Jackson Hole, Wyoming. At a rodeo a man in a cowboy hat and sunglasses had approached her and asked about the conference. Miller didn't recognize him. "Judy, it's Scooter Libby," he'd said. Beyond that, she didn't know what he was trying to say.

Miller's testimony was another blow to Libby's alibi, contradicting his claim that he hadn't discussed Wilson's wife with Miller at their July 8 meeting and that he was unaware of Plame's identity until he learned it from Russert.

Miller returned to New York that evening and went to her office. Her notebooks from June and July were in a shopping bag under her desk; she went through them looking for notes of her July conversation, and found nothing. But then she looked in the June notebook, and there were pages of notes from a June 23 interview with Libby—something she hadn't mentioned to the grand jury. Among them was the notation "(wife works in bureau)?" The notes reminded her that she and Libby had met on the twenty-third and discussed the

Wilson affair, something she'd completely forgotten. She immediately called Bennett, who got the notebooks and turned them over to Fitzgerald.

Miller returned to the grand jury on October 12 to describe the June 23 interview. Seeing the notes had jogged her memory, and she now recalled their discussion in some detail. Libby had been "agitated" and "frustrated" about the Wilson mission and how it was being interpreted. Libby said Wilson's wife worked in the bureau, which Miller put in parentheses because it seemed an aside. The question mark probably indicated Miller was initially puzzled by the reference; she later realized the bureau meant the CIA. Miller had also written "Valerie Flame," "V.F." "Valery" and "Victoria Wilson" in the notebook, but she didn't think Libby had mentioned the name, and the notations may have come from other sources she couldn't remember.

"When you heard that," Fitzgerald asked, referring to Libby's mention of Wilson's wife working at the CIA, "was that the first time you associated Mr. Wilson's wife with the bureau at the CIA?"

"I don't remember if that was absolutely the first time, but it was among the first times I had ever heard that. I don't—I can't recall for sure."

But there were no notes from anyone else mentioning Wilson's wife prior to the Libby interview. "Is it fair to say that as you sit here today, you have no specific recollection of talking to any specific government official other than Mr. Libby about Wilson's wife working at the CIA during that time frame?"

"That is correct."

Miller officially returned to work at the *Times* on October 3, 2005. She made a speech hailing her incarceration and release from prison as a victory for press freedom, a claim greeted by polite but skeptical applause from her colleagues. As editor-at-large Jack Shafer wrote in *Slate*, "The real winner for anybody with eyes to read a newspaper is Patrick Fitzgerald."

SEVEN

"A Cloud over the White House"

O ver the next six weeks, Fitzgerald met frequently with the FBI agents and lawyers working on the case, reviewing the evidence and taking frequent polls on who, if anyone, should be charged with a crime. By now the targets had been narrowed to Armitage, Rove, and Libby. The FBI agents were unanimous that Armitage should be charged with violating something—if not the Intelligence Identities Protection Act, then for making false statements or mishandling classified information. Armitage knew or should have known that Plame's identity was classified—he read it in the confidential INR report, plainly marked "secret." But the lawyers disagreed. Armitage had insisted he never knew Plame was covert. The INR report might have been classified, but not everything contained in a classified report is a secret. Armitage maintained that in all his years of government service the name of a covert agent had never appeared in a written report, classified or otherwise. The statute was strict about knowledge of covert status, and it would be difficult, if not impossible, to prove guilt beyond a reasonable doubt.

Beyond that, there were significant practical obstacles making any prosecution under the statute difficult. The lawyers would have to prove that Plame was a covert agent. They'd have to delve into her top-secret work for the agency. Defense lawyers would need access to her employment records. All of this was classified information that might not be allowed in court. As one lawyer involved put it, "This is a lawyer's nightmare. It's like trying for a seventy-yard field goal with goalposts three feet wide."

The agents were also unanimous that Rove should be charged with false statements, and Fitzgerald seemed to agree. Rove denied being a source for Novak, saying only that he'd "heard" about Wilson's wife; he didn't say anything about speaking to Cooper until an e-mail forced his admission. The president himself flatly contradicted Rove's testimony about his conversation with the president. The investigators believed that Rove had lied to the president about his conversation with Novak. Fitzgerald gave Rove's lawyer, Robert Luskin, every indication that he was on the brink of asking the grand jury to indict Rove.

Luskin flew to Chicago and met with Fitzgerald for five hours, breaking only for a quick trip to a nearby Dunkin' Donuts. According to Luskin, Fitzgerald focused on the discrepancies between Rove's testimony and the accounts of others, including the president's version of the phone call in which he asked Rove point-blank if he had had any involvement in the Novak leak and had said Rove denied it. Luskin argued that Rove had never hidden the fact that Wilson's wife had come up in the discussion from others in the White House, so why would he lie to the president? Perhaps Rove's memory was better than Bush's.

But what seemed to have most troubled Fitzgerald was the belated discovery of the Cooper e-mail and Rove's prior insistence that he didn't remember any such conversation with the *Time* reporter. How could that be true if in January—months before the e-mail surfaced—Rove had asked his staff to scour their files for any e-mail contacts with Cooper? It was true Rove had made such a request, but Luskin explained it was at *his* behest, not because Rove himself had any memory of such a contact. Moreover, why would Rove volunteer at his first interview with the FBI that he'd discussed Valerie Wilson with Novak but conceal the disclosure to Matt Cooper? It didn't make any sense, Luskin maintained.

More broadly, Luskin argued that the alleged discrepancies in Rove's testimony didn't add up to any coherent narrative—in pointed contrast to Libby, whose story conveniently "wrote Cheney out of the narrative," as Luskin put it.

Fitzgerald and Eckenrode questioned Rove again on October 25. Fitzgerald told him then that he wouldn't be indicted that week. Still, as Rove later said, "I had become paranoid and didn't feel safe from the prosecutor's reach." Fitzgerald struggled to find proof that Rove had lied. The night before the grand jury term was to expire, and final decisions had to be made, Fitzgerald made a last call to Adam Levine, the former White House communications adviser, who was in Eden Prairie, Minnesota. Fitzgerald had found an e-mail indicating Rove had met with Levine just after his conversation with *Time* reporter Matt Cooper.

Did Levine remember their meeting? Had Rove mentioned Cooper's call? Was it important to Rove?

If Rove had mentioned it, Levine didn't remember it. Levine was getting ready to leave the White House at the time, and all he remembered was that he and Rove had talked about his future.

With Libby, the evidence of false statements and perjury seemed overwhelming. Focusing only on those charges, and not the protected identities act, rendered Plame's actual status irrelevant, sidestepping all the national security issues. Plame wouldn't even have to be a witness. Still, the discussions about whether to seek charges from the grand jury were extensive, focusing primarily on the fact that Libby had not leaked to Novak. The investigators knew they would be criticized for failing to indict anyone for the crime that had launched the investigation. And, like the Martha Stewart prosecutors, they'd be faulted for pursuing crimes like perjury and false statements that are supposedly rarely prosecuted. But Fitzgerald had his assistant, Randall Samborn, research the issue for the Northern District of Illinois since 2001, when Fitzgerald had become U.S. Attorney. Samborn found 31 cases of perjury and 153 of false statements. Not only was lying being prosecuted, it was nearly an epidemic.

The evidence from Ari Fleischer sealed Libby's fate. No one believed Libby could have remembered talking about the Miami Dolphins but not Wilson's wife. The lies were brazen; Libby had been reckless. The vote was unanimous—among agents and prosecutors alike—to seek an indictment.

In the end, Fitzgerald did what he thought was right, not what was politically expedient. He knew he'd be criticized no matter what he did. As he told his staff, "It's damned if we do, damned if we don't." It would have been easy to do nothing. But when the president said he wanted to get to the bottom of the matter, Fitzgerald took him at his word. Before any public announcement, he drafted a cover letter to President Bush. Attached were two memos: one summarizing the evidence against Rove, the other against Armitage. (Based on what is now known publicly, presumably these summaries focused on the admissions by both officials that they had leaked Valerie Wilson's identity, and, in Rove's case, his apparent failure to reveal his involvement when asked by the president.) Fitzgerald invoked a rarely used exception to grand jury secrecy, which permits disclosure in cases involving national security. To Fitzgerald, the fact that Bush still employed two people who had apparently divulged the identity of a covert CIA agent was an issue of national security. The message was implicit: Rove and Armitage wouldn't be indicted, but the president could still do the right thing and ask for their resignations.

Fitzgerald hand-delivered the letter to Bush's personal lawyer, Jim Sharp. "How's your client?" Fitzgerald asked. Sharp never used Bush's name, referring to him only as "my client." "My client could use a new staff," Sharp replied. He said he'd get the letter to Bush.

On October 28, 2005, just over two years after the investigation had begun, Fitzgerald stepped to the podium in a Justice Department auditorium, the great seal of justice prominent behind him. He announced that Libby had been indicted by the grand jury for obstruction, perjury, and false statements. Though there were five counts, they were based on two essential falsehoods, repeated by Libby numerous times both to FBI agents and to the grand jury: that he learned Plame's identity from Tim Russert (and had forgotten hearing about her from the vice president); and that he hadn't leaked or confirmed her identity to reporters, saying only that he'd heard such information from other reporters and didn't know if it was true.

A reporter asked:

"Mr. Fitzgerald, the Republicans previewed some talking points in anticipation of your indictment and they said that if you didn't indict on the underlying crimes and you indicted on things exactly like you did indict—false statements, perjury, obstruction—these were, quote/unquote, 'technicalities' and that it really was overreaching and excessive.

"And since, when and if they make those claims, now that you have indicted, you won't respond, I want to give you an opportunity now to respond to that allegation which they may make. It seems like that's the road they're going down. . . ."

Fitzgerald replied:

"I'll be blunt. That talking point won't fly. If you're doing a national security investigation, if you're trying to find out who compromised the identity of a CIA officer and you go before a grand jury and if the charges are proven—because remember there's a presumption of innocence—but if it is proven that the chief of staff to the vice president went before a federal grand jury and lied under oath repeatedly and fabricated a story about how he learned this information, how he passed it on, and we prove obstruction of justice, perjury, and false statements to the FBI, that is a very, very serious matter.

"And I'd say this: I think people might not understand this. We, as prosecutors and FBI agents, have to deal with false statements, obstruction of justice, and perjury all the time. The Department of Justice charges those statutes all the time.

"When I was in New York working as a prosecutor, we brought those cases because we realized that the truth is the engine of our judicial system. And if you compromise the truth, the whole process is lost.

"When I got to Chicago, I knew the people before me had prosecuted false statements, obstruction and perjury cases.

"And we do it all the time. And if a truck driver pays a bribe or someone else does something where they go into a grand jury afterward and lie about it, they get indicted all the time.

"Any notion that anyone might have that there's a different standard for a high official, that this is somehow singling out obstruction of justice and perjury, is upside down.

"If these facts are true, if we were to walk away from this and not charge obstruction of justice and perjury, we might as well just hand in our jobs. Because our jobs, the criminal justice system, is to make sure people tell us the truth. And when it's a high-level official and a very sensitive investigation, it is a very, very serious matter that no one should take lightly."

Libby resigned his White House posts immediately. Through his lawyer, Joseph Tate, he said, "I am confident that at the end of this process, I will be completely and totally exonerated." He moved swiftly to expand his defense team, hiring prominent criminal defense lawyers Ted Wells and William Jeffress. President Bush and Vice President Cheney both praised Libby's public service, expressed sadness over his resignation, and cited the presumption of innocence to which he was entitled. Cheney called Libby "one of the most capable and talented individuals I have ever known."

Libby was formally arraigned on November 3. He appeared in court on crutches due to a foot injury, and entered a plea of not guilty.

Several prominent Republicans helped organize a defense fund, the Scooter Libby Legal Defense Trust, to raise $5 million. Members of the steering committee included Senators Fred Thompson of Tennessee (who played a prosecutor on *Law & Order*), Alan Simpson of Wyoming, and Spencer Abraham of Michigan, along with former presidential candidates Jack Kemp and Steve Forbes.

Democratic senator Ted Kennedy, a fervent critic of the war, issued a statement:

> Today is an ominous day for the country, signifying a new low since Watergate in terms of openness and honesty in our government. This is far more than an indictment of an individual. In effect it's an indictment of the vicious and devious tactics used by the administration to justify a war we never should have fought. It's an indictment of the lengths administration officials were willing to go to cover up their failed intelligence, their distortion on Iraq's weapons of mass destruction, and their serious blunders on the war. It is an indictment of their vindictive efforts to discredit anyone who challenge their misrepresentations.

By contrast, on *Meet the Press* the Sunday before the indictment was announced, Republican senator Kay Bailey Hutchison waved off perjury charges as a "technicality" and struck a refrain that quickly became a rallying cry for Libby's defenders:

"I certainly hope that if there is going to be an indictment that says something happened, that it is an indictment on a crime and not some perjury technicality where they couldn't indict on the crime and so they go to something just to show that their two years of investigation was not a waste of time and taxpayer dollars. So they go to something that trips someone up because they said something in the first grand jury and then maybe they found new information or they forgot something and they tried to correct that in a second grand jury."

"But the fact is perjury or obstruction of justice is a very serious crime and Republicans certainly thought so when charges were placed against Bill Clinton before the United States Senate," Tim Russert countered.

Hutchison responded, "Well, there were charges against Bill Clinton besides perjury and obstruction of justice. And I'm not saying that those are not crimes. They are. But I also think that we are seeing in the judicial process—and look at Martha Stewart, for instance, where they couldn't find a crime and they indict on something that she said about something that wasn't a crime. I think that it is important, of course, that we have a perjury and an obstruction of justice crime, but I also think we are seeing grand juries and U.S. attorneys and district attorneys that go for technicalities, sort of a gotcha mentality in this country.

And I think we have to weigh both sides of this issue very carefully and not just jump to conclusions, because someone is in the public arena, that they are guilty without being able to put their case forward. I really object to that."

Considering the passions that the case had already unleashed, the media was restrained in its reactions, perhaps because the central mystery—Novak's sources—remained publicly unsolved. Nor, as Fitzgerald had emphasized, did the charges have any bearing on the merits of the war in Iraq, although, if true, the charges portrayed at least one high-level official who showed no reluctance to lie under oath. As Fitzgerald had anticipated, the failure to charge Libby with the original crime being investigated—leaking the identity of a covert agent—led some to dismiss the perjury and obstruction charges as "technicalities." The *Wall Street Journal* editorial page—for which Libby and his mentor Paul Wolfowitz had been sources, Libby told the grand jury—was predictably skeptical, while conceding that the charges were a "serious matter":

> Unless Mr. Fitzgerald can prove beyond a reasonable doubt that Mr. Libby was lying, and doing so for some nefarious purpose, this indictment looks like a case of criminalizing politics.

The *New York Times*, finally confronted with the reason why Miller's testimony was indispensable to the grand jury, was more muted in its support for her, defending its decision to support a reporter in jail, but no longer praising her defiance of a court order:

> Recently, *Times* executives have expressed regrets about some of the ways her case was handled. Reflecting on these events, we have no reservations about the obligation of this paper to stand behind our reporter while she was in jail. We also think Ms. Miller was right on the central point, that the original blanket White House waiver was coerced.

Like the *Journal*, the *Times* conceded that the charges "are very serious," and noted that

> the Republicans' attempts to belittle the charges are quite a switch, considering that many of these same politicians gleefully helped to impeach President Bill Clinton on similar charges in a much less serious context.

The *Washington Post* warned,

To criminalize such discussions between officials and reporters would run counter to the public interest.

That said, the charges Mr. Fitzgerald brought against Mr. Libby are not technicalities . . . No responsible prosecutor would overlook a pattern of deceit like that alleged by Mr. Fitzgerald. The prosecutor was asked to investigate a serious question, and such obstructions are, as he said yesterday, like throwing sand in the umpire's face.

A few days later, Eckenrode was recuperating from minor surgery and checked his phone messages. Among them was the distinctive voice of Richard Armitage asking Eckenrode to call him. He sounded worried, and said it was "quite important." When Eckenrode returned the call, Armitage said, "There's been a development," and asked to meet with him in person. He didn't want to say more on the phone.

Armitage had left the State Department in November 2004, over a year after disclosing his role in the Novak leak, at the same time Colin Powell resigned as secretary of state. Eckenrode and Fitzgerald met him at his office in Arlington, Virginia, where he now ran a private consulting firm, Armitage International. He looked nervous and uncomfortable, more than at their earlier meetings.

Armitage said that after the press conference announcing Libby's indictment, he'd received a voice mail from Bob Woodward, for whom Armitage had been a regular and reliable source. According to Armitage, Woodward told him, "I was watching the press conference about Libby. It strikes me, Dick, that everyone—Fitzgerald, the whole country—now thinks that Miller was the first reporter who was told about Plame. I always imagined you a truth teller. I have to remind you, if you don't remember, that you and I had that same conversation."

Armitage said the call had come as a "jolt," a reminder that he had indeed discussed Plame's status as a CIA agent while Woodward was interviewing him on June 13 for his subsequent book, *Plan of Attack*. "I fucked up again," Armitage told them. "Do you believe it?" He apologized for not mentioning it before, but said he had no memory of the conversation until Woodward called.

Fitzgerald had deliberately and carefully not gone on a fishing expedition with the press, seeking testimony only from reporters known to have talked to Libby, Rove, and Armitage, the known sources of leaks. Still, it was startling at this stage of the investigation to discover yet another leak. How many more might there be, conveniently forgotten by sources? He warned Armitage that he'd have to present this new evidence to the grand jury, and reconsider his decision not to seek an indictment against him.

"This is the last straw" with respect to Armitage, Eckenrode argued to Fitzgerald. He'd read a classified report that mentioned Wilson's wife, leaked her identity to two prominent reporters, one of whom he'd claimed to have forgotten.

Obviously the investigators had to talk to Woodward. Eckenrode placed a series of calls and left messages, but none were returned. Finally Fitzgerald heard from Woodward's lawyer, Howard Shapiro, at the firm WilmerHale. Much like Russert, Woodward agreed to a deposition, but not an appearance before the grand jury. Questions were confined to discussions about Plame with three sources who'd given Woodward waivers to discuss their otherwise not-for-attribution interviews: Armitage, Libby, and chief of staff Andrew Card. (Armitage, however, insisted that Woodward not reveal his identity outside the deposition; his identity as Novak's source and now Woodward's was still a closely guarded secret.) Placed in virtually the same position as Miller and Cooper, Woodward—the nation's foremost investigative reporter—and his lawyers, by agreeing to testify, sidestepped entirely the constitutional standoff that had resulted in Miller's going to prison.

When Fitzgerald and Eckenrode met Woodward at WilmerHale's offices on November 14, Woodward apologized for failing to return Eckenrode's calls. "That's a shame, because I was looking forward to meeting you in an underground parking garage," Eckenrode quipped.

Four days before Libby's indictment was announced, Woodward had been at the White House for an interview and bumped into Rove in the West Wing. Rove brought up the leak investigation, and referred to Novak's original source as the "alpha source." To Woodward, a navy veteran, "alpha" meant the letter *A*—Armitage's initial—and he assumed that was whom Rove was talking about. "You've got that right," Woodward said. Rove looked mystified. "Armitage," Woodward clarified. Armitage was Novak's initial source.

Rove's face lit up. "Armitage?" Rove stood up and cupped his hands like he was about to throw a football and spun around. "You've turned my world upside down!" he exclaimed. He hadn't guessed Novak's source, and was obviously thrilled that it was someone in the State Department—anyone but him.

Woodward told Fitzgerald and Eckenrode he'd called Armitage on Monday, October 31, after hearing Fitzgerald's press conference because he realized "this isn't right" and thought he had a duty to "set the record straight" and correct the impression that Miller was the recipient of the first leak. Woodward also thought he might persuade Armitage to go public, allowing him to break the news that Armitage was the still unidentified primary source for Novak's column. Armitage expressed surprise—not that he'd leaked Plame's identity to Woodward but at the timing. He said he thought the interview had been in July, after Novak's column. Woodward said it had been June 13. "I'm going to the prosecutor," Armitage responded. "I have to tell the truth." He told Woodward he could describe their interview to Fitzgerald but not write anything for publication.

Woodward had taped the June 13 interview, as he did most interviews. His lawyers handed over the relevant portion, which lasted about one minute, in which Armitage discussed Wilson's wife. It was a stroke of good luck—the investigators' first direct evidence of a leak, since Novak hadn't even taken notes. It was a remarkable exchange:

"What's Scowcroft up to?" Woodward asked.

"Scowcroft is looking into the yellowcake thing."

"Oh yeah? . . . What happened there?"

"They're back together," Armitage replied. "They knew with yellowcake, the CIA is not going to be hurt by this one—"

"I know, that's—"

"Hadley and Bob Joseph know," Armitage continued. "It's documented. We've got our documents on it. We're clean as a fucking whistle. And George [Tenet] personally got it out of the Cincinnati speech of the president."

"Oh, he did?"

"Oh yeah."

"Oh really?"

"Yeah."

"It was taken out?"

"Taken out. George said you can't do this."

"How come it wasn't taken out of the State of the Union then?" Woodward asked.

"Because I think it was overruled by the types down at the White House. Condi doesn't like being in the hot spot. But she [unintelligible]—"

"But it was Joe Wilson who was sent by the agency. I mean that's just—"

"His wife works in the agency."

"Why doesn't that come out?" Woodward asked. "Why does—"

"Everyone knows it," Armitage said, talking over Woodward.

"—that have to be a big secret?"

"Everyone knows. . . . Yeah. And I know [unintelligible] Joe Wilson's been calling everybody. He's pissed off because he was designated as a low-level guy, went out to look at it. So, he's all pissed off."

"But why would they send him?"

"Because his wife's a fucking analyst at the agency."

"It's still weird."

"It—it's perfect. This is what she does. She is a WMD analyst out there."

"Oh, she is."

"Yeah."

"Oh, I see."

"[unintelligible] look at it."

"Oh, I see. I didn't—"

"Yeah. See?"

"Oh, she's the chief WMD?"

"No she isn't the chief, no."

"But high enough up that she can say, 'Oh yeah, hubby will go,'" Woodward suggested.

"Yeah, he knows Africa."

"Was she out there with him?"

"No."

"When he was ambassador?"

"Not to my knowledge. I don't know. I don't know if she was out there or not. But his wife is in the agency and is a WMD analyst. How about that shit?"

The Woodward tape suggests that Armitage's motive was to use the information to distance the State Department and CIA from the White House—blaming the latter for the sixteen words and insisting "we" are "clean as a . . . whistle." While not using her name or suggesting explicitly that she was a covert agent, Armitage freely identified Wilson's wife as a CIA WMD expert, so much so that Woodward said he assumed she was not covert and that the information wasn't classified. It wasn't clear what Armitage meant when he said "everyone knows it"—the two seem to have been talking past each other at that point—but Woodward took it to mean that everyone knew Wilson was the former ambassador sent to Niger, not that everyone knew his wife worked for the CIA. Woodward didn't think this revelation amounted to much of a story. He said he'd passed on the information about Wilson's wife to his *Post* colleague Walter Pincus (who'd never mentioned this in his testimony to Fitzgerald, and subsequently denied that Woodward did mention it to him). Woodward said he'd also briefed *Post* executive editor Leonard Downie—and showed him a transcript of the Armitage tape. But no story resulted.

Woodward also described a lengthy interview with Libby on June 27, also for his book, but didn't recall any discussion of Wilson's wife. He said his four pages of notes made no mention of her, although in this instance he didn't tape the conversation. Nor did a tape of his subsequent interview with Andrew Card contain any mention of Wilson's wife.

In this regard, Woodward added nothing to the case against Libby. But the revelation threw new and unflattering light on Armitage. He had evidently turned to Novak after failing to generate any coverage from Woodward. Could Armitage really have forgotten such a conversation with Bob Woodward, a conversation Woodward himself clearly remembered? When confronted by Woodward, he hadn't claimed to have forgotten the conversation, only the date. (A material omission is also a criminal violation of Section 1001.) Fitzgerald and Eckenrode interviewed Colin Powell again, at his home, and Powell said Armitage had never told him about Woodward. Even Powell, a staunch Armitage defender, agreed it was hard to fathom that Armitage could have forgotten such an interview with Woodward. Powell added that the Woodward revelation had plunged Armitage into depression.

The date of Armitage's leak to Woodward seemed significant: just days after the State Department's INR report circulated identifying Wilson's wife as a CIA agent, and the day after Kristof's second column criticizing the vice president. It also established that it was Woodward, not Miller and certainly not Novak, who first learned of Plame's identity.

On November 19, Fitzgerald convened a new grand jury to continue investigating the Plame affair, and called Armitage to testify for the third time. Armitage told essentially the same story, which was that he'd forgotten the Woodward conversation until Woodward himself jogged his memory. He emphasized, as he had before, that he didn't know Wilson's wife was a covert agent.

Fitzgerald had already concluded that it would be difficult to prosecute Armitage under the protected identities act. Woodward's testimony hadn't changed that; indeed, he weakened the potential case by saying his impression was that Valerie Wilson was not covert. That left possible perjury or obstruction charges. However unlikely that Armitage would have forgotten the Woodward interview, he had come forward as soon as he heard from Woodward. Woodward never said he would publicly identify a confidential source without Armitage's consent. Armitage had also identified himself as Novak's primary source. He hadn't concocted a false story. On February 24, 2006, Fitzgerald wrote Armitage, "Absent unexpected developments, I do not anticipate seeking any criminal charges against you." He had barely escaped prosecution.

After a fifth appearance by Rove before the grand jury, Fitzgerald finally resolved the case against Rove. Fitzgerald sent Rove a letter on June 13 informing him no charges would be brought. Rove's lawyer, Luskin, issued a statement saying he hoped the resolution would end "baseless speculation" about Rove. Out of deference to the ongoing investigation, he said Rove would have no further comment.

Rove felt neither elation nor relief. "I was still in shock," he later said. Neighbors brought him a cake with the word "Congratulations" on top in blue icing. But soon after, with his name now cleared, he began thinking about leaving the White House. Perhaps it was time.

Fitzgerald informed Novak's lawyers that he was now free to discuss his role in the case. In fact, Novak had always been free to discuss it; nothing in grand jury secrecy rules prevents a witness from discussing his testimony. Miller and Cooper promptly disclosed their appearances, ignoring any request from Fitzgerald not to do so. But Novak's lawyer was probably shrewd to advise him to remain silent while the firestorm raged over whether journalists were bound to protect their confidential sources, since he had revealed his and testified before the grand jury long before the courts ruled against Miller, Cooper, and Russert. Given the vindictive mood in the press, Novak would likely have been eviscerated.

Novak described his decision to testify in a July 12 column: "When I testified before the grand jury, I was permitted to read a statement that I had written expressing my discomfort at disclosing confidential conversations with news sources. It should be remembered that the special prosecutor knew their identities and did not learn them from me." He named Rove in the column, but not his primary source because "he has not come forward to identify himself."

His identity was revealed in *Newsweek* in late August. In "The Man Who Said Too Much" Michael Isikoff solved the mystery, drawing on an account in *Hubris*, a book he cowrote with David Corn of the *Nation*. "'I'm afraid I may be the guy that caused this whole thing,' [Armitage] later told Carl Ford Jr., State's intelligence chief," Isikoff wrote. "Ford says Armitage admitted to him that he had 'slipped up' and told Novak more than he should have. 'He was basically beside himself that he was the guy that f–ed up. My sense from Rich is that it was just chitchat,' Ford recalls."

Armitage himself finally came forward and acknowledged his role in an interview with the *Washington Post*'s R. Jeffrey Smith that ran on September 8. He said he'd received permission from Fitzgerald to discuss his involvement and stressed that he'd never known Plame was a covert agent and had never before seen a covert agent's name mentioned, even in a classified document. The article concluded: "Armitage said he deeply regrets embarrassing Powell, the State Department, his friends and family, and the Wilsons." He said nothing about embarrassing or causing trouble for the CIA, the White House, Rove, or Libby.

The trial of I. Lewis "Scooter" Libby opened on January 23, 2007. The courtroom was on the sixth floor of the Prettyman building. It had taken four days to choose a jury. The defense team was looking for jurors who weren't hostile to the Bush administration or the Iraq War—no small feat in heavily Democratic Washington—and who were open-minded about the possibility of memory loss, which was already emerging as the centerpiece of Libby's defense. The nine women and three men who filed in included a singer, an art historian, a postal worker, a retired math teacher, a Web page designer, and, curiously, a *Washington Post* reporter who had worked with Bob Woodward. Ten were white, an anomaly in the heavily African American District of Columbia. It was a well-educated, reasonably affluent group that pledged to weigh the facts with an open mind.

The defense team was deferential toward Judge Reggie Walton, though not especially happy about his selection as the presiding judge. Walton was a

Reagan appointee with a reputation for being tough on criminals. A former college football player, he'd once jumped out of his car to subdue a man attempting to beat a cabdriver. Dark gray suits and white shirts were the order of the day for both prosecution and defense, with only their ties—Fitzgerald's a solid blue, Libby's a patterned tan—to distinguish their attire. Libby's hair was grayer than when he entered the White House, but he looked trim and had shed his crutches. His wife, Harriet Grant, sat directly behind him, and the two occasionally exchanged glances.

In preparation for the trial, Fitzgerald had read Libby's novel, *The Apprentice*. Apart from a few bizarre sex scenes (including copulation with a bear and a freshly killed deer), Fitzgerald was struck by how much of it was a cautionary tale about covering up a crime, which in the novel was a murder. It seemed ironic that Libby himself was now accused of covering up his leaks of Plame's identity.

"May it please the court, the defense team, the government team, members of the jury, good morning," Fitzgerald began. "It's Sunday, July 6, 2003. It's the last day of a three-day Fourth of July weekend. The fireworks are over, except a different kind of fireworks are about to begin. When people wake up, they open up the Sunday paper, the Sunday *New York Times*. On the page opposite the editorial page appears a column, a column written by a man named Joseph Wilson."

In his surprisingly dramatic narrative account, Fitzgerald walked the jurors through the complicated events that provided the backdrop for Libby's alleged crimes: the State of the Union address, the invasion of Iraq, the failure to find weapons of mass destruction, the finger-pointing among the White House, CIA, and State Department. "Let me stop right there and remind you of something very, very important," Fitzgerald said at one point. "You won't be asked to decide nor consider in this case whether or not the war in Iraq was made properly or not. That's just the background of this case."

As his narrative reached May and June of 2003, Fitzgerald alluded to the Kristof article in the *Times*, and claims by the unnamed former ambassador that his intelligence warnings had been ignored. "This got some attention. People in the government began asking questions. Who is this former ambassador? What did he do? Where did he go? Who sent him? The defendant was one of those people asking those questions." Fitzgerald detailed the incidents in which Libby was told explicitly about Wilson, his wife's position in the CIA, and her alleged role in sending him on the mission: from his conversation with the vice president, on June 10 or 11, to briefings by Marc Grossman, Bob Grenier, Cathie Martin, and Craig Schmall—five different government officials—by June 14. And Fitzgerald described Libby's interview with Miller on June 23.

Then came the Wilson column, and a "firestorm" ensued, Fitzgerald said. "The evidence will show that Mr. Wilson accused the vice president of allowing the president to mislead the country. . . . And it was on an issue that could not be more important: someone being accused of lying about the justification for war."

Noting that Vice President Cheney had carefully saved the article and underlined it, Fitzgerald said, "The vice president wasn't going to take it lying down, nor was the defendant. The defendant was the vice president's right-hand man. He was his chief of staff, and he also had the job of national security adviser to the vice president. The defendant worked very, very closely with the vice president on many issues, including the war in Iraq. Wilson's charges hit close to home."

Fitzgerald turned to the campaign to rebut Wilson's allegations: lunch with Ari Fleischer on July 7, the meeting with Judy Miller on July 8, the call to Russert on July 10 to complain about Chris Matthews, the Tenet statement on July 11, the trip to Norfolk and subsequent calls to Cooper and other reporters on July 12. And finally Fitzgerald mentioned the Novak column, only to dismiss it. "One thing should be very clear. Mr. Novak relied on two sources. Neither of those sources is the defendant."

"Let's move forward to the fall of 2003." Fitzgerald pointed out that this was when the furor shifted to who had "outed" a CIA agent, and a Justice Department investigation began. The new White House press secretary was deluged with questions about who was responsible. ("He should have brought a helmet to work," Fitzgerald opined.) Though he had cleared Rove of suspicion, he refused to go further and exonerate Libby. "As you can imagine, the defendant was not happy," Fitzgerald continued, and lobbied the vice president to intervene on his behalf. Cheney did, and McClellan cleared Libby on October 7. "But the evidence will show the defendant had a problem. He was involved in leaking information about Wilson's wife to reporters. He had talked to Judith Miller about it on June 23, 2003; July 8, 2003; and July 12, 2003. He confirmed it to Matt Cooper in that phone conversation from the air force base. And he also told it to the White House press secretary whose job it was to talk to the press."

In Fitzgerald's telling, this set the stage for Libby's lies, first to the FBI, and then, under oath, to the grand jury. "The White House had insisted that no one in the White House was involved, and anyone involved would be fired. And at the defendant's insistence the White House had told the world he had nothing to do with this. You will learn that, during that FBI interview, the defendant lied. He made up a story . . . his story was essentially this: I am learning from Tim Russert this information, and as I'm learning it, I'm saying, I don't know this. And then, as he takes the information and passes it on to the other reporters, he says, 'I am just giving you rumors from another reporter. I don't know if it's true.' The note found in his files showing that the vice president had already told him about Wilson's wife inconveniently undermined this story, so Libby simply said that he'd forgotten all that. He was learning the information all over again, as if it were new, from Tim Russert.

"Well what about Tim Russert? Tim Russert will walk into the courtroom during this trial, take that witness stand, swear to an oath and testify. Tim Russert will tell you that he did not tell the defendant on July 10, 2003, that Wilson's wife worked for the CIA."

Fitzgerald played several sections of the audiotape of Libby in the grand jury describing the Russert conversation and his interviews with Miller and Cooper.

"Members of the jury, the evidence you will see in this case from the witness stand will show you that the defendant knowingly and intentionally lied to the FBI and lied after taking an oath before the grand jury. This is not a case about bad memory. . . . Having a bad memory is not a crime. The defendant is not charged with having a bad memory. . . . The defendant knowingly and intentionally lied by trying to shift the information he gave to reporters away from where he really learned it and to blame it on a conversation with Tim Russert that never happened.

"Something important needed to be investigated: Whether the laws protecting covert agents and classified information have been broken. And to do that on behalf of the citizens, the FBI and the grand jury needed the truth. What the evidence will show is that the defendant obstructed that search for truth. The defendant lied to the FBI, and he stole the truth from the grand jury.

"Thank you."

Ted Wells stepped forward to deliver Libby's opening statement. "Scooter Libby is innocent. He is totally innocent. . . . He has been wrongly and unjustly and unfairly accused."

Wells moved swiftly to what the defense team considered the weakest element of the government's case: motive. Motive is rarely an element of a crime that must be proved, but without a plausible motive, few juries are convinced. Without being explicit, Fitzgerald had planted a notion of Libby's motive: once he'd lied to get his name cleared, he'd had no choice but to lose his job and face public humiliation, not to mention possible prosecution for leaking Plame's identity. Wells tried to counter this: "People do not lie for the heck of it. When somebody tells an intentional lie, it's because they have done something wrong. They are trying to cover something up. And what you will learn from the evidence is Scooter Libby had nothing to cover up. He was an innocent person, and there was no reason to lie."

Wells also did his best to distance Libby from other, far less popular figures in the White House, saying that "some people" in the White House—he later mentioned Karl Rove by name—may have "pushed" reporters to write about Wilson's wife, but not Libby. Libby was concerned about being "set up. He was concerned about being the scapegoat for this entire Valerie Wilson controversy."

Wells made clear that the essence of Libby's defense would be a weak memory. He argued that he would show that Libby's recollections of his conversations with Russert and other journalists were accurate, and the reporters were wrong. But even if Libby had been mistaken in his testimony, he had never lied. As Fitzgerald had conceded, a bad memory is not a crime. "I am here to defend Scooter Libby for three telephone calls. And as interesting as it is to be in a case with the backdrop of the war and to have all these people here, ultimately, what you are all going to have to focus on and decide is a very narrow question having nothing to do with the war, but about three phone calls, three reporters, what somebody recollected three months later, and what some other people recollected three months later where there are no notes, no recordings. He said/she said. . . ."

Returning to the issue of motive, Wells asked why Libby would make up a story about Tim Russert when it wasn't a confidential conversation and he knew investigators would ask Russert about it. Wells's answer: "It didn't happen.

Mr. Libby was a very busy man, but he wasn't stupid. Nobody's going to tell you he was a nut. It makes no sense."

This was a variation on the Martha Stewart defense argument: that the defendant was too smart to have done something so stupid as to tell a lie that could be so easily exposed. Why Libby told the Russert story was a question Libby himself might address if he testified—Wells had listed him as a potential witness, but hadn't yet said if he would take the stand.

Returning to the theme, Wells argued again that it made no sense for Libby to fabricate the Russert story. "That theory is both flawed and illogical." Libby had heard on July 11 from Rove that Novak was writing a story about Wilson's wife, so if he wanted to say he was hearing this from reporters, "all he would have to say is . . . 'I've heard that from Robert Novak' or 'I've heard a reporter has already written a story.' No need to make up any fake, phony story about Tim Russert. Mr. Libby told the truth as he recollected it. The entire premise, the theory of the prosecution's case that he had to make up Tim Russert, to put some reporter in between him and Miller and Cooper, it's just stupid, stupid."

Wells told jurors, "During this trial you will learn how the vice president of the United States ordered him to stick his neck in the meat grinder. But being in the meat grinder did not mean saying anything about Valerie Wilson.

"I want to conclude by saying what I said earlier. You promised you would be fair. Any feelings about the war in Iraq you would put to the side. You promised. The only way I lose this case is if somebody starts to interpret the evidence based on your feelings about the war. They have no evidence. They have no case. He is innocent and, at the end of this trial, I will ask you to return a verdict of not guilty on each and every count. Thank you."

Both prosecution and defense had pointed out that Libby was not accused of leaking Valerie Wilson's identity. And yet in both presentations it had emerged as a central issue. Crime or not, leaking the identity of a CIA agent could hardly be construed as a patriotic or heroic act. And if Libby had leaked—something for which the president had said he would be fired—he had a motive to lie and obstruct the investigation. Thus Wells went to some lengths to establish that Libby didn't know Valerie Wilson's status at the CIA and that he wasn't Novak's source—facts that Fitzgerald didn't dispute. But while arguing that Libby "didn't do anything," Wells never said flatly that Libby hadn't leaked Valerie Wilson's identity to other reporters.

Given the broad scope and complexity of the investigation, focusing as it did as much on Armitage and Rove as Libby, the prosecution's case was surprisingly concise. Fitzgerald didn't call Novak, Rove, or Cheney as witnesses. His goal was simply to prove that Libby had lied about the source of his knowledge about Valerie Wilson: it was Cheney, followed by other government officials and not hearsay from Russert. And he had lied about his conversations with Miller and Cooper. Fitzgerald orchestrated his case by calling a series of administration officials, then journalists Miller and Cooper. All would build to the prosecution's star witness: Tim Russert.

The sequence began with the State Department's Robert Grossman, followed by the CIA's Robert Grenier and Libby's briefer, Craig Schmall. All gave straightforward accounts of Libby's efforts to learn more about the Wilson mission in June 2003, after the Kristof article appeared. Grossman testified that he'd commissioned the INR report that described Wilson's wife, and briefed Libby on it: "I recall that I said there was one other thing I thought he needed to know, which was that Mrs. Wilson, or Joe Wilson's wife, worked at the agency. . . . I felt it was my responsibility to make sure that he had the whole context. I didn't think it was right to not tell him the whole story."

The CIA's Grenier also described telling Libby about Wilson's wife, recalling that he was pulled out of a meeting and handed a note telling him to call Libby. It stuck in his mind, because "I don't think I had ever been called out of a meeting with the director either before or since." He said he'd called Libby right away, and "I mentioned it only in passing. I believe I said something to the effect that—in fact, Ambassador Wilson's wife works there, and that's why—that's where the idea came from." Grenier hadn't initially told the FBI this, and said he only remembered it later, after reading in the press that Libby said he'd learned about Wilson's wife from reporters. Grenier said he remembered feeling guilty about having told Libby, since "it wasn't absolutely necessary for me to have said that, and that is information that we normally guard pretty closely." He'd called the FBI to expand on his earlier testimony.

Schmall testified that Libby had asked him about Wilson and his wife, and, unlike the other witnesses, he had notes on his briefing materials, dated June 14, 2003: "Why was the [ex-ambassador] told this was a V.P. office question, Joe Wilson, Valerie Wilson." He also recalled later discussing the leak of Valerie Wilson's identity with the vice president and Libby at the Naval Observatory, the official vice presidential residence. "People were saying that, well, this is really no big deal. There is no danger involved here. I thought there was a very grave danger to leaking the name of a CIA officer."

And then came Cathie Martin, the witness who worked most closely with Libby. She described walking in on Libby and the vice president to report on her conversation with the CIA's Bill Harlow. "He told me the former ambassador's name, his name is Joe Wilson. And apparently he was a chargé [d'affaires] in Baghdad, and apparently his wife works at the CIA." She didn't recall the date, but thought it likely it was June 11. She also described listening to Libby's end of the phone conversation with Matt Cooper. She didn't hear Libby say anything about Wilson's wife, nor did he say anything about other reporters. She did acknowledge on cross-examination that she took another call at one point, and so might have missed some of Libby's conversation with Cooper.

Four witnesses had successively established that they told Libby about Wilson's wife well before he had the conversation with Russert. The fifth was the vice president, according to Libby himself and his notes of the conversation. Cheney himself had claimed to have no memory of this, so there was no point in calling him as a witness. This put the defense lawyers in a difficult position. Their first line of defense had always been that Libby's version of these encounters was correct, and that there had been no discussion of Wilson's wife, and virtually no talk of Wilson and his mission. Could all four witnesses be mistaken? The fallback position was that if Libby was wrong, it was an innocent mistake and something he'd simply forgotten. But given Libby's preoccupation with the Wilson story, even pulling Grenier out of a meeting with Tenet, was this plausible?

As the person closest to Libby, Martin might have been the ideal witness to convey how busy Libby was, how preoccupied with more important events, and how bad his memory was on a host of topics and not only the subject of Wilson's wife. Martin did say that Libby was "busy . . . he was always busy. But I don't know what—I never knew precisely what he was doing. . . . He spent a good deal of time with the vice president." But that was it—she wasn't asked, nor did she offer, a single example of a Libby memory lapse. Nor did she offer any praise of Libby, leaving the impression, fairly or not, that she didn't hold him in especially high regard.

The highest-ranking administration witness was Ari Fleischer, the only witness to testify under grant of immunity. As the former press secretary, someone close to the president, he was able to place the Wilson controversy in the broader context of the war, the State of the Union address, and the Bush administration's credibility problem. The heart of his testimony, however, was the crucial July 7 lunch.

Fleischer was a devastating witness, since Libby could not have told him about Plame on July 7 if he heard it for the first time from Tim Russert three or four days later. Fleischer demolished Libby's alibi. The defense tried to establish an alternative scenario: that Fleischer could have heard about Plame from someone on Air Force One (specifically, Dan Bartlett) and not from Libby. That Fleischer then leaked Plame's identity to other reporters, including NBC's David Gregory, who could have told Russert. But Fleischer gave no evidence that anything like this had happened. Wells and Jeffress stressed his immunity deal and the fact that he had leaked Plame's identity to undermine his character. But neither had any direct bearing on his credibility about his lunch with Libby.

On the afternoon of January 30, jurors were finally introduced to Judith Miller, whose notoriety had by now eclipsed Libby's. Miller was no longer a *Times* reporter; her article describing her grand jury testimony turned out to be her last. Shortly after, the *Times* negotiated a severance package and she resigned. Her decision to testify was the last straw for many in the *Times* newsroom who were already skeptical of her reporting on Iraq. As Miller herself put it in a letter the *Times* published:

> Mainly I have chosen to resign because over the last few months, I have become the news, something a *New York Times* reporter never wants to be. Even before I went to jail, I had become a lightning rod for public fury over the intelligence failures that helped lead our country to war.

Wearing a black velvet jacket and fighting a cold, Miller gave a straightforward, detailed account of her three pivotal interviews with Libby—on June 23, July 8, and July 12. She recalled that Libby had told her about Valerie Wilson and her CIA status on the twenty-third, and again on July 8, with both instances reflected in her notes. Her memory was vague about the July 12 phone call, but she thought she told Libby that she wasn't going to do a story on Plame.

Miller also gave a matter-of-fact account of her initial refusal to testify: "I told [Judge Hogan] I could not do so, because I did not have a waiver from my source that I believed was voluntary and personal. So I could not comply." And she acknowledged that she'd forgotten the June 23 meeting until she discovered her notes.

The defense made much of this, suggesting this was the type of common memory lapse Libby might also have experienced. But otherwise, Wells and

Jeffress made little headway on cross-examination. Indeed, it's hard to believe that Libby ever wanted her to testify, since she was a doubly damaging witness. Not only had Libby leaked Plame's identity to her in at least two interviews, but the first of these came weeks before the Russert conversation.

"One of the jurors wants to know," Judge Walton interjected, "why did you make the decision to go to jail?"

"Because everything that I do and have done in Washington–all of my reporting depended on people coming to me and being able to trust . . . that I would protect them. And it wasn't until I was absolutely certain that I had a voluntary and personal waiver–written waiver from Mr. Libby–not something his boss had asked him to sign, but something that he had given me and I was able to talk to him about, and knowing that I could protect the other sources–I really felt that, as a professional and ethical matter, I had no choice. It was all my conscience would allow. I wasn't trying to be a martyr or make a stand. I was just trying to do the right thing vis-à-vis my sources, knowing that without that kind of trust, you can't operate in Washington when people can go to jail for even talking to you."

Miller was dismissed, and Matt Cooper took the stand. Cooper testified that he'd first learned about Plame's identity from Karl Rove, and that when he asked Libby about it, he said, "Yes, I have heard that too," or "Yes, I have heard something like that too," which Cooper took as confirmation.

"And did Mr. Libby indicate to you how he had–who he had heard the information from?"

"Not in any way, no."

"And did he at any time indicate that he had heard the information from reporters?"

"No."

The defense stressed that none of this was in Cooper's notes, nor was it in his memo to his editors at *Time*. Jeffress, in particular, zeroed in on a cryptic reference in his notes to "had something and the Wilson thing and not sure if it's ever." Cooper conceded he wasn't sure what the notes referred to. "I cannot account for that sentence we've been talking about. I do have a distinct memory of when we talked about the wife and what he said."

"Had Mr. Libby given you information confirming [that Plame worked for the CIA], that would be something you'd want your editors to know, wouldn't it?"

"I would think so."

"And isn't the fact that . . . everything that you've described that Mr. Libby said to you that day is in this memorandum except anything about Wilson's wife?"

"Yeah, the Wilson's wife thing is certainly not in the memorandum. I don't know if there is anything else."

"That is consistent, Mr. Cooper, with the fact that whatever Mr. Libby said to you in that conversation was not confirmation of anything, isn't it?"

"What I remember, Mr. Jeffress, distinctly over these three and a half years . . ."

"Are you answering my question or some other question?"

Fitzgerald quickly objected, but Jeffress had scored a point in what Wells later characterized, no doubt with some hyperbole, as the trial's "Perry Mason moment."

Cooper was dismissed; it seemed ironic that his and Miller's testimony, which had occupied thousands of hours of legal argument, multiple court filings, millions in legal fees, and caused a furor in the media, had amounted to just several hours.

To establish exactly what Libby had told investigators, FBI agent Deborah Bond testified extensively about the FBI's interviews with Libby on October 14—when Libby first told the Russert story and produced his notes from the earlier Cheney conversation—and November 26. Next Fitzgerald played the full audiotape of Libby's grand jury testimony—a rare public glimpse into the grand jury process. It was obvious that Fitzgerald was skeptical of the Russert story during the questioning; yet Libby never wavered. If anything, his recollection became more detailed and certain.

Libby's grand jury performance set the stage for Fitzgerald's star witness: Tim Russert. The courtroom, which had thinned out during the playing of the Libby tapes, was packed. Everyone following the trial knew it would ultimately turn on Russert's testimony: the "he said/he said" dimension that had figured so prominently in Wells's opening statement. Russert was not only a celebrity in his own right but also one of the country's most trusted and popular journalists. He wore a navy suit and light blue tie and was on crutches from a recent broken ankle.

Russert's testimony was also critical for what he and Libby didn't say. He testified that Libby called to complain about Chris Matthews; he'd handled it as a routine "viewer complaint" and suggested other people at NBC for Libby to call.

Fitzgerald asked, "During this phone conversation did you at any time . . .

discuss with Mr. Libby the wife of Ambassador Joseph Wilson, whether referred to as the wife of Ambassador Wilson or by the name Valerie Wilson or Valerie Plame?"

"No, that would be impossible because I didn't know who that person was until several days later."

"And did you tell Mr. Libby that Wilson's wife worked at the CIA during that phone call?"

"No."

"Did you ever tell Mr. Libby that all the reporters were saying that Wilson's wife worked at the CIA?"

"No, I wouldn't do that. I didn't know that."

Russert's direct examination lasted fifteen minutes. He testified with clarity and seeming certainty: not just that he didn't discuss Wilson's wife, but that he couldn't have. Could the defense shake this conviction?

Wells and Jeffress made an exhaustive effort to do so. In many hours of cross-examination they tried to establish that Russert could have heard about Wilson's wife from other NBC reporters, that he didn't like Libby and had been gleeful over his indictment, that he had concealed his initial willingness to answer the FBI's questions, and that his own memory was spotty: he didn't even remember appearing on the *Today* show to discuss the case:

"Do you remember saying to Ms. Couric, 'It's huge, Katie. This is the first time in 130 years, as we mentioned the other day, that a sitting White House official would come under indictment'? . . . Does that refresh your recollection that it occurred?"

"No. I don't question I said it. But I just don't remember it."

"Do you have a bad memory?"

"No, sir."

"Are you able to remember some things better than others?"

"Yes, sir."

By the end of his cross-examination, Russert remained unshaken. Fitzgerald's redirect examination was very brief:

"Did you take any joy in Mr. Libby's indictment?"

"No, not at all. And I don't take any joy in being here."

Fitzgerald rested the government's case, with the defense set to begin the following Monday. Vice President Cheney was scheduled to testify on Thursday, followed by Libby himself.

The defense team launched its case with a barrage of reporters. On February 12, jurors heard from five journalists in a single day. Three were from the *Washington Post*: Walter Pincus, Glenn Kessler, and Bob Woodward. Fitzgerald had previously interviewed all three without the *Post* raising any firestorm over the First Amendment. The others were David Sanger of the *Times* and Robert Novak. They all made the same point: they had spoken with Libby during the relevant time period and he had not talked about Wilson's wife. Pincus, however, said he had learned Plame's identity from Ari Fleischer on July 12, though Pincus wasn't one of the journalists with whom Fleischer recalled discussing the subject. Libby himself had told the grand jury he thought he'd discussed Plame with Kessler; Kessler said he had not. The collective testimony suggested that Libby was not on any systematic campaign to "out" Wilson's wife; he had ample opportunity to spread her identity among other reporters but hadn't.

Novak, the source of the entire controversy, finally got his day in court, testifying that his sources for the column that set the Plame affair in motion were indeed Armitage and Rove—old news that by now seemed anticlimactic. It seemed ironic that the reporter who had set Libby's prosecution in motion was now a witness for the defense. Novak said he was "absolutely confident" that Libby gave him no help on the Valerie Plame story; he wasn't even sure he had raised the matter with him. In this sense, Libby had always been correct: he was not a source for the Novak column.

Next the defense called John Hannah, who had been Libby's deputy for national security affairs, to establish that Libby was exceptionally busy and had a bad memory. He said that Libby essentially held two full-time jobs.

"Did you have an opportunity to observe how well he remembered things?"

"I did. I had experience with that."

"And what did you observe?"

"On certain things, Scooter had just an awful memory."

"Can you give us an example from your experience?"

"Times too many to count, I would come in to Scooter in the morning, and we would discuss an issue. I would give my views on it, give a policy recommendation, give an analysis, and show up six, seven hours later that evening, and have Scooter in a very excited fashion repeat back to me the analysis, the recommendations, and have no idea that I had actually told him that the very same morning. It was very striking."

Judge Walton pursued this theme with a few questions of his own:

"When Mr. Libby had memory lapses, what was said or done by you to trigger Mr. Libby's recall of the issues previously discussed but seemingly forgotten?"

"Again, it would often be the case that he was quite good at remembering ideas and concepts and arguments, and very bad at sort of figuring out where those arguments might have come from and how they might have come to him. So I think I would simply say, 'Yes, that's a great idea because I told you this morning.' "

"Would Mr. Libby deny, acknowledge, or debate that you had informed him of these particular matters earlier?"

"Never."

"Based upon your observations, were there things that Mr. Libby had a good memory about?"

"Again, it's hard. This kind of thing that I just described was a fairly regular pattern with Scooter, but he was certainly good at remembering his own arguments and key points—key factual points that he would want to be able to make in any kind of policy argument. He was very good at keeping those types of things in his head and keeping his arguments organized."

When the jurors returned from lunch, Ted Wells informed the court that the defense had released the vice president as a potential witness and that he had advised Libby himself not to take the stand. Judge Walton turned to Libby: "I'm sure you understand, based upon your discussions with your lawyers and the fact that you are a lawyer yourself, that you fully appreciate that, under the United States Constitution, you have the absolute right to testify in your defense."

"Yes, sir, I do."

"Understanding that right, is it your decision, after consultation with counsel, to not testify in this trial?"

"Yes, sir. I thank you for the concern. I will follow the advice of my counsel."

Despite eager anticipation, the defense case had taken less than two days of testimony. That neither Cheney nor Rove was called as a witness disappointed those hoping for what would have been an unprecedented examination of two of the most powerful and secretive members of the Bush White House. Their absence was especially glaring, since both were in a position to corroborate Libby's testimony that he told each of them at the time that he learned Plame's identity from Tim Russert. Indeed, had either confirmed that account, it would likely at least have raised a reasonable doubt about Russert's claim that no such conversation took place. As it was, no one other than Libby himself (before the grand jury, not at trial) had testified that such a conversation had taken place.

Peter Zeidenberg, one of Fitzgerald's deputies, delivered the closing argument for the government, and made the point succinctly that Libby "does claim that he forgot nine separate conversations with eight individuals over a four-week period about Joseph Wilson's wife. But he also invents out of whole cloth—absolutely fabricates—two conversations that never happened, his conversation with Matt Cooper and his conversation with Tim Russert. That, ladies and gentlemen, is not a matter of forgetting or misremembering. It's lying."

Zeidenberg pointed out that Libby discussed his pivotal conversation with Russert more than two dozen times during his grand jury testimony "and his testimony was not that he thought he probably or likely learned the information about Wilson's wife from Tim Russert, or he was pretty sure he learned it from Russert. He was unequivocal. He was certain. He remembers being struck by the news. He remembers what he was thinking when he was told this information by Tim Russert. . . . Mr. Russert has a clear memory of that conversation. Mr. Russert never talked to Mr. Libby about Wilson's wife. He never said 'All the reporters know about Wilson's wife.' It never happened. Mr. Russert didn't know about Wilson's wife. He read about Joseph Wilson's wife in the newspapers. That conversation never happened."

Despite Libby's allegedly weak memory, Zeidenberg noted that he had an excellent memory of many details, such as the conversation in which Rove told him about Novak. He accurately remembered many details of his conversations with Judith Miller. He remembered discussing the Miami Dolphins with Ari Fleischer. But what did he forget? "You will find, ladies and gentlemen, that there is a pattern of always forgetting the piece about Wilson's wife."

Zeidenberg concluded by focusing on motive. Libby had signed a statement agreeing not to disclose classified information. He knew that he would be fired "at a minimum . . . and think about the political damage." Moreover, Libby had gone to the vice president and asked him to get the White House to issue a public statement exonerating him. And he did get such a statement. The president and vice president had now put their credibility on the line for him.

"And now the FBI comes knocking. . . . Now he has a choice to make. He can tell the truth and take his chances with the investigation or he can lie. And ladies and gentlemen, he took the second choice. He decided to lie, and he made up a story he thought would cover him.

"When you consider all the evidence, we suggest the government has met its burden of proof and has established the defendant lied under oath to the grand jury and committed perjury. He made false statements to the FBI and he obstructed justice. We ask you to convict Mr. Libby on each count in the indictment."

The defense lawyers had the daunting task of raising doubts about all of the government's witnesses: five government officials who said they discussed Wilson's wife with Libby before Libby spoke to Russert, three—Fleischer, Miller, and Cooper—who said Libby told them about Wilson's wife, and one—Russert—who said he hadn't told Libby about Wilson's wife.

Russert understandably received much of Wells's and Jeffress's attention, since if the jury believed Russert, then Libby was guilty. Wells read a portion of Eckenrode's notes of his initial interview with Russert: "Russert does not recall stating to Libby in this conversation anything about the wife of former ambassador Joe Wilson, although he could not completely rule out the possibility that he had such an exchange."

Wells continued, "The statement that he could not rule it out is totally contrary from what he told you on the witness stand. And with respect to the counts involving Tim Russert, those counts rely almost exclusively on Tim Russert's testimony. He is a one-man show. There is no corroboration. It's what I mean when I say he said/she said. It's what Russert said he recalls and what Libby says he recalls. That's it."

Though not strictly relevant to the charges, Wells stressed what even the prosecutors had acknowledged was a weakness in the case, which was that Libby was not a source for the Novak article. He shrewdly shifted the emphasis to the real leakers—Armitage, Rove, Fleischer—none of them on trial.

It was up to Jeffress to discredit Miller, who'd said Libby had told her about Plame at least twice. And she had notes. "So here's Ms. Miller, who has a total lack of memory of any meeting on June twenty-third. She accidentally finds some notes, and all of a sudden she can tell you that Mr. Libby was agitated and about his demeanor and exactly what he said, and a perverted war of leaks and so forth and so on. It's pretty amazing, pretty amazing for somebody testifying about a conversation of which they had no memory for two years. . . . She's reconstructing by coming in here and testifying as if she has a clear memory of this meeting that occurred three and a half years ago. It's just not so."

Given her bad memory, she might also have been wrong about the July 8 conversation. Jeffress stressed that Miller talked to other sources about Wilson's wife—"She either can't or won't tell you the name of a single other source"—and that these sources, not Libby, might have been responsible for the entries in her notes. After all, she testified that the name "Valerie Flame" didn't come from Libby. "In a case that requires proof beyond a reasonable doubt, Judith Miller is not a reliable witness."

Jeffress also argued that making mistakes, even under oath, is not the same as lying. "It's not fair to flashback Mr. Libby's grand jury testimony. I mean, I know he said, 'Look, I think I told Matt Cooper that I didn't even know Wilson had a wife.' Well, you know, number one, it's obviously not so. Mr. Libby couldn't have been trying to hide anything. He already admitted that he heard from Karl Rove the day before about Mr. Wilson's wife. He admitted that he heard from Mr. Russert two days before or one day before about Mr. Wilson's wife. He's not trying to hide anything. . . . It wouldn't be fair to go down and pick some little statement that he made in the grand jury and say, Well, that's not true. You know he must have meant to lie."

Wells returned for the final summation, focusing on the weakness of circumstantial evidence and the memory defense. "There is no evidence that Libby was engaged in intentional lying as opposed to he just forgot like all of us forget things. All of us forget things. We misconstrue things. We misrecollect things. It happens to everyone. . . ."

Wells continued that "when all of this was going on in June and July, there [were] some of the most high stress moments in the history of the United States of America. This country, not only were we at war, not only did we have 100,000 kids on the ground in harm's way, but they hadn't found any weapons of mass destruction. The country was starting to turn against the Bush administration. The country was saying, hey, you lied to the American public. You lied in the State of the Union . . . we started off talking about Karl Rove and sacrificing Scooter Libby. That's written in the vice president's own handwriting. I say to you, Don't sacrifice Scooter Libby for how you may feel about the war in Iraq or how you may feel about the Bush administration. Don't sacrifice Scooter Libby.

"This is a man with a wife, with two children, and nobody has come in here and said, He's been a bad person, done anything wrong. He's a good person." At this juncture Wells was so emotional that he was fighting tears, and had difficulty continuing. "He has been under my protection for the last month. I give him to you. I ask you at the end of the case, vote not guilty on each and every count and give him back to me. Just give him back." As Wells sat down, he was sobbing.

Fitzgerald had the final word, and he used the opportunity to suggest that Libby's lies had prevented him—and the American people—from ever learning the whole truth about how and why Valerie Plame was outed, at whose behest, and whether it was part of a broader campaign to discredit an administration critic. "There is talk about a cloud over the vice president. There is a cloud over the White House as to what happened. Don't you think the FBI, the grand Jury, the American people are entitled to a straight answer?" . . . Libby "threw sand in the eyes of the grand jury and the FBI investigators. He obstructed justice. He stole the truth from the judicial system. When you return to that jury room, you deliberate, your verdict can give truth back. Please do."

As the jurors deliberated, it was clear that many of the defense arguments had struck home. They agreed that Libby was a fall guy for others, and wondered why Rove and others weren't charged. They thought Libby was polite and personable in his grand jury testimony and felt uncomfortable judging him. They accepted that he did have a weak memory for some things. They compiled a long list of "reasons to lie" and "reasons to tell the truth." But as they categorized the testimony on Post-it notes, the "arithmetic," as one juror later described it, seemed compelling: eight witnesses had described nine conversations in which Libby discussed Wilson's wife before he claimed to have heard it "as if for the first time" from Russert. "There was no wiggle room about it, unless you think all these people who work for the administration were lying," said Denis Collins, the juror who was the former *Washington Post* reporter. "One of the jurors said, 'If I am told something once, I am likely to forget it. But if I am told it many times, it is much less likely I will forget it. And if I tell it to someone else, that is even more unlikely.'"

The jurors carefully weighed the credibility of each witness and the motives each might have had to lie or misremember. When it came to Russert, the most important witness, they found him credible. He had no motive to lie; moreover, he didn't even know about Wilson's wife. The defense had never shaken him on that point or produced any evidence to the contrary. They also found Ari Fleischer credible. His admission that he leaked to reporters wasn't in his self-interest, and his immunity grant didn't protect him if he lied. They also believed Judith Miller, although some jurors found her "confused" and "stressed out," understandably, after eighty-five days in jail. Several jurors said they felt sorry for Miller, who looked thin and chilled on the stand, and felt the defense lawyers had been unfairly hard in attacking her credibility.

The jurors took five full days to deliberate. They weren't swayed by any aversion to the Iraq War or distaste for Bush or Cheney. Nor were they affected by Wells's emotional appeal or the fact that Libby hadn't leaked to Novak. Collins said that everything kept coming down "to one or two statements" and the fact that some of the most damaging testimony came from those closest to Libby—Cathie Martin and John Hannah.

The jurors took their first poll on count five, perjury, based on Libby's sworn testimony that all he knew about Wilson's wife he'd heard from reporters. ("All I had was that reporters are telling us that . . . I didn't know if it was true.") The vote was 9–2 to convict. The jurors slept on it, and the next day, those in favor of conviction suggested the other two try to persuade them that the government hadn't proved its case. "I just think he [Libby] was confused," said one. The other argued, "I just don't see why a man with that much intelligence and being a lawyer would lie." But they faced the same struggle that the defense team had: there was no actual evidence to support either hypothesis. When the jurors voted again, they were unanimous in favor of conviction on count five.

They spent most of their time on count three, which was Libby's account of his interview with Cooper. "We had a spirited back-and-forth," juror Collins recalled, but he, for one, was insistent that Libby be acquitted. "There were flaws in the FBI notes," he said. Although they were "minor things," and he thought they were "going to the correct place," they weren't sufficiently reliable. Once that was resolved, they moved quickly through counts one, two, and four.

On March 6, 2007, at 11:45 a.m., after ten days of deliberations, the jury notified Judge Walton that it had reached a unanimous verdict on all counts. Libby, his lawyers, his wife, the prosecution team, and a full press gallery hastily reassembled in the courtroom. As the jurors filed in, none looked toward Libby. "You may be seated," the judge said. "Has the jury reached a unanimous verdict in the case of *United States of America versus I. Lewis Libby*?"

"We have."

"As to count one of the indictment, charging obstruction of justice, is your verdict guilty or not guilty?"

"Guilty."

"As to count two . . . guilty or not guilty?"

"Guilty."

"As to count three . . . guilty or not guilty?"

"Not guilty."

"As to count four, perjury . . ."

"Guilty."

"As to count five, perjury . . ."

"Guilty."

"Do all of you agree with the verdict?"

"Yes, Your Honor."

Libby looked impassive as his wife wept briefly. A man seated next to her put his arm around her. Libby's sentencing was set for June 5, and the jurors filed out of the courtroom. It was all over in just ten minutes.

Nearly three months later, the participants gathered for the last time before Judge Walton. The defense had generated an outpouring of 150 letters on Libby's behalf, from an array of prominent supporters, especially from the cadre of neoconservative strategists who had made the case for war: Donald Rumsfeld, Paul Wolfowitz, Kenneth Edelman, Richard Perle. Others writing included Henry Kissinger, former World Bank head James Wolfensohn, and two retired generals.

"Truth matters, and truth matters above all else in the judicial system," Fitzgerald began. "When people walk into a courtroom and raise their hand and take an oath . . . the whole system depends on that. If we lose the truth from our judicial system, then the judicial system is lost." He continued, "Mr. Libby's prosecution was based not upon politics but upon his own conduct, as well as upon a principle fundamental to preserving our judicial system's independence from politics: that any witness, whatever his political affiliation, whatever his views on any policy or national issue, whether he works in the White House or drives a truck to earn a living, must tell the truth when he raises his hand and takes an oath in a judicial proceeding, or gives a statement to federal law enforcement officers. The judicial system has not corruptly mistreated Mr. Libby; Mr. Libby has been found by a jury of his peers to have corrupted the judicial system."

Wells said he agreed that truth matters. But that Libby's "good deeds" and "outstanding public service" should spare him a prison sentence. The "social stigma of being so publicly humiliated should factor in, to some extent . . . if you read the public coverage, it makes it seem like Mr. Libby was the poster child for all that has gone wrong with this terrible war. Mr. Libby, in addition to his family, really had two loves in his life: government service and practicing law." As a result of his conviction, he was losing both.

Now it was Libby's turn. Having opted not to appear as a witness, this was his chance to make a statement. Remarkably, he said almost nothing. He thanked the judge and the court for the many "courtesies" and the "kindness" he had experienced in the courthouse. "I am, for this, most grateful. But now I realize fully that the court must decide on punishment as prescribed by law. It is respectfully my hope that the court will consider, along with the jury verdict, my whole life."

Then he sat down. Libby had conspicuously failed to acknowledge guilt or offer any contrition—two key requirements for leniency. He remained stoic to the end.

Judge Walton acknowledged Libby's contributions, saying he'd played an "essential role" in "keeping this country safe since the events of 9/11." At the same time, the evidence "overwhelmingly" established his guilt. And though there was no evidence Libby knew Plame's covert status, he had a "unique and special obligation" to make sure revealing her name would not compromise her or any intelligence operations. "He surely did not make any efforts to find out" about her status at the CIA, Walton noted. He also stressed that "the investigation that was embarked on in this situation was extremely serious" and Libby's crimes constituted "serious behavior."

Ultimately Judge Walton concluded that the factors weighing in favor of Libby and those against him pretty much canceled each other out. He sentenced him to thirty months in prison, the low end called for by sentencing guidelines. He also fined him $250,000.

From the moment Walton imposed a prison term, speculation was rife that President Bush would pardon Libby. There was ample precedent: the president's father had granted full pardons to six members of the Reagan administration convicted in the Iran-Contra affair, including Secretary of Defense Caspar Weinberger. Still, it could be argued that they were acting in the national interest even if they broke the law; it was hard to say that Libby's offenses, which served to conceal his role in leaking Plame's identity, served any public interest.

Nonetheless, the vice president, Republican senators and representatives, and many prominent conservatives called for a pardon for Libby. Cheney was especially insistent. Especially irksome to Fitzgerald was Rudolph Giuliani, now a Republican presidential candidate, who had first hired Fitzgerald to work for him when he was U.S. Attorney in Manhattan. Then, Giuliani had advocated stiff sentences for those convicted of obstruction and perjury. Now he went on CNN to belittle Libby's conviction. Libby's sentence "was grossly excessive in a situation in which at the beginning the prosecutor knew who the leak was," Giuliani told Wolf Blitzer. "What the judge did today argues for a pardon because this is excessive punishment."

On July 2, a court of appeals ruled that reversing Libby's conviction on appeal was so unlikely that he should begin serving his prison term immediately. Within hours, President Bush issued a statement:

> I respect the jury's verdict. But I have concluded that the prison sentence given to Mr. Libby is excessive. Therefore, I am commuting the portion of Mr. Libby's sentence that required him to spend thirty months in prison. . . .
>
> The Constitution gives the president the power of clemency to be used when he deems it to be warranted. It is my judgment that a commutation of the prison term in Mr. Libby's case is an appropriate exercise of this power.

President Bush gave no explanation for his conclusion that Libby's sentence was "excessive"; it was, after all, the shortest possible within the sentencing guidelines. Fitzgerald firmly disputed Bush's characterization, saying, "An experienced federal judge considered extensive argument from the parties and then imposed a sentence consistent with the applicable laws. It is fundamental to the rule of law that all citizens stand before the bar of justice as equals."

Bush had seemed genuinely angered by the leak of Plame's identity and called for a thorough investigation, which is what he got. Although he commuted Libby's prison sentence, he didn't pardon him. He asked two lawyers to review the entire case and to interview Libby for his side of the story. They reported to the president that they could find no basis for overturning the jury's verdict. When Bush told Cheney his decision, the vice president was furious. As Bush wrote in his memoir, "He stared at me with an intense look. 'I can't believe you're going to leave a soldier on the battlefield,' he said. The comment stung. In eight years, I had never seen Dick like this, or even close to this." It was a rare rebuke to a vice president on whom he had placed so much trust.

Still, in the end Bush spared Libby a prison sentence, just as he failed to take any action against Rove or Armitage. The message seemed inescapable that in the Bush White House, loyalty trumped truth.

With the threat of a prison term removed, Libby abandoned his appeal, though not his claim that he was innocent and wrongly convicted.

The Wilsons themselves embraced the limelight, and each wrote books on their roles in the affair: *Fair Game*, by Plame, for which she received a reported $2 million advance; and *The Politics of Truth* by Wilson. The couple was featured in *Vanity Fair*, and *Fair Game* was made into a movie starring Naomi Watts and Sean Penn. Plame left the CIA in 2007, and she and Wilson moved to Santa Fe, New Mexico. "We're hopeful that we can get some respite from these people who subvert the Constitution and spin and lie," Wilson told the *Times*. Nonetheless, Wilson's central charge—that the president and vice president ignored his findings in Niger in order to make the case for war—turned out to be little more than speculation, and proved unfounded.

Robert Novak's book chronicling his fifty years in journalism, *The Prince of Darkness: 50 Years Reporting in Washington*, was published in July 2007. Novak pugnaciously defended his column identifying Plame as well as his subsequent decision to name his sources to the grand jury, while settling a host of old scores from slights real and imagined. Fittingly, Novak was interviewed by Russert on *Meet the Press*.

"What do you think happened, Bob Novak, with Scooter Libby?" Russert asked. "He said that he had heard about Valerie Plame from me, and I said that just wasn't the case. It never came up in our conversation. In the course of the trial, it became apparent that he had heard about Valerie Plame from the vice president, and then spoke to several government officials and several reporters before he even spoke to me. What happened?"

"I think he got—I think he had to get mixed up. Because he's not dumb, he's a lawyer, very smart fellow. I hardly know him myself. . . . He didn't tell me a thing. He was—he was not a good source, as they say. But I believe—I believe he got mixed up and . . . I don't believe it was willful lying or perjury. But the jury thought so and convicted him."

"What has this whole situation meant to you? You have been harshly criticized. Every time you're on *Meet the Press*, people say, 'Why would you

have a traitor on like Robert Novak, exposing the identity of a CIA agent?'
How do you deal with that?"

"Well, of course, I always say that . . . If anybody had said to me that
anybody was in danger, any secret operations were undermined, I would
never have used her name . . . it's been tough. . . . It was not a lot of fun for
me, the situation. I certainly don't want it to be my trademark."

In July 2008 Novak was driving his Corvette in downtown Washington
and hit a homeless man, knocking him onto his windshield and slightly injur-
ing him. A week later Novak was diagnosed with a malignant brain tumor. He
suspended his column but kept writing periodically, describing an outpouring
of goodwill that surprised and touched him. He died in August 2009 at age
seventy-eight. The *Times*'s obituary devoted the first paragraph to his role in the
Plame affair and Libby case.

Star witness Tim Russert continued to host *Meet the Press* and moderated
the February 2008 televised presidential primary debate between Hillary Clinton and Barack Obama, cementing his position as the country's most visible
political journalist and one of its most respected. In June 2008 he was recording
voice-overs for *Meet the Press* in NBC's Washington studios when he suffered a
massive heart attack and died. He was fifty-eight.

After leaving the *Times*, Judith Miller became a fellow at the conservative
Manhattan Institute, and in 2008 joined Fox News as a commentator and writer
for *Fox Forum*, focusing on national security. Despite her testimony in the
Libby case, she was warmly embraced by the neoconservative intellectuals who
had made the case for war in Iraq and had been close to Libby. In announcing her hiring, a Fox spokesman defended her reporting on Iraq's weapons of
mass destruction: "We've all had stories that didn't come out exactly as we had
hoped. . . . She has explained herself and she has nothing to apologize for."
While continuing to sound a hawkish note on defense and terrorism issues,
Miller surprised many by revealing that she was supporting Barack Obama for
president and has praised his record in blog postings.

Matt Cooper seems largely to have escaped the ire of colleagues that Miller
faced. He left *Time* to join *Portfolio* magazine, a Condé Nast business publication that failed in 2009. He subsequently joined the staff of the Financial Crisis
Inquiry Commission, and then the staff of *National Journal*. He separated from
his wife, Mandy Grunwald, in late 2006, not long after he testified before the
grand jury.

. . .

FBI special agent Jack Eckenrode finally got a conviction in a leak case, even if technically it wasn't for leaking. Still, he felt justice was done. "We had a duty to the country to discover if there was a conspiracy among senior administration officials to discredit Joe Wilson or anyone else who criticized the president's policies," Eckenrode said. "This was how it looked to me." Eckenrode retired from the FBI in March 2006 and subsequently joined State Street Corp., the large Boston-based bank, as its chief security officer.

Fitzgerald returned to Chicago and his full-time duties as the U.S. Attorney for the Northern District of Illinois, where he cemented his reputation for tackling tough, politically charged cases. In 2008, he announced that a Chicago grand jury had indicted former Chicago police commander Jon Burge on three counts of perjury and obstruction of justice for lying about his role in widespread torture of suspects over an extended period dating from the 1970s. Allegations that Burge had used electric shock, burning, and Russian roulette to extract guilty pleas from suspects led Illinois to suspend the death penalty and evaluate the conviction of every inmate on death row, leading to thirteen being exonerated. Then-governor George Ryan commuted all death sentences before being convicted and going to jail himself, thanks to Fitzgerald's investigation. The statute of limitations had expired for Burge's alleged crimes, but Fitzgerald investigated him for perjury after he testified in a civil suit that he neither used torture nor knew about it. He was convicted of all counts in June 2010.

Fitzgerald has also overseen the investigation, wiretaps, and subsequent indictment of then–Illinois governor Rod Blagojevich, who was charged with soliciting bribery and mail and wire fraud for trying to sell the U.S. Senate seat vacated when Barack Obama was elected president. A wiretap captured Blagojevich stating that a Senate seat "is a fucking valuable thing. You don't just give it away for nothing," a remark that prompted Fitzgerald to say that "Lincoln would roll over in his grave." Fitzgerald had Blagojevich arrested on December 9, 2008, with the investigation still pending, to prevent the governor from further corrupting the selection process. Blagojevich was subsequently impeached and removed as governor.

After two weeks of deliberations, on August 17, 2010, a divided jury convicted Blagojevich on just one of twenty-four counts—making false statements to the FBI. The *Wall Street Journal* editorial page seized on the result to deliver a scathing critique of Fitzgerald:

The Fitzgerald method is to abuse the legal process to poison media and public opinion against high-profile, unsympathetic political targets. . . . Mr. Fitzgerald implied that Mr. Libby had obstructed his investigation into who leaked the former CIA analyst's name, even though he knew from the start that the real "leaker" was Richard Armitage.

Somehow Fitzgerald found time to get engaged. He married Jennifer Letzkus, a Head Start teacher in Chicago, in June 2008.

R ichard Armitage remains the head of Armitage International, the consulting firm he founded after leaving the State Department, focusing on international business development and strategic planning.

Fighting back tears as he appeared with President Bush on the White House lawn, Karl Rove announced his resignation from the White House on August 13, 2007. He later said he'd begun to think of leaving the day Fitzgerald told him he was cleared in the Plame investigation. He said he'd offered to resign in the summer of 2006, but that Bush had waved off the idea and told him they'd walk out together on January 20, 2009.

Despite Bush's earlier insistence that he would fire anyone involved, the president never publicly rebuked Rove for his role or took any other action. He never again mentioned the phone call in which Rove had assured him the subject of Wilson's wife hadn't even come up in Novak's call, and that he hadn't been involved in leaking her identity. The president never responded to Fitzgerald's letter laying out the evidence that had nearly led to his indictment.

After leaving the White House, Rove joined Fox News as a commentator and began writing a weekly column for the *Wall Street Journal*. His memoir, *Courage and Consequence*, was published in 2010. In it he recalls that at a formal dinner in 2007, Colin Powell said there was someone he wanted Rove to meet, and introduced Richard Armitage. "Powell laughed and grinned broadly as Armitage and I awkwardly shook hands and said hello." These were Rove's concluding words on the Plame affair:

On November 4, 2005, I cut from the newspaper a photo of Scooter Libby and his wife in the backseat of a car on the way to his arraignment. I put it in my home desk drawer. I have looked at it frequently in the years since so as not to forget that moment. But for the work of a brilliant lawyer in unraveling and ending the quixotic obsession of a special prosecutor, there went I.

Libby now works for the Hudson Institute, which he joined in January 2006 as senior adviser, even before he went to trial. His lengthy Hudson Institute biography makes no mention of his trial or conviction. It does cite "Twilight of the Arabs: The Contest for Leadership in the Muslim World," which Libby coauthored, and which appeared in the *Weekly Standard* in February 2010. The article contains renewed warnings of the dangers of weapons of mass destruction and the need for U.S. engagement with Arab nations.

The case of *United States v. I. Lewis Libby* was filled with ironies. Novak's sources, Armitage and Rove, were never charged with any crime, although the FBI investigators were unanimous that they should have been. Fitzgerald, vocally criticized by Libby supporters as overzealous, could, if anything, be faulted for being overly cautious. He was scrupulously fair-minded, never disclosing anything about the evidence amassed on Rove and Armitage. In the end the only person involved who served any time in jail was not someone who leaked, but Judith Miller, a reporter. Perhaps the greatest irony is that Libby leaked Plame's identity and mounted a sophisticated campaign to refute what he believed were falsehoods leveled by Joseph Wilson. Libby insisted that all he and the vice president ever wanted was to get the truth out. And then he himself lied, repeatedly and under oath. To combat what he thought was a lie, he leaked—and then repeatedly lied about it.

It is tempting to think that had Novak never written his column outing Plame none of this would have happened. But then Matt Cooper might have gotten his "double super secret background" scoop, and it might have run in *Time* magazine, not just the online edition. The same furor might well have ensued. The White House and State Department leaks may not have been an orchestrated campaign, but there were so many that eventually Plame's identity was sure to have been exposed, which is presumably what Libby, Rove, Armitage, and Fleischer wanted.

Is it possible that Libby was innocent? There can be no doubt he leaked Plame's identity in an effort to discredit Wilson. But could he have forgotten all those times that someone other than Tim Russert told him about Wilson's wife? Is it possible Tim Russert did tell Libby about Plame and that "all the reporters" knew about her?

Libby continues to maintain his innocence, and Ted Wells, his lawyer, says he believes him. But Libby's testimony was not about memory loss. In contrast to that of his boss, Vice President Cheney, or Rove or even Armitage, Libby had excellent recall of many events, even small details. He didn't say he couldn't remember whether he told any reporters about Wilson's wife or he didn't remember how he'd heard about her or even, when confronted at the very beginning with the fact that Russert didn't back his story, that he might have simply gotten confused. Had he done so—even if he had simply taken the Fifth Amendment and declined to answer—he would never have been charged.

Instead, Libby created a parallel universe in which he professed he was certain about what had happened, a detailed narrative that conveniently absolved him from any responsibility for wrongdoing. In this he flagrantly violated the most fundamental rule of lying: stick as close to the truth as possible. Clumsy though they may have been, in this regard Martha Stewart and Peter Bacanovic were far more proficient. By inventing a fanciful conversation with Tim Russert—a conversation no one could corroborate—Libby left his defense lawyers a near-impossible task. In many ways Fitzgerald didn't want to indict Libby, and Comey picked him in part because Fitzgerald had the independence and credibility not to file charges if none were warranted. But Libby's lies were so flagrant he left the prosecutor with no choice short of dereliction of duty.

By contrast, both Rove and Armitage, whose leaks found their way into Novak's column, narrowly escaped prosecution by withholding information and then claiming lack of memory. Did Armitage really forget his interview with Bob Woodward? And Rove his leak to Cooper? Did Rove forget what he told the president of the United States, or did he lie, as Bush's testimony suggests? Without a trial of either, we're left to draw our own conclusions. But the FBI agents most familiar with the case thought they had lied and should have been charged. Fitzgerald declined to do so because he felt he couldn't meet the burden of proof, which is different from believing them to be innocent. His letter to President Bush made clear that he thought there should be consequences from their at best reckless disclosures and evasive testimony.

Perhaps, at the time, saying he learned about Wilson's wife from Tim Russert seemed like a small, even inconsequential lie. If so, it had vast consequences. It unleashed a chain of events that sent Judy Miller to jail and ended her career at the *Times*. Perhaps these events were the metaphorical "roots" that connected the aspen trees in Libby's letter to Miller. Libby must have known her testimony would help convict him. If so, urging her to testify so she could leave prison was a decent thing for Libby to do, something also in keeping with his character. But there's no escaping that he was the cause of her confinement.

Fitzgerald had never wanted a press showdown, but the case ended up being disastrous for the press, both in its immediate consequences and in the case law that emerged. Journalists will no doubt continue to debate the merits of the *Times*'s resistance and other organizations' cooperation with Fitzgerald. But with benefit of hindsight, Judy Miller should never have gone to jail. She and the press lost resoundingly in the court of public opinion. It seems safe to say the press won't get a shield law on the terms it wants from Congress. The legal opinion of even the judge most favorable to the press made clear that courts will never give journalists the absolute privilege from testifying they want, no matter what they promise their sources. News organizations have already reacted by limiting confidentiality agreements. Despite some of the dire warnings from absolutists in the press, leaks have continued apace, including masses of confidential documents on the war in Afghanistan. But who knows how many stories have gone unpublished? The magnitude of the effect on news gathering remains to be seen and may prove impossible to measure, but it has to have had a chilling effect. For that, reporters and the public that relies on them for information have Scooter Libby to thank.

Given the secrecy of the CIA's covert operations, it's impossible to assess what damage the leak of Plame's identity inflicted on the CIA, current or former covert agents, or any ongoing operations. The CIA has declined to discuss any repercussions. Still, a dozen CIA agents wrote a letter to Bush urging him not to pardon Libby, arguing that he had committed an irreparable breach of security.

Libby's conviction was also a further blow to the already weakened credibility of the Bush administration and further undermined public confidence in government. It's true, as both Fitzgerald and Wells argued, that the evidence in the case sheds no light on the merits of the Iraq War. It doesn't explain the failure to find weapons of mass destruction. It doesn't prove there was a coordinated effort to "smear" Joe Wilson directed by the vice president or other high-ranking officials. It didn't even explain who really sent Joe Wilson to Africa or why his conclusions were ignored. But the charges against Libby did show a dispiriting willingness to lie—repeatedly and under oath—at the highest levels of the government. If Libby lied about Plame, who else in the White House lied, and about what?

Armitage's and Rove's behavior, whether criminal or not, does not inspire any confidence. The bar for service at the highest levels of government should not be so low that it excludes only those who commit crimes that can be proved beyond a reasonable doubt. Bush should have fired Rove as soon as his role in the leaks became clear, not to mention that Rove lied to the president, if Bush's memory of their conversation is correct. Bush's failure to do so after saying he'd fire anyone involved in the leak exposed rank hypocrisy at the highest level, a disregard for truth hardly overcome by his refusal to pardon Libby. Armitage at least had the decency to submit his resignation. Colin Powell should have accepted it immediately.

In light of this sorry spectacle, could anyone be blamed for being cynical about the integrity of government officials? The loss in public confidence is incalculable.

Perhaps no one made this point more forcefully than former White House press secretary Scott McClellan, who had publicly exonerated both Rove and Libby. In his 2008 memoir, *What Happened*, he acknowledged that in doing so,

> I had unknowingly passed along false information. And five of the highest-ranking officials in the administration were involved in doing so: Rove, Libby, Vice President Cheney, Andrew Card, and the president himself. . . . Top White House officials who knew the truth . . . allowed me to repeat a lie.
>
> The goal was to prevent political embarrassment that might hurt the president and weaken his bid for re-election in November 2004. The motive was understandable, but the behavior was wrong—and ultimately self-defeating. And, in retrospect, it was all too characteristic of an administration that, too often, chose in defining moments to employ obfuscation and secrecy rather than honesty and candor.

Part Three

BARRY LAMAR BONDS

EIGHT

"I'm Keeping My Money"

B ar-ry, Bar-ry, Bar-ry!"
The chant rolled across AT&T Park in San Francisco, packed with
a sold-out crowd of 43,154 fans, as Giants slugger Barry Bonds, forty-
three, stepped to the plate on August 7, 2007. His massive chest and arms filled
out the white Giants uniform piped in black and orange and emblazoned with
the number 24, the same number Bonds's father, Bobby, had worn when he
played as a Giant. Hoping to catch a historic moment, thousands of flashes
popped like strobe lights as the Washington Nationals' pitcher Mike Bacsik
threw his first pitch, a ball. Pitchers were often reluctant to throw a strike pitch
to Bonds, fearful of the consequences.

Baseball fans had been riveted during the summer as Bonds moved within
striking distance of the all-time home run record, held since 1974 by the legendary Hank Aaron. The previous Saturday, in San Diego, Bonds had hit home
run number 755, tying Aaron. Now he was at home in San Francisco. Family,
friends, and baseball officials had gathered in eager anticipation. On Monday
night he had failed to get a hit. By the bottom of the fifth inning on Tuesday,
Bonds had already notched two base hits against the twenty-nine-year-old Bacsik. Each pitch triggered an explosion of flashbulbs and more chants of "Barry,
Barry."

With no men on base, Bacsik worked the count to 3–2. On the next pitch,
there was a gasp from the crowd as Bonds connected. It was a foul off the
first-base line. Then the pitcher threw a high-risk fastball, right over the plate.
Bonds responded with a full-powered swing, and there was a loud crack. Bonds

dropped his bat and thrust both arms into the air. He could feel where the ball was going. He watched as it soared 435 feet into the right-center-field bleachers.

A rare smile spread across Bonds's face and the crowd erupted. Fireworks were unleashed as Bonds briefly savored the moment, then made a triumphal tour of the bases, grinning broadly. As he touched home plate he again thrust both arms into the air in what he said was a tribute to his late father. His seventeen-year-old son, Nikolai, was the first to reach him as family and teammates rushed onto the field to hug him. The game came to a halt.

An announcer asked everyone to turn their attention to the stadium's huge video screen. Hank Aaron, now seventy-three, appeared to offer a gracious tribute: "It is a great accomplishment, which required skill, longevity, and determination. Throughout the past century, the home run has held a special place in baseball and I have been privileged to hold this record for thirty-three of those years. I move over now and offer my best wishes to Barry and his family on this historic achievement. My hope today, as it was on that April evening in 1974, is that the achievement of this record will inspire others to chase their own dreams."

Bonds's godfather, seventy-six-year-old former Giants teammate Willie Mays, considered by many to be the greatest player ever, joined Bonds on the field as Bonds took the microphone. "Thank you very much. I got to thank all of you. All the fans here in San Francisco, road and home, it's been fantastic. . . . I got to thank my family. My mother, my wife, Liz, my kids Nikolai, Shikari, and Aisha. I'm glad I did it before you guys went to school. Thanks for being here. I got to thank the Washington Nationals for your support. Thank you for understanding this day. It means a lot to me. My dad . . ." Here he choked up, fighting back tears. "Thank you . . . for everything . . . thank you."

After the game resumed, no one cared that the Giants went on to lose. Baseball commissioner Bud Selig called to congratulate Bonds. The Giants hosted a press conference, and Bonds changed into a black cap and T-shirt, both emblazoned with the number 756. He was flanked by his wife, children, and sister, whom he described as "my backbone—we're a close-knit family."

Bonds said he was especially moved by a call on Sunday from his mother, after he tied Aaron's record, saying she was just glad she was alive to witness the moment of her son's triumph. "Truthfully, my dad would have said, 'What the hell took you so long?'" Bonds said. "My dad was never satisfied with anything." By contrast, he said his mother had always supported and encouraged him, driving him to practice and to school, working at concession stands when he was a kid. "My mother was there when my dad was never there," he said.

Then a reporter mentioned that despite his achievement, some people thought the new record was "tainted." Bonds's gaze immediately darkened. "You've heard that word," the reporter continued. "Do you think this record is tainted?"

"This record is not tainted at all," Bonds said, his voice taut. "At all. Period." His gaze defiantly swept the room of reporters. "You guys can say whatever you want."

Barry Bonds was born in 1964 into baseball royalty. His father, Bobby, signed with the Giants that year, and went on to notch a string of records: the first player to join the "30/30 club" (thirty home runs and thirty stolen bases in one season), the second player to reach a career total of 300 home runs and 300 stolen bases, and league records for lead-off home runs. He played in three All-Star games and was most valuable player in 1973. As a Giant, Bonds was especially close to Willie Mays, and many anointed Bobby as the heir to Mays's mantle. Bobby often moved to center field when Mays wasn't playing, and after Mays retired, Bobby got the position. Mays, in turn, doted on Barry, who often came with his father to Candlestick Park wearing a child-size Giants uniform. Mays became Barry's godfather.

But Bobby Bonds's life and career were far more troubled than the statistics and expectations implied. He was sometimes moody and withdrawn, and was twice arrested for driving under the influence of alcohol. He never lived up to the tremendous promise he showed early in his career, let alone to the Mays legacy, and in 1974 the Giants traded him to the Yankees, the first of a succession of trades that took him to six more teams in as many years. He retired from Major League Baseball in 1974, when Barry was ten, his baseball hopes focused on his sons.

Bobby Bonds was rarely at home with his family in Bay Area suburb San Carlos during baseball season, especially after he was traded to the Yankees (the family never moved east with him). Barry Bonds later alleged his father was abusive to him, his mother, and his siblings, and that his father's drinking embarrassed him. Even as Bonds publicly lavished praise on his father's coaching and influence, he lamented his frequent absences and impossible demands.

Barry was obviously a natural athlete, excelling at sports, especially baseball, at mostly white Junipero Serra High School in San Mateo. "Everything was easy for me, all sports, when I was a kid," Bonds told *Playboy* in 1993. "I'd work half as hard as other kids did and I was better. Why work when I had so much ability?" Bonds was tall, lithe, and slender, with remarkable timing and coordination. The Giants drafted Barry as soon as he graduated from high school; instead he attended Arizona State, where he was an outstanding player for the Sun Rays. He was drafted by the Pittsburgh Pirates in 1985 after his junior year and never graduated.

The combination of such natural talent and a celebrity father meant Barry Bonds was never just another teammate, giving him a privileged status he alternately embraced and resented. At Arizona State, he showed up driving a new black Pontiac Trans Am muscle car, which he parked in the coach's reserved parking space. His coach, Jim Brock, described his star player in a *Sports Illustrated* interview as "rude, inconsiderate and self-centered," with an inability to make friends. Bonds violated curfew and was suspended; teammates initially voted not to let him return, even though he was easily their most talented player.

Bonds made his first major-league appearance in center field for the Pirates in May 1986. He was just twenty-two. His behavior continued to reflect a mix of defiance and entitlement. In one altercation, captured on a widely circulated video, Bonds yelled, "I'll make my own rules here," and told revered former Pirate Bill Virdon, the outfield coach, "Nobody's going to tell me what to do." Though he was twice named National League MVP, Pittsburgh fans and the sports press never warmed to him. He was often booed. The local press awarded him its "MDP"—Most Despised Pirate—award.

After a series of salary disputes, the Pirates offered Bonds a five-year, $25 million contract in 1992, which he rejected. Bonds had obvious star appeal for San Francisco, which promptly signed him to a six-year, $43.75 million contract to play left field. During his first season as a Giant, Bonds hit 46 home runs and captured another MVP award.

Kimberly Bell was twenty-four, working as a graphic artist at Adobe Systems and as a part-time model when she met Barry Bonds in the players' parking lot outside the ballpark in 1994. She and her friend Kathy Hoskins had just watched the Giants beat the Montreal Expos, and afterward Hoskins maneuvered her car into the players' parking lot, hoping to meet some of the ballplayers.

Kathy's brother Steve was Barry Bonds's best friend, and the Hoskins and Bonds families had been close since childhood. Kathy's father, Bob Hoskins, a defensive tackle for the 49ers, and Bobby Bonds were close friends. The families were neighbors in San Carlos, and after Hoskins died at age thirty-four, Bobby became a surrogate father for the Hoskins children. After Bonds returned to the Bay Area from Pittsburgh, he and Steve resumed their childhood friendship and became all but inseparable. Hoskins was part of his entourage at the stadium and in the clubhouse, served as something of a public relations adviser as well as business manager for Bonds-themed memorabilia and other products, and was Bonds's overall right-hand man. Kathy sometimes worked for Bonds as a personal shopper.

Bonds came over to Hoskins's car and was immediately smitten by Bell. "I want to know that girl," he said to Hoskins, who invited both to a barbecue in San Carlos the next day. Bonds took Bell for a ride in his new Porsche, then persuaded her to spend the night with him.

At thirty, Bonds was already the Giants' star center fielder. He was also married. He'd eloped to Las Vegas and married Susann (Sun) Branco, a Swedish bartender he'd met at a Montreal nightclub in 1987. The couple had a son, Nikolai, and daughter, Shikari. But by the time he met Bell, they were separated and embroiled in a bitter fight over the prenuptial agreement Bonds had Branco sign. Bonds also felt their interracial marriage had attracted criticism and damaged his standing in the African American community. They divorced in December 1994 and at Bonds's behest the Catholic Church annulled the marriage.

Bonds and Bell were soon steady companions, though they never lived together; Bonds kept his condo in exclusive Redwood Shores, while Bell had a small apartment in Mountain View. After his contentious divorce, Bonds insisted he never wanted to be married again, and Bell said she wanted to pursue her various career possibilities. But they typically spent two or three nights a week together when Bonds was in town. He had a key to her apartment and came and went freely. She often traveled with him on road trips, staying in an adjacent room sometimes booked by the Giants organization. He introduced her to his parents, his children, his agents, his teammates. He called her frequently, even obsessively, at work and at home. She dutifully kept all the recorded messages, which, at least at first, were filled with endearments as well as anxiety: "Where are you? And who are you with? I have called you all night on your cell and home."

Bell was in love with Bonds, and she made few demands, something she felt strengthened their relationship. He didn't feel pressured or tied down. Still, there were benefits besides the travel and the limelight when she was with him. He (or his friend Steve Hoskins) sometimes gave her envelopes containing thousands of dollars in cash; he bought her a new Toyota SUV when her car broke down; he paid for her breast augmentation surgery. Though he never claimed the relationship was exclusive, it nonetheless came as a shock to Bell when Bonds told her, in 1997, that a woman had moved into his apartment with him.

Despite his claims to Bell that he never wanted to marry again, the following year Bonds told her he was getting married. As Bell recalled the conversation, she asked, "Are you going to have children with her?"

"Well, she's gonna be my wife. I guess I have to let her have one," he'd replied.

Bonds and Liz Watson were wed in a lavish ceremony at the Ritz-Carlton hotel in San Francisco attended by 240 guests. Steve Hoskins was his best man. Bonds serenaded the bride, who was quiet, attractive, and unlike his previous wife or Bell, African American. A daughter, Aisha, was born in February 1999.

But Bonds showed the same selective approach to the conventions of marriage that he did the rules of his various teams. He and Bell were together the day before the wedding. The day he returned from his honeymoon, he showed up at Bell's apartment and said he didn't see why anything about their relationship had to change. But inevitably, the relationship did change. Bonds and Bell could no longer date publicly, nor could she travel openly with him on Giants trips (though she still did accompany him to many cities). During spring training in Arizona, Bonds rented a luxurious house in Scottsdale. Bell got to spend a week there with him, but had to leave when his wife and children arrived. But later, in 2001, Bonds offered to buy Bell a house of her own, and began funneling cash from the memorabilia business for a down payment, using Hoskins as a conduit.

Bell moved to Arizona, and over the years she learned to make accommodations. So, apparently, did Bonds's wife, Liz, a private, publicity-shy person, who can't have been under too many illusions about her husband's frequent absences. Still, she had their baby daughter to care for, as well as joint custody of his other two children.

The Giants were eager to portray their new star as fundamentally changed, more mature than the moody, self-indulgent young player who had alienated Pittsburgh. "I think he has changed, and I think, frankly, that his marriage has a lot to do with it," Giants owner Peter Magowan told *Oakland Tribune* reporter Josh Suchon. "He's got a lovely wife and lovely kids. He's a very good father."

Kimberly Bell, too, noticed that Bonds had changed, though not in the ways praised by Magowan. Little more than a year after his marriage, Bonds's physique had been radically transformed. He was no longer the slender athlete she'd met in the Giants' parking lot. His chest, shoulder, and arm muscles were huge. Even his head seemed swollen. He developed acne on his shoulders and back. He complained that his testicles had shrunk, and his sex drive faltered. He became even more moody and possessive, evident from the phone messages Bell recorded. Bell recalled standing with him in front of a mirror as the changes became increasingly visible. "Do I look bloated?" he asked, according to Bell. "Does it look funny? Do you think this is obvious?"

B arry Bonds started working out with Greg Anderson in 1998, the same year he married Liz. Anderson was a personal trainer at the World Gym near San Francisco International Airport, a spartan, cavernous facility that attracted hard-core weight lifters. Anderson was five-foot-ten and 225 pounds, muscular, with tattoos covering his arms and long sideburns, a hyper-masculine look favored by many weight lifters and bodybuilders. He and Bonds had grown up together in San Carlos, and according to Bonds, they "ran into each other" toward the end of the season and started talking about weight training.

That summer the nation was riveted by the rivalry between two power hitters, Sammy Sosa of the Chicago Cubs and Mark McGwire of the St. Louis Cardinals, as each pursued the single-season home run record of 61 set by Roger Maris in 1961. Suspense built as the lead changed back and forth throughout the summer. Finally McGwire hit the record-breaking home run on September 8, and went on to finish the season with a new record of 70 homers, 4 ahead of Sosa.

Amid the national adulation, the *New York Times* wrote an editorial noting that "a dismaying little chill" had accompanied the admission by McGwire that he had been using a substance called androstenedione, or "andro," as it was known to bodybuilders and other users. Though not prohibited by professional baseball, the substance—which was said to enhance testosterone production and thereby boost muscle size and strength—had been banned by both the NFL and the International Olympic Committee. Though stopping short of calling McGwire's record tainted, the *Times* called his use of the substance a cause for "grave concern," in large part because McGwire was a hero and role model to so many young athletes. McGwire pledged to stop using it.

As McGwire and Sosa made national headlines, Bonds seethed with jealousy, according to Bell and others, belittling the two players as "sluggers" with few other skills. When McGwire played in San Francisco, crowds gathered to watch him warm up. They grew so large that ropes had to be installed to keep them back. Bonds flew into a rage over the ropes, knocked them down, and ordered them removed, saying "not in my house."

Bonds was in danger of being eclipsed, and in an effort to keep up with the staggering pace being set by Sosa and McGwire, he'd already started more serious strength training. When it came to home runs, keen hand-eye perception and coordination were essential but not enough. Blasting a ball 435 feet took sheer muscular strength.

Like Bonds, Anderson had wanted to play baseball, and what he lacked in natural ability, he figured he'd make up for with strength. He lifted weights, first at a community college in the Bay Area, and then at Fort Hays State in Kansas, where he was recruited to play baseball. As with many bodybuilders, lifting weights seemed to become something of an addiction, the constant pursuit of "getting big," as much for its own sake as for enhancing his baseball prowess. He spent countless hours in the weight room, adding twenty pounds of muscle in his first year. He started using steroids, which weren't yet illegal and were widely available at gyms for serious bodybuilders.

Anderson had hopes he might be drafted by a professional baseball team, but when nothing materialized after his junior year, he left without graduating and returned to California. He naturally gravitated toward other weight lifters and bodybuilders, and after one of his friends bought the World Gym franchise, Anderson found his perfect milieu. He started a personal training business, Get Big Productions. His license plates read "W8 GURU." He used and dealt in steroids, refining his knowledge of their benefits and risks, even though they had been outlawed by Congress as potentially dangerous controlled substances in 1990. Penalties for illegal use and distribution were increased, and distribution of steroids and human growth hormone, other than for legitimate medical reasons at the direction of a physician, was made a felony. With the AIDS epidemic in full swing, and steroids a common prescription for the wasting disease often associated with the virus, there was an ample supply in the Bay Area.

Steroids are all synthesized or naturally occurring forms of the male sex hormone testosterone, which promotes muscle growth and inhibits pain associated with the body's breakdown of protein, permitting more frequent and strenuous exercise. But frequent use, especially at the high doses embraced by many athletes, has numerous adverse side effects, some largely cosmetic, others serious. Steroids have been linked to psychiatric disorders, depression, and suicide; to heart and liver damage; and to sexual dysfunction. Steroid use can cause severe acne, especially on the back and shoulders, hair loss, mood swings, and fatigue, and it can be addictive. Human growth hormone, a synthetic or natural protein, encourages healing and tissue growth, and is often used in conjunction with a steroid regimen. It, too, has been associated with numerous adverse side effects.

When Bonds reconnected with Anderson in 1998, he felt he needed to "push [my] body to a new level," as he put it, "and I liked Greg's philosophy. Because my other trainer was, like, three sets of legs, three sets of this . . . And Greg is more, sixteen sets of chest, more biceps, to really maximize and expand your muscle. And I liked that philosophy. And I admired that."

Anderson became Bonds's strength trainer, working out regularly at the World Gym; Bonds had separate trainers for running and stretching. Anderson was suddenly vaulted to a new level, from obscurity to training one of the nation's premier athletes. Anderson had never realized much financial success, living a hand-to-mouth existence and moving through a progression of small rental apartments. He had no formal agreement with Bonds, and probably would have provided his training for free, just for the thrill of working with Bonds and for the prestige. Still, Bonds gave him periodic payments, typically in envelopes containing $10,000 in cash. Bonds sold Anderson a barely used SUV that Bonds had tired of in a matter of days.

Anderson also got to travel with Bonds, joining him at spring training in Arizona (where he shared the house in Scottsdale with Bell) and on an All-Star trip to Japan. As part of Bonds's entourage, Anderson moved freely throughout the stadium and locker rooms, and got to know other professional players, even though Bonds seemed jealous and resentful of any attention he showed other players. Still, Bonds introduced Anderson to other professional players who were his friends, like Gary Sheffield and Jason Giambi of the Yankees, whom he met on the Japan trip. Bonds invited Sheffield to stay with him after the end of the 2001 season and said he'd help him with his workout regimen. Bonds introduced him to Anderson, and Sheffield ended up paying him $10,000. Giambi, too, become an Anderson client at Bonds's behest.

As Kimberly Bell had already observed, Bonds's physical transformation in 1999, the year after he started training with Anderson, was little short of amazing. He went from 185 to 230 pounds even as his body fat dropped. He looked like an NFL linebacker, not the trim young Pirate of just a few years earlier. His teammates started calling him "the Incredible Hulk."

But perhaps he had bulked up too fast, and the Anderson training regimen had been too intense. He tore an elbow tendon lifting heavy weights and was disabled for weeks. Then he pulled a groin muscle. He played in only 102 games in 1999.

None of this was lost on the Giants management. The next year, as the Giants moved into their new, state-of-the-art Pac Bell Park, they hired Stan Conte as head athletic trainer. Bonds quickly made it clear to Conte that he might be head trainer, but he wouldn't be training Bonds. He needed "special attention" from his own trainers. Bonds had his own area in the new clubhouse, separated from other Giants players by a wall of lockers, with a large-screen TV and vibrating lounge chair. His teammates nicknamed Bonds's private space "the kingdom."

Conte was immediately suspicious of Anderson, whose own physique and demeanor were practically a billboard for illegal steroid use. Conte asked Anderson for his résumé. Other than a high school diploma, it showed no training or other education that might qualify Anderson as a personal trainer, let alone as a strength trainer for someone of Bonds's stature. During spring training, Conte worried that Bonds was lifting excessive weights and risking further injury, but Anderson told him, "I'm doing what Barry tells me to." Conte tried to have Anderson banned from the Giants' clubhouse, to no avail.

Under Anderson's direction, Bonds adjusted to his new training regimen and physical condition. Despite Conte's worries, Bonds not only avoided injury, but at age thirty-five, when most players undergo an inevitable physical decline, he demonstrated increased strength and stamina. In 2000, he hit 49 home runs; in 2001 he nailed his career 500th. After a streak of home runs in Atlanta, a local reporter asked him how he could account for such a feat: "Call God. Ask him," Bonds replied.

As Bonds was closing in on McGwire's record, reporter David Grann visited him in the Giants' clubhouse several times for a profile that ran in the *New York Times Magazine*. At one session, Bonds was lounging shirtless in his reclining chair, and Grann admired his bulging biceps and sculpted abdominals. Steve Hoskins and Greg Anderson were standing nearby. "To stay in such condition he eats six specially prepared meals a day, consisting of fish, chicken, turkey, vegetables or, on rare instances, beef; each meal has 350 to 450 calories," Grann reported. "'Every month we take his blood and test his mineral levels to make sure they're in line so that if he's 10 milligrams off in zinc or 6 off in magnesium or 5 milligrams off in copper, that's what we replace,' Anderson explained. 'That's how he stays in such good condition.'"

Bonds was also featured in the June issue of *Muscle & Fitness* in what amounted to an advertorial for BALCO, the acronym for the Bay Area Laboratory Cooperative, founded by fitness-supplement guru Victor Conte Jr. Bonds told the magazine:

> I visit BALCO every three to six months. They check my blood to make sure my levels are where they should be. Maybe I need to eat more broccoli than I normally do. Maybe my zinc and magnesium intakes need to increase. Victor will call me to make sure I'm taking my supplements, and my trainer Greg will sit near my locker and stare at me if I don't begin working out right away. I have these guys pushing me.

Be that as it may, one of Bonds's teammates approached head trainer Stan Conte for advice about using steroids, which he was thinking of buying from Anderson, pointing to Bonds's success. Conte gave him what he called a "good lecture" on the unfairness and risks of steroid use. Though notoriously slow to address the issue, Major League Baseball had explicitly banned the use of steroids and human growth hormone in the 2002 Players Agreement, and random drug testing was scheduled to begin the following year. Though Conte wouldn't name the player, he also reported the incident to Giants general manager Brian Sabean, who'd done nothing about Conte's requests to have Anderson barred from the clubhouse. Sabean suggested Conte confront Bonds and Anderson—which Conte knew would be futile and would only turn Bonds against him. Nor did Sabean report the incident (he later said he was unaware of a major-league requirement that such matters be reported to the commissioner's office). Clearly, no one wanted to raise the delicate matter of Anderson's suspected use and distribution of steroids and risk Bonds's ire. Basically, Conte resigned himself to the status quo, which meant that Bonds was exempt from the rules that applied to everyone else. When the Giants' head of security asked during spring training in 2003 if he could help with the Anderson problem, Conte said, "the horse had already left the barn and there's no need to close the door now."

In 2002, the Giants signed Bonds to a five-year, $90 million contract. He was the highest-paid player in baseball history. He paid $8.7 million for a six-bedroom, ten-bathroom mansion in Beverly Park, a gated community in the Hollywood Hills, above Los Angeles. In May, Bonds passed McGwire's career home run total, then led the Giants to their first National League pennant since 1989. Anderson accompanied him to the World Series games in Anaheim. The Giants seemed well on their way to a world championship title, but Anaheim came from behind in game six and then took the series in game seven. The World Series champion ring Bonds coveted had eluded him.

Still, Bonds was again the National League MVP, and there was growing anticipation that he was poised to assault baseball's ultimate peak, the all-time home run record. At that year's MVP ceremony, slugger Reggie Jackson said, "Babe Ruth, Ted Williams, Henry Aaron. Sooner or later they'll have to end that list with Barry Bonds."

During spring training in Arizona the following March, Bonds encountered a fan wearing one of the baseball jerseys personally autographed by Bonds, part of the memorabilia business his friend Steve Hoskins managed. He didn't recognize the signature and was suspicious it was a forgery. He flew into a rage and accused Hoskins of various financial irregularities, threatening to turn Hoskins in to law enforcement authorities.

It had never been easy being Bonds's best friend, although Hoskins had endured plenty of abuse over the years without complaint, in return for the many benefits the relationship conferred. Like Bell, he'd observed the physical changes in Bonds, including his volatile mood swings and an increasing suspicion of Hoskins, leading to frequent arguments, culminating in the latest threats. Hoskins was convinced that steroid use was to blame.

According to Hoskins, he warned Bonds against steroids and tried to dissuade him, to no avail. Hoskins was so concerned he took the issue to Bonds's father, Bobby, hoping to enlist him in the effort to stop Bonds. But Bobby flatly rejected the possibility that his son might be using illegal performance-enhancing drugs. So, to provide the evidence that might persuade him, Hoskins arrived at the Giants' clubhouse in March carrying a concealed tape recorder. Perhaps, with their latest dispute and Bonds's threats fresh in his mind, he had less altruistic motives.

Anderson was in Bonds's area, as usual. Hoskins fell into conversation with him and activated the recording device.

"You know, um, when Barry's taking those shots, Dr. Ting [Arthur Ting,

Bonds's personal physician] said that one of, one of the basketball players . . . he was taking them shots, and doing it in his thigh . . . and he's . . . oh shit . . . it's fuckin' . . ." Hoskins began.

"Oh, I know. Yeah, you can't even, you can't even walk after that," Anderson said.

"Yeah, no, he said he had to go in and graft his—"

"Oh yeah, you know what happened?" Anderson interrupted. "He got uh . . ."

"He must have put it in the wrong place," Hoskins said.

"No, what happens is, they put too much in one area, and what it does, it'll, it'll actually ball up and puddle. And what happens is, it actually will eat away and make an indentation. And it's a cyst. It makes a big fucking cyst. And you have to drain it. Oh yeah, it's gnarly . . . Hi Benito [Santiago, the Giants' catcher, walked by] . . . oh it's gnarly."

Startled by Santiago, they started whispering. Hoskins steered the conversation back to Bonds. "He said his shit went . . . that's why he has to, he had to switch off of one cheek to the other. Is that why Barry didn't do it in one spot, and you didn't just let him do it one time?"

"Oh no. I never. I never just go there. I move it all over the place."

"Yeah, that's why he was like . . ." Hoskins laughed. "He was like, tell Greg if he's puttin' it in one fucking place, to tell him to move that shit somewhere else."

"Oh, no, no, no. I learned that when I first started doing that shit . . . sixteen years ago . . . because uh . . . guys would get gnarly infections . . . and it was gross . . . I mean, to the point where you had to have surgery just to get that fucking thing taken out."

Hoskins asked about the possibility Major League Baseball would start testing for drug and steroid use. "What if they decide that . . . I think, didn't they say they're going to test . . . um . . . they don't know. They're not testing the players yet. They're just doing random shit. So they're just going to get a percentage. And then after they figure out the percentage . . . then if it's high enough, then they'll do whatever."

"Well, what, what I understand is that, what they're doing is they're . . . um . . . they're, they did twenty-five players, random, supposedly, in spring training," Anderson replied.

"Oh, so you don't even . . ."

"And then, so those guys have already been tested twice. They got tested, then a week later they got tested again. Same guys. So what happens is, is those guys are pretty much done for the year."

"Okay."

"They don't ever have to get tested again," Anderson continued. "Now supposedly, there's gonna be three guys . . . excuse me, not three . . . one hundred and fifty guys tested during, random during the season . . . which he's going to be on that list, easy. . . ."

"Oh yeah, definitely."

"So, in that . . . after . . . but they're going to test him once, then test him again. And then after, he supposed to be . . ."

"But do we know?"

"Do we know when they're going to do it?"

"Yeah. Does he know?"

"I, I, I have an idea," Anderson said. "See I gotta . . . , where, where the lab that does my stuff, is this lab that does entire baseball . . ."

"Oh okay. Oh the same . . ."

"Yeah. So, they . . . I'll know . . . I'll know like probably a week in advance, or two weeks in advance before they're gonna do it. But it's going to be in either the end of May, beginning of June. It's right before the All-Star break definitely. So after the All-Star break . . . fucking, we're like fucking clear as a mother."

"Okay, so what you want . . . so they'll . . . the guys from Major League Baseball. . . . so baseball will tell, you'll know when they're gonna do it, but you don't know exactly if it's gonna be him."

"Right."

"Or will you know . . ."

"He may not even get tested," Anderson added.

"Right, that's what I'm saying."

"Because it's supposed to be computerized."

"But we just know if . . . he's gonna be . . ."

"He's gonna be. But the whole thing is . . . everything that I've been doing at this point, it's all undetectable," Anderson boasted.

"Right."

"See, the stuff that I have . . . we created it. And you can't, you can't buy it anywhere. You can't get it anywhere else. But, you can take it the day of and pee . . ."

"Uh-huh."

"And it comes up with nothing."

"Isn't that the same shit that Marion Jones and them were using?" Hoskins asked.

"Yeah, same stuff, the same stuff that worked at the Olympics," Anderson confirmed.

"Right, right."

"And they test them every fucking week."

"Every week. Right, right."

"So that's why I know it works. So that's why I'm not even trippin'. So that's cool."

The tape ended.

Hoskins evidently dropped any plans to play the recording for Bonds's father, who was struggling with lung cancer. As Hoskins became increasingly estranged from his former best friend, Bonds barred him from the clubhouse, fired him from the memorabilia business, and threatened to take evidence against him to the FBI.

Bonds's relationship with Kimberly Bell also reached the breaking point that spring. Although his cash payments to her for the house in Arizona had reached $80,000, mostly conveyed in cash by Hoskins, they had become increasingly sporadic and were dwindling as Bonds pursued an affair with a model he'd met in New York. He showed centerfold pictures of her he'd taken from the Internet to teammates. In May, when Bell's flight to San Francisco was late, Bonds was furious, put his hand on her throat, and threatened to kill her, she subsequently claimed. Other times, she says, he told her, "I'm gonna cut your head off and leave you in a ditch. And I'm glad nobody knows that you and I are tied this close together, because that way nobody will know it's me when I kill you."

Later that May, they saw each other in Arizona, and then Bonds called her from the airport as he was leaving. According to Bell, he told her he wanted her to "disappear . . . maybe forever."

The next day Greg Anderson called her, evidently to apologize on Bonds's behalf. She said she knew all about the woman in New York. Anderson asked what he should tell Bonds. Bell said she didn't care what he told him.

In June, Bonds and his personal business lawyer, Laura Enos, met with Hoskins at a conference room in Enos's office in an attempt to resolve Bonds's concerns over the memorabilia business. Enos subsequently told the *New York Times* that Hoskins said, "I have three doors. If you don't drop this memorabilia issue, I'm going to ruin Barry. Behind door No. 1 is an extramarital affair. Behind door No. 2 is failure to declare income tax. And behind door No. 3 is use of steroids. And I will go to the press and ruin Barry. His records will be ruined. He will never get into the Hall of Fame."

Hoskins hasn't publicly disputed Enos's account. Within days, Bonds took his complaints about Hoskins to both the U.S. Attorney and the FBI field office in San Francisco, which launched an investigation of Hoskins.

Despite his father's illness, the turmoil in his personal life, and the breach with his best man and best friend, during the 2003 season Bonds hit 45 home runs and was again named MVP.

At the end of the season, a clubhouse attendant found a sealed package of syringes in catcher Benito Santiago's locker. He took them to Giants trainer Stan Conte, who said he'd "take care of it." Conte and the other trainers discussed the implications, and decided to throw them away. Santiago was leaving the team to become a free agent in any event, and Conte said nothing further.

At 12:20 p.m. on September 3, 2003, a half-dozen Buick sedans ferrying twenty-four IRS agents and other investigators pulled into the parking lot of a strip shopping mall on Gilbreth Road in Burlingame, California. BALCO occupied a nondescript, one-story storefront with plate-glass windows and a stone veneer. Jeff Novitzky and two other agents entered through the front door, their handguns drawn, and moved quickly through the reception area, decorated with signed photos of some of BALCO's clients—Barry Bonds occupied pride of place. Through an open door Novitzky spotted Victor Conte, BALCO's founder and president, and James Valente, his right-hand man and vice president, at a fax machine. He walked up to them, told them federal agents were executing a search warrant for the premises, and asked them to sit in the reception area.

In Conte's vivid re-telling:

Three unmarked black cars come screeching into BALCO's front parking lot. More unmarked cars skidded up one behind the other on the frontage road. The six or seven cars were filled with a team of twenty-six IRS special agents, narcotics task force agents, FDA agents, and other armed law enforcement officers wearing flak jackets. The three of us watched in awe through the front windows as the agents rushed out of their cars, carrying assault rifles and handguns. They lined up in single file with great speed and precision and headed straight for our front door.

As they came inside the lead agent yelled, "Does anybody have a weapon?" All three of us were frozen in place as the agents charged in one after another and pointed guns directly at us.

They ordered us to put our hands up and walk slowly over and sit down in the three chairs along the wall in the front lobby. They instructed us to put our hands on our knees and not to move. We were swiftly surrounded by a semicircle of gun-packing police officers standing shoulder to shoulder. . . .

The lead agent yelled, "We're here to execute a search warrant." He then commanded other officers to "secure the building." Within seconds, we heard the loud noise of a helicopter hovering directly over the lobby entrance. The glass louvers above the front door started to rattle from the intense vibration of the chopper blades. We heard officers screaming loudly, "Anybody in there? Does anybody have a weapon?" as they stormed throughout the BALCO building. None of us had a criminal history, so the intensity of the raid was like using a laser-guided missile to kill a mosquito.

Conte concluded, "It was surreal."

As an investigator the thirty-two-year-old Novitzky preferred to work quietly, unrecognized, out of the limelight. But his six-foot-six height and shaved head made him stand out. He'd played basketball at nearby Mills High and at San Jose State, where he majored in accounting, and his father was a high school basketball coach. But a series of injuries and then back surgery kept him out of most games. He joined the IRS as an investigator right after college and was now in his tenth year with the IRS Criminal Investigation division, which functions much like the FBI. Since tax evasion is often linked to other crimes, like drugs and extortion, he often worked with other investigators.

After making sure the offices were secure, Novitzky returned to the reception area and, according to Novitzky, showed the three officers a copy of the search warrant, based on "probable cause to believe that Victor Conte Jr. and others are involved in a nationwide scheme to knowingly illegally distribute athletic performance-enhancing drugs, including anabolic steroids, a federally controlled substance, to numerous elite professional athletes at a local, national and international level."

The warrant represented more than a year's work for Novitzky, who'd painstakingly assembled a trove of evidence suggesting that BALCO, in addition to whatever legitimate business it engaged in, was actively marketing illegal steroids and human growth hormone to an astonishing array of top athletes. After an anonymous caller lodged allegations that "an individual" was distributing steroids "to players of a local professional sports team," the IRS and the U.S. Anti-Doping Agency (USADA) both launched investigations. Novitzky began working on the case in August 2002. As an athlete, the clean-cut, sportsman-like Novitzky wouldn't have dreamed of using drugs to cheat, and he seemed relatively naive about the use of performance-enhancing drugs in professional sports. He wasn't familiar with the extensive vocabulary that had developed among steroid users and distributors. That quickly changed.

Novitzky and other agents began searching BALCO's trash the very week they received the tip, and returned every Monday night thereafter. (The Supreme Court has ruled that searching trash without a warrant isn't unconstitutional or an invasion of privacy, since the material has been discarded.) A team kept BALCO's offices under surveillance. Conte was followed and observed. Novitzky monitored Conte's Internet postings in chat groups devoted to fitness and bodybuilding, in which he freely discussed the risks, benefits, and use of steroids. Novitzky used the information to obtain subpoenas and gain access to Conte's bank records and e-mail accounts, as well as medical trash removed from BALCO. Novitzky took a crash course in the science of steroids, consulting with Dr. Don Catlin at UCLA and Dr. Larry Bowers, senior managing director of USADA, in charge of testing for U.S. Olympic athletes. Novitzky had brought Bowers along on the BALCO raid for help in identifying substances they might discover there.

For someone warning, as Conte wrote in one e-mail, "be careful about how you say what you say," he was remarkably indiscreet. The trash yielded empty boxes and used vials of testosterone, various steroid compounds, human growth hormone, and empty boxes and used syringes and syringe wrappers—all in such quantities as to suggest the steroids were being injected on BALCO's premises. Novitzky described the haul of evidence as a "treasure trove of information."

Greg Anderson and a stream of elite athletes were observed coming and going from the offices; Anderson sometimes went directly from BALCO to Pac Bell Park (later renamed AT&T Park) and entered the Giants' clubhouse. E-mails contained sophisticated discussions of various steroid regimens and how to avoid detection with references to the "cream," the "gel," and the "clear." Financial records indicated Conte had withdrawn $480,000 in cash (over several years), and had directed various athletes to make payments into his personal accounts rather than BALCO's.

Various documents uncovered in BALCO's trash strongly suggested that

Conte and Valente were sending blood and urine samples to be tested for steroids to make sure that the drugs their clients were using wouldn't show up in
routine tests. The source of the samples was often identified only by a code, but
one bore the name Barry Bonds. The blood sample had been sent to LabOne in
Kansas. But an affidavit from Valente dated the next day swore that the sample
had been mislabeled, and was actually from Greg Anderson.

Novitzky also found a letter dated June 5, addressed to International Association of Athletics Federations (IAAF) and USADA testing personnel. The letter implicated some of the world's top track-and-field athletes, as well as their
celebrated coach, Trevor Graham, in illegal steroid use.

Novitzky summarized the evidence he'd gathered with his application for a
search warrant, concluding that "this affidavit has presented evidence of illegal
anabolic steroid and other athletic performance-enhancing drug distribution to
professional athletes, including the distribution of new, untested substances;
the use of the mail to purchase epitestosterone, a substance used in the fraudulent defeat of performance-enhancing drug tests" and various financial irregularities suggesting "illegal money laundering transactions." The application had
been granted the day before the raid.

According to Novitzky, he showed Conte a copy of the search warrant and
said he'd like to interview him. (Conte maintains he only saw the warrant
much later, after his interrogation.) He encouraged Conte by indicating that
"when someone cooperates from the beginning, they often receive a benefit,"
though he said the U.S. Attorney would make the decisions and he couldn't
make any promises. He told Conte he wasn't under arrest, and there were no
plans to arrest him that day. He said he wasn't required to say anything, and he
was free to stop the interview at any time. He could leave whenever he wanted.
(Since there was no arrest, there was no need to extend a Miranda warning.)
Conte indicated he understood, and agreed to be interviewed. He, Novitzky,
and another agent moved to a private conference room at the rear of the offices
while Valente and his wife waited in the reception area, even though the agents
told them they were free to leave. Word of the search quickly spread, and BAL-
CO's phones started ringing with calls from anxious customers and the press.

Conte, fifty-three, followed his own fitness regimen, but with his slender mustache and small wire-rimmed glasses, he looked more like a professor than an athlete. Conte was born in 1950 into a working-class family in

California's Central Valley. After attending a community college, he played in rock bands and wound up in San Francisco, where he studied Eastern philosophy, experimented with vitamin supplements, and like many others, dabbled in recreational drugs. He'd gotten into the laboratory business in 1984, when he worked for a lab in Santa Barbara, later buying the rights to the blood-testing equipment, which he used to found BALCO. He'd also launched a nutritional supplement business from the same office. A nutritional supplement, ZMA, was his biggest product.

According to Novitzky, Conte was remarkably forthcoming about his illegal steroids business and his customers, whom he described as "elite" athletes. He sold them two products—the "clear" and the "cream," both performance-enhancing drugs—"so they can increase athletic performance without getting caught by the testers." The "clear" is a clear liquid anabolic steroid that athletes take orally in small doses. Conte said he didn't know what was in it; he'd bought a supply from Patrick Arnold, an Illinois chemist, for $450 a couple of years earlier, and he was still selling it. The "clear," he said, "helps athletes with recovery." He told all his customers that "the clear" was a steroid, but if they were ever asked about it by anyone in authority, they should say it was "flaxseed oil."

The "cream" is a mixture of testosterone and epitestosterone that athletes rub directly on their skin. Tests for steroids look for a rise in the ratio of testosterone to epitestosterone; by raising both levels, the "cream" keeps the ratio in balance. Conte said he got the testosterone cream from a doctor in Texas and the epitestosterone from a large life-science company. Conte in turn sent the ingredients to a friend of Arnold's in Texas, who mixed them into the cream sold by Conte. Conte typically charged $350, and kept athletes on a "short leash," selling only small quantities at a time, and only delivering the drugs in person when the athletes came to BALCO's office. He said all such payments were deposited in his personal accounts.

According to Novitzky's notes of the interview, Conte didn't hesitate to name his customers: San Francisco 49ers and Oakland Raiders linebacker Bill Romanowski was the "first guy" to whom he sold illegal performance-enhancing drugs. Other NFL customers were Dana Stubblefield, Josh Taves, Barrett Robbins, Chris Cooper, Johnny Morton, and Daryl Gardner. He had many track-and-field customers, including Olympic medalist Marion Jones; her boyfriend, world hundred-meter record holder Tim Montgomery; English sprinter Dwain Chambers; and world champion sprinter Kelli White—all current or former members of Trevor Graham's Sprint Capitol USA club in North Carolina.

And then there were the Major League Baseball players: Gary Sheffield, Jason Giambi, Jeremy Giambi, Armando Rios—and Barry Bonds. Conte didn't charge Bonds for supplies; instead, he'd agreed to endorse ZMA.

As Novitzky wrote in his report of the interview:

> At the beginning of this Major League Baseball season, Greg Anderson, a personal trainer at Bay Area Fitness who works closely with several Major League Baseball players, brought in several of the players to BALCO in order to obtain the undetectable "cream" and "clear." This was done because of Major League Baseball's new drug-testing policy. Barry Bonds was one of the players that Anderson brought to Conte to obtain the "clear" and the "cream." Bonds takes the "clear" and the "cream" on a regular basis. The protocol for using the substances is two times per week for the "clear" and two times per week for the "cream." The athletes do this for three weeks, then take one week off.

Conte led the agents, joined by Bowers, to a nearby public storage locker where he kept his supply of the "cream," the "clear," other steroids, and files on customers—including an extensive file on Trevor Graham. They seized the contents.

At about 4:00 p.m., Novitzky beckoned Valente to the conference room, and repeated that he wasn't required to answer questions and could leave anytime. Valente had worked for Conte for fifteen years, investing in BALCO, staying in the background. He had more direct contact with Anderson and Major League Baseball players than Conte. Valente confirmed much of what Conte had said, and added some details on Anderson and Bonds. (Conte later disputed the accuracy of Novitzky's notes and maintains he never gave Bonds illegal steroids.) As Novitzky wrote in his report:

> Greg Anderson also provides human growth hormone and testosterone cypionate to his professional baseball clients. Anderson brought his baseball clients to BALCO this spring when Major League Baseball announced their new steroid testing policy. This was so Anderson could start giving them steroids that would not show up in drug tests. Among those baseball players brought to BALCO by Anderson was Barry Bonds. Bonds has received the "clear" and the "cream" from BALCO on a "couple of occasions." According to Valente, Bonds does not like how the "clear" makes him feel.

Other players that Anderson has obtained the "clear" and the "cream" for from BALCO are Benito Santiago, Gary Sheffield, Marvin Benard, Jason Giambi and Randy Velarde. Sometimes the substances are given to Anderson to give to the athletes and sometimes the athletes are given the substances directly.

Other agents searching the premises found numerous documents detailing BALCO's distribution and monitoring of performance-enhancing drugs for professional athletes. They included a ledger used for recording urine samples and test results, as well as a numerical coding system used to identify the samples. The entries showed that Bonds's urine samples tested positive for an injectable steroid, methenolone, three times in 2000 and 2001. His samples had tested positive for another injectable steroid, nandrolone, twice. Other test results showed elevated ratios of testosterone to epitestosterone.

By 5:45 p.m., armed with the disclosures about Anderson and Valente, agents obtained a search warrant for Anderson's house and car. After they finished with Valente, Novitzky and two other agents drove to Bay Area Fitness, where they found Anderson training several of his clients. His young son, Cole, was also with him. Novitzky didn't want to embarrass Anderson in front of his clients and his son, so he asked him to follow him to a private room.

Anderson seemed unaware of the day's drama at BALCO. Like the others, Novitzky told Anderson he wanted to interview him, but he wasn't being arrested and he was free to leave, even return to his workout clients. But his house was about to be searched, and he was welcome to go with Novitzky to observe and answer some questions. Anderson said his girlfriend, Nicole Gestas, who was also a personal trainer, was at the house, and she would probably "freak out," so he'd better go along. Anderson got a call on his cell phone while they were walking to the parking lot. "They're coming to do it," Anderson said, then hung up.

When they arrived at Anderson's home, at 1111 Bayswater Avenue, a rented two-story stucco house on a narrow lot, Gestas's 2003 Porsche was in the driveway. Anderson opened the front door, followed by Novitzky and several agents, and told Gestas, "The BALCO thing has followed me here."

Copies of the warrants arrived about 6:45 p.m., which Novitzky reviewed with both Anderson and Gestas. As they did, other agents opened the refrigerator and found steroids and syringes. More were in a kitchen cabinet. In another cabinet they found a safe with about $60,000 in cash.

Both Anderson and Gestas agreed to answer questions, and Novitzky and another agent went with Gestas to an upstairs bedroom as the other agents continued the search. Gestas told Novitzky she worked as a personal trainer at the Powerhouse Gym. She said she never knew Anderson used or sold steroids. Novitzky said flatly he didn't believe her; what about all the steroids and syringes in the refrigerator and cabinet? Gestas said they were "Greg's area and she never looked." She said she didn't know where he got the supplies, nor did she know anything about the cash in the safe. About the only thing she admitted knowing was that Anderson trained both Barry Bonds and Gary Sheffield. In other words, Gestas wasn't going to cooperate and was, in all likelihood, making false statements.

After finishing with Gestas, Novitzky returned to Anderson, who said he was willing to answer questions because "he felt he had done nothing wrong." He told Novitzky he'd become a certified trainer about sixteen years earlier, and worked full-time as a personal trainer. He said he'd worked with BALCO, which did blood testing, for a few years, and met Victor Conte through friends. Anderson said he gave "a small amount of steroids to people," and knew how to use them from his "bodybuilding days," according to Novitzky's memo. Anderson said he didn't make a profit from steroids, thought of himself as just a "middleman," and added, "I felt that if I didn't earn a profit, then I'm not a drug dealer."

Anderson said he'd grown up with Barry Bonds, and that Bonds was his first client who was a professional athlete. It was obvious Anderson owed Bonds for his entrée to the world of elite professional athletes. In addition to Bonds, Anderson said he was currently working with Gary Sheffield, Benito Santiago, catchers A. J. Pierzynski and Bobby Estalella, outfielders Marvin Benard and Armando Rios, and Jason Giambi.

At first Anderson insisted he only provided steroids to bodybuilders. Then he acknowledged he'd given them to a "few" professional athletes, but said he didn't want to name them. He'd given them both testosterone and human growth hormone, which he sometimes mailed using Federal Express. He claimed he "didn't really pay any attention" to the steroid distribution.

Anderson confirmed much of what Valente had told them about bringing his baseball clients to BALCO after Major League Baseball decided to initiate drug testing. He said he bought the "clear" and the "cream" from BALCO, paying cash, and he understood that the cream was a combination of testosterone and epitestosterone that would escape detection.

Novitzky pressed him to name his clients who were taking the "clear" and the "cream," but Anderson was evasive. He said he only gave them to "my little guys," adding that "drugs are a very minute part of my little guys." Novitzky asked who these "little guys" might be, and Anderson named Benard, Estalella, Rios, and Santiago. He said nothing about Bonds.

Anderson said the cash in the safe was money he'd been saving for years for a down payment on a house. He acknowledged taking cash payments from his workout clients that he put in the safe and didn't declare as income. But Novitzky doubted the cash had been accumulating for the years Anderson claimed. Would the serial numbers on the bills indicating their age bear out Anderson's claim? Anderson replied, implausibly, that he "rotated" the bills, so most were actually new.

Then Novitzky asked specifically about Barry Bonds. Anderson said Bonds had never taken either the "clear" or the "cream." Novitzky thought Anderson was lying, and said so. He warned him that any false statements would be taken into account in evaluating his cooperation, or lack of it.

At this juncture other agents interrupted the interview to tell Novitzky that they'd located a number of file folders, each bearing the name of a professional baseball player. Novitzky looked inside. Each file contained calendars with handwritten entries that seemed to record the dates, times, and quantities for administering performance-enhancing drugs, including the "clear" and the "cream." One of the folders was labeled "Barry Bonds." In addition to the calendar was a sheet labeled "Barry" and the notes "blood tests," "G," "depo test cyp 3 bottles off and reg. season," "clear and cream," and "Clomifed" (a type of steroid).

Novitzky showed Anderson the folder. Visibly nervous, Anderson said he'd better stop answering questions, because "I don't want to go to jail." He said he wanted to cooperate, but "didn't want to get himself into further trouble," Novitzky wrote in his notes of the interview. He refused to let the agents search his computer, which wasn't covered by the warrant.

Novitzky and his agents left at about 9:00 p.m., carrying with them numerous vials, many labeled to indicate they contained steroids; envelopes containing various creams; over a hundred syringes; alcohol pads; and assorted pills. Anderson said it was all for his personal use.

Two days later, on September 5, Novitzky and his team returned, this time with a warrant to seize Anderson's computers. They arrived at 7:25 p.m. Anderson's SUV was in the driveway, and they could hear the TV through the front door. But no one answered. They broke open the door and discovered no one home. About thirty minutes later, Gestas's Porsche pulled into the driveway, and she and Anderson got out. Novitzky walked outside to intercept them, and told Anderson another search was in progress. They were taking his computers because they'd discovered computer-generated invoices for steroids during the previous search. Anderson said he didn't know what Novitzky was talking about.

In the wake of the Novitzky-led raid on BALCO, San Francisco U.S. Attorney Kevin Ryan, named by President Bush to the post in 2002, had an extraordinary case on his hands that threatened to blow the lid off the long-suspected but hitherto secret world of illegal performance-enhancing drug use in professional baseball, football, and track. More than a score of elite athletes were implicated, including world-record holders, Olympic medalists, and Bonds, one of the best-known athletes in the world, bent on a new all-time home run record. It was, he later said, "the case of a lifetime." The son of an Irish immigrant, born in Alberta, Canada, Ryan was Republican, conservative, Catholic, a graduate of Dartmouth (where he played rugby) and the University of San Francisco School of Law. He'd worked as a prosecutor in Alameda County and then as a municipal court judge in San Francisco.

The BALCO investigation also posed extraordinary risks to any prosecutor. Many of the athletes were national icons, beloved and admired by fans. The San Francisco Giants were a hometown institution. They'd just represented the city in the World Series. However controversial Bonds may have been on road trips, in San Francisco he was a star. Ryan told the *San Francisco Chronicle* he stopped attending Giants games out of fear he'd be pictured on the giant screen—and booed, or worse.

From the beginning, Ryan had decided to focus on the manufacturers and distributors of illegal steroids—the dealers—and not the end users, much as drug prosecutions often target dealers rather than users. So a grand jury was convened to investigate Conte, Valente, and Anderson—not Bonds or any other athletes identified as BALCO clients. Although Ryan later said some of the things he learned about the Giants were "hard for me to stomach," he wanted to keep their names confidential and avoid any public disclosure.

In mid-September the grand jury issued subpoenas to about three dozen athletes named in BALCO documents, including Bonds.

Ten days after the raid on BALCO, Victor Conte had hired Sacramento defense lawyer Troy Ellerman, a lawyer who had handled a speeding ticket for his daughter. Ellerman was an unusual choice for a high-profile criminal case in San Francisco; he was better known in rodeo than legal circles. Ellerman was a former professional rodeo cowboy who still habitually wore a cowboy hat over his shaved head. He came from a rodeo family—they appeared professionally as the Flying Cossacks—and had been riding bulls since he was six. He'd served as a stunt double for Paul Hogan ("Crocodile Dundee") in the 1994 film *Lightning Jack*. In addition to his work as a lawyer, Ellerman was chairman of the board of the Professional Rodeo Cowboys Association.

Now, over the phone, Conte went on at length about the day's raid, offering a far more dramatic and colorful version than anything described in Novitzky's report. He'd repeatedly asked for a lawyer (at least ten times, he later said), but Novitzky had brushed aside his requests and simply moved to the next question. He hadn't been shown a search warrant until the raid was over. He insisted he hadn't named names of drug users; he'd only told Novitzky the names of some of his clients. Novitzky had asked him to wear a wire, and he'd said, "Absolutely not." He said he'd take responsibility for his own actions, but wouldn't cooperate in any way. Later, Conte said he was shocked by the inaccuracies he found in Novitzky's written report of the raid and said, "The government has not been truthful."

Ellerman brought in another more experienced lawyer from Sacramento, Robert Holley, to help out, someone he thought might impress a jury with his maturity and gravitas. The two had worked well together before, and Holley became the attorney of record for Conte, while Ellerman represented Valente. But as time passed, Conte began to wonder if his lawyers were adequate for such a complex, high-profile case in federal court in San Francisco. He called Ellerman and Holley his "hillbilly lawyers from Sacramento."

In the wake of Hoskins's ouster from his inner circle, Bonds had been relying increasingly for advice on one of his bodyguards, Daniel Molieri. As a former San Francisco police officer, Molieri knew Michael Rains, a criminal defense lawyer based in the East Bay who'd made his reputation defending accused cops. But defending police officers was far different from guiding a star of Bonds's magnitude through the maze of the BALCO investigation. Rains, in turn, lined up a friend of his to represent Anderson.

Rains responded to Bonds's subpoena by telling the prosecutors his star client would invoke the Fifth Amendment and refuse to testify. And, like Ari

Fleischer in the Libby case, Bonds was offered immunity in return. It was an extraordinary grant, one for which Ryan was subsequently harshly criticized, and which provoked disagreement among the government lawyers and investigators. After all, Novitzky had already amassed what seemed compelling evidence that Bonds had used illegal controlled substances. Bonds had also introduced other professional athletes to BALCO and to Anderson, who in turn used the drugs. Bonds was the biggest name in the investigation, a national role model, and prosecuting him for illegal steroid use would be a huge deterrent for other potential steroid users. But Ryan stood by the decision, and the assistant attorney general in Washington approved Ryan's request for immunity for Bonds.

Celebrated track coach Trevor Graham's was a distinctly American story of triumph over adversity. He was born in Jamaica, the eighth of nine children, and his parents had no choice but to leave him behind when they moved to the United States. He shuttled among relatives and struggled to find food before eventually joining his parents in Brooklyn.

Graham had excelled as a scholarship track star at St. Augustine's College in North Carolina, and won a silver medal for Jamaica at the 1988 Seoul Olympics. He was best known for his elite track club, Sprint Capitol USA, which he operated on the campus of North Carolina State University in Raleigh. His coaching was eagerly sought after by top runners, including Marion Jones, winner of five medals at the Sydney Olympics, arguably the most famous female athlete in the world. He was one of the few coaches with his own endorsement deal for Nike.

Earlier that summer, Novitzky had found a letter in the trash from Conte to the USADA. The letter detailed the once-close relationship between Conte and Trevor Graham and their falling-out. Graham had played a key role in introducing Conte to some of the world's top track stars, long before Greg Anderson brought Bonds to Conte. But during the spring of 2001, Conte became furious when he heard reports that Graham was siphoning off supplies of the "cream," the "clear," and other performance-enhancing drugs for use with other clients. The two had several bitter arguments, and Conte put Graham and Graham's clients on strict allocations, demanding an accounting of how the drugs were disbursed, further angering Graham.

"Trevor Graham, former coach of Marion Jones, is giving his IAAF and USATF athletes oral testosterone undecanoate from Mexico," Conte's letter began.

Trevor is having a friend . . . purchase this substance from his group in
Mexico . . . he routinely goes over the border to Mexico to make the
purchases. Oral testosterone undecanoate will clear the body and be
undetectable in urine in less than a week. . . . If a urine sample was collected
from any of Trevor's athletes within two days after a competition, they
would likely test positive for T/E ratio . . . If USADA or IAAF would be
willing to collect a urine sample from any of the athletes listed below,
a positive test result would be likely.

Conte evidently had second thoughts, considering that he was one of Graham's sources for illegal steroids. He never sent the letter, and threw it in the
trash.

While Conte fumed, Graham was presiding over a veritable soap opera in
North Carolina. In March 2001, after the Sydney Olympics, a nearly
distraught Jones had confided in Graham that she was separating from her husband, shot-put champion C. J. Hunter. Hunter had tested positive for steroids
and had withdrawn from the Sydney Olympics, which dragged Jones into the
steroids scandal and had caused strains in their marriage. Then Hunter started
"sleeping with" another of Graham's runners, Jones alleged.

The next year Jones started dating sprinter Tim Montgomery, another of
Graham's track star athletes. Montgomery had won a gold medal in Sydney as
part of the United States' 4x100 relay team. Jones and Montgomery moved in
together and continued training with Graham. In June, Jones gave birth to a
boy, Tim Montgomery Jr.

That same summer, Tim Montgomery, who was so slight his nickname was
"Tiny Tim," had visibly gained muscle. His stamina and strength also surged.
In Paris in September, he set a new world record in the hundred-meter. During
his victory lap, Graham joined him on the track to congratulate him. But Montgomery had spurned him, saying Graham had "nothing to do" with his victory, which he credited to another coach who was working closely with Conte.
Stunned, Graham had responded, "I hope you pass the drug test."

"I'll pass with flying colors," Montgomery replied.

Afterward, Graham called Montgomery and said he was releasing him from
the camp. "Who doesn't want to coach the world's fastest man?" Montgomery
asked.

"I don't," Graham replied.

Soon after, Graham and Jones argued about various training issues, and she sent Graham an e-mail terminating their contract.

C. J. Hunter, Jones's ex-husband, stayed in touch with Graham through all this. His positive drug test had effectively ended his career, and at one point he proposed to Graham that he become the track club's strength coach. Then, in the spring of 2003, Hunter showed Graham a syringe about one quarter full of a clear liquid. Hunter said this was a "magic potion" he'd gotten from Conte. Other top athletes "are all passing the tests and this is what they are using," Hunter told him. Hunter suggested Graham try it.

By this point Graham was furious with Conte, jealous of his relationship with Montgomery, and suspicious that Conte was behind his breakups with his star clients. Graham called Gene Cherry, a copy editor for the *Raleigh News & Observer* who'd written about illegal drug use in sports. Graham said he had information on steroid use by some top track stars on the West Coast that he wanted to convey to anti-drug authorities. Cherry referred him to Rich Wanninger, a spokesman for the USADA in Colorado. When Graham and Wanninger spoke, Graham implicated Conte, describing his operation in detail and his connections to West Coast track stars while making no mention of his own connections to Conte.

Graham also revealed he had a syringe containing one of Conte's undetectable steroid compounds, which he sent to Wanninger by overnight mail. Wanninger, in turn, sent it to a UCLA laboratory, which identified it as a previously unknown testosterone derivative. The scientists named it tetrahydrogestrinone, or THG. It was indeed a steroid, one that testers couldn't identify because they didn't know what to look for. UCLA scientists raced to create a testing protocol before the U.S. Track & Field Championships at Stanford that July, with several of Conte's clients competing. All the athletes' urine samples were held in reserve until the UCLA scientists completed the test. When they did, four athletes tested positive. All had won their events and were national champions. All were BALCO clients.

As prominent sports celebrities began streaming into San Francisco's Phillip Burton Federal Building, a hulking 1959 office building next to the Civic Center, the press staked out the building's entrances every Thursday, which was the day the BALCO grand jury was in session. Tim Montgomery arrived on November 4, hiding his face to avoid the photographers.

Unlike many of the athetes, Montgomery was disarmingly frank, perhaps because of his falling-out with Graham. Montgomery explained to the grand jury that C. J. Hunter had been married to Marion Jones, whose track coach was Graham. "And Trevor Graham is—he wanted to be known as the mastermind in chemistry also. So, before they had this real chemist, he was the person that provided—"

"Had the stuff," a grand juror interjected, according to the transcript of Montgomery's testimony.

"That had the stuff," Montgomery agreed. "And C.J.'s coach didn't, because everyone is not going to be willing to give you stuff or able to get the stuff. But Trevor had a connection to get the stuff. So C.J. had a relationship with Trevor—Trevor coaches sprinters, not shot-put."

"What do you think Trevor Graham's connection to getting the stuff was before he knew Victor Conte?" the grand juror continued. "Because if he hadn't had a relationship with Victor . . ."

"It was Memo had sent—a guy named Memo out of San Antonio."

Prosecutor Jeff Nedrow took up the questioning. "And when you say Memo, that's what you knew him as, M-E-M-O, is that correct?"

"Yes . . ."

"And how do you know that Memo was the connection for Mr. Graham?"

"Because I traveled out to San Antonio, Texas, myself."

"And did you meet Memo?"

"Yes, I did."

"What does he look like?"

"Heavyset Mexican guy."

"And based on your trip out there, did you get any information about where Memo would get whatever this stuff was that would come through to Trevor and then be given to the athletes?"

"Yes. His daddy was a horse doctor at a university. He was a teacher at a university over in Mexico. . . . He was, I guess, a veterinarian for the university or something. And so, most steroids, people use them on horses. And so he would get it in Mexico, send it over, send it to Trevor. And that's how it was."

According to Montgomery, Graham, far from the whistle-blower he appeared to be when he turned over the syringe to the USADA, had been importing and distributing steroids entirely apart from Conte. This added a whole new dimension to the case.

Later in his testimony, Nedrow returned to the subject of Conte.

"Did Mr. Conte ever give you or talk to you about norbolothone [a steroid]?"

"No."

"Did you ever hear . . ."

"I heard a name, but he never said that he had made a new thing. All I know about is the trenbolone."

"Did Mr. Conte ever provide you with human growth hormone?"

"Yes, he did."

"Okay. And how—approximately how often or how many times did he give you human growth hormone?"

"He would send you four vials a month."

"Okay."

"Each vial would last you one week."

"Okay. . . . Did he give you human growth hormone every month that you were working with Mr. Conte, the whole time?"

"Yes, he did."

"And so the totality of that time frame is about, let's see, you said . . ."

"Eight months. . . ."

"And the human growth hormone again is the banned stuff that's injected with a syringe actually in your body, correct?"

"Yes, it is."

"And did you take that?"

"Yes, I did."

"What about this EPO [the hormone erythropoietin] stuff, did he give you that stuff?"

"No. We had . . . decided that sprinters wouldn't need EPO due to the fact that you're not running as far. If I was running 200, then it may be good for me. But my hematocrit [the proportion of the blood consisting of red blood cells] was already good. So, he decided . . . He had sent it and I sent it back to him because we decided not to do it."

Prosecutors didn't ask Montgomery point-blank if he knew whether Jones was taking steroids, the "clear," or other performance-enhancing drugs, presumably out of deference to the fact that they were in a relationship and were new parents. But the same day that Montgomery was appearing before the grand jury, Marion Jones, accompanied by her lawyers, met Novitzky at a conference room in the Fairmont Hotel in San Jose, far from any reporters or TV crews. Like the other athletes appearing before the grand jury, Jones had immunity from prosecution as long as she didn't make any false statements.

Novitzky pulled out a plastic bag containing a vial of what looked like light olive oil. Had Jones ever seen or used it? No, she replied. Novitzky asked her again. In that moment, the *New York Times Magazine* later reported, she "thought about her years of training and her successes. She thought about her money, her sponsors, her family."

"No," she repeated.

According to Novitzky's subsequent report of the interview, this was just one of a series of categorical denials Jones made that day. Jones "stated, in sum and substance, that: (a) she had never taken athletic performance-enhancing drugs; (b) she had never seen and ingested a performance-enhancing drug, referred to as the 'clear,' and (c) she had never received any such items from Trevor Graham."

A month later, on December 4, Novitzky arranged to rendezvous with Barry Bonds, his lawyer, and a bodyguard about a mile away from the federal building and drive them into a parking garage in the building in an unmarked car. Bonds was wearing a well-tailored light gray suit and a silver tie. As they waited for traffic to get into the building, a few photographers managed to get a shot of Bonds in the car, which irritated him. More photographers were on the seventeenth floor, waiting outside the grand jury room.

Bonds and his entourage arrived about 10:30 a.m. for his scheduled 1:00 p.m. testimony. As they waited, Gary Sheffield was in the room, testifying under a similar grant of immunity. Benito Santiago was coming in right after Bonds. It was a full day for the prosecutors, Jeff Nedrow and Ross Nadel.

Before going in, Bonds met briefly with the prosecutors, with his lawyer Rains present, and they explained his immunity grant, stressing that nothing he said could be used against him as long as he told the truth. Then they went into the grand jury room and Rains had to wait outside, where he was joined by Bonds's wife and mother.

Nedrow reviewed Bonds's rights and went to some lengths to make sure that he understood the conditions of his immunity. "Now, there's an exception to what I just said," Nedrow continued. "And so let me make sure that that exception is clear. And that exception is that if it were to be the case that you were untruthful today—and I have no reason to think that you would be today, but I say this to every witness who comes in here—if there were a prosecution for perjury, false declaration, false statements or otherwise failing to comply with this accord, that would be a circumstance where these statements could be used against you. Do you understand that?"

"Yes," Bonds replied.

Nadel added, "Is there anything that you're unsure of with regard to the use of the immunity order compelling you to testify that we need to clear up?"

"No, none at all," Bonds said.

"What would you describe as . . . the athletic achievement you're most proud of?" Nedrow asked.

"My draft," Bonds answered without hesitating. "When I was drafted in 1985. There's no better achievement than fulfilling your goal."

It seemed odd that Bonds hadn't mentioned his home run record.

"You also in 2001, I think, set the single-season home run record, correct?"

"Correct."

"Mr. Bonds, I want to ask you some questions about the individuals we identified as the targets of this investigation. And let's start with Greg Anderson. How long have you known Greg Anderson?"

"Since we were children . . . fifth grade, sixth grade, somewhere around there."

"Besides providing you with advice on weight lifting systems, did Mr. Anderson provide you with anything else in connection with your working out with him?"

This was the first real test of Bonds's candor.

"Vitamins and protein shakes," he replied.

When pressed, Bonds acknowledged that Anderson had asked him for blood and urine samples, which he sent to BALCO, in order to "figure out what you're deficient in and be able to supplement that with vitamins or food intake. And I thought it was just a neat idea."

"Did you provide the blood samples directly to Mr. Anderson?" Nedrow asked.

"Yeah, I had my own personal doctor come up to draw my blood. I only let my own personal doctor touch me. And my own personal doctor came up and drew my blood and Greg took it to BALCO."

"What about the urine samples?"

"Same thing. Come to my house, here, go."

Nedrow asked the question again: "Did you ever get anything else from Greg besides advice or tips on your weight lifting and also the vitamins and the proteins that you already referenced?"

"At the end of 2002, 2003 season . . . my dad died of cancer, you know, and everyone knows that."

"Yes. I'm sorry about that."

"And everyone tries to give me everything. You got companies that provide us with more junk to try than anything. And you know that as well. I was fatigued, tired, just needed recovery, you know? And this guy says, 'Try this cream, try this cream.' And Greg came to the ballpark and he said, 'This will help you recover,' and he rubbed some cream on my arm, like, some lotion-type stuff, and, like, gave me some flaxseed oil, that's what he called it. Called it some flaxseed oil, man. It's like, whatever, dude. And I was at the ballpark, whatever, I don't care. What's lotion going to do to me? How many times have I heard that? 'This is going to rub into you and work.' Let him be happy. We're friends. You know?"

This sounded remarkably like the "clear" and the "cream"—both of which Anderson had told Novitzky he never gave Bonds.

"When did this happen for the first time?" Nedrow asked.

"Not until 2003, this season."

Bonds described what the "flaxseed oil" looked like, adding "and you would get, like, two drops underneath your tongue." Bonds opened his mouth, demonstrating. "Like this, you know, like, you ain't taking this whole thing." He pointed to the plastic vial. "It was this little bit right in here. And, you know, to me it didn't even work. You know, me, I'm thirty-nine years old. I'm dealing with pain. All I want is the pain relief, you know? And I didn't think the stuff worked. I was, like, dude, whatever. But he's my friend. You know?"

Of course, the "clear," assuming that's what it was, didn't relieve pain. It was a steroid, not a pain reliever. "Okay," Nedrow continued. "Had you ever taken flaxseed oil, by the way, before?"

"I never asked Greg. When he said it was flaxseed oil, I just said, 'Whatever.' It was in the ballpark. . . . You know, in front of everybody. I mean, all the reporters, my teammates. I mean, they all saw it. I didn't hide it. I didn't hide anything."

"Did you even know what flaxseed oil was at the time he presented it to you?"

"Not really. Not at all."

Nedrow asked if the oil had any effect, and Bonds said, "I told him, 'It's not doing crap. I'm still in pain. I'm still feeling the pain.'"

Then Nedrow showed Bonds the "cream."

"Yeah, this is that lotion stuff." He explained, "I said, 'I don't want to be addicted to anything. I don't want to be addicted to pain pills and stuff like this to take pain away.' There's got to be something that can loosen me up, you know, to take the arthritis pain away that I feel in the mornings when it's super cold. . . . And he said, 'Okay, let me check.' And he goes, 'Well, try this.' You know? And he rubbed it right here." Bonds pointed to the inside of his arm, near the elbow.

"And you didn't ask him what it was?"

"No."

"Did Greg ever talk to you about this cream actually being a steroid cream that would, you know, conceal steroids or testosterone in your blood?"

"No, no."

"Did Greg ever give you anything that required a syringe to inject yourself with?"

"I've only had one doctor touch me. And that's my own personal doctor. Greg, like I said, we don't get into each other's personal lives. We're friends . . . I don't talk about his business, you know?"

"Right."

"That's what keeps our friendship. . . . You know, I was a celebrity child, not just in baseball by my own instincts. I became a celebrity child with a famous father. I just don't get into other people's business because of my father's situation, see."

Nedrow asked, "Have you ever injected yourself with anything that Greg Anderson gave you?"

"I'm not that talented, no."

The prosecutors carefully went through the calendars marked with Bonds's initials, seized at Anderson's house. Bonds denied any knowledge of them, and said he had no idea what the letters G, E, or I stood for, or any other entries on the papers.

"Let me be real clear about this," Nedrow continued. "Did he ever give you anything that you knew to be a steroid? Did he ever give you a steroid?"

"I don't think Greg would do anything like that to me and jeopardize our friendship. I just don't think he would do that."

"Well, . . . did you ever take any steroids that he gave you?"

"Not that I know of."

"What do you mean, 'Not that I know of'?"

"Because I have suspicions over these two items right here." Bonds pointed to the "clear" and the "cream." But he said he only became suspicious after the raid and ensuing publicity. "I'm thinking to myself, What is this stuff?" But he said he'd never asked Anderson.

Bonds acknowledged introducing other players to Anderson, and stressed that he didn't trust the Giants' trainers, like Stan Conte.

"Did the Giants' training staff have any involvement in working with you with Mr. Anderson?"

"No way."

"Okay . . ."

"We don't trust the ball team. We don't trust baseball."

"Why not?"

"Because I was born in this game. Believe me, it's a business. Last time I played baseball was in college. I work for a living now."

The prosecutors turned to a urine sample that was dated 2000 and which had tested positive for two steroids. "So, I got to ask," Nedrow said. "There's this number associated on a document with your name, and corresponding to Barry B. on another document, and it does have these two listed anabolic steroids as testing positive in connection with it. Do you follow my question?"

"I follow where you're going, yeah."

"So, I guess I got to ask the question again. I mean, did you take steroids? And specifically this test is in November of 2000. So, I'm going to ask you, in the weeks and months leading up to November 2000, were you taking steroids?"

"No."

"Or anything like that?"

"No, I wasn't at all." Bonds said he'd never seen or heard about any such results. Anderson would take the samples, "and he'd say, 'Everything is fine.' I wouldn't think anything. And he'd say, 'Barry, I need you to eat this much food or I need you to take this much vitamins.' That was it. I trusted him, you know what I mean?"

It was almost 3:00 p.m. After a fifteen-minute break, the jurors reassembled, and Nedrow resumed, making little effort to conceal his skepticism. "I'm sorry, Mr. Bonds, but I have to ask because you are a professional athlete, and an enormously successful athlete, but your trust in Greg with these items that don't have packages on them and trusting in his word, without looking at these results, I mean, that's a lot of trust for somebody whose body is, as you said, your work, your life. Isn't it?"

"It's exactly right. You're right. I did trust Greg. And I have other people that have put stuff on my skin, too."

Nedrow showed Bonds a 2001 blood test indicating an extremely high level of testosterone, and Bonds said he'd never seen or heard of it either. He emphasized again that he didn't discuss such things with Anderson. "We were friends, we grew up together. I mean, he works in a gym. I could suspect what goes on in a gym. I don't work out in the richie gym where everybody is rich. I work out—"

Nedrow tried to get in a question.

"Can I finish?" Bonds asked. "I work in a dungeon gym. You know, my thinking of what they may be doing is their own business. That's what I'm saying. So, it never became a conversation. Because, you see a bodybuilder in a gym, how many bodybuilders going to tell you, 'This is all natural'? You know, they don't talk about it. Whatever, you know. They're only lifting weights."

At about 4:00 p.m. Nedrow got to his last question. "With what you've seen today, do you feel comfortable as you sit here today saying that you have never taken steroids?"

"I feel very comfortable, very comfortable," Bonds concluded.

Given the opportunity, several grand jurors asked questions of their celebrity witness, and they seemed especially interested in what Bonds had paid Anderson—$15,000 a year in cash, plus a bonus of $20,000, also in cash, after Bonds won the title for most home runs in a season. One asked, "Greg Anderson. When his house was searched, did he talk to you about the search?"

"I just asked him, 'What's it like getting your door blown down?' Greg right now is down, you know? He's a great guy. He's a really nice person and a very good guy, you know. . . . You just don't turn your back on somebody you've known for a long time. And I'm not turning my back on him."

"Another question," a juror added. "With all the money you make"—Bonds had earlier volunteered, unasked, that he was making $17 million a year—"have you ever thought of maybe building him a mansion or something?"

The question seemed to touch a raw nerve. "One, I'm black," Bonds answered. "And I'm keeping my money. And there's not too many rich black people in this world. And I'm keeping my money. There's more wealthy Asian people and Caucasian and white. There ain't that many rich black people. And I ain't giving my money up. That's why. And if my friends can help me, then I'll use my friends."

Nedrow seemed to think this line of questioning had gone far enough. "Actually, I think that's it for Mr. Bonds," he interjected. But a grand juror got off another question, about Bonds's endorsement of BALCO and its products in an ad that ran in *Muscle & Fitness* magazine.

"They gave those protein shakes and stuff to my father, you know, and my friends. And no one . . . they never charged us for anything. So it was a favor, for a favor. I didn't charge him for that thing. I didn't get paid for that or nothing. It was just, thank you."

"I would think the free publicity . . . just being seen in a picture is payment enough for BALCO, you know?" the juror observed.

"That's true. BALCO never charged me for anything. They never asked me for a penny, nor did I ever pay them anything. And it was, you know, it was the least [I] could do. When my dad was sick, they sent up protein shakes for my father. Some things are worth more than money. I thought they were doing something in kindness for my family. And to me that's priceless."

Bonds was getting emotional. "You're excused, Mr. Bonds," Nedrow said. "Thank you very much. You're free to go."

At 4:30 p.m. Bonds emerged from his interrogation, seemingly relaxed, chatting with several of the grand jurors. Outside, dusk was gathering. Bonds and his entourage left through the underground garage, where a waiting car drove them into a heavy rain.

NINE

"Everybody Is Doing It"

I n his 2004 State of the Union address, President Bush focused again on the ongoing war against terror. He sidestepped issues like Iraq's quest for weapons of mass destruction, which had caused such controversy the year before. On the home front, the president—an avid sports fan and former co-owner of the Texas Rangers—zeroed in on performance-enhancing drugs in professional sports:

> To help children make right choices, they need good examples. Athletics play such an important role in our society, but, unfortunately, some in professional sports are not setting much of an example. The use of performance-enhancing drugs like steroids in baseball, football, and other sports is dangerous, and it sends the wrong message—that there are shortcuts to accomplishment, and that performance is more important than character. So tonight I call on team owners, union representatives, coaches, and players to take the lead, to send the right signal, to get tough, and to get rid of steroids now.

A few weeks later, on February 12, 2004, Attorney General John Ashcroft personally announced the indictments of Conte, Valente, and Anderson at a Washington press conference televised live by ESPN. He was flanked by San Francisco U.S. Attorney Ryan, Novitzky, and other officials involved in the investigation. "The use of anabolic steroids in sports is a matter of great concern to the public," Ashcroft said. "And I believe that the integrity of sports will be reinforced by enforcement actions. I believe there is already a question in the mind of the public. And it's a question which is well founded given the indictment today."

Picking up on the president's message, Ashcroft stressed that "illegal steroid use calls into question not only the integrity of the athletes who use them, but also the integrity of the sports that those athletes play. Steroids are bad for sports, they're bad for players, they're bad for young people who hold athletes up as role models."

Ryan, in turn, said, "Like anything in life, true success must be earned. Nothing can replace hard work and dedication."

This was a lofty and important message, but once again, it focused exclusively on the athletes—the role models—not on anyone named in the BALCO indictment. Conte, Valente, and Anderson, as well as a fourth defendant, Remi Korchemny, a Russian track coach who had moved to the Bay Area and was seventy-one years old, were virtually unknown. The indictment identified six specific instances in which the defendants allegedly conspired to distribute steroids to two professional baseball players, two professional football players, and two track-and-field athletes. Two counts singled out the "cream" and the "clear," alleging they were "designer steroids" that would enable athletes to escape detection. To conceal their illegal activities, the defendants used codes and shorthand abbreviations ("C" was the "cream," for example), put the substances in unmarked plastic containers, provided athletes with false cover stories ("flaxseed oil"), and traded illegal drugs for product endorsements like Conte's ZMA. But no athletes were named.

Pressed by reporters on whether there might be additional indictments, Ashcroft responded, "We do not want to signal in any way that we are closing the book."

In San Francisco, the BALCO case was assigned to federal district court judge Susan Yvonne Illston, a 1995 Clinton appointee to the federal bench. A Stanford Law graduate and former trial lawyer who once defended the NFL in an employment case, she was praised by colleagues for a calm demeanor and keen intelligence, and had attracted little notoriety or attention in her eight years on the bench.

With the indictments of Conte and Valente, the BALCO investigation shifted to other potential dealers and distributors, especially coach Trevor Graham and his mysterious Mexican steroid source, identified by Tim Montgomery only as "Memo." Graham had evidently had second thoughts about cooperating since submitting the syringe and implicating Conte. When Novitzky called him for an interview, he'd hired a lawyer. Novitzky and another agent flew to North Carolina, and on June 8, they met at Graham's lawyer's office in Raleigh. Graham insisted that his wife, Ann, sit in on the interview. She was a detective for the Wake County sheriff's office, specializing in illegal drugs.

Novitzky took out a proffer agreement, which stated that nothing Graham said in the interview could be used as evidence against him except in a "prosecution for false statements, obstruction of justice, or perjury." Like the athletes who testified before the grand jury, Graham essentially had immunity as long as he told the truth, even though he was a coach, not a competitor, who'd been implicated both in testimony and by BALCO documents as a possible distributor of illegal drugs. His status was closer to Conte's and Anderson's than Montgomery's or Bonds's, and presumably he was only offered immunity because of his value as a potential witness against Conte. It was an unusual opportunity for Graham to come clean. His lawyer, Joe Zeszotarski, asked Graham and his wife to follow him downstairs for a private conference before Graham began answering Novitzky's questions, where he presumably stressed the importance of telling the truth.

When portraying himself as a whistle-blower, an advocate for playing by the rules, Graham was expansive.

The notion that Graham was a law-abiding idealist who wouldn't tolerate the use of illegal performance-enhancing drugs by his athletes permeated the interview, perhaps because his wife was sitting nearby. Graham worried openly that cooperating with the authorities, which he'd done by turning in the syringe, would lead to retaliation. "Graham is concerned for his family," Novitzky wrote, and that "Hunter and Conte were going to harm him physically."

According to Novitzky's notes of the meeting, "Trevor Graham stated that as a coach he felt that he has always 'done the right thing.'" Players he suspected of using illegal drugs he kicked out of his training camp. As for his most famous clients, he said he "never physically observed Tim Montgomery taking drugs," that he "never saw or heard of Marion Jones taking any illegal performance-enhancing drugs," and "brought nothing with him to Sydney for Marion Jones. . . . The only thing Graham ever gave Marion Jones was Gatorade, protein, and potassium for cramps."

Graham described a visit he made to BALCO headquarters in November 2000, at Montgomery's behest, to meet Conte, who was working closely with Montgomery on what they called Project World Record. While he was there,

Graham maintained, "there was no talk of performance-enhancing drugs in his presence during his entire time at BALCO," Novitzky wrote. "He stated that there was no talk about nutrition, clear, EPO, growth hormone, insulin, or testosterone."

Then Novitzky got specific. He showed Graham calendars from a folder labeled "Marion Jones" that was seized in the BALCO raid. Like the others, the calendars contained codes for various illegal drugs as well as quantities and schedules. There were handwritten notes on them. Graham said he knew nothing about the calendars and had never seen them. Novitzky asked specifically if any of the handwriting on them was his, and Graham said no. Then Novitzky read from Jones's grand jury testimony, in which she said Graham had ordered various blood tests for her. She had also identified Graham's handwriting on the calendars.

It was an awkward moment. "Graham reiterated that he never ordered any tests for Marion and none of the handwriting on the calendars in her folder was his," according to Novitzky's notes.

Confronted with Federal Express receipts sent to Graham by "Vince Reed," the pseudonym used by Conte when he was shipping illegal drugs, Graham said he hadn't known what was in the packages and simply handed them to Jones at the track.

How did he know a package from "Vince Reed" was supposed to go to Jones? Novitzky asked.

Because "BALCO" appeared somewhere on the box, Graham answered.

But why would Conte use a pseudonym and then put "BALCO" on the package? "Graham did not have an explanation," Novitzky noted.

Indeed, Graham didn't have an explanation—at least, not a plausible one—for any of the documents Novitzky produced. Eventually Graham contradicted himself on some points, conceding, for example, that he was aware that Conte was testing Jones's blood and urine samples.

Then Novitzky shifted away from Conte and BALCO. Who was "Memo"?

This should have been a warning to Graham: How could the agents know about Memo, who had nothing to do with BALCO? It isn't clear why Graham's lawyer failed to interrupt the interview at this juncture, but Graham plunged ahead.

"Memo" was a shot-putter from Laredo, Texas; Graham said he didn't know his full name. Through a mutual friend, a pole-vaulter Graham knew only as "George," Memo had contacted Graham for help getting into St. Augustine's

College, where Graham had trained. This was the extent of their relationship. According to Graham, he "never set up any of his athletes with drugs obtained from Memo," Novitzky wrote. "Graham is not aware of any of his athletes getting drugs from Mexico. Graham has no connections with a Mexican laboratory. The only contact Graham had with Memo was over the phone, when he was trying to assist him with entry into St. Augustine's. Graham last spoke with Memo on the phone in approximately 1997. Graham knows that Memo's father is involved in a medical profession."

Novitzky dutifully recorded Graham's answers, nearly all of which had already been flatly contradicted by Tim Montgomery.

As Novitzky later described his reaction, Graham "threw a bit of a wrench into the equation in that these were not the answers based upon the evidence we were seeing and hearing that we were expecting. Any time you have another witness come forward and contradict what they told you, you have some extra work to do to figure out who is telling the truth. In regards to Marion Jones and her grand jury statements that she had never knowingly taken athletic performance-enhancing drugs, we were really thinking and hoping that Mr. Graham would be the link that would really advance that investigation. And when he told us he had no knowledge of her use, that it was not true that he was using this Memo character to set up any of his athletes with drugs, at that period of time we, obviously, had a lot more work to do in terms of the Marion Jones investigation as well."

In early June 2004, the USADA formally accused Tim Montgomery and three other sprinters—but not Marion Jones—of illegal use of performance-enhancing drugs and said it would seek to prevent them from competing in the upcoming Athens Olympics. The primary basis for the charges was the documents Novitzky had gathered in the BALCO raid, as well as the memo of Conte's interview, in which he admitted providing Montgomery with steroids. Those documents had been shared with USADA officials at the urging of Congress, and parts of some of them, including Novitzky's memo, were quoted in both the *San Francisco Chronicle* and the *San Jose Mercury News*. Jones rushed to defend Montgomery. "I support him, and believe in him, and I have no doubt that if a fair process is applied, then Tim will be racing for gold in Athens this August."

Montgomery had already admitted obtaining the drugs from Conte before the grand jury, but publicly, his lawyer, Cristina Arguedas, emphatically denied it, insisting there was "no evidence" Montgomery had used banned drugs.

By now, the *San Francisco Chronicle* had staked out a dominant role covering BALCO, both as a hometown story and as one of national significance. It had become a full-time beat for Mark Fainaru-Wada, age thirty-nine, a sports reporter who'd grown up in Marin County, and Lance Williams, fifty-three, an investigative reporter born in Ohio. Fainaru-Wada had just moved to the investigative team before the BALCO raid; at the time, he'd never heard of BALCO or Conte. Soon the sprawling story took over their lives. Fainaru-Wada says they went to bed every night "panicked" that they'd be beaten by rival reporters.

Fainaru-Wada was deeply skeptical of Montgomery's asserted innocence. He'd been in touch with the voluble Victor Conte since being assigned to the story, and now he e-mailed Conte a copy of Arguedas's press release and said people did not really know the whole story "because so much remains under seal." Later that day, Fainaru-Wada sent another e-mail to Conte asking for Conte's thoughts regarding the press release, and noting that it will "be interesting to see if and when that comes back to bite them."

Conte responded that "Tim is dumb for trashing me like that. If his attorney does not know the scoop about his grand jury testimony, then she is not as smart as I have been told that she is by Robert Holley [Conte's counsel]. Why set him up for a total fall when the truth comes out? And you can bet your last dollar that it will."

That same night, in an e-mail he characterized as "off-the-record," Conte tantalized Fainaru-Wada, writing that "I would say at this point the only way the athletes' grand jury testimonies will come out is at trial. Unless I just give you a copy of the indexed CD-ROM that contains all thirty thousand pages of evidence. How would you like that? Just kidding."

Soon after Montgomery's latest declarations of innocence, someone who had a copy of the transcript allowed Fainaru-Wada to read Montgomery's secret testimony and copy parts of it. In the *Chronicle* on June 24, Fainaru-Wada and Williams quoted directly from Montgomery's grand jury testimony in a front-page scoop headlined "Sprinter Admitted Use of BALCO 'Magic Potion'":

Tim Montgomery, the world's fastest man, told a federal grand jury he used human growth hormone and a steroid-like "magic potion" provided by the alleged ringleader of the BALCO steroids scandal, the *Chronicle* has learned. The admission contradicts his recent public denials.

The reporters also revealed that Montgomery had implicated his and Jones's former coach, Trevor Graham:

> Montgomery testified that Graham provided steroids to athletes, including one-time shot-put champion C. J. Hunter, Jones's ex-husband, who retired in 2000 after testing positive for steroids. Montgomery said Graham had a connection in Laredo, Texas, who got the drugs from a horse veterinarian in Mexico.

That prompted an emphatic rebuttal by Graham's lawyer, Zeszotarski: "The accusations reported to be made by Mr. Montgomery in his grand jury testimony are false and baseless. Trevor Graham has never distributed steroids or any illicit substance to anyone, and is in no way involved in any such matters. Trevor has told the Government this fact, and has truthfully answered all of the Government's questions."

A separate article by the reporters the same day focused on what Montgomery had said about Barry Bonds:

> Federal prosecutor Jeff Nedrow asked whether, on his visits to BALCO, Montgomery had seen any "traditional anabolic steroids," as opposed to the "clear," the substance he said Conte gave him in exchange for a ZMA endorsement. Montgomery replied that in a locker above BALCO's weight room, Conte kept several steroids, including Winstrol, also known as stanozolol. . . . Montgomery said Conte didn't give Winstrol to Olympians because it was so easily detected in drug screenings. "You would definitely get busted off of them steroids," he testified. Instead, Montgomery said Conte gave Winstrol to athletes in sports in which drug testing was lax or nonexistent.
>
> "Mr. Conte has athletes from baseball to football to–professional bodybuilding to, to–you name it," Montgomery said.
>
> "Any sport there is, Mr. Conte got someone in it . . . he would brag on Barry Bonds, he would brag on Ronnie Coleman," he continued, referring to the 2003 "Mr. Olympia" bodybuilder.
>
> The prosecutor asked: "Did he say he gave any steroids, Winstrol or any of the other ones to Mr. Bonds?"
>
> "Yes, he did," Montgomery replied.
>
> "Did he say specifically which ones?"
>
> "Winstrol," Montgomery said.

The extensive quotations from Montgomery's grand jury testimony were not only a bombshell for what they said about the use of steroids by some of America's top athletes but also shattered the grand jury's secrecy. It is a federal crime for any government lawyer or investigator to disclose grand jury testimony except in very limited circumstances. Copies of Montgomery's testimony, as well as that of other grand jury witnesses, had been provided to defense counsel under a strict confidentiality agreement that all the lawyers had signed. Violating such an order would be criminal contempt of court.

The next day, Judge Illston ordered U.S. Attorney Ryan's office to launch an investigation into the leak and report back in three weeks. Conte's lawyers seized on the opportunity to accuse the government of improper leaking. Anderson's lawyer called for a grand jury investigation into the leak and said the defendants were being denied their right to a fair trial. Troy Ellerman, Valente's lawyer, told the *San Jose Mercury News* that "the government continues to leak information, and they continue to put their case together one lying idiot at a time," and told the prosecutors they were "unadulterated punks." The prosecutors, in turn, denied they were responsible.

In their investigation, government lawyers questioned everyone from clerical workers to IRS agents to prosecutors and defense lawyers with access to the grand jury transcripts. They got nowhere. Everyone with access to the transcripts—two dozen people in all—signed declarations under penalties of perjury that they had not been the source of the leak. Someone had to be lying.

Since she was first identified as a BALCO client, Marion Jones had adopted an aggressive posture of denial. In May she attended an Olympic Team Media Summit in New York for star athletes expected to compete later that year at the Athens Summer Olympics. "I know that I've always been drug-free, I am drug-free and I want to continue to be drug-free," she told reporters. She also went on the offensive, warning that "if I make the Olympic team, which I plan to do in Sacramento, and I am held from the Olympic Games because of something that somebody thought, you can pretty much expect that there will be lawsuits. I'm not just going to sit down and let someone or a group of people or an organization take away my livelihood because of a hunch, because of a thought, because of somebody who is trying to show their power."

The campaign climaxed in June with publication of Jones's autobiography, *Life in the Fast Lane*. The book contained the declaration "I am against

performance-enhancing drugs. I have never taken them. I will never take them,"
and the phrase appeared inside the book in large red capital letters. Jones
described her shock and bewilderment when she learned from media reports
that her husband, C. J. Hunter, had tested positive for steroids in Sydney. Without mentioning Trevor Graham by name, Jones also described an "anonymous
coach" who sent the sample that was linked to BALCO, run by "C.J.'s pal
Victor Conte." She implied that she was an innocent bystander who'd been
dragged into the BALCO affair only because of her relationship to Hunter.

This was all too much for Hunter. Although he and Jones had signed a
nondisclosure agreement at the time of their divorce, he thought the book was
a flagrant violation on Jones's part, and so he felt free to respond. He spoke first
to Novitzky and then, on July 8, to the grand jury. Jeff Nedrow and another
assistant U.S. attorney, Haywood Gilliam, did the questioning:

"Did you and Miss Jones receive shipments of the 'clear'?"

"Yes."

"At your house in North Carolina?"

"Yes."

"Who were those from?"

"They were from Victor [Conte], but he would label it as Vince Reed. Anytime he sent anything that I guess was illegal or banned, he would never put his
name on it. . . ."

Gilliam showed Hunter a vial about half full of a clear yellowish liquid and
a syringe. "Is that familiar to you?"

"Yes."

"What is that, as far as you can see?"

"It appears to be the 'clear.' That's the way it was packaged. That's identical
to the way it looked. Earlier on when we received this, we didn't have a syringe.
We didn't need a syringe with it because in the beginning you just drank it. . . ."

"Do you remember about when the syringes started coming with it?"

"I believe it was right round the time he switched from the norbolethone
to the THG. . . . It was after Sydney because he had said that he thought everybody had that in Sydney. They were on to that in Sydney, something like that,
so it was time to switch to something else."

"And who was telling you this?"

"Victor."

"And he said that to you directly?"

"Um-hum . . ."

"Based on your personal knowledge, did Miss Jones see these vials when they arrived by FedEx at your house?"

"Yes."

"Do you remember how often shipments like this would come?"

"He sent so many shipments . . . originally he sent it to Trevor [Graham] and then I guess they had a little rift or whatever, and he didn't trust Trevor because he felt that Trevor was giving the 'clear' to other athletes, you know, taking some of Marion's and giving it to other athletes. So that's when he started sending it to the house. . . . There would be one dose per container. He only wanted to send a limited amount. So that's the way he set that deal up. . . ."

"So, now, talking about the 'clear,' to your knowledge did Miss Jones use the 'clear' at any point during your marriage?"

"Yes."

"When was the first time you can recall her using it?"

"The first time was around Sydney . . . it was an apartment, it wasn't technically a hotel, where she would use it where it was in the refrigerator along with everything else."

"How would she use it?"

"At that time, like I said, you would drink it. And then there would always be a little residue left and his instruction was to put a little bit of water in there, mix it around, and drink."

"When you say 'his' instruction, you mean Victor?"

"Victor through Trevor at that point."

"So you were getting instructions from Trevor about putting some water in it and swirling it and drinking it?"

"Right."

"How many times can you remember firsthand seeing Miss Jones use this 'clear'?"

"It's quite frequently. That was the one thing she used the most . . . it was a common occurrence, common to the point where nothing really stands out except for Sydney . . . that is where I really remember seeing it . . ."

"How did the 'clear' that you said you saw Miss Jones taking in Australia get there?"

"Trevor brought it."

"How do you know that?"

"Trevor packed everything. He didn't want Marion to carry anything."

"And how did he get it?"

"Well, either Victor sent it to him, or at the time that he and Victor weren't doing so well, he'd send it to us and we'd give it to him. But he always carried everything. Whether he went to Sydney or whether we went to California, he carried everything. Once we arrived he would, you know, he would give it back to her."

"So, do you remember when you were in Australia Trevor specifically coming by and dropping things off?"

"Yeah, he came by and put it in the fridge."

"And 'it' being the 'clear' and some of these other . . ."

"The 'clear' and the growth hormone."

"Based on your observation, did Miss Jones know what this was, this 'clear'?"

"Yeah. I mean, she knew before I knew . . ."

"Did she ever refer to it as flaxseed oil?"

"No, no. Victor made a comment, and I think Trevor made the comment, that if anybody ever asks you what it is, say flaxseed oil because I guess it looks just like flaxseed oil. I've never seen flaxseed oil, but that's what he said."

The prosecutors shifted from the "clear" to human growth hormone. "Did you ever see Miss Jones inject herself with human growth hormone?"

"Yes," Hunter replied.

"When?"

"In Sydney."

"And what were the circumstances . . . ?"

"I mean, just in the room when it was time for her to take it and she took it."

"How?"

"Subcutaneously with the syringe."

"She injected herself?"

"Yeah . . . pulled it out of the vial and did, you know . . ."

"And was she actually drawing the hormone out herself?"

"Yes, um-hum."

"Were there ever instances in which you injected Miss Jones with growth hormone?"

"At first because she didn't like needles. . . . She knew what it was and what had to be done. She just didn't like to do it. Trevor would tell me what to do, I showed her how to do it, and she did it from that point on. . . . When she would inject herself, she would go to that bathroom so she could use the mirror. Then I rarely, if ever, went in there with her. But, I mean, I know what she did when she went in there."

Hunter's testimony was devastatingly candid, in contrast to so many other BALCO witnesses. Not only was it consistent with what the investigators had learned from Montgomery and others, but Hunter was a direct eyewitness to Jones's injections of illegal drugs, and to both Conte's and Graham's involvement.

Jones was allowed to compete in the 2004 Olympics, presumably without benefit of performance-enhancing drugs, but qualified only in the long jump and as part of the 4x100 relay. She managed a fifth-place finish in the jump and fumbled the handoff in the relay. She was in tears when interviewed after the race, saying her performance was "extremely disappointing. Words can't put it in perspective."

E fforts to settle the Conte case with some kind of plea bargain had gone nowhere, especially as testimony implicating Conte and Valente mounted. Conte's lawyer had taken the case directly to President Bush. In June, in a letter copied to Attorney General Ashcroft, Holley wrote:

> Mr. Conte is willing to reveal everything he knows about officials, coaches
> and athletes in order to help to clean up the Olympics. . . . In return,
> Mr. Conte asks that he not be forced to plead guilty to money laundering
> (a crime which he insists he did not commit) and that he be guaranteed
> a sentence of straight probation for both he and Mr. Valente. Quite frankly,
> what Mr. Conte has to offer in terms of real value to this country is worth
> far in excess of any possible sentence in the pending criminal case.

Predictably the effort went nowhere, and the Olympics had come and gone without any assistance from Conte. But now the grand jury leak and other coverage offered another angle: prejudicial pretrial publicity, and a possible grounds for dismissing the government's case, especially if leaks to the *Chronicle* could be pinned on the government lawyers or investigators. As Conte said in an e-mail to Fainaru-Wada after his story about Montgomery's testimony, "Maybe you have done me a big favor."

Citing prosecutorial misconduct and other alleged transgressions, the defendants moved to dismiss the indictment on October 8. Holley and Ellerman asserted that

> While these charges were pending, without any notice to any defendant in
> the case at bar, or this Honorable Court, the government simply turned

over all relevant police reports and discovery in the case to private individuals in Congress who in turn disseminated them to members of USADA who in turn, for whatever reason, gave them out to private individuals, athletes whom they were investigating, and to their counsel.

Almost all of it found its way into the hands of the media, who had a field day with it. The media reveled in the release of Mr. Conte's disputed "Memorandum of Interview," which says that he turned on the athletes whom he had helped and befriended over the years. Mr. Conte said that he did not do so but who would listen? The information literally generated thousands upon thousands of articles all over the United States, not to mention the rest of the world. Defense counsel sometimes received up to forty or fifty telephone calls per day from members of the news media trying to get a story. And the name BALCO became a household word synonymous with illegal steroid distributions.

And the leaks kept coming. Filed already with the Court and by reference made a part hereof is a list of a mountain of *San Francisco Chronicle* articles slandering Mr. Conte and all appearing to come from government sources. Every single news leak sank the ship of the defense in the case at bar a little bit deeper and slandered Victor Conte and the other defendants to the point where they are afraid to even go out in public. Someone has even leaked grand jury testimony for which there is a Court order prohibiting the same. And the testimony was devastating to Mr. Conte and his business and is much disputed although the time for challenging it still lies in the distant future. . . .

Neither Mr. Conte, nor any of the other defendants in this case can ever receive a fair trial. It's not just that finding an impartial jury anywhere in this country would be difficult, but a fair trial requires a fair and even atmosphere within which to have that trial. The world believes Mr. Conte is not only guilty but the non-thinking public thinks of him as some sort of villain—guilty until proven innocent—all to the benefit of the prosecuting government. And much if not all of it caused directly by a government which does not appear to care a whit whether or not these defendants ever receive a fair trial. One might even call it a "trial tactic."

Ellerman told the *New York Times*: "The jury pool has been infected, and our right to a fair trial has been jeopardized. It's alarming. Things are spinning out of control."

The case had undeniably generated intense media coverage. But apart from the fact there was still no evidence the government had leaked anything, the approach had one major problem: Conte himself. Virtually from the day the government raided his offices, Conte had been agitating to take his case directly to the public, an impulse his lawyers had vigorously discouraged. Still, Conte had sent a stream of e-mails to Fainaru-Wada and other reporters covering the story, with tantalizing hints of more revelations to come, like his allusion to the CD-ROM. Far from shunning pretrial publicity, he appeared to revel in it. By exposing the extent of illegal drug use in sports, even his own role as a purveyor of banned drugs, perhaps he could emerge as a reformer.

Conte says he stopped listening to his lawyers, and opted to make his own decisions. He was avidly courted by television newsmagazines *60 Minutes*, *Dateline*, and *20/20*. All staged elaborate efforts to secure his exclusive cooperation. He chose *20/20* because ABC could offer him a tie-in to sister network ESPN. Conte agreed to write a first-person account for *ESPN* the magazine and appear on *20/20* in a prime-time interview, both of which would appear the first week in December. With this bold stroke, Conte evidently felt he could reverse over a year of negative publicity. "A lot of people had lied about me publicly," Conte said. "I said to myself, The best thing I can do is tell the truth, and come out publicly and set the record straight."

In many ways Conte was a natural for TV: provocative, combative, willing and even eager to shock his audience. ABC assigned Martin Bashir, best known for an on-air interview of Michael Jackson that caused the pop star to be investigated for child molestation, to interview Conte.

"Did you feel there was a moral problem when you realized that if you wanted to compete, you had to cheat?" Bashir asked.

"The answer is no," Conte replied. "It's not cheating if everybody is doing it. And if you've got the knowledge that that's what everyone is doing, and those are the rules of the game, then you're not cheating. . . . Did I feel that I was doing something different than other athletes and coaches and trainers had done throughout the entire history of the Olympic sport? The answer is no."

"And does that mean that just in principle you would feel no shame, because everybody was doing it?"

"You know, Martin . . . the Olympic Games are a fraud. Okay? It's almost like, what I'm here to tell you right now is that not only is there no Santa Claus, but there's no Easter Bunny or Tooth Fairy either . . . I mean, the whole history of the Olympic Games is just full of corruption, cover-up, performance-enhancing drug use. It's not what the world thinks it is."

"It's a fraud?"

"It's a fraud."

Conte may have considered this revelation a public service, but he also freely acknowledged distributing illegal drugs that wouldn't show up in tests, including the "clear."

"You were still breaking the law," Bashir pointed out. "This was a criminal activity. Did that ever bother you?"

This was Conte's opportunity to assert a defense, or at least proclaim his innocence. Instead, he replied, "If you're asking me, did I know there were risks involved? Yes, I did."

Although Conte had denied in court that he'd implicated any of his clients in his statement to Novitzky, he freely did so in an interview intended for national TV. Marion Jones: "She did the injection with me sitting right there next to her." As for her grand jury testimony, "If she said she didn't use drugs, then she lied." Tim Montgomery: "If you're asking if it [his training regimen] included illegal activity, the answer would be yes." Bill Romanowski: "Did I help Bill in certain ways? Yes."

And then he got to baseball and Barry Bonds:

"I did give 'clear' and 'cream' to Greg Anderson, yes," Conte acknowledged.

"And who is Greg Anderson's number one client?"

"His number one client is Barry Bonds."

"So is it possible, that some of the 'clear' and 'cream' that you gave, without any strings attached, to Greg Anderson may have found its way to Barry Bonds?"

"It's possible. I can't say that it's not possible."

Bashir asked Conte about the raid on BALCO. "I knew that this was coming," Conte said. "I knew that they were on to me. I knew that they were going to come crashing through the door like they did that day. And I almost didn't care because I also knew that that would give me the opportunity to be sitting right here talking to you, telling the truth to the world. And the world deserves to hear the truth."

During the week before the show aired, ABC began running promotional spots that showed excerpts of some of Conte's more provocative comments. The spots coincided with a hearing before Judge Illston on December 1, where

Conte's lawyer, Holley, reiterated his claim that publicity and government leaks were denying Conte his right to a fair trial. "We've been slandered from one side of the world to the other," Holley maintained.

When he finished, prosecutor Jeff Nedrow pointed out that Conte was about to go on national television. Judge Illston seemed incredulous. "I didn't know until it was too late," Holley lamely responded.

Later that month Judge Illston rejected the defendants' motion to dismiss, stating they had presented no evidence that anyone from the government had leaked anything.

As Conte was being interviewed for *20/20* and writing his manifesto for ESPN, Fainaru-Wada's source again allowed him to review grand jury transcripts and copy passages. This time he offered far more than just Montgomery, giving Fainaru-Wada access to transcripts of testimony from baseball stars Bonds, Giambi, and Sheffield. Baseball—the national pastime—was a much bigger story than track, even with stars like Jones and Montgomery involved.

It was too much material for one story. The *Chronicle* led with Giambi. "Giambi Admitted Taking Steroids" was the front-page headline in the *Chronicle* on December 2. Like Bonds, Giambi had been granted immunity for his testimony, which occurred on December 11, 2003. He acknowledged that he was already taking a steroid—Deca Durabolin—when he met Anderson during the players' trip to Japan. "So I started to ask him: Hey, what are the things you're doing with Barry? He's an incredible player. I want to still be able to work out at that age and keep playing. And that's how the conversation first started."

The next day, December 3, it was Bonds's and Sheffield's turn. "What Bonds Told the Grand Jury" led the *Chronicle*'s front page: "Barry Bonds told a federal grand jury that he used a clear substance and a cream supplied by the Burlingame laboratory now enmeshed in a sports doping scandal, but he said he never thought they were steroids, the *Chronicle* has learned." Fainaru-Wada and Williams quoted extensively from the Bonds grand jury transcript, and it was obviously they'd had direct access to it, as well as various documents Bonds had been shown during his testimony. "I never asked Greg what the products contained. When he said it was flaxseed oil, I just said, 'Whatever,'" Bonds testified.

That same day, the *Chronicle* revealed a raft of other testimony before the grand jury. Another headline was "Sheffield's Side: Slugger Testified Bonds Told

Him to Use 'the Cream' and 'the Clear,' Saying, 'Don't Ask Any Questions, Just Trust Me.'" As the headline suggested, Sheffield was more ambiguous about what he knew than Giambi or Montgomery had been, but more forthcoming than Bonds. He said he'd gotten the "clear" and the "cream," as well as pills called "red beans," while he was staying with Bonds after the 2001 season. But Sheffield said he didn't know they were steroids; the "cream" was something that would help his arthritis, and the "clear" and the pills were nutritional supplements to ward off injury. That, at least, was what Anderson had told him. Sheffield said he didn't feel the substances did him much good, and Bonds proved a demanding and difficult host. They soon had a falling-out over a rental car, Sheffield said, and he left, returning to his home in Florida. But Bonds kept after him to pay Anderson. Sheffield paid the trainer about $10,000.

Without quoting directly from any grand jury transcripts, the *Chronicle* also reported that former Giants Armando Rios, Benito Santiago, and Bobby Estalella had also admitted using performance-enhancing drugs.

That afternoon, Valente's lawyer, Troy Ellerman, had a conference call with Jeff Nedrow, the chief prosecutor, and Novitzky. Ellerman was staying at the Mirage Hotel in Las Vegas, where he was attending a professional rodeo conference. Ellerman said he wanted to apologize formally for earlier blaming Novitzky and the government for leaks in the case. Although he and Bob Holley, his cocounsel, had genuinely believed Novitzky was the source of the leak, "I know that is not the case now," he said, according to Novitzky's notes of the call. Ellerman said he suspected Conte himself was the source. "Victor is doing things on his own." Ellerman added that he thought "it is our obligation as human beings to apologize to Novitzky." Still, Ellerman and Holley neither withdrew nor amended their motion to dismiss the charges on grounds of prosecutorial misconduct.

Coming just a day after the hearing about pretrial publicity, the timing of the latest leaks couldn't have been a greater affront to Judge Illston and her stern warnings about confidentiality. This time she wasn't content to let Ryan's office undertake another ineffectual inquiry. She referred the issue to the Department of Justice and called for a full-scale investigation, using all the resources of the U.S. government. The Justice Department in turn referred the matter to the U.S. Attorney in Los Angeles, since prosecutors in San Francisco were among the possible suspects. The hunt for Fainaru-Wada's source began in earnest.

· · ·

The *Chronicle*'s revelations set off a national furor. Senator John McCain called for congressional hearings and stricter testing in baseball. The revelations dominated the national media. The next day, *Washington Post* sports columnist Thomas Boswell singled out Bonds:

> Bonds won four straight National League most valuable player awards, two batting titles and set the all-time single-season records for home runs, slugging percentage, on-base percentage, walks and intentional walks. All those records are now a steroid lie. Without Anderson's illicit help, there is no reason whatsoever to believe Bonds could have approached, much less broken, any of the all-time marks for which he lusted so much that he has now ruined his name. Throw every record that Bonds has set in the past four years into the trash can that history reserves for cheats.

The *20/20* episode featuring Conte aired the same night as the *Chronicle*'s story on Bonds, December 3. Conte was furious about the timing, convinced that Fainaru-Wada, or more likely his source, had deliberately sabotaged his television interview. Still, Conte delivered quite a performance. He freely admitted his own guilt and implicated his clients. (In response, Jones not only reiterated that she'd never used illegal drugs, but sued Conte for libel and $25 million in damages.) Ed Williams, a lawyer representing several track stars, told the *New York Times* that Conte "has essentially pled guilty to the charges. There are no facts to be tried. All they have to do is roll the video and say, 'Is this you?' I don't know what his motives are. I haven't spoken to his psychiatrist, and he ought to have one."

Victor Conte wasn't the only person connected to the BALCO case who was talking to national television. In February 2005, Bonds's ex-girlfriend Kimberly Bell appeared on the Fox News program *At Large with Geraldo Rivera*, accompanied by Aphrodite Jones, an author working with Bell on a book still in search of a publisher, tentatively titled *Bonds Girl*. As Bell told Rivera, she had demanded that Bonds honor his agreement to buy her the house in Arizona or pay her the two years' salary she lost by moving there, either of which amounted to $157,000. Instead, Bonds had offered her $20,000 and wanted a confidentiality agreement, an offer she found insulting.

Did Bonds admit using steroids? Rivera asked.

"Yes, he did tell me," Bell replied. "He told me between '99 and 2000 that this is something that he was doing."

Aphrodite Jones elaborated: "He told Kimberly Bell that he used steroids, because he had an arm injury, Geraldo. And he used it, in his words, not the way everybody else used it, that he wasn't shooting anything up. Kimberly, perhaps you can say it exactly the way Barry told you."

"The way he explained to me was that what he was using was helping him recover quicker from his injuries. And that as a result of that, it caused the muscles and then the tendons to grow at a faster [rate] than the joint could handle."

"All right," Rivera said. "So he never used, specifically, the word steroids?"

"Oh, no, he used the word steroids. He said this was something everybody was doing."

"Are you a gold digger, Kimberly?"

"Absolutely not. I had a great job at this time. . . ."

"What do you think of Barry Bonds in the pursuit of the home run title?" Rivera continued. "Should it be tarnished by what you saw?"

"Absolutely."

"Tell us."

"There are a lot of fans out there paying a lot of their hard-earned money to go watch these players play. And to know that they are making millions off of what is essentially a lie. It's kind of sad."

"And as you sit there tonight, you say that Barry Bonds's prowess as a hitter, as a slugger is a lie?"

"Some of it, yes. Everything after, I'd say, 2000."

Shortly after the interview, Bell heard from Novitzky. On March 17, she, too, appeared before the grand jury, testifying for three hours under a grant of immunity. The government subpoenaed all her phone records, recorded messages, bank records, and correspondence with Bonds. She told the grand jury the saga of their relationship, about the financial arrangements, and the threats, the changes to his physique and sexual behavior.

That same month, the quest for the elusive "Memo," Trevor Graham's alleged Mexican connection, brought Novitzky and another agent, Erwin Rogers, to the campus of Texas A&M University in Kingsville, a town just south of Corpus Christi. C. J. Hunter had told them Memo's real name and spelled it for them, and knew he was at one of two universities in Texas. University police led them to Memo's dorm room, where they intercepted Angel "Memo" Heredia when he returned from a workout at the gym. "You're Angel," Rogers said, introducing himself and Novitzky.

Heredia was heavyset, with the build of a shot-putter. He had dark, neatly clipped hair and a trim goatee. "You're Erwin," Heredia replied. He already knew Rogers and Novitzky were looking for him. Heredia and Rogers had spoken by phone in December, after the agent left his card at Heredia's sister's house, where Heredia had been living, and Heredia called his number.

Rogers asked Heredia if his nickname was "Memo."

"No," Heredia replied.

Did he know anything about performance-enhancing drugs?

"No," Heredia replied. (Both answers were blatant lies. "I was afraid," he later said.)

The agents reassured Heredia that he was only being questioned as a witness, and that he'd never be prosecuted as long as he told the truth. Heredia assessed the situation and agreed to talk. He was eager to finish his degree in sports and science and didn't want to be deported to Mexico.

Heredia said he'd first spoken to Trevor Graham by phone in 1996. "I told him that I could get pretty much everything in Mexico; that it was very easy to get certain things, and whatever things were not available, I could get them from twenty-two different countries, no problem," Heredia said. In December, Graham and two of his athletes made the twenty-two-hour drive from Raleigh to Laredo and stayed with Heredia.

Then Heredia produced what seemed a trump card for the government: a photograph of him and Graham in Heredia's bedroom. It was seemingly irrefutable proof that Graham had lied when he said he'd never met Heredia in person. Other photos from the visit showed Graham at the local track.

After that visit, Heredia and Graham dealt with each other over the phone. In one call, Graham introduced Heredia to Montgomery. "He told me that he wanted me to take care of them, to put them on the gold plan. That the money was not an issue, they wanted to get the best things available. The most important is to remain undetectable for the drug testing toward Olympics," Heredia later testified. And he had extensive conversations with Graham about a drug program for Marion Jones.

Shortly after the Sydney Olympics, Heredia and Graham had fallen out over money, with Heredia claiming Graham owed him $20,000–$30,000.

Despite being an illegal drug dealer and an illegal immigrant, Heredia was a godsend to the government, with valuable firsthand testimony against Graham and Jones. He hired a lawyer and repeated his story to the grand jury in San Francisco, this time under a grant of immunity. The government helped him obtain a work visa. He also told the agents he'd be willing to operate undercover and wear a wire.

During the summer, he met and spoke to Graham at a track meet in Eugene, Oregon. He also taped calls with Graham in which he discussed the investigation. Graham was obviously wary, and never directly acknowledged dealing in steroids. But according to a government summary of the tapes, they clearly had a "long-standing relationship," contrary to Graham's statements that they barely knew each other; Graham assured Heredia that he'd told the authorities "nothing," confirmed that Heredia had "said no" when asked about Graham's athletes, agreed with Heredia that they both needed to "deny the whole thing," assured Heredia that he "had Heredia's back," and told Heredia they'd have nothing to worry about as long as Heredia "said nothing" if they "put him on the stand."

Still, Heredia wasn't an ideal witness. He'd told the agents he stopped dealing drugs in 2004, but in October 2006, Rogers called and asked, "Hey, are you still dealing drugs? We have been working with you for two years. Are you still dealing?"

"I'm not going to answer that unless I still have the immunity I had from the grand jury," Heredia replied.

Heredia felt bad about cooperating. "Even at the last moment, I felt I was betraying my oath, the underground oath among athletes," he later said. "What hurt me was that deep down, I didn't want to put all this stuff on the table. I truly felt sad about it."

In January 2005 Troy Ellerman, the lawyer for Valente and Conte, was named commissioner, or chief executive, of the Professional Rodeo Cowboys Association and moved to the association's headquarters in Colorado Springs.

Although Ellerman still represented Valente, his responsibilities on the case had waned, which made it possible for him to move to Colorado and make just the occasional trip back to the courthouse in San Francisco. Victor Conte had proved vexing both as a client and as a defendant. As a client, he had repeatedly defied his lawyers' advice. Bob Holley had resigned (Conte says he was fired) after Conte's *20/20* appearance and his awkward exchange with the judge, and Conte hired new lawyers with no ties to Ellerman or Holley. As a defendant, Conte had initially cooperated with Novitzky, freely answering questions the day of the raid. Then he had abruptly reversed course, denying he had named his clients, accusing Novitzky of dishonesty, refusing further cooperation. And then he had implicated many of his clients on national television.

Even without the mounting testimony of witnesses before the grand jury recounting how they'd obtained illegal steroids from Conte and his own admissions, it was obvious from the documents seized in the raid that Conte was guilty. Apart from his legal gamesmanship and reckless accusations against the government, Conte had never disputed the essence of the charges. He may never have told the whole truth, but he didn't lie about his steroid distribution. His codefendants, Valente and Anderson, had kept quiet and stayed in the background. But their fates were inextricably linked. They, too, had essentially acknowledged their guilt the day of the raids.

Interest in the trial, which had been set by Judge Illston for September, focused more on the professional athletes likely to be called as witnesses than it did on the outcome, which seemed a foregone conclusion. Would Bonds and Jones, the two biggest names, repeat their grand jury denials on the witness stand? Would a score of other top professional athletes from track, baseball, and football have to admit steroid use? Unlike a secret grand jury proceeding, any trial would be public. Given the government's focus on steroid distributors and not users, any trial of Conte, Valente, and Anderson was likely to have the perverse effect of becoming a de facto trial of steroid users.

As his letter to President Bush indicated, Conte wanted a plea bargain. Considering the overwhelming strength of their case, it's hard to see why prosecutors would have had any interest in anything but a straight plea, unless Conte, Valente, and Anderson could aid the ongoing investigation into other potential defendants. In this regard, Anderson had great value as a potential witness in any perjury case against Bonds, and Conte and Valente had some value in perjury cases against Jones and Graham. But their lawyers rejected any notion of cooperation. No proffers—statements indicating what their clients would say if called to testify—were made.

So it came as a surprise to most when U.S. Attorney Kevin Ryan announced, on June 15, that Conte and Anderson would plead guilty to just two counts—conspiracy to distribute steroids and money laundering—and Valente would plead to just one, distributing steroids. The other forty counts were dropped. Prosecutors would recommend sentences of just four months in prison for Conte and probation for Valente. They would make no recommendation for Anderson. The recommendations did not depend on any cooperation from any of the three men. Anderson's lawyer, Anna Ling, said he would "never" cooperate with the government by naming athletes. "It's not in his character," she said.

Conte maintains that he essentially dictated the terms on which he would plead, and that he and his codefendants were able to extract such lenient pleas because they had so much evidence of misconduct by Novitzky and other agents, which his lawyers were prepared to demonstrate in an evidentiary hearing. Novitzky "never served me with a search warrant; he lied about that. In his memo, he said I made a confession; he lied about that. Eighty percent of his memo is conjecture. I certainly never mentioned any athletes using drugs," Conte said. He was also influenced by Martha Stewart's sentence, which may have been less of a deterrent than Judge Cedarbaum had anticipated. "After watching how quickly her time in prison seemed to pass, I decided that I would be willing to accept a similar split sentence of four and four," Conte later wrote.

Ryan defended the decision by noting that federal penalties for steroid distribution were light, and that the maximum sentence any of the men faced if convicted at trial was a year. He called for Congress to enact stiffer penalties. In the meantime, he issued a statement denouncing athletes who cheat.

But Ryan's statement again focused on athletes—not distributors—and no athlete had been charged or even named by the government. As the *San Francisco Chronicle* noted in an editorial:

> If the goal of the prosecution was to cleanse professional sports of steroids and other cheating substances, as Ashcroft suggested, the Justice Department came up short. None of the defendants who admitted to conspiring to sell steroids would name the recipients of illegal substances—and the plea deal will ensure that many of the details of the investigation will never be heard in open court.

In December, Conte and Anderson began their terms in federal prison, four months and three months respectively, followed by an equal amount of house arrest. Valente was placed on probation. The BALCO case itself was essentially over. Had witnesses before the grand jury testified truthfully—and had someone not leaked the transcripts of their testimony—it would have been over. For the athletes who used the steroids BALCO supplied it would have been over as well. As it was, the case all but disappeared. More than three years after the BALCO raid, Bonds retained his $17-million-a-year contract with the Giants and continued his pursuit of the all-time home run record. Even Giambi and Sheffield, who admitted they used steroids, emerged largely unscathed.

Then, in April 2006, Greg Anderson, still under house arrest, was subpoenaed to testify before a grand jury—this time for evidence that Bonds had committed perjury. Having already pleaded guilty and been sentenced for distributing steroids, Anderson was no longer at risk of prosecution—and hence couldn't invoke the Fifth Amendment and refuse to testify. Nonetheless, he was shocked that he was being asked to testify about Bonds's steroid use after being told that he didn't have to cooperate as part of his plea agreement. And he argued that leaks had undermined any confidence that his testimony would be secret. U.S. Judge William Alsup, assigned to Anderson's contempt case, swiftly rejected those arguments and ordered Anderson jailed until he agreed to testify or the grand jury term expired.

Anderson didn't have a First Amendment argument, nor did he argue for a common-law "trainer-client" privilege (though another trainer later did, unsuccessfully), but he had run into the same issue as Judith Miller: criminal law expects and demands that all citizens testify truthfully when questioned about crimes they may have knowledge of. Except for recognized privileges, such as priest-penitent and husband-wife, it doesn't matter that testimony may be demanded against a close friend, a client, or a benefactor. Loyalty may be a virtue, but it is irrelevant to a grand jury.

"We will wait and see how loyal [Anderson] wants to be to someone other than his government, his country," Judge Alsup observed.

The combination of his flamboyant personality and infatuation with the media had made Victor Conte an obvious suspect in the ongoing leak investigation. Even Ellerman, a member of Conte's own defense team, had blamed his client for the leaks. On January 26, Los Angeles–based prosecutors Brian Hershman and Michael Raphael, who been assigned to the leak investigation, had obtained a search warrant for Conte's home, where federal agents seized his computer.

Although the agents found extensive e-mail correspondence between Conte and Fainaru-Wada, it not only didn't prove that Conte had leaked the transcripts but, if anything, suggested he hadn't. In his e-mails to the reporter, Conte seemed angry about the leak. It's "sad I can no longer communicate with you," Conte wrote after their stories ran, although their correspondence soon resumed. He also seemed surprised that the *Chronicle*'s legal department had approved the stories, asking Fainaru-Wada whether it wasn't analogous to selling stolen property. "This is not something I can discuss in any way, other than to say we're fine," Fainaru-Wada had replied. Why would the source of the leak be criticizing the *Chronicle* for running it?

The investigation was at an impasse, short of asking the reporters themselves to identify their source. As the prosecutors reported to the court:

> The criminal violations at issue here strike at the very heart of the secrecy of grand jury proceedings and the integrity of the judicial system. An order of this United States District Court, the Honorable Susan Illston, was blatantly violated by a party to a criminal proceeding who leaked secret grand jury testimony to reporters for the *San Francisco Chronicle*. The perpetrator then baldly lied to the Court in a sworn declaration denying his or her involvement in violation of 18 U.S.C. § 1623. If the leaker is a government employee, this deliberate violation of a Court order and false declaration to the Court undermines the trust we place in our public servants, as well as the leaker's obligations under Federal Rule of Criminal Procedure 6(e). If the leaker was a defendant or defense counsel, this egregious conduct was compounded by moving to dismiss the criminal indictment based on false accusations that the government had leaked the grand jury transcripts, perpetrating yet another fraud on the Court.

The *Chronicle* reporters had turned their grand jury scoops into a book, *Game of Shadows*, published by Gotham Books on March 23. Two weeks before, *Sports Illustrated* ran an excerpt with a cover photo of Bonds and the headline "The Truth: Barry Bonds and Steroids." The book set off a renewed media furor over performance-enhancing drugs and professional baseball's foot-dragging on the issue. Fainaru-Wada and Williams were guests on *David Letterman*. The book attracted glowing reviews and vaulted onto best-seller lists, reaching number two on the *New York Times* list. But the timing of the book, as investigators were still trying to identify who leaked the grand jury transcripts, only strengthened prosecutors' determination to solve the mystery of the leak. To their credit, the authors didn't pull any punches to curry favor with a Justice Department trying to uncover their sources. The book took aim at U.S. Attorney Ryan and his decision to offer the BALCO defendants such a lenient plea bargain, noting that "from first to last, Ryan had seemed to want to limit BALCO's impact. He had decided to keep the names of the BALCO athletes secret. He had spurned USADA's pleas for help and threatened to prosecute the reporters for publishing the leaked files."

Soon after the book's publication, the prosecutors turned to the Justice Department in Washington, which in May authorized them to issue subpoenas to Fainaru-Wada and Williams. Both reporters invoked the First Amendment and refused to testify. As in the Libby case, the investigating agents had obtained signed waivers from all the lawyers involved in the case releasing the reporters from any promise of confidentiality from everyone with access to the transcripts. Each person with access also signed a sworn statement that he or she was not the source. Neither the *Chronicle* nor its reporters made any attempt to gain the consent of their source. In their view, they had promised to protect their source, and to identify him now, with or without a waiver, would be a breach of that promise with dire consequences for the source and, in their view, information gathering in general. They were in a different position than Judith Miller, who couldn't know whether or to what extent her testimony might damage her source. In their case, their testimony would obviously be damaging.

Barely more than a year after Miller was sent to prison, another major clash loomed between the courts and the press. Unlike the leaks by Libby, Rove, and Armitage, the *Chronicle*'s disclosures undeniably served a significant public interest: deterring the use of illegal performance-enhancing drugs by athletes. It corrected the U.S. Attorney's arguably misguided decision to protect the identities of the star athletes who had used illegal steroids. Publication of the names of people who were national role models had a far more deterrent effect than punishment of little-known figures like Conte, Valente, and Anderson, people few had heard of or cared about. The *Chronicle*'s stories had prompted congressional hearings and a long-overdue inquiry into rampant illegal drug use in professional baseball.

As the *Chronicle* editorialized:

> Journalists across the land have come forth in defense of *Chronicle* staff
> writers Mark Fainaru-Wada and Lance Williams, who are at risk of going
> to jail for doing their jobs. At stake is much more than the welfare of two
> decent men and diligent reporters who led the way on one of the big-
> gest sports scandals in recent history—the pervasiveness of steroids and
> other illegal performance-enhancing drugs at the highest levels of athletic
> competition. . . . Journalists have an obligation to pursue these stories and
> sometimes the only way to get them is by guaranteeing anonymity to their
> sources. A democracy that cherishes a free press must respect the need of
> journalists to make and keep such promises.

But Miller had never asked to be told Plame's identity. Libby had thrust
it upon her in an effort to discredit Plame's husband. In the BALCO case,
Fainaru-Wada had evidently used all his considerable persuasive powers to gain
access to the transcripts. In an e-mail to Conte seeking the CD-ROM containing all the secret grand jury transcripts, he wrote:

"So I checked my mail yesterday and I'm still waiting for that CD-Rom.
Figured you were gonna Fedex it to me. Perhaps it will arrive tomorrow. Or the
next day. Or the next. Or the next . . . OK, won't hold my breath. . . ." And, a
day later, "Frankly, I wanted to make a pitch about seeing some stuff and talking
about a few things. . . . As to our email exchanges, well, the only way they end
up in our paper is if/when you give me the green light. As with the CD-Rom,
waiting, waiting, waiting."

Raphael told the court that the reporters "were very likely participating in
a crime."

(The reporters counter that Fainaru-Wada was kidding around with Conte
in the emails, as Conte often did. Fainaru-Wada said he had "no belief or expec-
tation" that Conte would give him the CD-ROM or transcripts and wasn't
soliciting him to do so.)

The day of the hearing on the journalists' motion to quash the subpoena, a
crowd of journalists wearing T-shirts emblazoned "Sportswriters for Freedom of
the Press" marched outside the courthouse. Both Fainaru-Wada and Williams
made statements to Judge Jeffrey White, the federal judge overseeing the leak
investigation. "I do not wish to spend even a minute in jail," Fainaru-Wada said.

"However, I cannot—and will not—betray the promises I have made over the past three years" to confidential sources.

Like other judges who considered the issue, Judge White was unmoved by the First Amendment or common-law appeals to the public interest. "When do we get to choose what laws we're going to obey?" the judge asked. He held the reporters in contempt and ordered them jailed. But he agreed to stay the order until the Ninth Circuit Court of Appeals heard their appeal.

Ordinarily the prosecutors might have objected, but Hershman and Raphael were relieved that the judge granted the stay. The point of their investigation was to find the leaker, not to put journalists in jail. Raphael (himself a former journalist) felt agitated at the prospect, as he later put it. Surely the prospect of a prison term would lead the reporters to reconsider their silence, just as Judith Miller had changed her mind. Or surely Fainaru-Wada's source would come forward, sparing the journalists a stay in prison. But the summer passed, and nothing happened.

TEN

"You're a Snitch"

In Colorado, Troy Ellerman was busy promoting rodeo activities and seemed to have landed in his dream job, one far from the drug dealers and petty criminals he'd represented in Sacramento before hitting the big time in the BALCO case. As Larry McCormack pointed out to him, Ellerman was a "rock star" in the world of rodeo. McCormack was a former sheriff's deputy who had worked for Ellerman as a paralegal, a private investigator, and an expert witness for the past six years, and was closely involved in the BALCO defense. McCormack also counted himself one of Ellerman's best friends. When Ellerman moved out to Colorado, McCormack accompanied him and became the rodeo association's head of human resources and then chief operating officer. They were so close that friends teased them they argued like a husband and wife.

In late March, Ellerman dropped into McCormack's office and tossed a signed copy of Mark Fainaru-Wada's and Lance Williams's new book, *Game of Shadows,* on his desk. "Mark said he wanted you to have this," Ellerman said.

McCormack was pleased that Fainaru-Wada had remembered him and was eager to read the book. He liked Fainaru-Wada. So did Ellerman. There in Colorado, Ellerman often complained about the press coverage of the rodeo association. "I wish I could get a reporter like Mark," he told McCormack. "He's honest and he does his homework."

Soon after the BALCO raid, McCormack, Ellerman, and Fainaru-Wada had met over lunch, which they ate outside at a park across from the old city hall in Sacramento. Ellerman had told the reporter that McCormack was the one he should be talking to, since no one knew more about the case. After that,

Fainaru-Wada often made the drive from San Francisco to see Ellerman, and sometimes he and McCormack shot the breeze.

McCormack read the book straight through. He noticed some details he'd revealed, though he wasn't mentioned by name or cited as a source, which was just as well. But what really caught his attention was one sentence referring to the U.S. Attorney: "Ryan wouldn't comment on whether there would be more indictments, other than to say he hoped to indict 'the individuals identified with the leaks.'"

The next day McCormack asked Ellerman if he'd read the book.

"No," Ellerman said.

"Well, you should." He read aloud the passage about Ryan and the leak.

Ellerman brushed off McCormack's concern about the reporters. "They'll never reveal their source," he assured him. Ellerman told McCormack, as he had several times before, that he'd spoken to a lawyer, who had assured him the First Amendment would protect them from having to name their source.

"Then why do they keep losing in court?" McCormack demanded. "Troy, I've been in this business a long time. From their lofty perch they can say they'll never give it up. They can cite the First Amendment. But you've got these white-bread, middle-class guys. When those big iron doors slam shut they're going to sing like canaries. And your chances are quadrupled because there are two of them. Your chances of their keeping their mouths shut—it ain't going to happen."

"Well, if that happens, you'll be here and I won't," Ellerman said.

"No, I won't," McCormack heatedly replied. "I'm also on the line here."

Ellerman looked at him with a narrowed gaze. It was as if Ellerman was considering for the first time that McCormack might be a problem.

Despite their close proximity, McCormack had never witnessed Ellerman give Fainaru-Wada a grand jury transcript. There were many things Ellerman didn't share with McCormack, and McCormack made it a policy not to get involved in things that didn't concern him. But it hadn't taken a genius to figure out what was going on. After Judge Illston launched the inquiry into the leak of Montgomery's testimony in June, McCormack confronted Ellerman. "You're going to get us in trouble. You shouldn't be doing this. And you should never have involved me in it. Keep me out of this crap." That's when Ellerman first told him he'd been assured by lawyers that he didn't have to worry.

After the much bigger leaks in December—right after visits to the office by Fainaru-Wada—McCormack was angry. How could Ellerman be so reckless?

Coming just days after the hearing on the June leak, Ellerman was all but taunting Judge Illston. But Ellerman laughed about it. He seemed to be enjoying the furor. "That's Troy," McCormack later said. "Troy played the game very loosely. He always walked a fine line."

Then the Justice Department had launched a formal investigation. McCormack read SFGate.com, the *Chronicle*'s website, every day for any news about the investigation. One day he heard from a former employee of Ellerman's who said the FBI had contacted him. He didn't know anything, but the investigation was widening. McCormack wondered how long it would be before the FBI called him.

After he read *Game of Shadows*, McCormack consulted a lawyer, who wasn't very reassuring. He told him about something called "misprision of felony," which is a crime under Title 18 of the U.S. Code:

> Whoever, having knowledge of the actual commission of a felony cognizable by a court of the United States, conceals and does not as soon as possible make known the same to some judge or other person in civil or military authority under the United States, shall be fined under this title or imprisoned not more than three years, or both.

As McCormack put it, this "scared the hell out of me." After this lawyer failed to devise a strategy for extricating McCormack, he hired Chris Wing in Sacramento. Wing told him it wasn't enough to just be a witness to a crime; to be charged with misprision, there had to be some overt act of concealment. "I think you're okay," Wing said, which reassured McCormack somewhat. Still, what would he say if the FBI called him? He wasn't going to lie, which was yet another crime.

As the leak investigation continued, McCormack's close personal and professional relationship with Ellerman deteriorated. Ellerman had proposed moving the rodeo hall of fame from Colorado to New Mexico, a move backed by then-governor Bill Richardson and several million dollars in New Mexico revenue bonds. McCormack thought the idea was fiscally irresponsible, and they argued strenuously about it. Then Ellerman held a board meeting and excluded McCormack, which angered McCormack.

Soon after the board meeting about the move, Ellerman "berated" McCormack over the budget, then "stormed out" of his office. After that, Ellerman told McCormack he had a "shitty attitude," slammed a binder on McCormack's desk, and backed him into a corner, glaring at him in a "menacing" manner, according to a complaint against Ellerman and the rodeo association McCormack later filed in a Colorado court (the suit was subsequently settled). Though the two had often argued, this was unlike anything McCormack had experienced. McCormack feared for his safety. He got on the phone to a friend and said if Ellerman threatened him again, he was going to take a ceremonial shovel Ellerman kept in his office and "smack him in the side of the head." The phone call was secretly recorded, as were several others in which McCormack allegedly threatened inappropriate behavior. Although McCormack claimed he was just letting off steam ("we're cowboys, for God's sake"), he was fired on August 30 for what the association characterized as issues of "anger management, decision making, use of alcohol, and financial mismanagement."

As these matters were coming to a head, McCormack instructed Wing, his lawyer, to approach the authorities. Wing called the FBI. A week later, on September 8, Steven B. Merrill, the FBI's lead agent on the leak case, called Raphael in Los Angeles. There had finally been a break: McCormack claimed that Ellerman was Fainaru-Wada's source and had shown him the grand jury transcripts. Merrill and Raphael quickly arranged a conference call with McCormack. Was he credible? What was his evidence? And why was he coming forward now?

McCormack described his work for Ellerman during the case and recounted his dealings with Fainaru-Wada. He said he'd confronted Ellerman after the June leak, and said he knew it was wrong "from the get-go." McCormack said he was worried that he might be potentially liable for the leak. He acknowledged that he'd had a falling-out with Ellerman, and had just been fired from his job at the rodeo association. But he insisted he'd been thinking of coming forward long before that dispute. He worried that if the reporters decided to name their source, and implicated Ellerman, he might face liability as Ellerman's accomplice. He specifically mentioned "misprision of felony"—a crime so obscure even the prosecutors weren't familiar with it—and he also said he thought it was unfair that the reporters would have to go to jail, when it was Ellerman who violated the law.

Given the timing of McCormack's revelation, just days after being fired, Raphael wasn't so sure McCormack's motives were all that pure. Nevertheless, McCormack's disclosures were detailed and plausible. It bolstered his credibility that McCormack said he had not actually seen Ellerman show Fainaru-Wada any grand jury transcripts, nor had Ellerman explicitly admitted doing so. Still, they would likely still need testimony from the reporters to prove the case against Ellerman, which didn't resolve the issue of the reporters' having to testify or going to jail.

Now Raphael was even more relieved that the reporters' prison sentence had been stayed pending appeal. The prosecutors had represented to the court that they had exhausted all possible leads—and now a promising one had materialized. Did the judge—and the reporters—need to be told that circumstances had changed?

Since the reporters were in no imminent risk of imprisonment, the lawyers decided to continue the investigation, using McCormack as an undercover source. McCormack readily agreed to be wired and secretly record Ellerman. He'd done the same thing countless times as a law enforcement officer, and he even showed Merrill, the FBI agent, how to install the wire.

Despite their recent estrangement, McCormack and Ellerman were still in touch, and McCormack called him and said he had some files he needed to drop off. On October 5 the two met in the parking lot outside Ellerman's office, and McCormack started moving the files from his truck into Ellerman's van. Wearing his wire, McCormack said he'd been to see a lawyer and he was still nervous about the leak investigation. Ellerman told him to stop worrying, that the reporters would never talk. "I went and talked to Fainaru-Wada," Ellerman said, according to a transcript of McCormack's recording. "I went right to him. He is not going to say a word . . . and I made sure he wasn't going to say a word about you or me."

"I have to worry about my livelihood," McCormack said, now that he was out of a job.

Suddenly it seemed to dawn on Ellerman that McCormack was a threat. He swore. "Are you trying to take me down? You're a goddamned snitch."

"I don't play the snitch game, Troy," McCormack responded. "But if I am, what does that make you?"

Ellerman broke off the conversation and went back to his office. People outside his office heard him throwing and smashing things.

McCormack felt terrible. Whatever had happened between them, Ellerman was still his friend. He felt he'd just betrayed him.

When Raphael listened to McCormack's tape, he was convinced Ellerman was the reporters' source. The comments only made sense if Ellerman was; he never denied it or asked McCormack what he was talking about. The tape was probably enough to corroborate McCormack's testimony. Still, Ellerman never said point-blank that he'd given Fainaru-Wada the transcripts. He and Merrill decided to try for more.

On October 31, Merrill and two other agents met with Ellerman at his office in Colorado Springs. Now that he was the prime suspect, and not just one of twenty people with access to the transcripts, they wanted to ask him more pointedly what he knew about the leaks and observe his demeanor. They again warned him that any false statement is a federal crime. According to Merrill's report of the interview, Ellerman denied leaking anything and tried again to blame Conte. "Ellerman stated it would not have been worth ruining his career by leaking this FGJ [federal grand jury] material. Ellerman stated representatives of the *San Francisco Chronicle* never tried to 'hit him up' to leak these materials . . . Ellerman stated he does not know 'for sure' who leaked BALCO FGJ materials to the media, however, Ellerman thinks Conte leaked BALCO FGJ materials."

The moment the FBI agents left, Ellerman called McCormack. "I need to talk to you," he said. "I need you to come over here right now."

"I can't. I've got things to do," McCormack said, resisting.

"I need you to get over here," Ellerman repeated, his voice strained.

"Dude, I don't work for you anymore," McCormack reminded him. Then he relented. "Okay, give me a few minutes."

Merrill called McCormack. "He's gonna call you."

"He just did."

They agreed he'd again wear a wire.

When McCormack arrived, Ellerman's demeanor had changed. He was scared. He turned on the TV and turned up the volume. He told McCormack the FBI had just been back.

"Where's this thing going to end?" McCormack asked.

Ellerman argued again that the reporters would never talk and neither of them had anything to worry about if they kept their mouths shut. But now he sounded like he was trying to convince himself. McCormack was amazed that it still hadn't dawned on him that it was too late—that McCormack had already talked.

"Troy, you've got to clear this up," McCormack said. "Why don't you just come forward?"

"I can't," Ellerman said. "I've looked at the sentencing guidelines and there's no way I can work this out. I'll go to prison. If I have to go to prison, I'll kill myself."

Much of this recording was obscured by the sound of the television in the background. Still, the FBI managed to capture key passages and put excerpts from both recorded sessions on a CD.

The FBI asked McCormack to try making a third recording, but this time he balked. Merrill had been transferred to New Delhi, replaced by a less experienced agent McCormack considered a "clown." He was also evidently having second thoughts about his extensive cooperation, and how it might look in the close-knit rodeo community. He'd started working with a nonprofit organization based in Phoenix, Cowboys for Kids, which introduces disadvantaged children to rodeo activities. The new agent suggested McCormack call Ellerman and say the FBI was coming to interview him. What should he say?

McCormack drew the line. To him, this was an effort to entrap Ellerman in yet another crime: inducing McCormack to make a false statement. "Look," McCormack told the agent. "What he did, he did. But I'm not going to get him into more trouble. I told you he did it, now you prove it."

"Are you saying you feel sorry for this guy?" the agent asked.

"You goddamn well better believe I do," McCormack said indignantly. "He's my best friend."

At this juncture Raphael asked for a closed hearing with Judge White. Over their protests, the *Chronicle*'s lawyers were excluded. Raphael disclosed the break in the leak case as well as some excerpts from McCormack's undercover tapes of Ellerman. Judge White seemed annoyed about not being informed earlier, but Raphael assured him that had the reporters been in jail, he would have told him immediately. The judge agreed they should continue the investigation.

Even as grand jury testimony to the contrary mounted, Trevor Graham continued to insist that he was a whistle-blower about steroid use in track and field, not a perpetrator. But by now, an astounding twenty-five of Graham's athletes had tested positive for steroids—a highly incriminating pattern. Many of them had come forward to testify that Graham gave them performance-enhancing drugs and introduced them to Heredia, including Antonio Pettigrew, an Olympic medalist who was also godfather to Graham's daughter. Pettigrew had initially lied to agents, and then recanted when warned he was risking a prosecution for false statements. Once he was granted immunity, Pettigrew said Graham had called him and said, "You don't have to say anything, just be quiet."

Even though Graham had sworn that he hadn't spoken to Heredia since 1997, Novitzky had collected phone records that showed more than a hundred phone calls between the two from 1998 to 2001 alone. And while Graham had insisted he'd never met Heredia, prosecutors had Heredia's photograph showing the two together, as well as testimony from the two athletes who'd accompanied Graham to Texas for the face-to-face meeting with Heredia.

On November 2, the grand jury investigating BALCO in San Francisco indicted Graham on three counts of making false statements to Novitzky when he said that he "never set up any of his athletes with drugs obtained from Source A," when he said he had "never met Source A in person," and when he said he had "last contacted Source A via a phone call in approximately 1997." Source A, of course, was Angel "Memo" Heredia.

The Wrangler National Finals Rodeo, rodeo's biggest annual event, started the first week in December in Las Vegas. The FBI told McCormack that they were going to confront Ellerman, but he begged them to hold off. He argued that arresting Ellerman then could disrupt the entire event and affect the livelihood of hundreds of participants. The FBI agreed. McCormack and his wife attended, and despite their recent problems, McCormack felt Ellerman treated them like royalty, giving them VIP seats in the front row and inviting them to dinner with him and the show's chairman. It was as though nothing had come between them, but "it was all smoke and mirrors," McCormack says.

Four days later, on December 13, FBI agents pulled up at Ellerman's house in Colorado Springs in the early morning. After he came to the door, they played the CD containing excerpts from the tapes and told him McCormack would testify against him. They added that McCormack didn't want him to call. "Tell him not to call me, either," Ellerman said. He said he wanted to speak to a lawyer, and the agents left.

Ellerman hired Scott Tedmon, a lawyer he knew in Sacramento, but as a criminal defense lawyer himself, he knew the game was over. Tedmon entered into plea negotiations on Ellerman's behalf, and Ellerman admitted he had leaked the grand jury transcripts and then lied repeatedly about it. He resigned his post with the rodeo association and withdrew from the California bar. He gave the government almost everything it wanted, which was a guilty plea to four felonies: two counts of contempt of court, one of obstruction of justice, and one of filing a false declaration under penalty of perjury. In return, the government agreed not to seek a prison term greater than twenty-four months.

As Raphael subsequently told the court:

The entire judicial system relies on the integrity of its proceedings and the lawyers' duty of candor with the court. Defendant repeatedly violated this duty in order to avoid having his own criminal behavior exposed. To make matters worse, defendant then sought to capitalize on his criminal conduct by filing a motion to dismiss an indictment returned against his client, which he knew was frivolous and, if granted, could result in his client, who later pled guilty, going unpunished. For an experienced criminal attorney, who has been practicing for a decade, to engage in such deceitful and self-motivated criminal behavior in the course of a high-profile federal prosecution is shocking. Indeed, there are few, if any, other examples of an attorney committing such blatant crimes in the course of litigating a case.

The BALCO prosecutors in San Francisco also submitted a blistering memo:

Mr. Ellerman attempted to use his own illegal dissemination of the grand jury transcripts to destroy the government's prosecution of this case [BALCO] and . . . to destroy the professional and personal reputations of the law enforcement professionals involved in the investigation. . . . Mr. Ellerman's obvious indifference to the impact his false accusations might have on the reputations and lives of others is one of the more unsettling and disturbing aspects of this conduct.

Of course, the greatest potential impact was on the *Chronicle* reporters, who were preparing to go to jail to protect Ellerman's identity. Fainaru-Wada tried to explain to his children that he might be going to prison in order to protect someone, and that not everyone who goes to prison is a bad person. As Raphael noted, Ellerman "used the media's belief that it has a 'reporter's privilege' against a grand jury subpoena to cover up his crimes, and he was willing to have reporters go to prison for him."

The reporters got the news that Ellerman had confessed to being their source when an AP reporter called them for comment on Valentine's Day. They declined to comment on any relationship with Ellerman. They were relieved, but experienced a range of emotions. It wasn't the vindication in a precedent-setting court of appeals ruling they'd hoped for.

"I didn't want to go to prison and I was relieved to be done with the situation," Fainaru-Wada said. "By the same token, this was not how this was supposed to end. I felt like everyone who helped us and took risks for us were whistle-blowers in the truest sense. The idea that the government was now prosecuting somebody . . . I wasn't celebrating. Lance and I had lunch the next day. We were mostly decompressing. We were shell-shocked."

In court Ellerman's lawyer offered no excuses for Ellerman's behavior, but countered that "Mr. Ellerman has been living in a mental and emotional prison for the past three years. Since he committed these acts, Mr. Ellerman has been punished beyond measure by having to live with the guilt, torment and uncertainty of where his life was headed."

In a handwritten letter to the probation officer assigned to write his presentence report, Ellerman said he had been going through "severe difficulties" in his life when he leaked the transcripts and then lied about it, and attributed his lapse in judgment to cocaine and alcohol abuse, the pressure of the high-profile BALCO case, and unspecified "pressure" from Fainaru-Wada:

> I was weak and caved to the pressures that under normal circumstances
> would not have phased [sic] me. When I let the reporters view the
> grand jury transcripts I made the mistake of my life. It was certainly
> not calculated or premeditated. I gave no thought as to why or what
> I was doing. I did not plan or calculate the consequences of my decisions,
> good or bad. In my depressed, drugged-out mind the training and the line
> between right and wrong no longer existed.

His lawyer said Ellerman offered these details as "an explanation, and not as an excuse" and that he "understands his actions were offensive and an affront to the judicial process as a whole . . . Mr. Ellerman is genuinely remorseful."

Judge White rejected the plea agreement as too lenient. He wanted a longer term than the twenty-four-month cap the prosecutors had agreed to, and told them to come back in a month. Then, on July 2, President Bush commuted Scooter Libby's sentence, which became the centerpiece for Ellerman's plea for leniency. Like Libby, Ellerman was a lawyer convicted of false statements. Unlike Libby, Ellerman had leaked information about steroid use in professional sports, not national security information. Moreover, Ellerman acknowledged his guilt, pleaded guilty to four felonies, and expressed remorse. "Mr. Libby took the government all the way through a jury trial and as far as defense counsel knows, Libby has never publicly acknowledged any wrongdoing on his part," Tedmon argued.

But Judge White made short shrift of that argument. "If Mr. Ellerman is dissatisfied with his sentence, he should seek a commutation from the president," said Judge White, himself a Bush appointee. He also criticized Bush for commuting Libby's sentence after his administration had urged judges to adhere to federal sentencing guidelines. "Under the president's reasoning, any white-collar defendant should receive no jail time, regardless of the reprehensibility of the crime," he noted.

The subsequent hearing put the government in the odd position of defending Ellerman, arguing that twenty-four months was an adequate prison term, and urging the judge to give him credit for coming forward and sparing the reporters a prison stay.

"He didn't come forward. He was caught," White tartly observed. "Mr. Ellerman . . . I really want to hear right out of your mouth what was going on in your mind at the time you did these crimes."

Ellerman replied, "When they asked me time after time after time to see these transcripts and I allowed it, I did not measure that in my mind . . . I should have had the courage to stand up and tell cocounsel that I'm the one that leaked the information. But when you lie it's difficult to come forward and tell the truth. What I should have had the integrity to do I didn't have the backbone to stand up and say 'I did it.' I didn't and it took on a life of its own. Once you lie you have to continue to lie.

"I'm glad this is exposed. I don't have to pack this around anymore. I'm glad that I can get rid of this and do my time and live a productive life. . . . I lied, I filed a false declaration. I didn't have the courage to come forward and stop the lying. I didn't do it and I apologize. I'm prepared to be sentenced. I'm sorry for what I've done. I can't undo it, Judge. But I can make you a promise. I can be a better father, be a better son, and be a better husband, and I can be a better citizen and lead a productive life."

Ellerman was fighting back tears. "That's all I can offer you right now is to be better. I can't undo my crime," he concluded.

Judge White said he'd ponder Ellerman's statement over lunch. When he returned, he seemed to have softened his views slightly. He said he had seriously considered sentencing him to a prison term longer than that called for by the sentencing guidelines, but had decided on thirty months—just six months longer than the maximum under his original plea agreement—followed by three years of court supervision. "If you can't believe what the lawyers say, you have no basis for finding the truth, no basis to follow the law, and the system breaks down," White said.

S everal weeks later, on August 2, 2007, Marion Jones and her lawyer, Richard Nichols, sat down with two federal prosecutors, E. Danya Perry and Daniel Levy, this time in New York. Agents from the Immigration and Customs Enforcement agency joined them. Jones was now living in Austin, Texas, with her new husband, Obadele Thompson, another Olympic track medalist and a native of Barbados. Her name was now Marion Jones-Thompson. She was pregnant. She'd come to the interview voluntarily, not under subpoena, and not as a suspect but simply as a potential witness. She didn't have an immunity agreement, since she wasn't suspected of any wrongdoing and there didn't seem to be any need for one. As in California, all she had to do was answer truthfully or, if she chose, decline to answer at all. The prosecutors and agents were hoping she could help them.

This investigation had nothing to do with BALCO, except for some of the people involved, including Tim Montgomery, the father of her first child.

For all his charm and athletic prowess, Montgomery had caused Jones a whirlwind of trouble and heartbreak. His promising track career had nosedived since his grand jury testimony and Ellerman's subsequent leaking of the transcript, in which he admitted using illegal drugs. He failed to qualify for the Athens Olympics. The USADA imposed a four-year ban on him in 2005, and Montgomery announced his retirement. He was stripped of his medal and world record. Worse, his fees—$60,000 per race—and endorsement contracts—$575,000 a year from Nike alone—evaporated. His relationship with Jones had suffered under financial and other strains, and the two had separated in the summer of 2005, leaving Jones to raise their two-year-old son. She, too, was having financial problems, and a bank foreclosed on the $2.5 million house in Raleigh where she and Montgomery had lived.

Then, in April 2006, Montgomery had been arrested and accused of depositing $775,000 in bogus checks, for which he received a commission of $20,000 as part of a sprawling money-laundering and counterfeit-check scheme that defrauded banks of nearly $6 million. The checks were part of an expanding investigation, initially launched by the Department of Homeland Security, of Douglas Shyne and Natasha Singh, a couple who appeared to be at the center of the ring. They'd generate stolen, altered, or counterfeit checks, have their accomplices deposit them into their accounts, then funnel the proceeds, minus a generous commission, back to them. Steven Riddick, a sprinter who'd won a gold medal on the U.S. relay team in 1976, had enlisted Montgomery in the scheme. He'd gone on to coach both Montgomery and Jones. An ex-convict who knew Shyne from prison, in turn, had introduced Riddick to Shyne.

Now Montgomery's involvement in the check scheme had landed Jones back before federal prosecutors. They showed her a check from Nathaniel Alexander for $25,000 made out to her. Her signature was on the back, and the check had been deposited into her account. Alexander shared an office with Riddick—they were close friends—and Alexander was having an affair with another track star, a close friend of Jones. Jones seemed genuinely surprised, and said she knew nothing about the check. As for her signature, she said her secretary had a stamp that she sometimes used to sign Jones's name. She said she knew nothing about any check scheme involving Montgomery.

Then the prosecutors obtained records from Wachovia that included a $200,000 check made out to Montgomery that was deposited into a business account for which Jones had been added only days earlier as an officer and cosigner. On September 5, Jones returned for another meeting at the Manhattan U.S. Attorney's office. Pressed on the issue of the newly discovered check and account, Jones broke down, sobbing, acknowledging that she did know about the checks. "I loved him. He was the father of my child," she said of Montgomery. "I just wanted what was best for my child."

Jones recalled now that she'd loaned Montgomery $50,000 for attorneys' fees, and the $25,000 check from Alexander represented partial repayment. She remembered that Montgomery had sold his car, a "big, pink, souped-up Lincoln," as she described it, and had a check for $25,000 made out to her. She didn't know anything about the source of the $200,000 check (which, in any event, had bounced) but had agreed to be an officer and cosigner on the account, which was intended to benefit their son.

Jones was an impressive witness, so much so that the prosecutors listed her as a witness for the upcoming trial of Montgomery. The prosecutors had prepared a detailed script of questions and answers, including her innocent explanation for the $25,000 check. Then, just a week before trial, they got a letter from Montgomery's lawyer alleging that Jones was a "bald-faced liar," and if they had any doubts, they should contact the prosecutors in the BALCO case.

Perry and Levy called Matt Parrella and Jeff Nedrow, who said she'd lied in her grand jury testimony. They showed the New York prosecutors the calendars of her doping regimen and made clear that she'd lied to them repeatedly.

Meanwhile, investigators contacted Montgomery's North Carolina car dealer, the one who had indeed handled the sale of Montgomery's custom pink Lincoln. The story had a kernel of truth to it—but the car had been sold more than a year before Jones deposited the $25,000 check, shattering her story.

The prosecutors were taken aback. As one participant said, "We pride ourselves on some ability to tease out the liars from the truth tellers. It's a part of our job. A lot of it is by amassing facts, a part of it is a gut thing. How believable is someone? How good is someone at lying?

"She was world-class. She created a whole story she seemed to believe. She can be very convincing. She's physically attractive, an amazing smile, open expression. She's well spoken, smart. She comes across really well. You want to believe her. But she was going to get up in front of twelve jurors, take an oath, then lie about the whole thing, with the same coldness and ease that she'd lied to us. People commit perjury all the time, but not with this level of calculation and confidence."

Jones was abruptly removed from the potential witness list. And the following week, Montgomery agreed to plead guilty to the check scheme, and implicated Jones as a coconspirator.

Prosecutors asked Jones for another interview on April 8. This time the tone had changed. As Danya Perry later told the judge in the case, "We came to have some serious questions about her credibility, and the truth of the story, and we reached out to counsel. We suggested that criminal counsel was necessary. And we were very clear that we did not believe her story."

This time, Jones brought with her an experienced criminal lawyer from North Carolina. She dropped the pretense she knew nothing about the check scheme. She admitted that she'd lied in the previous two interviews. The sale of the pink car was a fabrication. Sobbing once again, she insisted she'd lied to protect Montgomery, her child's father, and Riddick, her former coach. But she had willingly entered into the check scheme as a participant.

Levy and Perry contacted the California prosecutors and suggested offering Jones a plea that would resolve both investigations—two counts of making false statements in each case—and Parrella and Nedrow readily agreed. Faced with the prospect of fighting cases on two coasts, and with the overwhelming evidence in the check case, Jones capitulated. She finally admitted using the performance-enhancing drugs she had so long denied.

Jones appeared before Judge Kenneth M. Karas in the federal courthouse in White Plains, New York, on October 5. At the outset Judge Karas reminded Jones that she had taken an oath to tell the truth, and thus, any answers to his questions would be subject to the penalties of perjury. "Perjury is intentionally lying under oath. If you were to do that today, you could be prosecuted separate and apart from the charges contained in the information. Do you understand that?"

"Yes, Your Honor," she replied.

And then, at the judge's request, she described her crimes in her own words, albeit reading from a statement that had been carefully crafted in conjunction with her lawyers. "In September 2000, before the Sydney Olympics, [Trevor] Graham began providing me with a substance he referred to as flaxseed oil, which I had never taken before, but I trusted Graham and I did not ask any questions. At Graham's direction I took this substance orally. He told me to put it under my tongue for a few seconds and then to swallow it. I consumed this substance several times before the Sydney games and continued using it afterward. Graham told me not to tell anybody anything about what he was giving me or my workouts or my training.

"I continued using this substance through to July 2001 when I stopped using Graham as my trainer. After I left Mr. Graham and stopped taking what he was giving me, I noticed a difference in how I felt physically. I realize now that while I was with Graham, I was able to train more intensively, I had quicker recovery periods, and achieved better times and results in part due to my use of this substance.

"By November 2003, I realized that Graham had given me a performance-enhancing drug. On November 4, 2003, I was interviewed in San Jose, California, in the presence of my then attorneys as part of the BALCO investigation by Internal Revenue Service agent Jeff Novitzky. During that interview, Agent Novitzky showed me a substance that he referred to as 'the clear,' which I recognized as the substance given to me by Mr. Trevor Graham. Agent Novitzky asked me if I had ever seen this substance before and whether or not I had ingested it. I told him that I had never seen the substance and that I had never ingested it. These were both lies, Your Honor, as I knew at the time that the substance that Agent Novitzky showed me was the same as that provided to me by Mr. Graham, which I ingested from September 2000 to July 2001.

"During that same interview, Your Honor, Agent Novitzky asked me if I had ever taken performance-enhancing drugs. I answered that I had not. This was a lie, Your Honor, as I knew at the time that I had taken the substance provided to me by Mr. Trevor Graham."

"Did you know what you were doing was illegal?" the judge asked.

"Yes, sir. I did."

So this was Jones's new story, what her lawyers characterized as a soul-searching, courageous admission of guilt: She hadn't known what she was taking; she'd been told it was flaxseed oil; she had somehow deduced on her own that it was a performance-enhancing drug only after the Olympics and after her performance declined; and, remarkably, that this substance, what Agent Novitzky had called the "clear," was the only performance-enhancing drug she'd ever taken—and orally, at that.

Judge Karas turned to Matt Parrella, the assistant U.S. attorney from San Francisco from the BALCO case, and asked if he thought there was "any need" for further explanation.

The answer was painfully obvious. Victor Conte (on national television), Jones's former husband C. J. Hunter (in sworn testimony), and Tim Montgomery (in a statement to prosecutors) said that they were present when Jones injected steroids; Hunter had actually administered the shot. Jones's drug calendar seized in the BALCO raid indicated a regimen of "E," or erythropoietin (EPO); "C" (the "clear"); "G" (human growth hormone); and "I," insulin, some administered by injections. Blood-test results confirmed a surge in red blood cells associated with EPO use. In her earlier conversations with Perry and Levy, Jones had admitted most of this. Now, under oath, she was backpedaling from the truth.

"No, Your Honor," Parrella replied.

Outside there was a battery of camera crews and a crowd of reporters. Flanked by her lawyers, Jones made a statement from the courthouse steps:

> Good afternoon, everyone. I am Marion Jones-Thompson, and I am here today because I have something very important to tell you, my fans, my friends, and my family.
>
> Over the many years of my life, as an athlete in the sport of track and field, you have been fiercely loyal and supportive toward me. Even more loyal and supportive than words can declare has been my family, and especially my dear mother, who stands by my side today.

And so it is with a great amount of shame that I stand before you and tell you that I have betrayed your trust. I want all of you to know that today I pleaded guilty to two counts of making false statements to federal agents.

Making these false statements to federal agents was an incredibly stupid thing for me to do, and I am responsible fully for my actions. I have no one to blame but myself for what I have done.

To you, my fans, including my young supporters, the United States Track and Field Association, my closest friends, my attorneys, and the most classy family a person could ever hope for—namely my mother, my husband, my children, my brother and his family, my uncle, and the rest of my extended family—I want you to know that I have been dishonest. And you have the right to be angry with me.

I have let them down.

I have let my country down.

And I have let myself down.

Jones returned the five medals she'd won at the Sydney Olympics. Her seven relay teammates were ordered to return their medals too (a decision they successfully appealed). The International Olympic Committee formally stripped Jones of all medals and titles won since 2000. She announced her retirement from track and field during her speech on the courthouse steps, and in any event was suspended from competition for two years. Public condemnation was swift. The head of the International Association of Athletics Federations said, "Marion Jones will be remembered as one of the biggest frauds in sporting history."

Her lawyer later characterized the reaction: "She's been tarred and feathered. She has been pilloried, pummeled, savaged, dragged through the public square. It has been a public shaming and really a global shaming."

Based in part on the sanctions and public reaction, Jones's lawyers appealed for leniency when she came before Judge Karas for sentencing on January 11, 2008. Besides the usual glowing character references and the plight of her two young children (her second son had been born in July), they stressed her courage, honesty, and strength of character in coming forward with the truth. Henry DePippo, one of her lawyers, told a poignant anecdote about his wife's goddaughter, a high school runner, who told him over the Christmas break that Marion Jones was her hero. How could that be? DePippo had asked her. "And she said, well, because she made a mistake, and she told the truth. And, Judge, I think that's what this is really all about."

"She's admitted the truth," DePippo concluded. "She's disavowed her denials. She's done it in a sincere and respectful manner."

Parrella, too, stressed that "probably the most important thing for us in the Northern District of California investigation . . . was really to set the record straight. We believe we've done that."

"Well, can I probe that a little bit?" the judge asked. He'd reviewed the drug calendars seized in the BALCO raid, which were attached to the government's sentencing memo. The memo itself concluded that Jones's "use of performance-enhancing drugs encompassed numerous drugs (THG, EPO, human growth hormone) and delivery systems (sublingual drops, subcutaneous injections) over a substantial course of time. . . . Her false statements were focused, hoping not only to deflect the attention of the investigation away from herself, but also to secure the gains achieved by her use of the performance-enhancing substances in the first place. The false statements to [Novitzky] were the culmination of a long series of public denials by the defendant, often accompanied by baseless attacks on those accusing her, regarding her use of these substances."

As Judge Karas said to Parrella, "I mean you say it's all clear to you now. I don't read the response to your submission as acknowledging that these doping calendars, as you call them, have been admitted by this defendant."

"That is correct," Parrella acknowledged.

"But when you say it's all come clean, I'm not sure I follow."

Parrella didn't really answer, and said he'd rely on the government's sentencing memo, which laid out her extensive drug use.

Judge Karas returned to this issue as he explained the factors he considered in determining Jones's sentence. "I hope you're right, Mr. DePippo. I hope that your wife's goddaughter can keep her faith in Ms. Jones-Thompson. . . . But I have to say, and I'm sorry to say, that I do have some doubts about the truthfulness of the entirety of Ms. Jones-Thompson's statement before the court under oath."

The judge then read extensively from the transcript of Jones's statement, beginning with "I didn't know if it was flaxseed oil . . ."

When he finished reading, the judge continued, "I think the statement that troubles me the most is, 'After I left Mr. Graham and stopped taking what he was giving me, I noticed a difference in how I felt physically.' The statement, I think, is at odds with common sense.

"Athletes at Ms. Jones-Thompson's level understand that the difference between winning and losing, between all-time greatness and just being very good, is measured in micro units. And in fact, the difference between the fastest time of all in the hundred-meter dash and the ninth-fastest time is three-tenths of a second . . . And what the Court was told under oath is that Ms. Jones-Thompson realized in hindsight, nearly two years after she stopped taking performance-enhancing drugs, that the changes in her training regimen and the effectiveness were not as high after she stopped taking what she was told was flaxseed oil. And that's a very difficult thing to believe; that a top-notch athlete, knowing the razor-thin margins separating the best from the others, would not be keenly aware and very careful about what he or she would put in his or her body and recognize the effects immediately on their performance. . . . I am troubled, quite frankly, by the statement."

While the judge conceded that it was not for him to say that Jones's statement had been proved false beyond a reasonable doubt, he all but said she had committed perjury—again.

He also stressed the broad harm that her lies had inflicted. "Athletes in society have an elevated status. They entertain, they inspire, and, perhaps most importantly, they serve as role models for children around the world, kids who wait in line to get autographs of their favorite athlete. They wait in line just to see them walk by. They stay up late . . . so that they can watch them compete somewhere around the world and the country. They spend money to see them in person, buy products they promote, buy their jerseys. And from these top athletes, all of us, but particularly children, can learn the value of hard work, of dedication, teamwork, sportsmanship, and how to lose and to win within the rules and with dignity."

Jones had doubly broken those rules: by using illegal drugs, participating in an illegal check scheme, and then lying about both. "It sends all the wrong messages to those who follow the athletes' every move," Judge Karas observed. "The choice to not play by the rules was compounded by the choice to break the law."

Under the circumstances, Judge Karas said, he considered imposing a sentence greater than called for by the federal sentencing guidelines, which suggested a prison term from zero to six months. Instead, he imposed the maximum—six months—to be followed by two years of supervised release during which Jones should "get the message out to kids that it's wrong to cheat and then lie about the cheating. And I think that will do a world of good."

. . .

I n San Francisco, Kevin Ryan had the satisfaction as U.S. Attorney of seeing
the grand jury leak case solved—but not Jones's guilty plea, let alone the culmination of the BALCO investigation his administration had launched. Ryan
resigned in February 2007, one of seven U.S. Attorneys targeted by Alberto
Gonzales, the former White House counsel who had succeeded Ashcroft as
attorney general. The resulting furor over whether they were improperly ousted
for partisan political reasons (and whether Gonzales was truthful about the
reasons) largely excluded Ryan. There seemed little doubt that Ryan was told
to resign for cause.

Over fifty experienced prosecutors had quit under Ryan's regime. As John
Hemann, a prosecutor who served on the Enron task force, wrote in an open letter:

> There are problems in the office now that have not existed in kind
> or magnitude since I got here in 1995. It is no solution to deny these
> problems exist. People in the office—lawyers and staff—are unhappy and
> frustrated. People outside the office are critical and, increasingly, derisive.

Another prosecutor wrote to the Justice Department, describing an office
"in crisis," and faulted Ryan for "gross mismanagement," according to excerpts
of the letter subsequently published in the Bay Area *Recorder*, a legal paper. At
a meeting conducted as part of a formal Justice Department audit, attorneys
in the office disparaged him as isolated, inflexible, and disengaged from the
agency's work. Ryan had stalked out afterward, according to a detailed account
in the *San Francisco Weekly*.

After announcing his resignation, Ryan told *USA Today* that the BALCO
investigation would continue. "When I leave, this won't just fall off the map.
The infrastructure is in place. We have good prosecutors on it. A good review
process. Good institutional knowledge. So when I move on, there are those that
can carry forward with it without a problem."

But many wondered. Witnesses kept showing up at the grand jury, including Giants trainer Stan Conte and others from the Giants' staff, but the press
had largely abandoned staking out the federal building. As Bonds approached
Hank Aaron's all-time home run record, the case receded into the background.

And then Bonds had done it, hitting number 756 on August 7, setting off
fireworks and a citywide celebration. Baseball commissioner Bud Selig, under

fire for dragging his heels on confronting steroid use in professional baseball, called Bonds to congratulate him. So did President Bush, despite the concerns about steroid use he expressed in his State of the Union address. San Francisco mayor Gavin Newsom gave Bonds the keys to the city.

In the following weeks Bonds added six more home runs and finished the 2007 season with a record career total of 762. On November 15, 2007, a month after Jones's guilty plea, two months after his record-shattering home run, and nearly four years after testifying before the grand jury, the Justice Department issued a short press release:

> A federal grand jury in San Francisco indicted Barry Lamar Bonds, age forty-three, of Beverly Hills, California, with four counts of perjury, and one count of obstruction of justice.
>
> Bonds is charged with knowingly and willfully making false material statements, regarding his use of anabolic steroids and other performance-enhancing substances, while under oath during his testimony before the federal grand jury that was conducting the investigation into the Bay Area Laboratory Cooperative ("BALCO"), and with obstructing justice in the same investigation.

Specifically, the indictment charged that Bonds had given "false" and "evasive and misleading" testimony to the grand jury when he answered:

> "Not that I know of," when asked if he had ever taken steroids;
> "No" and "No, I wasn't at all," when asked if he had taken steroids during the weeks before November 2000, when a blood test showed high levels of testosterone;
> "Not at all," when asked if he was taking steroids in December 2001, when a urine test was positive for two steroids;
> "No," when asked if he was taking flaxseed oil or the "cream" or any other steroid in January 2001;
> "No, no," when asked if anyone other than his personal physician, such as Anderson, had ever injected him;
> "Right," when asked to confirm that Anderson had never given him anything to be taken by injection;

"No," when asked if Anderson had ever given him human growth
hormone, and "No," when asked if Anderson had given him either
human growth hormone or testosterone;

"Not that I recall," when asked if he had gotten anything other than
vitamins and proteins from Anderson during 2001, when a calendar with the initials "BB" indicated he was taking a full regimen of
performance-enhancing drugs.

Hours after Bonds's indictment, Greg Anderson was released from a federal
prison in Dublin, California. He'd been there just over a year while the grand
jury deliberated. Now that it had finished its work and indicted Bonds without
Anderson's testimony, there was no reason to keep him in jail. Of course, his
predicament was far from resolved. He'd likely be subpoenaed again if and
when Bonds came to trial. Then the ordeal would start again. But for now he
was free.

As Anderson walked out, other inmates gave him a standing ovation. Paula
Canny, a longtime friend and one of his lawyers, picked him up and took him
to dinner at the Black Angus, a nearby steak house. Anderson said nothing to
waiting reporters, but Canny told the *New York Daily News*, "In America the
only thing worse than being a cheat is being a snitch. He's never going to say
anything–not because of Barry but because of Greg."

Bonds entered a not-guilty plea on December 8. A horde of fans applauded
as he emerged from the courthouse, with many clutching baseballs for him to
autograph. "I love you, Barry," shouted one man.

Trevor Graham's trial began on May 19, 2008, delayed in part by the resignation of Zeszotarski, his lawyer, who said Graham wasn't paying his bills.
He was replaced by a court-appointed lawyer, William Keane, who alternately
portrayed Graham as a courageous whistle-blower for sending in the syringe,
and the government's star witness, Angel Heredia, as a manipulative, schem-
ing, drug-dealing liar who would do anything the government wanted to avoid
prosecution and protect his immigration status.

Even so, the government's case seemed overwhelming and was widely seen
as a preview of the Bonds trial. Novitzky was a key witness, and he held up well
on cross-examination. The government had the photo of Graham with Heredia
in Laredo, seemingly proof that Graham had lied when he said he never met

him. There were the phone records showing over a hundred calls between Graham and Heredia during the period Graham said they'd never spoken. Prosecutors Matt Parrella (who had also handled the Jones case) and Jeff Finigan played the tapes of Graham that Heredia had recorded.

Five major athletes, among them sprinters Antonio Pettigrew, Jerome Young, and Dennis Mitchell—all Olympic gold medalists—testified in detail that while working with Graham he had encouraged them to use banned steroids, introduced them to Heredia, and then monitored their drug use and the results. Mitchell testified that Graham himself had injected him with illegal drugs on two occasions.

In his closing argument, even Graham's lawyer, Keane, had conceded that Graham had indeed met Heredia in Laredo, but said he had simply "misspoken" rather than lied when he denied doing so. He argued that that none of Graham's alleged lies were material to the investigation. The athletes were falsely trying to blame Graham, make him a scapegoat, to minimize their own culpability. He renewed his attack on Heredia, saying he was a "publicity hound" who "says he's got a book agent." When he claimed to have stopped dealing in steroids in 2004, but wouldn't answer Rogers's question about whether he was still dealing in 2006, he was obviously lying. "Clearly, he is still dealing drugs," Keane said.

Suspicion of government authority runs deep in the San Francisco jury pool, and Keane's argument that the government was relying on an admitted drug dealer troubled several jurors. Still, as instructed, they put aside their feelings about Heredia and concentrated on the evidence. They voted overwhelmingly—but not unanimously—for conviction on all three counts. One juror, who worked for the post office, pronounced Graham "guilty as hell."

There was unanimous agreement about the phone calls. But Frank Stapleton, the foreman, a fifty-nine-year-old owner of an art supply business, refused to convict Graham on the other two counts. Despite the photograph showing Graham and Heredia together, he argued that Graham's denial they'd ever met was a slip, not a deliberate lie. He thought Heredia was a liar about everything, and the other athletes all had some kind of grudge against Graham, and were also lying. But Stapleton was mostly offended that it was Graham on trial rather than Heredia. "To me, Angel Heredia was the evildoer," he says. "They should have gone after him instead of Trevor Graham. He seemed like a good guy, a working guy, and his wife took time off to be with him. But they chose to go after him."

Stapleton concedes that strictly speaking, Graham may well have been guilty. "In a court of law, you're asked to make judgments based on the law. I went beyond the parameters," he acknowledges.

Others jurors were furious with Stapleton, and one bluntly called him an "asshole." But he wouldn't budge. After four days the jurors told Judge Illston that they could only agree on one count, of lying about the telephone calls. It was a remarkable verdict under the circumstances, a triumph for Keane and Graham and a setback for the prosecutors.

Immediately after the verdict, Judge Illston came into the room where the jurors were still assembled. "I just want to thank you all for your service," she said. "But how in God's name did this happen?"

"We didn't have anything to do with this," several protested, pointing to Stapleton.

"I just didn't think this was fair," Stapleton told the judge. "Why did they bring this guy to trial? This is a guy that works for a living. I think our government did the wrong thing."

Afterward, Stapleton distributed a statement making his sentiments clear:

On this case and speaking only for myself I will say that the government was bound and determined to make an example of the defendant. To achieve their goal they felt it necessary to do a deal with a true devil, an untruthful drug dealer and illegal immigrant who is walking the streets of America, free and presumably still plying his trade with impunity.

I hope this verdict satisfies the Justice Department's lust for blood in this matter and that there will be no retrial. When deciding what to do I hope they consider that while the facts in this case are very similar to those in the Scooter Libby trial, Mr. Graham cannot count on the president of the United States to commute his sentence.

Victor Conte finished his four months in prison and four months of home confinement in 2006. The *Contra Costa Times* called his sentence "the wrist slap heard far and wide." Conte painted over the BALCO signs after the curiosity seekers and tourists showed up, with some bodybuilders posing for photographs with their shirts off. He closed the business and moved to another location, where he runs SNAC, an acronym for Scientific Nutrition for Advanced Conditioning. Conte wrote a book, *BALCO: The Straight Dope on Steroids, Barry Bonds, Marion Jones and What We Can Do to Save Sports*. It was scheduled for publication in February 2009 but was withdrawn by the publisher because, Conte says, no company would provide libel insurance.

Conte sounds almost disappointed that he hasn't been called as a witness in any of the BALCO trials. "They're afraid of me," he says, referring to both the government and the defense lawyers. "I'm too unpredictable." He avidly follows every development in the investigation, and remains convinced that he was a victim of government leaks and that Novitzky lied about what he said after the BALCO raid. Still, he says there's no point in dwelling on the past, and he's trying to put the case behind him.

Conte say he feels he did what he could to rid sports of illegal drugs, and now uses his considerable expertise about nutrition and fitness only toward lawful ends. He is again training elite athletes, focusing now on professional boxing. He has been working with Nonito Donaire, the world bantamweight champion, and was on hand when Doniare won the title against Wladimir Sidorenko in December 2010.

Jim Valente finished his period of home detention and works for a telecommunications company in Silicon Valley. He is listed as a witness in the Bonds trial, and will testify that Anderson provided him with blood and urine samples for a number of athletes, including Bonds, according to the government witness list.

Troy Ellerman served sixteen months in prison after having his sentence reduced for attending a substance-abuse program. As required by his sentence, he began giving lectures to law students. Hastings College of Law professor John Diamond said Ellerman told students that "in the heat of litigation or the heat of battle one can be tempted to cross the line." According to Diamond, he was "totally apologetic. He thought his conduct was indefensible." Ellerman and his wife returned to Sacramento. He and Larry McCormack, who works for a security firm in Stockton, California, have had no further contact.

Chronicle reporters Mark Fainaru-Wada and Lance Williams have never discussed their relationship with Ellerman or confirmed that he was their source. They and the *Chronicle* have been honored with the George Polk Award, the White House Correspondents' Association's Edgar A. Poe Award, and the Edward Willis Scripps Award for Distinguished Service to the First Amendment. Both left the *Chronicle*, Fainaru-Wada for ESPN and Williams for the Center for Investigative Reporting.

Special agent Jeff Novitzky left the IRS in 2008 and joined the FDA, where he has continued to pursue illegal steroid cases. His highest-profile target appears to be Lance Armstrong, the celebrated seven-time Tour de France cycling champion and cancer survivor who has repeatedly denied using any performance-enhancing drugs. A grand jury in Los Angeles is investigating drug use in professional cycling. Novitzky is scheduled to be a witness at Bonds's trial, and will testify about the BALCO raid, according to the government. He will also describe how Bonds's "false statements in the grand jury influenced the criminal investigation of Conte and Anderson."

Unlike Conte or Marion Jones, Trevor Graham never admitted guilt or expressed any remorse. He had also put the government through a full trial. As prosecutors argued, "When confronted with questions about his involvement in doping elite athletes—and with the protection of immunity that he demanded from his statements—the defendant repeatedly lied to investigators in a premeditated and calculating way. . . . Instead of supporting the athletes he coached and encouraged to dope, he called them liars and forced many of them to testify at a public trial. To this day, the defendant absolutely refuses to take any responsibility for what he did."

At Graham's sentencing hearing on October 21, 2008, Judge Illston conceded that the government had introduced "compelling evidence" that he had distributed illegal steroids and then lied about it. But she said she saw no reason why Graham should suffer a stiffer penalty than Conte, whom she described as the "mastermind" of the BALCO conspiracy, and who had only gotten a prison sentence of four months. She may also have been swayed by his probation report, which stressed his childhood poverty in Jamaica and glowing tributes to his character, personal qualities, and devotion to his family. She sentenced him to one year of home detention to be followed by five years of probation and a $5,000 fine.

At the time of his sentencing, his lawyers said Graham was driving a bus for special-needs children in North Carolina. Nike terminated his endorsement deal. The USADA imposed a lifetime ban on his participation in any track-and-field event, the first time it had ever imposed such a ban on a coach. In May 2010 Graham sued the USADA in North Carolina for $30 million, saying the agency had "slandered my name for all the world to see." Graham denied ever supplying any athlete with illegal performance-enhancing drugs. The USADA said the suit was meritless.

Marion Jones was released from prison in September 2008. As part of her community service, she gave lectures to high school students, recounting her rise and fall and the perils of lying under oath. Still, she continues to deny injecting any performance-enhancing drugs, sticking to the story she told at her sentencing. While still on probation, she went on *Oprah* and reiterated that "I thought I was taking a supplement. . . . Never knowingly did I take performance-enhancing drugs." When *New York Times Magazine* contributing writer Maggie Jones asked her in 2010 how she could square that claim with statements by Hunter, Montgomery, and Conte that they witnessed injections, she replied, "I don't know why they made the decision to say or do certain things—what I say is true. And people can believe it or not."

Though banned from track and field, Jones had played basketball in college, and she returned to professional sports in 2010, joining the WNBA's Tulsa Shock. In October she published a book, *On the Right Track*, and embarked on a national publicity tour. Publisher Simon & Schuster described the book as "the candidly told story of how Marion came to grips with her lies and the consequences of her actions, and how she found meaning in all of it."

While still awaiting sentencing in the check-fraud scheme, Tim Montgomery was arrested in Virginia Beach for possessing and selling heroin. As Montgomery later told ESPN reporter Mike Fish, "I had been around bad people the whole time. When this all happened, I had to turn to them because I was trying to get some money. . . . I made money, yeah. That's just part of the game on the street. That's part of the business. A lot of money is made in drugs. . . . The simplest way to raise the money that came to mind was to sell drugs."

Montgomery pleaded guilty and was sentenced to five years in prison. "What we find here is someone who has wrecked his life," a prosecutor told the judge. Montgomery entered the federal prison camp in Montgomery, Alabama, in 2008. He told ESPN reporter Fish that he's had no contact with his son and that a letter he sent Jones went unanswered. As for Jones's ongoing claims she never knowingly used performance-enhancing drugs, he said, "She is a great actor. She doesn't believe in reality. She thinks she can say something and make it stick. And like most athletes, the first thing we say is 'I'm not guilty.' "

Despite her appearance with Geraldo Rivera, Kimberly Bell failed to find a publisher for *Bonds Girl*. In November 2007, Bell told her story again and posed for six pages of photos in *Playboy*. "A lot of people have said a lot of rotten things about me," she said. "It comes to a point where you have to defend yourself," she told the *New York Daily News*. The photos are "tasteful. They are not sleazy in any way at *Playboy*. Why not do the pictures? I'm thirty-seven years old and they made me feel beautiful." She said she hopes to go back to school, get an education degree, and teach middle school.

Bell is identified as a witness in the Bonds trial who will testify that Bonds "told her that he was taking steroids prior to the 2000 Major League Baseball season," will identify "changes in the defendant's body" after 2000, and will describe occasions when Bonds and Anderson were together.

After the 2007 season, Barry Bonds and his family lived in the gilded seclusion of their Beverly Park mansion high above Los Angeles. In February 2010, his wife, Liz, filed for divorce, citing irreconcilable differences. She said the marriage had ended in January and they were no longer living together. She asked for custody of their daughter and said their assets would be divided pursuant to a prearranged agreement.

The San Francisco Giants didn't offer Barry Bonds a contract when his expired after the 2007 season. Nor did any other major-league team after he was indicted in November, despite reports that Bonds was willing to sign for $400,000 a year, a small fraction of the $17 million he was earning under his previous contract. He didn't play in any of the ensuing years. In his mid-forties and out of practice, it seemed his controversial but still celebrated career as a professional baseball player was over.

In February 2009, Judge Illston ruled that substantial parts of the government's case against Bonds—the positive drug tests and the alleged doping calendars seized at Anderson's house—could not be admitted unless Anderson testified that the samples were in fact from Bonds and that the calendars referred to Bonds. Without Anderson's testimony, she ruled that the evidence would be inadmissible hearsay. Anderson's lawyer reiterated that Anderson would never testify.

The ruling set back the case over a year, while the government appealed the decision to the Ninth Circuit Court of Appeals. A divided court upheld Illston's ruling, setting the stage for Bonds's perjury trial—sometime in 2011.

Could Bonds be innocent? Did he use no performance-enhancing drugs other than what he believed to be flaxseed oil and a pain-relieving cream, and then only after 2002, as he testified under oath?

Bonds is constitutionally entitled to a presumption of innocence in any trial, and to convict, the government must prove him guilty beyond a reasonable doubt. But these are requirements that apply to jurors. There is nothing to prevent everyone else from reaching a judgment based on the undisputed facts and common sense.

And those facts are extensive. Although the calendars and drug tests were excluded from evidence, Hoskins turned over to the government the tape he made of Anderson in the locker room, and Judge Illston ruled it admissible. (The FBI investigation of Hoskins's handling of the Bonds memorabilia business hadn't resulted in any charges.) So was a positive drug test of Bonds obtained by the USADA. According to the government's witness list, Kathy Hoskins, Steve Hoskins's sister who worked as a personal shopper for Bonds, will testify that she saw Anderson give Bonds an injection. Steve Hoskins and Bell will testify that Bonds admitted using steroids. Professional baseball players Marvin Benard, Jason Giambi, Jeremy Giambi, Armando Rios, and Benito Santiago will testify that they received illegal drugs from Anderson and were told what they were and how to use them. Doctors will describe Bonds's physical changes and their ties to steroids.

The critical question, of course, is not whether Bonds used steroids—he admitted in his grand jury testimony that he used what appear to be the "clear" and the "cream." It's whether he lied when he said he used nothing before the end of the 2002 season, used no other illegal performance-enhancing drugs, and didn't know what the "clear" and the "cream" were. For this to be true, Bonds would have to be unusual among Anderson's clients whose files were found in his house, since others acknowledged that the calendars reflected their scheduled drug use and that Anderson explained it to them.

In this regard, Judge Karas's statement to Marion Jones applies with equal force to Barry Bonds: "That's a very difficult thing to believe; that a top-notch athlete, knowing the razor-thin margins separating the best from the others, would not be keenly aware and very careful about what he or she would put in his or her body and recognize the effects immediately on their performance."

And, of course, there was Bonds's remarkable physical transformation over the period he is alleged to have used drugs, which was on display for every fan to see.

Major League Baseball has imposed no sanctions on Bonds. He still holds the all-time home run record; Commissioner Bud Selig has said he needs "more evidence" before he would consider restoring the title to Hank Aaron. But in declining to hire an athlete at the peak of his career, when he had just set the all-time home run record, Major League Baseball effectively rendered its verdict on Bonds. And so have the fans.

The ball Bonds hit for his record-setting home run was caught in the stands by a tourist from Queens, New York, who sold it in an online auction for over $750,000. After Bonds's indictment, the winning bidder, fashion designer Marc Ecko, set up a website for voters to decide its fate, and ten million people voted. The verdict: brand the ball with an asterisk and donate it to the Hall of Fame.

Part Four

BERNARD L. MADOFF

ELEVEN

"Keep Your Eyes on the Prize"

T homas Thanasules paused as he sifted through a pile of e-mails he'd gotten from Renaissance Technologies, arguably the most successful hedge fund in the world. "Please keep this confidential," one said. "I have kept this note to a restricted circulation," read the reply.

What was so secret? It was April 2004, and as a young compliance examiner for the Securities and Exchange Commission in New York, Thanasules was struggling to keep up with the burgeoning number of new investment vehicles known as hedge funds. Hedge funds themselves weren't new–Long-Term Capital Management, whose near collapse in 1998 triggered a global financial crisis, was a hedge fund, and the earliest example dates to 1949. But in the wake of the dot.com bust and technology bubble, their popularity had exploded. The funds were generally open to a limited number of wealthy investors; could pursue a broad range of investment strategies, many of them risky; and charged both a management fee and a percentage of the gains, or incentive fee. Other than that, they had little in common. They engaged in a myriad of investment styles and approaches. They'd gotten their name because many of them took both long and short positions, thereby "hedging" against a market downturn. (More traditional mutual funds can't short, or bet on market declines.)

After the technology bubble burst in 2000, triggering a collapse in stock prices and a recession, investors poured into anything that promised to protect them from a downturn. Institutions, long accustomed to a straightforward buy-and-hold approach divided between stocks and bonds, embraced hedge funds as something that would protect their endowments, and billions in new money poured into the secretive funds. Scores of new billionaires were minted, seemingly overnight. The fees were exorbitant, but clients didn't mind as long as their gains surpassed alternative investments and helped smooth out volatility, as many hedge funds did.

Some of the most mysterious of the funds were the so-called quantitative, or "black box," funds, which used complex computer programs, often created by MIT-trained PhDs, to guide and execute strategies. Renaissance Technologies had soared to the top of this secretive world. RenTec, as it was known to traders, was founded in 1982 by James Simons, an MIT- and Berkeley-trained mathematician who six years earlier had won the prestigious Oswald Veblen Prize in Geometry. As chairman of the math department at the State University of New York at Stony Brook, he had built the school into one of the world's top centers for geometry. Then in 1976 he quit abruptly, saying he was seeking new challenges, and began using sophisticated mathematical models to invest in markets. He hired theoretical physicists, philosophers, statisticians, mathematicians like himself—but no MBAs. They worked at a gated, leafy estate in Setauket, near Simons's home on Long Island, far from the clamor of a Wall Street trading floor. They gathered for tea and wide-ranging intellectual conversation every Friday afternoon. The atmosphere was more like Harvard's senior common rooms than the hurly-burly of a Wall Street trading floor. Simons had little or no interest in traditional fundamental investing, the kind practiced by investors like Warren Buffett. What interested him were statistical anomalies that could be exploited and used to predict even tiny market moves in virtually every asset that is traded. His was the ultimate black-box trading operation.

Renaissance had several funds; its best known, the Medallion fund, was largely restricted to Simons himself and other Renaissance employees. Medallion had racked up astounding average returns of over 30 percent per year, and *Forbes* estimated Simons's worth in 2004 as $2.5 billion (he earned an estimated $1.5 billion in 2005 alone). The fund's assets under management had surged to over $5 billion. Nat Simons, James's son, ran the Meritage fund, a sister fund that was run from offices in San Francisco. Meritage was a so-called fund-of-funds, meaning that it invested its assets in a variety of other hedge funds, which added diversity and helped lower risk. Meritage, too, was largely restricted to Renaissance employees.

Given its prominence, size, and remarkable returns, which were hard to fathom given the difficulty of consistently beating the market averages, RenTec had naturally attracted the interest of the SEC. Hedge funds themselves weren't directly regulated by the SEC or anybody else, but they had to abide by securities laws. The SEC had asked RenTec for numerous documents and records, including internal e-mails. So far Thanasules hadn't found anything suspicious, but as he sifted through Meritage's assets, he discovered that Meritage didn't simply invest directly in other hedge funds, like most funds-of-funds. It had entered into a so-called total return swap with another fund-of-funds, HCH Capital, effectively paying HCH for the returns and risk associated with one of its investments. So far it looked like it had been a very profitable investment for Meritage, since the fund it had swapped into had delivered extraordinarily consistent and quite high returns. It looked like it had never had a down quarter, even after the technology bubble, and only a handful of down months. Meritage had to gain access to the fund using a swap, because the fund was so successful and sought-after that only the chosen few were allowed to invest, handpicked by the fund's manager. Given Simons's reputation and track record, most funds would have been thrilled to have Meritage among its investors. But when Meritage tried to invest, Bernard L. Madoff had turned Simons down.

The name Madoff meant nothing to Thanasules. But from the RenTec e-mails, he could tell that Madoff was a subject of concern to the people there, who were, after all, some of the most sophisticated people in the hedge fund world. Since they were only indirect investors in the Madoff fund, they didn't get account statements or have direct contact with Madoff, relying instead on what they could learn from HCH and other sources. They didn't really know what strategies Madoff used, or how he earned such consistent returns—more consistent than even their flagship Medallion fund. On November 13, 2003, Nat Simons wrote an e-mail to his father and other investment committee members:

> We at Meritage are concerned about our HCH investment. First of all,
> we spoke to an ex-Madoff trader (who was applying for a position at
> Meritage) and he said that Madoff cherry-picks trades and "takes them
> for the hedge fund."

This alone was a red flag, since cherry-picking is illegal unless the practice is fully disclosed to investors. Cherry-picking consists of executing many trades, and then allocating the most profitable ones to favored investors, inflating the returns at the expense of others.

The e-mail continued:

> He said that Madoff is pretty tight-lipped and therefore he didn't know much about it, but he really didn't know how they made money. Another person heard a similar story from a large hedge fund consultant who also interviewed an ex-trader. The head of this group told us in confidence that he believes Madoff will have a serious problem within a year. . . .
>
> Another point to make here is that not only are we unsure as to how HCH makes money for us, we are even more unsure how HCH makes money from us; i.e., why does [Madoff] let us make so much money?

Here Simons was evidently referring to the fact that Meritage charged investors a percentage management fee plus a percentage of the gain, but Madoff charged zero percent, and only a modest four-cents-per-share trading commission.

> Why doesn't he capture that himself? There could well be a legitimate reason, but I haven't heard any explanation we can be sure of. Additionally, there is a $4 billion Madoff pass-through fund (Fairfield Sentry) that charges 0 and 20% and it's not clear why Madoff allows an outside group to make $100 million per year in fees for doing absolutely nothing (unless he gets a piece of that). [A pass-through, or "feeder," fund raises money from investors and then simply invests it in another fund, in this case Madoff, making no investment decisions of its own.] The point is that as we don't know why he does what he does, we have no idea if there are conflicts in his business that could come to some regulator's attention. Throw in that his brother-in-law is his auditor and his son is also high up in the organization and you have the risk of some nasty allegations, the freezing of accounts, etc. To put things in perspective, if HCH went to zero it would take out 80% of this year's profits.

More red flags, especially if Madoff's auditor wasn't really independent. (Simons was wrong about Madoff's auditor, but his point was well taken. The auditor, David Friehling, wasn't Madoff's brother-in-law, but he was a close

Madoff family friend, a one-man operation in suburban New Jersey, and an investor in Madoff's fund—a blatant conflict of interest.) Moreover HCH—Madoff—accounted for an astoundingly high percentage of Meritage's profits, especially for an operation that was supposed to be diversified. Simons suggested pulling out of the HCH position entirely:

> Perhaps the best reason to get out is that we don't really expect to make an outsized return on this investment. Sure it's the best risk-adjusted fund in the portfolio, but on an absolute return basis it's not that compelling (12.6% average return over the last three years). If one assumes that there's more risk than the standard deviation would indicate, the investment loses its luster in a hurry.
>
> It's high season on money managers, and Madoff's head would look pretty good above Eliot Spitzer's mantel. [Spitzer was then New York's aggressive attorney general.] I propose that unless we can figure out a way to get comfortable with the regulatory tail risk in a hurry, we get out. The risk reward on this bet is not in our favor.
>
> Please keep this confidential.

Troubled by the suggestions in Simons's e-mail, Thanasules looked for a reply, and found one written the next day by Henry Laufer, a former math colleague of James Simons at SUNY Stony Brook who now held the title of "chief scientist" at Renaissance. "I share the concern at Meritage about the HCH investment," Laufer began.

> In Nat's note, I am most worried about the new information in the statement that "Madoff cherry-picks trades and takes them for the hedge fund." We at Renaissance have totally independent evidence that Madoff's executions are highly unusual. . . . In all, I very much agree with the sentiment "It's high season on money managers, and Madoff's head would look pretty good above Eliot Spitzer's mantel."

A week later, Paul Broder, RenTec's risk manager, reported the results of some further work he'd done on the Madoff exposure. He'd examined the account statements from investors in Madoff's funds, and compared them to the strategy Madoff said he used: a "split-strike forward conversion" strategy, as Madoff had told both clients and Michael Ocrant, a reporter for *MAR/Hedge*, a hedge fund industry newsletter, who'd raised questions about Madoff in a 2001 article "Madoff Tops Charts; Skeptics Ask How":

> Skeptics who express a mixture of amazement, fascination, and curiosity about the program wonder, first, about the relative complete lack of volatility in the reported monthly returns.
>
> But among other things, they also marvel at the seemingly astonishing ability to time the market and move to cash in the underlying securities before market conditions turn negative; and the related ability to buy and sell the underlying stocks without noticeably affecting the market.

Another article in *Barron's*, "Don't Ask, Don't Tell," by Erin Arvedlund, raised similar questions. "Even adoring investors can't explain his steady gains," she reported.

Although it sounds sophisticated, the split-strike strategy is a relatively simple options strategy used by many traders and fund managers to reduce risk. Madoff bought stocks—he described them as a "basket" of stocks mirroring the S&P 100, which are the most liquid, large-capitalization stocks. Then he protected the portfolio from falling prices by buying a put on the S&P 100 index (known by its trading symbol, the OEX). A put is like insurance, since it gives the buyer the right to sell an index representing the underlying stocks at the designated strike price. To pay for the puts, Madoff sold calls on the basket of stocks. Calls give the buyer the right to buy the underlying stocks at the strike price. By selling calls on his stocks, Madoff sacrificed any further gains if the stock prices went above the strike prices.

Buying puts to reduce or prevent loss while selling calls that limit gains is called a "collar," one of the most common options strategies. But by reducing risk and incurring additional transaction costs, the strategy usually produces lower long-term returns than an unhedged strategy. Although it may smooth out returns, it will sharply underperform market averages in a strong bull market. In a bear market, it may outperform, but will still have trouble showing gains, since the strategy is a hedge, not a bet on declining prices. So many investors were using the strategy that, by 2004, returns had shrunk. So the fact that Madoff used the split-strike strategy didn't impress Broder. On the contrary, it made Madoff's high returns even more mysterious.

Broder had compared Madoff's account statements to volume and pric-

ing data on the OEX options that figured so heavily in Madoff's strategy. He
summarized his findings in an e-mail:

> I have kept this note to a restricted circulation. I had some further
> conversations . . . on the Madoff data. I also looked at some daily volume
> data on and around the OEX option transaction dates as indicated by
> Madoff's statements. I was specifically trying to address the question of
> how big a fund base can Madoff trade with this strategy by focusing on
> the option volume numbers.
>
> 1. Recall that Madoff's strategy involves a collar, that is a put and a
> call. The volume numbers provide total calls executed on the OEX and
> total puts. In the two independent sets of statements . . . the strikes were
> always the same for both accounts. Make the generous assumption that
> 50% of the volume was in the most liquid strike . . . By this measure
> Madoff could only do $750m[illion]. That is with him doing 100% of the
> option volume in his chosen strike (with the generous 50% assumption).
> Let's assume that he spreads it over 3 days—so we get to 2.1bln—still far
> short of the target numbers.

In others words, assuming Madoff accounted for *all* of the trading volume
in the most liquid strike price, and allocating 50 percent of his contracts to that
strike price, he could only account for $750 million in assets, when Madoff was
believed to be managing $15 billion.

> 2. Another important point: In every case . . . the options strike
> (call) is the one closest to the close in the underlying market. Of course
> the market is not known until the close!! Does this mean that all the
> options are done almost at the close?
>
> 3. The volume does seem to spike on the days when Madoff
> is executing by a factor of 3-4. This must produce deterioration in
> execution prices—and for 15bln!
>
> 4. When we examined the issue before, we concluded that maybe
> he does the options in the OTC market. [The OTC, or over-the-counter
> market, consists of direct trades between two parties. Since it's a private
> transaction, the trades aren't reported on any exchange.] We have spoken to
> several market makers in OTC equity options. [A market maker maintains

buy and sell prices for securities and other assets at which it will enter into a transaction, thereby providing liquidity and "making a market" for buyers and sellers.] Recall . . . that Madoff had said it was necessary to spread trades over several days—why if you are doing OTC? [Large orders typically move price, which is why they would be spread over several days on an exchange. But two private parties could do a trade of any magnitude at an agreed price.]

5. Recall point 2. This would indicate that the OTC options would also have to be done at the end of the day (to get a strike near the close). Are we to believe that the market makers would take on $15bln of market risk at the close? Of course they might (might!!!) be willing to take the options risk if Madoff provided the market hedge in the underlying (i.e., they did the whole package with Madoff) but we already know that the trades in the underlying, compared with the closing prices, would leave the OTC counterparty showing losses (as our account always shows gains).

6. Of course ALL of our trades are with Madoff as the principal—so our option positions are OTC with Madoff so he can choose to use any strike, and any total volume he chooses, but the risk must be covered somewhere if he is doing the trades at all?

So we need an OTC counterparty (not necessarily a bank) who is willing to do the basket of the options plus the underlying with Madoff at prices unfavorable for the OTC counterparty—in 10-15bln!!!

Any suggestions who that might be?

None of it seems to add up.

And it wasn't just the massive but strangely undetectable volume of Madoff's trading that made Broder suspicious. The prices at which he bought, sold, and executed options were amazingly profitable. Madoff's ability to predict when to buy and sell stocks was better than anyone Broder had ever encountered. As he later put it, "I knew it wasn't possible because of what we do." The Renaissance officials also noticed that Madoff didn't consistently follow a split-strike conversion strategy. Sometimes he withdrew from the market entirely, moving his accounts to all cash. Essentially he was market timing—a notoriously difficult quest—and he was doing this, too, with extraordinary success, managing to get out of the market in exactly those months when the split-strike strategy would have generated losses. "We had no idea . . . how he managed to do that,"

RenTec's Laufer later said. "We didn't understand what he was doing. We didn't understand how he was doing what he was doing."

And if Renaissance executives couldn't figure out what Madoff was doing, who could? To Thanasules, the e-mails raised a host of troubling questions and carried extra weight because they came from Renaissance. He called the compliance officer at RenTec, who said that Meritage had reduced its exposure to Madoff, though not because of the concerns expressed in the e-mails. Still, Simons later said that "we were very worried about the position" and cut it in half because of the concerns expressed in the e-mails. He added that they would have eliminated it entirely except for one reason: they understood that the SEC had examined Madoff and given him a clean bill of health. But eventually they got rid of it entirely.

Armed with copies of the e-mails, Thanasules went to his supervisor, branch chief Diane Rodriguez. The facts they alleged—a nonindependent auditor, incomprehensibly consistent returns with near-perfect timing, and, most of all, Broder's inability to identify any trading volume or counterparties essential to execute the strategy—led Thanasules to wonder "whether Madoff is doing these trades at all," as he described his thinking. On April 20, he sent an e-mail to Rodriguez:

> Good afternoon, Diane.
>
> I wanted to inform you I have started reviewing the e-mails they provided. Certain e-mails have come to my attention that appear to raise questions about another entity, Bernard L. Madoff Investment Securities. As far as I know right now Madoff is a registered broker-dealer.

He attached two of the e-mails and continued:

> Diane, these are some e-mails I have reviewed. At this point I spoke to the compliance officer regarding Madoff who informed me that they have reduced their investment in this vehicle but not due to anything referenced in the aforementioned e-mails. At this point I do not know any further details, however, I am currently putting together a request list, asking for due diligence folders, type of information they receive regarding their investment, etc. Anyway, I will call you in a few minutes to hear your thoughts. Thank you.

Rodriguez, in turn, passed the e-mails to her superior, Dorothy Eschwie, who referred them to Robert Sollazzo, who was co-head of the broker-dealer examination program. He responded to Eschwie on May 11:

> We believe this matter is worthy of an examination when resources permit. Since the trading appears somewhat complex, we will have to assign an experienced examiner who has a sophisticated knowledge of options. When the time is right we will strike.
>
> The story, especially the consistent high returns earned over an extended period, makes you wonder.

Eight months later, Sollazzo referred the Madoff case to John Nee, the division's assistant director. Nee had been working at the SEC since 1991, shortly after his former employer, Drexel Burnham Lambert, imploded in the wake of the Michael Milken junk bond and securities fraud scandal. (Nee worked at Drexel as a mutual fund accountant, not in Milken's Beverly Hills junk bond operation.) Sollazzo also recruited two young examiners, Peter Lamore and William Ostrow.

Sollazzo especially wanted Lamore, since he was one of the few examiners who had firsthand experience working for a hedge fund and trading options, and had waited to begin the examination until Lamore was available. Lamore was stocky, with neatly clipped brown hair. He had the upright demeanor of a military man, and he'd spent five years in the U.S. Coast Guard after graduating from the Coast Guard Academy. After earning an MBA degree at New York University, he'd worked for two years at Millennium Partners, a large hedge fund run by Israel Englander, and had worked as a trader at several smaller firms before joining the SEC in late 2003. In the ensuing year he'd worked on just four broker-dealer examinations. Ostrow had more experience, having been at the SEC for five years. He joined the agency right after graduating from the New York Institute of Technology with a degree in finance.

Lamore and Ostrow started with Thanasules's and the Renaissance e-mails, along with the articles from *MAR/Hedge* and *Barron's*. Lamore read the Renaissance e-mails carefully, making notes in the margins, as well as the articles, raising specific questions about who might be on the other side of Madoff's trades. But Ostrow read only "snippets," as he later recalled, and in his years as an examiner had come to be skeptical of what he considered "tips," which he felt should be taken with a "grain of salt." Unlike Thanasules, who'd called the Renaissance compliance officer, they didn't get in touch with anyone at Renaissance to ask for any more information about Madoff, the e-mails, or the status of the fund's exposure to Madoff. Lamore believed SEC policy was to take questions directly to the firm being examined, not to outsiders, so as not to fuel rumors that a firm might be under investigation.

The name Madoff meant little to either Lamore or Ostrow, although both knew that his firm was a large market maker. But they were soon impressed with his stature in the industry. Ostrow sent Lamore an entry on Madoff from Hofstra University's alumni website:

> The same year as his graduation from Hofstra, Bernard L. Madoff, Class of 1960, founded a successful investment firm that bears his name. Madoff Securities currently ranks among the top 1 percent of U.S. securities firms and is the third largest firm matching buyers and sellers of New York Stock Exchange and NASDAQ securities. While building his firm into a significant force in the securities industry, Bernard and his family have been deeply involved in leading the dramatic transformation that is currently underway in U.S. securities trading.
>
> Bernard has been a major figure in the National Association of Securities Dealers (NASD), the major self-regulatory organization for U.S. broker/ dealer firms. He is credited with being one of the five broker/dealers most closely involved in developing the NASDAQ Stock Market. He has served as chairman of the board of directors of the NASDAQ Stock Market as well as a member of the board of governors of the NASD and a member of numerous NASD committees. Bernard has also served as a member of the board of directors of the Securities Industry Association. . . .
>
> Bernard is a trustee of Yeshiva University and a member of the board of directors for City Center. He and his wife, Ruth, reside in Manhattan and are active in numerous philanthropic causes. They have two grown sons, Mark and Andy, who are actively involved in the family business.

Ruth; Madoff's brother, Peter; and his niece, Shana, were also involved in the family business. Ostrow forwarded another article to Lamore, called "The Madoff Dynasty," which extolled the family ties:

"All of his family members grew up with this being our lives. When it is a family operated business you don't go home at night and shut everything off, so you take things home with you, which is how all of us grew up," says Mark Madoff, director of listed trading at Madoff Securities.... "What makes it fun for all of us is to walk into the office in the morning and see the rest of your family sitting there. That's a good feeling to have."

Madoff often told the story of starting the firm with $5,000 he'd saved as a lifeguard at the beach in Far Rockaway and from installing underground sprinkler systems. Ruth, whom he'd met in college, worked as the fledgling firm's bookkeeper. Madoff's firm was a broker-dealer, meaning it acted both as a middleman, handling trades for others (a broker) as well as buying and selling for its own account (a dealer). Madoff handled trades for customers who wanted to trade when the stock exchanges were closed, or who wanted to trade away from the exchanges, especially since Madoff not only charged lower commissions than the members of the exchanges, but actually paid customers (like Fidelity and Schwab) to steer their order flow to his firm. It was a high-volume, very low-margin, and not very glamorous business. Indeed, by the time the SEC examiners started doing their research, Madoff Securities was paying so much to secure orders, its margins so slim, that it was actually losing millions of dollars a year on its broker-dealer business. It was subsidized by the least known of Madoff's operations, one never mentioned in descriptions of the firm, which was an investment adviser business in which Madoff indicated he invested money for a few hedge funds and institutions. His returns from that business were so reliable that he became known to the fortunate few who invested with him as "the Jewish T-bill."

This division had started sometime in the 1960s, initially managing money for Madoff's family and friends. Madoff had never registered with the SEC as an investment adviser, which requires hedge funds and investment advisers to make detailed books and records available for inspection, and makes it unlawful "to engage in any act, practice, or course of business which is fraudulent, deceptive, or manipulative." But it exempts firms with fifteen or fewer clients, which presumably was why Madoff had never registered.

While stressing his philanthropy, Hofstra, Madoff's alma mater, said nothing about his extravagant spending and luxurious lifestyle. According to the IRS, he reported income of $250 million per year from 1998 to 2007. He owned a duplex penthouse on East Sixty-fourth Street in Manhattan with four bedrooms and five bathrooms; a palatial house with a two-story veranda, five bedrooms, and seven bathrooms on the Intracoastal Waterway in Palm Beach; a sprawling shingled "cottage" with pool on 1.2 acres of prized beachfront property in Montauk, Long Island; and an apartment villa in exclusive Cap d'Antibes on the French Riviera. There he sometimes kept his fifty-six-foot yacht, *Bull*, which featured teak decking and a hydraulic elevator. He kept two other boats in Palm Beach, a thirty-foot Runabout Sport, *Sitting Bull*, and a twenty-four-foot Maverick, *Little Bull*. The Madoffs were fixtures at the Palm Beach Country Club; he also belonged to the Atlantic Golf Club in Bridgehampton on Long Island, the Breakers Palm Beach Country Club, and the Trump International Golf Club in West Palm Beach. His club expenses alone totaled just under $1 million a year, paid as a business expense by Madoff Securities. To reach his far-flung homes and clubs he owned a half-interest in a private jet. He drove no fewer than six luxury vehicles: a Range Rover, two Mercedes S550s, a Mercedes SUV, a Lexus, and a Cadillac. Ruth had her own Mercedes convertible.

Madoff's firm was located on Third Avenue, in the heart of Manhattan's East Side business district, in an oval-shaped, thirty-four-story building known as the Lipstick Building. Madoff's operations occupied three floors, seventeen through nineteen. When Lamore and Ostrow arrived at Bernard L. Madoff Securities on April 11, Madoff himself came into the lobby to greet them. Madoff looked like Wall Street royalty, wearing a custom-tailored suit and crisp white shirt, his hair cut modishly long and swept back from his receding hairline. According to Madoff, Ostrow was wearing a baseball-style jacket with the word "Enforcement" emblazoned on the back, which annoyed Madoff. What would employees and customers think? But Madoff said nothing to betray his reaction. (The SEC disputes Madoff's claim that Ostrow was wearing such a jacket. It insists that the enforcement division doesn't use any such jacket and that no examiner would wear one.)

The examiners were impressed that Madoff himself—the head of the firm—was handling their examination. Usually it was the compliance officer, or someone else designated to act as a liaison with the SEC. The logical person would have been his niece, Shana Madoff, Peter's daughter and the firm's general counsel and compliance officer, but Lamore and Ostrow had almost no contact with her.

Madoff didn't know why they were there, and they hadn't wanted to tip their hand. Lamore and Ostrow may have been a little unsure themselves.

They'd been given the Renaissance e-mails as a starting point, and they had the *MAR/Hedge* and *Barron's* articles. Contrary to policy, no branch chief was assigned to supervise them. They'd never been given any formal instructions, nor had they drafted any planning memorandum. Ostrow thought the exam would evolve "just sort of as the exam progressed, notes were taken and e-mails were exchanged."

After two days of gathering documents and reconciling account statements, they had their first official interview with Madoff. They hadn't seen anything that suggested he was running or advising any hedge funds, so Ostrow asked a basic question: "Do you do a retail business?"

"No," Madoff answered. "I don't manage money."

Madoff insisted that his firm was simply a market maker and traded for its own accounts. It didn't generate investment advice or execute strategies. As Ostrow later put it, "According to Bernie there was no investment advisory business."

This was an astounding proposition, since the premise of the Renaissance e-mails was that Madoff was managing money for hedge funds (including them) and generating returns that seemed impossible to explain. And what about all the feeder funds that the published reports said were funneling money to Madoff? If Madoff was simply a market maker, there was no reason for Ostrow and Lamore to be there.

Neither believed him, but Madoff managed to divert them from this line of inquiry, regaling them with stories about Wall Street trading and the evolution of the business. Afterward, Lamore e-mailed a colleague to report that the interview lasted over two hours and ended after 6:00 p.m. But he made no mention of Madoff's startling claim, and seemed in a lighthearted mood. "Was there a storytelling class when you attended Hofstra because this guy has a story about everything? . . . Does everyone miss me in the office yet?" he wrote.

Ostrow reported Madoff's strange denial to Nee, who asked for a list of the feeder funds that supposedly funneled money to Madoff for investment.

Although Ostrow said he often found Madoff to be charming, within a week, relations were deteriorating. Madoff thought Ostrow was "obnoxious," a "total asshole," a "blowhard," and "an idiot," he later said. Ostrow kept asking for reams of computer data and was "doing things that made no sense," Madoff thought. Lamore reported that during a meeting on April 20, "it was disconcerting how angry he [Madoff] became. I mean, his veins were popping out of his neck . . . and he just repeatedly said, 'What are you looking for?' And his voice got increasingly loud and the veins were popping out." (Madoff confirmed that "I almost came to blows with him.") Lamore turned Madoff's question around, asking Madoff what he thought they should be looking for. "Front running," Madoff replied. "Aren't you looking for front running?" (Front running is the illegal practice of trading ahead of pending customer orders, knowing how those orders are likely to affect market prices. It is a form of insider trading.)

"Just to make you aware of the current situation," Ostrow e-mailed Nee that day, "Bernard Madoff is getting increasingly agitated regarding our examination. He keeps insisting on knowing exactly what we are looking for. He repeatedly mentions front running as something we should be looking for. He thinks our request for order and execution data is outrageous."

Of course, the fact that Madoff himself was urging them to examine front running was probably a sure sign that they wouldn't find anything.

A week later, in a meeting with both Bernie and Peter Madoff, the examiners returned to the basic question of whether Madoff managed money for anyone outside the firm. "Never," Madoff flatly replied. Peter said nothing to contradict him. Questioned about the issue of his options trading, Madoff said he no longer traded options. If correct, this meant he couldn't possibly be executing any split-strike conversion strategy, which depended entirely on options trading. The examiners were baffled.

A week later, Lamore reported that in examining some of Madoff's trading records he'd come across some large transactions involving Barclays, the large London-based bank, and asked Madoff about them. Madoff had gone off to consult with his staff, and reported back that Barclays simply "clears for the brokers in London." (Clearing is a back-office activity that arranges for payment and delivery of shares once orders are executed.) Lamore asked Madoff if the London office managed any money for outsiders, and Madoff again insisted that neither London nor any other Madoff office did any investment management for outside investors. "We are not that kind of firm," he insisted. As for the London activities, "It is my money," Madoff asserted, invested solely for his personal account.

Lamore doubted this. In response, Nee sent Barclays a letter asking for all trading by or on behalf of Madoff or any of the feeder funds by Barclays. Lamore responded by e-mail: "I'm ready to call his bluff on his refusal to admit the money-management side of the business, so your document request is perfect timing."

Nee responded, "If you think the timing is right, question him about it whenever you want."

Lamore assumed that Barclays would disclose the trading on behalf of Madoff's feeder funds, and said he wanted to wait until they heard back before confronting Madoff. "Also, I think it would be a good idea to be ready to speak with the funds as soon as possible after he denies involvement with them. I suggest we shoot for . . . May 24, 2005, to confront him as well as be ready to speak to the funds."

Barclays responded on May 16. Although Madoff had an account at the bank, "no relevant transaction activity occurred . . . there were no other customer relationships identified at Barclays Capital Inc." Far from what they expected, Barclays said Madoff did no trading whatsoever, either for his own account or for anyone else.

The SEC examiners didn't know what to make of it. The Barclays letter noted that Madoff had an account with Barclays' UK affiliate, and Nee assumed Madoff must be trading there or through a foreign broker dealer. But he never asked Barclays UK for any trading records. The prospect of approaching European banks for information seems to have flummoxed the SEC examiners, even though the SEC has a division devoted to dealing with foreign financial institutions and governments. And no one tried to reconcile Barclays' disclosure that there was no trading activity with the large transactions Lamore had spotted in the records.

By late May, Lamore and Ostrow had been on the Madoff premises for nearly two months. They spent the entire time in a conference room, and neither ever ventured onto the seventeenth floor, which is where Madoff indicated that routine back-office tasks were conducted. Madoff continued to regale them with stories about the evolution of Wall Street, which Lamore found simultaneously "captivating" and "distracting," and impressed Lamore with his "incredible background of knowledge." Madoff dropped names of SEC officials he knew and mentioned that he was on the "short list" to be the next SEC chairman. Two weeks before the chairman's appointment on June 2 Madoff shared with them the confidential information that Christopher Cox would be selected.

At the same time, Madoff was clearly growing impatient with their presence. On May 24, Lamore spoke to Madoff and e-mailed Ostrow, "He wants an idea of when we are going to finish the exam. He is getting more aggressive about trying to find out. I told him that we would speak to him tomorrow and based upon our questions and requests he should have a better idea. . . . Again, be ready for his badgering about us leaving."

The next morning, Lamore reported on what turned out to be a two-hour meeting with Madoff. Madoff had again taken off on long-winded explanations of the firm's automated trading program. "Once he started he couldn't stop," Lamore lamented. "He started to trash the SEC exam program for not having a full understanding of time slicing, automated market-making trading, spending time reviewing e-mails . . . I defended the program by explaining our mission. Anyway, I look forward to speaking to him regarding the hedge fund issue which he has opportunistically failed to mention to us."

The examiners' planned showdown with Madoff took place on the afternoon of May 25. Ostrow leaned back in his chair with his hands behind his head. His manner and appearance reminded Madoff of the disheveled fictional TV detective Lieutenant Columbo.

"So, tell me about this article," Ostrow said. He showed Madoff the *MAR/Hedge* report.

Madoff glanced at it. "So, what about it?"

Ostrow pointed out that both it and the *Barron's* article flatly contradicted Madoff's repeated claim that he didn't advise any hedge funds or manage their money. With the articles on the table in front of him, Madoff abruptly reversed himself. "We do execute trades on behalf of brokerage firms and institutions which include a number of hedge funds," he now acknowledged. "They use a model—algorithm—that we developed." At first he said there were just four hedge funds using the model, and named Fairfield Sentry, Thema, Tremont, and Kingate Global. But then he said there were actually fifteen clients, including two corporate accounts, but all of them were foreign. (Firms don't need to register with the SEC as investment advisers if they have fifteen or fewer clients or if they are foreign.)

Lamore and Ostrow asked Madoff how the model worked. Madoff said he developed it eight years earlier (in 1996) and that he was the only person allowed to execute trades using it. He said he used a computer server separate from the firm's market-making activities. He called the strategy incorporated in the model a split-strike conversion strategy, but described something quite different: a "basket" of about fifty stocks used to replicate the S&P 100, but said it was a "long only" position with no options trading or selling short. He said the model had stopped using options about a year before. Instead, Madoff timed the market, trying to buy at bottoms and sell at peaks, moving in and out of the market based on "momentum signals" and—remarkably—his "gut feel" about where the market was headed. As the examiners wrote in the subsequent report of the interview, Madoff was "adamant" that he "uses his gut feel to enter and exit the market."

Madoff also volunteered that he did all his trading through European brokerage firms in the early morning before the market opened in New York. Clients using this strategy had committed about "six to seven billion" to the strategy and his firm earned four cents a share as a trading commission, but otherwise received no management or advisory fees. He added that the high volume of the trading meant the model sometimes took several days to implement the strategy, whereas it used to be possible to do it in a single day. On the other hand, he also said the high speed at which the model could execute the strategy was a "competitive advantage," which seemed contradictory.

Lamore and Ostrow were flabbergasted that all this information was only now being volunteered, after Madoff had repeatedly and flatly denied that he had any outside clients. Why hadn't he disclosed any of this earlier in their exam? And Lamore was puzzled: Why would it take Madoff several days to execute his equities trading? He of all people should have known that automated trading made it possible to trade almost any volume in seconds, especially highly liquid S&P 100 stocks.

Madoff said that since he received a commission of four cents a share, and no management or incentive fee, he didn't consider himself an investment adviser or his customers as "clients," within the meaning of the examiners' questions. At this juncture, before they could really absorb this highly technical and dubious distinction, Madoff effectively pulled the rug out from under them.

He said he had already disclosed all of this trading to the SEC about a year and a half earlier, when the SEC's Office of Compliance Inspections and Examinations (OCIE), a separate Washington-based operation whose primary mission is to detect fraud, examined him. "Lori Richards has a whole file I sent her with this info," Madoff said. "They have it." (Richards was a compliance official with the OCIE.)

Ostrow and Lamore were embarrassed that this was the first they had heard if it. "Well, it's a big organization. We don't talk to each other," Ostrow responded. Madoff sensed he had them at a disadvantage and adopted a "condescending" tone, as Lamore later put it, "sort of the tone he took like when I didn't understand algorithmic trading." Ostrow and Lamore were reduced to asking whom Madoff had dealt with besides Richards so they could follow up. He mentioned John McCarthy and said he'd provide copies of his correspondence with his SEC contacts.

A ny material false statement made to an SEC examiner is a felony, just as it is when being interviewed by the FBI. Despite the fact that Madoff had changed his story, in effect admitting that his earlier statements to Ostrow and Lamore had been false, neither the examiners nor their superiors appear to have given any serious thought to immediately referring the Madoff case to the U.S. Attorney's office for further investigation. Nee, their supervisor, later said that Ostrow and Lamore "felt they were lied to by Mr. Madoff on numerous occasions." But he didn't consider pursuing any false statement partly because, like perjury cases, they're hard to prove. "Oh, it was suspicious," Nee later acknowledged. "But, you know, it's hard to get inside someone's head about why they're saying what they're saying. But yes, it was suspicious."

Nee seems not to have focused on the fact that very few people lie simply for the sake of lying, especially when they're under oath or participating in an official inquiry, as Madoff was. If he was lying, as both Ostrow and Lamore believed, what was he covering up? Surely not front running, which he was urging them to investigate, knowing they would find nothing. Despite the bombshells that Madoff had lobbed—that he was managing and trading six to seven billion dollars for hedge fund clients, after denying having any such clients; and that he was "timing the market" based on his "gut feel"—Ostrow and Lamore as well as their superiors were diverted by the embarrassing disclosure that, as one put it, "the left hand didn't know what the right hand was doing" at the SEC.

Nee sent an e-mail to McCarthy at the OCIE the day after the Madoff interview. "Our major focus has been the possibility that Madoff is using his vast amounts of customer order flow to benefit the $6 billion in hedge fund money that we believe he manages [i.e., front running]. In initial inquiries about managing outside money and supplying 'black box' models (algorithms, etc.) to outside accounts he either denied it or was evasive." He asked McCarthy if the OCIE had any information.

In a conference call five days later, McCarthy and other OCIE officials confirmed that they had indeed investigated Madoff, and although it was still an open investigation, "for all intents and purposes it was finished." They hadn't reached any conclusions or issued a final report, which Lamore thought was strange. It also struck him that the Washington officials kept stressing how important Madoff was. Ostrow noted that "I don't know who said it, someone from OCIE basically, 'He's a very powerful person, Bernie, and you know, just remember that.' But basically just, 'He is a very well-connected, powerful person.'" But the OCIE officials said they'd turn over all their work papers from the investigation.

Ostrow and Lamore turned back to the startling admissions from Madoff, asking for more documents and trading records for the hedge fund accounts. Ostrow ran a search for the term "Madoff" on a Bloomberg terminal and uncovered an intriguing reference to what appeared to be another Madoff feeder firm, Auriga International. According to the Bloomberg description, Auriga was "an open-end investment company incorporated in the British Virgin Islands. The fund's objective is to purchase shares in Auriga International Ltd., which itself invests on a leveraged basis into discretionary accounts with B. Madoff Securities, a New York broker dealer which employs an option trading strategy described as 'split-strike conversion.'"

Oddly, Madoff had never mentioned Auriga. Ostrow and Lamore decided they'd test Madoff's candor, and see if he produced anything related to Auriga after they asked for documents for all his hedge fund and feeder fund clients. He didn't. Ostrow e-mailed Lamore, who was on the Madoff premises, saying that "if Bernie stops in" he should ask him about Auriga. Lamore did, and Madoff seemed mystified. He said he'd never heard of the firm, although he added it "could be an investor through one of the feeder funds." "That's weird," Ostrow responded, "because Bloomberg reports Auriga has discretionary accounts with B. Madoff." But then he explained the discrepancy away: "Maybe it was a few years ago or it could be a feeder fund." No one contacted Auriga.

Madoff's claim that he timed the market successfully using his "gut feel" also attracted renewed scrutiny. Market timing is the investment equivalent of alchemy: no one has ever figured out how to do it consistently. Indeed, efficient market theorists maintain that the movement of stock prices is a random walk that can never be predicted with any consistency. And yet the Renaissance e-mails had noted Madoff's high returns and amazing consistency, with an extraordinary ability to exit the market entirely in down quarters.

Lamore, Ostrow, and their supervisors were all skeptical. In another encounter with Madoff, Lamore pressed him on what he meant by his "gut feel." Madoff cited his "observations of his trading floor in New York, what his

European contacts were telling him, and what he reads in industry papers and publications." Lamore later said that "I thought his gut feel was, you know, strange, suspicious. . . . I kept trying to press him. I thought there was something else. I thought he was getting some sort of insight into the overall broad market that other people weren't getting. So I repeatedly sort of pressed him on that. I asked Bernie repeatedly over and over again, and at some point, I mean, I'm not sure what else to do."

Madoff's production of requested documents was sporadic and often incomplete, but he did turn over monthly statements for two of the feeder funds—Kingate Global and Kingate Euro—as well as a list of brokers who executed trades based on the model. The statements showed no transactions at all over the requested time period. "It seems clear as mud to me," Lamore wrote Ostrow.

Both Lamore and Ostrow were feeling some pressure—both from Madoff himself and from their superiors—to wrap up the site examination, which was now entering its third month. Despite the many unanswered questions, the investigation had now jelled, at least in Nee's mind, into an investigation of front running. Lamore e-mailed Nee on June 2 that, after reviewing the Kingate records provided by Madoff, he didn't see any signs of front running:

> I don't believe the retail customer order flow information from Madoff's market-making business has anything to do with his hedge fund model. Essentially, he got long the S&P 100 for the hedge funds January 20 through January 24, 2005, and sold the S&P 100 (flattened out) March 10 through March 15, 2005. There was no activity in April 2005. Granted, his purchase & subsequent sale timing was excellent (buy low & sell high), but he held the basket for approximately six weeks. Therefore, I don't believe that he is using any short-term signals that would come from his retail order flow. I suspect that he is extremely well connected to European order flow information through his brokers (and possibly the investors in his fund) and is timing the market based on that information rather than his retail order flow information.

Ostrow and Lamore were still trying to find out who executed Madoff's hedge fund trades, and what was going on in his London office, which apparently oversaw the trading. They'd also discovered that Madoff's vaunted market-making operation was losing millions of dollars a year, and all the firm's profits were apparently coming from the hedge fund business, which Madoff had concealed until just a few weeks before. At the very least, Ostrow thought Madoff should be required to register as an investment adviser.

Nee disagreed. He later said an "examination cannot go on forever . . . we really didn't have the luxury to look at any conceivable area which might have a securities violation." On June 7 he sent an e-mail urging Ostrow to "keep your eyes on the prize," which was front running.

Two days later, the OCIE delivered all its work papers from the Madoff case—nine categories of documents and records. By now, the air was rapidly draining from the investigation. Lamore thought he "may have glanced" at the files. Ostrow said he didn't recall reading any of them and noted that he and Lamore had "already returned from the field." Nor did Nee or any of their supervisors examine the files.

If they had, they would have seen a complaint about Madoff dated May 2003 from a highly regarded manager of a fund-of-funds, who asked to remain anonymous. He had considered an investment with a Madoff feeder fund, and actually met with Madoff to discuss his strategy. Madoff had described the split-strike conversion, and told the hedge fund manager he traded the OEX options on the Chicago Board of Options Exchange (CBOE). "Well, I found something exceptionally odd about that," the manager had reported. He asked Madoff, "How are you doing that? Because I don't think there's enough volume on the Chicago Board of Options Exchange for you to get that sort of coverage for the amount that you're managing."

Afterward, the manager called the CBOE to check on volume, and "the problem is, the volume was never there for Madoff. So that was problem no. 1 for me. Problem no. 2 was, I called up buddies of mine around the street and I asked them all if they were trading with Madoff. And nobody was. Nobody was doing these OEX options. And, in fact, the funny part about it was they all said, yeah, I hear that he's doing all these trades but, you know, we don't see it anywhere. . . . And so, for me, the biggest issue was the fact that I couldn't reconcile a big part of that strategy. And the information that [Madoff] told me on the surface seemed to be false."

Another complaint received by the OCIE had alleged that Madoff was front running, and despite the hedge fund manager's questioning whether any trades actually existed, the OCIE team had decided to focus exclusively on the issue of front running, a decision made by McCarthy because "that was the area of expertise for my crew." Also in the files was a letter from Madoff himself stating, "Neither Madoff Securities, nor any person or entity affiliated with Madoff Securities, manages or advises hedge funds" and "we have no interest in becoming a manager or adviser to hedge funds." The split-strike conversion strategy was simply something the firm executed on behalf of institutional clients; it was their strategy, not Madoff's. Ostrow and Lamore now knew, by Madoff's own admission, that all of this was false.

Madoff had produced numerous records, including various client statements with trade data, showing numerous options trades, which undercut his claim that he'd stopped trading options a year before. Like Ostrow and Lamore, the OCIE staff had numerous unanswered questions. They suspected Madoff was in fact creating and executing his split-strike conversion strategy for hedge fund clients and was lying or misleading them. They expanded the investigation from front running to whether Madoff should have to register as an investment adviser. But then the OCIE's priorities had shifted to issues involving mutual funds. The team was reassigned while the Madoff investigation remained open but dormant. There were no conclusions or final report.

One SEC staff member bumped into Shana Madoff at an industry conference in St. Louis in March 2005, just weeks before Ostrow and Lamore had begun their visit to Madoff's offices. He'd sent an e-mail to another member of the Madoff team at OCIE. "What is the status of the Madoff hedge fund thingy?"

The reply: "Deady. We never found any real problems."

Ostrow was eager to continue the investigation, and was planning visits to Fairfield Sentry and other Madoff feeder funds. He was especially eager to see how the split-strike conversion strategy could be executed without Madoff trading options. Madoff's latest explanation had been that the hedge fund clients themselves put on a hedge by trading options. But the glossy brochures they prepared for clients made no mention of this. Did they really trade the options, and if so, how did this fit into the strategy? He and Lamore had never discovered whom the mysterious European brokers were who supposedly executed Madoff's trades, nor did they know the identity of any of his counterparties when he traded option contracts. Indeed, they'd never spoken to anyone except Madoff himself, who they thought was lying, and a handful of people at his firm who had no involvement with the hedge fund operation. In fact, none of the issues raised by the Renaissance e-mails—which had set the investigation in motion—had been resolved.

On June 16 Nee met with Ostrow and Lamore and directed them not to visit or contact any of Madoff's feeder funds. Ostrow recalled that Nee warned them that Fairfield "is a $7 billion customer and if you go and raise red flags there and they go ahead and pull all of their money from Bernie and we're wrong, then we'll be sued personally or the SEC itself." (Nee denied that fear of lawsuits was a factor, but acknowledged, "We'd have to be very careful about going to a hedge fund client.") Nee told them it was time to end the examination and move on to their next assignment. As he explained, "There's no hard and fast rule about field work, but field work cannot go on indefinitely because people have a hunch or they're following things."

Ostrow and Lamore completed their report on Madoff on September 8, 2005. It cited three minor technical violations they'd discovered in Madoff's market-making operation.

Ostrow was demoralized by the experience. "It's frustrating when you're out there for three months, lied to every day, and you try relaying that, and you try to get it across that, how can this be? . . . We asked him specifically, 'Do you manage money?' Like, we asked it eight different ways and six different languages, and you know, got the same 'no.' . . . We still knew and felt it was highly suspicious and just odd, and the whole story, there were inconsistencies that were unsettling."

In October 2005, the SEC's David Bergers e-mailed colleague Michael Garrity that an "informant" was coming in. "We'll tell him he has an hour but he'll go over," Bergers predicted. Bergers and Garrity worked in the SEC's Boston regional office, Bergers in enforcement and Garrity as the branch chief for investment advisers and investment companies. Garrity, in his late forties, had worked as a journalist in Connecticut, New Jersey, and Philadelphia before going to law school, and had been with the SEC since 2001. Bergers told him his informant's name was Harry Markopolos. Garrity had never heard of him, but Bergers said he was someone "connected to the industry" who was worth listening to.

Later that month, the Boston officials met Markopolos in a satellite office of the SEC on Boston's Tremont Street. Markopolos was fifty-one years old, with tousled dark hair and a slender build, analytical and talkative, at least about the kinds of arcane financial transactions that fascinated him. His wife had a similar bent and worked in compliance for an investment firm. Markopolos had worked for several years as an options trader and then chief investment officer at a Boston financial firm, Rampart Investment Management. He'd recently left there, and was now an independent forensic accountant, often hired by lawyers and financial firms to ferret out evidence of fraud. Madoff had come to his attention years before when fellow options traders challenged him to match Madoff's reported returns. Markopolos repeatedly tried, and failed, to replicate Madoff's results using a split-strike conversion strategy, something Markopolos was very familiar with as an options trader. The strategy could smooth out returns, softening market downturns, but it still put a cap on gains in bull markets and generated losses in bear markets. Markopolos couldn't get anywhere near Madoff's returns or his consistency. If not quite an obsession, the quest became an ongoing preoccupation, something that intrigued and mystified Markopolos.

The more he'd learned about Madoff, the more convinced Markopolos had become that he was a fraud. He thought the Madoff operation had all the signs of a Ponzi scheme—a fraudulent investment operation that pays investors from their own money and that of subsequent investors, and not from any actual investment profits. It was named for a charming early twentieth-century swindler, Charles Ponzi, who promised investors a 50 percent profit within forty-five days. Markopolos had first approached the SEC's Boston office in 2000. He'd met with Ed Manion, a young accountant, and a more senior administrator, Grant Ward. When the meeting was over, Ward seemed uninterested and dismissive. Manion told Markopolos, "He didn't understand a damn thing we said." Although Ward told Manion he'd refer the complaint to the New York office, he apparently never did. (Ward left the SEC soon after and later said he didn't even recall meeting Markopolos. But Manion had stayed in touch and kept encouraging Markopolos to keep tabs on Madoff.)

Now, five years later, Markopolos had heard that Madoff was trying to borrow money at high interest rates in Europe. As they grow, requiring ever-larger amounts of new capital to meet redemptions, all Ponzi schemes eventually implode, and Markopolos thought this meant that Madoff's operation might be close to running out of cash. He didn't really want to get involved—indeed, he feared for his and his family's safety—but the collapse of a multibillion-dollar hedge fund might trigger a financial crisis. He'd felt obliged to act, and had drafted a detailed, twenty-page analysis. At the meeting with Bergers and

Garrity, he handed out copies of his report, and the headline was certainly an attention-getter: "The World's Largest Hedge Fund Is a Fraud." Given his previous failure to trigger the SEC's interest, he wanted to make it provocative. Garrity quickly scanned the opening paragraphs:

"I am the original source for the information presented herein," the submission began. Noting that he wasn't an insider or a whistle-blower, the author said:

> My observations were collected firsthand by listening to fund-of-funds investors talk about their investments in a hedge fund run by Madoff Investment Securities LLC, an SEC registered firm. I have also spoken to the heads of various Wall Street equity derivative trading desks and every single one of the senior managers I spoke with told me that Bernie Madoff was a fraud. Of course, no one wants to take undue career risk by sticking their head up and saying the emperor isn't wearing any clothes.
>
> I am a derivatives expert and have traded or assisted in the trading of several billion $US in options strategies for hedge funds and institutional clients. I have experience managing split-strike conversion products both using index options and using individual stock options, both with and without index puts. Very few people in the world have the mathematical background needed to manage these types of products but I am one of them. I have outlined a detailed set of red flags that make me very suspicious that Bernie Madoff's returns aren't real and, if they are real, then they are certainly generated by front running.
>
> Due to the sensitive nature of the case I detail below, its dissemination within the SEC must be limited to those with a need to know. The firm involved is located in the New York region.
>
> As a result of this case, several careers on Wall Street and in Europe will be ruined. Therefore, I have not signed my name on this report. I request that my name not be released to anyone outside this SEC region without my express written permission. The fewer people who know who wrote this report the better. I am worried about the personal safety of myself and my family. Under no circumstances is this report or its contents to be shared with any other regulatory body without my express permission.

Markopolos walked the SEC officers through some of his key findings, sometimes going to a whiteboard to illustrate points or do some simple calculations. Garrity didn't know much about options or trading strategies, and had never heard of a split-strike conversion, but Markopolos found him curious and open-minded.

Markopolos had organized his report around twenty-six key "red flags" he'd identified. He said it was possible, though unlikely, that Madoff was achieving his results by front running the order flow in his market-making business. The more likely scenario was that he was running a giant Ponzi scheme. Markopolos estimated that Madoff had anywhere from $20 to $50 billion in assets, making it the world's largest hedge fund. He noted that Madoff didn't identify his operation as a hedge fund, "although it acts and trades like one." Although Markopolos had no direct contact with Madoff, he did have the advantage of Fairfield Sentry's account statements over fourteen and a half years and had spoken to numerous Madoff investors, both in the United States and in Europe.

Just about everything Markopolos had found out about Madoff's fund was suspicious. Unlike virtually all other hedge funds, the only fee Madoff charged investors was a four-cents-per-share trading commission. Meanwhile, the feeder funds that gave him their money (and did nothing else to generate returns) charged the typical 1 or 2 percent of assets and 20 percent of any gains. Why would Madoff charge so little, leaving all the spoils for the feeder funds? (This was the same issue that had puzzled the Renaissance officials.) Markopolos had never heard of another fund with such a fee arrangement. Why would he leave the fees to others "unless he was a Ponzi scheme?" Markopolos asked.

Like the Renaissance executives, Markopolos was baffled by Madoff's claimed reliance on a split-strike conversion strategy. Markopolos offered a detailed explanation of it to the SEC officials, since Garrity wasn't familiar with it. He stressed that "there are not enough index option put contracts in existence to hedge the way Madoff says he is hedging," that it was "mathematically impossible" for Madoff to earn such consistent returns, with only seven "extremely small" losses in fourteen and a half years, and that other funds pursuing a split-strike conversion strategy didn't have anywhere near the consistency or level of Madoff's returns.

Markopolos said that a London-based fund-of-funds he spoke to was considering a Madoff investment, and asked to conduct a performance audit of Madoff's returns. Madoff refused, saying only his accountant could audit the results in order to preserve the secrecy of Madoff's model. "The number of hedge funds that have relied on fake audits has got to number in the dozens," Markopolos pointed out. Markopolos was also troubled that apparently only

Madoff family members were privy to the investment strategy, asking, "Name one other prominent multibillion-dollar hedge fund that doesn't have outside, non-family professionals involved in the investment process. You can't, because there aren't any."

Markopolos also provided performance data from Fairfield Sentry from 1990 to 2005, the *Barron's* article, and a list of French and Swiss money managers and private banks with investments in Madoff's hedge fund. (He added that there were undoubtedly dozens more.) "The only way these returns are real is if Bernie Madoff is an alien from outer space who has perfect foreknowledge of what the capital markets are about to do," Markopolos said.

"Investors don't want to have to trade against aliens," Garrity quipped.

Garrity and the other officials were impressed by Markopolos's analysis, even though some of it was repetitive and Markopolos himself was long-winded and "sometimes he starts out in the middle of things," as Garrity put it. Garrity also interrupted with numerous questions. Markopolos was also a "bounty hunter," someone hoping to be paid for a tip that uncovers an insider trading fraud, so he had a motive to expose Madoff (the law prohibiting insider trading allows for bounties to be paid for successful tips, but doesn't apply to Ponzi schemes). And he had no direct evidence, only information from feeder funds about Madoff's tactics and results.

Still, Garrity thought Markopolos was credible and he was intrigued by the suggestion that the Madoff operation might be a huge Ponzi scheme. As he came to understand the split-strike conversion strategy, he agreed with Markopolos that it couldn't generate the results attributed to Madoff. Walter Ricciardi, the Boston office's chief administrator, was a former general counsel for PricewaterhouseCoopers, and he was especially concerned by the lack of an independent auditor.

Garrity was eager to pursue the investigation. He'd never gotten such a detailed tip with such potentially far-reaching ramifications. "It was intriguing . . . fundamentally interesting," he said. "It's the kind of thing I get excited about." He didn't think it would be all that difficult to investigate. If Madoff were running a hedge fund of the magnitude Markopolos had suggested, there would be evidence of the massive trading necessary to carry out Madoff's strategy. He'd simply go to the DTC (the Depository Trust Company, which clears and settles trading in securities), the CBOE, and other options exchanges, or, if Madoff traded options over-the-counter, to his trading counterparties, to verify the timing and prices of the trades. "If this was taking place in our jurisdiction I'd have teams in there tomorrow tearing the place apart," Garrity told Markopolos.

But Ricciardi felt the case should be referred to New York, since Madoff was based in New York and much of the investigation would have to be conducted there. Offering such a potentially high-profile case to New York might also be seen as a goodwill gesture that would help ease the rivalry that often sprang up between the two offices. But Ricciardi noted in an e-mail, "Let's try to make sure that NERO [the Northeast Regional Office in New York] recognizes the potential urgency of the situation. By the way, auditors are required to be independent. You cannot have an independent audit performed by a relative."

TWELVE

"Some People
Feel the Market"

In New York, Markopolos's report was assigned to Meaghan Cheung, a branch chief in the enforcement division, and Simona Suh, a staff attorney. "Here's a new case for Simona," Doria Bachenheimer, a lawyer and the enforcement staff's assistant director, wrote to Cheung. "Do you want to come by and we'll call John Dugan to see what he can tell us?" Dugan was the head of enforcement in Boston.

Both Cheung and Suh had graduated from Fordham Law School in New York City, Cheung in 1999 and Suh in 2001. Cheung had never heard of Madoff, even though he was a cofounder of NASDAQ and a prominent industry executive whose niece, Shana, often organized and participated in conferences dealing with SEC compliance.

Suh had worked at the SEC for only nineteen months, but was considered one of the agency's best young lawyers. After Fordham, she'd landed prestigious judicial clerkships and worked at Cravath, Swaine & Moore, one of the country's most prominent firms, as a junior associate on the Enron case. Suh did some Internet research on Markopolos, which she forwarded to Cheung. There wasn't much available, but she included a quote from Markopolos: "I can teach you how to spot fraud and what to do about it, so you aren't in the hot seat."

"I have some qualms about a self-identified independent fraud analyst, but who knows," Cheung responded, betraying an almost immediate skepticism of Markopolos.

In early November, at Garrity's suggestion, Markopolos called Cheung to say he was the informant on the Madoff case, and offered to help.

Cheung acknowledged she'd read his report, but then fell silent. Her tone was cool.

Markopolos asked if she had any questions. She didn't answer.

"Well, do you understand derivatives?" Markopolos persisted.

"I did the Adelphia case," she replied, sounding offended.

Markopolos pointed out that Adelphia was an accounting fraud, not a Ponzi scheme based on an alleged options trading strategy. Adelphia had nothing in common with Madoff.

Cheung said she didn't need to understand derivatives because the SEC had a staff of PhDs who did.

Markopolos started arguing that academic PhDs didn't necessarily understand the world of options trading. Cheung didn't respond. Markopolos felt this was going nowhere, that he "had to draw every sentence out of her," and "she acted as if I were insulting her intelligence."

"Is there anything you need from me?" he concluded.

"If we do, we'll call you."

Markopolos was furious. He called Manion, his longtime SEC contact in Boston. "Your agency sucks," he told him. "Your people are beyond incompetent."

Given the traditional rivalry between Boston and New York, Manion surmised that New York probably thought Boston had dumped a dead-end case on them, and was treating it accordingly.

Nor did the *Barron's* and *MAR/Hedge* articles make much of an impression on Cheung, even though they echoed much of what Markopolos was saying. She noted that they dated from 2001, and for all she knew, Markopolos had just gotten his information from them and "rewrote it," as she later said. A problem for both Cheung and Suh was that Markopolos wasn't a true whistleblower who could make a case for them. He didn't work for Madoff, nor was he a Madoff investor. He had no direct, firsthand knowledge of fraud. It was all inference, albeit based on detailed information he'd obtained from some of Madoff's customers.

Since Madoff had been investigated only months before by the New York office, Cheung and Suh's boss sent an e-mail to John Nee saying, "We're going to look into this." Nee forwarded it to Lamore with a two word comment: "Oh no!"

"Ironically, I thought of Madoff as I went to sleep last night," Lamore responded. "I would be more than happy to sit down with anyone . . . I don't think we missed anything."

The fact that the enforcement division was looking into Madoff so soon after the regional office had concluded an examination with only minor technical violations seemed to put Nee and Lamore on the defensive. For a renewed investigation of Madoff would inevitably be an investigation of them.

A week later Cheung sent a copy of Markopolos's report, "The World's Largest Hedge Fund Is a Fraud," to Lamore, who forwarded it to Nee and Ostrow. "These are basically the same allegations we have heard before," Lamore commented (although no one previously had stated directly that Madoff was running a Ponzi scheme). And even though Markopolos would earn a bounty only if insider trading was involved, and not if Madoff was running a Ponzi scheme, Lamore added, "The author's motives are to make money by uncovering the alleged fraud. I think he is on a fishing expedition and doesn't have the detailed understanding of Madoff's operations that we do which refutes most of his allegations. Any thoughts?"

Nee agreed that a "Ponzi scheme or directly trading on order flow doesn't [seem] likely from what we've seen."

"I must admit I was a bit spooked when you forwarded me the string of e-mails from the Boston and New York SEC offices (Ponzi scheme getting ready to crash), but after having just read the 'informant's' analysis I feel much better he is incorrect," Lamore replied.

Given that Markopolos was alleging a Ponzi scheme as the most likely explanation—something Lamore and Ostrow never seem to have seriously considered, let alone investigated—and was casting doubt on the level and consistency of Madoff's returns—and Lamore and Ostrow, by their own admission, had never figured out how Madoff achieved his returns—it's hard to know on what grounds Markopolos's analysis made Lamore feel better. Still, despite his skepticism, to his credit Lamore e-mailed Cheung that "to refute all his allegations, we may need to request some documentation from one or more of the funds-of-funds."

After speaking to Lamore, Suh felt it was clear that he and Ostrow had not focused on whether Madoff was running a Ponzi scheme. Cheung, on the other hand, came away with the impression that the examiners had looked into all the issues Markopolos raised and found nothing, and conveyed that message to her superiors.

. . .

On October 1, the enforcement division's office of Internet enforcement received an e-mail from a "concerned investor":

Dear SEC:

I was a former client of one of Madoff Financial's "hedge funds." . . . I am deeply concerned that Madoff is running a very sophisticated fraudulent pyramid scheme. I came to this conclusion shortly after I joined Madoff as a client in 1999. When I tried to get a better understanding of their operation and get some financial data, they refused. Their response to me was, "If you don't like your returns, then get out." After a short period of time, I decided to withdraw all my money (over $5 million). . . .

I know that Madoff also has a broker dealer which they [use] to run all their trades. Although I cannot point to anything concrete, their return of 12% to 18% annually over the last 20 years or so tells me something is wrong there. Believe it or not, I don't think they had a losing year. I also know firsthand that they "guarantee" a certain percentage annual return for some clients who put in more than $100 million. I know at least 3 people in Palm Beach who have actually borrowed money—great sums of money—to put into Madoff because of this "guarantee."

I know that the Madoff Company is very secretive about their operations and they refuse to disclose anything. If my suspicions are true, then they are running a highly sophisticated scheme on a massive scale. And they have been doing it for a long time. I suspect that their scheme has not collapsed because they control the amount of redemptions. I only hope I am wrong but given the recent blowups around the country, more and more I think of Madoff's operation, more and more it seems fishy.

I know I have not provided too many concrete facts but I only wish I had them. If you can look into their operation, perhaps it will reveal a greater truth.

An enforcement attorney searched the SEC's database for "Madoff" and found nothing. No one in the enforcement division had entered the Markopolos complaint into the SEC's computer system. The e-mail made it through several layers of authority before it languished, forgotten, among the Internet division's archived records.

. . .

D espite the initial skepticism over Markopolos's report, Cheung, Suh, and Lamore followed up on Lamore's suggestion to contact a feeder fund, and made an appointment to interview Amit Vijayvergiya, known as Vijay, a managing director and head of risk management at Fairfield Sentry, Fairfield's largest feeder fund.

Fairfield's general counsel, Mark McKeefry, asked Suh if it was okay for them to talk to Madoff first, and surprisingly Suh didn't object. Vijayvergiya and McKeefry had a conference call with Madoff on December 19.

"Obviously, of course, this conversation never took place. Okay?" Madoff said when he got on the phone (although it turned out that the entire conversation was recorded, in part because Madoff typically spoke so fast that they had trouble taking notes).

Madoff was clearly at pains to make sure that Vijayvergiya told the SEC that Madoff Securities was not an investment adviser nor was it required to register as one with the SEC. Throughout the call, he essentially dictated to Vijayvergiya what he should say, and Vijayvergiya repeatedly responded "Right," "Okay," and "Good."

"We never want to be looked at as the investment manager or that we are out, you know, soliciting or doing any marketing for the fund," Madoff emphasized. "We are the executing broker for these transactions and you use a proprietary trading model . . . that has certain parameters built in that have been approved by you."

Still, Madoff had a problem. Fairfield Sentry's Madoff trading records were filled with options trades, and Madoff had just told Ostrow and Lamore that he no longer traded options. Fairfield even had a document from Madoff indicating that options were part of the proprietary model, which Madoff said was actually a few years out-of-date. "Options are no longer part of the model," he said. "The options are separate and there are standing instructions for the model . . . so if you ever get into any conversations about the model, it's for the equities. That's important, okay?"

"Okay, good," Vijayvergiya responded.

"Any time you say you have something in writing they ask for it. . . . So the best thing to do is just say it's a phone call. That's what we said it is. . . . No one pays attention to these types of things or who calls or who doesn't or who remembers who calls," Madoff continued. Meanwhile, he assumed the focus of the call would again be front running. "You guys are not part of the execution piece of this. The concern they have with any strategy is, does anybody know it ahead of time? Because then . . . there's the possibility for someone to front run an order."

Madoff's phone rang, and he put Vijayvergiya on hold. After a few moments he came back on the line.

"I'm sorry, if I get any more solicitations for charity I'm going to kill myself. As I was saying . . . that's the major concern that these people have and probably why they want to know who is it that's implementing the strategy . . . and probably the most important issue is Madoff is the one who's implementing the strategy."

"And how many people are on the team now?" Vijayvergiya asked.

"I'm the only one that can make the decision. . . . I'm the only one that pulls the trigger. Or if I'm not there someone else, but I'm always there. But this kind of information is not information that you have any reason to have," Madoff stressed, and hence, should not be volunteering to the SEC. Vijayvergiya shouldn't get into any details about Madoff's trading strategy. "The less you know about how we execute, the better you are . . . you could, you know, if they ask, do you know if Madoff has Chinese walls, you could say, yes, . . . Madoff has been in business for forty-five years, he executes a huge percentage of the industry's orders, he's a well-known broker. We make the assumption that he's doing everything properly."

At this juncture Madoff looked over a written list of points he'd prepared.

"Okay, so we don't market. You don't know the exact amounts we trade for others. We're the executing broker. We don't do any other business with you. There are terms and conditions on the options just like the equity. Yup, and the options are not part of the model anymore."

Next he read over Fairfield's marketing materials, which vaguely described Madoff's investing approach and promised consistent monthly returns. "Don't say consistent monthly returns," he lectured. They were a little too consistent.

"Okay, you can delete that," Vijayvergiya said.

But then Madoff seemed unable to resist boasting about them and his unique strategy. "And the purpose of the strategy is to take advantage of an upward move in the market, all right?" he said. "You're buying the securities that are basically going to move with the S&P. That basket of securities can be hedged using broad index options, you know, to put a collar to limit the risk of the strategy. . . . We'll hedge it with a broad base index with certain parameters below the market, they have to be out of the money, you know, on both sides and so forth. But again, that is not something, so you understand, that they . . . You're not the one that's implementing the strategy and you're not even the one that determined if this is a great strategy or not. I mean this fund has been using this strategy for fifteen years."

"Right," Vijayvergiya responded.

"This strategy was put on long before you even showed on the scene," Madoff continued, evidently warming to his subject. "The skill of Madoff is to know when to get into the market and get out of the market," he said, speaking of himself magisterially in the third person.

"I wouldn't anticipate that will be something the SEC is interested in . . ." Vijayvergiya said.

Madoff warned they might ask about anything. "These guys come in to do a books and records examination and they, you know, they ask you a zillion different questions, and we look at them sometimes and we laugh, and we say, are you guys writing a book? We're good market timers. . . . If they ask, you know, do you know how Madoff decides when he's going to go in the market and out of the market, which is a question people always ask me, I'd say, 'I'm not going to share that information with you.' There's all sorts of, obviously, black-box technology, momentum models, and all sorts of things that tell us when to get in and out of the market."

"I know the options are all OTC at this stage," Vijayvergiya mentioned.

"Yeah, those are done with derivative dealers."

"Dealers, okay . . ."

"Basically European bank and derivative banks, dealer banks," Madoff added. "You don't want them to think you're concerned about anything. With them you should be, you know, casual. . . . What else, what else, what else," Madoff continued, as if thinking aloud. That seemed to be it. "Okay . . . great, Amit. Take care."

Madoff's first words—"this conversation never took place"—should have been a red flag. (A spokesman for Vijayvergiya responds that Madoff was always so secretive that he didn't find Madoff's initial comment jarring and took it as an "off the cuff" remark.)

Madoff also tried to get Vijayvergiya to accept the proposition that options trading was no longer part of his proprietary model, although they always had been. He also didn't want Vijayvergiya saying that anything was in writing (such as the document indicating options trading was part of the model). And Madoff's explanation for his vaunted ability to time the market, filled with vague references to "black box models" and "momentum," lacked any credible detail. In any event, Vijayvergiya wasn't supposed to know anything about that.

Vijayvergiya dutifully followed through with his SEC interview on the after-noon of December 21, so much so that Cheung, Suh, and Lamore were all sus-picious that he'd worked out his statements with Madoff in advance—in Suh's words, that he was "prepped." According to Fairfield's notes of the interview, Vijayvergiya explained the split-strike strategy and said, "The equities piece of the strategy is done by a proprietary model and 'black box' technology . . . whereas the options piece is more broad based and not proprietary. Therefore there are separate documents for each. . . . The price and timing decision is made by Madoff employing a sophisticated model and technology. We do not have any input to the price or timing decision. . . ." To his credit, Vijayvergiya defied Madoff and acknowledged, when asked, that he had spoken to Madoff before the interview, although he gave a truncated version of the conversation: "The substance was, do you know what the conversation with the SEC might concern? We talked about our relationship. . . . The whole thing was more of a courtesy call." (Nor did Vijayvergiya disclose there was a tape of their call.)

Vijayvergiya also testified correctly that options trading was an essential part of the Madoff strategy, whether or not they were part of the model. Yet Madoff had told Lamore and Ostrow that he'd stopped trading options entirely—not that he'd removed options from his model—and that the clients executed their own options trades. This didn't escape Lamore, who noted the next day in an e-mail that "I'll be writing up my notes from the Madoff/Fairfield Greenwich Group (FGG) conference call that I participated in yesterday. Also, I'm going to provide the attorneys with a list of differences (lies) from what we were told and provided during the Madoff exam vs. what we learned about Madoff's opera-tion from various documents provided by FGG and during the conference call yesterday." And Bachenheimer, the enforcement staff's assistant director, wrote, "The Madoff investigation took an interesting turn. Contrary to what Madoff told our exam team, he is trading options for at least one hedge fund." Now the enforcement division itself recognized that Madoff had lied—yet evidently didn't consider referring the matter to the Justice Department.

Not only was Madoff plainly trading options for Fairfield, but when Lamore analyzed the Fairfield statements, he had concluded that "the number of S&P 100 index options traded by Madoff, purportedly over-the-counter, is an order of magnitude greater than the total exchange-traded volume for these options," Suh wrote Cheung.

Lamore added, "According to Bernie Madoff, all equity transactions occur in Europe . . . and clear through Barclays capital. . . . I believe that we should find out more about the counterparties to these transactions and the agreements/arrangements between Madoff and the counterparties."

By now, Lamore was worried that Madoff might be running a Ponzi scheme. Suh assured him that they were demanding that Madoff produce documents identifying who had custody of assets for all his customers as well as contracts with his counterparties to the options contracts. "Sounds good. I'll sleep better with the answer to this question," Lamore responded.

In response, Madoff provided a write-up of his strategy and a list of customers, and voluminous customer account statements and balances, but no original documents, no indication of who held custody of the assets, and no contracts with counterparties. Suh called Madoff and asked for an explanation. Madoff said he had no written contracts with any counterparties, but he promised to identify them as well as the asset custodians.

Neither Suh nor Cheung had any experience with over-the-counter options trading, which in fact required detailed documentation and extensive paperwork. Suh asked Lamore for help analyzing the account statements, but Lamore wrote back, "I don't have clean answers to your questions. However, I do believe your questions go back to the custody of assets issue. Where are the assets held and where does BLM [Madoff] settle the trades (wiring instructions)?"

"Thank you—I am glad I am not the only one confused," Suh said.

"Ha. No problem. It's very confusing to me as well," Lamore e-mailed back.

Despite their shared confusion, on January 23, 2006, a little over three months after receiving Markopolos's report, Suh and Cheung concluded there was enough evidence to open an informal investigation. In a status memo summarizing the investigation, Suh noted that Madoff had "misled" the examination staff in a prior investigation and withheld information. "The staff is trying to ascertain whether the complainant's allegation that BLM is operating a Ponzi scheme has any factual basis."

Now that the Madoff case had been designated an informal investigation, it was finally entered into the SEC's database, and the staff could issue subpoenas and take sworn testimony. The first witness they called was Frank DiPascali Jr., an unassuming forty-nine-year-old with neatly cropped dark hair and a medium build who spoke with a distinct Queens accent. At Madoff Securities he held the lofty title of chief financial officer, but functioned as chief administrative officer for Madoff's investment services business, overseeing computer operations and a staff of about twenty who occupied the seventeenth floor of Madoff's offices.

DiPascali had gone to work for Madoff at age nineteen, a year after graduating from a parochial high school. His next-door neighbor in Howard Beach, Queens, a working-class neighborhood in the far outskirts of New York City, was Madoff's secretary, who recommended him for an entry-level part-time job as a research clerk. He enrolled at St. John's University and Brooklyn College, but dropped out of both. In thirty years he'd never left the Madoff firm, and everything he knew about markets and trading he'd learned there.

His résumé was unusual for a top officer at a leading hedge fund, but his was also a classic all-American success story. DiPascali now lived in a five-bedroom home with a pool on seven acres in affluent Bridgewater, New Jersey. He owned two black Mercedeses, one a sedan, the other an SUV, and a sixty-one-foot Viking sportfishing boat, the *Dorothy-Jo*, named for his daughter and his wife, Joanne. DiPascali earned $2.6 million in 2006 (over $4 million the next year) and was also an investor in Madoff's fund.

On January 26 DiPascali arrived at the SEC's offices, now in Three World Financial Center, just across the street from its former location in the World Trade Center. He came alone, but had been briefed by Madoff. Suh and Lamore were hoping to get a clearer idea of how Madoff generated his returns, how the split-strike conversion strategy worked, and where and how all these trades took place. Suh told DiPascali he had the right to be represented by a lawyer and that failure to tell the truth was a crime. He testified under oath.

"Have there been instances in the past ten years where Mr. Madoff's overall returns have been negative?" Suh asked him.

"I don't believe so," DiPascali replied. "For the year, no. For any particular period of time, definitely, but not over the course of a year. No. I don't remember one."

"How does the firm—"

"I don't want to interrupt you, but keep in mind that there have been market corrections that have occurred. We are not in the market all the time. We are in the market for short periods of time."

Suh pressed for a better explanation of the firm's market timing, and DiPascali made clear that the firm's success depended entirely on Madoff.

"How do you decide when to get out of the market?" Suh asked.

"How do I decide when to get out? Two ways, I guess. The model will dictate when to get out because correlation will break. So when you got in was dictated by the model. When you get out is dictated by the same entry parameters as when you got in. If that breaks, you gotta bail. If it didn't break, then you can hold on. Now, you may have a situation where it doesn't break, but he [Madoff] decides that he doesn't like the market, so he will bail. Those are the only two ways it can happen."

Cheung intervened, asking, "Is there anybody else at Madoff, the company, who can make these judgment calls other than Mr. Madoff?"

"No."

"What happens when he goes on vacation?"

"He is never on vacation. Bernie Madoff is available twenty-four hours a day, seven days a week, three hundred sixty-five days a year, anywhere on the planet."

This should have been a red flag, since the failure to take a vacation is a classic symptom of fraud. Nearly all Wall Street firms require employees to take two consecutive weeks of vacation.

"He is not a young man," Suh observed.

"I am fearful of that, let me tell you. . . . That often worries me. I would imagine that he has contingency plans in effect with his brother and his sons. Whether this strategy will continue to be as successful as it has in the past under a different . . . with someone else's helm, if you will. . . . Like I said, I am a salaried employee. I admitted to him, I don't have the ability to do what he does. I am a numbers cruncher. I didn't do it well when I traded for him for a couple of years, I couldn't trade my way out of a paper bag. I can't call market direction. I am not his replacement by any stretch, you know."

As Madoff had told Ostrow and Lamore, DiPascali also testified that the options counterparties were European.

"I wanted to make sure that the basket [of S&P 100 equities] is put on during a trading day and the options are put on subsequent to the basket?" Suh asked.

"The basket is put on during the European trading day. The options are put on prior to the New York open and after the European trading day is ended, when I am complete."

"The people that you execute your equities with, are they the same broker-dealers that you execute the options with?"

"No, they are not."

"None of them are the same?"

"People I execute the equities with, you are talking about European contra side dealers?"

"Yes."

"No, no."

"About how many derivatives dealers do you deal with?"

"Derivatives dealers, twenty, maybe two dozen. It's not five and it's not thirty. It's probably eighteen, nineteen, twenty."

Suh also tried to pin down whether there were written records of the options trades.

"I have the entry database that comes back from the dealers that is accessible in any format I want to look at it," DiPascali said. "Trade date, dealer, I want to look at it by price, symbol, by any sort of mechanism." Madoff himself, DiPascali explained, communicated with the dealers by "telephone. They affirm back to me by computer."

Later she asked, "You mentioned confirmations and account statements that you sent to customers. . . . Who is in charge of generating them and sending them to customers?"

"The computer actually gets all the information, spits it out and a printer—one of the operators is told to print me that file and they print it out. There are not that many statements."

So there *were* options trading records, contrary to what Madoff had said.

After more questions in this vein, Suh said she wanted "to switch gears and talk about the customers in the institutional business. What kind of customers does this business have? Who are they?"

"Who are they, I guess there [are] about twenty, the largest of which would be Fairfield, which I guess is an offshore hedge fund. I am thinking some of the names, what they do. They are either a hedge fund or some sort of European institution. They are not natural people like a client would be, Joe Schmo."

"Any rough idea how much [Madoff] is managing?"

"Ten, eleven billion dollars."

Toward the end of DiPascali's testimony, Suh asked an open-ended question: "To your knowledge, are there any aspects of the business that give you concern that maybe something improper is going on?"

"No, no," DiPascali replied. "The guy is the straightest shooter in the world."

The next day, Lamore e-mailed Suh with what he called some "rambling thoughts regarding Madoff."

I meant to ask Frank why the strategy is implemented only in Europe and during European trading hours and not New York time? What if there is breaking news having a huge impact on the market such as 9/11? I am still puzzled that Bernie is able always . . . to find counterparties willing to trade options in the size that he needs to for the strategy without freaking out the market. Talk about having difficulty finding liquidity–try calling a large broker-dealer in the U.S. with such a huge options order. I am confident that you would move (scare) the market. Maybe the counterparties are able to hedge themselves, somehow, but I don't see how.

He followed up with another note: "I don't know what I'm thinking, but it seems weird to me that the counterparties aren't the bulge bracket firms (Goldman, Merrill, Lehman . . .) Instead they are smaller, more obscure firms. . . ."

Suh responded, "Excellent points. We can pursue them with Bernie, when we take his testimony," though she cautioned they wouldn't be doing so until they had exhausted other sources. But then she largely dismissed his questions. "On the options trading issue, we probably will not be able to get any help from the dealers, since they are all overseas . . . if we had any *real* reason to suspect some kind of wrongdoing in Bernie's market timing decisions, I would send a document request on the issue, but I am not sure how much stress we want to put on him if all we suspect is disclosure problems. I will talk to Meaghan about it. We can definitely question him about it."

This was the first indication that the enforcement staff's focus was shifting from the Ponzi scheme questions to the far more modest issue of whether Madoff needed to register his investment advisory business. Suh later acknowledged that despite Madoff's glaring inconsistencies and failure to produce records, "at that time I think the view was that there's probably nothing there and that this would be primarily a registration and disclosure case."

Even so, Suh forged ahead. Despite Madoff's claims to the contrary, DiPascali had made clear there were computer-generated records of the options transactions (yet another glaring inconsistency on Madoff's part). In February, Suh sent another written request to Madoff for account documents and trading records for his hedge fund clients as well as for his options counterparties. This time Madoff responded that he traded through his own broker-dealer, the Depository Trust Company, the Bank of New York, and Barclays. He provided a six-page list of four broker-dealers who handled equities trades and twelve, all overseas, who were the options trading counterparties, including UBS in

Switzerland and the Royal Bank of Scotland. But he provided none of the records DiPascali had described and Suh had specifically requested.

Suh also sent a lengthy e-mail describing the Madoff investigation to Vance Anthony, an economist in the SEC's Office of Economic Analysis in Washington, where many of the PhDs Cheung had told Markopolos about worked. She also sent Fairfield Sentry account statements and a copy of the *Barron's* article, and asked for help analyzing the returns. Two months later, after getting no response, she called and prodded Anthony. They spoke on the phone and Suh forwarded more materials. Anthony later said he "clicked on them to look and see what they were but I didn't do anything else." Suh heard nothing further.

In early May, having wasted several months waiting to hear from the Office of Economic Analysis, Suh drafted document requests to the Bank of New York and Barclays, unaware that Ostrow and Lamore had already contacted Barclays, which had said Madoff's account showed no trading activity. Suh also called Madoff himself to clarify which accounts at DTC, Bank of New York, and Barclays were specifically for his hedge fund business. Madoff said that "all three accounts are not solely for the institutional trading but for all BLM business," according to Suh's notes from the call. However, he agreed to produce account statements for "BLM account 290003 per BMadoff, this one is solely for the institutional trading."

Someone with even a rudimentary knowledge of the securities business should have known that a broker-dealer cannot commingle customer assets with those of the firm. SEC Rule 15c3-3 requires broker-dealers to segregate customer assets. Yet Suh seems to have attributed no significance to Madoff's response. Indeed, although she was in the process of drafting document requests to the clearing and custodial banks Madoff had identified, she and Cheung decided to hold off sending the requests until they had a chance to question Madoff directly.

But Suh did speak to Susan Tibbs, the director of market regulation at the Financial Industry Regulatory Authority (FINRA), which monitors over-the-counter options trading. Tibbs had examined FINRA's records for S&P 100 index option trading on one day when Lamore had indicated heavy volume on Madoff's part. But Tibbs reported there were no S&P 100 index options traded that day over-the-counter. Unless Madoff had failed to report the trades—or they were fictitious, either of which would have been illegal—the only possibility would have been that they were traded through Madoff's London operation, which didn't have to report trades to FINRA.

Three days later, on Friday, May 19, 2006, Madoff arrived at the SEC's New York office. Like DiPascali, Madoff came alone, unaccompanied by a lawyer.

He was wearing a white shirt and a dark gray suit and conveyed the confidence and poise of someone who had reached the pinnacle of Wall Street. An hour before he arrived, Suh had called Bachenheimer to ask "how to confront him with the fact that he lied."

Madoff sat on one side of a conference table, across from Cheung, Suh, and Bachenheimer, all enforcement attorneys, as well as Stephen Johnson, another SEC investigator. Lamore was also at the table. It was the first time Madoff had been required to leave his home turf in midtown, and to testify under oath. He swore to tell the truth and stated his name, Bernard L. Madoff. Suh led the questioning, reminding Madoff that he had a right to be represented by a lawyer and that failure to tell the truth was a crime.

As he had before with Lamore and Ostrow, Madoff recounted at length his humble origins, his rise on Wall Street, the history of trading commissions and how the firm came to "execute" trades for hedge funds. He rarely missed an opportunity to digress on an irrelevant topic, such as the intrusion of television screens onto trading floors. While he described various "models" he relied on for making trading decisions, he stressed that "It's not autopilot . . . I can listen to a conversation with my traders on how they feel. I can look and see how nervous my trading room is at a particular time or CNBC for example is a very important tool today. It's something I used to laugh at. I used to ridicule everybody for looking at that, my traders looking at it. We put the screens into the trading room. We had them all over the trading room, you know, television screens. In those days, CNBC just had a bunch of people that were promoting stock like this idiot [Jim] Cramer, whatever his name is. I can't stand that guy. There were all these guys, Dan Dorfman, I'm showing my age, but whenever he said anything, people would race in and buy the stock, so we had our television screens."

"Let's get back to the point," Suh said. "If you could, please explain what makes you the trader?"

"Forty-some-odd years of experience," Madoff answered. "To me that's the best answer I can give you. . . . You have to understand, I'm not saying trust me. I'm saying I've been in the business for forty-six years. I have a relationship with the regulators and the firms in general in the Street, and I have never, ever–I know the rules and regulations better than most people because I drafted most of them. The bad news is if I violated them, I can't say I didn't know, I was ignorant. I know what the rules are. I go to great pains to stay within those. There's plenty of ways you can make money in the business doing the right thing. You don't have to look to do the wrong thing. We document our traders all the time, and that's why in forty-six years, we've never had any sort of regulatory issue with our firm–"

Suh interrupted. "So I guess the answer to the question–the question was what makes you a good trader, and you said experience. Is that pretty much–"

"It's experience and using what tools are available to me which are perfectly open, legal tools to use," Madoff continued. "The advantage I have and the reason I don't need to be represented by lawyers is I'm not doing anything wrong."

Cheung stepped in, pressing him on the question of why he charged clients only a modest trading commission. "I think the obvious question is why are you leaving the money on the table? I mean you're making returns for somebody else to make 20 percent of, and you're getting $.04 a share. I could see, if I were your sons, asking why you were doing that."

In a rambling answer Madoff expressed his misgivings about the hedge fund business generally ("the bloom is off the rose in that area"), and said specifically that he didn't like the need to raise capital and meet with investors ("I'm not much of a marketing person or a sales person, quite frankly.") He continued, "My sons don't like this business either, that end of the business, and part of it is I guess they feel that I don't like it. It's not that I don't like it. I certainly like the money. . . . There are lots of businesses that we didn't go into over the years, and most of them were mistakes not going into them. We certainly had opportunities along the road to do that."

Madoff seemed eager to discuss the split-strike conversion strategy and proprietary model that was uniquely his creation. He likened it to cooking using a blender: "So I'm saying that you're cooking a meal. You put in carrots and oranges and a whole bunch of stuff. You put it into a blender. If you let it run for two minutes, it's going to have one consistency. If you let it run for three seconds, it's going to be a different consistency and so on and so forth. Depending on what you're looking for, everybody is looking for different things, so people design their systems to say I don't care about this stuff, I care about that. Again, I don't attach too much importance to the information that flows out of that stuff. It's available to anybody. It's not unique data. It is a–people are always trying to ask me what makes a good trade or why you can trade better than other people and so on. It's the same thing. We are proprietary traders and market makers. Some guys have more guts than others. Some of them are just stupid. They don't get frightened when they should be getting frightened. Some people feel the market. Some people just understand how to analyze the numbers that they're looking at. Everybody is different." But Madoff, clearly, was one of those people who could "feel" the market.

Early in the interview Suh tried to clarify the issue that had come up with Tibbs, the FINRA official, about whether Madoff traded his options contracts through his London office, thereby avoiding having to report the trades to FINRA. Suh asked what role the London office played in the trading.

"None whatsoever," Madoff answered.

Lamore was surprised. After all, Madoff had told him that all the trades were handled in London and cleared through Barclays. "Are they involved with the equities at all?" he asked.

"They're the liaison on the selling side, but not on the trading side, no," Madoff replied, whatever that meant.

"And how are the equity trades cleared?"

"The equity trades are all cleared through us because they're U.S. securities."

Suh continued, "Now going to the options trades, how are those trades executed?"

Madoff launched into an explanation. "The options trades, orders are placed based upon the conditions. We put out an order to buy thirteen thousand contracts with—basically what we do is we go ahead, once we buy the basket shares, we determine what the price of that, we're looking to hedge it. Basically there are a dozen derivatives dealers that participate in the process, and what we basically do is I'll call up and say I'm interested in buying—very typically what I say is, I'm looking to buy this put at this price and size. Come back to me. I'll put that out with all of these dealers. That's the way it's typically done, and then they come back." He continued at length in this vein, reminding Lamore why he had always been such an exasperating witness.

Madoff seized on a question about electronic orders for his options contracts to deliver a long and irrelevant soliloquy about block trading: "Typically the way it works is you call up a block—somebody wants to trade a hundred thousand shares of stock, so they'll call around a couple of block desks and say, listen, I'm a buyer of IBM in size at this point . . ."

Suh and her colleagues struggled to keep Madoff on point, but to a remarkable degree he was able to avoid answering directly and instead lecture them on the basics of the securities business. Still, they persisted.

"You mentioned that there was a group of dealers to whom you put out this indication of interest each time. Generally, with how many of them do you end up trading in each execution?" Suh asked.

"Within the basket, we're probably interacting with forty, close to fifty."

"That's for equities and options?"

"Equities. Options is a dozen."

"A dozen. Do all of them end up trading usually?"

"Pretty much . . . yes . . ."

"What is the rationale for going to the over-the-counter market rather than the exchange?"

"Everybody goes to the over-the-counter market on options. That's the way the market is. The over-the-counter market is just really the institutional—that's the marketplace. I mean, you can trade on the floor. You could. Then you'd be trading during the U.S. hours, which you don't want to do and you don't want to—there's really not the liquidity in the option market. It's improving, but it's not where you would want to go. . . ."

The assertion that "everybody" uses the over-the-counter market was preposterous on its face. The Chicago Board Options Exchange alone trades millions of equity options contracts a day. But Suh moved directly to a critical matter: "Who are the counterparties to the options contracts?"

"They're basically European banks," Madoff replied.

"Why foreign dealers rather than U.S.?"

"Because I'm dealing with their time zone, and that's where my contacts are with. Most of them happen to be the big derivatives dealers anyhow."

But major U.S. banks also trade in Europe during European business hours, and an over-the-counter trade can be done anytime, even if it is handled in the United States.

"With the options trades, is there any documentation generated?"

"Yes, there's an affirmation that's generated electronically, and there's a master option agreement that's attached to that that's also electronic."

This was startling, since Madoff had earlier told Suh there was no documentation of the options trading. "And the electronic affirmation stores data for each trade with each particular dealer?" Suh asked.

"Correct."

"So if you wanted to find out with whom you bought these contracts on a particular day, that's where you would go."

"Right."

After taking a break for lunch, Suh asked Madoff why he didn't just run a hedge fund, charging the usual annual fee and performance fee, instead of leaving that to his feeder funds. Remarkably, Madoff said his results weren't high enough to justify opening a hedge fund, even though they were, in fact, quite high by any measure, and his answer begged the question of why a fund-of-funds would want to invest its clients' money with him.

"You mentioned the returns, that they're not high enough to justify setting up a hedge fund," Suh continued. "They also are remarkably consistent. They have low volatility, and there are fairly few periods when they're down. I'm sure you're aware of people wondering, how can this happen? What's your answer to that?"

This promoted another long response, filled with digressions. "Well, let me just say that I pay no attention to what other people say or try to figure out," Madoff began, "because I've been in this business a long period of time, and I've learned that everybody is always busy trying to figure out what everybody else is doing and how they do it, and the only people that do that are the people that don't know what they're doing, quite frankly, so a lot of us in the trading community sit around at times and laugh about these types of questions, and how anybody does anything. If somebody understood the strategy, when somebody says it has low volatility, how come, you'd say because that's what the strategy is, to have low volatility."

At this juncture Madoff seized the opportunity to attack Erin Arvedlund, the author of the *Barron's* article critical of him. "I'll give you an example. There's stupidity out there. There was an article written years ago about this strategy. I remember the lady that wrote it who was fired from *Barron's* or wherever it was. [In fact, she was not fired.] She did a number of stupid articles. The issues that were . . . about being low volatility, she got it from some other article, and she totally misquoted, but the point is they compared it to a fund called Gateway." And then he launched into a long analysis of Gateway's returns. When he finally returned to the subject of his own unusually consistent returns, he concluded, "It is absolutely not surprising, the performance and the strategy is what you would expect it to be if you understood the parameters of the strategy, and that's all I can tell you, but any academic that looked at it would tell you that."

Suh shifted again to the issue of who handled Madoff's trades, and he acknowledged that they were all cleared and settled through the Depository Trust Company. This time he said the assets and trading for hedge fund clients were segregated in a separate account from all other activity by Madoff acting as a broker-dealer.

"There are codes that are attached to the activity that say whether it's held for the firm or whether it's held in seg."

"You mean in segregated?" Cheung asked.

"Segregated."

"Do you remember what those codes are?"

"No."

"But DTC would know."

"Yes."

"And what kind of report does the firm get from DTC on the transactions in this account?"

"Everything gets generated online to the firm on a daily basis. That's the way the DTC works now. As a clearing corporation, you get data on everything, the transactions and all that sort of stuff."

"And in the DTC account, the activity that's in the segregated account, that's solely institutional trading business and solely what's perceived as the strategy we've been discussing."

"Right."

This flatly contradicted what Madoff had told Suh only a few weeks earlier on the phone, which was that all the trading was in a single account. Moreover, this was a significant admission, since all Madoff's trading for hedge fund clients could be verified with one request to the DTC.

Suh shifted to another line of questioning. "Are there any other accounts for which you trade the split-strike conversion strategy that we've been discussing?"

"No."

So there could be no misunderstanding, Bachenheimer asked explicitly, "Mr. Madoff, do you personally trade money for anybody else?"

"What do you mean by 'anybody else'?" Madoff asked.

"Is there anybody else who provides you capital to invest and you trade on their behalf, whether it be an individual, an entity, a partnership, a corporation, your neighbor, anything or anyone?"

After insisting for years that he only managed money for a few institutions, Madoff allowed that there might be some so-called friends and family accounts, and Bachenheimer asked him to provide a complete list.

Finally Suh got to the confrontation with Madoff she'd discussed with Bachenheimer that morning. "Do you recall an examination conducted by our staff last summer of your firm?"

"Yes."

"Do you recall discussing the institutional trading business with Mr. Lamore?"

"Yes."

"Do you recall telling Mr. Lamore in substance that because of the complexity of incorporating options into the investment strategy of the institutional trading business, you stopped utilizing options as of January 1, 2004?"

"I said that the—what?"

"Do you recall telling Peter that as of January 1, 2004, you no longer incorporated options into the strategy for the institutional trading business?"

"I said they're not part of the model," Madoff stated as Lamore sat incredulous across the table. "The options are not deemed to be part of the model. I did not say—my recollection certainly is not that I said that the accounts don't use options anymore to trade. I said the options, that the options were taken out of the model, and they're not part of the model anymore."

"So what change were you referencing in that statement?"

"Well, they used to be part of the model. As a matter of fact, the change in the trading authorization directive, originally it had the options as part of the model." This coincided with the story he'd told Fairfield's Vijayvergiya to tell the SEC.

Suh continued, "Do you recall telling Mr. Lamore in substance that since that change, as of January 1, 2004, the clients may hedge the strategy themselves but that you did not discuss or provide any guidance to clients for hedging the strategy?"

"No."

"You do not recall making that statement?"

"I recall saying what I just said, that they were part of the model, that they were no longer part of the model, but I remember specifically saying that the options are still used to hedge the transactions."

Lamore was furious at Madoff's testimony, which implied that Lamore had either lied about or misstated his previous accounts of Madoff's answers. "I just remember sitting there in the testimony thinking he's lying," Lamore later said. "It was just remarkable to me." According to Ostrow, Lamore "was jumping up and down at the attorneys and letting them know about all the discrepancies." Suh, too, thought Madoff was lying. "Madoff wasn't truthful and I knew he was not giving us full information," she said. And clearly, Madoff had withheld the names and number of his customers, which grew every time they asked him about it. "Bernard Madoff misled NERO examination staff earlier this year about the nature of his trading strategy," Suh subsequently e-mailed a colleague.

On June 7 Madoff e-mailed the SEC staff a list of not just a few, as he'd implied, but eighty-six previously unmentioned friends and family accounts. When Suh called demanding to know why he hadn't provided the names before, he said he didn't consider the accounts "discretionary," whatever that meant. "He has a Clintonian definition of discretionary," Cheung commented.

"Or anything," Suh responded. "It still is not clear to me on what grounds he didn't disclose these accounts when we had that 'is there anything else' exchange of letters."

Madoff's testimony was replete with contradictions. He said he maintained segregated accounts with DTC; previously he'd said there was just one account. He said he traded options over-the-counter through the New York office, not in London, as he'd told Lamore before. He said he had electronic records of the options contracts; earlier he'd said no documentation existed. And with a firsthand witness who could contradict him sitting at the table, he had baldly denied he had told Lamore that he'd stopped trading options. Just about the only consistency was his assertion that "some people can just feel the market," a proposition that was, as Markopolos had asserted, dubious on its face.

Lamore thought there was enough to refer the case to the Justice Department immediately. At the least, Madoff was lying under oath, which begged the question of why. As Lamore put it, "So I'm sitting there thinking, You got to be kidding me. I mean, this is huge. This guy just lied on the record to your face." But the enforcement lawyers, especially Cheung and her superior, Bachenheimer, didn't seriously entertain the possibility. As Ostrow put it, "Peter [Lamore] was extremely upset that the [enforcement lawyers] weren't taking seriously the fact that everything was a lie. There were so many contradictions to what Bernie said in testimony or [DiPascali] said to what we were told on our exam." Suh later explained, "Meaghan [Cheung] did not think that this was likely to lead to an enforcement action or this was likely to lead to anything." Lamore was assigned to other matters and had no further involvement in the Madoff investigation.

At the least, the contradictions cried out for further investigation. A few relatively simple inquiries should be able to resolve the fundamental questions. The Depository Trust Company, as Madoff himself acknowledged, could verify the equities trading and demonstrate that the hedge fund assets were held in a segregated account. Now that Madoff had identified the dozen options counterparties, the enforcement staff had only to contact them to verify the massive number of contracts that Madoff traded. They needed to follow up on Madoff's promise to provide the "electronic" records of the options trades. Some simple fact-checking could establish whether over-the-counter options trades typically generated any paperwork or whether Madoff's assertion—that options volume in the over-the-counter market far exceeded that on the exchanges—was true. These tasks fell to Simona Suh.

But by now, the focus of the Madoff investigation appears to have shifted away from Markopolos's original attention-getting allegation—that Madoff was running a massive Ponzi scheme—to the far more technical issue of whether Madoff needed to register as an investment adviser. The staff was no longer even looking at front running. As Suh described the evolution of their inquiry in an e-mail in April:

> We initially began looking at BLM's institutional trading business because of suggestions in the press that the returns reported by BLM's customers were too good to be true and that BLM could be engaging in some improper conduct, such as front running or false reporting of returns. So far, we have not found evidence of any such wrongdoing. It does appear to us, however, that BLM's institutional trading business is actually [an] investment advisory business and that BLM should be registered with the Commission as an investment adviser.

Nonetheless, Suh did follow up on at least some of the outstanding issues from Madoff's testimony. She spoke by phone with Susan Geigel, director of legal and regulatory compliance at the DTC. This was a critical call, but later, Suh didn't remember making it, didn't remember the name of the person she spoke to, and had difficulty remembering the outcome. Suh seemed confused about just what the DTC did and how it maintained records, and solicited advice from Lamore about what questions to ask. He didn't seem to know any more than she did. When they did speak, Geigel apparently indicated there was only one account for Madoff at DTC, through which all the firm's trading was routed. Thus, Suh concluded it wasn't feasible to confirm any specific trades for Madoff's hedge fund clients, since they were commingled with the broker-dealer's trading.

This was a startling assertion whether or not it was true the DTC couldn't identify specific hedge fund transactions. (Geigel said she could have identified trades in specific stocks if Suh provided the CUSIP [Committee on Uniform Securities Identification Procedures] number, a nine-digit code that identifies every security, and which would have appeared on Madoff's trading records.) Commingling client funds in one account is illegal. It also undercut Madoff's claim that the accounts were segregated and that DTC would supply the account number for his institutional and hedge fund trading. And apart from whether any accounts were segregated, it didn't occur to Suh to check whether total trading volume or equities holdings in the single Madoff account on any given day matched the trading volume reported to Madoff's clients. For example, the Fairfield Greenwich account statement in Suh's possession showed that Fairfield held $2.5 billion in S&P 100 equities as of January 31, 2005. But DTC records showed that on the same date, the Madoff account with DTC held less than $18 million.

Considering her DTC approach at a dead end, Suh made no further inquiries. She didn't report the conversation to Cheung, who in turn never asked Suh whether she'd followed up with DTC, Bank of New York, or any other custodial or clearing entity.

Suh also commenced efforts to obtain trading records from the European banks Madoff had identified as his options counterparties. Ordinarily the SEC's Office of International Affairs (OIA) handled such requests, but Cheung advised her to contact their U.S. subsidiaries. "I hate the OIA—they are probably the slowest part of our bureaucracy, and that is saying a lot," Cheung noted.

UBS resisted, saying Suh would have to ask the parent in Switzerland. But Royal Bank of Scotland said it would provide the information, provided Madoff signed a consent letter giving his permission. In July an RBS lawyer drafted a letter for Madoff to sign and faxed Suh a copy. It was a significant step forward in the investigation, the closest anyone at the SEC had gotten to an actual counterparty to Madoff's options trades. If Madoff signed the letter, they'd get the records. If he refused to sign, it was anther red flag, a serious indication something must be amiss. Suh told the RBS lawyer that as a "courtesy," she might call Madoff to let him know he'd be getting the request.

Suh reported this development to Cheung, who said it was no longer anything they should pursue. "I spoke to Meaghan [Cheung] about it and asked whether we should pursue this, and she said no," Suh later recalled. (In response, Cheung said, "I don't believe that I unilaterally said, 'Stop it, we're done, that's enough.'" But Cheung's superior, Bachenheimer, said she had no recollection of Cheung ever raising the issue with her and couldn't imagine why Cheung didn't have RBS send Madoff the letter.) Cheung herself was later unable to recall why she blocked the effort, but it may have reflected what had become her single-minded focus on getting Madoff to register as an investment manager. "One possible reason is that given the scarcity of resources and the difficulty of obtaining such records, it made more sense" to pursue the investment manager issue "rather than persist in an investigation which thus far had not uncovered evidence of a Ponzi scheme," she later said—despite the fact that an enormous amount of evidence had surfaced. It may also have reflected her conviction, almost from the beginning, that the Madoff investigation wasn't going to lead to anything.

Whatever the reason, on July 27, Suh left a message for the RBS lawyer and, according to her phone log, "told him that we decided not to pursue the request at the moment and asked him not to send the letter to Madoff unless he hears from us again." He never did.

On August 10, 2006, Madoff agreed to register with the SEC as an investment adviser. He initially hired a lawyer, Brandon Becker, to dispute the enforcement staff's conclusion, but didn't seriously resist. Suh didn't pursue any other open issues from Madoff's testimony. The letter from RBS was never sent. Madoff never produced any electronic records of options trading, as he'd promised. "I overlooked that," Suh later admitted. "I kind of assumed we were done." Suh may also have been preoccupied by the fact she was pregnant with her first child. She went on maternity leave soon after Madoff agreed to register.

Suh returned to work in January 2007. While she was gone, a letter dated April 26, 2006, to the SEC chairman, Christopher Cox, had been forwarded to her attention:

Dear Sir:

Your attention is directed to a scandal of major proportion which was executed by the investment firm of Bernard L. Madoff, 885 Third Ave., New York, NY.

Assets well in excess of $10 billion owned by the late Norman F. Levy, an ultra-wealthy long time client of the Madoff firm, have been "co-mingled" with funds controlled by the Madoff Company with gains thereon being retained by Madoff. . . .

This is an extreme example of uncontrollable greed which should be investigated by the proper authorities.

Sincerely,
A concerned citizen.

Norman Levy, the chairman of Cross & Brown, a commercial real estate

firm in New York, and the owner of a vast real estate empire, had died at age
ninety-three in September 2005. Levy's offices were in the Lipstick Building
with Madoff's; Madoff was named an executor of his estate; and Madoff published a tribute to Levy in the *New York Times* after his death: "I'll cherish our
relationship forever." Suh checked the list of eighty-two individual friends and
family accounts that Madoff had provided. Norman Levy wasn't among them.

Suh reported this omission to Cheung, and called Brandon Becker, Madoff's
lawyer. No one contacted Levy's daughter, Jean Levy-Hinte, or son, Francis, who
oversaw the Betty and Norman F. Levy Foundation. Becker spoke to Madoff,
and reported to Suh that "Bernie says he has not managed money for Norman F.
Levy." Cheung wrote Suh: "Then I think we are done and do not have to worry
any further."

On January 11, Suh began gathering the Madoff files so she could formally
close the investigation. "I guess I can't wait to lay this case to rest," she e-mailed
a colleague. But closing the investigation was hardly a high priority. It was
inactive but still technically open six months later, when Markopolos, showing
remarkable persistence, sent another e-mail to Cheung:

"Hello Meaghan,

"Attached are some very troubling documents that show the Madoff fraud
is getting even more brazen. . . ."

The attachments were promotional materials from another hedge fund, the
Wickford Fund, which was leveraging an investment in Fairfield Sentry, which
in turn invested in Madoff.

"When Madoff finally does blow up, it's going to be spectacular, and lead
to massive selling by hedge funds, funds-of-funds, as they face investor redemptions," Markopolos warned.

No one at the SEC had ever figured out how Madoff managed to generate
his returns. But Cheung considered the Madoff case "for all intents and purposes" to be closed. Markopolos received no response.

Finally, on November 20, 2007, more than two years after Markopolos
had contacted the Boston office, Bachenheimer sent a brief letter to Becker,
Madoff's lawyer:

"This investigation has been completed as to Bernard L. Madoff Investment
Securities LLC and Bernard L. Madoff, against whom we do not intend to recommend any enforcement action by the Commission."

Madoff did register as an investment adviser. In a form he filed with the

SEC, he said Bernard L. Madoff Investment Securities had between eleven and twenty-five clients with assets of $17.1 billion.

On December 11, 2008, FBI special agent Theodore Cacioppi and another agent arrived at Madoff's apartment building on East Sixty-fourth Street at 8 a.m. They were hoping to interview him, and perhaps obtain a confession. But they brought no arrest warrant. He and his colleague identified themselves to the doorman, and Madoff invited them up to his apartment, where he greeted them in the marble-floored entry hall with a sweeping, curved staircase. He was wearing a robe and slippers, and seemed nervous. Madoff said he knew why they were there. "We're here to find out if there's an innocent explanation," Cacioppi said.

"There is no innocent explanation," Madoff replied.

Madoff led the agents into his study; they passed Ruth Madoff, who was elegantly dressed and seemed remarkably composed under the circumstances. And then, without any prompting, Madoff confessed: He had "traded and lost money for his clients," it was "all his fault," he "paid investors with money that wasn't there." Madoff said he had already admitted this to his brother, Peter, and his two sons, Mark and Andrew. Now he was "broke" and "insolvent," and "it couldn't go on," according to Cacioppi's notes of the meeting. The confession lasted forty-five minutes, and when it was over, Madoff seemed both "relieved and defeated," in Cacioppi's recollection.

Cacioppi told Madoff he'd have to accompany him to the courthouse that morning, and told him what not to wear: no belt, tie, or shoes with laces. No overcoat. Cacioppi waited for Madoff to dress, then escorted him to the car, where two other agents drove them to the FBI's Manhattan field office at 26 Federal Plaza. Only then did he call a lawyer, Ira Sorkin.

As all Ponzi schemes do eventually, Madoff's hedge fund business had collapsed under the weight of massive redemption requests. It had survived far longer than most, probably because most of his feeder funds and wealthy investors didn't need the money and few wanted to get out of an investment that brought them such generous and steady returns. But then Lehman Brothers had collapsed, the stock market plunged, and investors were suddenly panicking. They wanted security above else, and started pulling back from hedge funds and alternative investments of every variety. Existing investors wanted their money out, and potential new investors vanished. Among the feeder funds, Fairfield

Greenwich alone wanted to redeem $7 billion. On paper, Madoff's investors owned $65 billion in assets. In reality, Madoff had less than $300 million.

Madoff had tried to pay what little was left to favored employees, friends, and relatives. He transferred $15.5 million to his wife, Ruth. Two days before, he had told his son Mark that he wanted to pay employee bonuses in December, rather than the usual February. He'd written out $173 million in checks. Mark thought this seemed odd, reported it to Andrew, and the next day the brothers met with their father in his office to ask about it. Madoff calmly said he'd recently made some profits on "business operations" and it seemed a good time to distribute them.

This made no sense—Wall Street was reeling from the Lehman collapse and its aftermath. Bonuses were being slashed. Mark and Andrew knew that Madoff ran an investment advisory business located on the seventeenth floor and separate from the broker-dealer and market-making business. He'd always been cryptic about it, keeping the financial statements "under lock and key," according to Mark. The brothers thought that Madoff had about $8 billion to $15 billion under management. The first week in December, Madoff had told Andrew about Fairfield's request to withdraw $7 billion, said he was "struggling" to meet it, although he thought he'd be able to. And now, just days later, he wanted to pay out $173 million in bonuses?

When pressed, Madoff's façade crumbled. He was overcome by emotion and had trouble composing himself. Finally he said he "wasn't sure he'd be able to hold it together" if the discussion continued at the office.

Madoff and his two sons retreated to Madoff's apartment, where Madoff broke down and sobbed. He was "finished," he said as his sons listened in stunned silence. He had "nothing. It's all just one big lie." He admitted that "basically, it's a giant Ponzi scheme." He thought the total losses would be about $50 billion.

Madoff said he'd already confessed to his brother, Peter. He planned to turn himself in in a week, and in the meantime wanted to give the $200 million–$300 million he had left to employees, family, and friends. In other words, he wanted to continue the fraud and deprive his investors of what little they had left. Mark and Andrew went to a lawyer at Paul, Weiss, Rifkind, Wharton & Garrison, who immediately contacted the U.S. Attorney's office. FBI agent Cacioppi debriefed the brothers the next morning, and then Cacioppi went to arrest their father.

. . .

Given the multitude of lies Madoff had told the SEC, there was no reason to believe that the statement he filed as an investment adviser was any different. One of Madoff's (and DiPascali's) more flagrant lies was that they had only fifteen to twenty clients, all of them hedge funds and institutions. Contrary to Madoff's assertion to Becker and the SEC, Norman F. Levy had not only been a mentor and father figure to Madoff; he'd been one of his earliest and most important clients. His foundation's $244 million in assets were invested with Madoff.

Madoff, in fact, had 4,800 clients with reported assets under management of $64.8 billion. These included the large feeder funds like Fairfield Greenwich, which in turn had many thousands of clients. *Time* magazine estimated that the total number of Madoff victims worldwide would reach three million people.

As the shock waves from Madoff's arrest emanated from Manhattan to Long Island; Greenwich, Connecticut; Palm Beach; London; and Madrid, and then rippled throughout the financial system, the damages and victim toll mounted. Though hedge fund investors were supposed to be wealthy and sophisticated (the main reason they aren't regulated more intensively), Madoff's victims came from every walk of life, from Hollywood royalty like Steven Spielberg and Jeffrey Katzenberg to retired schoolteachers and police officers. Tragically, many had all their assets invested with Madoff and stood to lose their life savings.

On March 12, 2009, Madoff appeared before U.S. district court judge Denny Chin in the same building where Martha Stewart was tried. He wore a dark gray suit, a white shirt, and a lighter gray tie, his silver-tinged hair swept back from his forehead. He looked thinner, but still distinguished. The twenty-fourth-floor courtroom in the federal courthouse in lower Manhattan was packed with lawyers, reporters, and many of Madoff's victims. Madoff stood before the judge. He was charged with eleven felony counts: securities fraud, perjury, false statements, and eight related charges.

"How do you plead, guilty or not guilty?" Judge Chin asked.

"Guilty," Madoff answered in an almost inaudible voice.

"Try to keep your voice up," the judge admonished him. "Mr. Madoff, tell me what you did."

"Your Honor, for many years up until my arrest on December 11, 2008, I operated a Ponzi scheme. . . . I am actually grateful for this first opportunity to publicly speak about my crimes, for which I am deeply sorry and ashamed. As I engaged in my fraud, I knew what I was doing was wrong, indeed criminal. When I began the Ponzi scheme I believed it would end shortly and I would be able to extricate myself and my clients from the scheme. However, this proved difficult, and ultimately impossible, and as the years went by I realized that my arrest and this day would inevitably come. I am painfully aware that I have deeply hurt many, many people, including the members of my family, my closest friends, business associates, and the thousands of clients who gave me their money. I cannot adequately express how sorry I am."

Madoff said his scheme began in the early 1990s, during a recession, and that clients had given him their money expecting him to outperform the market. He promised to use his split-strike conversion strategy to achieve superior results and instead simply deposited their money in Chase Manhattan Bank, periodically withdrawing it to meet redemptions and for his own purposes. Apart from the window dressing of Madoff's strategy, it was a simple Ponzi scheme.

Madoff readily acknowledged that perjury and false statements were essential to continuing the scheme. "I knowingly gave false testimony under oath" during his 2006 SEC interrogation and "filed false and misleading certified audit reports and financial statements with the SEC." When he was finally required to register as an investment adviser, "I falsely and intentionally certified under penalty of perjury that [I] had custody of my advisory clients' securities. That was not true and I knew it."

Madoff stressed that his fraud was confined to Bernard Madoff Investment Securities, his hedge fund advisory business, and not the market-making or proprietary trading aspects of Bernard Madoff Securities, in what seemed an obvious effort to shield his employees and family members. And then he was done. "I hope I have conveyed with some particularity in my own words the crimes I committed and the means by which I committed them."

Judge Chin accepted Madoff's plea and revoked his bail. Madoff was handcuffed and led outside to a hallway and the adjacent Metropolitan Correctional Center, the federal prison in lower Manhattan, to await sentencing.

On December 16, SEC chairman Christopher Cox had announced an internal investigation into the SEC's failure to detect the Madoff fraud, and referred the matter to David Kotz, the SEC's inspector general. Kotz, age forty-two, a lawyer and Cornell graduate, had served in a similar capacity for the Peace Corps. He'd joined the SEC a year earlier, well after the investigation of Madoff had been closed. After months of negotiations with Madoff's lawyers, Madoff had agreed to be interviewed, and on the afternoon of June 17, Kotz and a colleague from the SEC arrived at the Metropolitan Correctional Center. Madoff wore the standard-issue orange jumpsuit and was flanked by his lawyer, Ira Sorkin, and one of Sorkin's associates. Sorkin warned his client that he was under oath and his only obligation was to tell the truth—not that it mattered much, given the magnitude of the crimes to which Madoff had already confessed.

Madoff was expansive and seemed almost eager to unburden himself of the secrets he had held so long. He complained that the prosecutor "misunderstood" things he'd said, and as a result, there was a lot of misinformation about his case. Still, "I'm not saying I'm not guilty," he said.

The Ponzi scheme had been going on so long Madoff had trouble remembering exactly how it had started. But as best he could recall, he'd begun in 1992. Originally he pursued a common, low-risk strategy trading convertible securities. But so many hedge funds piled into the strategy that returns soon shrank to practically nothing. "I made commitments for too much money and then I couldn't put the strategy to work," he told Kotz. "I had a European bank, I was doing forward conversion, they were doing reverse conversion." He hadn't promised any specific returns, but thought he'd equal his typical returns. "When that didn't happen, I thought, Fine, I'll just generate those trades and then the market will come back and I'll make it back . . . and it never happened. It was my mistake not to just be out a couple hundred million dollars and get out if it." But there were actually trades, albeit money-losing ones. Soon after, Madoff conceived his split-strike conversion strategy, but there were never any trades. Madoff said he simply deposited clients' money into an account at Chase Manhattan Bank, and his back office on the seventeenth floor generated fake trading statements.

Madoff said he was "astonished" that the SEC's enforcement investigation hadn't exposed his fraud, and added there were two times when he "thought the jig was up": during the on-site exam by Lamore and Ostrow, because he thought they'd check with third parties, and when Suh asked him for his DTC account number, and he assumed the SEC would go to the DTC. "I thought it was the end game, over," he said. "Monday morning they'll call DTC and this will be over . . . and it never happened. After all this, I got away lucky." Still, he knew it was just a matter of time, and if not this time, then the next. "This was the nightmare I lived with," he said.

Madoff indulged his disdain for Lamore and Ostrow, referring them dismissively as "two young fellows" who "didn't understand what they were looking for." He was especially annoyed by Ostrow, who "came in here like Columbo" and wasted his time looking at canceled checks. He said he was "astonished" they didn't go to either the DTC or his purported trading counterparties. "It would've been easy for them to see," he said. "They didn't do any of that . . . if you're looking at a Ponzi scheme it's the first thing you do." He readily acknowledged lying to them when he said he didn't manage money, but said, "At this point I was trying to conceal." He added, "After two months, they found two or three nitpicky things, and they were wrong about those things."

As for the enforcement investigation led by Cheung and Suh, he said he thought they asked the right questions, and even got his DTC number. At his deposition, "it was obvious they thought something was amiss." But they never asked him about his accounting firm, which surprised him. And the idea that he was running a massive Ponzi scheme seemed "inconceivable to them." He thought this was "probably because of the reputation I had." They'd think, "Why would this guy do a Ponzi scheme? Of course they'd be shocked it was a Ponzi. They'd be astonished."

Madoff didn't hire a lawyer, he said, because "I didn't think I needed one. I had good answers for everything." Indeed, he seemed eager yet again to extol the virtues of his split-strike conversion strategy. He said everything he'd told Lamore, Ostrow, and the enforcement lawyers about his computer model was true. Even so, "You still need to have a gut feel. It's a combination of technology and a trader's feel, and I was a good trader." He continued, "Credible people knew it could be done or else they wouldn't be clients. All you have to do is look at the types of people I was doing this for to know it was a credible strategy. They knew the strategy was doable, and they knew a lot more than this guy Harry," referring to Markopolos. Madoff was contemptuous of Markopolos, who thought he was some kind of "seer," Madoff said, when in reality he was a "joke in the industry," someone who was just "jealous" of Madoff.

It was almost as if Madoff had forgotten he'd never actually executed any such strategy, and that it only produced the returns it did because fake records were generated with benefit of hindsight and perfect market timing. At one point, Madoff even insisted the client statements he generated, copies of which he'd given the SEC, weren't false, evidently because such trades could have been executed.

"Wait a minute," Kotz interjected. "Weren't those documents false?"

"No," Madoff said.

"If you provided documents that showed trading activity, and you didn't conduct any, wouldn't that be false?" Kotz asked.

Madoff paused. "Yes, I guess I can see how you might see it that way," he conceded.

Kotz had agreed in advance not to ask Madoff questions about who else knew about or participated in the fraud, since investigations into that question were continuing. But Madoff repeatedly volunteered that his wife and family members knew nothing. Kotz did ask if Madoff was worried when DiPascali was subpoenaed to testify, and Madoff said, "No, he didn't know anything was wrong, either."

Madoff said he "was worried every time" he heard from the SEC and "it was a nightmare for me," because "it was very basic stuff. I wish they had caught me six years ago, eight years ago. I got myself into a terrible situation. It's a nightmare . . . the thing I feel the worst about besides the people losing money is that I set the industry back. I'm very proud of the role I played in the industry," he said. "Of course I've destroyed that now."

Madoff's lies hadn't stopped in prison, despite his lawyer's admonition that he was under oath. He had not acted alone, as he'd insisted, nor was DiPascali an innocent bystander. DiPascali was intimately involved in nearly every aspect of the Ponzi scheme. He oversaw execution of the fictitious split-strike conversion strategy, made sure the phantom trades and volume—chosen by DiPascali with benefit of hindsight to achieve the desired returns—corresponded to actual prices and trading on exchanges, made sure that the phony returns matched what Madoff had promised his clients, and generated thousands of pages of fake trading records and account statements. The reason it took Madoff "several days" to "execute" the equities trades, which had puzzled Lamore, wasn't because modern trading platforms couldn't handle the volume, as Madoff had implied. It was because there wasn't enough real volume on any given day to cover the massive volume Madoff pretended to be trading, should anyone try to match his purported trades with actual volume. Madoff, who could barely use a computer himself, anxiously called DiPascali several times a day for updates on the fake strategy's results. Madoff had coached DiPascali before his 2006 testimony, and DiPascali admitted that virtually everything he told the SEC at Madoff's behest was a lie.

Madoff returned to Judge Chin's courtroom for sentencing on June 29. Nine of his victims spoke, and it was an extraordinary outpouring of grief, loss, betrayal, and anger. They called Madoff a "monster," a "beast," "the most despised person in America," and tearfully described the devastation he'd inflicted on their lives. But they made clear their anger wasn't directed only at Madoff. They also felt their government had failed and betrayed them.

Maureen Ebel, a sixty-one-year-old widow: "I have lost all of my life's hardearned savings because our government has failed me and thousands and thousands of other victims. . . . The Securities and Exchange Commission, by its total incompetence and criminal negligence, has allowed a psychopath to steal from me and steal from the world."

Carla Hirschhorn, a physical therapist: "Since December 11, 2008, my life has been a living hell. . . . We were devastated by the SEC failure to uncover Madoff's fraud and its continued stamp of approval behind Madoff over the decades of his crime."

Miriam Siegman, sixty-five years old, living on food stamps: "Victims became the byproduct of his greed. We are what is left over, the result of stunning indifference . . . of politicians and bureaucrats."

Sheryl Weinstein, former chief financial officer of Hadassah, forced to sell her home: "We, the victims, are greatly disappointed by the agencies that were set up to protect us. . . . The SEC appears to have looked the other way on numerous occasions."

With the echoes of their voices still in the room, Judge Chin offered Madoff the chance to speak. He rose and faced the judge, his back to the audience.

"Your Honor, I cannot offer you an excuse for my behavior. How do you excuse betraying thousands of investors who entrusted me with their life savings? How do you excuse deceiving two hundred employees who have spent most of their working life working for me? How do you excuse lying to your brother and two sons who spent their whole adult life helping to build a successful and respectable business? How do you excuse lying to and deceiving a wife who stood by you for fifty years and still stands by you? And how do you excuse deceiving an industry that you spent the better part of your life trying to improve? There is no excuse for that, and I don't ask any forgiveness."

Madoff said again that when he started the Ponzi scheme, he thought he'd soon extricate himself, and meant no harm. But as the scheme grew, "I couldn't admit that failure and that was a tragic mistake. . . . I live in a tormented state now knowing all the pain and suffering that I have created . . . I will live with this pain, this torment, the rest of my life. I apologize to my victims. I will turn and face them," which he did. "I'm sorry," he said. "I know that doesn't help you." And then he sat down.

Lisa Baroni, an assistant U.S. attorney, spoke for the government. "This defendant carried out a fraud of unprecedented proportion over the course of more than a generation. For more than twenty years he stole ruthlessly and without remorse. Thousands of people put their trust in him and he lied repeatedly to all of them. . . . He destroyed a lifetime of hard work of thousands of victims. And he used the victims' money to enrich himself and his family, with an opulent lifestyle, homes around the world, yachts, private jets . . .

"This was not a crime born of any financial distress or market pressures. It was a calculated, well-orchestrated, long-term fraud, that this defendant carried out month after month, year after year, decade after decade. He created literally hundreds of thousands of fake documents every year. Every time he told his clients that he was making trades for them he sent them trade confirmations filled with lies. At every month end he sent them account statements that were nothing but lies. . . . In doing so he drove charities, companies, pension plans and families to economic ruin.

"In sum, for running an investment advisory business that was a complete fraud, for betraying his clients for decades, for repeatedly lying to regulators to cover up his fraud, for the staggering harm that he has inflicted on thousands of people—for all of these reasons and all the reasons Your Honor heard so eloquently from the victims, the government respectfully requests that the Court sentence the defendant to 150 years in prison . . . that ensures he will spend the rest of his life in jail."

Judge Chin began by saying he would try to reach a "just and proportionate sentence," unswayed by "all the emotion in the air." But, "objectively speaking, the fraud here is staggering." However calculated, the monetary losses "are off the charts by many fold. . . . The breach of trust was massive. Investors—individuals, charities, pension funds, institutional clients—were repeatedly lied to. . . . Investors made important life decisions based on these fictitious account statements—when to retire, how to care for elderly parents, whether to buy a car or sell a house, how to save for their children's college tuition . . . Mr. Madoff also repeatedly lied to the SEC and the regulators, in writing and in sworn testimony . . . to cover up his scheme.

"In a white-collar fraud case such as this, I would expect to see letters from family and friends and colleagues. But not a single letter has been submitted attesting to Mr. Madoff's good deeds or good character or civic and charitable activities [nor were any relatives in the courtroom]. The absence of such support is telling."

Judge Chin acknowledged that given the seventy-one-year-old Madoff's life expectancy of twelve or thirteen years, any sentence greater than twenty years was largely symbolic. "But symbolism is important. . . . Mr. Madoff's crimes are extraordinarily evil" and took "a staggering human toll. . . . The message must be sent that in a society governed by the rule of law, Mr. Madoff will get what he deserves, and that he will be punished according to his moral culpability."

As for the victims, Judge Chin noted that they came from all walks of life, and cited letters from a retired forest worker, a corrections officer, an auto mechanic, and an eighty-six-year-old retired New York City school secretary. He said he was "particularly struck" by one woman who told him she went to see Madoff after her husband died of a heart attack. Two weeks before, her husband had given the couple's entire savings to Madoff. Madoff had put his arm around her. "The money is safe with me," he'd said.

"More is at stake than money," Judge Chin continued. "The victims put their trust in Mr. Madoff. That trust was broken in a way that has left many—victims as well as others—doubting our financial institutions, our financial system, our government's ability to regulate and protect, and, sadly, even themselves.

"Mr. Madoff, please stand."

Madoff rose, steadying himself with his hands on the table in front of him.

"It is the judgment of this court that the defendant, Bernard L. Madoff, shall be and hereby is sentenced to a term of 150 years."

David Kotz completed his investigation of the SEC's various Madoff investigations and issued a detailed and unsparing 457-page report in August 2009. It should be required reading for every current and future staff member of the agency. Kotz concluded that there was no "misconduct" or inappropriate influence exerted on any individual staff member. Rather, the staff "never took the necessary and basic steps to determine if Madoff was misrepresenting his trading," and "there were systematic breakdowns" in the investigation, which, if anything, seems an understatement. The SEC's entire approach to investigating fraud needs a thorough overhaul, starting with training its enforcement staff on the rudiments of securities trading. Beyond Kotz's report, the Madoff failure suggests a broader problem of culture at the agency: there was simply no zeal for exposing wrongdoers. Too many just wanted to close cases. They narrowed the investigations to minor technical issues rather than confront the possibility of massive fraud. They didn't reach out to the Renaissance officials and treated Harry Markopolos as a meddlesome fortune-seeker who was making their lives more difficult. They seemed more interested in proving him wrong than in catching criminals. They didn't seem to care about the public they were hired to protect.

Still, for all the missteps by the SEC, it came amazingly close to catching Madoff. Thomas Thanasules deserves a promotion and recognition for spotting the Madoff issues in the Renaissance e-mails and bringing them to the attention of his superiors. Michael Garrity and others in the Boston office also showed genuine enthusiasm and an investigative bent. Would that their instincts had extended further into the agency.

When Simona Suh was on the phone with the compliance officer from the Depository Trust Company, she was only one question away from exposing the biggest fraud in history: What was Madoff's total trading volume in his DTC account? And had she allowed the Royal Bank of Scotland to send the letter it had already drafted, that might well have established that Madoff had no counterparties, and that the options trades were fake. She came close to exposing the Madoff fraud. But then, incredibly, she stopped. Meaghan Cheung had evidently already made up her mind that the investigation was a "fishing expedition," as she later put it, and getting an eminent Wall Street figure like Madoff to register as an investment adviser was accomplishment enough.

Ostrow and Lamore, for all their inexperience, were also well on their way to contacting Madoff's alleged counterparties when John Nee pulled the rug from under them. And Lamore wanted to pursue perjury charges, but was brushed aside by the enforcement lawyers, who of all people should have taken Madoff's false statements seriously. Had the case been referred to the U.S. Attorney's office for a perjury and false statement investigation, the scheme would almost certainly have been uncovered. As Eckenrode demonstrated in the Libby case by immediately calling Tim Russert, the first step in any perjury investigation is to test the suspect's veracity by verifying information attributed to others. After Madoff was arrested, the SEC was able to verify his fraud with just one phone call to the DTC.

John Nee remains an assistant director in the SEC's New York office. He has declined comment on all aspects of the investigation. Meaghan Cheung left the SEC in September 2008, before the Madoff scandal broke, to care for her two children. In her only public comment since, she told the *New York Post*, her eyes "tearing up":

"Why are you taking a mid-level staff person and making me responsible for the failure of the American economy? I worked very hard for ten years to make a career and a reputation, and that has been destroyed in a month."

As of late 2010, two years after the Madoff scandal broke, the SEC had taken no disciplinary or other measure against anyone involved in the various Madoff investigations. The SEC officials' collective failure is, as Madoff himself put it, astonishing. It will surely rank as one of the greatest regulatory failures ever, not just because of the size of the fraud, but because it was staring them in the face.

James Simons, the founder of Renaissance, whose 2004 e-mails set the investigation of Madoff in motion, directed $8 million of the state university's money to Madoff while he was chairman of the Stony Brook Foundation. Stony Brook was thus one of Madoff's first investors, at a time when Madoff denies the fraud had even started. The university and Simons were also powerful drawing cards for other investors. The *Wall Street Journal* reported that in 2004, soon after the Renaissance e-mails raised questions about Madoff, the university withdrew $3.5 million at Simons's behest, and that Simons had urged that the entire investment be liquidated. Other members of the board overruled him. Neither Simons nor anyone else at Renaissance ever raised concerns with the SEC. Simons retired from Renaissance in 2010 with a net worth estimated by *Forbes* at $8.5 billion.

When news of Madoff's arrest broke, Harry Markopolos was waiting for his sons at karate practice. His years of skepticism and perseverance had been vindicated. Soon television crews were camped on his front lawn, and as he later put it, "my phone never stopped ringing." "I was living on adrenaline. I couldn't sleep." Markopolos was profiled on the front page of the *Wall Street Journal* on December 18; a Hollywood producer told him he could get him $1 million if he appeared on *Oprah* (an approach he rejected) and he appeared on *60 Minutes*. He testified in Congress. Markopolos went overnight from being an obscure accountant who was rebuffed by the SEC to the star of a real-life Frank Capra movie, "Mr. Markopolos Goes to Washington." In 2010, Markopolos published a book about his experience, *No One Would Listen*.

· · ·

Frank DiPascali appeared before Judge Richard J. Sullivan in federal district court in Manhattan on August 11, 2009. "I am standing here today to say that from the early 1990s until December of 2008 I helped Bernie Madoff and other people carry out the fraud that hurt thousands of people. I am guilty and I want to explain a little bit about what I did and how I want everybody to know that I take responsibility for my conduct," he said.

"Judge, I started working for Bernard Madoff Investment Securities in 1975 right after I graduated from high school. I was a kid from Queens. I didn't have a college degree. I didn't know anything about Wall Street. I ended up spending the next thirty years working for Bernie Madoff and his firm. . . . During that first fifteen or so years, I watched Bernie Madoff and other people at the firm. I learned how the securities industry worked, or at least how it worked in the Madoff universe. I thought I worked for a prestigious and successful securities firm.

"By 1990 or so Bernie Madoff was a mentor to me and a lot more. I was loyal to him. I ended up being loyal to a terrible, terrible fault. . . . From at least the early 1990s through December of 2008, there was one simple fact that Bernie Madoff knew, that I knew, and that other people knew but that we never told the clients nor did we tell the regulators like the SEC. No purchases or sales of securities were actually taking place in their accounts. It was all fake. It was all fictitious. It was wrong and I knew it was wrong at the time, sir."

DiPascali specifically addressed the issue of perjury: "On January 26, 2006, at Bernie Madoff's direction, I lied to the SEC during testimony I gave under oath in Manhattan about the activities of the Madoff firm."

Were these in fact false statements? Judge Sullivan asked. And did DiPascali know at the time they were false?

"Yes, Your Honor," he replied. "I knew at the time I was describing it, it was entirely fraudulent."

"You did this to mislead the SEC?"

"Yes, sir."

"For what purpose?"

"To throw them off their tracks, sir."

"Did you have the sense they were on the track?"

"Yes, sir. . . . Your Honor, while this was going on, I knew no trades were happening. I knew I was participating in a fraudulent scheme. I knew what was happening was criminal and I did it anyway. I thought for a long time that Bernie

Madoff had other assets that he could liquidate if the clients requested the return of their money. That is not an excuse. There is no excuse. I knew everything I did was wrong and it was criminal and I did it knowingly and willfully. I regret everything that I did . . . I don't know how I went from an eighteen-year-old kid happy to have a job to someone standing before the court today. I can only say I never wanted to hurt anyone. I apologize to every victim of this catastrophe and to my family and to the government. I am very, very sorry."

DiPascali signed a cooperation agreement with the government. His sentencing was deferred until the investigation of Madoff family members, employees, and others was complete.

A court-appointed trustee liquidated Madoff Securities. All of Madoff's assets were sold, including the houses, the yacht, and the boats. Madoff agreed to surrender $170 million in personal assets and investments, and his wife, Ruth, gave up $80 million pursuant to an agreement that allowed her to keep $2.5 million. By late 2010 Irving Picard, the trustee overseeing Madoff's estate, had recovered about $1.5 billion for Madoff's victims, a small fraction of the $65 billion they thought they had. Picard filed thousands of suits seeking a total of about $50 billion, but many defendants, such as JPMorgan Chase, vowed to fight the allegations and the trustee seemed likely to recoup only a fraction of the victims' losses.

Picard filed a lawsuit claiming $200 million against Madoff's brother, Peter; his sons, Mark and Andrew; and his niece Shana, who, according to Picard, earned a combined $141 million during the last six months before Madoff's arrest. Their assets, which include luxurious multimillion-dollar Manhattan apartments, were frozen pending resolution of the case. Ruth also agreed to a freeze of her remaining assets. Madoff continues to insist that none of them knew anything about his fraud, though given his track record, it's hard to take such claims seriously.

After their father's confession, Mark and Andrew Madoff had no further contact with him, nor, on advice of their lawyer, did they speak to their mother. Friends said Mark was especially distressed by the proliferating lawsuits, his inability to find work on Wall Street, and speculation that he and other family members knew about his father's fraud. On December 11, 2010, the two-year anniversary of Madoff's confession, Mark Madoff committed suicide by hanging himself with his dog's leash. His wife was out of town and his two-year-old son was sleeping nearby. His lawyer said Mark "was an innocent victim of his father's monstrous crime who succumbed to two years of unrelenting pressure from false accusations and innuendo."

Bernie Madoff entered the federal prison in Butler, North Carolina, a minimum-to-medium-security prison northwest of the Raleigh-Durham area, on July 13, 2009. The facilities are sufficiently comfortable that the camp has earned the nickname "Camp Fluffy," and it is known for its medical facilities.

Judged by the duration and magnitude of his fraud, Madoff would seem the most cunning and skilled of liars. That's what David Kotz assumed when he began his investigation of the SEC's failure to expose Madoff. "I assumed Madoff was a genius, a master, that nobody would have had a prayer of figuring him out," Kotz said. But in fact, Madoff was no better than average, if that. Written records flatly contradicted his lies, had anyone bothered to check them. He repeatedly changed his story on numerous points: whether he did or didn't trade options; whether his accounts were or weren't segregated; whether he did or didn't man-age money for individuals; who did or didn't handle his trading; how many cli-ents he had and how much money he managed. Madoff had the temerity to lie about what he said to Lamore to Lamore's face. "He wasn't a good liar," Kotz concluded. "He couldn't keep his story straight. He was no evil genius."

In the end, it's impossible to quantify the damage Madoff's lies did, not just to his immediate victims but to an already fragile financial system or to stock prices, which plunged to new lows in the months after his arrest. By December 2008 the economy was already in recession and stock prices were falling precipi-tously. But Madoff's lies further shattered public confidence in the stock mar-ket, which surely cost investors untold billions in additional losses. His crimes also undermined public trust in financial institutions and the government's ability to regulate them, an incalculable loss that is still being suffered by us all.

Madoff hasn't given any press interviews since entering prison. *New York* magazine reporter Steve Fishman interviewed numerous inmates for glimpses of his life there, finding that Madoff was a celebrity among the prisoners and blamed his victims for pushing their money on him. "I carried them for twenty years, and now I'm doing 150 years," Madoff complained to another inmate, Fishman reported.

After prison authorities informed Madoff about his son's suicide, his lawyer said Madoff wouldn't seek permission to attend any funeral "out of consider-ation for the family's privacy."

Conclusion

P erjury clearly poses a threat to the judicial system and the administration of justice. But the importance of truth—and the risks posed by perjury—transcend even an institution as vital as the judicial system, as I hope the stories of Martha Stewart, Scooter Libby, Barry Bonds, Bernie Madoff, and their victims make clear. False statements have a direct, immediate, and often devastating impact, not only on those who make them but on those closest to them, their friends and families; on their colleagues, allies, and supporters; on all who rely on their word; on the ideals of fair play, integrity, and trust to which people of goodwill everywhere aspire; and ultimately to the very moral fabric of the society in which we live.

There are, of course, circumstances in which lying, even lying under oath, is not only justified but morally imperative. Surely no one would expect the Dutch family that concealed and protected Anne Frank from the Nazis to answer truthfully that a Jewish family was living in the attic, even if lying to the Gestapo was a crime. But such occasions are extraordinary. As Harvard distinguished fellow Sissela Bok demonstrates in her penetrating philosophical analysis, *Lying,* such cases are probably even more rare than most of us realize. Lies and deceptive practices "are not immutable," she concludes. "In an imperfect world, they cannot be wiped out altogether; but surely they can be reduced and counteracted. . . . Trust and integrity are precious resources, easily squandered, hard to regain. They can thrive only on a foundation of respect for veracity."

To the extent that any of the characters in this book offered any justification for their lies, the most common was loyalty. Peter Bacanovic told Douglas

Faneuil that he would never betray Martha Stewart. Scooter Libby may have lied to protect a White House besieged by criticism. Greg Anderson initially lied, and then refused to testify, even after being jailed, to protect Barry Bonds. Even Bernie Madoff lied after his Ponzi scheme collapsed to protect his collaborator DiPascali and, perhaps, his wife and family members. They evidently expect to be admired for this behavior. There's no question that close kinship of whatever sort—father and son, employer and employee, professional and client, even trainer and athlete—can promote deep and lasting bonds. But do they justify lying under oath? Surely not. To elevate loyalty over truth is to revert to the rule of the tribe or clan, where power and brute force decide all conflicts. It seems fitting that a group of prison inmates would give Anderson a standing ovation for his silence.

And shouldn't loyalty be reciprocal? What concern—let alone loyalty—did Peter Bacanovic or Martha Stewart show toward Douglas Faneuil, whose life to them seemed to be little more than collateral damage? What loyalty has Barry Bonds shown Greg Anderson, who went to jail on his behalf? Why hasn't Bonds publicly demanded that Anderson testify and tell the truth instead of insisting that Anderson is to blame for the fact that he unwittingly used creams that turned out to be steroids? And what favors did Bernie Madoff do for Frank DiPascali, who came to him an impressionable eighteen-year-old and now faces the prospect of life in prison?

Troy Ellerman never offered any justification for deceiving the court about leaking grand jury testimony to the press, but perhaps he could have appealed to a higher cause, which was the public's right to know about steroid use and cheating in professional sports. But that confuses the act of leaking information with lying about it. Ellerman didn't have to answer whether he was the reporters' source. He certainly didn't have to submit a sworn affidavit. If pressed, he could have invoked the Fifth Amendment, which is every citizen's right. If he truly believed in his cause, he could have acknowledged that he defied the order of confidentiality and taken his case to the public. Instead, having done the deed, he took the cowardly approach, which was to lie about it, and place two reporters at imminent risk of jail. Ellerman could have been speaking for many of the characters in this book when he told the judge, "Once you lie you have to continue to lie."

To return to the question I posed at the beginning: Why did these accomplished, celebrated, successful, wealthy leaders and role models risk so much by lying under oath? Why did they do it?

It's possible, as clinical psychologist Martha Stout argues in *The Sociopath Next Door*, that highly successful people are in fact *more* likely to lie and take risks than average people. The American Psychiatric Association defines "deceitfulness" and "manipulativeness" as essential elements of an antisocial personality disorder as well as "lack of remorse after having hurt, mistreated, or stolen from another person." Sociopathic personalities "have a greater than normal need for stimulation, which results in their taking frequent social, physical, financial, or legal risks," Stout writes, and many succeed. "Characteristically, they can charm others into attempting dangerous ventures with them, and as a group they are known for their pathological lying and conning, and their parasitic relationships with 'friends.'" It doesn't take a sociopath to manifest many of these same traits, as some of these examples make clear.

Other people are also more likely to assist successful, famous people in lying under oath. In each of these examples, enablers played a significant role. David Marcus, the in-house lawyer at Merrill Lynch, had every reason to be suspicious of Bacanovic, whether or not he had the mistaken belief that the government would "look the other way" if they delivered the Waksals on a "silver platter." Perhaps he and other Merrill officials were simply unwilling to confront a successful broker, let alone their office's most celebrated client.

In another glaring abdication of responsibility, if Libby can be believed, he tried to tell Vice President Dick Cheney the full details of his interaction with reporters on the subject of Valerie Plame, and Cheney held up his hand, indicating he didn't want to hear about it, embracing a "don't ask, don't tell" policy. Cheney should have gotten the facts and immediately ordered Libby to disclose the full story to the Justice Department, thereby sparing the administration a far worse scandal—Libby's trial and conviction—than the Plame affair, which would have soon blown over. And President Bush, when confronted with evidence that his top aide Karl Rove had lied to *him*—did nothing.

Barry Bonds's alleged use of illegal steroids seemed obvious to trainers in the Giants organization, to management, and should have been obvious to team owner Peter Magowan and baseball commissioner Bud Selig. No one wanted to confront him or jeopardize the box-office appeal of a home run king. Even now, after a perjury indictment against Bonds, Selig claims he needs more evidence before restoring the crown to its rightful owner, Hank Aaron.

Madoff benefited from a bevy of enablers who were only too happy to reap the hundreds of millions in fees he generated for them while his lies persisted. Any doubts were evidently overwhelmed by Madoff's reputation, his track record, and above all, his sure and steady returns. Fairfield Greenwich's managing director, Amit Vijayvergiya, conferred with Madoff two days before his testimony and then followed the party line, failing to mention that Madoff began by stating "this conversation never happened." Nor did he volunteer the document indicating that options actually were part of the model, or at least had been until Madoff said otherwise. Fairfield had the detailed trading records indicating that Madoff moved in and out of the market with extraordinary timing, yet never seriously challenged Madoff's vague, even ludicrous, explanations for his success. A Fairfield spokesman counters that Vijayvergiya "respected–worshipped might be too strong a word–Madoff," which was understandable based on Madoff's reputation, stature in the industry, performance record, and the thousands of trading records Vijayvergiya had reviewed. "He believed everything Madoff said," and had no reason to suspect otherwise, the spokesman said.

Other feeder funds should also have known what was obvious to Markopolos, Renaissance, and others, which was that Madoff's returns were too high and consistent to be true and there wasn't enough trading volume to support his purported strategy. Even the Renaissance officials, who were skeptical of Madoff and withdrew their own investment with him, failed to take their suspicions to regulators.

These cases also illustrate that criminal defense lawyers have much to answer for. To his credit, Rove's lawyer Robert Luskin promptly revealed a damaging e-mail and had Rove amend his earlier testimony that he didn't speak to *Time*'s Matt Cooper. But other defense lawyers allowed their clients to lie in circumstances where they knew or should have known they were doing so. Lawyers are ethically bound to withdraw from representing clients they know are lying under oath. But the prevailing standard seems to be that unless defense lawyers know to a 100 percent certainty that their clients are lying, they are free to turn a blind eye.

A society that depends only on prosecutors and the judicial system to curb perjury will never succeed. It must be stopped when it happens, by others who recognize it for what it is and condemn it. It requires a capacity for moral outrage. We need more Harry Markopoloses.

But the ultimate responsibility for lying rests with the liar. In Martha Stewart's case, despite thousands of pages of testimony and exhibits, we still don't know whether lying was Stewart's idea, or whether she was going along with a scheme proposed by Peter Bacanovic, or some combination of the two. They both had motives–Bacanovic to protect his job, Stewart to avoid insider trading charges–but the penalties for perjury were far worse. Bacanovic lost his job,

Stewart her trading profits, and they both went to jail. Morvillo's argument that the conspiracy amounted to a "conspiracy of dunces" may have lacked legal force, but it rings true. It's not only abundantly clear that Bacanovic and Stewart lied and obstructed justice, but they weren't very good at it.

"There's no doubt in my mind that it was Peter who had the idea to lie and cover up," Faneuil hypothesized when I asked what he thought. "The very first time Judy [Monaghan] confronted me, I called Peter immediately. My impression is that I was the one who told Peter there was an investigation that was beginning. Right when I told him, he freaked out and started lying. 'Tax-loss selling.' This was right after Judy confronted me. Was the trade solicited? Was it? Peter freaked. He lied. By the time he talked to Martha, he'd already lied to Merrill and to me. My guess is Peter lied from the start.

"Of course, Martha had an inclination to lie, too. It's very hard for people to understand how high-powered, super successful people could be so brazenly off base. How could they have had such bad communications about something so important? But for me it's easy, knowing Peter, to picture them freaking out, and talking at one another, and not listening. I wouldn't be surprised that at their breakfast, and over the phone, they were confident they were on the same page and had come up with a plan. But neither one of them ever listens. I can picture them so easily. The way Peter spoke, nothing could penetrate. Even if she interrupted him, Peter would just bite his lip until he could get the next word in. It's not hard to imagine how they blew it so badly."

Why would Scooter Libby have lied? Libby was clearly a successful, hardworking, and highly intelligent person. Perhaps he could have reasonably counted on reporters refusing to testify, even Russert, although they weren't speaking in confidence when he called to complain about Chris Matthews. Libby knew he wasn't a source for the Novak column, and if that's all the investigators were looking for, he could have deflected them long enough for Novak's sources to be exposed. Then he would have been in the clear.

But he knew the investigators were looking at other leaks—a *Washington Post* clip about the scope of the investigation was in his files. Even if Russert remained silent (and by his second interview, he and his lawyer Tate both knew that Russert had contradicted him), Libby had to assume that other administration officials would undermine him—even his closest aide, Cathie Martin. Was it simply too late at that point for him to admit he was wrong?

The letters to the judge urging leniency for Libby paint a detailed picture of his personality: someone intensely hardworking, with routine fourteen- and sixteen-hour days; someone well organized, even-keeled, unfailingly civil and polite. They also suggest someone who is a workaholic, a perfectionist, sensitive to criticism. The zeal with which he sought public exoneration from the White House press secretary indicates how important his reputation was to him. For Libby to tell the truth—that he knew Plame's identity and leaked it to Judith Miller and confirmed it to Matt Cooper—after he told the vice president he hadn't, and had gotten the press secretary to publicly exonerate him, would not just have cost him his job and his credibility in the White House. It would have cost him his self-esteem.

Perhaps Libby's perjury was yet another instance of loyalty trumping honesty. When Patrick Fitzgerald suggested that there was a "cloud over the White House," he was clearly referring to Vice President Cheney. In Libby's telling, the campaign to retaliate against Wilson and "out" his wife as a CIA agent was set in motion by other reporters, not his boss. Yet Cheney's notes on the Wilson op-ed piece, Libby's admission that he first learned Valerie Wilson's identity from the vice president, and Libby's admission that it was "possible" the vice president had suggested on Air Force Two that he call reporters point to the possibility that Cheney initiated the campaign, and that Libby was covering for him. If so, it's no wonder that Cheney argued so forcefully for a presidential pardon—and saw Bush's failure to do so as leaving a "soldier on the battlefield."

Barry Bonds would have been a justly celebrated athlete without using steroids; as he himself asserted, no drug has been invented for hand-eye coordination. But he would never have been the greatest baseball player ever; he probably would never have overtaken Sammy Sosa and Mark McGwire (McGwire has admitted using steroids and Sosa reportedly tested positive, although he denied using them), and he would never have dethroned Hank Aaron as the all-time home run king. Bonds seems to have been afflicted both by privilege—born into baseball royalty, as he put it—and a sense of racial inferiority. The rules, such as they were, didn't apply to him, whether it was his parking space in college or fidelity in marriage. Nor, evidently, did they apply before the grand jury, where Bonds was at no risk of prosecution as long as he told the truth. Apart from living with his own conscience, which gives no sign of troubling him, Bonds—alone among the major characters in this book—has escaped any serious consequences.

How could it be that with the combined investigative resources of the FBI, the IRS, and the Justice Department, it took the government four years to obtain an indictment of Bonds? Or that even by 2011—eight years after the raid on BALCO's headquarters—Bonds had still not come to trial?

Bonds and the other BALCO cases are a vivid illustration of the threat that perjury and false statements pose to the judicial system: they essentially paralyze it and render it dysfunctional.

From the beginning, the BALCO investigation was marked by false statements and perjury on a massive scale. Critical witnesses lied, dissembled, or refused to answer. Greg Anderson's false statements and subsequent refusal to testify posed enormous obstacles for the investigators. If Anderson were to testify fully and honestly, he would essentially be the only witness needed at Bonds's trial. He could go a long way toward exonerating him, or he could all but prove his guilt.

No wonder, then, that prosecutors have diverted enormous amounts of time and resources toward securing Anderson's testimony, including pursuing contempt charges and Anderson's imprisonment, all unavailing. Further proceedings—and more years of litigation—loom should Anderson continue to defy subpoenas. Meanwhile, prosecutors have opted to go forward against Bonds without Anderson, even with a much weaker case.

Even with grants of immunity protecting them from liability for anything except perjury, other critical witnesses lied. Marion Jones pleaded guilty to two lies in the BALCO case, but she told many more. Prosecutors had to turn from the original targets of the investigation—suppliers like Conte and Anderson—to a perjury investigation. Even then, Jones would probably still be under investigation and continuing her denials if she hadn't gotten involved in a brazen and amateurish check fraud scheme—and then lied about that too.

How many others lied at some point in the investigation? Trevor Graham lied flagrantly and put the government through a costly and time-consuming trial. Nearly all the track athletes interviewed in the Graham case initially lied. In stark contrast to Douglas Faneuil, who had to plead guilty to a crime once he recanted his testimony about Martha Stewart, none of them were charged. Nor has Angel Heredia faced any sanctions for either his lies or his brazen steroid dealing. The government even helped him with his immigration status.

Alone among people in this book who lied, Faneuil demonstrated character, integrity, and courage by coming forward with the truth for no other reason than that his conscience demanded it. He was yelled at, castigated, handcuffed, and forced to plead guilty, albeit to a misdemeanor. His life was shattered. Given Faneuil's experience, why would anyone in a similar position come forward? When lying is prosecuted only selectively—when a Faneuil is punished and Heredia and other athletes lie with impunity—injustice results. The system is corrupted.

And then there is Bernard Madoff. His motive for lying is uniquely self-evident: his entire career was a lie. Giving credence to Adolf Hitler's admonition in *Mein Kampf* that people "more readily fall victim to the big lie than the small lie," the SEC officials who examined him simply couldn't believe it was all a giant Ponzi scheme. Like all creators of Ponzi schemes, Madoff claimed he was soon going to recoup his losses and return to the straight and narrow. He claimed he wished he'd done so when the losses were only a few hundred million dollars.

This doesn't ring true. To the extent his lies took on lives of their own, Madoff seemed to revel in them. He created a vast illusion of a successful investment firm with a potent top-secret trading formula. He flaunted the trappings of wealth and luxury. He cultivated the admiration and envy of his peers. He lied repeatedly and flagrantly every time he was questioned by the SEC, committing a felony each time. His oath to tell the truth meant nothing.

But what may be most disturbing is that Madoff's fraud—and the countless lies that supported it—continued unstopped for twenty years, ensnaring thousands of additional unwitting victims as it metastasized like a virulent cancer. Madoff was not an especially good liar. The SEC officials Ostrow, Lamore, and Suh knew he was lying. Their superiors Meaghan Cheung and John Nee knew or should have known, given the evidence, and they should have pressed the issue with officials higher up. The consequences of their failure to pursue perjury charges were staggering. At the time of his sworn testimony in 2006, Madoff purported to have approximately $20 billion under management. By the time his scheme collapsed, he had $65 billion. Failing to pursue his lies cost innocent victims another $45 billion.

The SEC lawyers brushed Madoff's perjury aside and seemed worn down by the prospect of proving a case. Perhaps they'd been lied to so often they'd become inured and jaded. Nee and Cheung seemed primarily interested in wrapping up the investigation and moving on, not in uncovering any wrongdoing. Considering that their primary mission is to protect the public and uncover fraud, they showed a striking lack of enthusiasm when confronted—not just once, but repeatedly—with evidence of wrongdoing on an unprecedented scale. On the contrary, they seemed eager to vindicate their own preconceptions and disprove the complaints. They just didn't seem to care that Madoff lied. Indifference is the enemy of virtue.

I asked David Kotz, the SEC's inspector general, if the SEC had *ever* referred a perjury or false statement case to the Justice Department for further investigation unrelated to an underlying securities fraud, and he said he could think of none. "Normally the SEC doesn't investigate false statements," Kotz said, "but false statements are serious issues and they should be referred and prosecuted." Of course, referring a perjury case doesn't mean there is no underlying crime, as Madoff vividly illustrates. But the SEC seems to have ignored the fact that perjury and false statements are crimes in and of themselves, often with tragic consequences.

There is no way to know how many other instances of perjury have gone unprosecuted, but anecdotal evidence suggests the number is legion. Madoff may be an extreme example, but is hardly an isolated case. The failure to prosecute perjury, and the resulting widespread perception that there is little risk in committing it, has only exacerbated the problem and bred widespread contempt for the law.

Ultimately, the reason why people at the pinnacle of their careers—respected, acclaimed role models like Martha Stewart, Scooter Libby, Barry Bonds, and Bernard Madoff—committed the crimes of perjury and false statements seems only too obvious: they thought they could get away with it. As long as perjury goes uninvestigated, unprosecuted, and unpunished, the problem will get worse. In Bill Clinton, America had a president who committed perjury, and in his successor George W. Bush one who condoned it by commuting Libby's sentence. What message does this send, both to Americans and to the rest of the world? The Obama administration—any administration, Democratic or Republican—needs to reaffirm the rule of law, the importance of truth, and embark on a sustained, visible, and public campaign to hold accountable those who commit perjury and false statements.

We appear to be on the brink of becoming a society where perjury is the norm. One assistant U.S. attorney told me, "I came to work every day expecting to be lied to. The only question was how good they'd be at it." As these stories make clear, perjury has infected virtually every aspect of American life. We lionize those who win, and turn a blind eye to cheating. We demand perfection and withhold forgiveness. We promote self-interest at the expense of others. The consequences are devastating.

Lying under oath that goes unproven and unpunished breeds a cynicism that undermines the foundations of any society that aspires to fair play and the rule of law. It undermines civilization itself.

ACKNOWLEDGMENTS

I am grateful to everyone who helped make this book possible in ways both large and seemingly small, starting with numerous sources who gave generously of their time and trusted me with what were in many cases sensitive personal disclosures.

Ann Godoff, my editor at Penguin Press, was a wonderful sounding board and provided just the right amounts of encouragement, patience, understanding, and good judgment while steering this manuscript to publication. Thanks also to her assistant, Lindsay Whalen; associate publisher, Tracy Locke; assistant director, publicity, Yamil Anglada; senior vice president for legal affairs, Alex Gigante; outside counsel, Gary Mailman; and cover designer, Evan Gaffney.

My agent, Amanda Urban, provided much needed advice, wise counsel, and encouragement from the inception of the idea for this book until the final manuscript and beyond.

Damian Fowler was my research assistant, working diligently and cheerfully far longer than I'm sure he anticipated. He contributed enormously to the book.

DowJones/*SmartMoney* magazine provided a professional home for much of my work on this book, and I'm especially grateful to editor Jonathan Dahl. My longtime assistant Julie Allen helped in countless ways on an almost daily basis.

I also appreciate the encouragement of my colleagues at Columbia University School of Journalism, especially Sylvia Nasar, Irena Stern, Bill Grueskin, Dean Nicholas Lemann, and Sam Friedman, who first drew my attention to the

Barry Bonds case. I'm also grateful to my co-teachers and fellow authors from the Columbia Business School, Jonathan Knee and Bruce Greenwald.

My friends and family encouraged me and bore with me throughout this project, often providing sound advice, but even more important, offering a refuge from the sometimes stressful and solitary work of writing a book. I'll only mention a few—Steve Swartz, Jane Berentson, Arthur Lubow—among the many who deserve recognition. Thanks also to Michael and Jane, my brother and sister, and their wonderful families. I'm especially grateful to my parents, who inculcated the values that have permeated my work as a journalist. I know my mother remembers a flagrant lie I told while in the second grade—and the "tangled web" that unfolded. Fortunately it proved an invaluable lesson at a young age.

Finally, I can never adequately repay my partner, Benjamin Weil, for sustaining me in every conceivable way through the years of this project. In the words of Troy Ellerman, I can only try to be better.

This book is based primarily on firsthand reporting consisting of hundreds of interviews and a review of thousands of pages of documents, including trial transcripts, grand jury transcripts, FBI interview notes, and other investigative materials. In each of these cases I was able to draw upon transcripts and notes of interviews in which the major characters, as well as many others, lied under oath or to a U.S. government official. That's because many ordinarily secret transcripts of grand jury testimony, notes of FBI interviews, and other original source materials were made public in the course of judicial proceedings. I also made several successful requests pursuant to the Freedom of Information Act. I've identified these transcripts in the notes that follow, but not for every citation, which would be needlessly voluminous.

This book is also based on numerous interviews. Many of them were on a background or a not-for-attribution basis, and I'm grateful to those people who were extraordinarily generous with their time. Given that all of these cases are or were matters of criminal investigation, many sources were not free to speak for attribution. Where a source is quoted directly, that person spoke on the record. However, statements made to me, as the author, should be distinguished from dialogue, which is based on reporting like any other fact. Dialogue and thoughts attributed to many characters in this book often come from other sources, such as their lawyers or other confidants, or from their testimony or interviews by law enforcement officials. Readers should bear in mind that remembered dialogue often differs in its exact wording from actual transcripts or recordings, even when it is the subject of sworn testimony. To an unusual degree, many of the quoted statements do come directly from transcripts or recordings. In quoting from these materials I have generally corrected grammatical errors and deleted various verbal tics and repeated words and phrases, as I would in quoting a source. I have not used ellipses to indicate such minor deletions.

I'm not going to burden the reader with names of people who were asked but declined to be interviewed, with the exception of the four major characters themselves. Through their lawyers, Martha Stewart, Scooter Libby, Barry Bonds, and Bernard Madoff declined to be interviewed. Their reliability as sources would have been compromised in any event, for obvious reasons.

Following are published sources on which I relied:

INTRODUCTION

xi Perjury in the common law: William Blackstone, *Commentaries on the Laws of England*, vol. 4 (Oxford Press, originally published 1769).

xi–xii Perjury in the U.S.: Jessica Fischweicher, "Perjury," *American Criminal Law Review*, spring 2008; Charles Doyle, "Perjury Under Federal Law," *CRS Report for Congress*, December 27, 2007.

xiii Former president Bill Clinton's false statements: Ken Gormley, *The Death of American Virtue* (Crown, 2010).

PART ONE: MARTHA STEWART

Legal Documents
United States of America v. Martha Stewart and Peter Bacanovic, 03 Cr. 717 (MGC).
Indictment.
Trial transcript.
Government exhibits 6, 52, 53, 54, 130, 131, 206, 81, 78, 33, 38, 40, 125.
Government exhibit 285-A, SEC transcript, Peter Bacanovic testimony, File No. NY-6971.
Securities and Exchange Commission v. Samuel D. Waksal and Jack Waksal, 02 Civ. 4407 (NRB)
    Second Amended Complaint.
United States of America v. Samuel Waksal, Indictment 02 Cr. 01041 and related docket entries.

8 *From humble beginnings:* Christopher M. Byron, *Martha Inc.: The Incredible Story of Martha Stewart Living Omnimedia* (Wiley, 2002).

9 *bizarre ethical lapses:* Geeta Anand, Jenny Markon, and Chris Adams, "Biotech Bust: ImClone's ex-CEO Arrested, Charged with Insider Trading," *Wall Street Journal*, June 13, 2002; Andrew Pollack, "For ImClone Drug Entrepreneur, a Past of Celebrity and Notoriety," *New York Times*, January 24, 2002; Geeta Anand, "Four Prestigious Labs Ousted Waksal for Questionable Work," *Wall Street Journal*, September 27, 2002.

10 *development of Erbitux:* Catherine Arnst, "The Birth of a Cancer Drug," *BusinessWeek*, July 9, 2001.

13 Martha Stewart homes: James T. Madore, "Stewart's Lucrative Living," *Newsday*, July 3, 2002.

14 *Stewart could be rude:* Christopher M. Byron, *Martha Inc.* (Wiley, 2002); Jerry Oppenheimer, *Martha Stewart: Just Desserts: The Unauthorized Biography* (Morrow, 1997).

18 *"Isn't it nice . . .":* Mariana Pasternak, *The Best of Friends: Martha and Me* (Harper, 2010).

29 The article Peikin read: Andrew Pollack, "House Panel to Investigate a Cancer Drug and Its Maker," *New York Times,* January 19, 2002.

55 Martha Stewart's sale of ImClone shares: Theresa Agovino, "Subpoenas Issued in ImClone Case," Associated Press, June 6, 2002; Chris Adams and Geeta Anand, "Martha Stewart Sold ImClone Shares—Timing Raises Questions, but There Is No Indication She Knew of FDA's Decision," *Wall Street Journal,* June 6, 2002.

76 *Faneuil was a "jittery Judas":* Christopher Mason, "The Loyalist," *New York,* May 15, 2004.

78 *"I have made terrible mistakes":* Constance L. Hays, "Ex-ImClone Chief Admits Some U.S. Charges," *New York Times,* October 16, 2002.

78 *magnums of Château Lafite Rothschild:* Robert Kolker, "Sam Waksal Was Right All Along," *New York,* March 23, 2009.

114 *"I have done nothing wrong":* Reuters, "The Martha Stewart Trial: A Message from Martha Gets a Quick Wording Change," March 6, 2004.

114 Jurors appear on *Dateline NBC:* "Profile: Martha Stewart. After the Verdict; Martha Stewart Jurors Discuss Her Trial and Their Verdict," NBC News, *Dateline NBC,* March 7, 2004.

115 Deletion from Martha Stewart's letter to the judge: Constance L. Hays, "Five Months in Jail, and Stewart Vows, 'I'll Be Back,'" *New York Times,* July 17, 2004.

116 *"I'll be back":* Brooke A. Masters, "Martha Stewart Sentenced to 5 Years in Prison," *Washington Post,* June 16, 2004; "The Verdict on Martha," CNN transcript, Associated Press, July 16, 2004.

116 Bacanovic sentencing: Erin McClam, "Bacanovic's Life Ruined, His Lawyer Says at Sentencing," Associated Press, July 16, 2004.

116 Stewart discusses her trial, sentencing, and future: *20/20,* ABC News transcript of interview by Barbara Walters, July 16, 2004.

117 Pasternak's relationship with Stewart after the trial: Pasternak, *The Best of Friends: Martha and Me.*

118 Stewart's life in prison: Laurie P. Cohen, "Captive Audience: In Federal Prison, Stewart Caters to a New Crowd," *Wall Street Journal,* March 3, 2005.

119 Bacanovic's relationship with Stewart after the trial: Landon Thomas Jr., "The Broker Who Fell to Earth; She Came Roaring Back; He Is Quietly Roaring," *New York Times,* October 13, 2006.

120 Bacanovic's fate at Fred Leighton: Lindsay Pollock and Philip Boroff, "Jeweler Esmerian Fights Merrill to Stop Reckless NY Auction," Bloomberg, April 14, 2008.

In addition to the transcripts, in describing the Stewart trial I relied on Henry Blodget, "Dispatches from the Martha Stewart Trial," *Slate,* November 20–December 23, 2003; January 26–February 20, 2004.

PART TWO: I. LEWIS "SCOOTER" LIBBY

Legal Documents

United States of America v. I. Lewis Libby, 2005-cr-00394-RBW.
Indictment.

Trial transcript.

I. Lewis Libby, grand jury testimony transcript, March 5 and 24, 2004.

Government's sentencing memorandum.

Various exhibits including government exhibits 10, 50, 51, 104, 401, 532, 540.

Transcript of Bob Woodward and Richard Armitage conversation, Defense Exhibit DX511.

FBI Memorandum of Interview, Richard B. Cheney, May 8, 2004.

Other Court Documents

In Re: Grand Jury Subpoena, Judith Miller, United States District Court for the District of
Columbia, No. 04-3138, consolidated with 04-3139, 04-3140, Appeals from the United
States District Court for the District of Columbia.

http://www.justice.gov/usao/iln/osc/legal_proceedings.html.

Affidavit of Patrick J. Fitzgerald, August 27, 2004, Case No.: 04-3138.

Affidavit of Patrick J. Fitzgerald, November 18, 2005, Case No.: 05-cr-00394-RBW.

Books and Articles

In addition to testifying, many participants in the Libby case wrote books describing their involvement, which I have used in many cases to describe their thoughts, reactions, and statements. These
include:

Ari Fleischer, *Taking Heat: The President, the Press, and My Years in the White House*
(HarperCollins, 2005).

Scott McClellan, *What Happened: Inside the Bush White House and Washington's Culture of
Deception* (PublicAffairs, 2008).

Robert Novak, *The Prince of Darkness* (Crown Forum, July 2007).

Karl Rove, *Courage and Consequence* (Threshold Editions, Simon & Schuster, 2010).

Joseph Wilson, *The Politics of Truth* (Carroll & Graf, 2004).

Valerie Plame Wilson, *Fair Game* (Simon & Schuster, 2007).

124 Text of President Bush's 2003 State of the Union address: *Washington Post*, January 28,
2003.

125 Full text of Powell speech to UN: "A Policy of Evasion and Deception," *Washington Post*,
February 5, 2003.

126 *I'm told by a person:* Nicholas Kristof, "Missing in Action: Truth," *New York Times*, May
6, 2003.

130 *documents were forged:* Seymour Hersh, "Who Lied to Whom?" *New Yorker*, March 31,
2003.

131 *"extremely sloppy":* Walter Pincus, "CIA Did Not Share Doubt on Iraq Data," *Washington
Post*, June 12, 2003.

132 *"I don't believe":* Nicholas Kristof, "White House in Denial," *New York Times*, June 13,
2003.

132 *New Republic* article: Spencer Ackerman and John B. Judis, "The First Casualty," *New
Republic*, June 19, 2003.

135–38 Novak and Wilson on *Meet the Press:* Novak, *The Prince of Darkness*; Wilson, *The
Politics of Truth*.

137–38 Joe Wilson with Andrea Mitchell: *Meet the Press* transcript, July 6, 2003; *Hardball*
transcript, MSNBC, July 8, 2003.

140–41 Fleischer's reactions: Fleischer, *Taking Heat*.

144 *"Let me be clear about":* Statement by George J. Tenet, director of Central Intelligence,
CIA Press Release, July 11, 2003.

147 The CIA's decision: Robert Novak, "Mission to Niger," *Washington Post* via Creators Syndicate, July 14, 2003.

148 *In the avalanche:* Matt Cooper, "Follow the Yellowcake Road," *Time,* July 9, 2003; and "A War on Wilson?" July 17, 2003.

149 *It took two* Newsday *reporters:* Timothy Phelps and Knut Royce, "Columnist Blows CIA Agent's Cover," *Newsday,* July 22, 2003.

150 *Congress called for an inquiry:* "Iraq Intelligence–Public Forum," transcript, Joseph Wilson et al., Pacific Views, August 21, 2003; Wilson, *The Politics of Truth.*

152 *At Cheney's behest:* McClellan, *What Happened.*

152 *"2 Disclaim Leaking Name of Operative":* New York Times, October 4, 2003.

153 Bush comments on CIA leak: "Remarks Following a Meeting with Business Leaders and an Exchange with Reporters in Chicago," George W. Bush, Weekly Compilation of Presidential Documents, WCPD, September 30, 2003.

155 *On September 28:* Mike Allen and Dana Priest, "Bush Administration Is Focus of Inquiry," *Washington Post,* September 28, 2003.

156 *The next day:* "Investigating Leaks," *New York Times* editorial, October 2, 2003.

163–66 Rove's recollections: Rove, *Courage and Consequence.*

182 *When Novak arrived:* Novak, *Prince of Darkness.*

210 *contracts contrary to public policy:* William Lawrence Clark, *Handbook of the Law of Contracts* (Cornell University, 1914).

211 *"The law can't distinguish":* Tom Scocca, *"Times's* Judy Miller, in Contempt, Says She Won't Budge," *New York Observer,* February 18, 2007.

212 Pearlstine recollections: Norman Pearlstine, *Off the Record* (Farrar, Straus and Giroux, 2007).

212 Cooper's decision to testify: Matt Cooper, "Valerie, Scooter and Me," *Portfolio,* April 16, 2007.

213 *The spectacle of a* New York Times *reporter:* Adam Liptak, "Reporter Jailed After Refusing to Name Source," *New York Times,* July 7, 2005.

215 *Miller might have taken a courageous stand:* Carol D. Leonnig, "Jailed Reporter Is Distanced from News, not Elite Visitors," *Washington Post,* September 17, 2005; Cindy Adams, "Judith Miller's Survival Guide," *New York Post,* 2005.

217 *The call lasted ten minutes:* Judith Miller, "My Four Hours Testifying in the Federal Grand Jury Room," *New York Times,* October 16, 2005.

219 *"The real winner":* Jack Shafer, "The Case for Patrick Fitzgerald," *Slate,* March 13, 2007.

223 *Fitzgerald stepped to the podium:* "Transcript of Special Counsel Fitzgerald's Press Conference," courtesy of FDCH e-MEDIA, *Washington Post,* October 28, 2005.

224 *Libby resigned:* Eric Schmitt, "Indicted Aide Had Been 'Cheney's Dick Cheney,'" *New York Times,* October 30, 2005.

225 Senator Kennedy's reaction to indictment: U.S. Fed News, October 28, 2005.

225–27 Editorial reaction: *Meet the Press* transcript, NBC, October 23, 2005; "Hot Topic: Obstruction for What," *Wall Street Journal* editorial, October 29, 2005; "The Case Against Scooter Libby," *New York Times* editorial, October 29, 2005; "Mr. Libby's Indictment," *Washington Post* editorial, October 29, 2005.

232 *Novak described his decision:* Robert Novak, "My Leak Case Testimony," *Washington Post* via Creators Syndicate, July 12, 2006.

233 Armitage identified as Novak's source: Michael Isikoff, "The Man Who Said Too Much," *Newsweek,* September 4, 2006; Michael Isikoff with David Corn, *Hubris: The Inside Story of Spin, Scandal and the Selling of the Iraq War* (Crown, 2006); R. Jeffrey Smith, "Armitage Says He Was Source of CIA Leak," *Washington Post,* September 8, 2006.

251 Libby conviction: Kate Phillips, "A View from the Libby Jury Box," *New York Times*, March 6, 2007.

254 Giuliani comment: Wolf Blitzer, CNN transcript, June 5, 2007.

254 Bush's decision to commute Libby's sentence but not pardon him: George W. Bush, *Decision Points* (New York: Random House, 2010).

255 Russert interviews Novak: *Meet the Press*, NBC transcript, July 15, 2007.

257 Blagojevich verdict: "Blagojevich 23, Fitzgerald 1," *Wall Street Journal*, Review and Outlook, August 19, 2010.

Also mentioned in the text:

Lewis Libby, *The Apprentice* (St. Martin's Press, 1996).

Bob Woodward, *Plan of Attack* (Simon & Schuster, 2004).

PART THREE: BARRY LAMAR BONDS

Legal Documents

United States of America v. Barry Lamar Bonds, 07-0732 SI.

Indictment; grand jury testimony; related docket entries.

U.S. Opposition to Defendant's Motion *in Limine* to Exclude Evidence.

Unsealed government exhibits; various trial memoranda.

United States of America v. Victor Conte et al., 04-0044-SI.

Indictment; Novitzky declaration; affidavit of Special Agent Jeff Novitzky.

Valente testimony transcript; IRS memoranda of interviews with Conte, Valente, Anderson, and Korchemny; trial motions to dismiss.

Grand jury transcripts of Tim Montgomery, C. J. Hunter, GJ Investigation, Northern District, California.

United States of America v. Marion Jones, 05-Cr-1067.

Indictment; sentencing memoranda; affidavit of Jeffrey Novitzky; transcript of plea hearing; transcript of sentencing hearing.

United States of America v. Troy Ellerman, 07-0080-JSW.

Sentencing memoranda; related affidavits; transcript of sentencing hearing.

United States of America v. Fainaru-Wada et al., 06-xr-90225-JSW.

In re Grand Jury Subpoenas to Mark Fainaru-Wada and Lance Williams; various motions; Hershman Declaration.

United States of America v. Trevor Graham, 06-0725-SI.

Indictment; trial transcript; sentencing memoranda; presentencing report.

McCormack v. ProRodeo Hall of Fame and Museum of the American Cowboy, Inc., et al., Colorado District Court, 1:2007cv01228, complaint and answer.

Books, Articles, and Other Sources

SFGate.com, the website of the *San Francisco Chronicle*, compiled all of the paper's BALCO coverage from December 21, 2003, through February 5, 2009, in "The BALCO Investigation: A Special Report" (www.sfgate.com/barrybonds/). Most of the articles are by Mark Fainaru-Wada and Lance Williams. I found this an indispensable resource and relied on it for many dates and details.

268–71 Barry Bonds/Kimberly Bell biography: Mark Fainaru-Wada and Lance Williams, *Game of Shadows* (Penguin, 2006); "The Barry Bonds Interview," *Playboy*, July 1993; Joan Ryan, "A Career of Conflict: Giants Slugger Bonds Is Still Trying to Forge His Identity," *San Francisco Chronicle*, February 17, 1997.

271 *"I think he has changed"*: Josh Suchon, *This Gracious Season* (Winter Publications, 2002).

271 *"Do I look bloated?"*: Michael O'Keefe, "Barry Bonds's Ex-Mistress Details Star's Steroid Use, Temper," *New York Daily News*, Oct. 3, 2007.

274 *"Call God. Ask him"*: David Grann, "Baseball Without Metaphor," *New York Times Magazine*, September 1, 2002.

279 *Hoskins evidently dropped any plans:* Josh Peter, "Bonds and Hoskins' Tale of the Tape," Yahoo! Sports, February 23, 2009.

279 The conference room meeting with Hoskins: Duff Wilson, "Ruined Friendship Could Imperil Bonds," *New York Times*, July 13, 2006.

280 FBI investigation of Hoskins: Sam Walker, "On Sports: Barry Bonds's Other Campaign—Slugger Says Bats, Jerseys Aren't Authentic, Jolting a Market," *Wall Street Journal*, May 19, 2006.

289 On Kevin Ryan: Mark Fainaru-Wada and Lance Williams, "Prosecutor Reflects on BALCO Firestorm," *San Francisco Chronicle*, June 17, 2007.

290 *Now, over the phone:* Victor Conte, unpublished ms., "BALCO: The Straight Dope on Barry Bonds, Marion and What We Can Do to Save Sports," p. 134.

290 Conte's description of the BALCO raid: Conte, unpublished ms., pp. 161–62.

296 *"She thought about her money"*: Maggie Jones, "What Makes Marion Jones Run?" *New York Times Magazine*, April 30, 2010.

303–4 Ashcroft press conference: CNN transcript, *Anderson Cooper 360 Degrees*, February 12, 2004.

308–9 *San Francisco Chronicle* stories: Mark Fainaru-Wada and Lance Williams, "Sprinter Admitted Use of BALCO 'Magic Potion'"; "Track Star's Testimony Linked Bonds to Steroid Use/Montgomery Said BALCO Owner Named Slugger," *San Francisco Chronicle*, June 24, 2004; Fainaru-Wada and Williams, *Game of Shadows*.

310 *Since she was first identified:* Liz Robbins, "Track and Field; Jones Will Sue if Barred From Games," *New York Times*, May 17, 2004.

310 *The campaign climaxed in June:* Marion Jones and Kate Sekules, *Life in the Fast Lane* (Melcher Media, 2004).

314 *Jones was allowed to compete:* SI.com via Reuters, "Friday: Bad Day for U.S.; New Dawn for China," August 28, 2004.

315 *Ellerman told the* New York Times: Carol Pogash, "Lawyers Are Frustrated by Leaks in BALCO Investigation," *New York Times*, December 3, 2004.

316–17 Conte on TV: *20/20* transcript, Victor Conte interviewed by Martin Bashir, ABC News, December 3, 2004.

318 *It was too much material for one story:* Mark Fainaru-Wada and Lance Williams, "Giambi Admitted Taking Steroids," *San Francisco Chronicle*, December 2, 2004.

320 *The* Chronicle's *revelations:* Thomas Boswell, "The Truth Lies in Numbers," *Washington Post*, December 4, 2004.

320 *The 20/20 episode:* Jere Longman, "In Conte's *20/20* Talk, Legal Experts See a Risk," *New York Times*, December 11, 2004.

320–21 Kimberly Bell on *Geraldo: At Large with Geraldo Rivera* transcript, "Barry Bonds' Alleged Mistress Speaks Out," Kimberly Bell interview, August 8, 2005.

323 *Heredia felt bad:* David Walsh, "Angel Heredia, the Whistle-Blower," *Sunday Times* (London), May 11, 2008.

325 *Chronicle* editorial: "Government as Editor," *San Francisco Chronicle* editorial, September 20, 2006.

350 *Over fifty experienced prosecutors:* Martin Kuz, "Untouchable," *San Francisco Weekly*, October 4, 2006.

350 *After announcing his resignation:* Bob Nightengale, "Outgoing U.S. Attorney Trailed BALCO and Bonds," *USA Today,* January 31, 2007.

352 *Hours after Bonds's indictment:* Christian Red, "Greg Anderson Faces More Jail Time, Refuses to Spill Juice on Barry Bonds," *New York Daily News,* November 20, 2007.

354 *"the wrist slap":* Eric Gilmore, "Wrist Slap Is Heard Far and Wide," *Contra Costa Times,* July 16, 2005.

355 *Troy Ellerman served:* Nathaniel Vinton, "Troy Ellerman, Lawyer Who Leaked BALCO Testimony, Tells Law Students He's Sorry for His Actions," *New York Daily News,* October 17, 2009.

356 *Marion Jones was released:* Maggie Jones, "What Makes Marion Jones Run," *New York Times Magazine,* April 30, 2010.

357 Marion Jones on *Oprah:* "The Oprah Show, Former Olympic Medalist Marion Jones's First Interview After Prison," October 29, 2008, on www.oprah.com.

357 *Though banned from track and field:* Marion Jones, *On the Right Track* (Howard Books, Simon & Schuster, 2010).

357 *Montgomery pleaded guilty:* Mike Fish, "The Fastest Man in the Prison Yard," ESPN.com, September 22, 2009.

PART FOUR: BERNARD L. MADOFF

Legal Documents

United States of America v. Bernard L Madoff, 09 Cr. 213 (DC), March 10, 2009.

Plea Allocation of Bernard L Madoff—statement to the court, March 12, 2009.

Madoff sentencing transcript.

SEC v. Bernard L Madoff, Bernard L Madoff Investment Securities LLC, December 11, 2008.

Victim impact statements, June 15, 2009, U.S. Department of Justice.

United States of America v. Frank DiPascali, Criminal Complaint 09 Cr 764 (RJS).

Plea transcript, August 11, 2009.

United States of America v. David G. Friehling, 09 Cr 700 (AKH).

"Investigation of Failure of the SEC to Uncover Bernard Madoff's Ponzi Scheme."

David Kotz, Report No. OIG-509, U.S. Securities and Exchange Commission Office of Investigations, August 31, 2009, and supporting exhibits, especially:

OIG (Office of the Inspector General) Exhibit 13, interview transcript, Thomas Thanasules, March 26, 2009.

OIG Exhibit 36 & 37, interview transcript, William Ostrow, May 5, 2009.

OIG Exhibit 38, interview transcript, John Nee, May 6, 2009.

OIG Exhibit 48 & 49, interview transcript, Peter Lamore, May 14, 2009.

OIG Exhibit 53, interview transcript, Simona Suh, May 27, 2009.

OIG Exhibit 55, interview transcript, Doria Bachenheimer, June 3, 2009.

OIG Exhibit 56, interview of Meaghan Cheung, June 4, 2009.

OIG Exhibit 104, memorandum of interview of Bernard Madoff, June 17, 2009.

OIG Exhibit 216, e-mails produced by Renaissance Technologies to the OIG.

OIG Exhibit 267, interview transcript, Bernard Madoff, May 19, 2006.

Commonwealth of Massachusetts Office of the Secretary of the Commonwealth, Securities Division, in the matter of Fairfield Greenwich Advisors LLC, Docket No. 2009-0029, Transcript Fairfield Exhibit No. 1.

367–68 *A week later:* Michael Ocrant, "Madoff Tops Charts, Skeptics Ask How," *MAR/Hedge,* May 2001.

368 *Another article:* Erin Arvedlund, "Don't Ask, Don't Tell," *Barron's,* May 7, 2001.

374–75, 379–81, 420, 425 Madoff's operations and his victims: James Bandler and Nicholas Varchaver with Doris Burke, "How Bernie Did It," *Fortune,* May 11, 2009; Mark Seal, "Madoff's World," *Vanity Fair,* July 31, 2009.

387–94 Harry Markopolos described his involvement in the Madoff investigation in congressional testimony and a book: Testimony of Harry Markopolos before the House Committee on Financial Services, February 4, 2009; Harry Markopolos, *No One Would Listen* (Wiley, 2010).

426–27 Madoff sentencing: David Glovin, Patricia Hurtado, and Thom Weidlich, "Bernie Madoff Gets 150 years in Jail for Epic Fraud," Bloomberg, June 29, 2009; victim impact statements.

428–29 On Meaghan Cheung: Lorena Mongelli and Dan Mangan, "The SEC Watchdog Who Missed Madoff," *New York Post,* January 7, 2009.

429 *James Simons, the founder of Renaissance:* Aaron Lucchetti and Jenny Strasburg, "Simons's Notion: All In, Then All Out," *Wall Street Journal,* February 25, 2009.

432 *Madoff hasn't given any press:* Steve Fishman, "Bernie Madoff, Free at Last," *New York,* June 6, 2010.

CONCLUSION

433 *There are, of course, circumstances:* Sissela Bok, *Lying: Moral Choice in Public and Private Life* (Vintage, 1999).

434 *To return to the question:* Martha Stout, *The Sociopath Next Door* (Broadway, 2006).

436 *Lawyers are ethically bound:* New York State Bar Association, Rules of Professional Conduct, Rule 3.3. The New York Rules closely follow the American Bar Association's Model Rules of Professional Conduct.

INDEX

Aaron, Hank, 265–66, 350, 359
Abrams, Floyd, 203–4, 207, 211–12
Adams, Chris, 55
Addington, David, 170
Agovino, Theresa, 55
Alexander, Nathaniel, 343
Allen, Mark, on sources for Plame's
    identity leaks, 155, 164–65, 175
Alsup, William, 326
Anand, Geeta, 55
Anderson, Greg
    and BALCO steroid distribution,
        282, 285–89
    and Bonds's steroid use, 274–79
    Bonds's testimony about,
        297–301
    as Bonds's trainer, 271–73, 287, 297
    charges/sentencing, 324
    indictment of, 303–4
    post-BALCO, 352
    raid of home, 286–89
    steroid use/distribution, 272, 275–79,
        286–89, 318–19
    taped by Hoskins, 276–79
    testimony against Bonds, 326

Anthony, Vance, 405
Apfel, David, Stewart-Bacanovic trial,
    95–97, 101, 103–4
Archer, Lord Jeffrey, xiv
Arguedas, Christina, 308
Armfield, Kirk, 167
Armitage, Richard
    and criminal charges, 208, 220,
        228, 232, 260
    grand jury testimony, 231–32
    Plame, learns about, 174
    Plame's identity leaked to Novack
        by, 158–59, 173, 183, 233
    Plame's identity leaked to Woodward
        by, 227–32
    post-Libby trial, 258
Armstrong, Ann
    legal counsel for, 56
    post-trial, 117–18
    and sale of ImClone shares, 12,
        28–29, 32, 35, 39
    Stewart-Bacanovic trial, 97
    Stewart's assistant, role as, 12
    and Stewart's tampering with
        evidence, 33–34, 97

Armstrong, Ann (*cont.*)
  as witness against Stewart, 63–66,
    111–12
Armstrong, Lance, 356
Arnold, Patrick, 284
Arvedlund, Erin, Madoff exposure by,
  368, 410
Ashcroft, John
  and BALCO arrests, 303–4
  resigns from Plame investigation,
    181–82
Auriga International, 382
Ayres, David, 181

Bacanovic, Peter
  background of, 8
  charges against, 84
  communication with Martha, post-
    sale, 26, 28–29
  communication with Martha, pre-
    sale, 7–8, 11–12
  competence as money manager, 15
  cover story for Martha, 20–26, 35,
    40–42, 45–46, 107, 436–37
  evidence, tampering with, 45–46,
    65–66
  Faneuil coerced to protect, 20–23, 27,
    46–48, 50, 57
  Faneuil hired by, 4–5
  firing of, 61, 75
  ImClone investigation, initial, 19–21
  ImClone shares, initiates sale, 6–8,
    11, 17, 101
  plea negotiation, 79–80
  post-trial, 119–20
  relationship with Martha, 8, 15,
    47–48
  relationship with Waskal, 8, 10
  SEC questioning of, 26, 38–44
  trial of. *See* Stewart-Bacanovic trial

Bachenheimer, Doria, and Madoff
  investigation, 392, 399, 406, 411
BALCO investigation, 289–338
  athletes indicted. *See* Bonds, Barry;
    Graham, Trevor; Jones, Marion
  athletes suspended, 307–8, 342
  and BALCO operation. *See* Anderson,
    Greg; Conte, Victor, Jr.; Valente,
    James
  First Amendment issues, 328–30, 332
  grand jury testimony, 293–302, 311–14
  immunity for witnesses, 291, 295–96,
    305, 318, 321, 323, 337
  media coverage, 308–9, 314–21,
    327–28
  testimony leak, investigation/
    conviction, 333–42
  testimony leak to press, 309–10,
    314–20, 326–30
BALCO raid, 275, 280–89
  athletes named, 284–85, 287–88
  Bonds name in, 285–86, 288
Baroni, Lisa, 426
Bartlett, Dan, 185
Bashir, Martin, 316–17
Bay Area Laboratory Cooperative. *See*
  entries under BALCO
Beatty, Christine, xiv–xv
Bell, Kimberly, and Barry Bonds,
  268–71, 279, 320–21, 357–59
Bellel, Zeva, and ImClone case, 4, 24,
  100–101
Benard, Marvin, steroid use, 286,
  287–88, 359
Bennett, Robert, as Miller's legal
  counsel, 215–16
Ben-Yehuda, Sabina, 78–79
Bergers, David, 386–87
Blackstone Group, 18
Blagojevich, Rod, 257

Blatt, Greg, 30

Bok, Sissela, 433

Bonadio, Jason, 51

Bond, Deborah
  Libby trial testimony, 243
  Plame's identity leak investigation,
      155, 167, 170

Bonds, Aisha, 270

Bonds, Barry
  achievements as athlete, 265–67, 268,
      274, 276, 280, 350–51, 359
  Anderson as trainer, 271–79, 287, 297
  arrogance of, 268, 272, 438
  background of, 267–68
  BALCO endorsement by, 275, 302
  BALCO raid, named in, 285–86, 288
  Giants signing/salary, 268, 276
  grand jury testimony, 296–302, 318
  home run record by, 265–67
  Hoskins threatened by, 276, 279–80
  immunity granted to, 291, 296
  indictment/charges, 351–52
  and Kimberly Bell, 268–71, 279,
      320–21, 357–59
  legal counsel for, 290–91
  media reports against, 320–21
  memorabilia business of, 276, 279
  perjury, motives for, 435, 438–39
  perjury trial, future of, 358, 438–39
  physical/personality changes, 271,
      274, 276
  post-indictment, 358–59
  steroid use, 274–80, 309–10, 321
  wives/children of, 269–70

Bonds, Bobby, 265, 267, 276, 279

Bonds, Nikolai, 269

Bonds, Shikari, 269

Boswell, Thomas, 320

Bowers, Dr. Larry, 282, 285

Branco, Susann, 269

Brock, Jim, 268

Broder, Paul, 367–70

Brown, James A., xiv

Browne, Lord John, xiv

Brune, Susan, 64

Burge, Jon, xv, 257

Bush, George W.
  administration, and perjury, 225–26,
      435, 441
  interviewed by U.S. Attorney, 201–2
  on investigation of Plame's identity
      leak, 153
  Iraq War, false basis of, 123–26,
      137–38, 140
  Libby's positions with, 127
  Libby's sentence commuted by,
      253–55, 340–41
  Rove and Plame's identity leak,
      questions about, 164–65
  Rove/Armitage resignation, request
      by Fitzgerald, 221–23
  on steroid use, 303

Byron, Christopher, 14

Cacioppi, Theodore, 418–19

Card, Andrew, 151, 228, 231

Catlin, Dr. Don, 282

Cedarbaum, Miriam, Stewart-
    Bacanovic trial judge, 85, 101,
    113–17

Central Intelligence Agency (CIA),
    Wilson's mission attributed to,
    132–33, 142–43

Chambers, Dwain, 284

Cheney, Dick
  defensive maneuvering by, 200–201
  as enabler of perjury, 435
  grand jury testimony, 197–201
  Kristof's article, reaction to, 129–30
  Libby denies leak to, 195–97

Cheney, Dick (*cont.*)
  on Libby pardon, 254–55
  Libby's conversations about Plame
    to, 138–39, 145, 166, 174, 178,
    195–96, 438
  mentioned at Libby's trial, 235, 239,
    240, 250
  mission to Niger initiated by, 126–
    31, 137–38
  National Intelligence Estimate
    declassified by, 141–42, 170
  Novak's article vindicates, 147–48
  office of, 128–29
  relationship with Libby, 127–28
  vindicates Libby via McClelland,
    152–53, 166, 235
  Wilson's mission denied by, 130,
    132, 134, 139–40, 143, 171
Cherry-picking, and Madoff, 365–67
Cheung, Meaghan, Madoff
    investigation, 392–96, 399–402,
    428–29, 440
Chevalier, Jeff, xiv
Chin, Denny, Madoff trial judge, 420–
  21, 425–27
CIA operative, leak to press about. *See*
    Libby, I. Lewis "Scooter"; Libby
    trial; Plame in CIA, leak
    investigation; Wilson, Joe
Clemens, Roger, xv
Clinton, Bill
  and perjury, xiii, 225, 441
  and Wilson, 135–36, 158, 162,
    183, 225
Cohen, Howard, Plame's identity
    leaked by Novak to, 161
Collins, Denis, 250
Comey, Jim
  on crime of perjury, xii
  ImClone investigation, 63–66, 70

Plame's identity leak investigation,
    180–82, 208
  and Stewart's plea negotiation, 79–84
Conte, Stan
  Anderson, suspicion about, 274, 275
  Giants' steroid use ignored by,
    275, 280
Conte, Victor, Jr.
  athlete-customers of, 284–85
  background of, 283–84
  as BALCO founder, 275
  and BALCO raid, 280–85
  book authored by, 354–55
  charges/sentencing, 324
  grand jury testimony leak, 308–10,
    314–20, 326–27, 329
  indictment of, 303–4
  legal counsel for, 289–90
  media presence of, 316–20
  post-BALCO, 354–55
  reports to authorities about, 293
Cooper, Chris, 284
Cooper, Matt
  as focus of investigation, 155
  grand jury testimony, 205–7, 212–14
  Libby trial testimony, 242–43, 249
  Plame mentioned in article of, 149
  Plame's identity leaked by Libby to,
    145–46, 149, 171, 172, 178, 194,
    206
  Plame's identity leaked by Rove to,
    209, 214–15, 221
  post-Libby trial, 256
  refusal to reveal sources, 177
  on White House sources, 149, 155
  Wilson's mission, article on,
    148–49
Cosby, Bill, 85
Cox, Christopher, 421
Cuti, John, 31, 34, 64

DeLuca, Heidi
  and ImClone case, 23, 25, 37, 50, 77
  as Stewart-Bacanovic trial witness,
    102–5, 110
DePippo, Henry, 347–48
Dickerson, John, 185
Dion, John, Plame's identity leak
    investigation, 157, 159, 172
DiPascali, Frank, Jr.
  background of, 401
  Madoff investigation, 400–403, 424
  role in Ponzi scheme, 424–25
Donaire, Nonito, 355
Duberstein, Kenneth, 183

Ebel, Maureen, 425
Eckenrode, John C.
  background of, 154–55
  leak cases, frustration with, 154–55
  Plame's identity leak investigation
    by, 154–80, 183–85, 192, 202,
    227–31
  post-Libby trial, 257
Ecko, Marc, 359
Ecrivo, Eva, 85
Edelman, Eric
  on Kristof's article, 128
  Plame, learns about, 132
Edwards, John, perjury by, xiii
Ellerman, Troy
  and grand jury testimony leak, 319,
    326, 331–42
  perjury versus higher motive, 434
  post-BALCO, 355
  rodeo involvement, 290, 323,
    331–34
  as Valente's legal counsel, 290, 310,
    314–15, 319, 323–24
Enablers, of lying/perjury, 435–36
Enos, Laura, 279

Erbitux
  FDA approval, 119
  FDA rejection, 10–11, 19, 25, 36
Eschwie, Dorothy, 372
Estalella, Bobby, steroid use, 287–88,
    319

Fainaru-Wada, Mark
  BALCO coverage, 308–9, 318,
    327–28
  book authored by, 331
  Ellerman's leak to, 331–42, 339–40
  First Amendment issue, 328–30
  post-BALCO, 355
Fairfield Sentry
  Madoff feeder fund, 366, 386,
    389–90, 403
  SEC investigation of, 396–99
False statements under oath. See Perjury
Faneuil, Douglas
  background of, 4–5
  courage and integrity of, 416–17, 439
  firing of, 61, 75
  guilty plea/court appearance, 67–74
  Gutman's legal advice, 27–28, 49,
    58, 77
  ImClone shares sold by, 3–8,
    11, 16–17
  immunity, absence of, 61, 67,
    69–70, 117
  and initial investigation, 19–22
  loyalty, perjury based on, 27, 46,
    48, 70
  media coverage of, 73, 75–76
  Pickholz as legal counsel, 58–60, 67–75
  plea negotiation, 67–72
  pressure to protect Bacanovic, 20–23,
    27, 46–48, 50, 57
  rudeness by Martha to, 13–14, 16
  sentencing, 116–17

Faneuil, Douglas (*cont.*)
  as Stewart-Bacanovic trial scapegoat,
    86–87, 109–11
  as Stewart-Bacanovic trial witness,
    76–77, 87–97
  stress suffered by, 24–25, 27, 46–51,
    68–69
  truth, confesses to, 59–62
  U.S. Attorney questioning of, 48–50
Farmer, Catherine, ImClone
    investigation, 35, 53, 62, 66, 69
Federal Bureau of Investigation (FBI),
    and leak about Plame's identity. *See*
    Plame in CIA, leak investigation
Fifth Amendment, versus perjury, 63,
    70, 184, 260, 434
Finigan, Jeff, 353
First Amendment
  and BALCO investigation, 328–30,
    332
  grand jury testimony, conditions
    for journalists, 157, 203–4, 210,
    213–14, 326, 330
  invoked by Fainaru-Wada and
    Williams, 328–29
  invoked by Miller, 207–8, 213–17
  and Plame's identity leak
    investigation, 178, 180, 203–4,
    208, 210, 245
  privileges and press, 178, 180, 210
Fishman, Steve, 432
Fitzgerald, Patrick
  background of, 63, 180–81
  Libby's trial, 234–36, 239,
    243–44, 250
  as Plame's identity leak investigation
    head, 180–82
  post-Libby trial, 257–58
  Rove/Armitage resignations, request
    for, 221–23

See also Plame in CIA, leak
    investigation
Fleischer, Ari
  immunity granted to, 184–85,
    240–41, 250
  interviewed by U.S. Attorney,
    184–86
  leaks to media about Plame, 185
  Libby denies leak to, 179, 189
  Libby trial testimony, 240–41
  Plame's identity leaked by Libby to,
    140, 184–85
  refusal to reveal sources, 175
Foster, Vince, 161
Friehling, David, as Madoff auditor,
    366–67
Fuhrman, Mark, xiv
Fuks, Zvi, 78–79

Gardner, Daryl, 284
Garrity, Michael, 386–91, 428
Gebhardt, Bruce, 154
Gestas, Nicole, 286–89
Giambi, Jason
  grand jury testimony, 318
  steroid use, 272, 285, 286, 287,
    318, 359
Giambi, Jeremy, steroid use, 285, 359
Gilliam, Haywood, 311
Giuliani, Rudolph, 180–81, 254
Glotzer, Helene, ImClone
    investigation, 22, 26, 35–36,
    39–41, 49–50, 54–55, 63–66
Goldberg, Alan, 5–7, 38
Gonzales, Alberto, 159, 201, 350
Graham, Trevor
  background of, 291
  BALCO investigation testimony,
    305–7
  dispute with Conte, 291–93

immunity granted to, 305
immunity negated by lying, 356
indictment of, 337–38
and Memo, 306–7, 322–23, 337–38, 352–53
post-BALCO, 356
self-described whistleblower, 293, 305, 337, 352
sentencing, 356
split with Jones/Montgomery, 292–94
steroid distribution to trainees, 283, 284–85, 291–94, 312–13, 337–38, 345–46, 353
trial of, 352–54
Grann, David, 274–75
Grant, Harriet, 127, 234
Greenwood, James, 56
Gregory, David, 185
Grenier, Robert
  Libby trial testimony, 239
  Plame's identity leaked to Libby by, 130–31
  position of, 130
Grossman, Marc
  interviewed by FBI, 173–74
  Libby denies discussion with, 179, 188
  Libby trial testimony, 239
  Plame, learns about, 173–74
  Plame, tells Libby about, 128–29, 131, 174
  relationship with Wilson, 173–74
Gutman, Jeremiah
  background of, 25
  as Faneuil's legal advisor, 27–28, 49, 77
  as Stewart-Bacanovic trial witness, 101–2

Hadley, Stephen, 141–42
Hamilton, James, as Novak's legal counsel, 161, 182
Hannah, John, Libby trial testimony, 245–46
Harlow, Bill, CIA denies Wilson mission, 132–33, 139
Haskell, Rob, and Faneuil/ImClone case, 4–5, 17, 24, 46–47, 89, 100, 120
Hedge funds
  popularity among wealthy, 363
  quantitative "black box" funds, 364
Hemann, John, 350
Heredia, Angel "Memo"
  BALCO investigation, 304, 306–7, 321–23, 337–38, 352–53
  immunity granted to, 323
Hershman, Brian, 326–27, 330
Hirschhorn, Carla, 425
Holley, Robert
  as Conte's legal counsel, 290, 314–15, 318
  as Valente's legal counsel, 323–24
Hoskins, Bob, 269
Hoskins, Kathy, 268–69, 359
Hoskins, Steve
  and Bonds memorabilia business, 276, 279–80
  and Bonds trial, 359
  relationship with Bonds, 269–70
  tapes Anderson, 276–79
Hunter, C. J.
  grand jury testimony, 311–14
  on Jones steroid use, 312–14
  steroid use, 293, 311
Hunter, Rielle, xiii
Hussein, Saddam
  uranium deal in Niger claim, 129, 136

Hussein, Saddam (*cont.*)
  weapons of mass destruction claim,
    123–26
Hutchinson, Kay Bailey, 225–26

Icahn, Carl, 51
Illston, Susan Yvonne, BALCO trial
    judge, 304, 310, 317–18, 324,
    332–33, 354, 356, 358–59
ImClone investigation
  accused in. *See* Bacanovic, Peter;
    Faneuil, Douglas; Stewart, Martha;
    Waksal, Aliza; Waksal, Harlan;
    Waksal, Jack; Waksal, Sam
  grand jury, 50
  Merrill Lynch, initial discovery,
    18–28
  SEC in, 22, 26, 35–44, 53–55, 120
  trial related to. *See* Stewart-Bacanovic
  truth confessed in, 59–62
  U.S. Attorney in, 29–37, 61–63
ImClone Systems
  Eli Lilly acquisition, 119
  Erbitux FDA approval, 119
  Erbitux FDA rejection, 10–11, 19,
    25, 36
  founding of, 9–10
  stock price decline, 16, 19, 29
Immunity
  for Faneuil denied, 61, 67, 69–70, 117
  granted in BALCO case, 291,
    295–96, 305, 318, 321, 323, 337
  granted in Plame case, 184–85,
    240–41, 250
  granted in Stewart case, 66
  negated by lying, 250, 295, 296–97,
    344–47, 356, 439
  and proffer, 33, 184, 305
Intelligence Identities Protection Act,
    150, 155, 220

Iraq War, false information and
    Bush administration, 123–26,
    137–38, 140
IRS Criminal Investigation, steroid
    distribution. *See* BALCO
    investigation; BALCO raid
Isikoff, Michael, 233

Jeffress, William, as Libby's legal coun-
    sel, 224, 241–44, 248–49
Johnson, Stephen, 406
Jones, Aphrodite, 320–21
Jones, Kimberly, xiv
Jones, Marion
  book authored by, 310–11, 357
  coach of. *See* Graham, Trevor
  immunity granted to, 295
  immunity negated by lying,
    344–47, 439
  and Montgomery's check scheme,
    343–44
  as natural liar, 344, 357
  post-BALCO, 356–57
  sentencing, 349
  steroid use admitted by, 345–47
  steroid use denied by, 296, 310–11,
    320, 345–46
  steroid use exposed, 284, 312–14,
    317, 346
  sues Conte, 320
Jones, Paula, xiii
Journalists. *See* First Amendment; Press;
    individual journalists; *individual
    publications*
Judicial system, as enabler of perjury,
    438–41

Karas, Kenneth M., 345–49
Kaye, Judith, xv
Keane, William, 352, 353

Keller, Bill, 211
Kelley, David, 70, 82, 83, 180
Kennedy, Ted, 225
Kessler, Glenn, 145–46, 171, 194
Kilpatrick, Kwame, xiv–xv
Kingate Euro, 383
Kingate Global, 383
Korchemny, Remi, indictment of, 304
Kotz, David, SEC/Madoff
    investigation, 422–24, 427–29,
    432, 440–41
Kristof, Nicholas
    impact of article, 129–30
    on Iraq War, false basis of, 126–27,
        129–30, 132
    on Wilson's mission to Niger,
        126–28, 132

Lamore, Peter
    background of, 372
    Madoff investigation, 372–86,
        394–96, 399–404, 411–13, 422–23,
        428
Laufer, Henry, 367, 371
Leaks to press
    cases involving. See BALCO investi-
        gation; Libby, I. Lewis "Scooter"
    leak as federal crime, legal code on,
        150
Letterman, David, 57
Levine, Adam
    interviewed by FBI, 175
    Matthews, efforts to influence, 143
    Rove blames leak on, 165, 175,
        221–22
Levy, Daniel, 342, 344
Levy, Norman F., 416–17, 420
Lewinsky, Monica, xiii
Libby, I. Lewis "Scooter"
    background of, 127–28

Bush commutes sentence, 253–55,
    340–41
Cheney talks about Plame to, 138–
    39, 145, 166, 174, 178, 195–96,
    438
Cheney vindicates via McClelland,
    152–53, 166, 235
classified information, initial respect
    for, 132
Kristof's article, reaction to, 128
leak investigation. See Plame in CIA,
    leak investigation
loyalty, perjury based on, 438
Matthews (Chris) reports on, 143
news media, efforts to influence,
    142–44, 160, 169
perjury, motives for, 435, 437–38
personality traits, 437–38
Plame's identity leaked to Fleischer
    by, 140
Plame's identity leaked to Miller by,
    134–35, 142, 146
Plame's identity leaked to Novack
    by, 146
Plame's identity revealed to,
    130–31, 174
post-trial, 259
relationship with Cheney, 127–28
relationship with Miller, 133–34
trial of. See Libby trial
Libby trial, 233–53
    charges against Libby, 223
    closing arguments, 247–50
    defense witnesses, 244–46
    jury and judge, 233–34,
        251–53
    Libby's defense fund, 224–25
    opening statements, 234–38
    prosecution witnesses, 239–44
    verdict and sentencing, 251–53

Ling, Anna, 324
Long-Term Capital Management, 363
Loyalty
    perjury based on, 21–22, 48, 326,
        433–34, 438
    versus truth, and Bush
        administration, 255
Luskin, Robert, as Rove's legal
        counsel, 162, 165, 209,
        221, 436
Lying
    under oath. See Perjury
    and sociopathy, 435
    and special circumstances, 433
    and successful persons, 435

McCain, John, 320
McCarthy, John, 381–82
McClelland, Scott
    book authored by, 262
    Libby vindication statement, 151–53,
        166, 262
McCormack, Larry, and grand jury
        testimony leak, 331–38
McGwire, Mark, 271–72
McKeefry, Mark, 396
McTiernan, John, xv
Madoff, Andrew
    assets frozen, 431
    Madoff's confession to, 419
Madoff, Bernard
    background of, 373–74
    collapse of scheme, causes of,
        418–19
    family members in business, 373
    in-house auditor for, 366–67
    market-maker claim, 376, 383–84
    market timing claim, 380, 382–83,
        398, 401–2
    perjury, motives for, 440

Ponzi scheme exposed. See Madoff
        investigation
    prison life, 432
    wealth/lifestyle of, 374–75
Madoff, Mark
    Madoff's confession to, 419
    suicide of, 431–32
Madoff, Peter
    assets frozen, 431
    in Madoff's business, 373
    Madoff's confession to, 419
Madoff, Ruth
    and Madoff arrest, 418
    in Madoff's business, 373–74
Madoff, Shana
    assets frozen, 431
    in Madoff's business, 373, 375
Madoff investigation
    assets, recovery of, 431
    audit and family members, 389–91
    Barclays transactions, bogus,
        377–78
    DiPascali pleads guilty, 430–31
    Fairfield Sentry, SEC questioning,
        396–99, 436
    feeder funds, 366, 382, 383, 389–90,
        420
    impetus, complaints about Madoff,
        363–71, 384, 395, 416
    impressions of Madoff by
        investigators, 376–78, 408
    inconclusive inquiries, 381–82,
        385–86, 395, 428
    Madoff confesses to family, 419
    Madoff on SEC incompetence,
        422–24
    Madoff pleads guilty, 420–21
    Madoff questioned during, 376–81,
        406–13, 422–24
    Madoff's arrest, 418–20

Madoff's lies/contradictions during,
    376–80, 385, 396–99, 408–17,
    420, 432, 440
Madoff's sentencing, 425–27
Markopolos identifies Ponzi scheme,
    386–96
money management, Madoff's
    denial, 376–77, 386, 396
options trading, Madoff's denial, 377,
    380, 385, 396, 398, 399, 404, 412
perjury, motives for, 435–36
Ponzi scheme, Madoff's description
    of, 421–22
Ponzi scheme suspected by
    authorities, 400, 404–5, 412–17
SEC Compliance Office
    examination, 380–82, 384
SEC failure in, 421–25, 427–29,
    440–41
split-strike forward conversion
    strategy claims, 367–68, 370, 377,
    379, 389, 407, 422
trade publications question returns,
    367–68, 379, 393, 410
Vijayvergiya coached by Madoff,
    396–99
Madoff Securities. See Madoff, Bernard;
    Madoff investigation
Magowan, Peter, 271
    as enabler of perjury, 435
Magrino, Susan, 14, 57
Manion, Ed, 387, 393
Marcus, David
    as enabler of ImClone perjury, 435
    ImClone investigation, 19, 22,
    27–28, 32, 38, 60, 102
Markopolos, Harry
    background of, 387
    book authored by, 429–30
    credibility issue, 393
    as hero, 436
    Madoff Ponzi scheme, identifies,
    386–96
    Madoff view of, 423
    post-Madoff, 429–30
Martha Stewart Living Omnimedia,
    ImClone case and share price, 31,
    56–57, 79, 119
Martin, Cathie
    implicates Libby, 166, 172, 189
    interviewed by FBI, 166
    job of, 128
    Libby trial testimony, 240
    Plame, learns about, 132
    Wilson's mission exposed, efforts to
    contain, 139–40, 145–46
Martin, David, 139
Matalin, Mary, 143, 191
Matthews, Chris
    interviewed by FBI, 161
    on Rove's comment Plame as "fair
    game," 160, 164
    uranium sale story, Libby efforts to
    stop, 143, 160, 169, 176, 191
Mayfield, Jenny, 171
Mays, Willie, 266–67
Mendelsohn, Dr. John, 10
Merrill Lynch
    as enabler of ImClone perjury, 435
    ImClone insider trading, discovery
    of, 18–28
    ImClone trades, learns truth, 59–60
    See also Bacanovic, Peter; Faneuil,
    Douglas
Milberg Weiss, xiv
Miller, James, 81–82
Miller, Judith
    background of, 133–34
    fights grand jury subpoena, 207–8
    grand jury testimony, 217–19

Miller, Judith *(cont.)*
    invoked by Miller, 207–8, 213–17
    jailed, 213–17
    Libby denies leak to, 190
    Libby permission to testify to,
        216–17, 261
    Libby trial testimony, 241–42,
        248–49
    National Intelligence Estimate given
        to, 142, 170
    Plame's identity leaked by Libby to,
        134–35, 142, 146, 218–19
    post-Libby trial, 256
    relationship with Libby, 133–34
    WMD, writings on, 134
Millerwise, Jennifer, 129
Mitchell, Andrea
    Libby withholds information from,
        171, 193–94
    refusal to reveal sources, 177
    reports on Wilson mission, 137–38,
        142
Mitchell, Dennis, 353
Molieri, Daniel, 290
Monaghan, Judy, ImClone
        investigation, 19–22, 89
Montgomery, Tim, 284
    athletic career, decline of, 342
    barred from Olympics, 307–8, 342
    grand jury testimony, 293–95
    heroin conviction, 357
    illegal check scheme, 342–44
    post-BALCO, 357
    steroid use, 292–93, 322
Morton, Johnny, 284
Morvillo, Robert
    background of, 63
    Stewart-Bacanovic trial, 87, 98–99,
        110–13
    and Stewart's plea negotiation, 82–84

Nadel, Ross, BALCO investigation,
    296–97
National Intelligence Estimate (NIE),
    142, 170
Nedrow, Jeff, BALCO investigation,
    294, 296–302, 309, 311–13, 319,
    344
Nee, John, Madoff investigation, 372,
    377–78, 381, 383–84, 386, 393,
    428–29, 440
News media. *See* Press
New York Times
    First Amendment specialist for,
        203–4, 207, 211
    Kristoff on false basis for Iraq War,
        125–26
    Miller as correspondent, 133, 241
    and Miller's refusal to reveal sources,
        207–8, 211, 213, 226
    on Plame's identity leak, 152–53,
        156–57
    Wilson's piece on WMD lie, 137,
        234–35
Nichols, Richard, 342
Novak, Robert
    background of, 135–36
    book authored by, 255–56
    death of, 256
    as focus of investigation, 155
    grand jury testimony, 232–33
    interviewed by FBI, 161–62
    interviewed by U.S. Attorney,
        182–84
    Libby trial testimony, 245
    Plame in column of, 146–47, 150
    Plame identity leaked by Libby to,
        146
    Plame's identity leaked by
        Armitage to, 158–59, 173,
        183, 233

Plame's identity leaked by Rove to, 144, 163, 183–84, 202
Plame's identity leaked to Cohen by, 161
refusal to reveal sources, 161–62, 182
view of Wilson, 138, 158, 161–63
on White House sources, 147, 150, 156
Novitzky, Jeff
BALCO raid/investigation, 280–89, 303, 319, 321–23
post-BALCO, 355–56
testimony of athletes to, 295–96, 305–7
Nussbaum, Andrew, 30–31

Ocrant, Michael, 367–68
O'Donnell, Rosie, 85, 100
Olson, Ted, 181
Oppenheimer, Jerry, 14
Ostrow, William
background of, 372
Madoff investigation, 372–86, 412, 422–23, 428
Owens, Richard, 81

Parrella, Matt, 344, 346, 348, 353
Pasternak, Mariana, and Stewart/ImClone case, 13, 14, 18, 25, 66, 97–100, 117
Paterson, David, xv
Patrick, Sharon, 14, 56
Pearl, Steven, 34, 65
Pearlstein, Norman, 211–12
Peikin, Steve, 29–30, 61–63
Pellicano, Anthony, xv
Pendergest-Holt, Laura, xv
Perez, Julia, 6, 20

Performance-enhancing drugs case. See BALCO investigation; Bonds, Barry; Steroids
Perjury, 433–41
Bonds's motives, 435, 438–39
and Bush administration, 225–26, 435, 441
conclusion about cases, 433–41
defense lawyers' allowance of, 436
enablers of, 435–36
false statements, forms of, xii–xiii
Fifth Amendment as alternative, 63, 70, 184, 260, 434
immunity negated by lying, 250, 295, 296–97, 356, 439
and judicial system, 225, 438–41
legal code for, xii
legal penalty for, 187
Libby's motives, 435, 437–38
loyalty-based, 21–22, 27, 48, 326, 433–34, 438
Madoff's motives, 435–36, 440
motives for, 435, 441
punishment, history of, xi–xii
recent examples of, xiv–xv
as restriction of free speech, 210
SEC cases, absences of, 440–41
selective prosecution of, 225, 439
Stewart's motives, 436–37
warning before testimony, 187, 345, 401, 406
and white-collar crime, rise in, xii–xvi
Perret, Emily, 17
Perry, E. Danya, 342, 344
Pettigrew, Antonio, steroid use, 337, 353
Phelps, Timothy, on Plame identity security breach, 149–50
Picard, Irving, 431

Pickholz, Marvin
Faneuil and truth, initiation of,
58–62, 102
and Faneuil guilty plea, 67–75, 117
Pierzynski, A. J., 287
Pigozzi, Johnny, 14, 25
Pincus, Walter, uranium deal story by,
131–32, 168, 198
Plame, Valerie
book authored by, 255
as CIA operative, 140, 147
identified as CIA operative. See
Libby, I. Lewis "Scooter"; Plame in
CIA, leak investigation
Libby learns about, 130–31
Plame in CIA, leak investigation
Ashcroft resigns from, 181–82
Bush's testimony, 201–2
charges, questions about, 220–23
Cheney's testimony, 197–201
contempt citations for reporters,
210–12
exposed, news media involved. See
Fleischer, Ari
FBI/Eckenrode investigation,
154–80
FBI interviews, 160–80
final incriminating testimony,
217–19
First Amendment issues, 178, 180,
203–4, 208, 210, 245
grand jury testimony, 186–219,
231–32
Justice Department launches, 150–51
Libby convicted. See Libby trial
Libby questioned by FBI, 167–72,
177–80
Libby's credibility, holes in, 172, 174,
176–77, 179–80, 185–86, 197, 205,
218–19

Libby's grand jury testimony,
186–97
Libby's indictment/charges, 223
Libby slips about leak, 170
Libby's resignation/indictment, 224
media coverage, 225–27
media support of, 156–57
news media connections. See Cooper,
Matt; Matthews, Chris; Miller,
Judith; Mitchell, Andrea; Novak,
Robert; Russert, Tim; Woodward,
Bob
press cooperating with, 204–7,
212–15
press refusal to cooperate, 161, 175,
207–8, 213–17
"subjects of," 186, 209, 220
U.S. Attorney Fitzgerald
investigation, 180–208
waivers releasing sources from
confidentiality, 182–83, 200, 202,
204, 210–13, 216, 228
White House connections.
See Armitage, Richard;
Cheney, Dick; Fleischer,
Ari; Libby, I. Lewis "Scooter";
Rove, Karl
Ponzi scheme
elements of, 387, 418, 421
and Madoff. See Madoff, Bernard;
Madoff investigation
Porz, Jim, 21, 75
Posner, Elana Waksal, ImClone shares
sold by, 7, 19
Powell, Colin
and Armitage leak, 158, 231
weapons of mass destruction claim,
125–26
Powers, Marc, Faneuil and truth,
initiation of, 58–62, 88–89

Press
  Fainaru-Wada and Williams invoke
    First Amendment, 328–29
  First Amendment and BALCO case,
    328–30, 332
  First Amendment and Plame's
    identity leak, 178, 180, 203–4, 208,
    210, 245
  First Amendment privileges, 178,
    180, 210
  grand jury testimony, conditions
    for, 157, 203–4, 210, 213–14,
    326, 330
  Miller invokes First Amendment,
    207–8, 213–17
  waivers releasing sources from
    confidentiality, 182–83, 204,
    210, 228, 328
  See also individual journalists and
    individual publications
Proffers, conditions of, 33, 184, 305

Quantitative "black box" funds, 364
Quattrone, Frank, 79

Rains, Michael, as Bond's legal counsel,
    290–91, 296
Raphael, Michael, BALCO investigation,
    326–27, 330, 334–37, 339
Ray, Robert, xiii
Renaissance Technologies
  complaints about Madoff by, 363–
    71, 428–29
  Madoff rejects business of, 365
  Medallion and Meritage funds,
    364–65, 371
Ricciardi, Walter, 390–91
Rice, Condoleezza, 127, 129
Richards, Lori, 380–81
Riddick, Steven, 343

Rios, Armando, steroid use, 285, 287–
    88, 319, 359
Robbins, Barrett, 284
Rodriguez, Diane, 371–72
Rogers, Erwin, BALCO investigation,
    321–22
Romanowski, Bill, 284, 317
Rove, Karl
  Bush questions about leak, 201–2
  calls Plame "fair game," 160, 164
  and criminal charges, 221, 232, 260
  FBI suspicion about, 165
  grand jury testimony, 208–9, 232
  interviewed by FBI, 162–66
  Plame mentioned to Libby by, 144,
    164, 169–70, 193
  Plame's identity leaked to Cooper
    by, 209, 214–15, 221
  Plame's identity leaked to Novak by,
    143–44, 163, 183–84, 202
  post-Libby trial, 258–59
  resignation of, 258
  Wilson blames leak on, 150–51,
    160–61
Royce, Knut, on Plame identity security
    breach, 149–50
Rumsfeld, Donald, 127
Russert, Tim
  death of, 256
  denies leaking information, 176–77,
    205, 236
  grand jury testimony, 205
  interviewed by FBI, 175–77
  Libby blames leak on, 168–72, 176,
    177–78, 186, 188–92, 195–97
  Libby complains about Matthews to,
    143, 169, 176, 191–92, 204–5
  Libby trial testimony, 243–44, 248
  Novak's interview with, 255–56
  relationship with Novak, 135–36

Ryan, George, 257

Ryan, Kevin
  background of, 289
  BALCO investigation, 289–91,
    303–4, 324
  resignation of, 350

Sabean, Brian, 275

Sacharoff, Laurent, 53

Samborn, Randall, 222

San Francisco Chronicle
  BALCO leaks, First Amendment
    issue, 328–30
  Fainaru-Wada and Williams
    BALCO coverage, 308–9,
    318, 327–28

Sanger, David, 170

Santiago, Benito
  grand jury testimony, 296
  steroid use, 280, 286, 288, 319, 359

Sarbanes-Oxley reforms, xiii

Savarese, John
  background of, 31
  as Stewart's legal counsel, 31–33,
    55–56

Schachter, Michael
  background of, 30
  ImClone investigation, 35–37,
    49–50, 65
  Stewart-Bacanovic trial, 97–101,
    104–8
  and Stewart's plea negotiation,
    81–82

Schimpfhauser, Brian, reports ImClone
  stock sales, 18–19

Schmall, Craig
  Libby questions about Wilson to,
    131–32
  Libby trial testimony, 239

Schwarzman, Steve, 18, 25

Securities and Exchange Commission
  (SEC)
  ImClone insider trading
    investigation, 22, 26, 35–44,
    53–55, 120
  and Madoff scheme. *See* Madoff
    investigation

Selig, Bud
  and Bonds' steroid use, 266,
    350–51, 359
  as enabler of perjury, 435

Seymour, Karen
  and Faneuil's plea negotiation,
    68–70
  ImClone investigation, 63, 65
  Stewart-Bacanovic trial, 86, 89–94,
    106, 117
  and Stewart's plea negotiation, 83–84

Shapiro, Howard, 228

Shapiro, Neal, 143

Sharkey, Kevin, and Stewart/ImClone
  case, 13, 18, 56, 66, 118

Sharp, James, 201, 223

Sheffield, Gary
  grand jury testimony, 296, 318–19
  steroid use, 272, 285, 286, 287

Shelby, Richard, 155, 160

Shyne, Douglas, 342–43

Siegman, Miriam, 425

Simons, James
  Renaissance Technologies, 364–71
  suspicion about Madoff, 365–67, 429
  trading methods, 364

Simonyi, Charles, 14

Singh, Natasha, 342–43

Slansky, Jill, ImClone investigation, 22,
  24, 26, 35, 38–43, 49–50

Smith, R. Jeffrey, 233

Snyder, Stephen, ImClone
investigation, 19, 21–22
Sociopaths
and lying, 435
traits of, 435
Sollazzo, Robert, 372
Sorkin, Ira, 418
Sosa, Sammy, 271–72
Stanford, Robert Allen, xv
Stapleton, Frank, 353–54
Steroids
actions/side effects, 273
Anderson use/distribution, 272, 275–79
clear and cream types, 284
production/distribution. See entries
under BALCO
undetectable, 284, 293, 304
use/distribution, legal prohibition,
272, 303–4
Stewart, Alexis, 8, 114, 119
Stewart, Martha
background of, 8, 13
as brand, impact of investigation on,
31, 56–57, 79
charges against, 84
company. See Martha Stewart Living
Omnimedia
cover story, 20–26, 35, 40–42, 45–46,
436–37
cover story weakness, 26, 32, 37, 43,
51–53, 56, 64–65, 104–8, 115
evidence, tampering with, 33–34,
64–65, 97, 112
evidence supporting crime,
63–66, 79
friendships of, 14, 117–19
frugality of, 13, 25, 82
ImClone shares sold by, 16–17, 106
and initial investigation, 20–23

and insider trading charge, 66, 76,
80–82, 84
media coverage, 57
Morvillo as legal counsel, 63, 82–84,
110–13
negative personality traits of, 13–14, 16
perjury, motives for, 436–37
phone logs, truth in, 31–32, 51–53, 105
plea negotiation, 79–84, 118
post-trial, 118–19
testimony about ImClone sale,
31–32, 35–37, 52–53
trial of. See Stewart-Bacanovic trial
U.S. Attorney questioning of, 30,
33–37
and Wachtell legal group, 30–33, 62–63
Waksal's relationship with, 8, 25, 35
wealth of, 13, 118–19
Stewart-Bacanovic trial, 85–120
Armstrong as witness, 97
Bellel and Werring as witnesses,
100–101
defense closing arguments, 108–13
defense presentation, 86–105
defense weaknesses, 115
DeLuca as witness, 102–5
Faneuil as witness, 87–97
Faneuil attacked during, 86–87
Gutman as witness, 101–2
immunity for witnesses, 66
jury, 85–86, 114–15
Pasternak as witness, 97–100
prosecution closing arguments,
106–8, 113
prosecution witnesses, 63–66
social support for accused, 76, 85
Stewart brands proceedings, 85
verdict and sentencing, 113–17
Stout, Martha, 435

Strassberg, Richard, Stewart-Bacanovic
trial, 86–87, 101, 109–10
Stubblefield, Dana, 284
Suh, Simona, Madoff investigation,
392–96, 399–417, 422–23, 428
Sullivan, Richard J., 430–31
Szady, Dave, Plame's identity leak
investigation, 157

Taft, Will, 157, 159
Tate, Joseph, as Libby's legal
counsel, 167, 172, 177, 186,
195, 207, 224
Tatel, David S., 209–10
Taves, Josh, 284
Tedmon, Scott, 338
Tenet, George, and weapons of mass
destruction claim, 125, 144
Thanasules, Thomas, Madoff
investigation, 363–71, 373, 428
Thomas, Evan, 146, 171, 194
Thompson, Obadele, 342
Tibbs, Susan, 405, 408
Time
Cooper at, 145, 256
and Cooper's testimony about Libby,
177, 205–7, 212, 214–15
First Amendment specialist for,
203–4
on Plame's identity leak, 155, 211
on Wilson op-ed, 145, 148–49, 171
Ting, Dr. Arthur, 276–77
Townsend, Fran, 158, 163

U.S. Attorneys' Offices
BALCO investigation, 289–91
ImClone investigation, 29–37,
61–63
Plame's identity leak investigation,
180–208

Valente, James
and BALCO raid, 280–83
charges/sentencing, 324
indictment of, 303–4
post-BALCO, 355
Velarde, Randy, 286
Vijayvergiya, Amit
as enabler of perjury, 436
and Madoff investigation, 396–99,
436
Virdon, Bill, 268
Vulcans, 127

Wachtell Lipton Rosen & Katz, as
Stewart's legal counsel, 30–33,
62–63
Waivers, releasing sources from
confidentiality, 182–83, 204, 210,
228, 328
Waksal, Aliza
ImClone investigation testimony,
53–54, 78
ImClone shares sold by, 5–7, 18–19,
54–55
Waksal, Harlan
ethical problems of, 9
as ImClone CEO, 55
ImClone shares sold by, 29
See also ImClone Systems
Waksal, Jack, ImClone investigation
testimony, 53–54, 78
Waksal, Sam
arrest of, 57
background of, 8–9
cover story of, 54–55
debt of, 10–11
ethical problems of, 9, 11, 78
ImClone, founding of, 9–10
ImClone shares sold by, 5–7, 19, 29
phone logs, truth in, 54

pleads guilty/sentencing, 77–78
relationship with Martha, 8, 25, 35
resignation from ImClone, 55
SEC questioning of, 54–55
testimony about sale, 54–55
See also ImClone Systems
Walton, Reggie, Libby trial judge,
    233–34, 252–53
Wanninger, Rich, 293
Ward, Grant, 387
Washington Post
    Pincus on Wilson trip to Niger,
        131–32, 168, 198
    Plame outed by Novak, 147, 155, 158
    on Plame's identity leak, 175, 185,
        196, 227, 233, 245
Watson, Liz, 270
Weinberg, Rick, ImClone investigation,
    49–50, 58–59
Weinstein, Sheryl, 425
Wells, Ted, as Libby's legal counsel,
    224, 237–38, 243, 248–50, 252
Werring, Eden, as Stewart-Bacanovic
    trial witness, 100–101
White, Jeffrey, 329–30, 340–42
White, Kelli, 284
Williams, Ed, 320
Williams, Lance
    BALCO coverage, 308–9, 318,
        327–28
    book authored by, 331

Ellerman's leak to, 331–42
First Amendment issue, 328–30
post-BALCO, 355
Wilson, Joe
    background of, 136
    book authored by, 255
    credibility, assault on, 141–42,
        146–47, 155
    interviewed by FBI, 160–61
    Libby learns about, 129–31
    Meet the Press interview, 137–38
    mission to Niger by, 129–30,
        136, 160
    mission to Niger findings by, 160
    Rove blamed by, 150–51,
        160–61
    statements on leak, 150
    Times op-ed by, 137–39, 234–35
    Valerie Wilson, leaks about. *See*
        Libby, I. Lewis "Scooter"; Plame in
        CIA, leak investigation
Wing, Chris, 334
Wolfowitz, Paul, 127, 226
Woodward, Bob, Plame's identity
    leaked by Armitage to, 227–32
Wright, Susan Weber, xv

Young, Jerome, 353

Zeidenberg, Peter, 247–48
Zeszotarski, Joe, 305, 309, 352